ECONOMIC PROGRESS
AND
PROBLEMS OF LABOR

ECONOMIC PROGRESS
AND
PROBLEMS OF LABOR

SECOND EDITION

FRIEDRICH BAERWALD

Professor of Economics
Fordham University

INTERNATIONAL TEXTBOOK COMPANY

An Intext *Publisher*

Scranton, Pennsylvania 18515

International's Series in Economics

1SBN 0-7002-2315-0

Library of Congress Catalog Card Number: 70-122538

Foreword to Second Edition

Five years have elapsed since the manuscript of the first edition was written in 1965. In the comparatively short span of time since then many developments have occurred in wage structures, employment policies, industrial relations and in social security and welfare systems. As a result this second edition represents far more than an "updating" of the materials offered originally. The economic setting began to change. Wage-productivity relations became unbalanced. Overall productivity gains declined as the war production and service sectors increased, but money wages rose sharply. However in early 1970 real purchasing was down and unemployment was back to 5 percent. These unfavorable developments demonstrate the need for the emphasis on the conditions of full employment to be found in this text. Another development has been the increase of a special type of collective bargaining in the public sector. A new chapter —17—has been added dealing with these new problems. Other recent developments such as the frequent difficulties in contract ratification have been considered in some detail.

When the text was written originally the Economic Opportunity Act of 1964 had just gone into effect. In this edition the experience with this legislation has been reviewed and changing concepts of employability have been noted. The minimum income proposals submitted by the Nixon Administration in August, 1969, have been incorporated and evaluated.

While whole chapters especially in Part IV; "Collective Bargaining" have been rewritten completely, the last two paragraphs of the text are unchanged. They hinted in 1965 at developments which burst upon the American and world scene three years later. It is hoped that the approach used in the text may make a contribution to the renewal of confidence in the possibility of dealing with labor problems rationally, academically, and without bias.

Friedrich Baerwald

New York, N. Y.
June, 1970

v

Foreword to First Edition

While this text was still in an early planning and discussion phase, a symposium of eminent labor economists was published under the challenging title: "Are Labor Courses Obsolete?"[1] In the course of this debate a number of points were made which correspond to my own thinking. For a long time I have held the view that the treatment of the various topics of the economics of labor must be balanced. For this reason I agree with those who feel that a textbook in this discipline, while paying proper attention to those aspects of the development of labor unions which are relevant today, should not itself be primarily a longer or shorter history of labor unions.

Actually in a text on labor economics equal stress must be placed on the institutional and the economic aspects of all issues coming under analysis. Such an approach necessitates a careful study of the labor market and of the problem of achieving or maintaining reasonable levels of full employment. When the labor market deteriorates, wage structures, collective-bargaining procedures, and social security are deeply affected. As the writing of this text got under way, unemployment still averaged more than 5 percent of the civilian labor force. When it was completed, the national average had dropped to less than 4 percent. While this may be taken as indication of the validity of the aggregate-spending approach to overcome "cyclical" unemployment, there will be general agreement that the situation does not permit complacency, and that labor economics, far from assuming that the problem of full employment has been solved permanently, must point out the serious in balances which remain in the labor market.

Labor economics as a particular aspect of institutional economics must certainly deal with the basic aspects of organized labor so far as it affects the market structure and more specifically the labor market. Further-

[1]Arthur M. Rose, Jack Barbash, George B. Schultz, Arthur H. Meyers, and Neil W. Chamberlain, "Are Labor Courses Obsolete?" *Industrial Relations, A Journal of Economy and Society*, vol. 4, no. 1 (Oct. 1, 1964).

more, it must deal with industrial relations and particularly with the methods emerging of handling such problems as job security and company pensions.

The main emphasis in this text, however, is on the economic foundation and on the interrelationship of all issues usually treated under the general title of Economics of Labor. Collective bargaining cannot take place in a vacuum. It must be brought into context with the structural changes occurring on the labor market. Wage structures cannot be treated adequately without relating them to unit labor cost and unit labor requirements. The problem of job security eventually grows into the more general question of social security and the strength it must derive from the growth and development of the economy.

One participant in the above-mentioned symposium, Charles A. Myers, has stressed the desirability of international comparisons, especially of industrial relations systems. To include such a study in this text has been my intention from the very beginning. However, in doing so I was guided by the general desire to maintain a balance in the overall treatment of all topics. A really intensive comparative study in this area would require specialized monographs which, in my opinion, would have to take into consideration more than just labor relations. Differences in these systems are related to different basic attitudes towards the role of government. In this text international comparisons have been extended to the area of social security. Even today, after the Social Security Amendment of 1965, the United States is in this respect a slightly underdeveloped country. Hence, references to more advanced solutions, especially in the area of old-age insurance and of health insurance, seemed to be indicated.

Throughout the text ample use has been made of the abundant data published by the United States Department of Labor. In the treatment of the theory of employment and of the labor market use was made of the continuing research in macrodynamics, which has been going on under the direction of the author at Fordham University. The establishment study of productivity in a steel mill in Germany which is referred to in the text was carried out originally with a Rockefeller grant in 1953–54. A follow-up study also used in the text was carried out at the same plant in 1961–62.

I should like to express my appreciation to Professor John W. Leonard of the University of Arizona and Professor Glenn W. Miller of the Ohio State University for their careful scrutiny of the manuscript and their constructive suggestions. Mr. Edward Corrigan of Fordham University read the manuscript and prepared the questions and discussion topics. Many thanks are due Justinian F. Rweyemamu, who translated the employment-spending ratios shown in Sec. 13-4 into the mathematical statement contained in the appendix to Chapter 13. While this argument strengthens the verbal and statistical statements dealing with these ratios, the message of this part of the book can also be understood without the appendix. René Scharf designed the graphs and Mr. Charles O'Donnell of Iona College, New York compiled the index.

Owing to a combination of circumstances this text had to be produced while I was committed to a full teaching schedule. For this reason I am particularly obligated to Mrs. Ethel Gore and to Mr. Joseph Mittaga for having submitted so patiently and efficiently to my "dictation." Finally, thanks are due to the students in my courses on the Economics of Labor. They are a challenging audience and on many occasions the educational process has been reciprocal.

FRIEDRICH BAERWALD

New York, N.Y.
November, 1966

Contents

PART II   WAGE DETERMINATION AND WAGE STRUCTURE

PART III   EMPLOYMENT, UNEMPLOYMENT, AND THE
LABOR MARKET

The Development of Social-Welfare Expenditures. Social Welfare Expenditures and the Income Flow. Transfer Payments in Social Security. Trust Funds in Social Security. Selected Bibliography. Questions for Discussion.

Old-Age Insurance Benefits and Retirement. Scope and Adequacy of OASIS and DI. Methods of "Dynamizing" Old-Age Insurance. Selected Bibliography. Questions for Discussion.

The General Scope of Unemployment Compensation. Financial Status of Unemployment Insurance and the Issue of Experience Rating. Some Suggestions for Improvement in Unemployment Insurance. Unemployment Insurance and the Labor Market. Selected Bibliography. Questions for Discussion.

A Survey of the Development of Medical Care Expenditures. Voluntary Health Insurance. Foreign Experience with Compulsory Health Insurance. Health Insurance for the Aged. Towards a Universal Health Insurance for the United States. Workmen's Compensation. Selected Bibliography. Questions for Discussion.

The Welfare Sector and the Gross National Product. Public Aid Programs: Their Development up to 1969. The Reform of Public Aid Programs. Leads and Lags in the Economic Status of American Labor. The Perils of Success in Social Policies. Selected Bibliography. Questions for Discussion.

ECONOMIC PROGRESS
AND
PROBLEMS OF LABOR

Part

I

PERSPECTIVES

In these four introductory chapters the scope of the study of labor economics is outlined. The changing settings within which economic problems of labor arise are discussed. This involves a study of the great changes in the size and composition of the labor force which have already occurred and will continue to take place. The present status of organized labor is analyzed. The progress in economic well-being of the vast majority of people is demonstrated, as well as the new problems of poverty arising in an industrialized society.

Introductory Survey

1-1. SCOPE AND PURPOSE OF THE ECONOMICS OF LABOR

In approaching a field of study such as labor economics it is important to obtain a clear overview of the area it covers and of its more important features. In the advanced industrialized society of the United States the vast majority of people participating in the labor force make their living as wage and salary workers. They outnumber by a ratio of about five to one the farm owners, business proprietors, and independent professionals such as lawyers and medical doctors. Labor economics deals with the conditions, institutions, and procedures which shape the income, standards of living, employment, social security, and industrial relations of this largest segment of the labor force.

The inclusion of all wage and salary workers in this study makes it clear that our investigations will not be confined to production or "blue-collar workers." One of the outstanding features of contemporary industrialized society is its ability to increase output of industry and agriculture while the share of production workers in the total labor force is declining. By the same token, employment of office or "white-collar workers" has risen steadily. To confine a treatment of labor economics to industrial workers would narrow the field, and vast sectors of the employed population would be left out. Furthermore, the earnings of blue- and white-collar workers are closely interrelated. While a large proportion of white-collar workers are unorganized, their wages, hours, and fringe benefits are influenced to a considerable degree by the spillover effect of collective bargaining.

An investigation of the impact of collective bargaining on wage structures and on relations between labor and management is, therefore, an important phase of labor economics. But our study cannot be confined to these problems and procedures. In an economic system characterized by a preponderance of employees, organized and unorganized, the problem of continuous employment is of paramount significance. The general rise in affluence has not lessened the dependence of the large majority of people on a steady flow of income, which is derived from work for others, for corporations, individual proprietors, and government agencies.

The labor market and the conditions that shape the level of its activity is a central topic of labor economics. A study of the real problems of such dramatic labor conflicts, as a strike against newspapers or in a metropolitan transit system, brings out an "iceberg" issue. It is the attempt to protect workers against the effects of automation and mechanization. Labor economics must come to grips with the submerged parts of this gigantic problem. For this reason a discussion of the theory and problem of employment must be part of a comprehensive treatment of this field of study.

The economic well-being of the vast majority of people having reached retirement age is predicated on the effectiveness of public and private social insurance systems. A complete survey of labor economics must deal with these important institutions, their operations, benefits, and their ultimate dependence on the general state of the economy. Although many topics which must be discussed in labor economics will also come under analysis in more general studies of economic principles, labor economics deals with all these issues in a special way. This statement requires further explanation.

1-2. THE TWOFOLD ASPECT OF LABOR: MANPOWER AND HUMAN RESOURCES.

In general economic analysis labor is presented to us as a factor of production. As such it ranks with land, capital, and entrepreneurship. The theory of distribution is concerned with factor returns. Thus wage theory will try to establish the relations between what labor contributes to the total value of production and what it receives back in the form of income of wage and salary earners. Labor, because it is a factor of production, is therefore an important component part of total factor cost. Changes in the cost of this factor may have a great bearing on the employers' demand for labor and on the way in which management tries to arrange the various factors so that they will bring about the best possible returns. If labor only had this one aspect of a factor of production requiring the necessary outlays for its use, labor economics as a more specialized discipline would not be necessary.

Obviously, however, labor is more than a factor of production. It is not one-dimensional. Labor is embodied in people who are part of the community in which they work, who group together to advance their interests, who are motivated by aspirations for themselves and their families. This is the social dimension of labor. Labor economics must deal with this two-dimensional condition. In fact, one of the main concerns of labor economics is to emphasize the two dimensions of labor and to establish this frame of reference for all inquiries into the field of labor economics.

The *first dimension* of labor as an essential *factor of production*, has individual as well as macroeconomic aspects. In classical economics it was clearly understood that labor as a factor required a continuous reproduction of the energy expended in the work process and it was also stressed that the labor force must receive an aggregate income sufficient for its continuous renewal and replacement. Today even on this pure "factor of production" approach level these requirements to assure mere reproduction of the factor labor would be considered inadequate. Through the various phases of the joining together of capital and labor in the process of production, total output per unit, that is to say, productivity, increases and economic equilibrium and progress can be maintained only if the income of labor reflects these advances in technology and output. This will be one of the main topics to be treated in our study of the economics of labor, especially in the field of wage and employment policies.

The *second dimension* of labor emanating from the identity of labor as a factor with a person embodying it and who is involved in a total social situation with its values, conflicts, models of work performance, behavior patterns and manners of living, leads to the concept of the manpower available in a labor market as *human resources*. This implies more than the "labor supply," its quantity and quality available at a given moment. Human resources in this sense also embody potentials of development, the possibility of increasing and uncovering skills of those participating in the labor force, of creating new motivations and incentives for work performance. This dynamic view of manpower as human resource must permeate the treatment of all facets of the economics of labor.

It has already been stressed that in our contemporary society blue- and white-collar workers fall under the concept of "labor." There is, however, one distinct group of employees that does not come within the scope of labor economics—the executives or managers. In fact American Labor Relations Legislation insists on a clear cut separation between management and employees. The Taft-Hartley Act of 1947 took foremen out of the employee group and assigned them to management. This meant that foremen usually rising from the rank and file of employees could no longer claim the right to bargain collectively because they were now considered the lowest link on the chain of management.

The distinction between management and labor is insisted upon although family owned and controlled enterprises have become the exception rather than the rule in many sectors of the economy. Technically speaking, top executives and all management personnel of corporations are employees working under contracts and subject to dismissal.

Management is directing the enterprise. It has the prerogative of setting production schedules and prices, deciding on further investments, and last but not least determining how many workers shall be employed. While the settlement of these questions falls within the province of management, mature industrial relations require open lines of communications with labor as these decisions are in the making.

This need for communication is particularly felt in relation to the impact of technological innovations on levels of employment in the various shops and departments of an enterprise. The setting of wages and other conditions of work is the joint responsibility of labor and management. In collective bargaining, managerial employees and representatives of the wage and salary earners face each other at opposite sides of the table. A clear distinction between labor and management is drawn, although technically speaking, executives and employees share the same status of working not for themselves but for the owners of the enterprise.

1-3. EARLY PROBLEMS OF INDUSTRIAL LABOR

When the first Industrial Revolution got under way in the eighteenth century it replaced human energy to an ever-increasing degree with other sources of power such as steam and electricity. But at first there was little precedent for dealing with the new kind of labor represented by industrial workers. They were without roots in the mushrooming industrial communities and had neither experience nor economic power to resist low wages and long hours.

In preindustrial days work situations in agriculture, in the shops of master craftsmen, and in the offices of merchants were carefully structured. While under the feudal system farmers had to carry heavy burdens in terms of rent payments and labor services, they had their roots on the estate, were identified with it, and could improve their own situation by careful cultivation of the land allotted to them. Similarly in the small-shop setting of the guilds and mercantile enterprises masters and owners were in continuous close contact with the people working for them. Prior to the industrial revolution the work situation was family-centered. Apprentices and journeymen joined the household of the masters. The factory system brought about a basic change in the relations between work and other aspects of daily living. The factory represented a sharp separation of shop and home. The workday became standardized. Rigid discipline enforcing punctuality of workers and setting production targets was introduced.

The workers attracted by the seemingly high cash wages of industry experienced a complete change in their way of life. Whereas they had been embedded in the small village community or in the face-to-face relationships with masters who ran their own shops, the work setting now became more impersonal. Working hours were completely detached from all other aspects of living. Work itself became shop-centered. This change from the family-centered to the shop-centered pattern of employment was bound to bring about an almost exclusive emphasis on an impersonal aspect of labor as a pure factor of production. In the absence of effective labor organization—which made its appearance only much later—individual workers would actually or potentially compete with each other for jobs which were usually scarce if compared with the multitude of newcomers seeking employment. In such a situation wages would be set at a level which seemed barely acceptable to those in most desperate need of immediate employment. In some industries, especially textiles, women and children were considered better factors of production than grown-up men. The workday was extremely long and little attention was paid to industrial hygiene and safety.

Almost from the start of modern industrialism critical voices were raised denouncing these conditions and demanding improvements through legislation. Throughout the nineteenth century social reformers advocated (1) restrictions on the employment of women and children, (2) factory inspection as a means of alleviating the health and safety hazards of working in factories, and (3) a raising of extremely low wages. As early as 1819 the first Factory Act was passed in England forbidding employment of children below the age of 9 in the newly developing industrial enterprises. This legislation had been sponsored by Robert Owen (1771–1858). This early English industrialist was also a great advocate of structural reforms of the newly emerging system of industry. While his utopian colony which he founded in 1825 in New Harmony, Indiana, was a failure, the consumers cooperative he started in Rochdale, England in 1847 set the pattern for similar organizations especially in Europe. Throughout the 19th Century Royal Commissions were engaged in detailed studies of the operation of the Poor Laws, on working conditions especially the length of the work day and the employment of children. Writers such as the husband and wife team Sidney and Beatrice Webb spent their whole life in the exploration of labor conditions and the advocacy of industrial democracy. They also wrote extensively on the history of labor.

Among the American pioneers in the field of labor economics was Professor J. R. Commons, (1862–1945). He was a strong advocate of unionism at a time when collective bargaining was rejected by most large scale industrial enterprises as a method of establishing standards of pay and work for employees. A historian of labor in the United States, he was also instrumental in the progressive labor legislation adopted by Wisconsin especially in the areas of workmen's compensation and unemployment insurance. At various times he served prior to World War I with the Wisconsin Industrial Commission and with Federal committees studying labor problems and industrial relations.

The efforts made by the writers mentioned here and by many others were not without success. By the end of the 19th Century already substantial improvements in the condition of the working class were noticeable. As early as 1841 Friedrich Engels, who, like Robert Owen, was connected with the textile industry, had published his "Condition of the Working Class in England." It was a detailed description of the dismal living conditions of industrial workers in the newly developing factory towns in England, of their low wages, poor housing conditions and the prevalence of alcoholism, tuberculosis, and other diseases among the working poor. Fifty years later in 1891 Engels, now a septuagenarian, wrote a preface to a new edition of his early work conceding that towards the end of the 19th century some of the conditions which he had described in his original publication of 1841 had been alleviated. This was an important admission of a writer who had been a life long associate of Karl Marx and to his end remained a radical Socialist expecting the turnover of the capitalistic system by the proletariat.

By the end of the 19th Century the labor movement had gotten underway in all industrial countries. Operating through trade unions and especially on the European continent also through socialistic parties it stressed the solidarity of workers and began to struggle for social recognition and better social status of the industrial workers. Over the long haul these concerted efforts were successful.

The history of industrial relations in the twentieth century can be summed up as the gradual acceptance of a two-dimensional aspect of labor. This dualism has found its expression in legislation by protecting in specific ways the inherent right of labor to organize and to bargain collectively. There emerged a new status of labor as both an individual and a collective entity.

Today workers are aware of their rights. Labor organizations are coequal with other bodies representing segments and interests of the economy. If we understand by "the establishment" the sum total of social institutions and groups which through their interaction shape the course of events and the structure of society, then we must recognize that organized labor is very much a part of it. Labor's road from the rank of outsiders or groups without established status to full-fledged participants in the economic process demonstrates its rapid social progress.

In a sense, labor economics is a study of the conditions that have made this progress possible and of the requirements that must be met in order to secure these gains, and to relate them to all the other aspects of the functioning of the economy. But new problems emerge as labor moves to higher plateaus of income, employment security, and social acceptance. Hence a study of labor even in the advanced industrial society of the last third of the twentieth century is also of necessity an inquiry into new problems of labor.

1-4. PROGRESS AND PROBLEMS OF LABOR

In the early decades of the nineteenth century coinciding with the first Industrial Revolution there was a widespread opinion that the laws of the labor market prevented a rise of wage levels beyond mere subsistence. Economists like John Stuart Mill argued that the only way to improve the lot of the working class was through education, for education would make workers more responsible, bring about a smaller family, and thereby spread total wage allocations among fewer individuals.

Socialists of the nineteenth century took a different view. They demanded and hoped for a complete change of the economic system, especially a transfer to society of privately owned means of production. They maintained that so long as capitalism, or production for profit, continued, the conditions of industrial workers could not improve. According to the socialists, this low ceiling on wages and living standards transformed workers into "proletarians" because there did not seem to be even a long-run hope of improvement for later generations. Socialism emerging from capitalism in the course of ever-deepening crises was considered the only way in which this proletarian condition could be eliminated and the standard of the working class bettered.

It is important to note that both defenders and critics of capitalism formulating such pessimistic theories were refuted by the actual development of modern industrialism. The increased concern for the working conditions and well-being of labor shown by social-reform legislation in the later part of the nineteenth century, and the growing strength of the labor movement in the period prior to World War I had already brought about gradual changes for the better. After that conflict and continuing through the period after World War II an acceleration of the progress of labor took place. In this sense the history of labor is a history of the progress of labor. Let us illustrate this assertion in more tangible terms.

We have stressed that in the initial period of the factory system working hours were very long. Prior to World War I the average work week in manufacturing in the United States was 50 hours; It is now about 40 hours with the legal mandate of paying time-and-a-half for each hour after 40 hours. While hours were shortened, the spendable income, that is to say the wages that workers retain after the withholding of income taxes and contributions to Old-Age and Survivors Insurance had risen steadily. Measured in constant 1947-49 dollars the net real spendable weekly earnings of workers with three dependents were $39.76 in 1939. In 1959 they had climbed to $64.49 in the manufacturing industries. In this period, therefore, a very noticeable increase in the real wages of industrial workers has occurred.

If we take an even longer period into account we observe still more clearly the enormous improvement in the income of labor. In 1914 average weekly earnings of production workers were $10.92: in 1966 they had risen to $111.92. This means a ten-fold increase in current dollars. The consumer price index in constant 1957 to 1959 dollars stood at 35.0 in 1914 and at 113.1 in 1966. That is to say cost of living had risen three times while wages in manufacturing increased ten times.

A study of income trends in New York State, released in March 1970, projects that by 1980, 48 percent of the households will have incomes of $15,000 and more. This forecast includes the earnings of residents in prosperous "dormitory suburbs" peopled by managers in business and finance, professionals in engineering, research, high level teaching and also skilled labor. On the other hand even at that time 14 percent of the family units will have incomes of $4,000 and less. They will in the main live in the cities. Thus their poverty will become more easily apparent than the affluence of the suburban wage and salary earners and higher professional and executive employees.

Nor was this improvement confined to this group of the labor force. Real wages and salaries throughout the economy show the same upward trend, although some groups experienced a lag in the general advance. More important is the great improvement in working conditions other than pay. Paid vacations are now in effect for large segments of the labor force. Group hospital insurance, while still not of the scope known in other advanced industrialized countries, has been extended to the majority of wage and salary earners. A smaller segment of employees, especially those employed by large enterprises, can also expect company pensions. In 1968 average weekly gross earnings of production workers in all manufacturing industries had risen to $122.50, and was considerably higher in many heavy industries. In the primary metal industries these earnings were $146.23, in railroad transportation $143.05, in chemicals and allied products $130.64. These earnings have lifted a large proportion of industrial workers to a middle-class economic status, enabling many of them to become homeowners, to have automobiles and modern household appliances and send their children to college.[1] However, the progress of labor can no longer be measured in these purely economic terms. Throughout our study of the economics of labor we will encounter the phenomenon of the transformation of the labor force, the upgrading of work requirements through the ever rising needs for technical and professional workers, for programmers and employees engaged in advanced operations, research and accounting. Simultaneously, not only the demand for but also the supply of labor doing routine work in factories and offices is declining. For instance, in 1969 the garment industry in New York found it increasingly difficult to obtain

---

[1]*The American Workers' Fact Book*, U.S. Department of Labor (Washington, D. C.: U.S. Government Printing Office, 1960), Table 36.

machine operators because the graduates of vocational schools preferred to go into designing and similar jobs requiring personal imagination and initiative. Many large and prestigious banks also found it difficult to staff departments engaged in necessary routine work because young people were reluctant to go into dead end type of careers. All this illustrates the progressive dynamism underlying labor towards the end of the twentieth century. Even in the Soviet Union it became apparent that the new and better educated generation was reluctant to go into manual work. Hence there as well as in Western advanced nations labor shortages develop not only at the top but also at the bottom of the occupational structure.

Even more significant psychologically is the changed social status of labor, and especially of organized labor. This improvement is maintained even while trade unions are losing to some degree their share in the total number of wage and salary earners. But labor organizations and their leaders have now been recognized as part and parcel of our complex contemporary society in which varied interests are strongly organized, and are continuously engaged in a struggle to protect and to advance the interests of those they represent in an ever-expanding economic structure.

Labor's new status does not mean that groups of employers and individuals in these organizations do not experience some emotional resistance to the still comparatively novel fact that they have to deal with organized labor, or that labor leaders have completely forgotten an original antagonism to management. However, representatives of both groups know that they have to deal with each other. Mature management understands that the times in which they could unilaterally determine working conditions and wages are gone; labor leaders know that they have to work within the given but ever-changing structure of the economic system. But the fact that the nineteenth-century prophets of despair were mistaken must not lead to the facile assumption that all labor problems have been solved or are on the way to a solution. The great strides that labor has made must not blind us to the very real problems that lie ahead.

Most labor problems of an advanced industrialized society that is characterized by mass production and consumption, rising real wages and rising standards of living can be reduced to a common denominator—the emergence of an economic system in which by far the greater part of the national income is derived from current employment rather than from such proprietary assets as land, personally owned businesses, stocks, bonds, or savings. The security of the individual in periods of unemployment, sickness, and old age is safeguarded only to a small extent by the property he owns. He may have a house in his name and all the other goods characteristic of a high standard of living, but these assets do not produce an income. Inasmuch as they require constant renewal, they presuppose a steady flow of earnings. Only active participation in the labor force guarantees the level of income required to maintain an established standard of living. Equally important, for the overwhelming majority of people, is the fact that only the claims they acquire during their activities as wage and salary earners for old-age benefits and company pensions can assure them of some minimum comforts upon retirement. It is therefore not the security of privately owned property but the stability of employment which establishes life-long economic well-being for most people in our industrialized society.

From these general considerations two conclusions follow. First, a study of labor economics must extend over the lifetime of wage and salary earners, dealing with problems encountered by many in their attempt to enter the job market and by those leaving it for retirement. It must also be concerned with temporary losses of income during the productive years as they occur in periods of sickness or unemployment. Secondly, labor economics must pay close attention to the economic conditions conducive or detrimental to the maintenance of high employment and income stability in a period of a rapidly rising labor force and the ever-increasing spread of advanced mechanization and automation.

Labor economics cannot confine its interest to those who became unemployed after they had been working for a considerable period of time. Already prior to World War II a considerable proportion of young people up to age 24 were unable to gain any kind of regular work experience. Fifteen years after the end of that war this condition returned on an even larger scale. As a result of the increase in population, larger numbers of young people looking for their first regular jobs got trapped in this state of nonemployment. An analysis of the causes of this condition and a study of current policies to deal with it has become an important part of the study of labor economics. One remedy which was suggested and largely put into effect a long time ago was compulsory retirement of older workers. It was maintained that their withdrawal from the labor force would increase the turnover of jobs, thereby improving the outlook for those fighting for an entry into the employed labor force. But this policy has been only partially successful.

Retirement, even with earned public and private pensions, means for the large bulk of the older people in the United States a drastic transition from middle- to low-income levels. The introduction of hospital insurance and Medicare for people 65 and over has lessened the impact of protracted illness. However, the problem of maintaining a steady ratio between old-age benefits and current wages and salaries has yet to be solved in this country. A continuation of the current tendency toward an accumulation of more and more retirees in the lowest income groups, reducing their aggregate purchasing power to a minimum, may in due time endanger the rate of growth required to maintain stability of employment unless something is done about it.

Higher earnings, shorter hours, and vastly improved working conditions give evidence of the steady progress that labor has made since the inception of the industrial revolution. A good deal of this advance is due to better management, higher educational attainments of workers, and collective labor agreements. However, a vast measure of these improvements is attributable to improved technology—that is to say, the systematic and continuous application of ever-deepening scientific insights to the design of machinery. Without technology, the great increases in the production of goods and services—in fact the transition to a mass consumption society— would not have been possible.

One indication of the impact of technology is the rising productivity of labor measured in output per worker or per man-hour. But there is another side to this type of progress. In many sectors of the economy aggregate production has risen at a much faster rate than employment. While new employment opportunities are continuously being created in the area of public and private services, the concern for job security—the protection of existing and future jobs against the inroads of progressive mechanization and automation—has developed into a major problem of labor. Nor is it possible to deal with it merely in terms of monetary macroeconomic analysis. A study of the labor market is necessary to discover and analyze these areas where severe unemployment already persists or is threatening to develop. This emphasis on the reverse side of the impressive picture of labor's progress does not imply that the problem of technological unemployment cannot be solved. It merely stresses that it should not be ignored and that dealing with it is the concern of labor economics.

There is another aspect of the progress of labor which posits difficult problems. Although organized labor comprises only about one-third of the wage and salary earners, collective bargaining takes place in all the strategic sectors of the labor market, establishing patterns for the terms of employment of large groups of the unorganized employees. In the first part of this century, once the issue of whether or not management ought to recognize and deal with organized labor had been settled affirmatively, new problems of labor-management relations began to appear almost everywhere.

Collective bargaining is most firmly established in industries where management and labor have grown stronger in the course of time. This is particularly true of the industries such as steel, automobile, printing, contract construction, and transportation. Both partners to the management-labor relationship have gained financial strength and staying power, which has made the negotiation of new contracts more difficult. The pressure on management to come to speedy agreements is lessened by the leadership that giant firms have gained in their industry and their markets, and by careful financial and other preparations which both sides are now able to make in anticipation of an impending conflict. The changes in the economic environment within which the procedures and processes of collective bargaining take place must be carefully considered. Furthermore, the impact of collective bargaining on the wage structure, and the relation of collective bargaining to economic growth and stability, are important aspects of the problems of labor economics.

The road of progress of labor in modern society is marked by many signposts indicating how problems were solved. But economic progress is not only a problem-solving occurrence. It is continuously creating new problems, especially those of employment, security, and labor-management relationships, most recently in the public sector. This perspective underlies the treatment of labor economics in this book.

1-5. SOURCES OF RESEARCH AND STUDY IN LABOR ECONOMICS

The vast increase in the employed labor force, the buildup of social security systems, and the accumulation of experience with collective bargaining have given a great stimulus to the development of sources of information for research and studies in the field of labor economics.

The United States Department of Labor was established under the Taft administration in 1913. Its main publication, the *Monthly Labor Review,* gives current labor statistics on employment, labor turnover, earnings and hours, consumer and wholesale prices, work stoppages, and work injuries. In addition, each issue contains monographic studies covering virtually all issues of labor economics including frequent reports of labor conditions aboard. The same department publishes detailed monthly statistics on employment and earnings.

In 1962 Congress passed the Manpower Development and Training Act. This law makes it mandatory on the President to submit an annual Manpower Report. The first report was transmitted to Congress in 1963 and proved to be a highly significant new source of information about the labor market of the United States. In 1946 the Employment Act was passed. It stipulated the annual submission of an Economic Report of the President. The statistical material contained in the appendices of this report are of particular value for long-run analyses because most of the series published there are carried back to 1929. Indexes of output per man-hour in certain industries have been added in recent years to the wealth of information offered in these reports—information that is of great significance to labor economics.

Although the Social Security Administration was originally affiliated with the Department of Labor, the scope of its operations has become so large that it has been taken out of this jurisdiction and put under the Department of Health, Education, and Welfare which was set up in 1953.

This administration publishes every month the *Social Security Bulletin*. In each issue Current Operating Statistics of old-age and survivors' as well as unemployment insurance are given. Furthermore, there is a regular reporting of the various programs of public assistance.

This listing of official sources of information is not meant to be exhaustive. It indicates, however the enormous amount of information that continuously flows to those who deal with these problems on the academic level of teaching and research. If we add that most states, through their departments of labor, release information dealing with labor conditions under their jurisdiction, the amount of facts and figures available appears in its true perspective. It must be clearly understood that most of the information to which reference is made here is collected and published in order to fulfill a requirement of the law and to inform Congress and other legislative bodies so that they can use it in evaluating existing and proposed legislation.

Above and beyond this gathering of data, these agencies of the government are involved in continuous specialized research activities. It is obvious that they have more personnel and money available than can be generally obtained by researchers in the private sector of the economy, whether in business or in universities. However, research in labor is not and can never be a monopoly of government. One of the main functions of labor economics is to continously test and reexamine current assumptions with regard to wages, employment, security, and industrial relations. While much of the official data is most helpful in this process, the researcher and scholar outside of government often have to regroup these series, search for significant relationships between them, and outline and explore areas not covered by these reports and studies to which research has to be extended. Furthermore, the important academic function of system and model building—the setting up of meaningful frames of reference for continuous inquiries so that the abundantly available facts about labor and its place in the economic structure become intelligible—is one of the important preoccupations of the labor economist.

This preoccupation must be free of prejudices and prejudgments. This is a difficult requirement because through their involvement in relations between labor, management, government, and the economic structure, most issues in labor economics are subject to the controversies of the labor marketplace. A treatment of these problems on the academic level requires partisanship of the highest type, namely partiality for the common good.

SELECTED BIBLIOGRAPHY

Drucker, Peter. *The Future of Industrial Man: A Conservative Approach* (New York: New American Library, 1967).

Ferkiss, Victor C. *Technological Man: The Myth and the Reality* (New York; George Brazillen Inc., 1969).

Galbraith, John Kenneth, *The New Industrial State* (Boston: Houghton Mifflin Company, 1967).

Harrington, Michael. *The Other America: Poverty in the United States* (New York: The Macmillan Company, 1962).

Merton, Robert K. *Poverty in Affluence* (New York: Harcourt, Brace & World Inc., 1970).

QUESTIONS FOR DISCUSSION

1. The fact that labor has two dimensions, one social and one as a factor of production, imposes certain special features on a comprehensive study of labor economics. Why is this so, and what are some of these special characteristics?

2. The gradual evolution of the shop-orientated conditions of employment as opposed to the family or guild system brought significant changes in the structure of the labor force and on the conditions of employment. Discuss at some length, the nature and implications of these changes.

3. The social and economic well-being of labor is not merely a question of high hourly wages. Cite some of the other factors of importance in this respect.

4. Many nineteenth-century economists predicted a dismal future for labor and for the bulk of society in general. Clearly, experience has shown them to be in error. Indicate the nature of their reasoning and the areas in which their argument has failed to stand the test of time.

Chapter
2

The New Labor Force

The wage and salary earners with whom we are concerned represent the greatest part of the labor force. In 1969 the total labor force had risen to 82.3 million people, of whom more than 70 million were wage and salary workers. A proper understanding of many issues in labor economics requires a clear understanding of the concept of the labor force, it composition, the structural changes it has undergone, and the various types of educational and occupational achievements to be found among wage and salary earners. Furthermore, an assessment of the employment outlook and the problem it posits on the labor market and for society as a whole will become much clearer if trends of growth and change can be projected to a point in the future. We will take up these topics in the order indicated.

2-1. THE CONCEPT OF THE LABOR FORCE

In order to ascertain the size of the working population, it is necessary to set up some definitions which can serve to classify the various groups of a population and place them either in or outside the labor force. What the labor force is depends therefore to some degree on definitions representing a general judgment about what is considered a normal relation to the world of work in a given society. In our advanced industrial system the employment of children outside their homes is frowned upon. For this reason the labor force does not include the population under 16 years. On the other end of the age scale, people who have permanently retired and do not even hold part-time jobs are outside the labor force. The whole working population, however, is included. For this reason the armed forces are part of the total. The large bulk of people are of course in the civilian labor force, which also comprises those working for local, state, and Federal governments. Those working on their own account as business or farm proprietors or in any other self-employed capacity are counted in the labor force, which therefore includes employers as well as employees.

There remain large numbers of people over age 16 who are not in the labor force. Among them are full-time housewives whose actual workday may be much longer than that of factory or office workers but who do not seek outside employment. Another large group not counted into the labor force consists of full-time students. This creates some statistical problems during the summer months because of the assumption that a large proportion of high school and college students seek employment during this period of the year. A sudden increase each year of the total labor force occurs in June, July, and August. When classes are resumed in September, the labor force is reduced somewhat. Since not all these students are able to obtain summer work, unemployment tends to rise during the vacation season and to decline in September. In 1965 it was reported, however, that employment had risen by 1.5 million between June and July. The impact of projects under the Economic Opportunity Act of 1964 had made itself felt in the statistics.

It must be clearly understood that the unemployed are part of the labor force. They are included in the totals at all times. We have already seen that the labor force comprises the working population. Now the chief criterion of membership in the working force is not actual employment alone but also the active search for employment of those who are currently not working. If they did not look for a job shortly before the call of the employment census taker visiting households in the population sample, they are not considered unemployed due to their "resignation" from the labor force. In this connection it does not matter whether the household member has never worked before or whether he is an experienced worker who has lost the job he had held, let us say, for twenty years. Great emphasis is being placed on evidence that the unemployed are currently seeking employment. People may be counted in the labor force who have been laid off as a result of shutdown of enterprises in localities where alternate opportunities of employment are manifestly absent, but did not look for work because there was none.[1] Generally active members—those who have made an effort to find employment in the most recent past—are counted in the labor force, and since the concept of unemployment is tied to participation in the labor force, those without a job who do not measure up to this *activity standard* are not counted among the unemployed. Whether or not these classifications and definitions are adequate to deal with the labor market as it evolves in a period of rapid structural and technological change is a question that will be taken up in Chapter 12 in connection with a discussion of full-employment policies.[2]

The concept of the labor force refers to the "noninstitutional population," that is to say it does not consider people in jail or in mental hospitals

[1]"How the Government Measures Unemployment," Bureau of Labor Statistics Report No. 287 (November 1964).

[2]*Manpower Report of The President* (Washington, D.C.: U.S. Government Printing Office, 1964).

and other places where it is impossible for them to participate in civilian employment. However there is a considerable group of men age 18 to 64 who are not in the labor force.[3] It is important to stress that these males do not include those several hundred thousand men in the age group 25 to 44 mostly nonwhite which were missing in the 1960 census although the Bureau of the Census assumes that they must be somewhere.

In 1968 53.3 million men and women over 16 years of age did not participate in the labor force. Naturally the largest group of the nonparticipants consisted of women numbering 41 million. Now, of the total nonparticipants in 1968, 4.5 million, or 8 percent indicated a desire to take a job although they had not looked for employment in the four weeks preceding the interview. A more detailed analysis of these nonparticipants will give us additional insights into current concepts of the labor force in the United States. In the study by Paul O. Flaim of this group it is reported that 46.8 percent of men indicating that they were willing to accept employment were actually in school. In fact 83.5 percent of the age group 16 to 19 said they wanted jobs although they were attending school. Naturally the percentage of those not participating in the labor force but desiring work is declining rapidly as we study the responses of older age brackets. Particularly significant from the viewpoint of employment policies, especially for recent attempts to give training and job opportunities to people who used to be considered unemployable, is the fact that among the nonparticipants 16.7 percent men and 14.2 percent women were not in the labor force in 1968 because they thought "they cannot get work." While the youngest age groups from 16 to 24 do show only a low percentage of people who believe that they cannot obtain employment, the percentage rises significantly for men 25 to 34 years of age where it is 17.5 percent. In the same age group only 10.3 percent women are not part of the working population because they think they cannot get work. Naturally as we move to the higher age brackets we find that the percentage of nonparticipants who believe that they will be rejected by employers is increasing rapidly. So far this group of "discouraged" people who give themselves a zero rating in terms of employment opportunities has been analyzed without reference to race. A racial breakdown indicates that the percentage of people who are not participating in the labor force because they think they cannot find employment is generally twice as high among the nonwhites as among the whites.

Obviously we have here a group of people at the margin of the labor force. Intention to work is, as we have seen, not the equivalent of "seeking work" as understood by our current concepts of the labor force. Consequently this fairly large group is also not considered as unemployed.

---

[3]*Monthly Labor Review*, July 1969, pp. 3 ff.

2-2. THE COMPOSITION OF THE LABOR FORCE

The total labor force of the United States is increasing steadily. In the ten years from 1958 to 1968 it rose from 70.2 million people to 82.3 million. The average increase in that period was, therefore, about 1.2 million people per year. Actually the annual growth was below that average up to 1963. Thereafter there was an acceleration of the growth rate due to the entry into the labor force of young people born during the "baby boom" after World War II. Throughout the 1970's the annual increase is projected at around 1.5 million additional participants in the labor force each year.

The total labor force comprises the Armed Forces and the civilian labor force. For a considerable period from 1958 to 1965 the Armed Forces were held at a numerical level of about 2.7 million. By 1968 the Armed Forces had risen to 3.535 million men.

Of the total labor force of 82.3 million in 1968, 78.7 million were in the civilian labor force. The largest part of this group consisted of wage and salary workers who numbered 68.1 million employees in 1968. The rest of the civilian labor force, 10.6 million, consisted of farm owners, proprietors of nonincorporated businesses, of lawyers, medical doctors and other independent professionals and artists. Among the self-employed the greatest decline occurred among independent farmers. Their number dropped from just under 5 million in 1947 to 1.9 million in 1967. In the nonfarm sector the number of self-employed dropped in the same period from 6 million to 5.2 million. After World War II the self-employed still represented about 20 percent of the labor force. In the late 1960's they were down to less than 15 percent. Wage and salary workers with whom labor economics is primarily concerned represent, therefore, now more than 85 percent of the civilian labor force.

The labor-force *participation rate* indicating the percentage of the population who are either currently employed or seeking employment is also of significance. Over the years it has not changed substantially if we take the total labor force. The participation rate of both sexes was 58.9 percent in 1947. Twenty years later in 1967 it had risen slightly to 60.6 percent. No substantial change is projected even for the year 1980. However within this almost constant rate interesting shifts have occurred. There have been declines in male participation rates. Most dramatically this has occurred both among single and married males 65 years and over. Single men of this age group participated at the rate of 40.2 percent in 1947 and at the much lower percentage of 16.2 in 1967. The corresponding figures for married males over 65 were 54.5 percent in 1947 and 28.8 percent in 1967. Labor-force participation also dropped for males up to the age of 24 and for females 20 to 24 years of age. To a certain extent this indicates the much larger proportion of young people who continue their full time education especially on the postgraduate level. While total labor force participation of single females remain almost unchanged between 1947 and 1967 there was a very sharp increase in the labor force participation of married women. This is most strikingly the case for women in the 45 to 64 age bracket where the participation rate more than doubled from 18.4 percent in 1947 to 40.4 percent in 1967. The total labor force participation of married women rose from 20 percent in 1947 to 36.8 percent in 1967. In evaluating these figures it is, however, necessary to take into account that people who are working only part time, in fact as little as a few hours a week, are considered as participants in the labor force. Part-time work is heavily concentrated among female wage and salary earners especially in the higher age bracket.

These shifts in labor force participation reflect major institutional and social changes which are still going on in American society. The sharp drop of participation of males 65 years and over shows that the Social Security Act of 1935 with its retirement age of 65 and later amendments which reduced it to 62 has had a great impact. Actually in many lines of work this has led to compulsory retirement of people reaching that age. The low labor-force participation rate of this old age group does not mean that these people are affluent. As we will see in Sec. 4-4, a considerable proportion of these retirees are in the poverty sector of the American economy.

2-3. STRUCTURAL TRANSFORMATION OF THE LABOR FORCE

In the past twenty years there has been a decisive change in the employment patterns of the labor force. Whereas in 1947 blue-collar workers still outnumbered white-collar workers, the reverse was true in 1969.

It will be noted that in the period covered in Table 2-1 white-collar workers increased by 14 million, whereas blue-collar workers gained less than 4 million. Between 1947 and 1967 the number of employed persons rose to 16.6 million. It is evident that production work contributed only a small fraction of the gain in employment, especially if we also take into account the sharp drop in farm workers indicated in Table 2-1.

Another aspect of the structural change in the labor force is the rapid increase in nonproduction workers in manufacturing industry. It more than doubled between 1947 and 1967 in durable-goods manufacturing. This indicates that while more and more can be produced with only slight increases in employment of blue-collar workers, it takes more and more people to handle the clerical work and the administration of business enterprises experiencing such an expansion of physical output. Within the blue-collar group significant changes have taken place. Table 2-2 shows a sharp cutback of unskilled and farm laborers and an upgrading of industrial workers. The percentages given relate to the share that these occupational groups have in the total labor force.

TABLE 2-1
EMPLOYMENT BY MAJOR OCCUPATIONS, 1947 AND 1967
(thousands)

Occupation	1947	Percent	1967	Percent
Total employed	57,843	100.0	74.372	100.00
White-collar workers	20,185	34.9	34.232	46.0
Professional, technical, and kindred workers	3,795	6.6	9.879	13.3
Managers, officials, and proprietors, except farm	5,795	10.0	7.495	10.1
Clerical and kindred workers	7,200	12.4	12.333	16.6
Sales workers	3,395	5.9	4.525	6.1
Blue-collar workers	23,554	40.7	27.261	36.7
Craftsmen, foremen, and kindred workers	7,754	13.4	9.845	13.2
Operatives and kindred workers	12,274	21.2	13.884	18.7
Laborers, except farm and mine	3,526	6.1	3.533	4.8
Service workers	5,987	10.4	9.325	12.5
Private household workers	1,731	3.0	1.769	2.4
Service workers, except private household	4,256	7.4	7.556	10.2
Farm workers	8,120	14.0	3.554	4.8
Farmers and farm managers	4,995	8.6	1.970	2.6
Farm laborers and foremen	3,125	5.4	1.584	2.1

Adapted from *Manpower Report of the President* (Washington, D.C.: U.S. Government Printing Office, 1967). Table A7.

If we now consider jointly the trends indicated in the tables given here, we come face to face with a serious problem created by the structural change in the composition of the labor force. Without doubt Table 2-2 demonstrates clearly an important aspect of the progress of labor. The share of craftsmen and operatives, that is to say skilled and experienced workers has shown an increase at least until 1950. On the other hand the demand for laborers, primarily unskilled workers, has dropped very substantially and with increasing speed in the last few decades. This situation is further aggravated by the steep decline in the employment of farm laborers. With the up-

TABLE 2-2
PERCENT DISTRIBUTION OF SKILLED WORKERS AND LABORERS, 1900–1959

Major Occupation Group	1900	1910	1920	1930	1940	1950	1959
Craftsmen, foremen, and kindred workers	10.5	11.6	13.0	12.8	12.0	14.1	13.1
Operatives and kindred workers	12.8	14.6	15.6	15.8	18.4	20.4	18.1
Laborers, except farm and mine	12.5	12.0	11.6	11.0	9.4	6.6	5.7
Farm laborers and foremen	17.7	14.4	11.7	8.8	7.0	4.4	3.9

Adapted from *The American Workers' Fact Book*, U.S. Department of Labor, Washington, D.C. (1960), Table 11.

grading of the labor force, the greater proportion of craftsmen and operators among the blue-collar workers and the shift to a predominantly white-collar force, educational attainments are assuming an ever-increasing role in the makeup and employment opportunities of the labor force. More and more substandard educational achievements prove to be obstacles in obtaining employment or in reaching higher levels within the occupational structure. The time of the self-made man may not have come to an end in the United States. But such a person had better have a good educational record if he is to embark on a meteoric career. Table 2-3 shows the relation between occupational groups and years of schooling.

TABLE 2-3
OCCUPATIONS AND MEDIAN YEARS OF SCHOOL COMPLETED
1948 AND 1967

All Occupations, Both Sexes	1948	1967
Professional, technical, and kindred workers	16.0	16.3
Managers, officials, and proprietors, except farm . . .	12.2	12.7
Clerical and kindred workers	12.4	12.5
Sales workers.	12.3	12.5
Craftsmen, foremen, and kindred workers	9.7	12.0
Operatives and kindred workers.	9.1	10.8
Private household workers	8.0	8.9
Other service workers, ...	9.0	11.5
Laborers, except farm and mine	8.0	9.5
Farmers and farm managers.	8.2	9.1
Farm laborers and foremen	7.6	8.6

SOURCE: *Manpower Report of the President* (April 1968), Table B-12.

It should be noted that Table 2-3 indicates that a large proportion of craftsmen, foremen, and operatives have either a complete high school education or have gone substantially beyond the elementary school level. Furthermore, a comparison with 1948 shows that the median years of schooling of men increased by 1.9 years between 1948 and 1967. In our advanced industrial society it seems that the success of people during their working life is to a large extent determined by what they do before entering it. Apparently the method of "learning by doing" has lost much of the significance it once had. On the other hand rising educational *requirements* do not necessarily mean higher standards of educational processes and *levels*.

These higher educational requirements are also reflected in the rapidly rising percentages of young people enrolled in high schools and in colleges. In 1959, 79 percent of the population 14 to 17 years old was enrolled in high school. In 1966 this percentage had risen to 84.6 percent. In the age group 18 to 24, 16.7 percent was enrolled in college. Seven years later college enrollees represented 25.1 percent of the population in that age group.[4] This rapid expansion of high school and higher education is due to trends which began to assert themselves very strongly in the 1950's. Differences in years of schooling completed translated themselves into great disparities in median income of people in the labor force. This is shown in Table 2-4.

TABLE 2-4

MEDIAN INCOME OF PERSONS AGE 14 AND OVER, BY COLOR, SEX, AND EDUCATIONAL ATTAINMENT, 1958 AND 1961

Color, Sex, and Year	Years of School Completed				
	Elementary School		High School		College
	Less than 8 Years	8 Years	1 to 3 Years	4 Years	1 Year or More
Male					
Total: 1958	$1,905	$3,214	$3,594	$4,548	$5,702
1961	2,090	3,452	3,865	5,052	6,235
Percent change, 1958–61	9.7	7.4	7.5	11.1	9.3
White: 1958	$2,076	$3,276	$3,774	$4,654	$5,810
1961	2,303	3,617	4,090	5,155	6.379
Percentage change, 1958–61	10.9	10.4	8.4	10.8	9.8
Nonwhite: 1958	$1,447	$2,328	$2,224	$2,994	$3,679
1961	1,554	2,505	2,427	3,381	4,246
Percent change, 1958–61	7.4	7.6	9.1	12.9	15.4
Female					
Total: 1958	$711	$909	$867	$2,036	$2,429
1961	791	950	994	1,938	2,342
Percent change, 1958–61	11.3	4.5	14.6	−4.8	−3.6
White: 1958	$765	$924	$927	$2,095	$2,394
1961	817	955	996	1,965	2,395
Percent change, 1958–61	6.8	3.4	7.4	−6.2	*
Nonwhite: 1958	$663	$863	$839	$1,330	$2,365
1961	709	919	988	1,566	2,410
Percent change, 1958–61	6.9	6.5	17.8	17.7	1.9

*Less than 0.05 percent.
SOURCE: *Monthly Labor Review* (May 1963).

Table 2-4 shows that income from employment is predicated more and more on educational achievements. For these reasons "dropping out" of school has become a very serious matter with wide economic and social implications. It has been estimated that during the 1960's there will be about 7.5 million dropouts who will be trying to find jobs.[5] In former decades almost all of these workers would have been absorbed into employment.

[4] Denis F. Johnston, "Education of Adult Workers in 1975," *Monthly Labor Review*, April, 1968.

[5] *Manpower Report of The President* (Washington D.C.: U.S. Government Printing Office, 1964), Chart 32.

The narrowing of opportunities for those with a minimum of formal education is aggravating the problem of structural unemployment.

The employment opportunities of young people with college and post-graduate degrees are still improving. In the public sector, Federal employment in major professional occupations is increasing at a rapid rate. The Manpower Report for 1965[6] estimates that employment in Federal agencies of mathematicians and mathematical statisticians will have climbed to 5.615 in 1968, a percentage increase of 58.4 percent over 1964. Social scientists, especially economists, psychologists, and social workers, were slated for an increase of 16 percent in the same period. For other professional occupations, engineers, accountants, and attorneys substantial increases in Federal employment were forecast.

The rapid rise in public employment, especially on the state and local level enhances further the need for higher educational attainments. While Federal civilian employment was only from 2.2 million to 2.7 million between 1957 to 1967, employees of state and local government increased during the same period from 5.4 million to 8.3 million. In fact this type of civilian public employment was far greater than gains of employment in that ten year period in manufacturing and in all other categories, blue- and white-collar alike.

We have seen in Sec. 2-1 that *activity* is the main criterion. People who regularly work overtime as well as those who are only working a few hours a week or are seeking part time employment are equally considered as members of the labor force. It is important to analyze part time employment in some detail.

2-4. PART-TIME EMPLOYMENT

There are a considerable number of people who are only looking for part-time employment and others who through no fault of their own are actually working part time only for economic reasons. In 1967 the number of people in both groups exceeded ten million. This amounted to almost 15 percent of total employment in that year. The extent of part-time employment by sex and color will be shown on Table 2-5.

As can be seen from Table 2-5 no great changes have occurred in voluntary part-time employment. These figures represent that part of the labor force which does not plan to work full time. Actually the highest incidence of male part time employment is in the age group up to 24 years. As we have already seen in the preceding section there has been a steep increase in the number and ratio of people up to 24 years who continue their schooling. As a result the proportion of males in this group who are working part time has risen significantly from 6.3 percent in 1957 to 10.8 percent in 1967.

[6]*Op. cit.,* Table 17.

TABLE 2-5

VOLUNTARY AND ECONOMIC PART TIME EMPLOYMENT BY SEX AND RACE
1957 AND 1967

	1957	1967
Voluntary.	100	100
Male .	34.5	32.9
Female .	65.5	67.1
White.	88.5	89.4
Nonwhite.	11.5	10.6
Economic		
Male .	65.0	59.8
Female .	35.0	40.2
White	82.7	81.1
Nonwhite.	17.3	18.9

SOURCE: Arranged from Tables A-20 and A-23, *Economic Report of the President* (April 1968).

On the other hand longer attendance at high schools has led apparently to a decline of voluntary part-time employment of teenagers. It dropped significantly for males and females, for the former from 14.2 percent in 1957 to 9.7 percent ten years later and for the latter from 10.1 percent to 7.8 percent. Whereas voluntary part-time employment for males drops sharply for the age group 25 to 64 years it is high for females in the same age groups, 23.7 percent in the 25 to 44 year range and 19.8 percent in the 45 to 64 category.

Part-time employment for economic reasons is, of course, influenced by the overall level of economic activity. Male part-time economic employment rose from 65 percent in 1957 to 68 percent in 1960 but then dropped to 59.8 percent in 1967. On the other hand female part-time employment for economic reasons rose from 35 percent in 1957 to 40.2 percent in 1967.

It is important to note already here that the part-time unemployment rate is far higher than the unemployment rate of those who are working full time. In 1968 the part-time unemployment rate was more than twice as high than the full-time unemployment rate. The latter was 3.1 percent whereas the former was 6.5 percent.

2-5. LABOR-FORCE PROJECTIONS TO 1980

Forecasting the growth of the labor force is perhaps less difficult than making predictions in other areas of economics. The simple reason for this relative certainty and precision is the fact that nobody enters the labor force prior to reaching age 16. Since the number of children born each year is known, it is easy to forecast what the population 16 years old and over will be ten or fifteen years hence. Assumptions must also be made about the full-time school population, age 16 years and over, about the excess of entries into the labor force over withdrawals due to retirement or death, and about labor-force participation rates. Furthermore, the future trend in the labor-force participation rate must be assessed.

As we have seen in Sec. 2-2, there has been a steady increase in the proportion of women in the labor force. Such a development is certain to raise the labor-force participation rate. On the other hand, this may be upset by the increasing length of the period in which young people are full-time students in schools and colleges and a tendency towards earlier retirement of older people. These factors must be taken into account in the analysis of Table 2-6.

TABLE 2-6
LABOR-FORCE PROJECTION TO 1980
(thousands)

Years	Total Labor Force	Labor-Force Participation
1960	73,081	57.4
1964	76,971	56.5
1970	85,999	57.5
1975	93,646	57.8
1980	101,408	58.3

SOURCE: *Monthly Labor Review* (February 1965), p. 130.

It should be noted that the labor-force participation rate, or the proportion of the total population involved in the labor market, is very high in the United States compared to countries in Western Europe. More significant even are the annual growth rates, 1.3 percent for 1960–64 and 1.8 percent for 1964–70. For the 1970's it will remain close to this level. We must also consider that these high rates of annual increase apply to a larger base each year. The rate for 1964 applied to a labor force of about 77 million, whereas the slightly lower rate for the period from 1975 to 1980 (1.6 percent per annum) will apply to 93.6 million and 101.4 million respectively.

The rapid growth of the labor force at a time when huge strides are being made in technology posits novel problems for labor economics and for general economic analysis. In times of scarcity, when output was limited by primitive tools, by inefficient methods of production, and by a shortage of adults in the prime of their productivity, a rapid increase in the labor force was the most important means of increasing aggregate output and income. In contemporary industrialized society it is still true that an increase in population is also a stimulus to an increase in employment. Expectations of an increase in family formation will encourage investment decisions in construction, necessitate additional outlays for school buildings and health facilities. A growing population requires other additional public and private services. But in a society in which production possibilities are increasing at a faster rate than employment opportunities, a rapid rise in the labor force creates new challenges. It can no longer be said that an increase in population produces by its very existence its own opportunities of employment. The new situation of the labor market must be faced with new perspectives. Before we turn our attention to these problems, it is necessary to develop further the already established principles of the economics of labor.

SELECTED BIBLIOGRAPHY

Bancroft, Gertrude. *The American Labor Force* (New York: John Wiley & Sons, Inc., 1958).

Hamel, Harvey R. "Labor Force Status of Youth," *Monthly Labor Review* (August 1965).

Margenn, Garth L. *The Manpower Revolution —Its Policy Consequences* (New York: Doubleday & Company, 1965).

Senate Committee on Labor and Public Welfare. *History of Employment and Manpower Policy in the United States.* 88th Cong., 2d Sess. Committee Print (Washington, D.C.: U. S. Government Printing Office, 1965), 2 vols.

QUESTIONS FOR DISCUSSION

1. Carefully define the concept of the labor force with special attention to who is included or excluded and why they are so classified.

2. Between 1947 and 1963 there was a significant structural change in the labor market relating to the relative numbers of white-collar workers, service workers, and farm workers. Account for these changes.

3. The relation between levels of education, employment, and levels of income is a highly positive one. In recent years, this relationship has taken on increasing importance. Account for this development and, looking to the future, evaluate the significance of it over the next decade.

4. The increasing rate of growth of the labor force over the next decade, combined with the ever-increasing rates of automation, has very special implications for the continued prosperity of the labor force as a whole. Discuss the implications of these trends in terms of employment policies of the past and those which seem to be required in the future.

5. In view of the data on the nature, size, and structure of the labor force which is given in Chapter 2, what preliminary conclusions can you reach with respect to the view that much of present unemployment is due to the very structure of the labor force?

Chapter
3

History and Current Status
of Organized Labor

At the start of our discussion of labor economics it was stressed that attention must be paid to the two dimensions of labor. Labor is a factor of production but is represented in the concrete by individual workers and labor unions. It is therefore necessary to outline the history and analyze some basic aspects of organized labor prior to coming to grips with specific problems of wages, employment, industrial relations, and social security. Before we proceed with a more detailed analysis of the current status and strength of organized labor in the United States, we must gain a wider historical perspective. Only if we adopt this point of view will we be able to understand the apparent paradox of labor's maintaining and even strengthening its role in the United States while its share of the total number of wage and salary workers is continuing to decline.

3-1. A BRIEF HISTORY OF AMERICAN LABOR

Until the period of the Civil War the United States was a predominantly agricultural country. Economic growth as expressed in the building of railroads, residential and business construction and the beginnings of large-scale industry, was dependent on a continuous stream of immigrants. Labor organization of some effectiveness developed first among the highly skilled printers. In 1835 the National Typographical Society was established in Washington. It tried to standardize rules governing apprenticeship, one purpose being to discourage the use of apprentices to reduce the wages of skilled typographical workers. Generally during this period spokesmen for labor demanded the limitation of the workday to ten hours. This proved to be successful in many areas in the eastern United States. In the late 1830's consistent pressure for higher wages also proved to be effective. Wages for skilled workers moved up to a level of $1.50–$2.00 a day.

Throughout the pre-Civil War period it was difficult to establish larger federations of labor on a permanent basis. The British "conspiracy" concept of labor organization—dating back to the fourteenth century and repealed early in 1825—was not applicable in the United States, at least not since the enactment of the Bill of Rights in 1791. Nevertheless, Management succeeded in hindering the growth of trade unions through large-scale blacklisting.

The Civil War speeded up industrialization in the United States and accelerated the transition from an agricultural to an industrial system. Shortly after the end of that conflict the first serious attempt to organize labor in the United States got under way. In 1869 the Knights of Labor was organized. It was conceived as a coalition of a large number of local unions and labor organizations. These units were expected to pay to the federation a per capita tax of 3 cents per year. Membership figures in this national organization fluctuated widely. For the year 1886 over 700,000 members were reported in good standing. Two years later this figure had dropped to about 220,000.

The Knights of Labor had two distinctive features which were to differentiate it in many respects from the trade-union pattern which later emerged in the American Federation of Labor. It tended towards the system of industrial unionism, trying to organize all workers in an industry regardless of skill. Furthermore, in its national conventions it concerned itself with demands for a fundamental reform of the economic structure. It asserted that the aggressive accumulation of wealth should be checked, and demanded replacement of the existing industrial structure by producers' and distributors' cooperatives. The influence of nineteenth-century European social thought was clearly in evidence. Producers' cooperatives into which workers were to be combined were advocated in the 1860's by the German labor leader Ferdinand Lassalle. Cooperatives had also been strongly recommended by John Stuart Mill in his discussion of alternatives to outright socialism as advocated in the *Communist Manifesto* of 1848. The Knights of Labor also advocated election of U. S. senators by popular vote rather than by state legislature, and a progressive income tax. These demands, considered extremely radical in the 1880's, were realized in the first administration of President Woodrow Wilson. The establishment of Federal and state agencies dealing with labor problems was also demanded. In 1884 a Federal Bureau of Labor was organized, but it was not until the administration of President Taft that it was elevated to the rank of a department of Cabinet stature. The Knights of Labor voiced opposition to the easy entry of immigrant workers. They also tended to favor arbitration of industrial disputes thus deviating strongly from later views of organized labor.

Not all labor activity in this post-Civil War period was concentrated in the Knights of Labor. In that period Anarcho-Syndicalism had considerable impact on certain segments of labor in the United States. Some splinter groups in New York and Philadelphia joined up with the International Working Peoples' Association which had been established by European anarchists. Generally these groups operating at the fringes of the struggling labor movement advocated "direct action" on plant or local level rather than the systematic and consistent pressure for improvement of working conditions that was the platform of trade unionism. These Syndicalists gained considerable influence in Chicago in 1884, eventually bringing about a general strike in which 80,000 workers participated. On May 4 of that year the "Haymarket Affair" erupted in which ten men were killed when a bomb had exploded at a mass meeting. As was to be expected, public opinion turned against the strike, and eight of its leaders were later indicted for having "incited to murder." Three of those convicted were executed in November 1887.

Toward the end of the 1880's the Knights of Labor lost a good deal of its membership and strength. The record of this first large-scale labor organization seemed to indicate that in this country the time for a mass union movement organized along industrial lines had not yet arrived. The "melting pot" had not yet operated long enough to enable a rather heterogeneous working population to support industrial unionism over longer periods of time and in the face of unstable economic conditions.

Some groups of skilled workers, organized on the craft-union principle, had remained outside the Knights of Labor. Among them were International Typographical Union, the Amalgamated Association of Iron and Steel Workers, and the Cigar Makers' International Union. In the late 1870's the desire grew strong among craft unions to establish a federation. A number of conventions, often with very small attendance, were held. Out of them there eventually emerged the American Federation of Labor (A. F. of L., later shortened to AFL). While the name of the new federation of craft unions appeared first at a convention in Columbus, Ohio, in 1886, the official date of birth has now been pushed back to a convention which was held on November 15, 1881, during which a "Federation of Organized Trades and Labor Unions" made its appearance.

Samuel Gompers, who as a very young man shortly after his arrival with his family from England had become interested in organizing cigar workers, became the first president of the AFL. The pattern of unionism which developed under his long leadership differed sharply from the more ambitious but short-lived organization of the Knights of Labor. The AFL adhered rigidly to the principle of craft unionism, making occupational affiliation and achievement rather than employment in a particular firm or industry a criterion of membership. If we consider the fact that in the formative years of the AFL only 10.5 percent of the labor force was classified as "craftsmen, foremen, and kindred workers," whereas 30.2 percent of the total labor force were laborers in industry and in agriculture and another 12.8 percent were operatives, it is apparent that the craft-union principle excluded a majority of production workers. However, this self-limitation proved to be beneficial for those workers who were sometimes called the "aristocracy of labor." A result of these policies was that membership in the AFL starting with about 200,000 in 1890 grew only slowly, reaching 1 million in 1903. World War I with its great demand on industrial production brought about a rapid rise in union membership. A peak was reached in 1920 with 4.2 million members. Thereafter a considerable decline set in which accelerated once the Great Depression, beginning in 1929, got under way. By 1932 the membership in the AFL was down to about 2 million out of 38.9 million employees.

The AFL in addition to emphasizing small but strong unions of craftsmen also pursued a policy of noninvolvement in party politics. Gompers thought that in this way labor would remain free to throw its support to candidates of either party according to the politician's record or promises in labor matters.

By the mid-1930's this pattern of the AFL as a federation of limited membership and politically neutral craft unions had prevailed for almost half a century. With the passage of labor-relations legislation encouraging collective bargaining, demands were voiced within the AFL to start organizing the hitherto neglected mass-production, semiskilled, and even unskilled laborers. A Committee for Industrial Organization (CIO) was set up to embark on large organizational drives in the steel, automobile, textile, and electrical industries, with a view of forming industrial unions. The leaders of this committee (especially John L. Lewis of the United Mine Workers, which originally operated within the framework of the AFL) soon developed policies and procedures that were disapproved by the more traditional labor leaders of the Federation. Eventually the CIO became the Congress of Industrial Organizations, breaking away from the parent organization and establishing itself as a rival national labor federation.

As a result of the organizational drive of the CIO, union membership in the United States rose very rapidly after 1935. By 1940 it had almost reached the 9 million mark. Whereas in 1910 only 5.9 percent of the labor force had been organized, by 1940 the figure rose to almost 17 percent. As in the earlier wartime period, union membership increased sharply in World War II. By 1945 national and international unions in the United States had about 15 million members exclusive of Canadian workers. In the period after World War II the rate of growth slowed down, and after 1955 there was a period of stagnation, followed by a small but steady decline in union membership.

The organizational drives in the 1930's originally met considerable resistance on the part of management. There was violence in Chicago on Memorial Day 1937 in connection with the attempt of the Republic Steel Company to remain unorganized. Sit-in strikes were organized in a number of facilities of the automobile industry. However, organized labor prevailed in spite of a divided public opinion on the legality of such weapons of organized labor. Even before World War II industrial unionism was firmly established in the key industries of the United States. Meanwhile the conflict between the AFL and CIO continued. The ostensible issue which separated the AFL from the CIO in those days—craft unionism versus industrial unionism—was merely the verbal dressing for deep-rooted clashes of personality of union leaders engaged in a struggle for control over large organizations. In the late 1960's new differences developed between the president of the AFL–CIO and Mr. Walter Reuther, the President of the UAW, one of the original CIO industrial unions representing the automobile workers. This time the differences dealt more directly with basic concepts of what American unions are and should do. Mr. Walter Reuther was an advocate of a more dynamic, open kind of unionism, allocating personal and financial resources of organized labor to reach out more forcefully to the unorganized and to include in unions large groups of low wage workers. Mr. George Meany, the President of the AFL–CIO, showed little sympathy for these efforts. These continuing differences in American unionism with regard to the nature and scope of union activities require further investigation.

3-2. LABOR UNIONS AS A MOVEMENT AND ORGANIZATION IN THE UNITED STATES

Seen in the larger context of Western industrialized society, American labor has had some distinguishing characteristics in the past. Unlike trade unions in Europe it was not affiliated on a national level with a political party. Endorsements of candidates for political office were strictly on a temporary basis. Only in recent Presidential elections has organized labor changed this posture and endorsed Presidential candidates. American unionism understood itself as "business unionism." It was and of course still is concerned with the struggle to improve wages and working conditions through processes of collective bargaining. Working within the framework of a free economic system, American unions did not develop a counter-ideology to the free-enterprise system but tried to secure a greater share of the joint product of capital and labor for its members. Although there is a "working class" in the United States, people identifying with it as blue-collar workers nevertheless have a middle-class standard of living and outlook. Furthermore, the large number of the poor in the United States have rarely been included in the ranks of organized labor. For many, getting a job in a unionized industry would be a tremendous improvement and might actually point the way toward a rise not only in economic but also in social status.

Organized labor never developed socialistic platforms demanding a basic change in the ownership of industrial and commercial capital. But this acceptance of the free-enterprise system merely strengthened labor's drive to influence the labor market in its favor. Actually American unions have made greater demands on management and have received greater concessions than were obtained by organized labor elsewhere. Politically conservative in the generic sense of the word, American labor has been radical so far as goals of collective bargaining are concerned.

It would, however, be a great mistake to conclude that the prevalence of business unionism in American and its spread abroad after World War II eliminate from organized labor all dynamic aspects. Labor leaders like to refer to organized labor as the "labor movement."

Actually the group dynamics of trade unions justify this appellation. There is, first of all, a very definite *"in-group" feeling* in trade unions, fostering loyalty to the organization and a definite separation from the unorganized. Secondly, there is a high measure of *intergroup solidarity* in organized labor. These attitudes explain the great discipline of organized labor in strike situations. It would be difficult today to bring about a "back-to-work movement" among rank-and-file members against the wishes of union leadership, as happened in the steel strike of 1919. Provisions of the Taft-Hartley Act of 1947—such as voting on the last proposal of management in national emergency situations, which might have opened possibilities of turning the membership against strike leaders—simply have not worked out in this way. Strong identification of union members with their union and the ethics of labor solidarity are powerful aspects of American unionism, which to a certain extent overcome the negative effects of its inability to increase or at least to maintain the rate of unionization.

The "in-group" feeling is also manifest in the often very long job tenure of top union officials. Although organized labor in the United States has always been operating within the framework of business unionism, it has never adopted one practice characteristic of American business: the relatively rapid turnover of personnel in top management. Compulsory retirement usually at age 65 is standard for most large American corporations. It is rigidly enforced regardless of the accomplishments and the state of physical and mental health of the official. Presidents of corporations and other top officials do not even try to hold on to their jobs when the time for retirement comes. There is no compulsory retirement age for union officials in American labor in sharp contrast, for instance, to the German Federation of Labor where there is a non-negotiable retirement age of 65 for all top leaders. As a carry over of the period of struggle of unions in this country which now seems to lie very much in the past, many top union leaders give evidence of having as it were a proprietary attitude towards their jobs, they seem to feel that they own it and are somewhat entitled to it. As a result there is a tendency to consider opposition candidates pre-

senting themselves for top offices at conventions as rebels rather than con-
testants in a democratic process. Nevertheless, in the 1960's, opposition
candidates were able to unseat seemingly entrenched union leaders, for
instance, in the steel workers union and in the CIO electrical workers
union.

The group solidarity is particularly strong in the old established type of
craft unionism. Until recently, in a typical union in the building trades, new
members could be nominated only by an old member. In a particular instance of a craft union commanding very high hourly wages, a full-fledged
member holding a "union book" rather than a mere "permit" issued by the
union had exactly one opportunity during the entire span of his own membership to exercise his right of nominating a new member, for instance his
son. If he did not want to use it, he forfeited this chance for good. A nom-
inee would be placed on a waiting list. In due time he would be called to start
a formal apprenticeship. Eventually he would obtain a book in his own
right. Holders of books had priority in allocation of jobs but at all times
they were outnumbered by fellow-workers of the same trade who merely had
obtained work permits. It is obvious that this "father-and-son" type of
unionism had very great cohesion, and that it made it extremely hard for
outsiders to be accepted into the organization.

As we have seen, industrial unionism tries to incorporate workers in an
industry regardless of differences in skill and specialization. Entry into these
unions, in most cases initially with a temporary status, is much easier. This
type of unionism promoted in the 1930's by the Congress of Industrial Organizations experienced a rapid expansion during its organization drives in
the steel, automobile, and electrical industries. Nevertheless, in the merged
AFL-CIO, craft unions have a higher combined membership than industrial
unions.

The different structure of unions—craft unions and industrial unions—
is by no means merely an internal matter of organized labor in the United
States. The whole procedure of collective bargaining varies according to the
type of unionism involved in negotiations. Where industrial unionism prevails, negotiations take place between management and one union—either a
local, a district, or, in industry-wide bargaining, the national union itself.
Whenever craft unionism is dominant, management has to come to terms
with all the trades needed in its projects and operations. Failure to agree
even with one craft union frustrates the successful negotiations already concluded with other unions. Labor solidarity, however, prevents a start of
work until such time as the signature on the last contract has been affixed.

So far we have discussed some aspects of unionism which generate a high
degree of inner cohesion and solidarity within the ranks of organized labor.
Sometimes this is reflected in a certain "personality cult" of union leaders
who are, in many cases, more firmly entrenched than their opposite numbers

in business corporations. Although the selection of union officials is to a much larger extent based on democratic rank-and-file participation than it was originally, many unions present a closely knit image which seems to discourage changes in structure and in leadership. But let us turn now from the consideration of the internal aspects of unions to their impact on society at large.

We have stressed that union officials like to refer to the activities of their organizations as the "labor movement." Obviously in the United States where a labor party has never operated on a national level there is a tendency to equate a labor movement with organized labor. This identification is further enhanced by the legal definition of unions as "self-organizations of labor." They are the product of the unsupported effort of workers to combine and their struggle for recognition in collective bargaining and social status and are the exclusive agents in collective bargaining.

In the long decades prior to the enactment of labor-relations legislation in the 1930's, a large number of writers, social scientists, and political leaders fought for the recognition of the right of labor to organize effectively and for the creation of a legal setting that would enable organized labor to meet on something like equal terms with management. Many of these friends of the cause of labor were not part of organized labor yet helped prepare public opinion for its acceptance. Today the position of organized labor as a member of the establishment of well-organized interest groups is no longer seriously challenged. Attempts to turn back the clock of history through such proposals as the repeal of the section of the Clayton Act exempting unions from the antitrust laws have failed and are not likely to be revived.

While labor has achieved establishment status, it has remained rather stagnant so far as membership is concerned. In 1965 the industrial-union department of the AFL-CIO announced a renewed campaign to organize the "working poor," that is, those workers earning less than $3,000 a year, especially farm, laundry, hospital, hotel, restaurant, and service employees. They also pledged renewed efforts to organize the very reluctant white-collar workers.

Very little came out of these efforts. In the spring of 1969 after the United Automobile Workers—UAW had disaffiliated itself from the AFL–CIO a drive was undertaken together with the equally disaffiliated Brotherhood of Teamsters to activate organizational efforts to bring unskilled and lower paid workers as well as office workers into the ranks of unionism. In order to give structure to this new drive to organize the unorganized an *Alliance for Labor Action* was inaugurated. However it was stressed that this new group established by the two largest industrial unions in the United States which at that time had disaffiliated themselves from the AFL–CIO did not plan to set up a rival labor organization but tried to concern itself especially with such urban problems as "poverty, inferior education, unemployment and underemployment, overcrowding, sub-standard housing, inadequate health services, pollution and a rising crime rate."

In voicing concern about these problems the new alliance went beyond the limits which organized labor had set for itself traditionally. The more conventional view of the goals and objectives had been restated some years earlier by Mr. George Meany, President of the AFL–CIO, when he addressed the 50th Anniversary World Convocation of the National Industrial Conference Board under the title: "Labor Looks at Capitalism." To sum up the gist of that address one can say that Mr. Meany looked at capitalism and found it good. He praised the fact that the trade union movement helped to put workmen's compensation laws on the statute books of every state. There was no hint that the administration of such laws leaves much to be desired as was shown shortly thereafter in West Virginia. Mr. Meany fully endorsed the Civil Rights Act of 1964 and Voting Rights Act of 1965. However, he did not indicate the need to educate especially members of craft unions and foremen in the application of principles of fairness to minority groups. Mr. Meany also talked about Federal minimum wage legislation. He stated "my union (the plumbers) doesn't need this law," but he endorsed raising the minimum wages for "millions of people who are not members of unions, who need the protection of the minimum wage and an increase in the minimum wage. They have no other spokesman." Again there was no indication of any action other than endorsing legislation contemplated by the leadership of the AFL–CIO.

The basic attitude underlying policy concepts such as indicated in the address of Mr. George Meany quoted above affords an insight into the difficult problem of widening the base of unionism in the United States and extending its activities for the organization of the unorganized. Such an objective is particularly difficult to reach in the farm sector of the economy which even in the late 1960's was exempted from the provisions of the National Labor Relations Act. The difficulties resulting from that exclusion will be demonstrated now.

In recent years the attempt of farm workers in California, Florida, Texas and flower workers in Colorado to organize and to sign collective labor agreements with employers, especially grape growers, has drawn nationwide attention. Underlying these attempts is a basic fact that the National Relations Act does not apply to farm workers. As a result employers cannot be compelled to bargain collectively with representatives of farm workers although, of course, they can voluntarily negotiate with them and sign collective labor contracts. In the 1960's under the leadership of a Mexican-American, Cesar Chavez, a United Farm Workers Organizing Committee has been operating. Its main objective was to come to collective negotiations with grape growers. So far they have not succeeded and they are unlikely to do so as long as it remains certain that no farm workers will be taken into the coverage of the Taft-Hartley Act. Although at the insistence of the U.S. Department of Labor the number of "wet backs" or Mexican migratory farm workers coming to California illegally to do "stoop labor" on giant vegetable and fruit farms without a permit has been reduced drastically, farm operators still are using Mexican workers with a green card to do this work. The "green carders" are issued this paper at the border on their assertion that they have a job in the United States.

Lack of legal protection of the right to bargain collectively in the agricultural sector and the continuing competition of legal and illegal foreign labor are creating powerful obstacles for the attempts of Mr. Chavez to extend organized labor to the low wage workers in agriculture.

Actually the situation of the United Farm Workers Organizing Committee in the late 1960's is not unlike the condition in which labor in general found itself in the early decades of this century especially in mass production industries. While they had a right to organize, employers were under no obligation to negotiate with them and sign collective labor agreements. Furthermore, up to the period after World War I, there was large scale immigration of workers from Europe who were often forced to take low wage jobs in the many "sweat shops" of that era. As in that earlier phase of industrial relations in the United States, these difficulties have not prevented the farm workers organizing committee from making some headway in signing collective agreements. Contracts have been completed with some big processors especially with wineries, but not with fruit and vegetable growers.

Naturally spokesmen of employers especially of grape growers have denounced the organizing committee of Mr. Chavez, calling it even "a socialist civil rights movement." It was alleged that the organization was aided by "dogooder elements, beatnicks and socialist type groups." Actually the attempt to organize farm labor did find support outside organized labor including some members of the clergy and a grape boycott was widely publicized and had some impact.

The main support for the organizing drive has come from the AFL-CIO. The funds come in part from the Industrial Union Department, in part from the United Automobile Workers. But even in dealing with these problems top leaders of the AFL–CIO especially Mr. Meany and Mr. Reuther represented differences in philosophies of labor organization which contributed to the disaffiliation of the UAW from the AFL-CIO in 1968. Mr. Reuther demanded that the AFL-CIO should commit itself to a budget of about $5 million a year to assist farm workers to organize effectively; Mr. Meany felt that this would be excessive in view of the fact that farm workers did not enjoy the protection of their right to organize that nonfarm workers had had since the 1930's. On the other hand the AFL-CIO did not engage on an all-out drive to have labor legislation amended and extended to farm workers. This is in sharp contrast to the considerable effort which was made by the AFL–CIO to have Section 14–B of the Taft-Hartley Act repealed which gave states the right to ban union shop clauses. This attempt was not successful but this is no excuse for the general failure of the AFL–CIO to assume leadership in drives to improve legislation in favor of the underprivileged.

3-3. STRUCTURE AND MEMBERSHIP OF ORGANIZED LABOR IN THE UNITED STATES

Due to the self-imposed restriction to craft unionism, membership in the AFL, after a brief upsurge in World War I, remained low, until 1935. The drive for industrial unionism starting in that year increased total membership from 4 to 9 million in the short span of five years. It is important to keep in mind that these were years of high unemployment levels which are generally not considered as conducive to organizational drives. However, it was at that time that labor-relations legislation removed some of the obstacles to unionization—such as discrimination because of union membership, black-listing of unionists, yellow-dog contracts, and labor injunctions against union activities. When employment expanded rapidly after the outbreak of World War II, membership in unions climbed to 14 million in 1945. After that, membership continued to grow for some time but at a noticeably reduced rate. In the early 1960's union membership was above 17 million, a figure which also includes about one million members of unions in Canada. Table 3-1 gives a breakdown of union membership.

In Chapter 2 it was shown that since World War II a realignment within the labor force has taken place, with the result that white-collar workers gained numerical ascendency over blue-collar workers. If we bear this in mind while examining Table 3-1, the failure of organized labor to secure additional members in the rapidly expanding labor market sectors of trade, finance, and insurance, and the service industries becomes very striking.

Table 3–1 covers only membership in United States unions. Many unions however are "International" because they also have locals and districts in Canada. Between 1947 and 1953 the number of union members increased from 14.5 million to 17.1 million. In the early 1960's there was a substantial drop in membership as the United States economy went through the 1958–1961 depression and its aftermath. The membership figures given for 1966 indicate a recovery; actually they represent a peak in union enrollment. But this increase was far less than the growth of the employed labor force. As a result union membership as a proportion of the nonfarm labor force dropped from 34.0 percent in 1953 to 27.4 percent in 1966. While membership in the traditional unions has increased only slightly, public employees unions have grown considerably. Their status in 1968 is shown in Table 3-2.

TABLE 3-1
UNION MEMBERSHIP BY INDUSTRY, UNITED STATES, 1966
IN THOUSANDS

Industry	Actual Membership
All members	17,538
Goods sector.	13,433
Manufacturing.	7,794
Food, beverage, and tobacco	994
Clothing, textiles, and leather.	1,095
Furniture, lumber, wood, and paper	761
Printing and publishing	327
Petroleum, chemicals, and rubber.	522
Stone, clay, and glass	271
Metals, machinery, and equipment	2,635
Transportation equipment	1,189
Mining	297
Transportation, communication, and utilities	3,084
Construction	2,258
Service Sector	3,791
Wholesale and retail trade	1,242
Finance, insurance, and real estate	57
Services	918
Government.	1,574
Members, not classified elsewhere	314

SOURCE: *Monthly Labor Review*, September 1969, Table 1, Page 4.

TABLE 3-2
MEMBERSHIP IN PUBLIC EMPLOYEE UNIONS, 1968

Union	Membership
Special Delivery Messengers	2,073
National Alliance of Postal and Federal Employees	27,000
Post Office and General Service Maintenance	9,237
Post Office Motor Vehicle Employees	8,148
American Federation of Government Employees	199,823
National Federation of Federal Employees	80,000
ASCS County Office Employees	14,300
Rural Letter Carriers.	40,340
National Association of Government Employees	—
United Federation of Postal Clerks	143,146
National Postal Union	70,000
International Association of Fire Fighters.	115,000
Letter Carriers (AFL-CIO)	189,628
American Federation of Teachers.	125,000
National Education Association	1,081,660
American Federation of State, County and Municipal Employees . .	281,277
Postal Supervisors	31,700
Postmaster's League	18,000
Postmaster's Association	32,717
Post Office Mail Handlers	32,800

SOURCE: *Monthly Labor Review*, March 1969.

With the rapid rise of public employment, especially on the state and local levels, the unions of public employees assume increasing significance. The increase in membership in these labor organizations has contributed to stopping the overall decline of the ranks of organized labor. In recent years public employees have been granted in many states the right to bargain collectively and this has given a strong impetus to their organizational drives. However, public employees are not entitled to go on strike. Despite this clear legal prohibition, postal workers called a strike in March, 1970, in a number of areas. A "sick-in" of Air Traffic Controllers happening at the same time was carried out also in violation of the ban on strikes of employees of public authorities. In Chapter 17 of this book the new issues which have arisen in industrial relations in the public sector will be discussed in greater detail.

One reason for the failure of organized labor to maintain its share in the labor force is the structural transformation of the labor force and the shift from blue-collar to white-collar employment. In 1956, 12.8 percent of white-collar workers were members of unions. In the ten years between 1956 and 1966 the number of white-collar members of organized labor rose only by 276,000. In view of the very rapid increase of white-collar employment, this small rise in white-collar union membership meant that in 1966 only 10.5 percent of the white-collar workers were organized. The details of this significant development can be seen in Table 3-3.

TABLE 3-3
WHITE-COLLAR UNION MEMBERSHIP IN THE UNITED STATES
AS PROPORTION OF TOTAL UNION MEMBERSHIP AND WHITE-
COLLAR EMPLOYMENT, 1956–1966

Year	Union Membership (thousands)		White-Collar Union Membership as Percent of	
	Total	White-Collar	Total Union Membership	White-Collar Employment
1956	17,980	2,417	13.4	12.8
1958	17,506	2,143	12.2	10.7
1960	17,526	2,150	12.3	10.3
1963	17,050	2,242	13.1	10.1
1964	17,312	2,536	14.6	10.8
1966	18,391	2,693	14.6	10.5

SOURCE: Monthly Labor Review, January 1969.

As a result of the slow increase of union membership and the much faster rise of wage and salary workers the rate of unionization dropped from 30 percent in 1962 to 27.4 percent in 1966. In 1956 union membership as a percent of the total nonagricultural employees still had been 33.12 percent. It had been 24.8 percent of the total labor force. It is clear then that by 1966 the unionization rate had reached a low in the post-war period.

Since then there has been a very active unionization drive among public employees. Its effect will be to offset to some extent the declining share of organized labor in the private sector. However, in the public sector unions do not have the foremost right they claim in their dealings with private management: the right to strike. This has created new problems of labor relations in the public sector which will be taken up in Chapter 17 of this text.

The AFL–CIO had over 14 million members in 1966. This included at the time the 1.4 million members of the automobile workers. From the very beginning of its existence the AFL had been an organization of organizations. This federation of labor unions stressed the autonomy of its member organizations. Prior to the 1950's this even led to a hands-off policy of the federation with regard to such internal problems of organized labor as were created by the infiltration of underworld or radical political elements. Later this posture was changed and occasionally a union which was afflicted with this type of trouble was expelled from the AFL–CIO. At least in one instance, in the case of the International Longshoremen's Association in the 1950's, an attempt was being made to set up a rival union. This failed and later on the ILA was readmitted.

The AFL–CIO has an *Executive Council* in which the Presidents of the larger unions are sitting as members. In the 1960's there were 30 members of this top leadership group of the AFL–CIO. At the same time the Federation maintained 15 staff departments, most of them of an administrative nature such as accounting, investments, legal affairs, legislation, purchasing and supplies and public relations. However, there are also departments dealing with civil rights, community services, education, international affairs, political education, research and social security.

In 1966 there were 129 autonomous national and international unions affiliated with the AFL–CIO. Altogether there were about 60,000 local unions which were combined in these 129 labor organizations.

While typically labor organizations are structured *vertically*, that is to say from the local up to the national or international unions and further up to the Federation, there are also on the local or state level certain *horizontal* links. For instance there is a Labor Council for New York State which has considerable influence in labor and in political affairs. During the walk-out of the sanitation workers in New York City in 1968 this Council threatened to call a general strike if the governor would accede to the request of the mayor to use the National Guard for garbage removal. The governor rather than doing that injected himself into the dispute and assisted in reaching a settlement. In 1969 the Council came out in favor of one of the many candidates in the Democratic primary for the mayoralty election thereby yielding another example for the recent trend in organized labor to depart from its traditional neutrality in elections by endorsing particular candidates.

Despite the fact that total union membership has reached an all time high in the 1960's we have noted already that the rate of unionization has dropped. Since agricultural workers do not enjoy the protection of their rights to organize and to bargain collectively that the nonagricultural workers have obtained in the National Labor Relations Act of 1935 union membership must be measured against the total number of employees in nonagricultural establishments. Table 3-4 will show the post-war development of unionization as a percentage of the nonfarm civilian labor force and of nonfarm employment.

TABLE 3-4
RATE OF UNIONIZATION, 1947–1966

Year	Number of Members	As a Percent of the Civilian Labor Force	As a Percent of Non-Farm Employment
1947	14,526,400	24.5	33.1
1953	17,059,700	27.1	34.0
1963	16,193,900	22.5	28.6
1966	17,538,500	23.1	27.4

SOURCE: *Monthly Labor Review* (September 1969), p. 6.

In order to appraise the full significance of the trend indicated in Table 3-4 it is necessary to consider the rapid increase in the number of wage and salary workers. In 1947 they totaled 43.9 million. In 1966 their numbers had risen to 64 million nonagricultural employees.[1] That is to say that employees increased by about 20 million in the period under study here. However union membership as we can see from Table 3-4 increased only about 3 million in the same period.

Now it would be a great mistake to conclude from this declining rate of unionization that the influence of organized labor and especially the impact of collective bargaining on the nonorganized labor market has declined proportionately with lower unionization rates in the period after World War II. A study of modern highly organized and industrialized society shows that the influence of pressure groups on legislation and on the various sectors of the economy is not necessarily dependent on the number of members. For many years the number of people engaged in agriculture has been decreasing sharply. But at least up to the late 1960's this has made no difference in the ability of farm organizations to influence farm legislation and agricultural administration in the United States. The ability of organized labor to maintain and even enhance its position within the complex social structure of this country while its share in the nonagricultural labor force was declining significantly may also explain why labor leaders often give the appearance of being concerned more with organization maintenance rather than with all-out efforts to increase the

[1]Table B–27, Economic Report of the President, 1969.

rate of unionization. Another reason for this development is the structural transformation of the labor force and the emergence of a white-collar economy.

In view of the fact, already discussed in the preceding chapter, that blue-collar workers have become a minority in the labor force, it is important to explore some of the reasons why more than 85 percent of white-collar workers are either indifferent to unionization or are resisting it actively. Certainly these attitudes are not brought about by generally higher earnings of office workers below the executive level of business. Employees in insurance companies or in banks have substantially lower average weekly earnings than workers in the automotive industry or in machinery production. The aloofness of these employees from unionism cannot be explained by their superior material status. The reluctance of white-collar workers to join unions is based on the identification of many among them with management. These employees feel that joining a union is tantamount to forfeiting forever any chance of being raised to the level of management. This attitude persists even though discrimination because of union membership is an unfair labor practice and the right to organize is safeguarded by labor-relations legislation. That noneconomic considerations account for the resistance of white-collar workers to unionization is brought out further by some outstanding exceptions to this behavior. Airplane pilots do not strictly fall in the white-collar category and their earnings are well within the executive range of income. Nevertheless they are organized in a union.

The difficulty encountered in increasing the rate of unionization among office workers and employees of banks and insurance companies is also related to the growing significance of differentials in educational attainments on the labor market, as demonstrated in the preceding chapter. High school graduation, in many occupations now a key to entrance into the job market, seems to be compatible with union membership. There is, however, a widespread feeling that graduation from college lifts a person to a status in which collective action to improve conditions of pay and advancement is not required. This opinion seems to have a certain foundation in the hiring and promotional practices of private enterprise and public agencies.

As is well known a great deal of recruiting is carried out by private corporations on college campuses. Academic performance and the impression of a job candidate projected during an employment interview are among the most important elements in obtaining employment as trainees or in other forms in the private and public sector.

It is true that especially craft unions also offer prospective members the opportunity to present themselves for qualifying examinations. In fact this practice has spread in recent years in order to open up such unions for workers from minority groups desiring to join their ranks. However tests have also become of paramount importance for graduates of systems of

not want to end up in a state of "high-level stagnation." On the other hand to demand ever-increasing benefits merely because a new contract has to be negotiated can deteriorate into a reflex action type of behavior of unions which may retard rather than increase an overall growth in employment of the labor force as a whole.

Here a new test emerges for the "business unionism" approach of organized labor—does the great strength that organized labor has obtained not point to a widening of the framework of reference within which goals of collective bargaining are being formulated? Macroeconomic considerations ought to enter on the management as well as on the labor end of collective bargaining. The discussions in subsequent parts of this book will try to explore the underlying issues in greater detail.

3-5. ORGANIZED LABOR AND MINORITY GROUPS

The industrial revolution of the 19th century set in motion a large scale migration of labor generally in an east-west direction. Agricultural laborers, especially from Poland, moved to northwestern Europe where they found employment in the German, Belgian and French coal mining industry. A much larger migration took place across the Atlantic Ocean to the United States where throughout the 19th century the rapid build-up of railroads and industry depended on an ample labor supply which in part had to come from abroad. The gathering of these immigrants into effective labor organizations created in many cases unions in which one particular nationality predominated, at least at the beginning. Unions in the garment industry originally comprising a high proportion of Jewish workers coming from Eastern Europe retained for a considerable period a certain continental flavor by adopting European union practices such as providing adult education and at an early date, voluntary health insurance schemes. Eventually the nationality composition of these unions changed as more Italians sought employment in the garment industry. Other unions in construction had locals that were predominantly Irish, Italian, or German as the case might be. On the New York waterfront, locals of the International longshoremen Association have retained for a long time locals which were either strongly Irish as on the west side docks in Manhattan or strongly Italian as in Brooklyn. It is perhaps significant to stress in this connection that the founder of the AFL himself, Samuel Gompers, was not a native of this country but was born in England. Philip Murray, the second president of the CIO, was born in Scotland. While nationality differentiations were and to a certain extent are noticeable throughout the structure of organized labor in the United States it never carried the implication with it that immigrants as such and most certainly their children were excluded from joining unions in their field of work. However, this relative openness of unions did not apply to a considerable segment of native American labor, the Negroes.

Even in the 1930's there were a number of labor unions which had written racial restrictions into their constitutions. In 1955 when the AFL-CIO had been reunited into one large national labor organization they committed themselves to "rapid elimination of racial discrimination and segregation within unions." In the subsequent years this policy was implemented by all member unions. The Brotherhood of Locomotive Firemen was the last one to eliminate a restrictive provision from its constitution in 1963.

Even when a number of unions maintained an official policy of racial discrimination against Negroes and others engaged in policies which had de facto the same effect, there were in some areas unions which had segregated locals for blacks. This was the case, for instance, with the International Association of Machinists. Similar conditions prevailed in the old Hod Carriers Union. Segregated locals for blacks were found primarily in the South where in a number of localities this arrangement was underlined by local laws of the time prohibiting interracial meetings of all kinds.

With the growth of the automobile industry in the 1920's Negroes began to migrate to rapidly developing industrial areas on the Great Lakes. But this was at a time when labor organizations in the mass production industries were weak and the overwhelming majority of workers in the automobile and steel industries were unorganized. As a result the problem of union discrimination against black workers did not arise immediately as the percentage of nonwhite production workers began to rise gradually.

Greater difficulties have arisen in the field of craft unionism. In Sec. 3-2 we have already given an example of a closely knit union in the construction field where an "elite" of members are holding union books whereas the rest were issued "permits," which did not carry the important right of nominating one new member. In craft unions, especially in printing and in the building trades, *apprenticeship* served often a two-fold purpose. First it was designed to train new workers in all the skills of the trade. Secondly, it was used as a device to keep the supply of highly trained workers relatively scarce by restricting for any given period of time the number of apprentices. These long established practices were not motivated by racial discrimination because originally the question of the employment of nonwhites in these craft unions did not present itself with great urgency. But the restricted policies of craft unions limited the employment of many whites who would have liked to work in the occupations dominated by such unions. The result of these practices gained public attention in the 1960's in connection with the enactment of Civil Rights Laws. While those laws emphasized and began to enforce equality of employment opportunities regardless of race or national origin the extremely low participation of blacks in apprenticeship programs showed the wide gap between legal intent and social reality in this important field of labor organization. Until 1964 the

Plumbers Local from which Mr. George Meany, the President of the AFL-CIO sprang, was 100 percent white. The same was true for iron workers' locals in New York City. In California and in New York participation of blacks in apprenticeship programs was 1.9 percent and 2.0 percent respectively. On the other hand, the AFL Electricians Local 3 in Manhattan initiated a new apprenticeship program providing training opportunities for non whites amounting to 20 percent of the 1,000 apprentices.

In 1969 open conflicts broke out between overwhelmingly white construction unions in Pittsburgh and Chicago and black workers who began to picket construction projects where they were unable to find employment. Both groups engaged in demonstrations and counter demonstrations. Mr. George Meany denounced the proposal of spokesmen for black workers to admit a number of nonwhite apprentices corresponding to their share in the labor force because this would "water down" the value of the training procedure. In the same year the Federal Government used its leverage on public construction projects to have the construction industry and organized labor agree on a far greater employment of nonwhite workers in Federally financed building programs.

This policy became known as the "Philadelphia Plan." In 1970 a New York Plan was announced by the Building Trades Council providing in the first year of its operation training opportunities for eight hundred minority members of these unions. The complexity of the problems arising from these attempts to include nonwhites in apprenticeship programs of craft unions can be seen from the fact that this New York Plan was denounced by the local unit of the National Association for the Advancement of Colored People (N.A.A.C.P.) as a "hoax." It was alleged that under this plan skilled Negro craftsmen who were fully qualified but had been kept out of unions would be put into this apprenticeship program and would be earning only $80.00 a week. Without making a judgment on the merits either of the New York Plan or on the criticism of it, this controversy shows that it is very difficult to bring long established organizations to the point where they will make operational changes.

With rising educational standards or at least credentials of the greater part of the American labor force a continuation of de facto discrimination through restrictive devices in apprenticeship programs or in membership recruitment of union locals would be inconsistent with the necessity to maintain in the United States a labor force in which employment opportunities and advancement are not impeded by noneconomic factors such as racial discrimination.

3-6. REGULATORY LEGISLATION FOR UNIONS

In the free economic system of the United States there always seems to come a time when, after a rapid growth of economic bodies, restraining regulations are enacted. The Sherman Act of 1890 was designed to prevent the operation and the formation of trusts and monopolies and to preserve a high measure of competition among producers themselves. Business is under continuous control by the very fact that income-tax returns are examined scrupulously. There are elaborate rules with regard to allowable business and entertainment expenditures, annual write-offs, and other important aspects of business conduct.

As we have seen, the rise of organized labor was quite slow in this country until the mid-1930's. Labor, free to organize, selected a loose juridical form which did not subject it to the need of incorporation. This informal setup continued even after the great expansion in union membership which continued throughout the period of World War II. Actually the inner workings of unions differed considerably, the new CIO unions giving more evidence of union democracy especially in the election of national officers. Older unions in some instances held conventions only infrequently and in some cases had a system of co-option of new governors without the formality of elections. In other instances, elections were sometimes held under conditions which effectively discouraged possible dissenters or opponents. When large amounts of money began to flow into welfare funds, cases of financial mismanagement were not infrequent.

A good deal of these less than perfect conditions can be attributed to "growing pains." They are most certainly not inherent in the nature of a labor organization as such. More serious were cases of collusion between union officials and employers, leading to so called "sweetheart contracts" or agreements whereby not all of the contractual wage schedules had to be observed in the actual compensation of employees. Sometimes such deals were made at the expense of inexperienced workers, especially recent immigrants with little or no knowledge of English. While all these abuses were limited to a small fraction of organized labor and did not justify generalized accusations against trade unions, a majority of Congress decided that some regulatory legislation was indicated. This led to the Labor-Management Reporting and Disclosure Act of 1959, also known as the Landrum-Griffin Act.

The Landrum-Griffin Act tries to strengthen internal union democracy. Secret ballots are mandatory for the election of all union officers. Leaders of national and international labor unions must be elected every five years. Officers of subdivisions such as joint boards or councils must be elected for four-year terms. Local union offices must present themselves in elections every three years. Safeguards have also been established for unfettered election campaigns. Union funds cannot be used exclusively for the "administration condidate." There must be a sharing among candidates on an equal basis.

The Act has tried to emphasize the need for internal union democracy by a "Bill of Rights of Members of Labor Organizations." Equal rights of every member of a labor organization with regard to nominating candidates, voting in election or referendum, and attending membership meetings are guaranteed. The same is true of freedom of speech and assembly of union members. Dues and initiation fees of local labor organizations can be changed only by a secret ballot. So far as national or international labor organizations are concerned, changes in union fees and assessments must be submitted to regular conventions, or, if the case is urgent, to a special convention.

Unions retain the right to fine, suspend, or expel members. In case of nonpayment of dues no particular safeguards against improper or excessive disciplinary actions have been established. However, in all other cases written specific charges must be handed to the union member accused of violations. A reasonable time must be given him to prepare his defense, and a fair trial must be held.

This regulatory legislation obligates labor unions to make extensive reports to the Secretary of Labor. This does not mean only the filing of the constitution and other basic documents—for instance, the scale of initiation fees or fees for work permits—but also the submission every year of detailed financial reports. Not only are these financial statements to be reported to the Federal government, but copies must be given to each member of the union, and union members have the right to examine the books and records of their union. Union officers also have to file detailed reports of their financial status and transactions. This applies to reimbursement of expenses, loans extended by the union to officers and employees, and direct and indirect loans to business enterprises. Payments to wives and children of union officials from any employer also have to be reported. The main purpose of this provision, as of others to be discussed presently, is to prevent any collusion between labor and management.

The law also imposes duties on employers. They must report on payments or loans to a labor organization or such persons as agents and shop stewards. The purpose of these reports is, of course, the prevention of the payments and activities about which notice would have to be given to the Secretary of Labor.

In order to protect the rights of union members with regard to welfare and other funds set up by the union, the Landrum-Griffin Act requires all union officers occupying such positions of trust to be bonded. Embezzlement of such funds is a Federal crime punishable by a fine of $10,000 or five years in prison, or both.

Early in 1970 the Landrum-Griffin Act of 1959 was put to a severe test. In 1969 the United Mine Workers of America held an election for President of their organization. An opposition candidate Joseph A. Yablonski ran a vigorous campaign against the incumbent W. A. Boyle. The latter was re-elected by a decisive majority. Shortly thereafter Yablonski, his wife, and his daughter were slain in their home in Clarksville, Pa. The charges and countercharges resulting from that election led to an investigation by the U. S. Department of Labor of whether provisions of the Landrum-Griffin Act had been violated. The union cooperated in this procedure which led to an eight-count charge against the union. These charges will be summarized here only to illustrate the provisions of the Landrum-Griffin Act without prejudging the outcome of the proceedings against the union. The Department of Labor alleged that the union failed to provide adequate safeguards for a fair election; denied candidates the right to post observers at polling places; it failed to conduct elections in accordance with its own constitution; failed to elect its officers by secret ballot; denied members the right to vote for the candidate of their choice without being subject to reprisals; failed to hold elections in certain locals; used union dues to promote the candidacy of incumbent officers. Finally, the union was also charged with having failed to maintain records of financial expenditures such as required by the law.

It is easy to see why the Landrum-Griffin Act of 1959, like the Taft-Hartley Act of 1947, met with a good measure of criticism and resentment by organized labor. After all, business does not hold a monopoly on complaints about "government interference" and "excessive reporting." There is no doubt, however, that whatever restraints have been imposed on labor are no bar to the dynamic efforts aimed at increasing the scope of organized labor and its influence. Obstacles that have arisen on the road toward such dynamic development actually lie outside the area in which legislation is effective.

SELECTED BIBLIOGRAPHY

Broehl, Wayne G., Jr. *The Molly Maguires* (Cambridge, Mass.: Harvard University Press, 1964).
David, H. *The History of the Haymarket Affair* (New York: Farrar & Rinehart, Inc., 1936).
Estey, Marten S., Philip Taft, Martin Wagner (eds.). *Regulating Union Government* (New York: Harper & Row, Publishers, 1964).
Evans, Robert, Jr. *Public Policy Toward Labor* (New York: Harper & Row, Publishers 1965).
Lindsay, A. *The Pullman Strike* (Chicago, Ill.: University of Chicago Press, 1942).
Rayback, Joseph G. A History of American Labor (New York: The Macmillan Company, 1959).
Sultan, Raul E. *The Disenchanted Unionist* (New York: Harper & Row, Publishers, 1963).
Taft, P. *Organized Labor in American History* (New York: Harper & Row, Publishers, 1963).
Troy, L. *Trade Union Membership, 1897–1962.* Occasional Paper No. 92 (New York: National Bureau of Economic Research, 1965).
Ware, Norman J. *The Labor Movement in the United States 1860–1895* (New York: Random House, Inc., 1965).

Widick, B. F. *Labor Today: The Triumphs and Failures of Unionism in the United States* (Boston: Houghton, Mifflin Company, 1964).

QUESTIONS FOR DISCUSSION

1. What is the "labor movement," and how does this "movement" in the United States differ from similar events in the industrialized nations of Western Europe?

2. Define and distinguish between trade or craft unions and industry unions.

3. Account for the relative decline in union membership in the United States since 1956.

4. A number of factors seem to preclude any significant gains in union membership in the white-collar sector of the labor force. Cite these factors, and indicate their significance in terms of the future growth of unions in the United States.

5. Does the fact that union membership declined in recent years indicate that unions are now less effective?

6. Discuss recent problems of the inclusion of workers from minority groups into the ranks of organized labor.

7. Wage leadership, like price leadership, is said to be a "real" force in our economic environment. With respect to organized and unorganized labor, how does this institution manifest itself?

Concepts and Standards of Economic Well-Being

The conditions of compensation and of employment established in collective bargaining reflect the ever-changing concepts and standards of what constitutes the economic well-being of wage and salary workers. It was stressed in previous chapters that in an advanced industrial society characterized by production for mass consumption a current plateau of living standards is usually considered a stepping-stone for the next higher one. While this situation has generated a great deal of restlessness, the expectation of continuous improvement is consistent with the ever-rising production potential of the American economy.

Members of unions and a vast majority of the unorganized expect to obtain from employment more than high money wages. The drive for a shortening of the work week and for longer vacations adds to the demand for higher wages so that more discretionary income will be available for hobbies and other leisure-time activities. There is also an increasing concern among wage and salary earners about expenditures for a vastly stepped-up educational program for their children. Because these social and psychological structures underlie the dynamics of collective bargaining and of the wage structure in general, we must gain some insight into them before addressing ourselves to the more economic and institutional aspects of labor economics.

4-1. THE SOCIAL AND PSYCHOLOGICAL MEANING OF LIVING STANDARDS

Advanced modern society is progressively developing standards of living that are far above mere biological survival and subsistence levels. The fact that even in such an economic structure sizable pockets of poverty remain and that there are substantial numbers and groups of people who seem tied to extremely low levels of subsistence is no longer viewed as inevitable but is accepted as a challenge to concerted social action. The "War

Against Poverty," embodied in the Economic Opportunity Act of 1964, is evidence of the growing emphasis on the elimination of vast pockets of poverty which have become inconsistent with the progressive potential of the advanced industrial society of the United States.

The standard of living of a person or a family is an important element in his self-esteem, his social classification or status. The ownership and the use of material goods and of services has a double meaning. In the first place, it satisfies the "vital" requirements at a given time. Secondly, the way these needs are met in terms of housing, clothing, durable goods (including cars) and the level of schooling of children demonstrates the economic plateau that the family has reached, and very often indicates whether even higher levels are being approached. This second aspect of a standard of living becomes more important as the degree of vertical social mobility increases. For this reason living standards have a particularly profound significance in the United States, where it is easier than in more traditional societies to change social status through economic achievement. The wider the range of possibilities to rise within the economic structure, the greater the challenge to the individual to avail himself of these opportunities and to prove himself in the competitive struggle. So long as the economic system had to cope with a general condition of scarcity, being provided with the "necessities of life" seemed to be a satisfactory state for a large number of people. The United States was first among all nations to develop mass production of a great variety of consumer items. Especially in the period between the two World Wars it was far ahead in this respect of other nations, even those which had already achieved a fairly high level of industrialization. In more recent years the gap between this country and other nations of the Western world has been narrowed as American methods of mass production, marketing, management and advertising found wide acceptance in European countries. In appraising the psychological impact of manners of living in this contemporary setting, it must be realized that people live today in an environment in which they are constantly admonished to borrow, to spend, to expand the whole scale of their consumption habits.

Past generations had been brought up under diametrically opposed concepts. They were urged to be thrifty and to postpone to some extent current enjoyment of goods and services in order to accumulate savings out of which they could later purchase the type of things which are now available on credit. In this way their sacrifices, their self-discipline and industry would be rewarded eventually. In contemporary Western, consumer oriented society, instant satisfaction is promised through methods of financing homes, cars, household equipment, furniture and travel. All these goods and services can be delivered immediately after a small down payment and repayment is made not out of accumulated savings but out of current income. Far from advocating postponement of purchases until such time that the buyer can pay the full price, people are urged strongly to buy now and to spread the payments over a long period of time thereby committing their future income to meet these obligations.

In recent years, critics especially in the younger generation, have condemned the "materialism" implied in this steady bombardment of people with advertising messages and the ensuing striving of the masses to obtain immediate possession of newly advertised goods and gadgets. However, economically speaking, it must be pointed out that a modern peace time economy especially one which is not continuously being beefed up by rising defense expenditures requires an ever expanding consumer income in order to maintain the rate of growth necessary to ensure full employment and adequate utilization of production resources.

What constitutes a satisfactory standard of living is defined by prevailing social valuations. In a society like that of the United States these social concepts are dynamic. They conceive of standards of living continuously improving. This open-endedness leads to consumption habits in which existing goods such as homes, cars, household equipment are repeatedly exchanged for new ones. Up to the late 1960's these attitudes were supported by the fact that in spite of rising prices money income increased even more, thereby adding to the purchasing power of consumers. But in 1969 even steeply rising money wages began to lag behind even more rapidly increasing consumer prices.

In order to understand the problems of standards of living better, it is necessary to know some statistical concepts. These statistical classifications leave out two large groups of American households: the well-to-do and the poor. In 1966 when the Consumer Price Index was 113.1 percent of the base years 1957–1959, families with an income of $15,000 and over were classified as well-to-do. They represented 9.2 percent of all families in that year. At the same time 17.8 percent of the families had incomes ranging from under $1,000 up to $3,499 a year. This group was classified as poor. This leaves us with middle income families of various categories comprising 73 percent of household units in the United States. Within this middle class category we find the concept of a higher living standard.[1] In 1967 a family of 4 in this category of a living standard, residing in a metropolitan area needed an income of $13,367. Of this, $10,192 was allocated for family consumption and $2,043 for personal taxes. The rest was used for insurance, gifts and contributions, social security, disability and unemployment compensation taxes.

Moderate living standards for a similar spending unit did require a total budget of $9,243, with total consumption expenditures at $7,352 and taxes amounting to $1,092. Lower living standards required a total budget

---

[1]Jean C. Brackett "New BLS Budgets," *Monthly Labor Review*, April 1969.

of $5,594 with total family consumption expenditures at $4,591 and taxes of $419.00.

Before we try to evaluate these classifications of living standards in terms of the actual wage structure, it is important to stress that the incomes attached to the various levels of living refer to the whole family unit. They would include wages or salaries earned by the main bread winner, his wife, and also earnings of children living in the parental household. It follows that the *family income* of the principal wage earner may actually be in excess of his own yearly earnings and may place the whole family into a higher standard class than is indicated merely by the earnings of the wage or salary earner who is the head of the family. However, we will see presently that few wage and salary earners are likely to reach the "higher living standard" level despite the national publicity which is sometimes given to craftsmen such as plumbers or electricians whose annual earnings would place them into the well-to-do or $15,000 a year plus group.

The definition of living standards discussed above referred to 1967. Based on the gross average weekly earnings of production or non-supervisory workers in the same year, we find that most workers or salary earners would be placed somewhere between the lower and the moderate living standards. In January 1970 gross average weekly earnings of non-supervisory workers in finance, insurance and real estate were $111.37. It is clear then that this group of white-collar workers remained in the lower living standard category. The same was true of blue-collar workers in apparel and other textil products, of tobacco workers, of workers in retail trades and the rubber and leather goods industries. Steel workers on the other hand were heading towards "moderate living standards" and so were automobile workers. The former did have average weekly earnings of $159.01, the latter of $169.24 per week.

4-2. SPENDING PATTERNS AND LEVELS OF INCOME

We will see in Sec. 4-4 that among those who are officially classified as poor there are 1.5 million heads of families under 65 who are working full time. However, the overwhelming majority of nonagricultural wage and salary workers receive an income from their work which is way above the poverty level. This marks a decisive progress that labor has achieved in the 20th century. In the earlier phases of industrialization a large majority of the working class was still on a poverty level, defined in terms not of today but of the 19th century.

It has always been a deep belief of Americans that their standard of living generally speaking is higher than that of people in other countries. While the gap between this country and European countries has been narrowing, it is still true that in an international comparison of living standards the American manner of living of wage and salary earners is far more abundant than that of comparable occupational groups even in affluent European countries. Table 4-1 will give support to this statement by showing the increase in total per capita personal income in constant prices between 1965 and 1968. However in most countries in Western Europe, Social Security systems, especially health and old age insurance, are more effective than comparable systems in this country.

TABLE 4-1
TOTAL AND PER CAPITA DISPOSABLE PERSONAL INCOME
1965–1968

Year	Total (in Billions)		Total Per Capita (Dollars)	
	Current Prices	1958 Prices	Current Prices	1958 Prices
1965	473.2	435.0	2.432	2.235
1966	511.6	459.2	2.598	2.332
1967	546.3	478.0	2.744	2.401
1968	589.0	497.4	2.928	2.473

SOURCE: Table B-16, *Economic Report of the President*, January 1969.

It should be stressed that Table 4-1 deals only with disposable personal income. That means individual income taxes and contributions to social security have already been taken out of the gross earnings. The remaining net earnings represent the amount of money people can actually spend for consumption expenditures. While disposable personal income continued to rise, measured in constant prices, it did so at a slightly declining yearly amount each year since 1965. However, it would be erroneous to deal only with current earnings of consumers. We have already stated that installment credit is an important aspect of total consumer expenditures. Between 1960 and 1968 the total installment credit extended increased by more than 90 percent from 49.8 billion to 96.5 billion. This is a far greater increase in current dollars than the G.N.P. itself which rose from $504 billion to $861 billion in the same period. However, it is necessary to view the installment credit system in terms of the relation between credits extended and credits repaid in the same year. Occasionally, for instance in 1958, repayments exceed new extensions. Sometimes the excess of extensions over repayments is very small as occurred in 1961. Generally the excess of extensions over repayments tends to become considerable when the economy is forging ahead at a rapid rate. This will be shown in Table 4-2.

In order to complete the survey of the financial resources and liabilities available for consumer expenditures it is necessary to consider also outstanding mortgage debt on 1- to 4-family houses. This indebtedness rose very sharply from $141.3 billion in 1960 to $251.3 in 1968. While this

TABLE 4-2
INSTALLMENT CREDIT EXTENDED AND REPAID
1965-1968
(In Billions)

	1965		1966		1967		1968	
	Ext.	Rpd.	Ext.	Rpd.	Ext.	Rpd.	Ext.	Rpd.
Total	78.6	69.9	82.3	76.1	84.7	81.3	96.5	87.7
Automobile Paper	27.2	23.5	27.3	25.4	26.7	26.5	31.3	28.0
Other Consumer Goods Paper	22.7	20.5	25.6	23.2	27.0	25.5	30.4	28.0
Repair and Modernization Loans......	2.3	2.1	2.2	2.1	2.1	2.1	2.3	2.2
Personal Loans .	26.3	23.8	27.2	25.4	28.9	27.1	32.4	29.6

SOURCE: Table B-56, *Economic Report of the President,* January 1969.

represents a substantial increase it is far less than the rise in mortgage debt on commercial properties which more than doubled in the same period.

The favorable development of real purchasing power was halted in 1969 when consumer prices began to overtake wage increases. When prices rose very sharply early in 1969 a skilled worker in a mid-Western automobile plant, who with overtime had earned about $10,000 in 1968 and was, therefore, enjoying a moderate living standard, complained in an interview that the rise in prices created the following hardships for him and his wife: he had bought last year a new medium priced car in addition to the older car he was still using. Keeping up the payments of the new car became more burdensome as other costs of living rose sharply; he had planned to move out of his semi-detached home into a new house. It seemed that now he had to postpone this project; his wife now began to think actively about taking a job to supplement the family income. While this worker obviously had an income in the upper ranges of wage and salary employees, he could not escape the pressures brought about by ever rising aspirations in standards of living and increasing prices.

Spending patterns vary according to income. As we will see in Table 4-3 the structure of spending changes with income. It is interesting to note that early statistics in the 19th century already proclaimed a "law" called after the Bavarian Engel according to which household expenditures for food declined significantly relative to income as earnings rise. One of the difficulties of people having a low income in a society which continuously stresses improvements in standard of living and advertises new products is to maintain a rational pattern of spending. Actually, many people in the low income bracket deny themselves necessary food items and other essential expenses in order to purchase high priced consumer goods such as color television sets and other durable household gadgets. There is a cer-

TABLE 4-3
BUDGET ALLOWANCES FOR VARIOUS LIVING STANDARDS
(1967)

Components of Consumption	Lower Standard	Moderate Standard	Higher Standard
Percentage Distribution........	100	100	100
Food.................	34	29	26
Housing..............	27	31	34
Transportation	9	12	11
Clothing and Personal Care	14	14	14
Medical Care	10	6	5
Other Family .... Consumption.......	6	8	10

SOURCE: Arranged from Table 5, *Monthly Labor Review*, April 1969, p. 11.

tain distortion of the order of priorities within a limited spending pattern. This unhealthy trend is reinforced by the fact that even the lower income groups are continuously being solicited to sign papers obligating them to purchase expensive items on installment plans. If they fail to maintain the payment schedule the goods are repossessed. At this point these people are out of their money and also out of the things they tried to acquire in this manner.

The forceful sales campaigns on radio and TV that are part of the background noise in which many of us spend the waking hours lead to a distortion of priorities in the spending schedule, especially of families in the deprivation and poverty levels of income. In many cities welfare clients are not supposed to have TV sets. When a lookout in a tenement crowded with many people on relief spots the arrival of an investigator and sounds the alarm, TV sets are hastily silenced and covered so that they may not be noticed by the representative of the Welfare Department. While it is easy to understand that such sets can greatly relieve the boredom of people out of work, the payments for them cut down on essential food purchases and other important items.

People who are currently employed—especially blue-collar workers covered by collective agreements, but also many groups of office workers in business or government as well as such professional employees as teachers—can look forward to some increases in their earnings each year. These may take the form of deferred wage increases, salary increments, upgrading into higher job classes, or promotions. For these people installment credit offers little risk provided they keep track of their total commitments—which, however, a disturbingly large number of families fail to do. But in a real sense a job, almost any kind of job, is a form of collateral. This situation widens the gap between those who are working more or less the year round and full time, and the groups of people who are beginning to fill up the poverty brackets on the income scale because they are underemployed, unemployed, or overage. In this sense a reproduction of poverty is taking place while the society at large continues on a growth path of affluence. The fact that this new type of poverty has moved either to the fringes of the labor force where under-employment prevails or out of it altogether into the swelling ranks of the older population does not justify dropping this problem from the view of labor economics. We will have to return to it in the last section of the chapter.

4-3. OCCUPATIONAL PATTERNS OF INCOME

Economic well-being is not necessarily related to high income levels. In fact many people in the affluent-income classification are in various degrees of economic distress and rarely out of debt. Studies of budgets of upper-income suburban families have often shown that borrowing is required to meet Federal income-tax payments and that, generally speaking, as the rate of income increases the rate of expenditures rises somewhat faster. This paradoxical situation is often attributed to social pressures emanating from overly homogeneous suburban "dormitory" communities requiring membership in expensive clubs, frequent entertaining, and the desire to educate children in private schools. Actually many people in the income groups below statistical affluence are often better off because they are not under such pressures and can determine in greater freedom what their spending is going to be. Table 4-4 gives a detailed breakdown of median incomes of white and nonwhite male workers age 35–44. This age range is for a large number of wage and salary workers at the time when they have reached the peak of their earnings. Let us remember that a statistical median is a line dividing a population into two equal halves. This means that for all the figures given 50 percent earned more and 50 percent earned less than the monetary values attached to the various income brackets. The appearance of families rated with a poverty classification even in relatively high median ranges of income is a result of this statistical grouping. Of great interest is the information of the size of the families in the occupational groupings listed in the table.

It should be noted that Table 4-4 does not differentiate between employed and self-employed participants in the labor force. The top group, professional and technical workers, therefore contains, in addition to salaried employees, self-employed professionals such as medical doctors and lawyers. It is significant that the median income of this group whose members must undergo protracted periods of study is above that of managers and proprietors. This is attributable to the fact that, especially among the proprietors there are many individuals with very low earnings. On the other hand, managerial income will in many cases top the earnings of medical doctors. The fact that this group has been put into a classifica-

TABLE 4-4
MEDIAN INCOME BY OCCUPATION

Occupation Group	Median Earnings of Male Workers Age 35–44	Incidence of Poverty among Families with Employed Male Head	Percent of wives Age 35–44 of Employed Workers, with Specified Number of Children ever born.		
			0–2	3	4 or more
White males					
Professional and technical workers	$8,015	2	56	23	20
Managers, officials, proprietors, (except farm)	7,465	5	57	23	20
Sales workers..........................	6,325	3	60	22	19
Craftsmen and foremen	5,795	4	54	21	25
Clerical and kindred workmen	5,505	2	61	20	19
Operatives	5,075	9	52	20	27
Service workers........................	4,610	8	57	20	23
Nonfarm laborers	4,095	15	49	19	33
Farmers and farm managers.............	2,945	26	42	22	36
Farm laborers	2,020	43	35	17	48
Nonwhite males					
Professional and technical workers	5,485	12	65	16	19
Managers, officials, proprietors, (except farm)........................	4,655	21	57	16	27
Clerical and kindred workers............	4,630	13	61	14	25
Sales workers..........................	4,010	*	57	16	27
Craftsmen and foremen	3,885	21	52	13	35
Operatives	3,495	27	51	12	37
Service workers........................	2,970	25	57	13	30
Nonfarm laborers	2,825	45	48	11	41
Farm laborers	975	70	34	9	57
Farmers and farm managers.............	945	78	27	9	65

*Not available.
SOURCE: *Social Security Bulletin* (January 1965), p. 25.

tion covering also proprietors accounts for the low median value of earnings. The exceedingly low level of median farm income is due to the fact that there are still a large number of marginal farms in operation in the United States despite the continuous drop in the number of farms and in the share of the farm population in the total population. In the short period from 1960 to 1964 this percentage dropped from 8.7 to 6.7 percent. This table conveys information which has specific significance for labor economics and the general problem of economic well-being. We refer to the incidence of poverty among families with an employed male head and to the income differential between white and nonwhite males in identical occupational classifications.

At the $5,000-plus level of white operatives we encounter already an incidence of poverty at the rate of 9. For white nonfarm laborers this rate is 15. For nonwhite operatives the rate is exactly three times as high. For the same category of nonfarm laborers the incidence of poverty is also 200 percent higher than for the corresponding white group.

Table 4-4 demonstrates clearly that low earnings are associated with larger-sized families. These conditions of deprivation and poverty among low-wage workers with large families is not mitigated in the United States by family-allowance subsidies. In some countries such allowances for a worker with four children make up a considerable percentage of the hourly wage rate. In Italy they come to 28.32 percent; in Belgium to 32.57 percent; in France to 65.60 percent.[2] While it is true that in many instances wage rates are substantially lower in countries with generous family allowances than in countries where these schemes are less liberal or nonexistent, it is easy to see that the absence of such supports for large families of people who are employed in the lowest levels of earnings makes their hardship more onerous.

The Consumer Price Index reflects largely the typical expenditures at current prices of families enjoying living standards ranging from "lower to middle." A study of the development of these prices over a longer period of time is a graphic illustration of the progress of labor.

4-4. THE LONG RUN VIEW OF THE CONSUMER PRICE INDEX

Ever since 1913 the Bureau of Labor Statistics has compiled a consumer price index which is the basis for the evaluation of the purchasing power of the consumer. The main series going into the overall index are prices of food, housing, apparel and upkeep, transportation, medical care, personal care, recreation and reading and other goods and services. Every ten years a large sample of families is set up and forms are distributed in which all expenditures are to be written down, especially the types of food, clothing, cars and other items which are habitually purchased by families in the lower and moderate ranges of living in urban areas. The three last years of each decade become the base years for the monthly measuring of price changes of the items established in the sample study in the next decade. To illustrate: the Consumer Price Index for 1967 was 116.3; for 1968, 121.2; for January 1969, 124.1 as compared with the basis 57–59 = 100.

Although the Consumer Price Index dates back only to 1913, the BLS has estimated the basic items, food, rent, apparel and upkeep back to the year 1900 and has set up this limited Consumer Price Index on the basis of 1957 to 1959 = 100. It must be realized, of course, that in those early decades cost of transportation, medical care, personal care, reading and recreation

[2]"Impact of Automation on Employment," Hearings before the Subcommittee on Unemployment of the House Committee on Education and Labor, Government Printing Office, Washington, D. C. (1961), Table VII, p. 55.

TABLE 4-5
CONSUMER PRICE INDEX IN UNITED STATES CITIES,
1800 TO 1900. (1957–1959 = 100)

Year	Index All Items
1800	59
1810	55
1820	49
1830	37
1840	35
1850	29
1860	31
1870	44
1880	34
1890	32
1900	29

SOURCE: Table 104, *Handbook of Labor Statistics*, 1967, U. S. Dept. of Labor.

were of no significance to the income groups covered by the Consumer Price Index. A study of the development of consumer prices in the 19th century may be surprising to those who have lived only in times of rising prices. The BLS backward projection, however, shows that the 19th century was a "golden age" at least in one respect, namely, in the area of consumer prices. In order not to exaggerate the significance of this 19th century record of a secularly declining trend of consumer prices, it must be stressed that up to at least the middle of the 19th century the United States was a predominantly agricultural and rural country in which many farm families had only a tenuous relation with the market economy. It is interesting to note that after the War of 1912 and after the Civil War but not after the Mexican War there were flurries of a short-lived postwar inflation. The index rose to 73 in 1914 and starting from a much lower base, 31 in 1860, to 54 in 1865. It should be noted that the 1870's, a period of accelerating industrialization, was a time of declining consumer prices. The last two decades of the 19th century in which the advance of industry and of urbanization gained momentum, was a period of considerable stability of consumer prices with the period 1895 to 1899 unchanged at a level of 29 which was equal to the Consumer Price Index 50 years earlier in 1849. The record of the 19th century with its sustained growth of the American economy while consumer prices tended downward should give pause to late 20th century theorists who insist that "inflation" is the price we have to pay for continued economic development.

In the 20th century a post World War I peak of consumer prices was reached at the level of 62.3 in 1921. That meant a doubling since the beginning of the century. However, in 1933 the Consumer Price Index was down again to 45.1. It has been rising ever since with the greatest acceleration occurring in the 1960's. Whereas the Consumer Price Index rose from

83.8 percent in 1950 to 101.5 percent in 1959 it jumped from 103.1 percent in 1960 to over 125 percent early in 1969. The development of consumer prices in specific categories of spending was quite uneven. Medical care services had reached the 165 level in the spring of 1969 with no slowing down of the rate of increase in sight. Transportation services had climbed to 140. On the other hand food consumed at home stood at about 120.

In the first months of 1970 the Consumer Price Index rose at an accelerated rate, thereby putting an end for the time being to the continuous increase of workers' spendable income. Already in 1969 this income of workers with three dependents had declined slightly as compared to 1968. As a result, in 1970 unions made wage demands discounting future price increases. This practice contributes to a dangerous price spiral effect on wages.

4-5. THE PERSISTENCE OF POVERTY

We have seen in the first section of this chapter that in 1967 a total budget $5,915 was considered necessary to maintain a 4-person family on a "lower living standard." Moderate and higher living standards required much greater annual outlays. On top of this higher standard there is the "well-to-do" level of an annual income of $15,000 and over. In 1963–65 there were 5.4 percent of all families in this income bracket.[3]

On the other end of the scale are households below the "poverty level" or below the near poverty line. It is important to understand that according to current official definitions both lines are substantially below the income of the "lower living standard" of $5,915. In 1967 the poverty line for a nonfarm household of a 4-member family was set at $3,335; the "near poverty" income line was defined as being reached at an annual income of $4,345. We see, therefore, that the poverty line is about $2,600 a year below the lower living standard and the near poverty line is about $1,600 short of the lower living standard.

Actually households having an income which is so far below the lower living standard level must be considered as living in the poverty sector of the economy. It is no particular consolation for families to learn that they are defined as "near poor" rather than "poor" according to statistical definitions. The fact remains that their income does not enable them to participate fully in what is considered the American standard of living. Modern mass media of communication allocating so much of their time to advertising things representing that standard merely make the difference between poverty levels of living and the continuously improving manner of living of those in the prosperity sector more concrete and visible. Table 4-6 will show the extent of poverty and "near poverty" in 1966.

[3]Table 153, Handbook of Labor Statistics, 1967, U. S. Dept. of Labor.

TABLE 4-6
INCIDENCE OF POVERTY IN 1966

	Number	Percent
All Households		
Total	193,415	100.0
Poor	29,657	15.3
Near Poor	15,150	7.8
With Male Head		
Total	168,536	100.0
Poor	18,952	11.2
Near Poor	13,031	7.7
With Female Head		
Total	24,878	100.0
Poor	10,704	43.0
Near Poor	2,119	8.5

SOURCE: Arranged from Table 3, p. 6, *Social Security Bulletin*, March, 1968.

Table 4-6 covers the population of the United States without differentiation according to race. A breakdown into white and nonwhite households reveals that the incidence of poverty among nonwhites is 38.6 percent as compared to the national average of 15.3 percent for all households shown in Table 4-6. In the near poor category nonwhites have 11.9 percent of all families in their group whereas the incidence of near poverty is only 6.4 percent in white households.

In the Economic Report of January 1969 it is asserted that the percentage of poor households declined from 24 percent in 1959 to 16.2 percent in 1967. In the same period near poor households declined from 7.7 percent to 5.9 percent of all family units. The latter group may be considered as near poor but it would be difficult to assert that they do not live in the poverty sector. If we combine the poor and the near poor we find that according to the calculations of the Bureau of Labor Statistics the percentage of families living in the poverty sector declined from 22.1 percent in 1959 to 16.1 percent in 1967. In 1959 total unemployment was 5.5 percent of the civilian labor force; in 1967 the unemployment rate had dropped to 3.8 percent. This favorable development on the labor market can account to a certain extent for the declining incidence of poverty and near poverty. The poverty sector comprises heterogeneous groups. Table 4-7 will give a breakdown of the incidence of poverty according to age and race. Included are also the unrelated individuals.

Table 4-7 shows that the greatest incidence of poverty is to be found among unrelated individuals 65 years and over. It is highly significant also that in the same group of the near poor the incidence of this condition increased between 1959 and 1967 from 5.1 percent to 6.0 percent. This may be due to the fact that some unrelated individuals over 65 were "promoted" from the poor to the near poor sector during this period. But this

TABLE 4-7
INCIDENCE OF POVERTY BY AGE AND RACE, 1959 AND 1967

Incidence of poverty in percentage	1959	1967
Total households	24.0	16.2
Head 65 years and over	48.6	36.3
Unrelated individuals	68.1	53.4
Families	32.5	20.3
Head under 65 years	19.8	12.2
Unrelated individuals	36.8	27.0
White	32.9	24.4
Male	24.6	18.0
Female	39.1	29.0
Nonwhite	54.8	40.1
Male	47.1	29.4
Female	63.5	51.7
Families	16.8	9.5
White	13.4	7.1
Male	11.4	5.4
Female	35.9	25.3
Nonwhite	48.6	29.9
Male	42.1	20.9
Female	71.3	54.9

SOURCE: Economic Report of the President, 1969, Table 15.

does not change the fact that these people live as before in the poverty sector of the economy. As expected the incidence of poverty among nonwhite families is far greater than the incidence of poverty among white families. We see however that the poverty rate of nonwhite families dropped very sharply from 48.6 percent in 1959 to 29.9 percent in 1967. Since the Economic Report does not supply us with a racial breakdown of the near poor families, it is hard to make a judgment, to what extent the decline in nonwhite poverty families is due to their "upgrading" into the near poor category.

It is true that rising levels of employment lifted a substantial number of poor households headed by males out of the poverty sector. However, the facts remain that about three-fifths of the people living in the poverty sector are not employable. In the aggregate these vast numbers of people still in the poverty sector represent a substantial spending deficit on the one side and on the other the present way of allocating income to them especially through procedures of the various programs of public aid or through completely inadequate old age benefit schedules is wasteful.

As we will see in Chapter 25 of this text, plans have been proposed in 1969 to create more work incentives for people on relief and revise current procedure so that welfare allocations will not be cut in direct proportion to outside earnings of recipients of public assistance programs. It is, therefore, necessary to stress that among the families coming under the classification of poverty numbering over six million in 1966 there were 1.5 million headed by a male head under the age of 65 who was fully employed. We should note also that 70 percent of these men were white so that their low economic status as workers cannot be attributed to racial discrimination. We encounter here a sizeable group of "working poor" whose poverty is not attributable to either unemployment or unemployability but to wage scales which did not add up to yearly amounts above the poverty line for families.[4]

While it would be utopian to assume that poverty could ever be eliminated completely, we will discuss throughout the balance of this text wage, employment, and social security policies designed at least in the long run to reduce the poverty sector in the American economy to a more acceptable level. Its present size is inconsistent with the generally progressive character of the American economy.

A calculation was made for the year 1965 to ascertain the difference between the actual spending of families within the poverty line and the amount of aggregate expenditures necessary to lift them to a lower income which, however, would at least represent minimum levels of adequacy. The difference between actual and these hypothetical levels of spending of poor families was estimated to be $11.0 million in 1965 prices. In the meantime incomes and prices have gone up somewhat but the dollar amount of the deficit would still be about the same due to the fact that there has been a sharp rise in consumer prices since 1963. During the 1960's when the American economy became "overheated" as a result of the stepup of defense expenditures this implied deficit in aggregate consumer demands was more than upset by vast outlays for defense procurement. In the fiscal year 1968 this item alone was four times as high as the income deficit of poor families. It contributed substantially to establish higher levels of employment and of income both of wage and salary workers and of management. But this persistence of poverty in an economic structure characterized by continuously rising incomes and more elaborate manners of living of the majority is a potentially dangerous development. This is particularly so because poverty is not evenly dispersed throughout the country but is highly concentrated in urban centers, especially in "inner cities."

Table 4-8 presents the situation as it existed in 1965.

The condition shown in Table 4-8 demonstrates graphically that the great progress that labor had made has not eliminated serious social problems. This is a sobering thought. In the 1930's the opinion prevailed that the establishment of a comprehensive system of social security which will be taken up in Part V of this text in conjunction with policies designed to maintain full employment would reduce poverty to a very low level. While

[4]Mollie Orshansky; "The Shape of Poverty in 1966," *Social Security Bulletin*, March, 1968.

TABLE 4-8
THE POVERTY GAP—1965

	Poor Households		Dollar Deficit	
Type of Household	Number (in millions) 1965	Percentage Distribution 1965	Amount (in billions) 1965	Percentage Distribution 1965
Total.................	11.2	100.0	$11.0	100.0
Unrelated individuals ..	4.8	42.5	3.4	30.5
Men	1.3	11.4	.9	8.3
Women	3.5	31.1	2.5	22.2
Families..............	6.4	57.5	7.7	69.5
No children under age 18	2.2	19.7	1.7	15.3
Some children under age 18	4.2	37.8	6.0	54.2
With male head	4.6	40.7	5.1	46.3
No children under age 18....	1.8	16.1	1.4	12.5
Some children under age 18....	2.8	24.6	3.8	33.8
With female head....	1.9	16.8	2.6	23.2
No children under age 18....	.4	3.6	.3	2.8
Some children under age 18....	1.5	13.2	2.3	20.4

SOURCE: *Social Security Bulletin*, March 1968.

a considerable proportion of wage and salary earners who were in the lowest income ranges or who were unemployed a generation ago have experienced vast improvements in their economic status, a considerable sector of poverty remains. This is, as it were, the other coin of the general progress and one of the more disturbing aspects of this situation is that it does not seem to yield to the conventional remedies offered by social security legislation and employment policies. It, therefore, will be necessary to have a fresh look at these problems. This will be done in Part III of this text.

SELECTED BIBLIOGRAPHY

Katona, George. *Mass Consumption Society* (New York: McGraw-Hill Book Company, 1964).

Lauterbach, Albert. *Man, Motives, and Money* (Ithaca, N. Y.: Cornell University Press, 1954).

Murphy, Kathryn R. "Contrasts in Spending by Urban Families," *Monthly Labor Review* (November, 1964).

Orshansky, Mollie, "The Shape of Poverty in 1966," *Social Security Bulletin* (March, 1968).

QUESTIONS FOR DISCUSSION

1. Living standards are relative considerations, and any economic behavior

on the part of individuals which is said to be related to living standards must also be relative. Comment.

2. On the basis of the suggested "measures" to be used to designate persons living in poverty, do you feel that these concepts are adequate? Include concrete examples to support your position.

3. Poverty seems to be especially dominant in certain age, racial, and geographic groups. Cite these groups and give reasons for this concentration of poverty within these groups.

4. Discuss the macroeconomic implications of poverty in a highly industrialized nation like the United States.

5. The relative magnitude of discretionary spending on the part of individuals is often a workable variable for estimating standards of economic well-being. What is the nature of this relationship and what implications can be drawn from these observations?

6. The patterns of consumption over the "life cycle" have important implications in the light of ever-increasing life-expectancy figures. Comment on the nature of this relationship.

7. Is there any apparent relationship between the size of the family and the level of income? If so, what is the nature of this relationship and what are its implications?

8. Comment on the macroeconomic and microeconomic implications of relatively easy credit availability for members of the labor force.

9. From your knowledge of the "War on Poverty," specifically the Economic Opportunity Act of 1964, to what extent do you feel that such programs will successfully cope with this problem of poverty in the midst of the general affluence of the American people?

10. It has been estimated that poverty accounts for a deficit in aggregate income of approximately $11.0 billion. Assuming this deficit could be made up by outright government expenditures of this amount, what would be the short-run and long-run effects in terms of those individuals who presently account for this deficit?

Part

II

WAGE DETERMINATION AND WAGE STRUCTURES

Chapter

5

The Significance of Wage Theories

Wages in the broadest sense of the word are the price that management pays for the employment of the factor labor. When Economics started as a systematic inquiry into the workings of the economic system, the early writers in France and in England demanded the abolishment of most of the rules and regulations imposed ón the conduct of business by national and local governments and by guilds or privileged corporations. They criticized all interference with the "laws of the market" through elimination of competition and the fixing of prices and wages.

But in advocating the establishment of a free labor market, economists did have to give thought to the principles and the forces whose operation would set wage levels under such conditions of competition. If wages were no longer the product of local custom or regulation, just what would determine wage rates? It is in the context of this problem that wage theories developed.

In this chapter we will outline the main trends in wage theory from the eighteenth century to the present. At first sight some of these theories seem to have lost all relevance for an understanding of current wage problems. The question therefore may very well be asked whether a study of these theories is not really a waste of time. Obviously our answer is that it is not. Many issues—for instance, the relation between the growth of the population and of the labor force and wage levels which occupied the minds of early economists—present themselves today, although the answer to these problems are entirely different now. But on a more general level, wage theories are an important phase of labor economics because without them wage policies could not be formulated.

5-1. WAGE THEORIES AND POLICIES

In recent years *Economic Reports of the President* contained "guidelines" for wage policies. The purpose of these recommendations was to maintain or establish a balance between wages and prices. Actually two margins were considered. If wages went beyond the upper margin, it was feared that a wage-price spiral would be set into motion, thus initiating an inflationary trend. On the other hand, if wages lagged behind increases in productivity, a deficiency in aggregate income and spending was anticipated, which in turn could result in a slowdown of the economy.

It is obvious that these guidelines for wage policies, and especially for the setting of wages in collective bargaining, make a number of assumptions with regard to the structure of the market, the operation of the price system, the relations between wage rates and productivity, and the weight of wages in aggregate demand for goods and services. It is clear, then, that just as there can be no adequate monetary policy without a theory of money and credit or an effective employment policy without a theory of employment, it is impossible to formulate wage policies without having a prior understanding of wages on the level of theory. Although "practical men of affairs" in business and labor may be disinclined to pay too much attention to theories, they are more willing than their predecessors of a previous generation to concede their significance.

As we will see later in this chapter, there was a sharp break in the pattern of wage theories in the latter part of the nineteenth century. Whereas the earlier economists placed great stress on the supply of labor, especially on the impact of an increase in the number of people employed on wage levels, with the ascendency of the marginal utility theory of value the emphasis shifted to the demand for labor. Stressing demand gave a completely new aspect to economics, shifting the frame of reference from the macroeconomic to the microeconomic level, where it remained until the advent of Keynesian economics. But different though the wage theories of the early and latter part of the nineteenth century were, they had in common the objective of finding out how wages are determined on an unorganized labor market. In fact, as the practice of collective bargaining spread shortly before World War I, many economists felt that with the emergence of an organized labor market there was no point in pursuing wage theories any further. It was believed that this method of establishing wage rates ended the "determinacy" of wages, thereby making any scientific analysis pointless. Let us merely note that the linking of a scientific approach to determinacy reflects a stage of science that is no longer accepted by the natural scientists. It is equally obsolete in economics.

Actually during the lifetime of Adam Smith, who published his *Inquiry into the Nature and Causes of the Wealth of Nations* in 1776, and of David Ricardo, whose *Principles of Political Economy and Taxation* appeared in 1817, the labor market did not correspond to the model of an unorganized structure. Until 1825 "combinations of labor" were forbidden in

England. In the United States the Bill of Rights of 1791 abrogated this British legislation, which goes back as far as 1349. But it is clear that Smith, in line with his general argument for the abolition of all restraints on economic activities, was opposed to the Combination Laws. In his chapter on "Wages of Labour" he denounced combinations of masters who agreed among themselves not to raise wages. He mentions that these agreements were always reached in secrecy, whereas any attempt of workers to combine immediately brought about a call "for the assistance of the civil magistrate, and the rigorous execution of those laws which have been enacted with so much severity against the combinations of servants, labourers, and journeymen."[1]

Although an unorganized labor market really presupposes an absence of organization not only of labor but also of management, Smith and Ricardo investigated the principles of wage determination that underlay the establishment of wage rates if the labor market were completely competitive both on the supply and on the demand side. It was not until the early nineteenth century that the classical wage doctrine later described by the mid-nineteenth century German labor leader Ferdinand Lassalle as the "Iron Wage Law" was formulated in full. Before we turn our attention to this theory, which contributed very much to Thomas Carlyle's characterization of economics as a "dismal science," it is worthwhile to pay more attention to Adam Smith.

5-2. ADAM SMITH'S OBSERVATIONS ON WAGES

It would not be correct to attribute to Smith a clear-cut wage theory of the type developed by his successors early in the nineteenth century. However, Smith made some general observations on wages which, while neglected by later economists, are again seen in their true significance today. This pioneer of systematic economics stressed continuously the dynamic aspect of wealth. With regard to wages he asserted that it is "continual increase (of wealth) which occasions a rise in the wages of labour."[2] He refers to North America as an illustration of this thesis. He goes so far as to say that, in countries with a high rate of growth in which each year there is an increase in employment opportunities, there is no need for labor to organize. Clearly, then, in the eyes of Smith unionism is a device for preventing cutthroat competition of workers struggling to obtain scarce opportunities of employment. Although Smith viewed the prospects of labor very optimistically whenever the rate of growth of the system is very vigorous, he saw in the wage fund at any given time a limiting factor for the increase in employment and wages. However, this is a passing thought in Smith's treatment of

[1]Adam Smith, *Wealth of Nations*, Chap. VIII.
[2]*Ibid.*

wages. He never carried the wage fund theory, as it was formulated in the nineteenth century, to its ultimate, if fallacious, conclusion.

Adam Smith set a pattern of thought with regard to minimum levels of pay which was taken over by his successors. He emphasized that wages must enable the worker to start a family and to have enough children to perpetuate the "race of workmen." In this connection he observed that one-half of the children die before they reach the age of manhood. For this reason he was in favor of adequate wage rates in order to improve the prospects of survival of children born to workers. Generally speaking, Smith associated high wages with an increase in wealth and low wages with a condition of economic stagnation. It can be said that Smith's observations on wages were more in conformity with American thought and practices in the latter part of the nineteenth century than with concepts and policies prevailing in Europe at that time. We must turn our attention now to the emerging wage theories of the nineteenth century.

5-3. THE IRON WAGE LAW

It has been said that the whole outlook of Smith and one of his successors in France, Jean-Baptiste Say, was highly optimistic. Smith anticipated rapid progress in wealth and wages due to the ever more distinct "division of labor"—that is to say, specialization. While he mentioned a wage fund, he was not concerned about developing scarcities of the means of subsistence. All this changed with the appearance of "An Essay of the Principle of Population" by Thomas Robert Malthus, first published in 1799, which gained very wide attention and ran through a large number of editions in the early part of the nineteenth century. In fact, there are few instances in the history of the social sciences in which a new idea was accepted so fast by so many influential writers. Without reference to Malthus, the Iron Wage Laws cannot be understood. They cannot be refuted without taking issue with his "population law."

Taking note of the generally cheerful prognosis implied in the then novel science of economics, Malthus felt that it was necessary to voice a warning. In his opinion the possibilities of sustained economic progress were endangered by the rapid rise in population. In fact, the rate of population growth had been extremely slow throughout the Middle Ages. It had, however, gained considerable momentum in the eighteenth century. On the other hand, in Europe, and especially in England, no additional land seemed to be available for cultivation. Farming techniques, while fairly effective in most parts of Europe, appeared to be frozen and not subject to rapid improvement. In the light of these conditions Malthus asserted that populations have a tendency to outgrow food supply. Inasmuch as an imbalance between the rate of population growth and the rate of increase in agricultural output was likely to increase the spread of poverty, Malthus advocated a slowing down of population growth—primarily by motivating people to be more "responsible" and more continent.

These ideas of Malthus were soon integrated into the wage theories of the classical economists. In order to discuss these doctrines it is necessary first to explain the general frame of reference of classical economic theory. It was macroeconomic in scope, and more interested in long-run dynamic trends than in static analysis in which the time factor, or at least changes in time, was excluded.

David Ricardo is the best representative of this approach. With regard to wages, Ricardo made a sharp distinction between the market price and the "natural" or long-run average price of labor. Like the price of commodities, the market price of labor—that is, wages—was assumed to be subject to short-run fluctuations of supply and demand on the labor market. The natural price was conceived very much in the way in which Smith had already expressed it as the price required for the reproduction of the factor labor. This meant first of all the repletion of the labor energy expended by the individual worker so that his efficiency is restored; secondly, a standard of living of the family that would assure a continuous replacement by new workers of older ones who die or retire. In this connection it is important to understand that in the early nineteenth century the life expectancy of adults was very low. On the other hand, many children entered industrial employment before they had reached eight or ten years of age.

It is clear that the market price of labor was closely related to the rate of investment which in turn is an expression for and a cause of economic growth. But it is precisely at this point that the Iron Law aspect of the classical wage doctrine becomes apparent. According to Ricardo, a rise in real income of a worker's family is a self-defeating proposition. The moment such an improvement takes place, the size of the families will increase substantially and so will the number of workers in general, especially in a situation in which child labor is widespread. Before long the rise in real wages will have been canceled by a sharp rise in food prices and, at best, the income of the worker's family is brought down to the "natural" level.

We see here an early version of a "spiral" theory of the relationship between wages and prices. But in this case agricultural rather than industrial prices start the upward movement. It is not wages as such that initiate the rising price trend but the alleged causal relationship between higher wages, rapidly rising numbers of workers, and climbing living costs which prevent the maintenance of price stability during a long upswing of economic activity.

Projected into a secular frame, Ricardo presented a dark outlook for capital as well as labor. According to him, agriculture—at least in completely settled countries—could yield an increasing output only if factors of production and their prices were steeply increased. These higher prices reflecting the operation of the principle of diminishing returns would bring about a redistribution of income in favor of landowners, to the disadvantage of capitalists and workers alike. Rising food prices would compel employers to increase money wages which, however, would add nothing to the real purchasing power of the workers. By the same token, money profits would fall because, in Ricardo's opinion, profits are high when wages are low, and vice versa. It is for this reason that Ricardo forecast the tendency of profits to fall in the long run. Since the expectation of profits is essential for investment, an extrapolation of the trends of wages and profits that Ricardo predicted meant an ultimate stagnation within the economic system.

It must not be overlooked that this Ricardian analysis, which is logically consistent once the Malthusian premises are accepted, was sharpened to become a weapon in the great debate of his day—the repeal of the Corn Laws and the demand for counteracting the tendency of domestic farm prices to rise by importing cheaper agricultural products duty free.

The Iron Wage Law aspect of the classical wage theory was reinforced by the wage-fund doctrine of John Staurt Mill, whose *Principles of Political Economy* appeared in 1848 and remained for more than two decades the most widely acclaimed textbook on economics. In this work classical economics was said to have found its definitive expression. Mill accepted Malthus' population theory in full. In fact, he did not spend too much time in an exposition of this theorem, noting that it had been accepted by a majority of economists. While retaining the views of his predecessors, according to whom rising wages are associated with a rapid increase in family size, population, and labor supply—to be followed by inflation and a return to subsistence levels—Mill added the concept of a wage fund. At any given time, Mill asserted, the fund out of which wages can be paid and the means of subsistence available for the support of the workers are strictly fixed and limited. There is no possibility of an expansion. It follows that, if there is an increase in the labor force and in employment, the per capita share of a worker is bound to decline. The only way out, according to Mill, would be a prevention of a rapid increase in labor supply. This would enable the worker to retain or even to increase his share in the wage fund and to improve his standards of living.

Even during the lifetime of Mill the wage-fund theory came under heavy attack by W. T. Thornton. He pointed out that a prefixed wage fund available for the disbursement of wages does not exist in private enterprises, and that wages are paid out of current revenues or financial resources of business. The argument was presented so convincingly that Mill, in an article in the *Fortnightly Review*, conceded that the wage-fund theory was not tenable.

In spite of this retraction, the wage-fund theory was defended by J. E. Cairnes five years later, in 1874 in that writer's *Principles of Political*

Economy Newly Expounded. Two years later an American, Francis Walker, in his book *The Wages Question,* renewed the attack on the wage-fund theory and on the Iron Wage Laws in general. He was one of the first writers to link wages in a positive way with productivity, asserting that higher productivity of labor could lead to rising wages.

Since it has been stated earlier in this section that the Iron Wage Laws, with or without the wage-fund feature, stand and fall with the validity of the Malthusian population principle, it now becomes necessary to evaluate the doctrine of Malthus. Such evaluation is particularly urgent in a period of worldwide population explosion which has revived one of the main propositions of Malthus—that especially in emerging nations, population increases are so rapid that they nullify actual or potential advances in national income, wages, and economic well-being.

5-4. PROBLEMS IN THE RAPID GROWTH OF POPULATION

There was a time when population problems had been "read out" of academic economics. In his monumental work on business cycles, the late Joseph Schumpeter explicitly dismissed any considerations of changes in the rate of growth of the population and of the labor force as a legitimate topic in economic theory, even as related to economic development. Today the increasing focus on problems of economic growth has rekindled the attention of economists on population problems. While we will have to return to the question of the relation between changes in population growth and economic development in Part III, where we deal with the labor market and employment, it is necessary here to evaluate the Malthusian doctrines and their implications for wage and welfare policies in the light of historical experience.

That a local population can outgrow a local food supply in the absence of advancing methods of agriculture was graphically demonstrated in the Irish famine almost half a century after the appearance of Malthus' *Essay on Population.* There were no chemical or other means at hand to combat the blight that destroyed the potato crops. But inasmuch as Malthus did not assume agricultural improvements, the Irish crisis of 1848 seems almost to be a proof of his basic theorem. The Irish case is, however, at the same time also a refutation of this population theory. While many died, even more solved their difficulty by migration. This shows that a sharp distinction must be made between local food-population ratios and the worldwide situation.

Malthus did not foresee the agricultural revolution of the twentieth century, which started in the United States and after World War II spread with remarkable success to Western Europe. While large parts of the world, including the Soviet Union, are still far behind in the agricultural sector, food shortages and deficient diets that still plague the majority of mankind are not the inevitable result of a "natural law," but the specific product of a combination of cultural, political, and economic lags. These often extremely serious problems are subject to solution by rational economic and social action. This does not mean that such action will take place; it implies merely that the problem that Malthus saw in terms of a natural inability of land resources to increase yields concurrently with population growth no longer presents itself in the same terms today. The state of agricultural science and technology has advanced so rapidly that, in principle, agricultural-output lags can be overcome. Population growth and agricultural output might move at the same rate everywhere if the achievements of American agriculture in the twentieth century could be duplicated in other parts of the world.

But even if this transformation could be accomplished in time to take care of the doubling of the world population projected for the coming turn of the century, it would not solve the population problem. It would merely transfer the problem from the food sector of the economy to the labor market.

Agricultural output cannot be increased without the utilization of more effective fertilizers, more efficient machinery, and the merging of small farms into larger production units. Experience in advanced countries has shown that increases in farm productivity are linked inevitably with a sharp decline in farm employment. The very processes which enable agriculture to rise above the subsistence level and to produce those surpluses needed to meet the growing requirements of the nonfarm population and of industry also produce a surplus population. While a large number of these people have in the past been absorbed into the nonagricultural labor force, another proportion of the rural population no longer needed in farming is less fortunate. Their migration to cities creates, in many cases, large islands of poverty within the otherwise rising tides of prosperity. Thus it is possible in metropolitan areas for employment and unemployment to increase at the same time, and for a marginal labor force to develop which is either underemployed or not working at all. This condition cannot be overlooked in any assessment of the wage structure and the general state of the economy.

The Iron Wage Laws were based on an erroneous theory of population. They had serious implications for the whole outlook of the working class in the early phases of industrialism. These doctrines conveyed very strongly the idea that it was really futile for workers to push for higher wages, because wage increases were effective only for short periods and there was no escape from a return to a near-subsistence wage for the labor force in the long run. The concept of the "proletariat" as used by Marx and Engels was based on this alledged condition and their wage theories built around it. The proletariat in the Marxian sense consisted of large masses of industrial workers who were working extremely long hours at low pay, who were at the bottom of the income structure and who, most importantly, had no hope of ever improving their economic status. Furthermore, this condition was presented as being frozen not only for the current generation of industrial workers but equally so for their children.

It must be noted that the classical economists, especially Mill, while completely committed to this type of wage theory, were not blind to its social implications. It was only logical for them to advocate workers' education, especially with the goal of cutting down the size of the families in the lowest income groups, thereby relieving pressure on current budgets and future job opportunities.

5-5. SOME OBSERVATIONS ON MARXIST WAGE THEORY

In his overall approach to economics Marx used the conceptual structure of classical economics. Like Ricardo and Mill he assumed that labor units establish the scale of values that sets up the ratio at which goods are exchanged on the market through the intermediary of money. However, Marx rejected completely the population law of Malthus, maintaining that an economic system is always "producing" the population it needs. Furthermore, Marx tried to establish a link between wages and the total value of the product made by the workers whom the capitalist employed. He asserted that the worker should receive a wage equivalent to the final value of output at the point of sale. At this juncture Marx went back to classical wage theory and maintained that the worker merely receives a compensation covering his subsistence, including the needs for the continuous reproduction of the labor force. In a lengthy, repetitive presentation, he asserted that it takes only half a workday to produce the value equivalent of the subsistence wage, which is all that the worker receives. The capitalist however, compels the worker to stay in the factory for a full workday. What is produced in the second half of this day is the "surplus value" which is "appropriated" by the capitalist.

Exploitation, according to Marx, consists in the fact that the worker, generally speaking, receives an income which is only half of the value of the goods he has produced during a workday. The other half are profits, which, however, are termed "unearned income." While this is obviously wrong, it is only fair to point out that it was Adam Smith who equated manual or physical labor with "productive" employment. It is also true that the classical economists, while positing profits as the only effective motive for the accumulation of capital and thereby of economic growth, completely failed to show how this income share could arise in a competitive market economy in which the average long-run price was equal to the cost of production.

The exploitation theory of wages soon was challenged even by writers who accepted Marx's general propositions. Rosa Luxemburg pointed out early in the twentieth century that if the rate of exploitation really were as high in the advanced capitalistic countries as asserted by Marx, the economic system would have collapsed due to a small drop in aggregate domestic purchasing power. Engels himself in the foreword to a new edition of his early work, *Conditions of the Working Class in England,* conceded in 1891 that there had been substantial improvements in living standards of workers.

The fallacy of the surplus-value theory was tacitly admitted in recent changes in the teaching of economics in the Soviet Union. Early textbooks on Marxist economics, written and used in the 1930's asserted that, under Socialism, workers were actually receiving a wage which was equal to the value of their output. This was manifestly not so in a period when the income of farmers and industrial workers in the Soviet Union was kept extremely low in order to permit an accumulation of capital for the expansion of industry. For this reason the early textbooks on Marxian economics were withdrawn and a more realistic presentation given in newly composed teaching materials.

The exploitation theory of wages is generally conceded to be untenable. While exploitation is conceivable in underdeveloped economies, it cannot continue as a general wage pattern in rapidly growing systems, although it is possible that pockets of low-wage structures can develop and survive for a considerable period of time in such systems. There is, however, another aspect of Marx's wage doctrine which, while just as untenable as the exploitation theory, does offer some insights into issues involving wage theories and policies. We find this aspect of Marxist wage theory in the context of his "General Law of Capitalist Accumulation."[3]

We must always bear in mind that Marx's main work on economics has nothing to say about socialism. It deals exclusively with capitalism and the alleged laws of its inevitable development. Marx observes that at a certain economic level there is a great acceleration of growth. The surpluses are continuously reinvested so that the accumulation of capital, especially the building up of productive resources, assumes larger and larger proportions. Marx concedes that in this process money and real wages of workers are certain to increase, simply because there is such a strong demand for labor. But ultimately, according to Marx, there will be a sharp curtailment in labor requirements because the new capital equipment increases productivity and reduces the number of workers necessary for production. Unemployment rises and capitalism produces an "industrial reserve army." This group of unemployed exerts pressure on the wage levels of industrial workers. Their earnings return to the subsistence level and there is a general spread of poverty due to the contagious effects of technological unemployment.

At this point it becomes evident that Marx like all nineteenth-century wage theorists, was thinking in terms of an unorganized labor market. In his model of a capitalistic economy there are no labor unions capable of pro-

[3]Karl Marx, *Capital*, Chap. XXV.

tecting the wage rates of the employed against the pressures emanating from the masses of the unemployed. There is another significant aspect to this phase of the Marxist wage doctrine. While he saw rather clearly the trend toward increasing productivity of labor, he did not follow through with an analysis of the effect of this increase on cost and prices. He does not allow for the fact that at least to some extent, increased productivity must be translated into lower unit prices and a rising aggregate real income.

Marx posited an equivalence between wages and the value of the product of labor. We now turn to a wage theory which tries to show that this equivalence, which Marx said did not actually exist, may indeed prevail in explicitly stated circumstances.

5-6. THE PRODUCTIVITY THEORY OF WAGES

About a hundred years ago the Iron Wage Law was abandoned, as one result of the reorientation of economic theory from production and the conditions determining supply to consumption and the principles governing demand. The turntable for these shifting viewpoints was the concept of value. Whereas the classical economist used "labor," as the determinant of the rate at which goods were exchanged through the medium of price, the new economists of the 1870's asserted that value could be expressed only in terms of a process that established a link between an individual and the goods brought to the market. This link was "utility." In this perspective the law of supply and demand presented itself as the principle of diminishing utility. As more units of a particular commodity become available, each succeeding unit has diminishing utility. Eventually we come to the marginal unit, or the last additional one which is still desired. It has the lowest utility compared to all the preceding units. The marginal utility theory of value establishes that the value given to the marginal unit determines the value of all preceding units. The most desired unit will, in this way, be equated to the least desired—that is to say, the marginal unit.

The American economist J. B. Clark applied these concepts to develop in a systematic way his "Specific Productivity Theory of Wages" which is still the pattern used for the analysis of wages today.[4]

In discussing this theory it is important to bear in mind that Clark described carefully and explicitly the model of an economy in which wages tend to be equal to the product of labor. He was thinking in terms of a perfectly competitive market and a stationary economic system. The latter aspect means that, unlike the classical economists, he did not consider changes in labor supply or in productivity of labor, nor changes in capital equipment or consumer preferences.

---

[4]J. B. Clark, *The Distribution of Wealth* (New York: The Macmillan Company, 1902). See also P. H. Douglas, *The Theory of Wages* (New York: The Macmillan Company, 1934).

In such an economic system, just as in any other such structure, the employer or management wants to maximize profits. Under perfect competition this goal can be achieved only if all factors are continuously used to their full capacity. Clark applies the principle of marginal utility to labor. We encounter the marginal worker who is defined as the worker who contributes to the total value of output just what it costs to employ him. Let us assume that this worker earns $10 a day. If he is not employed, the daily revenue will be $990, whereas the maximum revenue of the firm is $1,000 per day. Hence this worker will be hired in order to maximize revenue, but his contribution to the total value of production is just the last increment needed to maximize it, which in turn is equal to his wage. In this way the worker contributes to production just what he is worth to the employer hiring him. The marginal worker is taken on because it is his contribution to total revenue which pushes the income to the maximum. Hence his wage is equal to what this worker contributes to the value of production. In a simple application of the principle of marginal utility, Clark shows that the wage which the employer is willing to pay to the marginal worker determines the wage of all other workers. The employer does not have to pay more to the first worker hired than to the marginal worker. Inasmuch as the latter receives a wage equal to his specific contribution to the value of output, all workers are paid according to the contribution of the factor labor to the value of output.

Obviously this type of analysis assumes that the demand is directed towards homogeneous labor units and is satisfied when the marginal unit appears. Clark realized of course that to bring labor with all its individual differences into such a scheme seemed to contradict common experience and observations. He tried to overcome this difficulty by finding a common denominator linking the most and the least important workers hired by an employer through the concept of their equal necessity in the process of production. Actually there is no reason why this type of analysis cannot be applied to various shops or departments of an enterprise without losing its general validity.

After World War II an extensive debate was conducted between Richard A. Lester and Fritz Machlup[5] as to whether or not management was exercising its demand for labor within the framework of the specific productivity theory. Lester's research seemed to indicate that marginal considerations did not prevail among businessmen in this respect, whereas Machlup held that the issue could not be settled merely by questionnaires and interviews with businessmen. In this controversy the fact was somewhat overlooked that the specific productivity theory as stated by Clark cannot be divorced from the abstract model outlined above for which the validity of this doc-

[5]Reprinted in Richard Perlman (ed.), *Wage Determination, Studies in Economics* (Boston: D. C. Heath and Company, 1964).

trine was asserted, so that actual conditions cannot be expected to conform to pure theory.

Clark was fully aware of the dynamic conditions of the real economy. This economy, even in Clark's day, was not perfectly competitive. There were continuous improvements in technology and productivity of labor was rising. In view of this, Clark himself would hardly have expected to find a business behavior corresponding precisely to the postulates of his model.

Nevertheless, the linking of wages to the product of labor, which is the main feature of the specific productivity theory of wages, is considered in an advanced industrialized system the most important aspect of the wage structure. Granted that employers do not consciously act according to the precepts of marginalism, the question is whether they should not act in this manner in order to assure a balance between factor cost, factor income, increasing factor output of labor, and prices. This problem of wage theory and policy remains even if full allowance is made for the fact that modern equipment and energy resources are the main reasons why output of labor continues to rise. We now turn our attention to these specific problems.

5-7. DYNAMIC IMPLICATIONS OF THE SPECIFIC PRODUCTIVITY WAGE THEOREM

Before entering into a discussion of the impact of rapidly changing methods of production on the interpretation of the productivity theory of wages, it is necessary to point out that "productivity" can be understood in two ways. First we can speak of value productivity. Applied to the factor labor, this involves the procedure employed by Clark. He compared the total money value of output to the last increment added to it by the marginal worker and the wage paid to him. Generally speaking, then, value productivity of labor is the ratio between the total value of output and the value of labor input.

The second method of measuring productivity consists in the concept of "output per man-hour." This would be a physical rather than a value concept of productivity. Given stable prices, value and physical productivity of labor will move in the same direction. While measurement of physical output and its changes over time in terms of production per man-hour presents certain technical and statistical difficulties, it is the physical rather than the value concept of labor productivity that is most commonly used today. This labor productivity is then being compared to wage rates. We will now proceed to show that the specific productivity theory of wages does not depend for its validity on a stationary model. It can proceed under assumptions of constant, decreasing, and increasing productivity of labor.

Total output is the joint product of capital and labor (K and L). The national income (Y) is produced by these factors and the way in which it is shared by them is written in the basic statement $Y = KL$. Now if the ratio between capital and labor is constant over a period of time, increases in output will require proportionate increases in K and L, with the result that the productivity of labor remains the same. This unitary relationship is written as $K/L = 1$. If there are labor-saving technological improvements, less labor is required per unit hour of output, and production can be increased without a proportional increase in the factor labor. This relationship is represented by $K/L > 1$. Conversely, if there is no possibility of improving machinery, increases in output can be brought about only by an increase in the factor labor. This would be represented by $K/L < 1$.

Figure 5-1 shows that wages change directly with labor productivity. [Wage rates (W) are plotted, on the vertical, labor units (L) on the horizontal axis.]

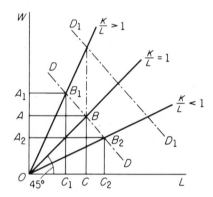

FIG. 5-1. Labor productivity, wage rates, and employment.

The line D-D represents a joint demand curve for labor and for the product resulting from the cooperation of K and L. The 45° line indicating a unitary relationship between K and L intersects with this demand curve at point B. The line O-C indicates the number of workers employed; the line O-A shows their wage rates. Now let us assume that there is a deterioration in capital equipment. In order to maintain the level of output, more workers, O-C_2, will have to be hired but their productivity is less than it was in the first case. We see on the vertical axis that their wages have declined by the distance between A and A_2.

Let us now consider the case of vast improvements in machinery and the resultant higher productivity of labor. We see that only the workers indicated by O-C_1 are required, but the wage of these workers has now risen to the level of A_1. It should be borne in mind that up to this point the analysis was carried out with the restraint of an unchanging volume of output so that the desired amount of productivity can be obtained with different numbers of workers according to what the K/L ratio is.

The graph also shows under what conditions the loss of employment brought about by increased productivity of labor can be offset. If the demand for the product increases to the extent shown by the position of the line D_1 -D_1 , the original employment indicated by the line O-C can either be retained or restored. We will have to deal with these problems in Part III when the conditions of full employment will be analyzed. It should be noted that in Fig. 5-1 total labor cost remains the same for all three K/L ratios shown. If labor efficiency is low, more workers are required, but their wages are low. This leads to a conclusion of great practical significance: *wage costs are not determined by wage rates but by unit labor costs.* Low wages do not necessarily imply low employment cost because of the low efficiency of labor associated with such a condition. Conversely, high wages may not actually lead to an increase in employment cost if the greater productivity of labor leads to a reduction in the unit labor requirements of output.

Seen in this context, it seems advisable to talk of unit labor cost (ULC) rather than wages in assessing the impact of changes in wage rates on prices and on employment. Figure 5-1 also points out a most difficult problem of labor economics. Certainly it does not operate within the time-honored scheme of relating low wages with high employment, and vice versa. But it does show that high wages reflecting increased productivity of labor occur in the context of a reduction of labor requirements if output remains the same after the introduction of innovations in production. This difficulty cannot be resolved within the framework of Clark's stationary state. It is also not subject to solution within the scope of the "once-over changes" of the K/L ratios shown in that figure.

In order to retain the level of employment O-C in Fig. 5-1 there must be an increase in output commensurate with the reduction in unit labor requirements. The line D_1-D would indicate this new level of output and the demand for labor derived from it. Whether such an increase in output is likely to occur is a question of utmost importance for labor economics. It cannot, however, be answered on the level of a wage theory. We will have to return to it in connection with our analysis of the problems of the labor market and of employment. At this point of our discussion we must direct our attention to the share of aggregate wages in the gross national product.

Many economists have discussed the apparent constancy of the share of wages in the national income. Figure 5-1 gives a general explanation of why we have good reasons to expect such behavior in wages. Inasmuch as higher wages are, through the mechanism of the wage-productivity relationship, associated with a smaller number of workers, and lower wages with a larger number, the basic relationship between wage and nonwage income remains the same, even though changes occur in the capital-labor ratio. This does not mean that the shares are mathematically fixed and are completely unchanging. However, a study of the relation between the compensation of employees and the gross national product over a long period shows a remarkable consistency.

Table 5-1 represents this relationship under two aspects. First there is shown the total compensation of employees. This series is equal to the total wage and salary bill rising out of the realization of the gross national product in a given year. The other series deals with wage disbursements. These represent the take-home pay before taxes but after withholding for social insurance and employers' contributions to private welfare and pension funds. Not shown in that table is the year 1929 when the difference between compensation and disbursements amounted only to $700 million. In the first year shown on Table 5-1 the difference had risen to $2.0 billion. Thirty years later in 1967 it amounted to $44.8 billion or more than 10 per-

TABLE 5-1

COMPENSATION OF EMPLOYEES AND WAGE AND
SALARY DISBURSEMENTS AS PERCENT OF GNP
1937–1967

Year	Compensation as Percent of GNP	Disbursements as Percent of GNP
1937	52.8	50.8
1938	52.8	50.5
1939	52.8	50.4
1940	52.0	49.5
1941	51.5	49.4
1942	53.6	51.6
1943	56.9	54.9
1944	57.4	55.3
1945	57.7	55.1
1946	55.9	53.1
1947	55.0	52.4
1948	54.4	52.1
1949	54.6	52.1
1950	54.2	51.4
1951	54.8	51.9
1952	56.2	53.3
1953	57.2	54.2
1954	57.2	54.1
1955	56.3	53.1
1956	57.8	54.3
1957	57.7	53.9
1958	57.8	53.9
1959	57.7	53.6
1960	58.3	53.9
1961	58.3	53.7
1962	58.1	53.4
1963	57.5	52.7
1964	57.7	53.5
1965	57.6	52.5
1966	58.2	52.6
1967	58.8	53.5

Computed from the *Economic Report of the President*, Tables B-1, B-12 and B-17.

cent of the wage disbursements. With the rise in contributions to old age benefits and the continuing very high allocations for private pension funds the discrepancy between total compensation and wage disbursements is bound to rise even further in the near future.

Now it is important to realize that the item compensation of employees represents the total labor cost of producing the GNP. We see that in a thirty-year period from 1937 to 1967 these total labor costs have risen by 6 percentage points or more than 10 percent. On the other hand actual disbursements rose only by 2.7 percentage points. The wage disbursements are identical with the gross earnings of wage and salary earners· out of which income taxes and the employees' share in contributions to social security are being withheld. If we take into account the fact that between 1937 and 1967 there has been a radical reduction in the number of self-employed farm operators and generally an increase in labor force participation, especially of married women, the 5 percent increase in wage disbursements as a percentage of the GNP actually amount to a striking stability of the share of wage payments in the national product. This becomes even more evident if we compare the 1947 and 1967 percentages shown in Table 5-1. This great stability of wage disbursements as a share of the GNP gives strong empirical support for the specific productivity theory of wages.

5-8. POLICY IMPLICATIONS OF THE SPECIFIC PRODUCTIVITY THEORY OF WAGES

We saw at the beginning of this chapter that wage policies suggested by government or advocated by labor or management are based on concepts of how the economic structure operates and how particular wage settlements are likely to affect the economic system. While the actual modern industrialized system, with its concentration of production and employment with fewer but larger firms and the resultant imperfectly competitive market structure, is far different from J. B. Clark's model, there is a general consensus today that wages ought to move within the margins indicated by Clark's theorem.

In other words, what was a theory of wages developed for the model of a stationary economic system has become a postulate for wage policies designed to fit into the growth requirements of steadily advancing industrialized economies. The Specific Productivity Theory of Wages as a guideline for wage determination seems to have found acceptance in the centrally planned socialistic economy of the Soviet Union. In outlining the five year plan 1966–70, Premier Aleksei N. Kosygin stated: "Wages must be placed in direct relationship to increases in labor productivity and growth of production."[6] He rejected the view hitherto held by Soviet leaders that wage

---

[6]Reported in the *New York Times,* April 20, 1965.

payments could be kept low even in periods of sharp rises in productivity because in the Soviet Union housing, transportation, and medical care take up only a small proportion of the wage-earner's income.

To recognize specific productivity as a guideline for wage setting is one thing; to achieve agreement on the application of this principle, another. During the negotiations for a new contract in the steel industry in 1965, management and labor both accepted the concept of productivity gains as a determinant for wage increases to be scheduled during the lifetime of the new contract. Management, however, used the average increase in productivity in all nonmanufacturing activities whereas labor derived its demand for higher hourly wages from productivity increases in the steel industry itself. Actually, this led to highly divergent standards. The management standard of productivity gains was 2 percent, whereas the union standard was 3.2 percent. In the theoretical model used by Clark there cannot be wide variations in productivity in an industry because perfect competition makes conformity to the least-cost combination of factors a condition of business survival. In an imperfectly competitive system, margins within which the productivity concept can be translated into dollars-and-cents figures of wage rates are greater. Actually the postulates of the productivity wage concept are not bound to the experience in a particular firm. Average values for the industrial sector as a whole might be adequate to achieve the intent of this wage policy.

Linking wage systems to productivity changes has the purpose of maintaining at all times a balance between the rate of change of the aggregate output of industry destined for the consumer sector and the aggregate income of wage and salary earners. In a consumer-oriented peacetime economy in which consumer expenditures are the largest aggregate in the gross national product, an equilibrium between rising output of goods and services and income is the minimum requirement for the economic system to maintain its forward momentum and avoid the always present danger of stagnation. In this sense wages and theories concerning the income of employees are concerned not only with the behavior of the share of labor within a given pattern of income distribution. Wage determination is part and parcel of the decision-making processes which affect the growth and progress of the economic system.

SELECTED BIBLIOGRAPHY

Clark, John B. *The Distribution of Wealth* (New York: The Macmillan Company, 1899).

Douglas, P. H. *The Theory of Wages* (New York: The Macmillan Company, 1934).

Hicks, John R. *The Theory of Wages*, 2d ed. (New York: St. Martin's Press, Inc., 1963).

Perlman, R. *Wage Determination, Market or Power Forces* (Boston: D. C. Heath & Company, 1964).

Rothschild, Kurt W. *The Theory of Wages* (Oxford: Basil Blackwell & Mott, Ltd., 1960).

Tolles, N. Arnold. *Origins of Modern Wage Theories* (Englewood Cliffs, N. J.: Prentice-Hall, Inc., 1964).

Weintraub, Sidney, *Some Aspects of Wage, Theory and Policy* (Philadelphia: Chilton Books, 1963).

QUESTIONS FOR DISCUSSION

1. Wage theories have been attacked as being useless in light of the existence of collective bargaining and other monopolistic institutions. Assuming that these institutions are real forces in the labor market, why then do we study wage theory?

2. Adam Smith cited a highly positive relationship between the specialization of labor and the wealth of nations. Given Smith's environment, what factors may have led him to such a conclusion?

3. Smith is not generally associated with a strict subsistence theory of wages as were his followers. Indicate the areas in which Smith held significantly different views on the plight of wages from his more prominant successors in the classical school.

4. The population theory of Malthus is essential to an understanding of the "Iron Law of Wages." State this theory and point to its implications for wage theory.

5. State the wage theory of David Ricardo.

6. The works of Malthus and Ricardo lead many persons to call economics the "dismal science." In the environment of classical economics, did this label seem fitting?

7. Indicate John Stuart Mill's contribution to Wage Theories and to what extent, if at all, he differed from earlier classical economists in this respect.

8. Indicate clearly and precisely the principal shortcomings of classical wage theory taken as a unit.

9. Although he worked in a different framework than did Ricardo, Marx reached much the same conclusions as the classical economists with respect to wages. Contrast the framework of Marx with that of the classical economists.

10. State the Specific Productivity Theory of Wages as given by J. B. Clark.

11. To what extent does the productivity theory of wages provide a workable framework for contemporary problems of wages and employment?

12. In terms of a macrodynamic theory, what important implications does the productivity theory hold in terms of employment policy?

Chapter

6

Wage Determination and Market Structure

In the preceding chapter it was explained that wage theories assume for purposes of analysis the existence of an unorganized labor market. Although collective bargaining has transformed the strategic sectors in which it is operating into an organized labor market, it is helpful to investigate the process of wage determination separately for these two types of market structures.

6-1. WAGES IN AN UNORGANIZED MARKET

Whenever employees representing labor supply and employers embodying the demand for labor face each other without the intermediary of a union, without such regulatory features as minimum-wage laws but also without such distortions in the demand for labor as racial discrimination, a free labor market can be said to exist. Obviously we have given here the outline of a model rather the description of actual conditions. Just as there has never been a full realization of a perfectly competitive commodity market, there has never been a completely unorganized labor market. But there have been and still are degrees of approximation to this model and they move closer to reality the further removed a labor-market area is from those of its sectors which are organized.

The marginal-utility theory has developed a simple method of analyzing the forces which shape the general level of wages in an unorganized labor market. The concept of utility is at the core of the argument which is being offered. Using a utility calculus on the supply side of the labor market, it is assumed that a person will accept employment only if, in his estimation, the utility of earning an income outweighs the disutility of having to go to work and expending one's labor energy. On the demand side of the labor market, the wage rate will be determined by the utility to the firm of hiring just one more worker. It follows that the general wage rate will be established by the marginal workers for whom the marginal wage offered by the employer is just high enough to induce him to change from a condition of nonemployment to employment and the marginal employer for whom the employment offer of the workers is just low enough to enable him to put them on his payroll.

In Fig. 6-1 a downward-sloping demand curve for labor is shown, indicating that the demand for the product of the firm is somewhat inelastic and that the utility of additional workers declines because of their diminishing contribution to the total revenues of their employer. This demand-supply diagram is given here in order to facilitate the analysis given later in this section.

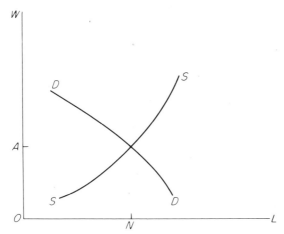

FIG. 6-1.   Wage determination in an unorganized labor market.

In this graph functional relations are assumed to exist between wage rates and demand for labor, *D-D*, and the supply of labor, forthcoming as wage rates change. Using the utility concept already explained, the shape of the labor-supply curve indicates that labor supply rises with increasing wage rates. The downward-sloping demand curve implies that demand for labor increases as wage rates decline. The point of intersection between the two curves determines the number of workers who will be taken off the labor market at the wage rate indicated by *O-A* on the vertical axis.

In the analysis of a perfectly competitive market which would be applicable also to an unorganized labor market, the word "determination" is to be taken rather literally. It means that if the forces of demand and supply on the labor market are entirely free to move according to principles of marginal utility, they must converge at precisely the point of intersection indicated in Fig. 6-1. From this point wage rates and number of workers employed follow with inevitability.

The fact that the completely unorganized labor market is merely a model does not detract from the value of insights which can be gained from a closer examination of the implications of Fig. 6-1. The slope of the demand curve for labor is shaped by the degree of elasticity in the demand for labor. If this demand is emanating from a labor-intensive enterprise—that is, a production system in which labor is the main factor—and if more units are required whenever output is to be stepped up, the demand curve will veer to the right. Conversely, in a capital-intensive enterprise, the demand curve for labor will slope steeply down to the left of the line *D-D*, because in such a case demand for labor is less elastic.

The graph assumes that more labor supply will become available as wage rates are increased. In fact, Fig. 6-1 shows that unless management is willing to pay the wage *O-A* it will not obtain the supply of labor it requires. The upward slope of the labor-supply curve is conditioned by factors which are to some extent operating outside the labor market. In economic systems in a state of transition from subsistence farming to industrialization wage rates have to be high enough to demonstrate that the utility of entering the labor market as industrial workers is greater than the benefit implied for remaining in the subsistence sector. Whenever labor supply is plentiful, even small increases in wage rates will bring about an increase in the number of people willing to work. In this case the labor-supply curve will flatten out. If there is a scarcity of labor, the curve will rise rather steeply to the left of the *S-S* curve in Fig. 6-1. These relationships show the impact of changes in the size of the total labor force on general wage levels.

It has been pointed out that the unorganized labor market under discussion here is a model. Before we turn our attention to an analysis of wage determination under collective bargaining, it is necessary to pay attention to certain built-in factors which prevent actual labor markets from achieving the ideal state of perfect competition even if there is no collective bargaining.

A major factor in the built-in imperfections of an unorganized labor market is time itself. In the normal course of affairs a job applicant is in more urgent need of employment than management is of hiring him. If a job seeker is in the position to postpone employment at a low wage rate in the expectation of obtaining a higher paying job at a later time, he will be on equal terms with the employer so far as timing is concerned, and the situation will move very close to perfect competition.

Another factor obviating the competitive model is the differentiation in the demand for labor and also in labor supply. This introduces rigidities in the labor market that cannot easily be overcome by wage adjustments. Especially in the short run, wage differentials will not serve as the mechanism through which specific supply and demand situations on the labor market can be brought into balance.

Finally, the demand-supply situation is influenced by levels of employment. In periods of more than seasonal unemployment, wage rates do not have to be raised in order to induce a jobless worker to accept employment at prevailing rates. Whereas on the contemporary labor market unemployment does not necessarily exercise a downward pressure on wage rates, the upward push of wages brought about by increases in the demand for labor will be held back so long as unused labor supply within the categories demanded by management remains available.

In the preceding paragraphs it was shown that there are elements in the very structure of the labor market which prevent it from coming close to the perfectly competitive pattern. If we bear this in mind we will also understand that the time-honored assumption that a freely moving wage rate could at all times equate supply and demand of labor has very limited validity. The idea that unemployment can easily be prevented or absorbed by a perfect "downward flexibility" of wage rates presupposes first of all the most complete type of perfect competition on the commodity market. Only in such an ideal state would lower wages be expressed in proportionally lower prices. Furthermore, it would have to be assumed that the overall employment structure is predominantly of the labor-intensive type discussed in this section, so that a substantial increase in employment would occur as wage rates drop. The concept of the equilibrating power of wages also assumes a very great elasticity of demand for the joint end product of capital and labor.

This aspect of the argument has indeed a good deal of plausibility, although it does not prevail ultimately. It is correct to assume that, as real income rises through a lowering of prices for a large number of goods, the income which is no longer claimed for the satisfaction of the demand for these commodities can now shift to hitherto unsatisfied wants. In this way, it is argued, there is no saturation point for aggregate demand even though such a plateau may have been reached with regard to many specific products. While the American economy in the 1960's seems to give support for this thesis, it must be pointed out that the rise in aggregate demand has been brought about not by a downward flexibility of wages but by rising wages. Furthermore, this development has not brought back fully satisfactory levels of employment. To sum up, a completely free wage rate unobstructed by such procedures as collective bargaining would still not establish perfect competition on the labor market. It also would not be a substitute for full-employment policies.

6-2. WAGE DETERMINATION IN ORGANIZED MARKETS

Generally speaking, an organized labor market exists whenever institutional structures modify the working-out of the forces of supply and demand as they behave in the perfectly competitive situation. From the viewpoint of the individual, unorganized worker the employer seems to "monopolize" the job market because of the time advantage, discussed in the previous section, that management has over employees. The banding together of workers into groups, eventually leading to the establishment of unions, has the purpose of overcoming through collective organization the weaknesses inherent in the situation of the individual employee on the labor market. In this sense unions represent the effort of workers to equalize the bargaining position of management and labor and to transform the legal equality shared by employers and employees into a de facto equality.

In order to achieve this condition a union must reach that level of effectiveness at which it can withold labor supply from being employed until such time as an agreement on conditions of pay and work has been obtained. This means that the union must be in a position to prevent workers from going to work at pay scales which are below what it is trying to negotiate. It is clear, then, that unionism becomes operative only when it is capable of determining under what conditions labor supply is either to be denied or to be given to management. Unionism eliminates the competition among unorganized labor for relatively scarce employment opportunities and replaces it with an aggregate supply whose price is to be determined through processes of collective bargaining. This procedure then implies the standardization of conditions of pay and work for all employees covered by the agreement. Furthermore, workers who were not yet employed at the time the contract was signed will automatically receive wages and other benefits in accordance with the collective agreement.

By channeling parts of the labor supply through its organization, by setting conditions for the availability of labor, unions establish areas on the labor market in which labor supply is joined together in aggregates and is handled in monopolistic manner. If it is the purpose of monopolistic behavior and practices to gain an advantage above and beyond what could be achieved in a perfectly competitive setting, then it cannot be denied that this is what unions have been trying to achieve and have actually obtained. It is quite obvious that unions attempt to do far more than to represent the general solidarity of their members; they are specifically oriented to achieve gains for organized labor above and beyond what is within the reach of the individual employee.

The organized labor market has, therefore, monopolistic elements on the supply side as well as on the demand side. The characterizing of this market structure as a bilateral monopoly is therefore entirely apt. One of the immediately discernible effects of this condition is the detachment of wage rates from short-run fluctuations on the labor market. Rates are established for the duration of the contract. This means, typically, a period of two years. In setting wages for such a longer period management and labor isolate themselves from the daily pressures and the ups and downs of an unorgan-

ized market.   In this way a stabilizing element is introduced in an area
which otherwise is subject to wide fluctuations.

Figure 6-2 shows the area within which wage agreements are likely to be
placed under collective bargaining.

The line *D-D* in Fig.   6-2 represents a normal, downward-sloping
demand curve for labor.   The upward-sloping supply curve for labor is cut
off long before it reaches point *D*, the intersection with the demand curve.
The empty space between the cutoff point of the normal labor-supply curve
and the intersection is brought about by organized labor.   When individual
workers are organized into a union, the combined labor supply is directed
towards an area marked by the rectangle *ABCD*.   Within this rectangle
there lie points below the line *AB* and above the line *DC* at which a wage
settlement can be reached.   The union will try to hold out for a point close
to the upper line, whereas management is likely to fight for a point close to
the base of the rectangle.   The rectangle indicates the range within which
bargaining will take place.   Unlike the situation shown in Fig. 6-1, there is no
one determined point for the establishment of a wage rate.   The wage settlement will be found somewhere in this circumscribed area of indeterminacy
shown in Fig. 6-2.

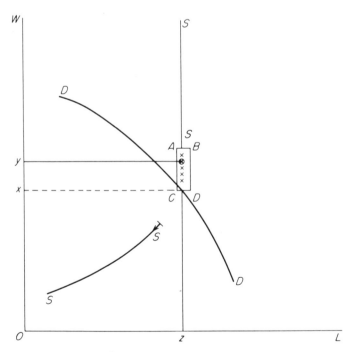

F{ɪɢ}. 6-2.   The area of collective wage determination.

Let us assume that a collective wage agreement is reached at the point circled in the illustration. On the vertical axis we can then measure the difference between the wage rate in an unorganized and an organized market. It is shown by the distance xy. We now turn to the most significant issue connected with this analysis. Figure 6-2 has been drawn so that the number of workers O-z on the horizontal line is the same under individual as under collective bargaining, although wages have been raised as a result of marshaling of labor supply through a labor union. This has been done in order to show as clearly as possible the effect of collective bargaining on wages. To that extent this illustration differs from Fig. 5-1.[1] In that figure relationships between changing productivity, wages, and employment were shown. That analysis was geared to long-run effects. Figure 6-2, on the other hand, presents a once-over change brought about by a transition from individual to collective wage determination. Even on purely analytical grounds, it is therefore possible to assume that in the very short run no changes in employment will result from collective bargaining, although there may not have been any increases in productivity offsetting the increased money cost of employment.

However, the schematic presentation in Fig. 6-2 showing higher wages without any change in employment, and therefore higher employment costs would not apply to industries in which there are continuous technological improvements and increases in labor productivity. Furthermore, the scheme does not cover a longer period of time in which higher unit labor costs may be offset by a rapid expansion in total output.

The analysis carried out here shows, however, that unions in pushing for higher wages may be faced with a choice between levels of wages and levels of employment. In most cases the decision is made in favor of higher wages. The reason is that these higher rates become effective immediately, whereas the effects on employment are either delayed somewhat or are contingent on factors that cannot be clearly identified at the time a contract is reached. The growing insistence on "job security" of employees in the course of collective bargaining negotiations—especially in the demand for longer vacations, more holidays, and "sabbaticals"—is an indication that union leaders are aware of the basic relationship between productivity, wages, and employment and are engaged in the difficult task of striving for higher wages while setting up a shelter for those currently employed through contractual reductions in annual working hours.

It will be noted that in this section dealing with the establishment of wage rates through processes of collective bargaining the concept of wage determination has been retained. Actually the setting of wage rates in an organized labor market gives "determination" a meaning which differs from

[1]See p. 86.

the free-labor-market model. Whereas in the latter the interaction of the forces of supply and demand reaches a determinate point which imposes, as it were, the wage rate and the demand for labor on employers and workers, the determination of wage rates under collective bargaining is an act of deliberate decision making. In this sense the process of wage determination is an activity where conscious wills rather than purely quantitative forces converge. This type of wage setting is closely related in structure to price setting under imperfect competition, which does not necessarily follow short-run fluctuations in supply and demand.

The fact that wage rates in collective agreements are established in this autonomous pattern does not mean that entirely arbitrary solutions are feasible or have any chance to survive in the longer run should they have been agreed upon. The area of indeterminacy shown in Table 6-2 outlines points of possible agreement which are generally clustered around the productivity wage level. Collective wage decisions falling outside this area are likely to be canceled either by accelerated rise in prices or, if they are below the floor, by decreasing aggregate income and employment.

So far we have talked in very general terms about the "wage rate." One of the most important effects of collective bargaining is, however, the extension of wages from a simple pay for the hour to an elaborate wage structure. These structures are explained in detail in Chapters 8 and 9. At this point in our discussion we will deal with this comparatively new development in a more general way.

6-3. GENERAL IMPACT OF COLLECTIVE BARGAINING ON WAGES AND LABOR UNIT COST

The question whether collective bargaining actually raises wages or has a neutral effect on them is still controversial.[2] In our treatment of this question we will show that collective bargaining not only has a tendency to raise wage rates somewhat but also adds additional money outlays to the payrolls, many of which are directly traceable to innovations in wage contracts. Whether or not these new features, such as paid vacations or shift differentials, cause unit labor cost to rise is, however, an entirely different question.[3] But let us first consider wage rates as such.

After the National Labor Relations Act had gone into effect in 1935, the drive to organize operators and other workers below the craft level got under way in major mass-production industries, especially in the steel, automotive, and electrical industries. This period in a way presented ideal conditions for the testing of the effect of collective bargaining on hourly wage rates: the consumer price index showed considerable stability be-

---

[2]See, for example, the papers by Robert Ozanne and John E. Maher, reprinted in *Wage Determination* (Boston: D. C. Heath and Company, 1963).

[3]See the discussion in Chap. 5. The topic is also taken up in Chap. 12.

tween 1936 and 1939 after taking a plunge from 59.7 in 1929 to 45.1 in 1933 (1957-59 = 100). There was, therefore, no reason why wages should be increased so far as living costs were concerned. Throughout the period unemployment as a percent of the civilian labor force remained extremely high. Although it had dropped from the catastrophic peak of 24.9 percent in 1933 to 14.3 percent in 1937, it rose sharply the following year and averaged 17.2 percent in 1939. With this abundant supply of labor, upward pressure on wage rates was nonexistent, and virtually millions of workers would have been happy to obtain employment at wage rates prevailing in 1935. If, therefore, there ever was a time when wage rates could be expected to remain practically unchanged, it was precisely this period from 1935 to 1939. Yet, as Table 6-1 shows, wage rates in durable-goods manufacturing, which includes the industries mentioned above, rose by 12 cents per hour when collective contracts were signed for the first time.

TABLE 6-1
AVERAGE GROSS HOURLY EARNINGS IN
DURABLE-GOODS MANUFACTURING, 1935–39

Year or Month	Durable Goods
1935	$0.571
1936	0.580
1937	0.667
1938	0.679
1939	0.691

SOURCE: *Economic Report of the President* (1965), Table B-28.

It is quite significant that the range of wage increase in nondurable manufacturing in the same period was much more narrow. In these industries in which collective bargaining did not spread very widely, wage increases were about 5 cents, or about 10 percent between 1935 and 1939, whereas they amounted to more than 10 percent in the durable-goods industries. In view of the stability of consumer prices this amounted to a substantial increase in real income of these workers. Nor was this increase in the hourly wage rate accompanied, in durable-goods manufacturing, by a decline in the average weekly hours of work. In fact these rose slightly from 37.2 hours in 1935 to 37.9 hours in 1939.

In the thirty years following the introduction of collective bargaining in mass-production industries the pattern established in that depression period continued. Collective bargaining still has the effect of bringing about somewhat higher wage rates than would otherwise prevail. In a period of accelerated growth such as the years after 1961, this means that workers covered by collective labor contracts will be ahead of nonunion workers in obtaining wage adjustments. However, the experience after World War II has shown that, especially in manufacturing industries, differences between union and nonunion situations tend to become less pronounced. There is a speeding up in this trend, as can be shown in Table 6-2. The median wage increase in manufacturing as well as in non-manufacturing industries was highest in the year 1965 when the impact of the vast increase in defense expenditures began to take hold of the American economy. The great jump from 1964 to 1965 in wages established in collective bargaining situations is particularly notable in the manufacturing industry.

Collective bargaining has an impact on the total wage structure. Its effect is not limited to those segments of the wage and salary earners who are members of unions. This can be seen clearly in Table 6-3.

TABLE 6-2
GENERAL WAGE CHANGES IN MAJOR COLLECTIVE
BARGAINING SITUATIONS
1960–1965

Year	Manufacturing				Nonmanufacturing			
	Median Adjustment		Median Increase		Median Adjustment		Median Increase	
	Cents	Percent	Cents	Percent	Cents	Percent	Cents	Percent
1960	8.7	3.2	8.9	3.2	7.4	3.3	7.5	3.3
1961	6.0	2.4	6.5	2.5	9.0	3.6	10.0	8.6
1962	5.0	2.4	6.8	2.9	10.2	4.0	10.2	4.1
1963	6.8	2.5	8.0	3.0	8.0	3.4	9.5	3.6
1964	5.7	2.0	6.0	2.2	10.0	3.6	10.0	3.6
1965	10.0	4.0	10.0	4.1	11.0	3.7	11.4	3.7

SOURCE: Table 64, *Handbook of Labor Statistics*, U. S. Dept. of Labor, 1967.

TABLE 6-3
AVERAGE MEDIAN WAGE CHANGES FOR UNION AND NONUNION
WORKERS IN MANUFACTURING, 1964

Classification	Adjustment		Increase	
	Cents	Percent	Cents	Percent
All manufacturing.........	5.0	2.2	6.6	2.7
All union.................	6.0	2.3	6.2	2.5
Major union..............	5.7	2.0	6.0	2.2
Nonunion................	4.5	2.0	7.1	3.2

SOURCE: *Monthly Labor Review* (October 1965).

While collective bargaining has a demonstrable impact on wage rates, it has become even more significant in introducing fringe benefits, from paid vacations to company pensions. These are discussed in Chapters 8 and 9.

There can be no doubt that the changes in wage rates, wage structures, and personnel needed to execute agreements induced by collective bargaining increase the money outlay for employment costs. But this fact alone does not determine whether collective bargaining brings about higher unit labor costs and higher prices. A sharp distinction must be made between *total money employment costs* and *unit labor cost*. If wages are raised at a time when no improvements in productivity or in the skill of labor occur, higher wages will not only bring about higher outlays for employment but also a corresponding increase in unit labor cost. However, if wages are raised in periods of increasing output per man-hour, unit labor cost can remain the same as they were before the round of wage increases. To equate higher wages with higher labor costs and with higher prices is a simplification of these relationships which appeals only to the semiliterate in the field of economic analysis.

We have shown in Table 5-1 that total compensation of employees as a percentage of the GNP rose by 6 index points, from 52.8 percent to 58.8 percent in the 30 year period from 1937 to 1967. However more than half of this increase is due to levies to be paid by employers on top of the wage disbursements especially for contributions to social insurance. This substantial increase in the total employment cost necessary to produce the Gross National Product is not attributable to collective bargaining but to legislation. If we now turn our attention to the share of wage and salary disbursements in the GNP in the 1937 to 1967 period we find only a 2.7 percent shift. However it should be noted that collective bargaining which became intensified in 1937 and thereafter cannot be blamed or credited for this increase for the very simple reason that in the years preceding 1937, wage disbursements actually were in the same range or even slightly higher relative to the GNP. Wage disbursements as a percentage of the GNP reached a high of 51.2 percent in 1932. They dropped to 50.7 percent in 1936. It should also be noted that their share dropped from 53.9 percent in 1937 to 53.5 percent in 1967 whereas at the same time compensation of employees as a percentage of the GNP rose from 57.7 percent to 58.8 percent.

The conclusion suggests itself that on the macroscale, where we observe distributive shares in the aggregate, collective bargaining has a neutral effect. This, however, does not mean that collective bargaining is unnecessary. A study covering the 1920's and published by The Brookings Institution in 1940[4] showed that especially prior to 1935 industry failed to raise wages in proportion to productivity gains. Other studies on an establishment level have confirmed that whenever collective bargaining becomes suspended as for instance in Germany during the Hitler regime, wages begin to lag behind the growth of productivity of labor.[5] It seems, therefore, that collective bargaining is necessary in a private enterprise system in order to insure that the postulate of the specific productivity

[4]Spurgeon Bell, *Productivity, Wages, and National Income*, (Washington, D.C.: The Brookings Institution, 1940).
[5]For references see next footnote.

theory of labor and, therefore, that wage level which is required for the maintenance of dynamic equilibrium is being preserved.

Whenever an industry is in the process of modernization and continuous adaptation to technical innovation, it is most likely that even substantial increases in employment costs will not bring about significant changes in labor unit costs. The reason for this is simple: while the collective agreement will force the employer to spend more for the employment of each worker—that is to say, unit of labor—fewer labor units are required for each unit of output. As was shown in Fig. 5-1, higher wages will increase the outlay for each worker without bringing about an increase in the aggregate labor cost. In industries which are continuously increasing the rate of mechanization and automation, unit labor costs are far less influenced by changes in wage rates than by levels of capacity utilization. An establishment study of one of the largest steel corporations in the United States[6] has shown that unit labor costs were highest in 1931 and 1932 when plant utilization had reached an all-time low. This period coincided with a sharp drop of wages from the preceding high of 1929. We find here a case where low wage rates were associated with high labor costs. If we follow the study through to the 1950's, we find that wage costs rose sharply while unit labor costs remained steady and were actually not higher in this establishment than they had been prior to World War I.

Although it can be shown that substantial improvements in wages and other working conditions do not necessarily lead to an increase in labor cost per unit, a word of caution must be inserted here. It was stated above that we must also take into consideration the elasticity of demand for the final product. In the case study referred to in this section, as well as in such industries as bituminous coal mining and construction, increased employment costs per worker (which, at least in the short run, were not completely offset by lower unit costs) were shifted to the ultimate consumer through higher prices. This was particularly true when these industries were operating in a sellers' market, where it could be safely assumed that demand for the products of these industries was inelastic. The same situation prevails only more so, in industries producing supplies for the government, especially for national defense. In the fiscal year 1968 $44 billion was spent with American industry for military procurement. The usual "cost plus" system of allowing for progress after cost does not create any incentive to keep employment cost low.

So far we have discussed only the case of an industry undergoing continuous technological improvements and with relative inelasticity of demand for their products. Collective bargaining has entirely different effects

[6]*Wages Productivity and Unit Labor Cost*, Economic Research Project No. 2, Fordham University, 1958; see also F. Baerwald, "Das Problem Der Lohninflation In Lichte Des Berichtes Der U. S. Steel Corporation Fuer Das Jahr 1956," *Soziale Welt* (Göttingen), 1958.

in labor-intensive industries with limited possibilities of mechanization. In such cases not only employment cost per worker but also employment cost per unit may rise steeply. This may lead either to actual layoffs or to a reluctance of employers to hire additional personnel as the possibility of increasing the volume of operations arises. The preference of Broadway producers for one-set, four-person plays illustrates the point made here.·

In manufacturing industries and in all other fields of production in which advanced mechanization or even automation is applied, wage rates must always be evaluated in terms of their impact on unit labor cost. When guidelines for collective bargaining were urged upon labor and management by the Council of Economic Advisors suggesting that they keep annual increases in wage rates to 3.2 percent there developed in the course of time a widespread disregard of these yardsticks which had been intended to assure maintenance of economic growth under conditions of price stability. The reason for this breakdown of the wage guideline policy can be seen easily in Table 6-4.

TABLE 6-4
INDEX OF OUTPUT PER MAN-HOUR, 1963–1968
(1957–1958 = 100)

Year	Total Private	Farm	Nonfarm Industries		
			Total	Manufacturing	Non-Manufacturing
1963	117.9	133.1	115.7	118.9	114.3
1964	122.5	135.5	120.0	124.7	118.0
1965	126.6	148.1	123.6	129.8	120.5
1966	131.4	152.9	127.7	131.6	125.4
1967	133.5	171.7	129.0	132.5	127.1
1968	137.9	172.1	133.4	136.2	131.9

SOURCE: Table B-34, *Economic Report of the President,* January 1969.

We leave out from further discussion the farm sector where productivity gains have been far greater than in any other part of the American economy. These enormous advances are due to the still continuing agricultural revolution. But we must disregard agriculture because it represents an ever declining part of the labor force. Furthermore, farm laborers are not covered by wage guidelines for the simple reason that they are excluded from the protection and the rights given to nonfarm workers in labor relations legislation. Turning now our attention to total nonfarm output per man-hour we note that this increased on the average of 4.3 percent per annum during the period in which the wage guide lines try to maintain the 3.2 percent per annum. In manufacturing the average annual increase in output per man-hour was close to 4 percent, again far in excess of the 3.2 percent yardstick.

By 1968 wage guidelines were dropped. This change in policy was not based on sound thinking. Wage guidelines in order to be effective must, of course, operate with correct statistical values which must be adjusted in a flexible manner to changing factual conditions. The mistake made with the guidelines of 1963 was that they incorporated in their average concept the recession years of the late 1950's in which productivity was low. An attempt to maintain this low productivity yardstick in a period in which the economy, output and output per man-hour gained considerable momentum showed very little adaptability on the part of the Administration.

More recently the confusion became compounded when President Nixon in October, 1969 issued a "Plea" to unions and business to exercise patience and self-discipline in the matter of wage increases. He stated, "New laws and new restrictions are not required if we treat with respect the law of supply and demand." It should be noted that this Presidential letter which was addressed to about 2,200 business and labor leaders came months after union contracts, especially in the construction industry, concluded in 1969 had provided for annual wage increases in excess of 7 percent. Experience has shown that "moral suasion" is no substitute for the type of economic reasoning which is embodied in guidelines representing valid figures on increases in productivity and taking into account the transformation of labor force and the equilibrium growth requirements of an advanced system having adopted the goal of maintaining full employment.

Let us now return to the core of the economic argument: the relation between output per man-hour, compensation per man-hour and unit labor costs. Table 6-5 will show that total labor unit cost began to rise sharply in the 1959 to 1961 recession and drop slightly as the economy started on its upswing.

TABLE 6-5

INDEXES OF OUTPUT PER MAN-HOUR, COMPENSATION PER MAN-HOUR AND UNIT LABOR COSTS IN MANUFACTURING, 1958–1964 (1957–1959 = 100)

Year	Output per Man-hour (all employees)	Compensation per Man-hour in Current Dollars (all employees)	Unit Labor Costs (all employees)
1958	99.1	99.9	100.8
1959	103.3	104.0	100.8
1960	103.8	108.1	104.2
1961	106.7	111.5	104.5
1962	112.6	115.7	102.8
1963	115.3	119.5	103.7
1964	119.6	123.3	103.1

SOURCE: *Monthly Labor Review* (September 1965).

The increase in unit labor costs shown in Table 6-5 continued after 1965 as will be shown in Table 6-6. This occurred because real compensation per man-hour in the total private nonfarm sector of the economy began to rise more rapidly than output per man-hour after 1965. It should be noted that we are referring here to developments in the production and in the non-production sector of the economy. As far as the development in manufacturing is concerned output per man-hour continued to rise at a greater annual rate.

TABLE 6-6

ANNUAL AVERAGE PERCENT CHANGES OF OUTPUT PER MAN-HOUR,
HOURLY COMPENSATION, AND UNIT LABOR COSTS PRIVATE NONFARM

Period	Output	Man-hours	Output Per Man-hour	Compensation Per Man-hour	Real Compensation Per Man-hour	Unit Labor Costs
1947–68	3.9	1.2	2.7	4.7	2.9	1.9
1957–68	4.7	1.6	3.0	4.4	2.7	1.3
1961–65	5.8	2.2	3.5	4.0	2.7	0.5
1965–68	4.3	1.8	2.4	6.4	3.0	3.9
1966–67	1.7	0.7	1.0	6.0	3.0	4.9
1967–68	5.2	1.8	3.3	7.3	3.0	3.9

SOURCE: *Monthly Labor Review* (June 1969).

In order to understand this departure of wage-productivity relations after 1965 from the long term trend of the preceding decade, it is necessary to realize that full employment, that is to say, overall unemployment of less than 4 percent of the civilian labor force was established in the United States only in 1966. On the one side hard core unemployment continued but on the other severe labor shortages developed in many skilled blue-collar and white-collar occupations. This shows that once full employment has been achieved relations between labor productivity, wages and unit labor costs have a tendency to become unstable thereby bringing about substantial increases in wages, labor costs and prices.

This instability is enhanced by the ongoing transformation of the labor force with its continuing relative decline of production workers and corresponding increase in nonproduction workers. Furthermore, the compensation of nonproduction workers in constant 1957–1959 dollars has increased faster than that of production workers as will be shown in Table 6-7.

We see from Table 6-7 that real compensation began to rise faster in the low productivity sector of the economy than in the high productivity sector as the white-collar economy emerged. If for the sake of the argument the term "wage-push inflation" is borrowed from those who are eager to use it in a most general way, this kind of effect seems to be located in the nonproduction worker sector of the labor force. Now it is this sector which in all likelihood will continue to increase as a result of mechanization and automation. The question will then arise whether the concept of output

TABLE 6-7
REAL COMPENSATION PER MAN-HOUR FOR
PRODUCTION AND NONPRODUCTION WORKERS
(1957–1959 = 100)

Year	Production Workers	Nonproduction Workers
1957	98.9	98.1
1958	99.5	97.3
1959	101.6	104.1
1960	103.9	105.6
1961	104.9	108.7
1962	107.3	112.7
1963	110.0	113.6
1964	112.1	116.1

SOURCE: *Monthly Labor Review* (September 1965).

per man-hour as used in current measurements of productivity can be retained.

If we consider production workers only, the evidence presented in the two preceding tables suggests strongly that the American economy is performing remarkably close to the expectations of the specific productivity theory of wages. However, the rapidly changing structure of employment, the transition from a blue-collar to a white-collar economy, and the increasing nonwage aspects of employment costs create doubts as to whether the old productivity concepts are still a valid frame of reference in the evaluation of wages. The far reaching impact of this transformation especially on problems of employment and economic growth will be discussed further in Chapters 13 and 14 of this book.

As the economy continues to make rapid advances in technology, the need becomes more urgent to keep in mind the great difference that exists between wages and employment costs. To assume that both are moving necessarily in the same direction would overlook not only the all-important factor of unit labor cost; it would also fail to take cognizance of the implications of the emerging white-collar economy of the United States.

SELECTED BIBLIOGRAPHY

Dunlop, John T. *Wage Determination Under Trade Unions* (New York: Macmillan Press, 1944).

Lester, R. A. "Reflections on the Labor Monopoly Issue," in *Journal of Political Economy* (December 1947).

Lewis, H. S. *Unionism and Relative Wages in the United States* (Chicago, Ill.: University of Chicago Press, 1963).

Reynolds, Lloyd G. and Cynthia H. Taft. *The Evolution of Wage Structure* (New Haven: Yale University Press, 1956).

QUESTIONS FOR DISCUSSION

1. Outline the determination of wages in an unorganized market, paying special attention to the forces that account for the supply and demand for labor and the mechanism which allows for equilibrium to be provided for and maintained.

2. Although a model of wage determination in a perfect market does not approach a "real world situation," it does provide some basic insights into the nature of the labor market. Indicate several areas in which these insights manifest themselves in the real world.

3. In contemporary society, would perfectly flexible wages, as suggested in the perfect market model, be likely to maintain full employment?

4. In terms of the supply-and-demand schedules, point out the significant differences between the wage determinates in the perfect and organized markets with special attention to the factors that account for these differences.

5. It has been said that the existence of collective bargaining makes wage rates indeterminant. State your opinion on this question.

6. The analysis of Chapter 6 points to the fact that unions may often be faced with a decision between advocating higher wages at the cost of greater unemployment. What are the factors which give rise to this situation, and what accounts for union preference in either direction?

7. It has been argued that unions do not really increase wages any more than they would have been increased in the absence of unions. State the opposing views on this question and give your own opinion.

8. Changing wage rates and wage structures have important implications for employment policy in that they affect unit labor costs. What preliminary insights into the nature of these relationships can be made on the basis of the analysis in Chapter 6?

9. It is said that if, over time, increases in wages are just equal to increases in productivity, unit labor costs should remain basically stable. Why is this held to be the case?

10. Discuss the impact of the emerging white-collar economy on wage-productivity relations.

Wages, Hours, Occupations, and Regions

The distinction between salary and wage earners continues to have practical significance. Usually people on salary are paid by the week, whereas wage earners are "hourly rated employees." By and large they comprise the group of blue-collar workers. The weekly earnings of this segment of labor are determined by two variables: the hourly wage rate and the hours worked per week.

Under the impact of collective bargaining, hourly wage rates are not subject to short-run changes, at least so far as "straight time compensation" is concerned—that is, the regular rate without such attachments as bonuses or overtime pay. On the other hand, weekly earnings can fluctuate widely due to the variation in the work week. These changes are often an immediate response to changing levels of industrial activity.

If we take a longer period into consideration, there has been a continuous rise in hourly earnings, whereas the weekly hours of work have declined somewhat. In 1929 the average weekly hours in manufacturing still were 44.2. In 1964 they had dropped to 40.7. On the other hand, average gross hourly earnings in manufacturing rose from $0.56 in 1929 to $2.54 in 1964. In the 1930's the average work week in manufacturing reached a low of 34.6 hours in 1934. The decline in hourly wages was far less. In 1934 they had declined only to $0.53, while as a result of the sharp curtailment of the work week, average weekly earnings in manufacturing had dropped from $24.76 to $18.20. Since World War II average gross weekly earnings in manufacturing have climbed steadily from year to year until they reached $122.51 in 1968.

7-1. MINIMUM WAGES AND MAXIMUM HOURS

Throughout the depression period of the 1930's organized labor insistently demanded the introduction of a 30-hour week on the theory that this might stretch employment opportunities and make more jobs available to more people. The Fair Labor Standards Act of 1938, popularly known as the Wages and Hours Law, did not respond to this demand. It established instead the 40-hour week. Actually few industries had work weeks of that duration at that time. On the other hand, working hours in wholesale and retail trade and in many service industries were substantially higher. But these occupations, because of their intrastate character, were not affected by the Federal law.

One important aspect of the legal establishment of a maximum work week is the emergence of the concept and practice of overtime pay. As long as there is no definition of what constitutes a normal work week it is difficult to talk of overtime. In the United States the normal overtime pay is "time-and-a-half." In some other countries such rates start with time and a quarter. Now it must be clearly understood that such requirements for extra pay were not intended originally to give a boost to the weekly earnings of employees. The prime purpose of overtime provisions is to discourage management from ordering overtime work. The higher rates for overtime hours are more designed as a penalty for employers than as a boon for workers. Obviously employment costs for the overtime hours are at least 50 percent higher than the straight-time wages. Ideally, management should not order overtime work at all but rather call in additional workers at straight-time rates if there is need to step up production.

The actual experience of recent years has shown that in many cases overtime pay is no deterrent to management. The experience of World War II when the average weekly hours rose to 45 in 1943 cannot, however, be taken as an example of this condition. The labor shortages of the war period left no other recourse but a substantial increase in the work week. Furthermore, "cost-plus" contracts in government procurement tend to deemphasize strict economy in business management.

It must be noted, also, that in recent years the average work week in the automotive industry was consistently longer than 40 hours, running to 42.7 hours in 1962, 42.8 hours in 1963, and more than 43 hours in 1964. The same pattern could be found in some sectors of the textile industry, such as silk and floor covering. If we take into account that in the manufacturing industries as a whole employment rose only insignificantly during the first five years of the 1960's whereas output came close to 150 percent of the 1957–59 base early in 1965, considerable doubt must be voiced about the continual validity of intended employment incentives of overtime pay. Actually the incidence of overtime is very unevenly spread throughout the nonagricultural private sector of the economy. Even after 1965 when unemployment dropped from 4.5 percent of the labor force in that year to 3.5 percent in 1969, average weekly hours declined from 38.8 in 1965 to 37.7

hours per week. But these low overall figures are the result of short working hours in retail trade—34.2-in. 1969—in nondurable goods manufacturing, and construction. On the other side overtime continued even in early 1970 especially in certain branches of machinery production. In January 1970 the hours in the metal working machinery industry still were 44.3; in machine tools, 43.0; and in special dies, tools and fixtures, 46.8. Printing trades machinery in January 1970 still had a work week of 43.1 hours. In aircraft parts the work week at the same priood was 43.0. On the other hand there had been a drop in the average weekly hours in motor vehicle production to 39.3 hours in January 1970 compared to 41.9 hours in January 1969. The example of the automobile industry given here shows that the work week follows with a certain lag the actual decline in output. It must be borne in mind that a cut in the work week, eliminating the time and a half feature of the overtime pay brings about a more than proportionate cut in average weekly earnings. In the automobile industry the average weekly earnings in January 1969 had been $173.47; in January 1970 they had dropped to $166.55. During the same period, however, the Consumer Price Index rose from 124.1 percent to 131.8 percent (1957–1959 = 100). It is easy to see then that a simultaneous elimination of overtime pay and a rise in consumer prices can bring about a noticeable decline in real income, or purchasing power of wage earners.

The original purpose of overtime pay has been also vitiated by a clause in some collective agreements with electricians' unions whereby the work week was cut to 25 hours with a certain number of additional "overtime" hours guaranteed. Guaranteed overtime would seem to be a contradiction in terms. Actually, such a practice is a device to increase average weekly earnings above and beyond what is implied in the straight-time hourly wage rate.

Table 7-1 establishes that in April 1969, 28.7 percent of the nonagricultural labor force worked 41 hours and over. The 22.3 percent who worked from 1 to 34 hours a week represent largely that part of the labor force on part-time employment. Here the differences between male and female workers are of particular significance.

While this use of the overtime device must be termed excessive, it is nevertheless important to see it in its proper perspective. Actually, at the end of December 1964, the average total working hours for the non-agricultural industries were almost standard, amounting to 40.1 hours. In subsequent years the average work week in manufacturing rose again to reach a high of 41.3 hours in 1966; however, in the durable goods industry the work week had risen in the same year to 42.1 hours. There was a decline in average weekly hours later in the 1960's. It should be noted, however, that this figure is arrived at by averaging out full time and part time workers. Table 7-1 illustrates this.

TABLE 7-1
PERSONS AT WORK BY TYPE OF INDUSTRY AND HOURS OF WORK
APRIL 1969

Hours of Work	Percentage of Distribution		
	All Industries	Nonagricul-tural Industries	Agricul-ture
Total at work..............	100.0	100.0	100.0
1–34 hours	26.9	26.4	39.1
1–4 hours	1.1	1.1	1.1
5–14 hours	5.3	5.0	11.0
15–29 hours	12.4	12.0	21.4
30–34 hours	8.1	8.2	5.6
35 hours and over..........	73.1	73.6	60.9
35–39 hours	6.0	6.0	6.1
40 hours	38.6	38.8	11.0
41 hours and over	28.6	27.9	43.8
41 to 48 hours	12.1	12.2	8.7
49 to 59 hours	9.2	9.0	12.7
60 hours and over ...	7.3	6.7	22.5
Average hours, total at work	38.7	38.6	41.0
Average hours, workers on full-time schedules	42.8	42.5	49.5

SOURCE: Table A-22, *Employment and Earnings*, U.S. Dept. of Labor, (May 1969).

Table 7-1 shows that in all industries 38.6 percent of the workers worked 40 hours: 27.6 percent worked between 41 and 48 hours whereas 26.9 percent of all workers worked from 1 to 34 hours per week. It is clear then that a considerable majority of the labor force, actually two-thirds were working 40 hours and more in 1969. This remains true even if agricultural work where working hours tend to be long is discounted and we concentrate only on nonagricultural industries. On the other hand we also see a considerable proportion of the labor force working only up to 34 hours per week with the greatest concentration in the 15 to 29 hours a week range.

Table 7-2 will show in detail voluntary part-time employment by males and by females in white-collar, blue-collar and service occupations. Throughout we will find that part-time employment is associated to a far greater extent to women than to men. It should be noted that Table 7-2 is dealing only with voluntary part-time employment. Obviously part-time employment even at standard wage rates is yielding a lower annual income than full-time employment. Therefore we find in this area of voluntary part-time employment that still increasing segment of the labor force whose purpose of being in the labor market is not so much to earn a living but to implement and add to the income of the family.

The Fair Labor Standards Act, in addition to putting a "ceiling" on the work week, also established a "floor" under hourly earnings. A 25-cent minimum was put into effect immediately. The law provided for a stepping-up of these minimum wages to 40 cents per hour over a period of seven

TABLE 7-2
VOLUNTARY PART TIME EMPLOYMENT, MALE AND FEMALE
APRIL 1969 IN PERCENTAGES

	Male	Female
White-collar workers...........................	6.8	22.6
Professional and technical.....................	6.6	21.6
Managers, officials, and proprietors.............	2.6	12.7
Clerical workers	10.6	19.6
Sales workers................................	13.4	46.7
Blue-collar workers	6.6	9.1
Craftsmen and foremen	3.0	12.2
Operatives...................................	5.9	8.5
Nonfarm laborers............................	18.3	20.2
Service Workers	21.1	39.0
Private household............................	64.4	56.5
Other service workers	20.5	32.7

SOURCE: Table A-26, *Employment and Earnings*, U. S. Dept. of Labor, (May 1969).

years. With the steep rise in the wages and prices in the 1940's these minimum wages soon became sub-standard but only in 1949 was the minimum wage raised to 75 cents per hour. In the early 1960's minimum-wage standards were increased to $1.25 and further increases were scheduled. In 1965 organized labor demanded raising the minimum wage to $1.75 per hour by 1968. However, Congress limited the minimum wage to $1.60 by that year.

In 1966 Congress passed an important Amendment to the Fair Labor Standard Act (FLSA). A new wage floor, setting the minimum hourly wage at $1.60 was established. It went into effect on February 1, 1967. It was estimated that this higher minimum wage raised the earnings of about 4.7 million employees who had received less than $1.60 an hour prior to the effective date of the FLSA Amendment of 1966. The aggregate increase in wages brought about by this upgrading of the minimum wage was figured at $1.1 billion a year.

Even more important than this increase of the minimum wage was a vast extension of coverage of the employees given the protection of the wages and hours law. Through this amendment, 3.1 million employees in the services were brought into the law, 2.4 million in government, 2.2 million in retail trade, 0.6 million in construction, and 0.5 million in agriculture. This extension of coverage affected employees of laundries, schools, hospitals, and hotels. However, in this area of employment, employees working in very small enterprises were still exempted. Among government workers maintenance workers in schools and more than 600,000 employees in state and local government hospitals were now protected by minimum wage legislation. Nevertheless even this 1966 Amendment which brought more than 9 million additional employees into the system still left 11.4 million without such protection. The overall effect of the minimum wage legislation can be seen in Table 7-3.

As can be seen from the last column of Table 7-3, the large bulk of agri-

TABLE 7-3
COVERAGE OF FAIR LABOR STANDARD ACT AS OF FEBRUARY 1967
(in thousands)

| Industry | Total | Covered Employees | | Not Covered |
		Total Covered	Included by 1966 Amendment	
United States.........	50,429	41,428	9,121	11,437
Agriculture, forestry and fisheries..................	1,517	477	460	1,040
Mining.....................	550	544	—	6
Contract construction	3,236	3,201	625	35
Manufacturing	17,481	16,903	69	578
Transportation, com- munications, utilities	3,823	3,751	112	72
Wholesale trade	3,133	2,368	143	765
Retail trade	8,690	5,060	2,210	3,630
Finance, insurance, real estate.....................	2,687	1,998	—	689
Services (excluding domestic service)..........	6,871	4,690	3,066	2,181
Domestic service	2,441	—	—	2,441
Government	—	2,436	2,436	—

SOURCE: Table 1, Edward C. Martin, "Extent of Coverage Under FLSA as Amended in 1966," *Monthly Labor Review*, (April 1967).

cultural workers still remains outside the coverage of FLSA. It should be noted that this group of labor is not only excluded from the protection of minimum wage legislation; it also does not enjoy the right to bargain collectively. The substantial number of employees still not included in retail and wholesale trade are attached to businesses whose dollar volume of business is less than $250,000 a year.

The income of wage and salary earners is, as we have seen in the preceding section, made up of two variables: the pay per hour or per week and the total hours or weeks which have been worked in a given period of time. As a result weekly earnings are of great significance because they are the product of hourly earnings and the number of hours worked per week. Since the work week is more subject to short run fluctuations than are hourly wage rates weekly earnings are bound to vary accordingly. This will be investigated in some detail in the next section.

7-2. WEEKLY EARNINGS IN VARIOUS OCCUPATIONS

During the depression of the 1930's average weekly hours of work declined sharply. They were 44.2 hours in 1929 and dropped to 34.6 hours in 1934. In 1939, after the 40 hour maximum work week had gone into effect the average weekly hours in manufacturing had risen only from the low indicated above to 37.7 hours. Hourly earnings in manufacturing dropped from 56 cents in 1929 to 44 cents in 1933. After that a sharp recovery and eventually an increase in average weekly hourly earnings set in reaching

63 cents per hour in 1939. It should be noted that this meant a substantial increase in real earnings because the Consumer Price Index on the basis of 1957–1959 = 100 had dropped from 59.7 in 1929 to 48.4 in 1939. But due to the sharp reduction in working hours gross weekly earnings in manufacturing in 1939 amounted to only $23.84 as compared to $24.76 in 1929. It must also be remembered, however, that unemployment in 1939 was extremely high, reaching 17.2 percent of the civilian labor force. Compared to 1929 about half a million fewer workers were employed in manufacturing in 1939.

After World War II average weekly hours in manufacturing for all industries fluctuated around the 40 hour normal maximum work week with notable exceptions only in the durable goods industries where in 1964 and 1965 the average weekly hours were 42. On the other hand average hourly earnings rose steadily. Table 7–4 analyzes the development of hourly wage increases for the years 1959 through 1966. It shows steady increases of hourly wages for organized and nonunion workers although the annual increases for the latter are somewhat smaller than those for union members.

TABLE 7-4
ESTIMATED HOURLY WAGE INCREASES FOR FACTORY PRODUCTION WORKERS
1955–1966

Year	All Factories	All Unions	Major Unions	Non-Unions
1959	$ .075	$ .079	$ .084	$ .061
1960	.076	.084	.09	.05
1961	.006	.088	.069	.02
1962	.045	.06	.065	.03
1963	.065	.007	.075	.06
1964	.055	.055	.055	.046
1965	.075	.08	.10	.063
1966	.085	.087	.099	.08

SOURCE: William Davie and Lily Mary David, "Pattern of Wage and Benefit Changes in Manufacturing," *Monthly Labor Review* (February 1968).

So far in this section we have discussed hours and earning patterns in manufacturing. Some of the more striking relations between hours and earnings have taken place in mining and contract construction. In bituminous coal mining for instance there has been a remarkable increase in the number of hours worked per week. Even in 1929 the work week in that industry was only 38.1 hours. It dropped as low as 23.3 hours in 1938. Throughout most of the period after World War II the work week in mining was substantially shorter than in manufacturing. Traditionally this was explained by the greater physical hardships connected with mining operations. In recent years operations in bituminous coal mining have been automated to a large extent and employment of production workers has been stabilized around 120,000 workers. But at the same time there was a substantial increase in the hourly work week rising as high as 41.4 hours in 1967 and generally maintaining itself slightly above 40 hours a week. In the late sixties, we find thorough modernization carried out in bituminous coal mining, a stabilization of employment after years of a steady reduction in the work force but also a more than 10 percent increase in the work week. Consequently the average weekly earnings in that industry kept miners among the top wage earners being exceeded only by those in contract construction. In January 1969, average weekly earnings in bituminous coal mining were $171.39; they had risen to $180.74 one year later. The corresponding weekly earnings for contract construction were $168.09 and $179.75. However the average hourly earnings in construction were substantially higher than in bituminous coal mining, $5.05 for the latter in January 1970 as compared to $4.37. As a result average weekly earnings in construction were higher than in mining in 1969 but the average work week was about 12 hours less in construction than in bituminous coal mining.

Although wage rates in various basic and durable goods industries are set in entirely different processes of collective bargaining, there is a certain tendency towards convergence of weekly earnings although time lags occur due to different contract termination dates. We have seen that in January 1970 coal miners in the bituminous field earned $180.74. But for coal mining in general weekly earnings were in the same month $177.86; working in blast furnaces and steel mills earned $165.65 in January 1970 and automobile workers $164.67 at the same time, as can be seen on Table C-2 of "Employment and Earnings," April 1969, published by the U.S. Department of Labor.

In spite of the fairly high weekly earnings in these three industries just mentioned average weekly earnings in manufacturing were still only $110.78. In order to demonstrate the wide gap in weekly earnings some high and some low levels in weekly earnings will be listed in Table 7-5.

TABLE 7-5
HIGH AND LOW AVERAGE WEEKLY EARNINGS OF PRODUCTION WORKERS

Occupation	February 1968	February 1969
Electrical Workers	$194.27	$204.91
Brokerage employees....................	159.83	182.60
Passenger car bodies	148.19	180.20
Petroleum refining	160.66	172.22
Handbags, leather goods	79.70	74.92
House furnishings......................	73.15	73.57
Poultry dressing.......................	66.77	70.95
Hotels, motels, etc.....................	58.00	61.95

SOURCE: Table C-2, *Employment and Earnings*, (April 1969).

Table 7-5 demonstrates the very large spread of weekly earnings ranging up to 100 percent. Generally an increase in weekly earnings is shown although it was quite limited in the low wage groups. In one instance, hand-
bags, weekly earnings declined sharply due to a drop of the work week
from 38.5 hours to 33.9 hours which nullified the increase in 14 cents per
hour between 1968 and 1969.

7-3. ACTUAL ANNUAL EARNINGS AND GUARANTEED WAGES

The census data for 1960 was used by the U. S. Labor Department to
study[1] the annual earnings of no less than 321 occupations. These range
from physicians, whose median annual earnings were found to be highest in
this survey, to newsboys, whose earnings—$550 median—were found to be
lowest in this analysis. Median annual earnings of laborers were $3.052 in
1959. That is, one-half of laborers earned more, but one-half of this group
earned less than this amount. The income of laborers was equated to 100.
This enabled the author to establish an earnings index. Physicians receive a
top ranking of 477. Managers, either self-employed or in banking and finance, scored 418. Professors and instructors reached 226, secondary
school teachers 193, other teachers 175.

After this excursion into the sectors of the professions and management,
let us return to the wage and salary earners. Workers in printing and publishing—for example, compositors and typesetters—earn an hourly wage
rate far above the average in manufacturing. The same is true of engravers.
But the median annual earnings of these two groups of craftsmen were in
the neighborhood of $5,800 in 1959, with a ranking of 189 and 188 respec-
tively on the earnings index. This comparatively low annual income is due
to the fact that about 20 percent of this group does not work a full year—
which is understood to be employment from 50 to 52 weeks.

The same condition prevails for many other experienced craftsmen.
Only 45.7 percent of the structural metalworkers had full-year employment
in 1959. Among the Teamsters, only 36.8 percent worked at least 50 weeks a
year. Longshoremen and stevedores showed an even smaller percentage of
full-time employment—42.5 percent, yet teamsters and longshoremen command very high hourly earnings.

In view of these very great variations in the number of weeks or days
worked during a year in the same occupation, considerable differentials in
annual earnings are characteristic of this type of employment. In fact, an informal differentiation according to income exists among workers all draw-
ing the same hourly wage. In such situations, what really matters for the

---

[1]Max A. Rutzick, "A Ranking of U.S. Occupations by Earnings," *Monthly Labor
Review* (March 1965).

individual workers and his family is not so much the wage rate as the way in which he is placed with regard to longer-term, or even year-round, employment opportunities.

It is in this area that the difference in the mode of pay and of employment between blue-collar and white-collar workers becomes rather pronounced. Clerical workers such as stenographers, secretaries, and office employees have a greater percentage of full-time employment than many categories of workers in manufacturing, construction, and transportation. Accountants and auditors with median annual earnings of $6,591 per year showed a full-year employment rate of 88.4 percent. Salaried managers with slightly lower annual earnings were employed the year round to the extent of 90 percent. It must be understood that this study is based strictly on the actual weeks spent in doing a particular type of job. Consequently it can be assumed that occupations with very low year-round employment opportunities will force those affiliated with them to look for other work in their off-season. For instance, athletes have only a 41.7 percent year-round employment rate. Hence they may also be working in other occupations listed in this survey. In this way their actual annual earnings are likely to be higher than is indicated by the earning index of their main occupational affiliation.

Once we leave the ranks of the professional, managerial, and technical occupations we encounter a large number of occupations in which a considerable proportion of all people work far less than 50 or 52 weeks a year. For instance, the year-round employment rate of such workers as assemblers is only 56.5 and of workers in manufacturing, 64.4. It is easy to see that the yearly earnings of many employees coming under such occupational classifications could be improved substantially if their employment could be extended to about 50 weeks a year.

To protect the income of workers against instability caused by seasonal fluctuations in weekly earnings, *guaranteed annual wage plans* have been in operation for some time in a number of companies. Under the Procter & Gamble plan, workers are guaranteed equal weekly pay regardless of actual working hours. This equalizes earnings in off-seasons and rush seasons. This is, however, an *income guarantee,* not a commitment of the company to provide year-round employment.

In 1965 the International Longshoremen's Association (ILA), secured a contract establishing a guaranteed annual wage income corresponding to a pay for 1,600 hours a year for all employees who had worked for at least 700 hours. Such payments are to be made at the end of the year. The next contract which went into effect in 1969 provided for an increase in the guaranteed annual wage income to slightly more than 2,000 hours a year. Here we encounter a genuine system of guaranteed annual wages. It is very similar to the year round system of compensation which had been demanded by the United Automobile Workers as early as 1955 but not incorporated in the collective contract either at that time or on later occasions. Instead "supplemental unemployment benefits" were inaugurated. They are discussed in some detail in Sec. 9-2.

It should be noted that the guaranteed wage system was introduced for longshoremen only after, over a period of years, there had been a very drastic reduction of the total number of workers attached to this type of employment. Employment in bituminous coal mining while not protected by an annual wage guarantee has also been stabilized, thereby providing for a far more steady income to miners only after a dramatic curtailment of employment. In the late 1960's only about 135,000 people remained employed in the bituminous coal industry.

The preceding analysis of a guaranteed annual wage has shown that such a system becomes workable only at the price of a considerable curtailment in employment. It is beneficial for those who succeed in remaining on the payroll. If the stabilization of employment can be brought about gradually by a phasing out of older workers and by a change of occupation of younger ones, the guaranteed annual wage can be obtained without causing too many hardships to those employees who will be excluded from its benefits.

7-4. OCCUPATIONAL WAGE RATES

In the course of time, occupational wage differentials have developed which have almost assumed an historical pattern. Collective bargaining, while contributing to a general upward push of wage rates, has not eliminated to any measurable extent the vast differences in pay scales. In fact in recent years a number of wage disputes, especially in the public sector, centered on the maintenance of such historical patterns of wage differentials. In a number of cities the police insisted on obtaining pay schedules keeping them somewhat ahead of those prevailing in the fire department. On the other hand employees of that department stressed that their wages should be equal to those of the police department pointing out that their work was just as responsible and often as dangerous as that of the policemen.

In the past when seasonal variations in employment on outdoor projects were far more pronounced than they are now, higher hourly wages rates were used to offset the shortness of the season. This was particularly true of the construction industry. Workers in the mining industry, especially coal mining, commanded a high hourly wage not only because of the strenuousness of the occupation but also because the work week was somewhat shorter than in manufacturing. On the other hand, wage rates in the lighter industries such as textiles, apparel, and leather always are considerably lower than in the heavy industries—steel, machinery, transportation equipment, and the like. This is expressed in the fact that toward the end of 1968 average hourly earnings in the durable-goods industries reached $3.11, whereas in non-durable goods they amounted only to $2.82. Among the lowest paid employees were those in the retail trade and in the services. Table 7–6 gives examples of high and low wage rates in a number of occupations. Furthermore, a five year period is covered by this study in order to point out the change that has occurred in most of these rates.

TABLE 7-6
SOME OCCUPATIONAL WAGE DIFFERENTIALS
(average hourly earnings)

Occupations	November 1963	November 1968
Contract construction	3.43	4.22
Passenger car bodies	3.46	4.29
Blast furnaces and rolling mills	3.33	3.83
Motor vehicles and equipment	3.34	3.81
Bituminous coal mining	3.16	4.09
Watches and clocks	2.09	2.48
Wood house furniture	1.92	2.40
Pens, pencils, office, and art materials	1.88	2.52
Poultry dressing and packing	1.53	1.96
Work clothing	1.47	1.92
Womens' ready-to-wear stores	1.45	1.92
Limited price variety stores	1.25	1.81
Hotels, tourist courts, motels	1.24	1.70

SOURCE: U.S. Department of Labor, *Employment and Earnings.*

Table 7–6 gives an indication of the wide range of occupational wage differentials. There is no reason to assume that the pattern of this spread will change significantly in the future. The persistent strength of wage differentials is shown clearly in the fact that over the five year period shown in Table 7–6 there was only one change in the ranking of hourly wages per occupation: whereas in November 1963, bituminous coal mining occupied the fifth place, it had moved to the third place in November 1968. But even this change reaffirms rather than denies the strength of established patterns of wage differentials. Actually the moving up of the wages of coal miners in the period between 1963 and 1968 restores them to a position which they usually had had, namely in the neighborhood of the top group, building construction.

The survival of considerable wage differentials, especially in those occupations commanding high hourly rates, is an indirect proof of the fact that wage rates operate rather imperfectly so far as the allocation of labor supply is concerned. Naturally there is a tendency of labor to move into high-wage occupations. If a large enough number of workers actually succeeded in obtaining jobs in high-wage industries, two things would occur: a slight decline in the rates of the high-wage industries, and a certain increase in wages of industries where rates are low. That is, there would be a tendency of wages to cluster far more closely around an average than is actually the case in the real labor market.

While certain actions of unions—especially the attempt to restrict the numbers of apprentices—have the effect of protecting high wages against the pressures of the labor market and to safeguard occupational differentials, some other union policies, especially in areas dominated by industrial unionism, have the opposite effect. Wage rates in primary metal industries, in metal working machinery, and in transportation equipment are virtually the same. But this is brought about by deliberate actions leading to collective agreements. The near identity of these rates is not the natural outcome of free forces on the labor market but the end product of difficult wage negotiations motivated by the desire of union leaders to draw even with their colleagues in some other unions and achieve near equality of earnings of members of their own organization.

In our survey of some occupational wage differentials we have already shown wage rates which, in November 1964, were just slightly above the minimum wage of $1.25 per hour set by Federal law at that time. This rule applies only to workers employed in interstate commerce industries. Wages below the Federal minimum are to be found primarily in intrastate industries, such as laundries and hotels and restaurants. For example, in 1960, when the New York State minimum wage was $1 per hour, the average hourly earnings of female clerks receiving materials in power laundries was $1.13 per hour. In the meantime, minimum wages in New York State have been raised in stages up to $1.25 per hour. Further increases in minimum wages, whether on the state or Federal level, would have to be very substantial in order to lift the earnings of workers in the service industries or in certain retail chains to a level of social adequacy. Nevertheless it must be realized that these low-wage industries are labor-intensive, have a high elasticity of demand for labor, and are therefore most likely to be affected by higher wages. In deciding on further raises in the minimum wage level, the desire to eliminate sweatshops must be accompanied by a concern for maintaining employment opportunities for workers who are most unlikely to find jobs in high-wage occupations.

There have been cases even in the 1960's when the pay scales for the lowest categories of municipal employment yielded a weekly income for the wage earner which was below the income level established for families of the same size by welfare departments. As a result such wage earners received supplementary public assistance. That is to say what the local taxpayer "saved" in terms of substandard pay schedules for certain city employees he had to spend for additional welfare expenditures as a tax payer for the state and the local government. To maintain extremely low wages and rely on supplementary welfare allocations to raise them to an acceptable minimum level is an abuse which already was denounced by David Ricardo early in the 19th century in his chapter "On Wages" in his *Principles of Political Economy and Taxation.*[2] Under the English Poor Laws this practice was prevalent especially during the Napoleonic wars when prices rose sharply while wages were frozen and collective bargaining still outlawed. Actually a supplementation of low wages by welfare allocations amounts to a subsidy to the employer, whether private or public, and simply has no place in any progressive economic system. In 1969 it was announced in New York City that wages of all municipal employees would be raised at least to the level where such supplementary payments would no longer be necessary.

7-5. REGIONAL WAGE DIFFERENTIALS

Wage rates in the same industries and occupations vary in different sections of the country. If such differentials are significant and persistent, they can induce a relocation of industry into lower wage areas. Such conditions have in recent decades brought about a certain shift in the textile industry from Northeastern to Southern states. To illustrate, in 1950 average hourly earnings of production workers in textile mills in Providence-Pawtucket were $1.33; in Chattanooga they were $1.19. In 1960 they were $1.72 and $1.50 respectively.[3] Similar differentials can be found between the Northeast and the South in apparel and related products. Nor are these differentials confined to the light industries. The average hourly earnings of production workers in electrical equipment were $2.78 in Pittsburgh in 1960 but $1.99 in Dallas. In the printing, publishing, and allied industries, average hourly earnings ranged from a top of $3.55 in San Francisco-Oakland to $3.08 in New York City to a low of $2.03 in Charlotte.

It should be noted that a comparison of regional wage differentials must be carried out strictly among identical occupational classifications. Such a study makes it possible to identify high and lower wage areas. The compensation of hospital workers is a particularly crucial problem. Hospitals complain about ever-increasing employment cost, whereas many categories of hospital workers actually draw a very low wage. Table 7-7 shows differences in average straight-time weekly earnings of male and female nursing aides. Earnings in New York City are equated to a base of 100.

The difference between the earnings of male and female nursing aides is significant. Whereas male hospital workers in Buffalo and Chicago earned

[2]Modern Library.

[3]Herbert Bienstock (ed.), "Employment, Earnings, and Wages in New York City," 1950–60, U.S. Department of Labor, Middle Atlantic Regional Office (Washington, D.C.: U.S. Government Printing Office, 1963).

more than their colleagues in New York, this was not the case for female employees.

So far the discussion has covered only differentials in wages within identical occupational classifications. We conclude this analysis of wage dif-

TABLE 7-7

AVERAGE STRAIGHT-TIME WEEKLY EARNINGS OF NURSING AIDES

Area	Men $63.00 (N.Y.C.) = 100	Women $57.50 (N.Y.C.) = 100
Boston............................	94	96
Buffalo............................	109	97
Chicago..........................	102	94
Cleveland........................	85	81
Minneapolis-St. Paul.............	100	100
Los Angeles-Long Beach..........	104	107
Portland, Oregon.................	96	98
San Francisco-Oakland...........	109	117

SOURCE: See footnote 2 on p. 93.

ferentials by showing differences in average earnings in manufacturing industries in a number of metropolitan areas. The average hourly earnings in such labor markets are determined by the "industry mix" in such regions. A preponderance of heavy industries or electronics and space-related types of production raises the average earnings as a whole. Light industries depress these average wages. In Table 7-8 ten metropolitan areas are shown. In the manufacturing industries, hourly earnings for New York City are quite low. This table will compare the years 1950 and 1960. The considerable changes in the ranking of metropolitan areas in that period is indicative of industry shifts, especially in the direction of southern California.

TABLE 7-8

AVERAGE HOURLY EARNINGS OF PRODUCTION WORKERS IN MANUFACTURING
INDUSTRIES IN TEN METROPOLITAN AREAS, 1950–60

Area	1960 Employment (thousands)	Average Hourly Earnings			
		Amount		Rank	
		1950	1960	1950	1960
Detroit	512	$1.80	$2.92	1	1
San Francisco-Oakland.......	199	1.71	2.79	2	4
Portland, Oregon............	64	1.68	2.53	3	11
Pittsburgh	291	1.62	2.80	4	3
Los Angeles-Long Beach	785	1.62	2.59	5	9
Buffalo	177	1.61	2.69	6	6
Sacramento	28	1.60	2.85	7	2
San Diego	68	1.60	2.73	8	5
Wilmington.................	57	1.59	2.60	9	8
New York City..............	954	1.57	2.26	10	30

SOURCE: See footnote 2 on p. 93.

This survey is concentrated only on manufacturing industries. The ranking of some metropolitan areas, such as New York City, would be quite
different if all occupations, especially banking and insurance, were included.
On the other hand, there is considerable variation in standard weekly hours
in office occupations. For instance, in many occupations such as duplicating
machine operator, classes A and B of keypunch operator, and stenographer,
the standard weekly hours in New York City are about 36, whereas in San
Francisco they are over 39.[4] As a result, the straight-time hourly earnings
in these occupations are somewhat higher in San Francisco than in New
York. This shows once again the great significance of the working hours on
weekly and even yearly earnings.

The data presented so far in this section are based on comparisons of
the years 1950 and 1960. While the hourly earnings shown in Table 7-8 have
long been superseded by substantial increases in wages discussed in some
detail in the third section of this chapter there has been no particular
change in regional wage differentials in recent years. This was brought out
in a detailed study of the New York State Department of Labor under the
title "Structure of Earnings and Hours in New York State Industries."[5]
This survey showed that the New York metropolitan area is actually a low
wage industrial complex. Of course it ranks highest in the earnings of the
nonmanufacturing sector including finance and insurance, medical and
legal services, contract construction and wholesale trade. Table 7-9 will
give a ranking of labor market areas in the State of New York based on an

TABLE 7-9

RANKING OF GROSS CASH WEEKLY EARNINGS IN NEW YORK STATE
LABOR MARKET AREAS
(Rank #1 = lowest median earnings)

Labor Market Area	Manufacturing	
	Durable Goods	Nondurable Goods
Nassau-Suffolk	7	2
Remainder of State	4	8
Binghamton	8	1
Utica-Rome	2	3
New York Metropolitan	3	5
New York City	1	6
Westchester-Rockland	6	8
Albany-Schenectady-Troy	11	9
Syracuse	5	10
Rochester	10	7
Buffalo	9	11

Source: Table A of the report quoted above.

[4]U.S. Department of Labor, *Occupational Wage Survey*, Bulletins No. 1385-36 and
13885-72 (Washington, D.C.: U. S. Government Printing Office).
[5]Publication B-163, Vol. 2, August 1968, Division of Research and Statistics.

"industry mix" concept. This statistical term represents the distribution of low and high wage industries in a particular area.

Table 7-9 shows the low standing of industrial wages in the New York metropolitan area. This is a reflection of the "industry mix" in that region. The total number of workers in the manufacturing industries in that area was 937,975 in March 1966 and their median earnings amounted to $2.38 per hour. However more than 247,000 workers were attached to the production of apparel and other textile products with median hourly earnings of only $2.09. Another 160,000 workers were employed in other nondurable goods manufacturing with half of their number earning more than $1.91 per hour and the other half earning less. In fact no less than 42.5 percent of that group earned less than $1.75 per hour in March 1966. On the other hand in the contract construction industry in the New York metropolitan area 45.1 percent of the workers earned more than $5.00 an hour at the same time.

At this highest scale of hourly compensation regional wage differentials are very significant. In other labor market areas, construction workers were in the $5.00 plus per hour bracket only to a small degree. For instance, in the Albany-Schenectady-Troy labor market area only 7.1 percent of the construction workers were in that category. In the Buffalo district 14.8 percent and in Rochester 11.5 percent.

In the model of a perfectly competitive, unorganized labor market, it can be assumed that regional wage differentials, especially the difference between high wage and low wage areas would set in motion a "natural" realignment of labor. People would always move out from low wage areas into labor markets where wages are higher. In reality this model proves to be correct in a general way. However, it must be realized that people migrating from rural areas, for instance the Southern part of this country and from Appalachia into metropolitan labor markets of the Midwest, the East and the Pacific coast augment that part of the labor supply which is available at very low hourly wages. Actually then these metropolitan labor markets, at least as far as production and service workers are concerned, attract labor supply not because of the very high wages paid in construction and in some sectors of the non-manufacturing occupations but precisely because there is a relative abundance of employment opportunities in low wage manufacturing and service types of employment.

SELECTED BIBLIOGRAPHY

Blackwood, James E. and Lily Mary David. "Hours of Work in the United States and Abroad," *Monthly Labor Review* (August 1963).

Greenbaum, Marcia L. *The Shorter Work Week* (New York State School of Industrial and Labor Relations, Bulletin, vol. 50).

U. S. Department of Labor, Bureau of Labor Statistics. *Employment and Earnings Statistics for the United States, 1909–1968*, Bulletin 12-6 (Washington, D. C.: U. S. Government Printing Office, 1966).

QUESTIONS FOR DISCUSSION

1. Since the depression of the 1930's there have been some attempts to legislate a degree of stability into the labor market, along with other efforts to spread out employment opportunities such as the legislation enacted governing overtime work and minimum wages. What reasoning and what ends give rise to legislation of this sort?

2. Differences in methods of pay, conditions of employment, and stability of earnings make earnings comparisons between job categories difficult and thus limit our insight into the all-important question of wage differentials. Relative to the above statement, indicate the nature of these differentials, and the implications thereof.

3. What are some of the important economic and noneconomic factors which may give rise to wage differentials such as those given in Table 7-6?

4. In low-wage, labor-intensive industries, indicate the possible effects of a hypothetical 50 percent increase in legal minimum wages.

5. What are some of the important economic and noneconomic factors that may account for regional wage differentials?

6. To what extent might regional wage differentials cause a movement of capital into the low-wage regions? Analyze this issue in the light of such developments as the movement of the textile industry from New England to the South.

8

Wage Incentives, Improvement Factors, Escalators

In the preceding chapter we were discussed in some detail average hourly earnings. These are largely determined by the straight-time rate established for particular job classes. However, in many industries, not all workers receive the same pay, even though classified under the same job description. This pay differential arises from incentive plans. The nature and scope of incentive pay will be discussed here in some detail. We will further turn our attention to the system of deferred wage increases which has been widely adopted after World War II. Lastly, changes in hourly wages rates through "escalator clauses" will be considered.

8-1. WAGE INCENTIVE PLANS

In the days prior to World War I organized labor, in addition to demanding the maximum work week, also campaigned strongly for the abolition of piece-rate compensation of workers. There were many industries in which it was feasible to measure the individual output of workers. One way to encourage higher output per man-hour was the incentive plan. In order to operate such a scheme it is necessary first to establish through time studies the average output of workers per hour. The straight-time hourly wage is geared to this performance level. Under the incentive system workers can obtain premium pay for exceeding the norm. In this way they are motivated to increase their individual output.

The opposition of unions to this system at a time when management was far stronger than labor was turned especially against the practice of "rate cutting." Once a higher output was obtained, the employer would declare that now he had proof that workers could produce more during one hour. This new level of output was made the new norm, more often than not without increase in straight-time pay. Incentives could be earned only if the new norm was exceeded. In this way labor felt that through the incentive pay it became involved in a continuous "speedup" and that they were working in a "sweatshop." In sharp criticism of these conditions unions were demanding a uniform wage rate for all workers in the same job classes.

Even today some union constitutions have articles stating opposition to incentive plans as a policy of the organization. Because organized labor had been so outspoken against the piece-rate system, in the early days of Communist rule in the Soviet Union uniform wages were paid in whatever industries existed there at the time. Soon it was found out that production did not rise above a minimum level. In a complete reversal the Communists introduced a steeply graduated incentive system, supplemented by premiums for all employees in case of a collective overfulfillment of production quotas.

Although American unions have never supported incentive systems with any enthusiasm, such plans are in force in a large number of industries, as shown in Table 8-1. However, piece-rate compensation is predicated on the measurability of individual output. A more collective way of rewarding a good performance consists of premium pay for full utilization of machinery and the avoidance of mechanical breakdowns.

Time studies carried out by industrial engineers have always been a highly sensitive area in industrial relations. In recent years unions have tried in some cases to use their own experts to check and counter the findings of management experts.

A study of incentive plans in effect in May 1958[1] showed that 27 percent of the production workers employed in the manufacturing industries were paid on an incentive basis. More recent studies have shown that incentive

TABLE 8-1
PERCENT OF PRODUCTION WORKERS PAID ON INCENTIVE BASIS

Industry Group	Capital Invested per Worker (dollars)	Percent Paid on Incentive Basis
Costume jewelry, buttons, and notions............	276	17
Women's and children's undergarments...........	326	52
Women's outerwear	326	63
Electrical equipment for vehicles	1,605	53
Knitting mills	1,865	64
Glass and glassware, pressed or blown	5,650	45
Carpets, rugs, and other floor coverings...........	7,910	40
Blast furnaces, steel works, and rolling mills.......	13,540	60
Industrial organic chemicals.....................	18,630	5
Industrial inorganic chemicals...................	18,700	8
Rolling, drawing, and alloying of nonferrous metals	29,100	33

SOURCE: *Monthly Labor Review* (March 1964), p. 275.

[1]Earl Lewis, "Extent of Incentive Pay in Manufacturing, "*Monthly Labor Review*, vol. 83, no. 5 (May 1960).

plans continue to be in force in a wide variety of industries. Table 8-2 will show the industries where, in the period 1963 to 1968, more than 50 percent of the employees were operating under an incentive system. The table will indicate for each occupation the time for which the percentages were established.

As can be seen from Table 8-2 incentive plans predominate in the garment industry in which it is easy to measure individual output of workers. The same would be true of the cigar industry. However, we also find that 66 percent of the production workers in basic iron and steel were on incentives. In that case the system operates through a bonus plan referring to the group performance of the team of workers cooperating on the basic steel making installations such as blast and open hearth furnaces, rolling mills and the like.

It is very difficult to give a quantitative expression of the addition to the straight hourly earnings brought about by the incentive payments. These payments differ from person to person and from enterprise to enterprise. In a study of average expenditures for supplementary employee remuneration published in the *Monthly Labor Review* for January 1962, incentive pay in manufacturing industries in the North Central states averaged out to 2.6 cents per hour. In all sections of the country these incentive premiums were far less than the additions to hourly earnings through daily, weekly, and weekend overtime work. As automation spreads, it is likely to reduce incentive pay because individual and even team output of workers will become less significant for the volume of production than the operation of the equipment itself. This fact does not lessen the role of workers in more or less automated production units. However, their function shifts more to the watching of signals reporting on the processes of production than on physical involvement in output itself.

TABLE 8-2
PERCENTAGE OF PRODUCTION WORKERS PAID ON AN INCENTIVE BASIS
SELECTED MANUFACTURING INDUSTRIES, 1963–1968

Industry	Percent U.S.A.
Work Clothing (Feb. 1968)	82
Men's and boy's shirts, except work and nightwear (April–June 1964)	81
Men's and boy's suits and coats (April 1967)	74
Footwear, except rubber (March 1968)	70
Women's hosiery (September 1967)	70
Children's hosiery (September 1967)	70
Basic iron and steel (September 1967)	66
Men's hosiery (September 1967)	65
Cigars (March 1967)	57
Leather tanning and finishing (January 1968)	53

SOURCE: *Monthly Labor Review* (July, 1969), Table 2, "Report on Incentive Pay in Manufacturing Industries."

8-2. DEFERRED WAGE INCREASES AND IMPROVEMENT FACTORS

Since the end of World War II there has not been a single year in which average hourly earnings have not risen. Until 1969 this rising trend has been maintained even in terms of constant dollars, which eliminate the distortions brought about by rising prices as they are indicated by the Consumer Price Index. While the trend is spread throughout the wage structure, in some industries the system of deferred wage increases provides for regularly scheduled increases in the hourly wage rate at a given time each year for the duration of a collective labor contract. In 1957 five million workers were scheduled for deferred wage increases. Although in more recent years the number of workers specifically covered by such a wage clause declined—for example, to 3.3 million in 1963—it is necessary to examine the concepts underlying deferred wage increases because the practice of scheduling annual wage increases has spread beyond contract clauses labeled deferred wage increases or improvement factor, shown in Table 8-3.

TABLE 8-3.
DEFERRED WAGE INCREASES IN 1963

Average Deferred Wage Increase (cents per hour)	All Industries Studied	Total Manu-facturing	Food and Kindred Products	Total Non-manu-facturing Studied	Ware-housing, Wholesale and Retail Trade	Trans-portation
Total..................	2,686	1,793	243	893	229	625
Under 5¢.............	188	104	7	84	7	76
5 but less than 6¢	196	123	34	73	10	62
6 but less than 7¢	573	522	81	51	27	17
7 but less than 8¢	873	792	42	81	39	35
8 but less than 9¢	129	72	14	57	40	11
9 but less than 10¢	123	44	13	80	28	48
10 but less than 11¢ ...	241	50	10	191	45	139
11 but less than 12¢ ...	208	15	13	193	9	180
12 but less than 13¢ ...	38	18	18	20	14	6
13 but less than 14¢ ...	33	16	—	17	—	17
14¢ and over..........	64	31	9	34	8	26
Not specified or not computed..........	19	6	2	13	3	10

SOURCE: *Monthly Labor Review* (December 1962), p. 1344.

There are two aspects to deferred wage increases. The first relates to the area of industrial relations as such, while the second has a macroeconomic significance. Mature labor relations would tend to stress stability. This goal can best be achieved through a longer duration of collective labor agreements. If such a contract has a running time of two years it must be assumed that, in the vigorously dynamic American economy, substantial gains in production, productivity, and income will occur. If, despite these changes, a union is to be persuaded to sign a longer-term contract, wage increases anticipating a yearly rise in productivity can be spread over the whole length of the agreement—so that, for example, for a three-year contract only one-third of the total scheduled wage increase would become due in the first year. The advantages of longer term contracts for the scheduling of production and for the overall steadiness of the economic system are so obvious that they need no further stressing. Equally important is the macroeconomic aspect of this wage system.

The practice of deferred wage increases first came into use about 1948. By that time a shift in the opinion of leading economists on the relation between increases in productivity and wages took place. The traditional viewpoint that gains in productivity ought to be translated into lower prices, while wages and profits remained on their previous monetary levels, was abandoned. It was clearly seen that such a relationship between productivity and prices was unlikely to occur under the now prevailing conditions of imperfect competition. But if prices could not be brought down in a proper proportion to increases in productivity, it seemed inevitable that under the assumption of unchanging wages the price of aggregate output would rise faster than aggregate labor income. If such a discrepancy continued over a longer period, it was argued, a deficiency of consumer income might develop which eventually could lead not to a spectacular crisis but to a new kind of economic stagnation.

Since a return to more perfectly competitive conditions did not seem feasible at the current phase of industrialization leading to ever-increased sizes of enterprises, the response to the downward inflexibility of prices was upward flexibility of wages. Once it was seen that productivity gains ought to be matched by increases in wage rates, the question arose as to what criteria should be employed in such a wage system. In the beginning, reference was made to estimated average increases in productivity per year in the nonagricultural sector. If it was found that such an increase averaged about 2.5 percent a year, then the scheduled deferred wage increases would provide for a similar percentage increase of the hourly wage rate.

Employers insisted that these increases should not be geared to actual gains or to specific industries and enterprises, but should be measured in terms of broad national averages. This attitude is understandable. If the deferred wage increases were known to reflect precisely the productivity gains in a particular enterprise, their amount and frequency might reveal information to competitors which management would like to keep secret.

Table 8-2 illustrates the operation of deferred wage increases in the more important manufacturing and nonmanufacturing industries to the exclusion of construction, service trades, finance, and government. This omission also explains the fact that in the survey only about 2.7 million workers were covered, whereas the total number of increases going into effect in 1963 was, as indicated above, 3.3 million.

It will be noted that, in the manufacturing industries, the heaviest concentration of deferred wage increases is in the 6–8 cents-per-hour range. Not all of the increases tabulated in Table 8-3 are construed as improvement factors directly related to productivity gains. It is also important to bear in mind that many wage increases occur through collective bargaining or otherwise each year which are not officially labeled as deferred increases or raises with respect to higher productivity. There is no doubt, however, that the system of deferred wage increases or other annual upward adjustment of wages has become widespread. In 1962 only 27 percent of production and related workers in manufacturing and selected nonmanufacturing industries did not receive a wage increase. All other such workers did. For 12 percent of these workers wage increases were between 9 and 10 cents an hour; 15 percent obtained raises between 10 and 11 cents per hour.[2] This general upward trend of wage rates is due not so much to increases in the cost of living as to the underlying general increases in output, productivity, and the gross national product. In fact, in the first five years of the 1960's the increase in consumer prices was kept within a narrow range, whereas the gross national product itself rose from $502.6 billion in 1960 to $622.3 billion in 1964. Although this development shows that the twin objectives of economic growth and relative price stability have been quite successfully approximated in the past, after 1965 distortions between wages and increases in productivity took place as we have already demonstrated in Chapter 6, Table 4. The contract in the steel industry concluded in 1968 and running into 1971 provided for an increase of 44 cents an hour for the three year period. In the first year the increase was fixed at 20 cents, for the two following years at 12 cents an hour. However, the package contained improvements in fringes such as a thirty-dollar-a-week vacation bonus and an improvement in supplemental unemployment benefits. By and large, the total increases in compensation of employees in the steel industry provided for in the 1968 contract amounted to annual raises of about 6 percent.

In a study of 1800 agreements covering 7.6 million workers conducted by the U. S. Dept. of Labor[3] it was found that in 944 cases, deferred wage increases only were written into the contract; another 266 agreements had such a clause and also a cost of living review requirement. Only this latter feature but not a deferred wage increase commitment was contained in

[2]George Ruben, "Developments Under Major Agreements," *Monthly Labor Review*, vol. 87, no. 1 (January 1964).

[3]Bulletin 1425-4, "Deferred Wage Increase and Escalator Clauses," U. S. Dept. of Labor, January 1966.

34 agreements. Less than one third of the 1800 contracts reviewed in this study had no provision for deferred wage increases or cost of living reviews.

The year 1969 witnessed steep wage increases exceeding the 6 percent pattern which had evolved in 1968. Contracts in the construction industry negotiated in New York City in 1969 provided for hourly wage increases of 48 cents for each year of the three-year contracts.

It is important to remember at this point that the original intention of deferred wage increases was simply to provide for the maintenance of an equilibrium between projected increases in productivity and wage rates in contracts covering two or three years. A detachment of the system of deferred wage increases from its original base of actual productivity gains and the application of deferred wage increases to the expanding low productivity sector of the economy is gradually bringing about an increase in total unit labor cost of the employment of production and nonproduction workers. This growing distortion of the relation between productivity of all employees—blue-collar and white—and their aggregate wages and salaries is due not to wage concessions to production workers in excess of the productivity gains which can be clearly demonstrated by an analysis of their output per man-hour, but to the continuing structural transformation of the labor force which leads to a narrowing of the high productivity sector of the economy and the spread of low productivity employment.

A discussion of "wage-push inflation" cannot concentrate on the content of wage agreements for production workers. It has to face the fact that an ever increasing proportion of the labor force consists of nonproduction workers many of whom are benefiting from the spill-over effects of collective bargaining into their employment relations. They receive higher compensation although their productivity increased at a low rate.

It should be noted furthermore that at least up to 1968 increasing unit labor cost did not interfere with the rapid rise in corporate profits. In the ten year period 1958 to 1968 they more than doubled, rising from 22.3 billion after taxes in 1958 to 51.0 billion in 1968. At the same time wage and salary disbursements rose by less than 100 percent from $239.9 billion in 1958 to $463.5 billion in 1968. This comparison is not meant to convey that aggregate wages were lagging behind. It demonstrates, however, that in the decade under analysis profits rose substantially faster than labor income despite the increasing labor cost brought about by the application of deferred wage increases to low productivity sectors of the American economy.

8-3. THE ESCALATOR CLAUSE

In Sec. 8-1 we established some relationship between the system of deferred wage increases and the desire to negotiate longer-term collective agreements. The same purpose led also to the adoption in many contracts of an escalator formula designed to preserve the real purchasing power of the money wages agreed upon in the contract. The word "escalator" was adopted to indicate that, in principle, wages could move up or down according to the behavior of the consumer price index. Actually there was only one period after World War II when the consumer price index dropped slightly. It fell from 83.8 percent in 1948 to 83 in 1949 (1957–59 = 100). Due to this development the downward escalator was put into motion in the automotive industry. Wage rates were cut by 1 cent an hour. At the same time, however, a deferred wage increase, or improvement factor, of 3 cents per hour was due so that, on balance, the workers gained 2 cents.

During the early 1950's the consumer price index rose sharply. As a result of scare buying of raw materials and consumer goods after the outbreak of the Korean War, the index rose from 83.8 in 1950 to 90.5 in 1951. Toward the end of the decade there was another substantial rise from 94.7 in 1956 to 101.5 in 1959. In between there was considerable price stability—actually less of a change than occurred in the 1960's. Because in the mid-1950's there was no hope of any substantial decline in the consumer price index, the actual upward escalator additions to the hourly wage rate up to that time were worked into a new basic hourly wage rate in many collective contracts.

In more recent years the escalator clause has been discontinued in a number of contracts. In the steel industry the 1960 contract put a ceiling on the escalator. Originally escalator increases were to be limited to 3 cents an hour for the duration of the contract. There were some slight modifications later, but the general tendency remained to deemphasize this wage feature. Table 8-4 shows the average increase in hourly wage rates based on the cost of living escalator in selected manufacturing industries 1959 through 1966. It should be noted that from 1965 to 1966 the escalator increase more than doubled, whereas in the period 1959 to 1964 the increase was only 1.3 cents per hour. This confirms the observation made in the preceeding section that after 1965 economic relations, especially wages and prices, became highly unstable. Nevertheless it would be quite erroneous to assert that the escalator clause as such is inflationary.

Inasmuch as there seems to be a good deal of confusion about escalators, the cost-of-living index, and inflation, we will further analyze this aspect of the wage structure.

The escalator clause as originally written into contracts provided for an increase in the hourly wage rate roughly on the following lines: for each half-point of increase in the consumer price index, hourly wage rates will go up by 1 cent an hour. Adjustments of this kind are usually made in the quarter after the change in the consumer price index has occurred. This means that these wage increases are made only if and when there has been a prior increase in the cost of living. There is actually no trace of a spiral between wages and prices in this procedure. The item "medical care" has gone up

TABLE 8-4
AVERAGE ESCALATOR INCREASES IN CENTS PER HOUR
1959–1966

Year	Increases
1959	2.0
1960	3.3
1961	2.5
1962	2.9
1963	3.0
1964	3.3
1965	4.0
1966	10.5

SOURCE: *Monthly Labor Review* (February 1968).

more than any other in the consumer price index but it would be hard to prove that this 20 percent rise over a period of six years can be traced back to a "wage-price spiral." Actually, the items of food, housing, and apparel, which represent the bulk of consumer spending, rose less than the composite consumer price index.

Unlike the deferred wage increases explained in the preceding section, tne escalator goes into action only *after* prices have risen. If they do not rise, then it remains dormant. It is therefore hard to see why so much opposition should arise against such a clause—which, if there is price stability, cannot be invoked, and, if there are measurable changes in the consumer price index, ought to be applied. It was mentioned that the word "inflation" was thrown into the controversy on the escalator clause. Here an additional warning is in order. The most unlikely behavior in any price system is a complete standstill. At any given moment prices will either move downward or upward. To call every upward movement of prices inflation is convenient, although this semantic practice has not brought greater lucidity to economic analysis. It would be better to eliminate slow changes in prices of modest range from the concept of inflation. This has often been called "creeping inflation," to distinguish it from "galloping inflation." However, it would be preferable not to refer to a slow annual rise in prices within the range of 1.5 to 2 percent as inflationary. Actually such a secular upward trend would be far less than annual increases in productivity and in output under contemporary conditions of progressive technology and economic growth.

Frequent reference has been made to the Consumer Price Index or CPI. This series actually goes back to the period of World War I. In the course of time it has undergone a number of definitional and technical changes.[4] One of the main adjustments has been the establishment of a source of income concept rather than an occupational classification of the heads of the

---

[4] "The Revised CPI Sample for the Consumer Price Index," *Monthly Labor Review* (October 1960), and "The Statistical Structure of the Revised CPI," *Monthly Labor Review* (August 1964).

household. However, the index still is concerned with the spending patterns of wage earners. For this reason only families whose income is derived at least 50 percent from wages and salary is included in the sample distributed through 50 sampling centers.

Periodically the spending habits of wage and salary earners are re-examined. With the rise of the earnings of blue- and white-collar workers, the scope of the typical family budget expanded. For this reason greater allowances had to be made in the CPI for automobiles and such discretionary expenditures as amusements, recreation, and education.

It should be noted that sales and excise taxes are included in the survey. The reason for this procedure is that these levies add to the price of the items on which they are due. This might lead to the paradoxical result that the consumer price index would go up in a period when anti-inflationary measures are put into effect. Such policies of austerity could lead to an increase in excise taxes in order to curtail aggregate spending for consumer durables and luxuries, in order to put brakes on a runaway boom. Interest rates also are worked into the consumer price index. They are also most likely to go up in connection with policies designed to prevent a further rise in prices. It seems, then, that the technical makeup of the consumer price index might counteract some efforts at restraining the upward push of prices, simply because higher excise taxes and interest bring about an increase in the consumer price index.

Wages will be adjusted to higher consumer prices whether or not escalator clauses are in effect. The difference between having or not having such a wage feature is not so much in the wage structure itself but in the area of industrial relations.

8-4. OBSERVATIONS ON REAL PURCHASING POWER

We have seen in Section 4-4 that in the 19th century consumer prices declined sharply in the first half of that period and showed remarkable stability for the rest of this era. It is easy to see then, that in that period an increase in wages always meant an increase in real income. Even without a rise in money wages, purchasing power increased when cost of living went down as occurred for instance between 1870 and 1880. This historical background explains the long standing union practice of always bargaining for higher money wages. When in the 20th century, especially after World War I, consumer prices remained high and continue to move up, the phenomenon of the "money illusion" appeared. This meant that union members and leaders continued to identify higher money earnings with increased purchasing power. As we have seen in the previous section, eventually the awareness of the frequent discrepancy between money wages and real wages grew and it led to the evolution of the escalator clause which has the purpose of stabilizing the purchasing power of the wage rate for the duration of a contract extending over several years. One would think that such a protection of purchasing power through escalator clauses would be in the interest of management as well as labor. It is, therefore, hard to understand why beginning in the late 1950's a management strategy emerged designed to cancel or at least limit the escalator feature in wage structures. The de-emphasis on escalator clauses in recent union contracts and the greater stress of organized labor on gaining substantial hourly wage increases spread over the duration of the contract has brought the country back to a situation which at one time was thought to have been settled: the continued complaints of organized labor that price rises have eliminated wage settlements which appeared favorable at the time of the negotiations and promised improvements in the real purchasing power of the take-home pay of workers. A union survey of the earnings of workers in manufacturing in two suburban countries came to the conclusion that very substantial wage increases granted in the period 1965 to 1968 had been reduced very sharply by the simultaneous decline in purchasing power. For instance workers in food and kindred products obtained in that three-year period, raises amounting to increases in weekly earnings of $22.22. But after considering price increases which as we have seen include taxes, this gain was reduced to $6.26 a week. In publishing and printing where in the same three-year period the wage rate in current dollars went up by $15.22 per week workers wound up with a loss in purchasing power of $3.66.

This survey corresponds to studies of the development of the real spendable income of factory workers between 1965 and 1969. In 1957–1959 dollars the average after-tax income of factory workers in the United States was $78.53. By 1969 it was $77.00. To a certain extent this reflects the surtax on individual incomes which was added in 1968. But the net result is that there has been no rise in real purchasing power for four years of this important segment of the labor force. If the American economy were less oriented towards the production of nonconsumer goods for defense and investment, the stagnation of aggregate purchasing power of this group of consumers would have translated itself into a considerable slowing down of the growth rate of the economy.

When management began to oppose the escalator clause in collective agreements, unions did not put up a great fight for its maintenance. Instead union strategy shifted to pushing for very substantial increases in hourly wage rates. An example for this was already given in Sec. 8-2. But as we have seen now these sharp increases in wages in current dollars merely were able to preserve the status quo in the purchasing power of wage and salary earners. In other words there was a great deal of motion in wage and price levels but this merely covered up a standstill. The question arises whether it would not have been better union strategy to fight for a retention of escalator clauses.

The upward push of prices precisely at a time when escalator clauses went out of fashion in many collective agreements is a factual refutation of the argument that such clauses are "inflationary."

Escalator clauses can eliminate from the agenda of collective bargaining the question of maintaining the originally established purchasing power of the hourly wage rate. Wherever such clauses do not exist or have been discontinued, more time has to be spent on reopening of contracts or re-negotiations of wage schedules. Since in the long run a decline in real wages is detrimental to the steady growth of the economy and is most unlikely to be accepted by labor without a struggle, the opposition against the escalator clause does not seem to be very soundly based on the facts of modern industrialized society. A longer view of the development of consumer prices is given in the next paragraph.

In fact the "money illusion" characteristic of union attitudes in the period between the two World Wars is still maintained in the tactics and public relations statements of management. There is still a tendency to identify higher money outlays for the compensation of employees with higher employment cost. It is, therefore, necessary to expand the traditional concept of real purchasing power which is usually identified only with the price of consumer goods used by typical household units of wage and salary earners to the price of labor itself. The real price of labor in any economic unit producing goods and services is, however, represented by labor unit cost. That is to say if an increase in money wages coincides with a reduction in labor unit requirements because of technical innovations the real price of labor of the purchasing power of management with regard to labor supply either remains the same or is rising. The undifferentiated use of such words as "wage push inflation" may be effective propaganda but it is poor economics for a progressive industrialized system.

It must be stressed, however, that the preceding analysis deals only with blue-collar workers. The ongoing labor force transformation and the resulting preponderance of white-collar and service workers and the increase in the low productivity sector of the economy have a tendency to translate on the macroscale higher money wages into higher unit labor cost. This structural change in the economy cannot be stemmed by opposition to the escalator clause which retains its validity even in this new setting. However, it gives a new meaning to cost inflation. This upward pressure on employment cost and prices is no longer offset in an almost symetrical manner by a decline in unit labor cost in the nonproduction sector of the economy. While automation increases labor productivity of production workers and continues to lower the employment cost in spite of higher wages and more elaborate wage structures, the same is no longer true of the majority of wage and salary earners in the nonproduction sector. This is the reason why the estimate for productivity increases for the 1970's for the labor force as a whole are lower than the actual increase in productivity for the 1960's which averaged 3.4 percent per annum.

Most of the wage features which are being discussed in this chapter and elsewhere in Part II of this text have originated in the production section of the economy and many of them have spread to the ever increasing white-collar sector. The cost inflation is, therefore, not traceable to the high wage levels in mining, construction and durable goods manufacturing but to the fact that through the spill-over effect these patterns of compensation inevitably spread to groups of employees with a far lower rate of productivity. The results are rising prices and at the turn of the decade from the 60's to the 70's an acceleration which must be called inflationary. While this tendency was particularly strong in the United States, the development was in fact noticeable throughout the world. This may be the price we have to pay for automation, the reduction in production worker employment and the maintenance of full employment through the expansion of the nonproduction sector.

It is only natural that this steep rise in Consumer Price Indexes has revived the complaints, so traditional with organized labor that gains in money wages were virtually being wiped out by increases in cost of living. In the view of Mr. Nicholas Kisburg, research and legislative director of the Teamsters Joint Council 16, New York, an increase of $30.43 in gross average weekly earnings in the construction industry in New York was reduced to 1.36. In order to arrive at this result the union spokesman deducted $13.21 from the increase attributable to higher taxes and $15.86 for "inflation."

The inclusion of excise taxes, for instance on gasoline, and of interest rates is a standard practice in the computing of the Consumer Price Index because obviously they influence the cost of living. It remains doubtful, however, whether direct taxes should figure in ascertaining the real purchasing power as contrasted to the money earnings of wage and salary earners. Throughout the period of steeply rising consumer prices, especially after 1965, personal savings continued to be substantially higher than at the beginning of the decade. They were 4.9 percent of the disposable personal income in 1960 but had risen to 6.9 percent in 1968. This was a drop from the 7.4 percent in the preceding year. With this comparatively high and stable rate of saving, the question arises whether higher taxes curtail consumer expenditures rather than savings. In view of the steady rise of consumer expenditures it appears that contrary to widely held views, tax increases do not so much slow down consumer spending but bring about a curb on personal savings. They dropped from $7.4 billion in 1967 to $6.9 billion in 1968. For this reason direct taxes should not be allowed in a calculus establishing the difference between an increase in money and in real wages.

SELECTED BIBLIOGRAPHY

Earl, Lewis. "Extent of Incentive Pay in Manufacturing," *Monthly Labor Review* (May 1960).
Keyseling, Leon H. *The Role of Wages in a Great Society* (Washington, D. C.: Conference on Economic Progress, 1965).
Ruben, George. "Deferred Increases Due in 1963 and Wage Escalation," *Monthly Labor Review* (December 1962).

QUESTIONS FOR DISCUSSION

1. On the whole, labor unions are against piece-rate compensation and incentive plans based on such pay systems. What factors account for this opposition?

2. In our contemporary industrial economy modified incentive systems still exist. One common plan allows for "incentive" pay for the minimizing of scrap losses during the productive process. Incentive plans such as this are usually viewed as highly beneficial to both labor and management. What accounts for the general acceptance of this particular type of incentive plan?

3. The gradual movement from mechanized industries to fully automated industries will probably reduce the relative importance of incentive pay in many industries. Why is this so?

4. At some length, define and analyze the concept of deferred wage increases, with special attention to their effects on collective bargaining agreements, macroeconomics, and labor market stability.

5. Contrast the concept of "escalator clause" with that of deferred wage increases.

6. Are escalator clauses inflationary? Why?

7. Using the 1962 or 1964 *Economic Report of the President* as a reference, analyze the relative importance of deferred wage increases in terms of the "Wage-Price Guideline."

Chapter

9

Fringe Benefits

As the working conditions of blue- and white-collar workers improve, more and more stress is placed on benefits connected with employment above and beyond hourly and weekly earnings. Indeed, in recent years workers very often have been more interested in fringe benefits than in a further increase in their current money earnings. In the last third of the twentieth century the scope of these benefits and the problem of job security seem to have displaced the old concern for ever-higher money income.

In assessing the progress of labor and the role played in its achievement by unions and by collective bargaining, increased attention must be paid to these issues. From a purely theoretical viewpoint of the specific productivity theory of wages, the argument could be developed that wage rates would move up even without union pressure whenever output and demand rises, but there can be no doubt that without collective bargaining fringe benefits would not have been granted to the extent that they have today—both in areas directly covered by union contracts and in nonorganized industrial relationships.

Fringe benefits cover a great diversity of topics. There are schemes dealing with compensation of periods when the employee is not actually performing any work. For some workers there is a system of supplemental unemployment pay; there is a whole bundle of welfare programs. Last but not least there are company pension plans in force for millions of employees. Furthermore, new approaches are discernible in some contracts to let employees share in productivity gains.

9-1. PAID VACATIONS, OTHER PAID ABSENCES, SEVERANCE PAY AND LAY-OFF ALLOWANCES.

Paid vacations are one of the most tangible signs of the great improvement in the total situation of wage and salary earners. Paid vacations were practically unheard of prior to World War I. Shortly before World War II they were initiated on a larger scale in some European countries. Today the vast majority of employees here and abroad have acquired rights to paid vacations. Among the side effects of this development is the emergence of tourism on a mass basis.

The length of the vacation varies with the length of service with a given company. Generally, graduated vacation plans prevail according to which employees with greater seniority are entitled to longer vacations. In Table 9-1 such a scheme dating from 1968 is given showing the relation between length of service and length of the period for which vacation pay was granted. It should be noted that in this particular scheme two weeks' vacation are due only to employees of five to less than ten years' seniority. The short vacation for employees with low seniority standing was accepted in exchange for the much longer vacation granted to long-time employees. It should be stressed that vacation plans define the time periods for which vacation pay has been earned for employees with different seniority ratings. That is to say, employees have an option between actually taking the vacation or just claiming the vacation pay which is due to them in consideration of their length of service.

TABLE 9-1
SENIORITY AND VACATION PAY IN A TYPICAL AGREEMENT

Seniority	Vacation Pay
1 to less than 2 years	1 week
2 to less than 3 years	1 week 1 day
3 to less than 4 years	1 week 2 days
4 to less than 5 years	1 week 3 days
5 to less than 10 years	2 weeks
10 to less than 20 years	3 weeks
20 years and over	4 weeks

SOURCE: U. S. Dept. of Labor, Bureau of Labor Statistics (June 1969), Bulletin No. 1425-9: "Paid Vacation and Holiday Provisions."

In some industries longer vacations are earned by employees having periods of service of five years or more. These *extended vacations*, sometimes called "sabbaticals" usually are given for thirteen-week periods every fifth year. As can be seen on Table 9-2 they are most widely spread in the primary metal industries but they have also found acceptance elsewhere.

It is obvious that the introduction of paid vacations (especially extended ones) increases somewhat the manpower requirements of an enterprise, although organizational and technological adjustments may minimize the impact of paid vacations on the total number of employees. Extended vacations have the effect of rotating in and out of the plant at any

TABLE 9-2
EXTENDED VACATIONS

	Agreements	Workers (in thousands)
All industries...............	76	584.2
Manufacturing	70	569.7
Ordnance and accessories	1	3.9
Food and kindred products	3	12.6
Chemicals and allied products.............	1	5.9
Stone, clay, and glass products	1	4.0
Primary metal industries	54	491.6
Fabricated metal products	4	11.5
Machinery (except electrical)	3	23.6
Transportation equipment	2	15.8
Instruments and related products..........	1	1.0
Nonmanufacturing...........	6	14.5
Mining, crude petroleum and natural gas production.............................	5	12.2
Utilities: Electric and gas	1	2.3

SOURCE: See Footnote in Table 9-1.

given moment a small but significant proportion of the work force. In this way manpower requirements are held at a somewhat higher level than would otherwise be the case. First experiences with this sabbatical system show that many workers had made advance plans for this long vacation period. These have ranged from house repairs to enrollment in adult education and school programs. It must be realized, however, that such extended vacations can be offered only by very large enterprises operating at low break-even points. Such vast schemes cannot be adopted by smaller firms or by industries which are labor-intensive and where employment costs are a very high proportion of total unit production cost.

Whereas vacation pay is given to employees who are scheduled to return to work, *severance pay* has been written into a number of collective contracts—for instance in the steel industry. These payments are due to workers who are laid off because of the closing of a plant or department of the company. For instance workers who have been with the firm for ten or more years are eligible for 8 weeks of severance pay; a 4-week allowance is paid to workers with at least three years of continuous service. Severance pay is given to workers who are laid off permanently, usually as a result of a reshuffling of production units in connection with modernization of facilities.

Although attempts are being made in many industries to "phase out" over a longer period workers no longer needed as a result of technical innovations, and to rely on a natural process of attrition to reduce the labor force to the new, smaller manpower requirements, there are extreme cases of a radical cutback in employment coupled with very generous severance pay. In the canning industry, where almost complete automation has displaced many production workers, some companies have agreed to paying 70 percent of the former weekly earnings to laid-off workers up to a maximum period of five years. In this case it is obvious that the full savings in employment costs connected with the introduction of automated equipment will become effective only with a considerable time lag. But despite the vast scope of this severance-pay arrangement, the investment in labor-saving machinery is bound to be most profitable in the long run. Severance pay is due only in cases of a permanent layoff of workers caused by modernization and reorganization of vast production systems. It prevails in capital-intensive industries in transportation and construction.

While severance pay is provided in many union contracts for workers whose employment is being eliminated as a result of the introduction of labor saving devices, in many cases union agreements today also provide for *layoff allowances.* These fringe benefits are not tied to technological changes but merely to reductions of personnel caused by general economic conditions. Usually no such allowance is payable if the employee has less than one year of service. But after one year a layoff allowance can be given in the form of one week's pay. These benefits rise rapidly in cases of layoffs of employees with ten years or more service. To illustrate, a worker who is being laid off for economic rather than technological reasons with fifteen years of service can receive a layoff allowance corresponding to twenty-four weeks of pay. Workers who have longer service can receive even more.

It is necessary to retain the proper perspective on the fringe benefits of severance pay and layoff allowances. Without doubt they have improved employment conditions substantially for those workers who are covered in such schemes. However, a study of the U.S. Department of Labor on "Severance Pay and Layoff Benefit Plans"[1] shows that only a minority of workers in manufacturing and nonmanufacturing is covered by such clauses as will be shown in Table 9-3 which is based on an analysis of 1773 agreements.

In the manufacturing industries the largest group of workers covered by severance pay and layoff benefits is in transportation equipment. They are followed by workers in the primary metals industry and in apparel and other finished products. Of the 3.3 million workers in nonmanufacturing shown in Table 9-3 almost 900,000 were in construction and 688,000 in transportation. It is also well to remember that the survey from which this study was compiled covered only major agreements. In 1963 almost 17 million wage and salary workers were employed in manufacturing but only 4.1 million of this total were included in the survey. However, it cannot be assumed that severance and layoff benefits are actually more fre-

---

[1]Bulletin No. 1425–2, March 1965, U.S. Dept. of Labor.

TABLE 9-3
SEVERANCE PAY AND LAYOFF BENEFIT PLANS IN
MAJOR COLLECTIVE BARGAINING AGREEMENTS, 1963
(workers in thousands)

Industry	Total number of agreements		No reference to severance pay or layoff benefit plans	
	Agreements	Workers	Agreements	Workers
All Industries	1,773	7,454.1	1,248	4,403.1
Manufacturing	1,023	4,137.1	646	1,805.1
Nonmanufacturing	750	3,317.0	604	2,598.0

SOURCE: See previous footnote.

quent than is indicated in Table 9-3 because the major collective bargaining agreements were covered in the study.

9-2. SUPPLEMENTAL UNEMPLOYMENT BENEFITS OR "SUB"

The purpose of supplemental unemployment pay is to maintain the weekly income of workers at a level of about 65 percent of their normal take-home pay during periods of temporary unemployment. These payments are added to the unemployment benefits to which the workers are entitled in the states where they are employed. If, for example, the total pay was $100 a week and the unemployment benefits amount to $50, then the supplemental pay would be $15 per week.

This system was first introduced in the automotive industry in 1955. Prior to this agreement there had been a well publicized demand by some unions for a *guaranteed annual wage*. Actually, this issue was raised originally during wage negotiations in the steel industry in the early 1950's, but the union did not insist on it when the 1952 contract was concluded after a lengthy strike. The demand for such a scheme was then picked up by the automobile workers' union at least a year prior to the expiration of the 1955 contract. Union spokesmen insisted that they were primarily interested in steady work for 52 weeks a year. The requested wage guarantee was to cover those weeks in which, for one reason or another, work could not be supplied by the company. The effect of the guaranteed wage plan, however, would have been to assure that all workers covered by it would receive 52 weekly pay checks. While this original demand did not go so far as to require employment guarantees, it nevertheless aimed at a commitment of a year-round income, amounting to a guarantee of annual earnings.

The supplemental unemployment benefits actually agreed upon are a compromise. The union did not insist on a guaranteed annual wage, and the companies promised the additions to the state unemployment-compensation payments. In order to meet these obligations, companies participating in this scheme set aside a certain amount per hourly pay to build up a fund out of which the supplemental benfits could be paid. There are differences in the calculation of the contributions being made by companies that have set up such supplemental unemployment schemes. Furthermore, actual cents-per-hour contributions range from 2 to 10 cents, the average being about 5 cents.[2] These variations are due to the fact that in some cases workers can obtain as much as 80 percent of their before tax earnings as benefits, whereas others receive benefits of 65, 62, or 60 percent of these earnings.

This scheme has not been widely adopted. Actually, in 1963–64, 174 plans covering 1.8 million workers were in force. Outside the steel and automotive industries, such plans have also been negotiated for rubber workers, the ladies' garment workers, and photoengravers.

Actually, fluctuations in employment have been less violent after World War II than in earlier periods. Modern scientific methods of business management have made it possible to schedule a production program more evenly over longer periods of time. Employment and income of production workers connected with large enterprises has become far more stable than formerly. For this reason the demand for a wage guarantee as described above, seems to have lost much of its urgency. The supplemental unemployment pay cannot be considered as having taken the place of a highly problematical commitment to guarantee 52 weeks of pay per year. Its effects merely soften the impact of unemployment and enable a worker who is laid off to continue meeting his commitments at least for the period in which he is receiving unemployment compensation.

The main objection to "SUB" is that it can benefit only a very small proportion of all employees. Furthermore, it tends to distract the attention of powerful labor unions from the need to update and improve unemployment compensation in the United States. This system of social insurance has never undergone the major structural changes required by a rational and efficient administration of the labor market. There is no doubt that unemployment compensation ought to be vastly improved, but supplemental unemployment pay is not the way to do this—because it cannot be applied to the vast majority of employees who are just as urgently in need of better unemployment benefits as the workers now eligible for this supplemental pay scheme.

These objections do not apply to another fringe benefit to be found in some contracts in the automobile and in the rubber industry under the name of *Short Workweek Allowances.* Such payments are provided for two types of situations. The first deals with a scheduled short workweek in connection with a reduction of production due to a decline in customer demand. In such a case workers are entitled to a total weekly compensation

---

[2]"Supplemental Unemployment Benefit Plans in Major Agreements," *Monthly Labor Review,* vol. 88, no. 2 (January 1965).

which would be the equivalent of what he would receive under the supplemental unemployment benefit scheme. An unscheduled short workweek deals with conditions where an employee returns during the week from a layoff or reports tardily after a recall. In such cases the pay can be limited to 50 percent of the average earnings of a normal work week.

In some industries, especially primary metals and transportation equipment in which frequently production units are closed down and others are opened at some distance, transfers of workers had to take place. In a study of 586 agreements in these two industries and also in contracts of teamsters, electrical and communication workers covering 3.5 million workers,[3] it was found that in 34.5 percent of the agreements *relocation allowances* were provided. They provide for moving expenses. It is significant, however, to note that in some cases such allowances are to be charged against an "Automation Fund." In other instances it was to be taken out of the reserves set up for supplemental unemployment benefits. Generally speaking these allowances apply primarily to transfers of workers who are retained in employment after their original job had been eliminated by technical innovations.

9-3. WELFARE PROVISIONS

In preceding sections substantial extensions of the wage structure were discussed. In the course of time, many wage contracts developed group life insurance and hospitalization plans. Furthermore, additional benefits in case of retirement and unemployment were instituted. The latter scheme has already been discussed in Sec. 9-2. Retirement plans assumed such importance that they are analyzed in greater detail later in the chapter. At this point it is necessary to give a total picture of the scope of all employee benefits and their development in recent years.

It should be noted that Table 9-4 gives an accounting of the fringe benefits paid out under the various schemes. Group life insurance has been increasingly adopted as an employee benefit feature. Contributions under such a group plan are comparatively low and consequently the premium-benefit ratio is in most cases very favorable. Payments under hospitalization and surgical plans have been going up in the period from 1959 to 1963.

It is also important to note that these voluntary health insurance schemes have to continue in spite of Medicare. This new scheme for people 65 years and over does not eliminate the necessity for wage and salary earners to continue their group health insurance policies. In fact, the added contributions to Medicare will bring about the situation that people in the active labor force will have to pay toward medical care for the aged while in

---

[3]Bulletin No. 1425–10, "Plant Movement, Transfer, and Relocation Allowances," U.S. Dept. of Labor, July 1969.

TABLE 9-4
ESTIMATED BENEFITS PAID UNDER EMPLOYEE-BENEFIT PLANS,
SELECTED YEARS 1950–1967
(thousands)

Type of Benefit	1950	1960	1963	1966	1967
Total..............................	$1,812.5	$7,848.5	$10,694.8	$14,420.4	$15,686.0
Benefits for all wage and salary workers					
Life insurance and death benefits......................	310.0	1,017.6	1,341.8	1,693.1	1,877.8
Accidental death and dismemberment...............	16.0	47.3	82.5	97.0	101.4
Hospitalization..................	477.5	2,355.0	3,312.4	4,312.0	4,526.3
Written in compliance with law	2.1	8.0	3.5	2.6	2.7
Surgical and regular medical	231.2	1,116.2	1,471.8	1,979.5	2,099.5
Major medical expense...........	—	427.0	752.0	1,136.0	1,306.0
Benefits for wage and salary workers in private industry					
Temporary disability, including formal sick leave	407.8	1,030.4	1,183.3	1,435.8	1,506.0
Written in compliance with law	54.3	196.1	198.2	208.7	222.4
Supplemental unemployment benefits......................	—	105.0	91.0	87.0	119.0
Retirement......................	370.0	1,750.0	2,460.0	3,680.0	4,150.0

SOURCE: *Social Security Bulletin*, (April 1969).

most cases they also have to carry the contributions to group health-insurance plans. Generally speaking, group life insurance and health insurance have added substantially to the overall security of wage and salary earners covered by these plans.

We now turn to private retirement pensions, which are another important feature in the overall security generated by contemporary wage structures. However, these plans raise serious questions with regard to the number of persons covered and the accumulation of funds deemed necessary to finance company pensions.

9-4. COMPANY PENSION PLANS

After World War I the system of compulsory retirement, especially in public service, was introduced in many European countries. The immediate purpose of such plans was to create a greater measure of turnover in jobs in order to create employment opportunities for war veterans. Eventually the idea of a definite retirement age gained hold in the United States, and in many cases corporations established rigid, impersonal criteria for the retirement of executives. This led to elaborate pension schemes for corporation officials. In addition to pension payments, such features as stock options were widely introduced to create economic security for retired corporation executives.

Prior to World War II small company pensions were also provided for production workers in isolated cases. After World War II organized labor began to push for company pensions. Originally management (for instance, in the steel industry) maintained that it was under no obligation to include company pensions in an agenda of collective-bargaining negotiations, and that if and when company pensions were to be provided for employees below the executive level it was to be done on a voluntary, noncontractual basis. However, after a fact-finding board set up by President Truman had made its report, it was ruled that the concept of bargaining in good faith covered the area of company pensions. Once this rule was established, bringing about a substantial broadening of the concept of labor-management relations, private company pension plans gained wide acceptance. The resistance of management to these schemes was negligible because the argument could not very well be advanced that executives needed company pensions but wage and salary employees did not.

In private industry these company pensions are in the vast majority of programs noncontributory. The employer either selects an insured plan or sets up a separate retirement pension fund. The outlays for the funding of these pension programs are operating expenses of the firm and as such they are tax-deductible. This feature has given considerable impetus to the rapid growth and accumulation of these funds. Before analyzing these developments in some detail it is necessary to discuss the general features of private pension plans.

A pension system must establish certain criteria for eligibility. Usually a company pension cannot be claimed unless the employee has accumulated twenty-five years of service. In many plans pensions increase rapidly with each year spent with the company beyond the twenty-five year minimum. It is easy to see that these necessary conditions for the operation of a pension system can create certain problems with regard to labor mobility. Wage and salary earners over age 35 may feel that they are frozen in their jobs, because any move might jeopardize their company pension. For this reason the system of *portable pensions* is now being considered, and has already been introduced in the steel industry. Under such a scheme, employees changing from one company to another in the same industry can "bring along," as it were, their pension rights. The service with the old company will be credited in the new company and the pension will be fixed under consideration of the total years of service in the industry.

Nevertheless, company pensions do have a tendency to cut down labor mobility of workers in their middle age to a certain degree. Furthermore, some employers are reluctant to hire people in this age group due to the relatively higher cost of including such employees in the company pension plan.

Pension systems in recent years have frequently been established in collective labor contracts. These legal instruments are signed by management and the authorized representative of employees. The question arose to what extent those collective contracts establish individual claims for employees. While they are covered by the agreement entitling them to company pensions, the enforcement of such rights on the part of individuals does present considerable difficulty. In general it is unlikely that pensions due to retired workers will be denied, but a further clarification of what an individual can legally do in such a case is still necessary. For a considerable period employees covered by pension agreements did not have *vesting rights.* If they withdrew from the company prior to reaching retirement age, they usually forfeited all claims. More recently vesting rights can be exercised in a growing number of contracts, and employees are being provided with some options. There can be lump-sum payments or reduced pensions earned up to the time of resignation.

It has been stated that most pension schemes in private employment are noncontributory. Employees are not called on to share in the cost of the program. For this reason many plans originally provided for a checking off of the Federal old-age pensions due to the retired employee from the amount of the company pension established in collective contracts or otherwise fixed. In recent years company pension systems have provided a more generous total retirement pay by lessening the amount of old-age benefits by which the company pensions themselves were reduced. The steel contract of 1960 limited the deduction to $80 a month. In the 1965 agreement this was cut to $60. To the retirement pay the wife's benefit would have to be added, but often she can claim her own social security pension based on her own employment credits.

It is obvious that company pensions make a substantial contribution to retirement income. However, it is necessary now to stress two aspects of these schemes. The first point to be made is that, at best, far less than half of the employed labor force is being covered. Secondly, the funding of these private company pension plans has led in a short period of time to an astounding accumulation of funds, both insured and noninsured. Table 9-5 gives a survey of private pension plans. Almost 16 million workers were covered by such schemes in the winter of 1962–63. Of this total number, about 5 million workers participated in pension plans not specifically mentioned in a collective agreement.

In 1962–63 total employment in manufacturing was about 17 million. As can be seen from Table 9-5, more than half of the wage and salary workers in manufacturing were covered by private pension plans. In the same year about 4 million workers were employed in transportation, of which roughly one-third was included in such private plans. When we come to wholesale and retail trade in which about 11.5 million were employed in 1962–63, we see that coverage by private pension plans drops to less than 10 percent of all employees. The same is true of service employment. In mining, about half of the workers were included in such private plans.

TABLE 9-5
DISTRIBUTION OF PRIVATE PENSION PLANS BY INDUSTRY GROUP AND
COLLECTIVE-BARGAINING STATUS, WINTER, 1962–63
(workers, thousands)

Industry	All Plans		Collective-Bargaining Status			
			Mentioned in a Collective-Bargaining Agreement		Not mentioned in a Collective-Bargaining Agreement	
	Number	Workers*	Plans	Workers	Plans	Workers
All plans studied	15,818	15,621	5,795	10,695	10,023	4,926
Agriculture, forestry and fisheries.................	75	26	15	18	60	8
Mining....................	316	327	43	242	273	86
Contract construction	449	1,072	384	908	65	164
Manufacturing	9,257	9,678	4,285	6,821	4,972	2,857
Transportation	673	1,286	384	898	289	388
Communications and public utilities............	849	1,270	314	1,042	535	228
Wholesale and retail trade ..	1,627	920	294	498	1,333	421
Wholesale trade.........	1,147	479	249	340	898	139
Retail trade	480	440	45	158	435	282
Finance, insurance, and real estate...............	1,853	733	22	78	1,831	656
Services..................	719	308	54	191	665	118

*Active workers in 1961.
SOURCE: *Monthly Labor Review* (July 1964).

It is doubtful whether the system of private pension plans can be substantially expanded beyond the scope which they had attained in the early 1960's. Large numbers of wage and salary workers in retail trade and in services are employed by smaller firms. As we will see presently, private pension funds require considerable outlays by management. They add to the employment cost, although considerable tax advantages accrue to firms making payments to their welfare funds. There is no doubt that these plans improve the retirement income of employees, primarily in large-scale enterprise. In view of these inherent limitations of private pension plans, the matter of financing such pension systems deserves particular attention.

As is seen in Table 9-6, the reserves of the pension funds multiplied more than eight times between 1950 and 1967, whereas the number of employees covered increased about three times. It should be noted that the number of covered employees listed in that table exceeds that given in Table 9-5 because in the latter tabulation employees of nonprofit organizations, and of the railroad retirement program are included. The noninsured plans are administered by trustees; the insured plans are underwritten by insurance companies.

In order to obtain a perspective on the significance of the data presented in Table 9-6, some comparisons are indicated. By 1967 the total

TABLE 9-6

PRIVATE PENSION AND DEFERRED PROFIT-SHARING PLANS ESTIMATED COVERAGE, CONTRIBUTIONS, BENEFICIARIES, BENEFIT PAYMENTS, AND RESERVES, 1950–1967

Year	Coverage, end of year (in thousands)			Employer contributions (in millions)			Employee contributions (in millions)			Number of beneficiaries, end of year (in thousands)			Amount of benefit payments (in millions)			Reserves, end of year (in billions)		
	Total	In-sured	Non-in-sured	Total	In-sured	Non-in-sured	Total	In-sured	Non-in-sured	Total	In-sured	Non-in-sured	Total[3]	In-sured	Non-in-sured[3]	Total	In-sured	Non-in-sured
1950	9,800	2,600	7,200	$1,750	$720	$1,030	$330	$200	$130	450	150	300	$370	$80	$290	$12.1	$5.6	$6.5
1955	15,400	3,800	11,600	3,280	1,100	2,180	560	280	280	980	290	690	850	180	670	27.5	11.3	16.1
1960	21,200	4,900	16,300	4,690	1,190	3,500	790	300	490	1,780	540	1,240	1,750	390	1,360	52.0	18.8	33.1
1961	22,200	5,100	17,100	4,770	1,180	3,590	810	290	520	1,910	570	1,340	1,960	450	1,510	57.8	20.2	37.5
1962	23,100	5,200	17,900	5,020	1,240	3,780	860	310	550	2,100	630	1,470	2,250	510	1,740	63.5	21.6	41.9
1963	23,800	5,400	18,400	5,300	1,390	3,910	880	300	580	2,280	690	1,590	2,460	570	1,890	69.9	23.3	46.5
1964	24,600	6,000	18,600	5,950	1,520	4,430	940	320	620	2,490	740	1,750	2,760	640	2,120	77.2	25.2	51.9
1965	25,400	6,300	19,100	6,720	1,740	4,980	1,030	360	670	2,750	790	1,960	3,180	720	2,460	85.4	27.3	58.1
1966	26,400	7,000	19,400	7,330	1,830	5,500	1,070	370	700	3,110	870	2,240	3,680	810	2,870	93.9	29.4	64.5
1967	27,600	7,800	19,800	8,040	2,010	6,030	1,150	390	760	3,420	940	2,480	4,150	910	3,240	103.8	32.0	71.8

SOURCE: *Social Security Bulletin* (April 1967).

reserves in the private pension funds had reached almost $104 billion. They exceeded by more than 400 percent the assets of Old-Age and Survivors Insurance trust funds. Whereas in 1950 these funds were still higher by more than $1 billion than the private pension reserves, by 1967 the latter system had surpassed the public old-age security reserves to the extent of $80 billion. In 1950 about 3.5 million primary beneficiaries received old-age benefits. In 1967 the number of beneficiaries was about 16 million, not counting dependents. In the same year 2.280 million former employees received private retirement pensions. In 1967 the total number of employees covered by private pension plans was 27.6 million. While it is difficult at any given moment to ascertain precisely how many individuals are covered by Old-Age and Survivors Insurance, it is safe to say that their number exceeds by at least two and one half times those included in private pension plans.

The rapid buildup of reserves in the 1950's and 1960's is certain to continue, because of the adherence of private pension fund administrators to the funding principle. That is, assets must be built up to the point where current and projected future private pension payments are secured by the dividend and interest income of the assets. It has been estimated that by 1970 these assets will far exceed $120 billion. But even in the early 1960's private pension funds had displaced such institutional investors as insurance companies, foundations, and other large-scale financial institutions from their leading ranks as investors. These pension funds now have assumed first place. They are well on their way to the one-third mark of the total public debt which in 1968 had risen to $358.0 billion.

Here we see a paradoxical side effect of the still increasing desire for social security. When Federal old age benefits were first introduced in the Social Security Act of 1935, there was considerable emotional opposition against the very idea of this type of public income maintenance scheme for people retired from the labor force. But very rapidly the idea of company pensions gained hold. Once the private sector became interested in company pensions and was given the opportunity to write off payments to private welfare funds, the system grew very rapidly and soon exceeded the amounts deposited with the trust fund of the much larger system of old age and disability benefit system (OASDI). Nevertheless primary social security benefits exceed in a significant way the median payment due to beneficiaries from private plans. This can be seen clearly from Table 9-7. In evaluating the private retirement plan benefits and social security payments, it must be remembered that the coverage of private pension plans is limited, comprising 27.6 million people in 1967 whereas in the public system virtually the total civilian labor force numbering over 77 million in the same year is included. While this broadens the basis of the revenue structure, it also implies a far greater eligibility rate of beneficiaries.

TABLE 9-7
PRIVATE PENSION AND PRIMARY SOCIAL SECURITY BENEFITS
1964 AND 1968

		Average Monthly Earnings		
		$350	$400	$450
Median private plan	1964	96.25	97.50	97.50
	1968	131.25	135.00	149.25
Primary social security	1964	116.00	127.00	127.00
	1968	140.40	153.60	165.00

SOURCE: Harry E. Davis, "Negotiated Retirement Plans—A Decade of Benefit Improvements," *Monthly Labor Review* (May 1969).

Whereas in 1967, 3.4 million former employees received private pensions, in the same year more than 12 million retired workers received primary benefits. Taking into account wives' and husbands' benefits, children's benefits and payments to widows, the total number of beneficiaries actually was over 21 million.

The great disproportionality between accumulated funds and benefit payments under private and under public benefit plans is based on the difference in principles of accumulation of reserved funds. The private pension plans are based on the *funding principle.* That is to say current and projected future benefits are to be paid out of the earnings of the invested funds. The latter are never to be used to meet claims. They must, therefore, be large enough to produce earnings sufficient to meet the insurance claims. Actually as can be seen from Table 9-6 employers' contributions to the private pension plans exceeded by about 100 percent current benefit payments. On the other hand in the public system in recent years the net contribution income exceeded cash benefits only slightly in 1968 by just $1.1 billion.

The application of the funding principle and the consequent rapid accumulation of private pension funds has led to a tremendous self-reinforcement of the financial strength of that part of the private sector which promises company pensions to its employees.

As can be seen from Table 9-8 in the early phases of the build-up of these private funds, investment in U.S. Government securities comprised 30.5 percent of the assets. But in 1967 these public issues were down to 3.1 percent of the total holdings.

It should be noted that Table 9-8 is dealing only with the noninsured private funds which, however, comprise about 70 percent of the total reserves. We see that in 1967 common stock holdings had become the largest category of assets thereby taking the place which had been held in 1960 by corporate bonds. If we consider the fact that median private plan benefits of retirees having average monthly earnings of $450 amounted to less than $150 the question arises whether the build-up of reserves for

TABLE 9-8
ASSETS OF NONINSURED PRIVATE PENSION FUNDS (BOOK VALUE)
AT END OF SELECTED YEARS, 1950–1967
(Amounts in Millions)

Type of Asset	1950		1960		1967	
	Amount	Percent	Amount	Percent	Amount	Percent
Total	6,452	100	33,135	100	71,818	100
Cash & Deposits..........................	264	4.1	546	1.6	1,184	1.6
U.S. Government Securities	1,966	30.5	2,683	8.1	2,246	3.1
Corporate Bonds........................	2,828	43.8	15,699	47.4	25,527	35.5
Preferred Stock	304	4.7	776	2.3	975	1.4
Common Stock	802	12.4	10,733	32.4	33,853	47.1
Mortgages..............................	102	1.6	1,301	3.9	3,935	5.5
Other Assets...........................	186	2.9	1,399	4.2	4,098	5.7

SOURCE: *Social Security Bulletin* (April 1969).

private pension systems does not come under "over-kill" patterns of financial and economic management. There is no doubt that this would not be tolerated in the public sector.

Employers' contributions to insured and noninsured private pension plans amounted to $8,040 billion in 1967, a 10 percent increase over the previous year. These contributions represent substantial tax advantages to the employer which originally were intended to encourage the setting up of private pension funds. It must be realized, however, that these contributions are also part of a cost and price structure of corporate goods and services. We see here a double effect of private pension plans as they are operating today. On the one side they are reducing the corporate tax liability; on the other side they are an additional factor strengthening the downward inflexibility of prices and actually contributing to their long run upward trend. The question must therefore be raised whether the funding principle used by private pension funds does not lead to increasingly severe distortions in aggregate allocation of resources and income flows.

9-5. SHARING IN PRODUCTIVITY GAINS

The vast majority of wage and salary workers do not participate in profit-sharing plans. The practice has been rather to emphasize continuous increases in basic pay rates as business conditions improve and profits rise and are maintained at satisfactory levels. There have been some attempts, however, to let employees share in gains made by management through progressive technology, including automation. Such gains are brought about by a sharp decline in unit labor cost. Because fewer workers are needed to produce a given volume of output, such savings can become substantial even if hourly wages of the reduced number of workers increase. In 1963 the Kaiser Steel Corporation made an agreement with the United Steel Workers of America inaugurating a long-range sharing plan.[4] The gist of this elaborate

[4] *Monthly Labor Review* (February 1963).

scheme is that based on the year 1961, "improvements in labor performance, material and supply usage, yield improvement and utilization of technological changes shall be measured." The gains resulting from these innovations shall be shared by management and employees. The computation of the employees' gross shares has been arranged in a most complex manner. One part of this share consists of 32.5 percent of the calculated net dollar gains. However, from this share certain deductions are to be made in order to set up a wage and benefit reserve. What is left can be used as an addition to earnings according to certain weights ranging from a factor of 2.0 to 8.0 for five categories of employees set up for the purpose of such a computation.

It remains doubtful whether this complex scheme can overcome the serious problems of employment and income security posed by automation. The agreement discussed here has established in Section A an "employment guarantee." However, this has been surrounded by so many escape clauses that it cannot be considered a real answer to the problem of labor displacement through automation. Actually, the system of deferred wage increases described in Sec. 8-2 of the present text, seems to be a more simple and effective response to the problem of maintaining a dynamic balance between productivity gains, wage rates, and aggregate levels of employment.

9-6. THE COST OF FRINGE BENEFITS

The elaboration of the wage structure from a simple compensation of workers by the day or by the hour into a complex system taking in all the features described in this and in the preceding chapter have added to the total employment cost. Unit labor costs already analyzed in Sec. 6-3 are being measured in terms of these total employment costs. Whether or not an improvement in fringe benefits brings about an actual increase in unit labor cost cannot be decided merely by adding up the outlays prorated per hour of compensated employment. At this point of our analysis, we are, however, concerned with the cost of the "package," above and beyond the straight-time hourly wage rate.

An estimation of the cost of fringe benefits, especially their impact on hourly labor costs is not a simple matter. In fact uncertainty and different calculations with regard to the money cost per hour of proposed changes in collective contracts are often creating impasses in labor management negotiations. For example the steel contract of 1965 provided incentives for the early retirement of workers. Management estimates of the higher retirement pay to be allotted to workers withdrawing from employment prior to reaching the mandatory retirement age were predicated on the assumption that many employees would take advantage of this opportunity. Union leaders assumed that most workers would forego this chance and would continue in employment as long as possible. Obviously their cost estimate of this fringe benefit was much lower. We have seen in the preceding section of this chapter that company contributions to insured and noninsured private pension plans are extremely high. This practice is reflected in substantial increases in the cost of fringe benefits rated per hour.[5]

While, in spite of these uncertainties, there is continuous reference especially by employers of the added cost per hour of fringe benefits, a more secure frame of comparison is the relation between employee benefit costs and payrolls. Table 9-9 will show this relationship for selected years from 1957 to 1967 as far as major benefits systems are concerned.

TABLE 9-9
SELECTED EMPLOYEE BENEFITS AS A PERCENT
OF GROSS PAYROLL,
1957–1967

Type of Benefit	1957	1963	1965	1967
Insurance and Welfare..............	2.3	2.9	3.0	3.2
Paid sick leave......................	1.2	1.3	1.3	1.3
Supplemental unemployment........	1.4	1.3	1.3	1.0
Retirement........................	5.1	4.6	4.4	4.8

SOURCE: *Social Security Bulletin* (April 1969).

Table 9-9 shows an important trend. While in the ten year period covered there substantial extensions have occurred in the scope of fringe benefits especially as can be seen from Table 9-4 in the area of Major Medical expense, the ratio of benefit payments to gross payroll remained virtually unchanged, rising only from 10.0 percent to 10.3 percent. There were actual declines in percentages in all fringe benefits with the exception of insurance and welfare. It can therefore be assumed that with a stabilization of the extent and coverage of fringe benefits, the ratio between payrolls and benefits will remain about the same as it has been in the latter part of the 1960's. It should be noted that retirement claims the largest share of employee benefits both in 1957 and in 1967.

It was mentioned above that a computation of benefit costs per hour is necessarily based on assumption some of which are somewhat uncertain. It is with this caution in mind that in Table 9-10 estimates of the cost per hour of such benefits are given. Increased money cost for fringe benefits add immediately to outlays of employers for compensation of employees but they are not converted at the same time into consumer expenditures. Thus the gap between total employment cost and gross earnings and dispos-

[5]See the detailed discussion in Lily Mary David and Victor J. Sheifer "Estimating the Cost of Collective Bargaining Settlements," *Monthly Labor Review* (May 1969).

able income of employees is widening as contributions to social security and allocations for fringe benefits increase. Table 9-10 deals only with production workers in manufacturing whose productivity has been increasing by more than 4 percent per annum between 1959 and 1966. That is to say output per man-hour increased by a much faster ratio than did hourly expenditures for fringe benefits as shown in Table 9-10. Even if we add the nonproduction workers into the overall development of productivity we find that on the basis 1957–1959 = 100 that output per man-hour in manufacturing rose from 103.7 in 1959 to 131.6 in 1966.

TABLE 9-10
AVERAGE HOURLY BENEFIT EXPENDITURES FOR
PRODUCTION WORKERS IN MANUFACTURING
SELECTED YEARS 1959–1966

	1959	1962	1966
Type of Expenditure	Cents Per Hour Paid For		
Insurance and Welfare	5.4	7.3	10.0
Paid Sick Leave.....................	2.3	2.5	3.0
Retirement	9.0	9.3	12.0

SOURCE: *Social Security Bulletin* (April 1969).

It should be noted that on an hourly basis just as in the comparison with the gross payroll expenditures for retirement are by far the largest component of average employer expenditures for employee benefits. The substantial increase in these costs since 1959 is partly based on the increase in contributions, employer as well as employee, to old age benefits. In addition contributions to insured and noninsured company retirement schemes are included in the computation of the cost per hour of these fringe benefits. Increases in the cost of benefits are likely to be absorbed by the continuous productivity gains of production workers so that their effect on unit labor cost is likely to be neutral. However the increasing white-collar sector with its low productivity will force unit labor cost for nonproduction workers up as outlays of employees for fringe benefits rise.

The preceding considerations show that in order to evaluate the substantial increase in employment costs brought about by the elaboration of the wage structure through fringe benefits and through legally imposed higher charges on employment for social security, they must be evaluated in the broader context of changes in productivity and the structural transformation of the labor force. The hourly cost for all benefit schemes shown in Table 9-10 increased from 16.7 cents in 1959 to 25 cents in 1966. In the same period corporate profits of all manufacturing corporations after taxes rose from $16.3 billion in 1959 to $30.6 billion in 1966. That is to say while expenditures for benefit plans for employees increased about 60 percent in current dollars of each year between 1959 and 1966, corporate profits in manufacturing almost doubled at the same time. It is clear then that the extension and improvement of fringe benefits did not interfere with a rapid rise of corporate profits. This means that those costs of fringe benefits which, especially as far as white-collar workers are concerned were not absorbed by productivity gains, were shifted to the customers of the manufacturing corporations, in the last analysis the private consumers and the government as buyer of industrial products.

SELECTED BIBLIOGRAPHY

Allen, Donna. *Fringe Benefits: Wages or Social Obligation?* (Ithaca, N. Y.: Cornell University Press, 1964).

Becker, Joseph M. *Guaranteed Income for the Unemployed—The Story of SUB* (Baltimore: Johns Hopkins Press, 1968).

Bernstein, M. C. *The Future of Private Pensions* (New York: The Free Press, 1964).

Dealing, Charles I. *Industrial Pensions* (Washington, D. C.: The Brookings Institution, 1964).

Farwell, Donald F., and Daniel L. Harbour. *Extended Vacations: An Innovation in Collective Bargaining* (Washington, D. C.: BNA, Inc., 1963).

Harbrecht, Paul R. *Pension Funds and Economic Power* (New York: The Twentieth Century Fund, 1959).

Hoffmann, J. Kenneth, "Provisions for Paid Sick Leave in Metropolitan Areas," *Monthly Labor Review* (February 1966).

McGill, Dan M. *Fundamentals of Private Pensions* (Homewood, Ill.: Richard D. Irwin, Inc., 1964).

Schother, Charles, Jr. "The Distribution of Profit Sharing Plans," *Southern Economic Journal* (July 1963).

U.S. Department of Labor: *Major Collective Bargaining Agreements* Bulletin numbers 1425-1210.

QUESTIONS FOR DISCUSSION

1. Outline the main features of the systems of paid absences and vacations as they exist today, and indicate how they relate to employment stability, employment costs, and the number of workers employed.

2. A system of guaranteed annual wages has never found widespread acceptance in the United States. In light of the rather significant issues involved in this question, what are the principal arguments for and against this type of employment program?

3. Indicate the nature of supplemental unemployment benefits as found in the Steel and Auto Industries and then evaluate the merits of these plans.

4. In some detail, outline the system of private company pensions as they exist in the United States and then critically evaluate this system of private welfare payment.

5. Portable pensions, such as those found in the Steel Industry, provide an important feature which helps to insure the most efficient use of our human resources, but such systems are not likely to find widespread acceptance. Why is this so?

6. Characterize the principal financial features of private pension plans and discuss their impact on the capital market.

7. Evaluate the relative merits of profit-sharing plans such as the one in operation at the Kaiser Steel Company.

8. The elaborate system of fringe benefits which make up such a significant part of labor costs require special attention in any analysis of relative wage movements, especially when wages are tied to productivity gains. Why is this so, and what are the important implications which arise from this situation?

9. Who ultimately pays the outlays of corporations for private pension plans?

Part

III

EMPLOYMENT, UNEMPLOYMENT, AND THE LABOR MARKET

Every economic aspect of labor is intimately related to the condition of the labor market, and especially to levels of employment. A study of these problems is therefore indispensable for an understanding of all issues in the economics of labor. In Part III we study first concepts of employment and unemployment and recent and discernible future prospects for employment. We then turn our attention to a careful study of the structure of the labor market itself, which must be analyzed on its own terms rather than by analogy with the commodity market. Only with this in mind do theories of employment, which will be taken up next, gain their full significance. In a rapidly changing economic system, levels of employment are intimately related to the variables which operate either in favor or contrary to the requirements of economic growth. This will be demonstrated in the chapter on "Macrodynamic Analysis of Employment." The last chapter of this part deals with economic goals and methods of employment policies.

10

Contemporary Problems of Employment and Unemployment

Modern industrialized society has developed a high degree of sensitivity about levels of employment. The fact that the overwhelming majority of the labor force consists not of self-employed but of employed wage and salary workers has created a great measure of dependency on the stability of employment. Only such a condition can assure a steady flow of income and maintain whatever affluence has been established for the many.

In the predominantly agricultural system of generations ago in which family-centered work arrangements prevailed on farms and in small shops, the proportion of the population actively engaged in the labor force was less than it is today. Furthermore, the more informal arrangements of work could adjust in a flexible manner to daily and seasonal changes in the work load without creating a formal condition of unemployment in slack periods. The modern industrial system with its rigid work schedules and its emphasis on a continuous, intensive work performance is less likely to carry workers on their payroll through times of low activities.

In addition, the complete separation of home and workplace whether factory or office, has largely contributed to the "visibility" of unemployment. If people usually have to leave home in order to work, the fact that they do not work immediately brings about a complete change in daily living arrangements and weekly income.

The whole outlook of modern industrialized society has created further psychological aggravations of unemployment. The various stages of the industrial and agricultural revolutions have strengthened the emphasis of competitive achievement. Individuals are expected to adjust continuously to changing standards of performance and to be engaged in economically productive activities.

While it is generally understood today that most people who are laid off cannot be blamed for it since they have been caught in impersonal economic

163

developments, the tradition of regarding renumerative activities as social justification for one's existence is still so strong that unemployment, in addition to bringing about a loss of income, often also leads to a decline of self-confidence. Whether or not the social value system applied to continuous involvement in productive work is consistent with the underlying contemporary trend toward automation and the continuous increase in output without a corresponding increase in employment is a question well worth asking. For the time being, however, social stress on economic activity dating back to the centuries in which, with tremendous effort, scarcity was transformed into abundance continues to dominate attitudes. As we proceed with our analysis of the labor market, the theory of employment, and employment policies it will be well to keep in mind this social and psychological context of employment problems. We will also see that the factors which make for full employment in advanced industrial systems are so structured that complacency about this problem because of high levels of employment after World War II would be short-sighted.

10-1. FULL EMPLOYMENT, OVEREMPLOYMENT, AND UNDEREMPLOYMENT

Because of the visibility of unemployment and its social and economic impact in modern society, governments, especially in the Western world, pursue the goal of full employment. In fact, the effectiveness of government and its policies are largely judged in terms of its ability to maintain reasonably high levels of full employment. In the early 1930's mass unemployment was one of the contributing factors in the breakdown of democratic government in Germany; in the United States it led to a radical break with the traditional hands-off policy of the Federal government toward employment problems. Even after World War II, when levels of employment remained consistently high, the underlying concern about the maintenance of full employment continued. In the 1960's new types of unemployment appeared in the United States which do not seem to yield to traditional employment policies. This led to the creation of the Office of Economic Opportunity in 1964, discussed in Chapter 14.

Full employment implies an overall balance between supply and demand on the labor market. Such an equilibrium must allow for certain margins if there is to be any flexibility and flow of labor. Normally at any given moment there will be a number of people who are in between jobs. Some of them may have resigned from their old positions in order to obtain more promising employment opportunities. Others may have been laid off because of a temporary shutdown of production, the closing of a firm or the removal of a company to another part of the country. All this amounts to saying that a certain fluctuation on the labor market—a condition often referred to as *"frictional unemployment"*—is considered a normal and healthy condition of the labor market. Such short term unemployment can be based on a variety of reasons. At any given moment there are people "between jobs." This group does not comprise only workers who have been discharged. A greater number of these people are not working because they are looking for a new job after they have given up their last employment for personal reasons; for instance, because they felt that they were trapped in a dead-end job without possibilities of promotion, or because they did not get along with supervisors or co-workers, or because the old job was too far away from their residence. People who leave jobs for this type of reason are in search of new employment. For this reason their condition is now often called *search unemployment*. It has been observed that this type of unemployment caused by "Quits" is highest when a condition of full employment prevails on the labor market. When there is a considerable measure of unemployment the "quit" rate drops because under these conditions people are more reluctant to take a gamble on the chance that they will find another job easily after leaving their present employment.

Other types of frictional unemployment occur in connection with temporary shutdowns of plants for the purpose of modernization or retooling. In such cases workers are usually told at what time they can expect a recall. Many workers will prefer short-term unemployment under such circumstances to searching for a new permanent job. This is particularly true when workers have earned seniority in their old jobs which they would lose by entering into a new employment relationship.

The various types of short-term unemployment discussed in the preceding paragraph are not incompatible with *full employment*. Inasmuch as 100 percent employment is not really desirable because it would create extreme rigidity on the labor market, the concept of full employment has always left some room for the various types of short-term unemployment. In the depression period of the 1930's the lowest level of unemployment was reached in 1937 when it represented 14.3 percent of the civilian labor force. In 1938 it had risen again to 19 percent. Its highest point had been in 1933 with 24.9 percent. It is easy to see then that economists immediately after World War II considered a 5 percent unemployment rate as still representing a general condition of full employment. In more recent years a 4 percent criterion has been applied. In most European countries where actually full employment has prevailed since World War II even lower percentages are in use. In the United States unemployment dropped below the 4 percent mark in 1966. The next table will show the development. In 1970 unemployment rose sharply.

These overall percentages of unemployment are the figures which are widely publicized each month and are taken as one of the prime indicators of the state of the American economy. It must, however, be clearly understood that these figures are national averages. In a country of the size and

TABLE 10-1
UNEMPLOYMENT AS PERCENT OF CIVILIAN LABOR FORCE

1960	5.6	1965	4.6
1961	6.7	1966	3.8
1962	5.6	1967	3.8
1963	5.7	1968	3.6
1964	5.2	1969	3.9

SOURCE: *Economic Report of the President* (1969).

diversity of the United States with its different regions, areas of concentration of the population and racial composition, these national averages simply do not tell the whole story. If too much is being made of these figures, entirely erroneous impressions could be created about the health of the social-economic structure.

The first correction which must be given to these over-all ratios of unemployment arises from the distinction between full-time and part-time status of the civilian labor force. Every issue the *Monthly Labor Review* supplies us with information on the incidence of unemployment on these two distinct groups of the labor force. We have seen in Table 10-1 that unemployment dropped to 3.8 percent in 1967. However, the unemployment rate of the full-time labor force was only 3.4 percent. The same rate for the part-time labor force was 6.9 percent. Now, in round numbers, there were 63 million people in the full time labor force in 1967 and 9.2 million in the part-time labor force. The latter figure comprises only those people who are voluntarily working part time. That is to say, they do not look for a full-time job and would reject full-time employment if it were offered to them. On the other hand, among the 63 million full-time workers there were over 2 million who were temporarily on part time because no full-time employment was available. It is easy to see why the unemployment rates for employees voluntarily working part time is much higher than the same rate for the full-time labor force. For many part-time workers this form of employment is the only one which they are willing to contemplate because they have other obligations such as housekeeping or study. For the same reason this segment of the labor force shows a higher rate of turnover. More important, however, is the fact that the statistical methods of counting the unemployed, which will be explained in greater detail in Sec. 10-6 will create a "case of unemployment," for instance for a woman in her mid-thirties who stayed home and took care of her children for the last 12 years but decides now to look for a part-time office job but has not found one just as the bell rings and an interviewer calls to find out who is working and who is unemployed in her household. If she tells him that she has not been working but has called an employment agency and will go down town next week for an interview, she will be reported as unemployed.

The over-all figures of the rate of unemployment naturally do not differentiate according to the racial composition and also the age composition of the labor force. Once, however, considerations of race and age are introduced into the analysis, wide divergencies of levels of unemployment from the average rate become apparent immediately. In 1961, 5.1 percent of white males over 20 were unemployed; the same nonwhite group showed unemployment of 11.7 percent. In 1968 the white group had an unemployment rate of 2 percent, the nonwhite group of 4 percent. Unemployment rates for the corresponding age groups of women were higher than those for males. But here also nonwhite unemployment was generally about 90 to 100 percent higher than white unemployment. Actually in grouping together all age groups and the two sexes the white rate of unemployment was 3.2 percent whereas the nonwhite rate was 6.8 percent.[1] The highest incidence of unemployment both for whites and nonwhites is in the age group 16 to 19 years. In both groups there is a substantial drop in unemployment once people reach the age of 20 years. This is particularly startling in the nonwhite group. While for the ages of 16 to 19 years the unemployment rate for nonwhites was 24.9 percent in 1968, it dropped for the same group to 5 percent in the categories 20 years and over. The decline in the white groups also was very drastic from 10.9 percent to 2.5 percent. While there has been justified concern about the high incidence of unemployment in the age group under 20, the sharp drop of unemployment once this bench mark has been reached should place the problem of juvenile unemployment into proper perspective. One reason for this sharp drop in unemployment rates is, of course, the termination of full-time education of large numbers of teenagers who were looking for part-time employment while attending school. Another reason is that employers are more willing to hire people 20 years and over than teen-agers. The question arises also at this point whether all of the teen-age unemployment which appears in our labor market statistics represents genuine and socially relevant cases of unemployment. There is no doubt, however, that a good deal of real "hard core" unemployment is to be found in the below-20 segment of the labor force.

We have seen that in a country of the racial and regional diversity of the United States, a general condition close to full employment[2] does not eliminate serious conditions of unemployment in certain local areas and in some population groups. In view of the high incidence of unemployment in certain age and race groups, it can even be doubted if a general 4 percent level of unemployment would eliminate the difficulties indicated above. We see already at this point that employment policies today are con-

---

[1]Table 5, *Manpower Report of the President*, January 1969.
[2]*Manpower Report of the President* (March 1965).

fronted with problems which defy solution in terms of conventional approaches to full employment. In order to gain an even wider perspective we must turn our attention to a condition of the labor market which does not exist in the United States but which must be taken into account in any comprehensive discussion of the various states of the labor market.

In many European countries experiencing the rapid rise in production after World War II, a general condition of *overemployment* has developed. Such a situation is characterized by the fact that the number of vacancies on the labor market by far exceeds the number of job seekers.

Such a condition is highly undesirable. Many pressures develop on already high-wage levels. "Labor pirating," or the hiring of workers currently employed by competitors under the promise of even higher than union wage rates, begins to spread throughout the labor market. Frequently union wage rates become mere minimum wages which will be topped by employers anxious to go ahead with production schedules. In European countries this condition of overemployment has led to the large-scale use of foreign labor, coming from the southern part of the continent. In Switzerland early in the 1960's the number of foreign workers reached 10 percent of the total population. In such a labor market the maintenance of price stability becomes very difficult. While large-scale unemployment as experienced in the United States during the 1930's has a tendency to keep prices low, overemployment is highly inflationary in character. However, if such a condition occurs in a peacetime economy, imposition of wage and price controls which are an essential part of the structure of a modern war economy cannot readily be effected.

Underemployment is characteristic of many developing countries. Employment opportunities are limited in one or two crop types of economy. A large number of people are needed for relatively short periods of time when the harvest has to be brought in. Between such peak periods of employment there is very little to do for agricultural workers. The total number of days they work during the year is small, thereby establishing the condition of underemployment. But even in advanced countries such as the United States, until recent years, certain types of work, especially on the docks, did fall into the category of underemployment. Many workers attached to this type of employment worked less than 1,000 hours a year. Although their hourly earnings were high whenever they worked, their yearly income was entirely inadequate. This type of underemployment on the docks has been substantially reduced during the past few years by a cutting down of the total labor force of longshoremen and the annual wage guarantee described in Sec. 7-3.

Underemployment in this sense is a relative concept. It signifies a level of year-round employment of a large number of people which is substantially below the national average. On the other hand, most people who are underemployed feel that they are committed to a particular industry or employer and therefore do not seek other work. While their workdays are few, they are not considered unemployed because they do not seek actively other employment opportunities during slack periods.

10-2. SEASONAL AND CYCLICAL VARIATIONS OF EMPLOYMENT

Levels of employment used to be influenced to a great extent by *seasonal* change. In the past many outdoor activities such as building construction were suspended almost completely during the winter. In the garment and fur industries as well as in the hotel and motel business, there were rush seasons followed by an extremely sharp decline in activity. People who were laid off in the off-season were considered as "seasonally unemployed." Even in the automotive industry there used to be sharp seasonal variations in output and in employment. Technical advances and managerial efforts have succeeded in reducing seasonal fluctuations of employment. Modern building methods make it possible to continue construction work virtually throughout the year; better scheduling of production has eliminated unnecessary peaks and troughs in automobile production. Nevertheless, some seasonal unemployment remains, but it is far less than it used to be a few decades ago.

Throughout the nineteenth century and up to the 1930's the business system was highly unstable. It went continuously through cycles with a duration of from seven to ten years. These periods were divided more or less evenly between downward trends and upswings. Unemployment which developed during the depression phase of the cycle was called *cyclical* unemployment. The cycle concept of unemployment implies that in the subsequent upswing of business, cyclical employment will be absorbed by the general rising trend. While levels of unemployment may reach large proportions during the depression, they will persist only in the medium-run period and will disappear altogether once the cycle pattern has run its course and a new peak of business activity has been attained.

It should be pointed out that the actual development of the labor market in the 1930's did no longer conform to this concept of an absorption of unemployment at the peak of business activities. Many economists are still inclined to consider economic developments between 1929 and 1937 as a typical business cycle. Equally, the sustained upswing in the American economy from 1961 to 1968 was compared to the upswing that took place between 1933 and 1937. Such comparisons, however, are quite misleading. In 1961 unemployment was at the relatively high level of 6.7 percent of the civilian labor force. It dropped to about 5 percent in 1965. At the peak of 1937 unemployment still stood at 14.3 percent of the labor force. Actually, the number of unemployed in that year averaged 7.7 million people. If the traditional cycle was operative at all during the 1930's, it was, unlike preceding upward trends, incapable of restoring even an approximation of equilibrium on the labor market.

Whether or not the 1930's experienced a traditional business cycle there is no doubt that after World War II the pattern of business fluctuations changed completely. The system still alternated between very high and somewhat lower levels of activity, but compared to the older pattern the amplitude of fluctuation became far less pronounced. Just as there were no very sharp declines in business activity, the drop in employment levels was far less drastic than it had been under the traditional cyclical behavior of the system in general and the labor market in particular. There are strong indications that the concept of cyclical unemployment is no longer an adequate analytical tool to study actual trends on the labor market in advanced industrial society.

This change in the behavior of the economic system in the second half of the twentieth century can be attributed to important changes in the market structure and in the methods of doing business. The larger the size of enterprises in key industries becomes, the wider is application of market and technical research to investment decisions. The greater availability of data on inventories and on consumer income and expenditures have also taken a good deal of guesswork out of business activities. The element of miscalculation, especially erroneous evaluations of short-run market developments which played a large role in generating business crises in the old cycle pattern, has been curtailed substantially. Furthermore, the much higher level of government spending, and the awareness of the business community that public expenditures may be stepped up in case of a lagging momentum in economic activities, have contributed toward a lessening of the swings of business fluctuations. The continued general use of the cycle concept must not becloud the fact that today it refers to less violent fluctuations of business than those characteristic of early phases of capitalism. But even these smaller declines create serious problems at a time when the demand for labor is undergoing qualitative changes and the labor force is increasing rapidly. Even a minor recession can generate dangerous lags in the growth pattern. For this reason we must continue to pay great attention even to short-run recessions.

10-3. PERSISTENT UNEMPLOYMENT

In the 1950's unemployment was usually of short duration. In 1954 no less than 63.1 percent of all unemployed were without a job for a period of less than 5 weeks. As is shown in Table 10-2 in 1957 persistent unemployment, that is to say, a period of joblessness of more than 14 weeks, prevailed only among 19.1 percent of the unemployed. With the onset of the recession in 1958 the share of persistent, long-term unemployment, rose to more than 30 percent of all unemployed. Until 1965 long-term unemployment remained consistently at a higher level than had been prevailing in the 1950's. However, as also shown in Table 10-2 in 1967 long-term unemployment dropped to 15.1 percent.

TABLE 10-2
PERSISTENT UNEMPLOYMENT—ANNUAL AVERAGES, 1957–67

Year	Number Unemployed (thousands)			Percent Distribution		
	Total	15 to 26 Weeks	27 Weeks and Over	Total	15 to 26 Weeks	27 Weeks and Over
1957	560	321	239	19.1	10.9	8.1
1958	1,452	785	667	31.0	16.8	14.2
1959	1,040	469	571	27.3	12.3	15.0
1960	956	502	454	24.3	12.8	11.5
1961	1,532	728	804	31.9	15.1	16.7
1962	1,119	534	595	27.9	13.3	14.6
1963	1,088	535	553	26.1	12.8	13.3
1964	973	490	482	25.1	12.6	12.4
1965	755	404	351	22.4	12.0	10.4
1966	536	295	241	18.6	10.3	8.4
1967	449	271	177	15.1	9.1	5.9

SOURCE: *Manpower Report of the President* (April 1968), Table A-16.

In order to gain a better insight into the significance of persistent unemployment it is necessary to study the occupational backgrounds of those who are out of a job for more than 15 weeks.

Table 10-3 shows that the incidence of long-term unemployment is particularly heavy among production workers, especially among operatives and laborers. The increasing share of service workers in 1967 as compared to 1957 is also of some significance. Generally speaking the table shows that long term unemployment is closely associated with segments of the labor force who have lower educational and occupational achievements. Quite notable is the increase in 1967 of the share of "persons with no previous working experience" in persistent unemployment. This requires some further investigation. According to the concept of the labor force as it was explained in Sec. 2-1 of this text, the labor force consists of two groups: those actually at work and those not working but seeking employment. Now, persons without previous working experience in order to be classified as long-term unemployed even for periods of more than 27 weeks are assumed to be people who are continuously trying to obtain a first job therefore changing their status from outside the labor force to seeking employment. Furthermore they must have reported, when the census taker came upon their household, that they have been busily

TABLE 10-3

PERCENTAGE DISTRIBUTION OF PERSISTENT UNEMPLOYMENT BY MAJOR
INDUSTRY AND OCCUPATIONAL GROUP—ANNUAL AVERAGES, 1957 AND 1967

Occupations	Unemployed 15 Weeks and Over		Unemployed 27 Weeks and Over	
	1957	1967	1957	1967
Total: Number (thousands)...............	560	449	239	177
Percent distribution	100.0	100.0	100.0	100.0
Professional, technical, and kindred workers................................	1.4	4.1	2.0	3.9
Farmers and farm managers	.3	0.2	.8	0.6
Managers, officials, and proprietors, except farm	3.1	3.8	3.5	4.9
Clerical and kindred workers...............	8.2	12.4	7.9	11.0
Sales workers	4.4	4.7	4.3	5.4
Craftsmen, foremen, and kindred workers................................	11.0	9.6	9.8	9.0
Operatives and kindred workers...........	31.8	26.6	30.7	25.1
Private household workers.................	2.8	1.8	2.8	2.0
Service workers, except private household ..	10.6	12.2	11.8	10.7
Farm laborers and foremen	2.4	2.1	2.4	2.3
Laborers, except farm and mine............	15.5	10.9	15.7	12.4
Persons with no previous work experience ..	8.4	11.6	8.3	11.8

SOURCE: *Manpower Report of the President* (March 1965), Table A-19.

engaged in looking for work. Obviously we are encountering here a bor-
derline segment of the labor force. By definition these people must have
been outside the labor force in the not too distant past. Yet they are
counted as unemployed although they have never worked.

Only those workers, however, are considered as long-term unemployed
who have been engaged in job-seeking activities at least during the last
four weeks prior to the visit of the census taker. If it becomes clear through
the questioning of members of the household that the person with work
experience who has been out of work for a considerable period of time has
not been active in the pursuit of work in that four week period he is considered as having withdrawn from the labor force. Such persons are often
called "*discouraged workers*." This term does not imply that they are too
apathetic to go out and look for work or that they lack a proper motiva-
tion. It rather indicates that these people have persistently failed to obtain
employment because they are considered "too old" or without specialized
experience in fields where there are vacancies or because the area where
they live has seen a decline in employment opportunities in general. These
people are unemployed in the fullest sense of the word if their condition
were to be evaluated according to social and economic criteria. Stastically,
however, they are not being counted because they do not measure up to the
standard of activity which is one of the prerequisites for membership in
the American labor force. Again by statistical standards, people who are
not in the labor force can by definition not be unemployed. It is, of course,

very difficult to obtain correct estimates of the number of discouraged workers in the United States. However, it is clear that from an economic point of view this group ought to be added to the numbers of long-term unemployment shown in Tables 2 and 3 of this section.

10-4. STRUCTURAL UNEMPLOYMENT

A good deal of the persistent, long-term unemployment which has been discussed in the preceeding section can be traced to structural changes of the labor market. Generally speaking there has been an upgrading of requirements in the demand for labor. Educational requirements are being stressed. The demand for craftsmen, foremen, engineers, managers and professional workers has increased while the need to employ operatives and laborers has declined sharply. This has led to the seeming paradox that "pockets of unemployment" remain in an economy where at the same time there is a severe shortage of qualified personnel of all kinds. This condition has given rise to the concept of "structural unemployment" which is said to prevail when the structure of the demand for labor, that is to say the composition of the categories of employees sought by management does not fit in with the structure of the various categories of available labor supply.

The concept of structural unemployment has gained considerable attention in the 1960's. It has been argued that this type of unemployment which does not seem to be susceptible to the old prescriptions for full employment such as appropriate monetary and fiscal measures, could be eliminated if demand for and supply of labor could be brought together. This led to attempts to train and upgrade labor supply so that it would be fit for employment. More recently it also has brought about changes in managerial attitudes and increased their willingness to employ at lease on a trial basis people who do not meet standard criteria of employability.

These novel employment policies will be discussed in greater detail in Chapter 14 of this book. It was, however, necessary to add to the preceding definitions of various types of unemployment the concept of structural unemployment in order to cover completely the field to which theories and policies are concerned must be applied.

10-5. PROJECTIONS OF EMPLOYMENT TO 1975

As demonstrated in Sec. 10-1, unemployment as a national average is today much smaller than in the ten years preceding World War II. Since 1961 the annual growth rate of the American economy has been far higher than in the decade of the 1950's. Nevertheless, considerable pockets of unemployment by region, age, occupational group, and race have remained— and seem to be rather intractable in reference to the usual methods of employment policies. It must be borne in mind that the labor force will continue to grow in the years to come. According to estimates made by the Bureau of the Census the total labor force in the United States will rise from about 83.9 million in 1970 to 99.2 million in 1980.[3] While this represents a significant decline in the percentage change of increase—18.3 percent—for the decade 1970–1980 over the increase of 21.1 percent in the preceding decade, due to the higher numbers of people to which these percentages have to be applied, the average annual increase of the labor force which was 1.46 million in the 1960's will rise to 1.53 million in the 1970's. That is to say that if during that decade the unemployment rate is to be kept at about the 4 percent level, there must be an annual increase in employment opportunities of at least 1.5 million jobs.

It must be understood that this projected employment is predicated on the assumption that there will be no slowdown in economic growth. Structural and persistent unemployment would rise very steeply if the growth rate dropped from 6 percent per annum to the 3 percent per annum pattern of the 1950's. The problems involved here will be explained further by a study of employment projections.

Longer-run projections of the development of the labor force contain a good deal of certainty. The age composition of the population is known. Children born today will, at the earliest, be counted into the labor force sixteen years from now. On the other hand, the rate of withdrawal from the labor force through death, retirement, or other reasons can also be estimated with a good deal of accuracy. It follows that labor-force projections can indicate within comparatively small margins of error what the labor supply is going to be like in the future.

It is far more difficult to make estimates concerning actual employment at some future date. Employment patterns are certain to be affected by changes in demand for workers—for instance, a shift from blue- to white-collar employment. Even more important is the impact of automation and other technological advances on unit labor requirements. While this indicates that output will continue to grow rapidly without a corresponding increase in the demand for production workers, projections of the *labor force participation rates* foresee a further increase. This rate was 57.4 percent in 1960. It is expected to rise to 60.2 percent by 1980. It is clear then that the maintenance of full employment is predicated on the continued increase in demand for technical, professional, and clerical workers and a corresponding transformation of the labor force in favor of nonproduction activities and generally speaking of higher types of employment. A projection of this further structural transformation of the labor force is given in Table 10-4.

Table 10-4 shows that in the projection of the development of major

---

[3]*Manpower Report of the President* (January 1969), Table E-7.

TABLE 10-4

EMPLOYMENT BY MAJOR OCCUPATIONAL GROUP, 1960–75

Major Occupational Group	Actual, 1960		Projected, 1970		Projected, 1975		Percent Change		
	Number (millions)	Percent	Number (millions)	Percent	Number (millions)	Percent	1960–70	1970–75	1960–75
Total................	66.7	100.0	80.5	100.0	87.6	100.0	21	9	31
Professional, technical, and kindred workers ...	7.5	11.2	10.7	13.3	12.4	14.2	43	16	65
Managers, officials, and proprietors, except farm........	7.1	10.6	8.6	10.7	9.4	10.7	21	9	32
Clerical and kindred workers ...	9.8	14.7	12.8	15.9	14.2	16.2	31	11	45
Sales workers........	4.4	6.6	5.4	6.7	5.9	6.7	23	9	34
Craftsmen, foremen, and kindred workers	8.6	12.8	10.3	12.8	11.2	12.8	20	9	30
Operatives and kindred workers ...	12.0	18.0	13.6	16.9	14.2	16.3	13	4	18
Service workers......	8.3	12.5	11.1	13.8	12.5	14.3	34	13	51
Laborers, except farm and mine.....	3.7	5.5	3.7	4.6	3.7	4.3			
Farmers, farm managers, laborers, and foremen ..	5.4	8.1	4.2	5.3	3.9	4.5	−22	−7	−28

SOURCE: *Manpower Report of the President* (March 1963), Table 28.

occupational groups to 1975 it was assumed that demand for professional managerial, and clerical workers will increase by a far larger proportion than that for production workers. In fact, only a 4 percent change is forecast for operatives. Farm employment is expected to decline even further. Projections for the gross national product made in the early 1960's indicated a one-trillion level for 1975, a 50 percent increase over 1960. However, as can be seen from this table, total employment is projected to rise only by 31 percent in the period 1960–75. Furthermore, this overall increase is calculated only on the assumption that employment of professional and technical workers will increase by 65 percent and clerical and kindred workers by 45 percent. This seems to be based on the expectation that automation in offices will not lessen but actually increase total employment in these occupational groups. These projections also imply a further drastic restructuring of employment patterns by industry divisions. Table 10-5 dealing only with nonagricultural wage and salary worker employment illustrates this.

Table 10-5 projects for 1975 a situation in which service-producing industries will exceed the goods-producing industries by almost 100 percent. It should be noted that all these forecasts are predicated on the assumption that full employment will be at least approximated throughout the whole period.

TABLE 10-5
NONAGRICULTURAL WAGE AND SALARY WORKER EMPLOYMENT
BY INDUSTRY DIVISION, 1960–75

Industry Division	Employment (millions)			Percent Change, 1960–75
	Actual	Projected		
	1960	1970	1975	
Total..........................	54.3	67.7	74.2	37
Service-producing industries........	34.0	43.7	48.8	44
Wholesale and retail trade........	11.4	14.0	15.6	37
Government....................	8.5	11.5	12.8	51
Service and miscellaneous........	7.4	10.2	11.9	61
Transportation and public utilities......................	4.0	4.4	4.5	13
Finance, insurance, and real estate....................	2.7	3.5	3.9	44
Goods-producing industries........	20.4	24.0	25.4	25
Manufacturing	16.8	19.2	20.3	21
Contract construction...........	2.9	4.0	4.4	52
Mining.......................	.7	.7	.7	—

SOURCE: *Manpower Report of the President* (March 1963), Table 27.

Whether or not these projected trends will materialize by 1975 depends to a large degree on conditions which must be clarified further by an analysis of the characteristics of the labor market, and of the overall framework of the economic system within which actual levels of employment are established at any given period. However, before we enter into these most important aspects of the problem of employment it is necessary to obtain some information on the methods which are being used in order to count the unemployed.

10-6. METHODS OF COUNTING THE UNEMPLOYED

In view of the great significance attributed to levels of employment and unemployment, it is necessary to realize that the statistical problem of enumeration which arises in this area is rather complex. It would be much simpler in the hypothetical case that all unemployed could be made to report at stated intervals with public employment services. If this could be done, it would be possible to have every month an actual count of all persons who are unemployed. Theoretically this would not require that all unemployed be either eligible for or currently receive unemployment compensation. For example, employable people receiving public assistance could also be required to maintain a regular contact with the employment service. Be that as it may, the fact is that no such arrangements exist in the United States and that therefore other devices had to be worked out in order to measure unemployment each month.[4]

[4]The method has been described in "How the Government Measures Unemployment," U. S. Bureau of Labor Statistics Report No. 312 (1967).

Since it is not feasible actually to count all the unemployed a very large sample of households has been set up. Out of the 3,128 counties in the country the Bureau of the Census has established 449 areas containing 863 counties and independent cities. Every month about 52,500 households are selected throughout the country which will be visited by an interviewer compiling information for the "household data" of employment. Each month one-fourth of the families are replaced with the result that no household will be visited by an interviewer more than four times in a row. However, the family will be re-visited after eight months and then it will be dropped from the sample permanently.[5]

Theoretically this procedure is unimpeachable; practically there are considerable difficulties.[6] To illustrate these problems we quote from a release of the U. S. Department of Labor referring to the difficulties encountered by the Bureau of Census in accounting for a considerable proportion of the nonwhite male population. If such situations arise in the house-to-house population census, it cannot be assumed that they are nonexistent in the monthly census of unemployment. The report states:

> In the urban Northeast, there are only 76 males per 100 females 20-to-24 years of age, and males as a percent of females are below 90 percent throughout all ages after 14.
> There are not really fewer men than women in the 20-to-40 age bracket. What obviously is involved is an error in counting: the surveyors simply do not find the Negro man. Donald J. Bogue and his associates, who have studied the Federal count of the Negro man, place the error as high as 19.8 percent at age 28; a typical error of around 15 percent is estimated from age 19 through 43. Preliminary research in the Bureau of the Census on the 1960 enumeration has resulted in similar conclusions, although not necessarily the same estimates of the extent of the error.

Perhaps such difficulties are unavoidable in a country the size and diversity of the United States. The sampling method of accounting for unemployment seeming the only feasible one, much depends on the way in which this monthly census of unemployment is taken.

Following sound interviewing techniques, the interviewed person is never asked directly whether he is unemployed. This must be inferred by the interviewer from answers to such questions: "Did you do any work at all last week, not counting work around the house?" or "Were you looking for work?" The latter question is of very great significance. According to the procedures adopted by the Bureau of Labor Statistics, "Persons are unemployed if they are looking for work and, of course, are not working at the same time." That is, people who are not working but also were not

---

[5]See Note 3 above.

[6]*The Negro Family.* Office of Policy Planning and Research, U.S. Department of Labor (March 1965), released for publication in the fall of 1965.

actively seeking a job at the time they are being interviewed are considered as not being part of the labor force.

In most cases there must be some tangible evidence that a person who did not work was actively seeking a job in order to qualify for a classification as unemployed. Such actions may consist of going to a public or private employment office, being interviewed by prospective employers, placing or answering advertisements and similar activities. However, there are certain cases in which such evidence is not required. For instance, a coal miner who has lost his job in his small mining town because the company has gone out of production, and who knows that it would be futile to look for other employment in his own community, would still be counted among the unemployed. On the other hand, teen-agers even without work experience, who have made some effort to get a job during the week prior to the interview but did not succeed, are included in the number of the unemployed.

The concepts employed for the definition of employment and unemployment are also applied to young people 16 years and over who attend school but are on vacation for the summer months. This is reflected in the estimated increases in the total labor force during this period and the sharp drop in September of each year. For instance, the total labor force in August 1968 was 83.8 million; it dropped to 82.1 million in September of that year. The corresponding figures for 1969 are 86.0 and 84.5 million.

Young people in the age group 16–21 who find summer employment are, of course, counted among the employed. In the summer of 1965 a "massive cross-country push" led by the Youth Opportunity Council was reported to have produced jobs at the rate of 10,000 daily. Former Vice President Humphrey, who headed this drive, reported to the President that 880,000 people of that age group had found summer work. About 300,-000 of these jobs were secured through a job finding campaign with private business firms. Twenty-six thousand young men and women were placed with the Federal government and 500,000 were enrolled in the Neighborhood Youth Corps. This concerted drive brought about a sensational drop in the unemployment rate of this age group from 18.5 percent in June to 12.3 percent in July. In subsequent years the large-scale enrollment of young people in the Neighborhood Youth Corps and other programs during the summer months continued. This has contributed to a substantial decline in unemployment of people in the age group 16 to 19 during the vacation period although the unemployment rate among people under 20 years of age has remained far higher than older people as will be shown in detail in Table 10-8.

Although it is sound statistical practice to list those young people who were given summer jobs by business firms or by government agencies as employed, to count among the employed young people enrolled in the Neighborhood Youth Corps or in the Job Corps set up by the Economic Opportunity Act of 1964 is a significant departure from practices of the 1930's, when participation in such government programs was not counted as regular employment.[7]

These changes in the methods of accounting for unemployment cannot be considered an improvement. They tend to blur the distinction between employment generated by the spending of consumers, business, and government, and by dealing with unemployment through special work projects. The spectacular decrease in unemployment between June and July 1965 must, therefore, be viewed with a good deal of skepticism, adding to the rather widespread criticism from professional economists of the tendency in the present methods to understate the actual scope of unemployment. This tendency applies particularly to the matter of persistent unemployment.

People who have been unemployed for a considerable length of time in small one company towns are not expected to expend futile efforts in finding new employment. However, the same is not true of unemployed residing in more differentiated areas. If the unemployed census taker comes across such long-run cases of unemployment in which the jobless worker has become discouraged and has not engaged in the job-seeking activities outlined above, there is a great likelihood that he will be considered as having "resigned" from the labor force. Since only participants in the labor force can, if the case occurs, be classified as unemployed, people experiencing persistent unemployment may also fall by the wayside in terms of unemployment statistics. Actual unemployment, especially in that category, may be understated; but the counting in the labor force of teen-agers who have been unsuccessful in finding employment may lead to some overstatement of unemployment in the lowest age brackets of the labor force.

With all these reservations, the fact remains that the reports on unemployment are indicative of its real trends and scope. We now turn our attention to these statistics.

10-7. THE SCOPE AND CHARACTER OF UNEMPLOYMENT

It was pointed out at the beginning of this chapter that the national unemployment rate, usually quoted in connection with an evaluation of the condition of the labor market in the United States, has only limited validity because it brings together in an overall average highly diverse categories with greatly varying incidence of unemployment. A breakdown of unemployment by sex, race, duration, age group, and occupation is necessary in order to enable us to come to grips with specific problems of the labor market, and to seek methods of mitigating the impact of unemployment on specific groups of persons. Table 10-6 gives a survey of the

[7]The scope of the programs is shown in Tables 20-2 and 20-3.

development of unemployment since 1947 and its impact on sex and race in general.

Table 10-6 shows that female unemployment rates, both white and nonwhite, are somewhat higher throughout the period from 1948–1964 with the significant exception of the recession period from 1958–1961 when unemployment rates of nonwhite males rose sharply. Generally, nonwhite unemployment rates are about twice as high as the corresponding rates for

TABLE 10-6
UNEMPLOYMENT RATES BY SEX AND COLOR
ANNUAL AVERAGES 1957–1967

Year	Total	White			Nonwhite		
		Total	Male	Female	Total	Male	Female
1957	4.3	3.9	3.7	4.3	8.0	8.4	7.4
1958	6.8	6.1	6.1	6.2	12.6	13.7	10.8
1959	5.5	4.9	4.6	5.3	10.7	11.5	9.5
1960	5.6	5.0	4.8	5.3	10.2	10.7	9.5
1961	6.7	6.0	5.7	6.5	12.5	12.9	11.9
1962	5.6	4.9	4.6	5.5	11.0	11.0	11.1
1963	5.7	5.1	4.7	5.8	10.9	10.6	11.3
1964	5.2	4.6	4.2	5.5	9.8	9.1	10.8
1965	4.5	4.1	3.6	5.0	8.1	7.4	9.2
1966	3.8	3.3	2.8	4.3	7.3	6.3	8.6
1967	3.8	3.4	2.7	4.6	7.4	6.0	9.1

SOURCE: *Manpower Report of the President* (April 1968), Table A-11.

whites. We now turn our attention to the duration of unemployment. As seen in Table 10-7, the duration of unemployment varies with business conditions. The higher the volume of business activity is the greater is the proportion of short-run unemployment of less than 5 weeks. This brings about a smaller rate of long-run unemployment of 15 weeks and over. On the other hand, the latter type of unemployment has had a tendency to increase its share in total unemployment since World War II.

As can be seen from Table 10-2, there were 454,000 unemployed of 27 weeks and over in 1960. With considerable improvement in the overall employment situation, there were nevertheless 482,000 people in this category in 1964. If we bear in mind that measurement of persistent unemployment is somewhat problematical because of the insistence on an activity concept of the labor force, we face here a hard core of unemployment—which might continue even when the general trend on the labor market is sharply upward.

One of the most difficult aspects of unemployment is its concentration in the younger age groups. Statistically and in fact this problem has been lessened slightly by the elimination of the age group of 14 and 15 years from the labor force. Before this went into effect in 1967 the male "unemployment rate" for these youngsters was reported for 1964 as 9 percent

TABLE 10-7
DURATION OF UNEMPLOYMENT—SELECTED YEARS, 1947–64

Year	Total	Less than 5 Weeks	5 and 6 Weeks	7–10 Weeks	11–14 Weeks	15 Weeks and Over		
						Total	15–26 Weeks	27 Weeks and Over
				Percent Distribution				
1947	100.0	53.3	8.6	13.1	8.2	16.9	9.9	7.0
1953	100.0	63.0	8.0	11.2	6.6	11.3	7.1	4.2
1960	100.0	45.7	8.2	12.7	9.0	24.3	12.8	11.5
1964	100.0	46.1	8.1	12.5	8.2	25.1	12.6	12.4
1967	100.0	54.9	9.3	13.3	7.3	15.1	9.1	5.9

SOURCE: *Manpower Report of the President* (April 1968), Table A-16.

whereas the total unemployment rate was only 4.7 percent. Table 10-8 shows that for the age groups 16 to 19 unemployment rates are substantially higher than the average for the labor force as a whole. But as can be seen from the same table unemployment has declined in these age groups in line with the general decline of total employment. It is also shown there, as was already indicated in Sec. 10-1 that unemployment rates of the age group 20 to 24 dropped sharply although they still are above the general level of unemployment. This again points up the fact that the twentieth year is very crucial with regard to a successful entry into the labor force.

TABLE 10-8
UNEMPLOYMENT BY SEX AND AGE, 16–24 YEARS, 1961–1967

Sex	Total 16 Years and over	16–19 Years		20–24 Years
		16 and 17	18 and 19	
		Unemployment Rate		
Male				
1961	6.4	18.3	16.3	10.7
1963	5.2	18.8	15.9	8.8
1965	4.0	16.1	12.4	6.3
1967	3.1	14.5	10.5	4.7
Female				
1961	7.2	18.3	15.1	9.8
1963	6.5	20.3	15.2	8.9
1965	5.5	17.2	14.8	7.3
1967	5.2	14.8	12.7	7.0

SOURCE: *Manpower Report of the President*, Table A-12 (April 1968).

Table 10-9 shows a completely different picture of unemployment rates for the age group 25–65 and over. It must, however, be remembered that these age groups, especially those up to 45 years, go back to a substantially smaller population base and, with reference to those born in the 1930's, to a very low birth rate. Furthermore, although unemployment is not widespread in the age group 45–64, it must be realized that people in this age

TABLE 10-9
UNEMPLOYMENT BY SEX AND AGE,
25–65 YEARS AND OVER, 1961–64

Sex	Unemployment Rate				
	25–34 Years	35–44 Years	45–54 Years	55–64 Years	65 Years and Over
Male					
1961	5.7	4.6	4.9	5.7	5.5
1962	4.5	3.6	3.9	4.6	4.6
1963	4.5	3.5	3.6	4.3	4.5
1964	3.5	2.9	3.2	3.9	4.0
Female					
1961	7.3	6.3	5.1	4.5	3.9
1962	6.5	5.2	4.1	3.5	4.1
1963	6.9	5.1	4.2	3.6	3.2
1964	6.3	5.0	3.9	3.5	3.4

SOURCE: *Manpower Report of the President* (March 1965), Table A-12.

group encounter great difficulties in finding a new job if for one reason or another they are separated from their present employment.

Tables 10-8 and 10-9 do not distinguish between white and nonwhite unemployed. In Sec. 10-1 it was pointed out that the incidence of unemployment is far greater in the nonwhite group than in the white group. Whereas total unemployment was 5.2 percent in 1964, it was 9.8 percent for the total nonwhite male and female labor force. It is at this point that the changing structure of employment makes itself felt in relation to unemployment rates. While total employment is rising, the demand for less skilled and especially for unskilled workers is declining. Disadvantages in educational opportunities and achievements are translating themselves into higher rates

TABLE 10-10
UNEMPLOYMENT RATES AND PERCENT DISTRIBUTION OF UNEMPLOYED
BY MAJOR OCCUPATION GROUP, 1967

	Unemployment Rate	Percent Distribution
Total Unemployed	3.8	100
Professional, technical, and kindred workers	1.3	4.5
Farmers and farm laborers	2.3	2.9
Managers, officials, and proprietors, except farm . .	0.9	2.3
Clerical and kindred workers	3.1	13.4
Sales workers	3.2	5.1
Craftsmen, foremen, and kindred workers	2.5	8.4
Operatives and kindred workers	5.0	24.5
Private household workers	4.1	2.5
Service workers, except private household	4.6	12.3
Nonfarm laborers	7.6	9.7
Persons with no previous work experience	—	14.5

SOURCE: *Manpower Report of the President* (April 1968), Table A-14.

of unemployment. This is clearly indicated by the rate of unemployment in various major occupations. Table 10-10 gives a breakdown.

As can be seen from Table 10-10, unemployment rates rise sharply above the average in the blue-collar field of operatives and laborers. It is extremely low in professional and technical employment and also below the average for such white-collar occupations as clerical and sales workers. It seems, therefore, that the labor market has a greater ability to absorb white-collar workers than to employ additional production workers. We must now turn our attention to these problems of the labor market.

SELECTED BIBLIOGRAPHY

Bairoch, P. and J. M. Limbor. "Changes in the Industrial Distribution of the World Labor Force, by Region 1880–1960" in *The International Labor Review*, (Geneva: October 1968).

Bureau of Labor Statistics, Agency for International Development. *The Forecasting of Manpower Requirements.* BLS Rept. No. 248 (Washington, D. C.: U. S. Government Printing Office, 1963).

Dernburg, Thomas and Kenneth Strand, "Hidden Unemployment 1953–62: A Quantitative Analysis by Age and Sex," *American Economic Review* (March 1966).

Keker, B. F. *Human Capital: In Retrospect* (Columbia, S. C.: University of South Carolina, Bureau of Business and Economic Research, 1968).

Neff, Walter. *Work and Human Behavior* (New York: Atherton Press, 1968).

Ross, Arthur M. *Unemployment and the American Economy* (New York: John Wiley and Sons, Inc., 1964).

Subcommittee on Economic Statistics of the Joint Economic Committee. *Measuring Employment and Unemployment* 88th Cong., 1st Sess., June 6 and 7, 1963 (Washington, D.C.: U.S. Government Printing Office 1963).

QUESTIONS FOR DISCUSSION

1. What is "frictional unemployment," and what special function does it perform toward a more efficient allocation of resources?

2. Aggregate figures which relate the extent of unemployment are often misleading in that they fail to relate the extent of unemployment within certain groups. In light of this, present a more useful and well-defined statement about current unemployment problems as they affect these certain groups.

3. Contrast the employment problem of Western Europe in the 1960's with that of the United States in the same period.

4. Characterize seasonal unemployment and indicate the reasons why it is somewhat less of a problem today than it was prior to World War II.

5. There are strong indications that the concept of cyclical unemployment is no longer totally adequate to explain unemployment of more than a short duration. Why is this so?

6. In some detail, define and characterize the concept of structural unemployment.

7. Labor-market projections such as the one given in Table 10-3 generally

point to a sharp increase in the numbers of persons employed in service industries, government, and in finance. Account for these expected developments.

8. Critically evaluate the more widespread methods used to count the unemployed.

9. Long-term or persistent unemployment presents an especially difficult situation in terms of the proper measures that may be taken to eliminate or reduce its existence and impact. What are these problems and what possible measures seem best suited to a more prompt solution to the problem?

Chapter

11

The Structure of
the Labor Market

Labor is not a commodity, and the labor market has characteristics which differentiate it from the commodity market. Under certain circumstances the behavior of supply and demand on the labor market is analogous to that of the general goods market. But since total supply of labor is not limited to current or long-run demand for its services, the analogy cannot be carried too far. Whereas levels of employment may fluctuate in the short run, the labor force, unlike commodities, does not adjust itself in a flexible way to changes in the volume of demand for its services. A surplus of commodities, piling up in inventories, can be liquidated below cost if need be. A labor surplus cannot be dealt with in this manner. Nor can shortages of labor supply be overcome in the short run if there is a basic scarcity of labor. It follows that the equilibrium on the labor market, a matching of labor supply and demand for labor, presents specific problems requiring analysis. Before we address ourselves to this task it is necessary to attempt to analyze the labor market simply in terms of an interplay between wage levels and levels of employment.

11-1. WAGES, PRICES, AND EMPLOYMENT

For a considerable period of time most economists held that the wage rate is the factor which balances supply and demand on the labor market in the short run, and even in the long run. Such an equilibrium wage rate was assumed to equate demand and supply at any given moment on the labor market because it is just low enough from the viewpoint of the employer to induce him to maximize employment in his firm—and at the same time just high enough to generate willingness of workers to accept employment. Thus a very close relationship appeared to exist between wage rates and levels of employment.

If some workers were not employed at the equilibrium rate, however, their unemployment was considered "voluntary," because apparently these workers chose to stay at home rather than to go to work at that equilibrium level. It was the great merit of John Maynard Keynes[1] to have proved to the economic scholars of his generation that there was indeed such a thing as "involuntary unemployment," a condition in which workers who were will-. ing to accept whatever wages were offered were nevertheless unable to find a job. This excess of labor supply over demand could not be eliminated even when there was a great downward flexibility of wages. Involuntary unemployment does not imply that wage rates, in general, have a neutral effect on levels of employment. They assume increasing significance as conditions of full employment are approached. Furthermore, wage differentials are one of the ways in which labor supply is allocated among various types of employment.

But if there is some degree of unemployment, it is not necessary for employers to offer higher wages in order to secure whatever supply of labor they require. If they offer employment to unemployed workers at prevailing wage rates they will obtain additional labor supply. It is only when full employment has been obtained that an upward pressure on wage rates will develop in response to still continuing demand for additional labor supply. Under these conditions an up-grading will take place of already employed, experienced workers into higher job classes carrying increased wage rates. This general uplifting of wage payments will affect also the wages of those hired additionally. If the labor supply in a given labor market is exhausted and many vacancies remain unfilled, this condition of overemployment is certain to inaugurate an interregional or international migration of labor. Usually this condition sets in motion a migration of people from rural, low-income areas. The large-scale migration of people in a general East-West direction in the nineteenth century and in a South-North direction after World War II illustrates this point. It also brings out a very important basic aspect of the labor market—the high degree of *regional* labor mobility. It is greater and to a certain extent easier to realize than *occupational* labor mobility.

Throughout the ages people have been willing to leave their homes either in search of better economic opportunities or in response to an intensive demand for additional labor arising in far-distant places. In this sense it is true that labor supply increases with high wages. By the same token, low wage areas lose some of their labor supply if they come within the range of high-wage impacts. It should be noted that these higher wages bring about primarily a relocation of labor supply, not an overall increase. They may augment the labor force where there is a demand for labor and shrink it in low-wage areas. Wages as such, however, have little bearing on the ultimate

[1]J. M. Keynes, *The General Theory of Employment, Interest and Money*, Chap. 2.

determinant of the size of the labor force, which is the population and its need to participate in the labor market itself.

In the past as well as today high wages have set in motion national and international shifts in labor supply. Interindustry wage differentials do have a different effect. Generally higher wages are an expression of the higher productivity of labor. In certain cases, however, they are also brought about by the great physical exertions required by such types of work as mining or loading or unloading vessels. To a certain extent these high-wage industries will attract labor supply. Especially will young workers try to find employment in such higher-wage industries. But the very fact that high wages are associated with high productivity establishes certain limits to an expansion of employment. Actually wages are high in most industries not as a result of an underlying shortage of labor but because output per wage earner is higher.

Low wage levels have two distinctly different effects on labor supply. The first of these impacts brings about an increase in labor supply by bringing to the labor market members of the household of a low wage earner who otherwise may remain outside the labor force. Wives of such wage earners may be looking at least for part-time jobs in order to augment the family income; children of the family may do the same or they may forego additional schooling in order to become full time wage earners. This aspect of the relation between low wages and labor supply makes inoperative the old assumption that if wages drop, a significant number of people will automatically leave the labor force because the utility of earning a modest wage is outbalanced by the disutility of having to work, using time and money for transportation and incidental expenses connected with going to work. It became clear in the 1930's that low earnings far from reducing aggregate labor supply did not prevent the steady growth of the labor force during that period.

Recently, however, the second effect of low wages has claimed wide attention. The argument is being advanced that low wages are a barrier to the reduction of hard core employment because the gap between a low wage income and relief allocations is too small. Now people who have managed to get on a specialized or a general public aid program such as will be discussed in Chapter 25 of this book will hesitate to accept usually unstable jobs paying not much more than the barest subsistence. A recent study of the New York State Department of Labor[2] has shown that while in March 1966, median hourly earnings in manufacturing in New York State in the nondurable goods industry were $2.27, 12.9 percent of the workers in that industry category earned less than $1.75 and an additional 14.5 percent earned less than $2.00 an hour. Among such industries were toys and sporting goods, costume jewelry and various leather goods. Naturally these low-

[2]Publication B–163, Division of Research and Statistics, Volume 1, May 1968.

wage occupations are located in industries that are employing more or less unskilled laborers or operatives. Relief recipients, for instance unwed mothers, could be fitted in this type of labor supply. But in order to be effective this would require a widening of the gap between a low wage income and relief allocations.[3]

The immediately preceding statement seems to be a validation of the traditional view that labor supply will increase as wages are being raised. It would seem to offer some verification to the neoclassical concept of voluntary unemployment outlined at the beginning of this section. However, it would be erroneous to generalize too much on the special situation discussed here when people are caught between two unpromising options: insecure employment at low wages or maintenance of the status as a recipient of public aid. In fact, relations between wage levels and levels of employment are far more complex than is indicated by the traditional concept of a general equilibrium wage rate having the effect of balancing at any given moment supply and demand on the labor market.

Built-in rigidities interfering with regional and occupational mobility of labor and with short run adjustments of unit labor cost and the impact of rapid technological change militate also against the uncritical acceptance of the *Phillips Curve* analysis of the relations between prices, wages and levels of unemployment. In its simplest terms, the work of Professor A. W. Phillips, based on statistical evidence extending to the 19th Century in Britain gives strong evidence that low rates of unemployment are associated with high prices and wages whereas low prices and wages coincide with low levels of employment and high rates of unemployment. It should be noted that these findings if valid, would make an additional and valuable contribution to the refutation of the neo-classical doctrine that full employment could be restored if wage rates were kept completely flexible and permitted to find their lowest natural level at which point demand for labor would rise steeply. We have seen earlier in this section that J. M. Keynes developed a forceful argument against the concept of "voluntary unemployment." Phillips shows that low prices and low wages far from being devices to increase aggregate demand for labor are actually associated with high levels of unemployment.

Phillips himself had suggested that his findings could be translated into policies attempting to manipulate price levels either for the purpose of establishing full employment or if there is a desire for price stability to permit some unemployment to develop. As a result during the 1960's policy options were debated in the United States in terms of "trading off" lower prices against some unemployment or vice versa. However, it is necessary to caution against "over-interpretation" of the statistical evidence which

[3]We will return to this problem in Chapter 25 in connection with the analysis of work incentives to relief recipients proposed by President Nixon.

led to the construction of the Phillips Curve. While these sweeping statements seem to be supported by historical statistical evidence at least to the 1950's in the United States, serious questions arise when wage, price and employment levels are made, as it were, functions only of the manipulation of short term fiscal and monetary policies. It is one thing to show, as Phillips has done, that high prices and wages are associated with high levels of employment and it is an altogether different assertion to say that historically or in the recent past high prices are directly traceable to low interest rates, easy credit and government deficit financing, and low prices are associated with high interest rates, credit restrictions and excess of income over expenditures in the public sector.

It is, of course, true that in the 1930's, for instance in the period 1931 to 1933, consumer prices dropped by 14.8 index points whereas unemployment rose by 21.7 points. But in 1937–1938 consumer prices dropped by less than one point whereas unemployment rose by 4.7 points. In this latter period, however, government deficits, and excess reserves of member banks of the Federal Reserve System were high and interest rates were kept low. While the 1930's proved out the Phillips Curve type of relationships between levels of prices, wages and employment, they do not supply convincing evidence that monetary and fiscal policies were effective in raising prices and increasing employment in that period.

More recent developments create doubts whether the Phillips type of relationship still exists. In 1957–1959 consumer prices jumped by 3.5 points. But unemployment which should have declined actually increased by 2.5 points. In 1966–1967 prices rose 3.2 points but the unemployment rate which should have declined remained unchanged.

The preceding considerations have shown that long range statistical evidence and generalizations based on it or a purely monetary macroeconomic analysis cannot be used as a substitute for a study of other factors which establish the behavior of demand for labor and of the supply on the labor market. We must, therefore, now address ourselves to these problems.

11-2. DEMAND FOR LABOR—GENERAL CONSIDERATIONS

So far in this chapter we have adopted the conventional term "wages" in order to establish some relationships between supply and demand on the labor market. It is important, however, to realize that from the viewpoint of the employer wage rates are significant primarily as part of total employment cost. The weight of these costs will vary with the type of production. In labor-intensive enterprises in which labor is the main factor of production and capital is less significant, the role of employment costs in total production cost will be more significant than in capital-intensive enterprise in which the principal factor of production is machinery. Increases in employment cost will have a greater effect in labor-intensive than in capital-intensive production units.

However we are not only interested in the short run behavior of the demand for labor. We have seen that the labor force itself is growing steadily. Furthermore in this longer run shifts in the demand for labor from production workers to nonproduction workers become significant. Actually in the 1950's the demand for white-collar workers began to exceed the demand for blue-collar workers. This trend assumes ever-greater significance because in speaking of the demand for labor, distinctions have to be made between the demand for production workers and for nonproduction workers. Before we analyze this difference in some detail, we will now present the rapid transformation in the employment structure in the United States between 1958 and 1967.

TABLE 11-1
EMPLOYED PERSONS 16 YEARS AND OVER, BY OCCUPATION

Year	Total Employed	White-collar	Blue-collar	Service Workers	Farm Workers
1958	63,036	26,827	23,356	7,515	5,338
1959	64,630	27,574	24,009	7,720	5,327
1960	65,777	28,516	24,067	8,031	5,163
1961	65,745	28,884	23,683	8,261	4,917
1962	66,704	29,632	24,048	8,383	4,639
1963	67,763	29,943	24,778	8,670	4,372
1964	69,306	30,866	25,231	8,890	4,219
1965	71,088	31,849	26,246	8,936	4,057
1966	72,896	33,065	26,952	9,212	3,667
1967	74,272	34,232	27,261	9,325	3,554

SOURCE: *Manpower Report of the President* (April 1968), Table A-9.

The preceding table demonstrates perfectly the great scope of the structural transformation of the demand for labor and, therefore, also of the labor force itself. While total employment between 1958 and 1967 increased by more than 11 million, the employment of farm workers declined by almost 2 million. One million of this decline is in the category of farm laborers who dropped from 2.555 million in 1958 to 1.584 million in 1967. It is well to keep these figures in mind because this falling off of demand for farm laborers at a time when total farm output increased by 16 index points demonstrates clearly the impact of progressive technology on the demand for labor. Inasmuch as many people who had been traditionally employed as farm workers had no alternative employment opportunities in their home environment, a good number of them migrated to the cities where they filled up pockets of unemployment. In a way hard core unemployment in urban areas is among other causes traceable to technological disemployment in the farm sector. This difficulty of workers no longer needed in farm production to find employment in other classi-

TABLE 11-2

WAGE AND SALARY WORKERS IN NONAGRICULTURAL ESTABLISHMENTS, 1958–1968

Year	Total Wage and Salary Workers	Manufacturing		Contract Construction	Transportation and Public Utilities	Wholesale and Retail Trade	Finance, Insurance, Etc.	Services	Government	
		Total	Mining						Federal	State and Local
1958	51,363	15,945	751	2,778	3,976	10,750	2,519	6,806	2,191	5,648
1959	53,313	16,675	732	2,960	4,011	11,127	2,594	7,130	2,233	5,850
1960	54,234	16,796	712	2,885	4,004	11,391	2,669	7,423	2,270	6,083
1961	54,042	16,326	672	2,816	3,903	11,337	2,731	7,664	2,279	6,315
1962	55,596	16,853	650	2,902	3,906	11,566	2,800	8,028	2,340	6,550
1963	56,702	16,995	635	2,963	3,903	11,778	2,877	8,325	2,358	6,868
1964	58,332	17,274	634	3,050	3,951	12,160	2,957	8,709	2,348	7,249
1965	60,832	18,062	632	3,186	4,036	12,716	3,023	9,087	2,378	7,714
1966	64,034	19,214	627	3,275	4,151	13,245	3,110	9,551	2,564	8,307
1967	66,030	19,434	616	3,203	4,271	13,613	3,217	10,060	2,719	8,897
1968	68,134	19,734	625	3,256	4,346	14,115	3,357	10,504	2,736	9,462

SOURCE: *Economic Report of the President* (January 1969), Table B-27.

fications of labor is also connected with the general shift of demand for labor from lower job classifications to higher ones.

Table 11-1 shows an increase of almost 4 million in blue-collar worker employment between 1958 and 1967. However, there was virtually no change in the employment of nonfarm laborers. In sharp contrast, the employment of craftsmen and foremen rose from 8.5 million in 1958 to 9.8 million in 1967. A similar upward shift of the demand for labor can be noted in the white-collar segment. There employment of professional and technical workers rose from nearly 7 million in 1958 to 9.9 million in 1967. We have already seen in Table 10-5 that the transformation of the demand for labor and of the labor force is expected to continue. Table 11-2 shows the development from 1958 to 1968. The trends shown there will be expressed in the actual mix of the demand for various categories of labor in the sectors of the economy, including government.

In analyzing demand for labor, it is necessary to distinguish clearly between the overall, aggregate demand for labor and the specific demand for labor in the various categories such as production, nonproduction and service workers. The aggregate demand for labor is brought forth by aggregate spending. If the latter is written as Y then the following simple functional relationship can be stated. Demand for labor-D_L can be written as

$$D_L = f(Y)$$

The significance and analytical value of this functional equation should not be overrated. It is, of course, a truism that as income and spending increases, employment will rise and if it decreases there will be a drop in the demand for labor and hence an increase in unemployment. These very general relationships have contributed very much to recent economic policy designs which assume that levels of employment can be influenced by the manipulation of aggregate spending especially through the devices of fiscal and monetary policies. While this is correct up to a certain point, it is necessary to dis-aggregate the overall demand for labor because the incidence of changes in spending is quite different on the various subdivisions of demand for and supply of labor. In fact the behavior of the demand for labor varies according to the general categories of workers to be employed. If we do not take into account these differences, which will be explored further in this chapter, we will not be able to come to grips with the problem of maintaining full employment in an advanced economy in which there is a high degree of technological change and a continuous transformation of the demand for labor transferring more and more participants in the labor force into the nonproduction sector.

In the next section we will take up the demand for production workers. This will be followed by a study of the demand for nonproduction workers.

11-3. DEMAND FOR BLUE-COLLAR WORKERS

Demand for production of blue-collar workers continues to be determined in the zone of marginal productivity. This can be clearly demonstrated by an inspection of the development of demand for production workers in manufacturing as it relates to output in manufacturing. As productivity in terms of output per worker increases, the demand for production workers declines per unit of output. This is clearly shown in Table 11-3.

TABLE 11-3
PRODUCTION WORKER EMPLOYMENT AND OUTPUT
IN MANUFACTURING INDUSTRIES—1957–1968
(1957–1959 = 100)

Year	Employment	Output
1957	104.7	100.8
1958	95.2	93.2
1959	100.1	106.0
1960	99.9	108.9
1961	95.9	109.6
1962	99.1	118.7
1963	99.7	124.9
1964	101.5	133.1
1965	106.7	145.0
1966	113.3	158.6
1967	112.9	159.7
1968	115.0	166.8

SOURCE: *Economic Report 1969* and *Monthly Labor Review.*

It should not be inferred from Table 11-3 that production workers are hired exactly at the margin. In fact, studies of variations in employment during depression and recovery periods have shown clearly that there is a "lagged employment effect." When production is curtailed, employment drops but not in the same proportion as output. As a result productivity measured in output per man-hour decreases in the depression phase of a cycle. Conversely when production picks up employment lags behind. In technically advanced production systems productivity reaches its peak at maximum utilization of plant capacity. As maximum utilization is reached, increases in output are achieved through overtime work rather than through the hiring of additional workers. Table 11-4 will show the lagged employment effect in a major steel plant of the United States for the period 1929–1939.

Table 11-4 shows the lagged employment effect both for periods of a declining production and for a rise in output. Between 1931 and 1935 the index of employment was consistently higher than the index of production. As a result output per man-hour dropped far below the level of 1929. In 1936 and 1937 the production index rose sharply but employment did not

TABLE 11-4
OUTPUT PER MAN-HOUR IN A LARGE STEEL PLANT—1929–1939

Year	Production Index	Employment Index	Man-hour Index	Output Per Manpower Index
1929	154	117	79	195
1930	118	116	73	162
1931	71	99	50	143
1932	35	75	38	125
1933	57	79	35	162
1934	61	87	38	159
1935	79	89	44	178
1936	119	102	59	202
1937	131	120	66	198
1938	66	93	40	166
1939	111	102	53	209

SOURCE: Primary: Annual Report of the Largest Steel Company whose data on their "Operating Story" and the "Financial Story" can be used to set up series of output per worker, output per man-hour and unit labor cost. With such outside information as "Index of Steel Prices and Production Workers" obtained from Government series of wage cost per unit of output of production workers can be developed. The index series of Table 11-4 are reproduced from "Senior Research Project No. 2: Wages Productivity and Unit Labor Cost." Available at the Library of Fordham University, New York. The study has also been published in a Journal of Labor Economics in Germany, *Soziale Welt*, 1958. An analagous study of a major steel plant in West Germany was published in the series "Soziale Forschung und Praxis" Volume 14 (J. C. B. Mohr Co., Tubingen, 1960).

rise in the same proportion. It must be remembered, however, that this behavior of the demand for production workers has to be identified with a very large steel corporation accounting for more than 30 percent of the output in the United States. The employer while not a monopolist operated in an imperfectly competitive market. Hence he was not under the same pressure as a perfectly competitive market situation would generate. Wherever the market structure is closer to perfect competition and is characterized by labor intensive rather than capital intensive production systems, the lagged employment effect will be minimized.

If we prescind from these medium term variations, marginal utility considerations govern the demand for production workers in the long run. That is to say as output per man-hour increases, the demand for labor declines. An outstanding example for this is given by the mining industry. Although output has been stabilized since 1965, employment continues to drop even though the rate of decline now is far less than it was in the 1950's. The most spectacular decline in employment is to be found in farming where output is continuing to rise while employment is falling rapidly. The number of hired workers on the farm dropped by almost 300,000 between 1965 and 1968 whereas output increased from 114 to 120 index points in the same period. (1957–1959 = 100.)

If we assume for one moment that the only demand for labor forthcoming would be for production workers, we could visualize the various conditions on the labor market for the case of a constant capital-labor ratio, of an increasing or a decreasing capital-labor ratio. These three cases are shown in Figure 11-1.

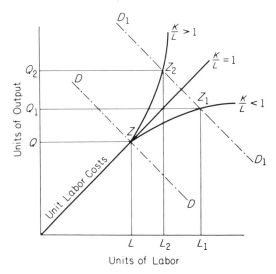

FIG. 11-1. Demand for labor and unit labor cost.

In Fig. 11-1 the unit-labor-cost curve shows a unitary behavior up to point Z. From then on it slopes upward to the left as the K/L increases to more than 1, and to the right as the K/L ratio becomes less than 1. Now if demand for output represented by line D-D increases so that it is now represented by the line D_1-D_1, it can be shown that at the point Z_2 the demand for labor, L-L_2 on the horizontal axis increases less than the units of output as can be seen in the distance Q-Q_2 on the vertical axis. At the point Z_1 the reverse relations obtain.

The main point to keep in mind with regard to demand for labor in general is that it is not determined by wage rates but by unit labor cost. By taking this into account it is also possible to consider even for shorter periods of time the impact of technical improvements, including automation, on the demand for labor. Now it must be realized that technical breakthroughs in production systems are predominantly associated with large sized firms. In fact the advance in technology itself is one of the prime reasons for the tendency towards ever larger units of production. This has important effects on the demand for labor. Already in 1956 almost half of the employment of wage and salary workers originated from less than 1 percent of the total number of firms employing workers. As is shown in Table 11-5, in 1956 there were slightly more than 500,000 firms employing 4 to 7 workers, giving in the aggregate 2.7 million employees out of a total of 40.6 mil-

TABLE 11-5
NUMBER OF FIRMS IN OPERATION AND PAID EMPLOYMENT
BY SIZE OF FIRM, 1956

Employee Size Classes	Firms in Operation January 1, 1956	Paid Employment, Mid-March, 1956
	Thousands	
All size classes	4,381.2	40,667
0 to 3	3,299.6	2,658
4 to 7	509.7	2,683
8 to 19	355.1	4,280
20 to 49	135.1	4,104
50 to 99	44.0	3,022
100 to 499	31.31	6,171
500 to 999	3.31	2,271
1,000 to 9,999	2.88	8,347
10,000 or more	.22	7,240
	Cumulative Percent	
0 or more	100.00	100.0
4 or more	24.69	93.5
8 or more	13.05	86.9
20 or more	4.95	76.3
50 or more	1.87	66.2
100 or more	0.86	58.8
500 or more	0.15	43.6
1,000 or more	0.07	38.1
10,000 or more	0.01	17.8

SOURCE: *Survey of Current Business* (September 1959).

lion accounted for. There were only 220 firms employing 10,000 workers and more. But these firms accounted for 7.2 million wage and salary workers.

The distribution of employment among firms of various sizes is of great significance for our understanding of the operations of the labor market in an industrialized setting. Table 11-5 gives full details. Although the last year covered by this study is 1956, there is no indication that since that time there has been a reversal of the trend indicated here.

As can be seen from Table 11-5, 0.23 percent of all firms operating in 1956 employed 17.548 million wage and salary workers out of 40.66 million in 1956. This small fraction of 1 percent of all employers accounted for 43.6 percent of all employment in that year exclusive of agriculture and government.

Generally this concentration of employment tends to stabilize the labor market to a greater extent than if employment were scattered among a much larger number of small firms. The economics of scale enable large firms to cushion the effect of a downward trend in activities at least in the short run. Productivity measured in output per unit of workers and man-hour is permitted to decline somewhat before layoffs are carried out. Generally attempts are made to maintain levels of employment by curtailing the work week. It is only in the longer run that large firms will proceed to a drastic curtailment in employment.

But what operates to the advantage of levels of employment when business is declining also puts a brake on the rapid expansion of employment in large firms when the volume of business is increasing. This trend has been very noticeable after 1961, when business activities rose sharply with a far less than proportionate increase in employment. By October 1965 the index of production in manufacturing industries had climbed to 150.4 on the basis of 1957–59 = 100. In the corresponding months of 1964 that index stood at 136.3. While output in this one-year period rose by about 10 percent, employment increased by only 5.5 percent in manufacturing—from 17.4 million in October 1964 to 18.5 million in October 1965.

Here we encounter the most serious impact of mechanization and automation on the demand for labor. The effects of these innovations cannot be measured in terms of the number of people who have been laid off. These figures are likely to be small in the short run because of the gradual "phasing out" of surplus workers, which is becoming standard practice in the United States. The decline in the demand for labor is more clearly in evidence in the lagging behind of levels of employment in periods of substantial increases in output.

Table 11-6 demonstrates this lag. The data incorporated in that table are taken from the "Big 500 Survey" which is published annually in the July issue of *Fortune* magazine. In that table information contained in the July issues of 1963 and 1964 has been combined and compared.

The year 1963 brought about very substantial increases in sales of major American corporations. This increase was headed by General Motors Corporation, whose sales went up by 12.6 percent. Employment increased, however, only by 5.84 percent. In the United States Steel Corporation the increase in sales was more closely related to increases in employment. Close relations between increases in employment and increases in sales can also be observed in International Business Machines Corporation. However, as shown in Table 11-6, in the majority of cases sales increased far more than employment.

Turning our attention now from the employment record of large-scale employers to the relation between wage and salary earners in manufacturing and changes in output, we find that the great upsurge in production characteristic of the 1960's was not accompanied by a proportionate increase in employment. In 1957, 17.2 million employees were attached to the manufacturing industries. At that time the index of industrial production stood at 98.1 percent of the average 1957–59 period. When this production index had risen to 131.5 percent in 1964, employment exceeded the 1958 level only by 100,000, or by 1.7 percent.

The 17.2 million employees who were attached to the manufacturing

TABLE 11-6

EMPLOYMENT AND SALES IN MAJOR CORPORATIONS IN THE UNITED STATES, 1962–63

Corporation	Sales		Employment		Percentage Increase in Sales	Percentage Increase in Employment
	1962	1963	1962	1963		
General Motors Corp.	14,640,241	16,494,818	604,718	640,073	12.6	5.84
Standard Oil Co.	9,536,877	10,264,343	150,000	147,000	7.6	2.00
Ford Motor Co.	8,089,617	8,742,506	302,563	316,568	8.0	4.62
General Electric Co.	4,792,733	4,918,716	258,174	262,882	2.6	1.82
Socony Mobil Co.	3,933,346	4,352,119	74,900	79,700	10.0	6.41
U. S. Steel Corp.	3,468,820	3,599,256	194,044	187,721	3.7	3.26
Texaco (The Texas Co.)	3,272,136	3,415,746	55,029	55,040	4.3	0.01
Gulf Oil Co.	2,836,292	2,977,900	46,900	53,200	4.9	1.34
Western Electric Co.	2,761,609	2,832,988	151,174	147,210	2.5	2.62
E. I. du Pont de Nemours Co.	2,436,352	2,584,593	93,159	100,468	6.0	7.85
Swift & Co.	2,494,553	2,473,450	54,200	52,400	8.0	3.32
Standard Oil Co. of N. J.	2,147,761	2,226,853	39,189	38,334	3.6	2.21
Standard Oil Company of California	2,150,934	2,202,512	43,281	43,764	2.3	1.09
Shell Oil Co.	1,960,733	2,128,637	33,908	32,191	8.5	5.06
Westinghouse Electric Corp.	1,954,480	2,127,307	109,966	115,170	8.8	4.73
Bethlehem Steel Co.	2,072,097	2,095,769	122,089	119,800	1.1	1.87
IBM Corp.	1,925,222	2,059,610	81,493	87,173	6.9	6.97
International Harvester Co.	1,837,468	1,957,371	102,230	106,230	9.0	3.91

Adapted from *Fortune*, July 1963–July 1964.

industry in 1957 were divided into 13.2 million production workers and 4 million nonproduction workers, that is to say, managers, supervisors, and clerical employees of various types. Now while in 1964 no more production workers were employed in manufacturing than in 1957, the number of nonproduction workers had increased by 1 million. Further increases took place at a slower rate in the subsequent years. By far the greatest part of the increase of nonproduction workers was concentrated in the durable goods industry especially in the electrical equipment, aircraft, instruments, and chemicals. This expansion of employment is associated with the ever increasing activities in "R. & D."—Research and Development, necessitating the employment of highly trained scientific and technical personnel.

The altogether different development of employment of production and nonproduction workers raises the question whether the demand for nonproduction workers can be analyzed within the same framework of utility, especially marginal utility, that seems to be applicable to production workers. While the demand for the latter seems to be definitely limited and actually is declining relative to total output, the demand for the former was apparently open-ended and steadily increasing in the 1960's. This requires further investigation.

11-4. DEMAND FOR WHITE-COLLAR WORKERS

As a point of departure for an analysis of the demand for white-collar workers it is important to stress that the structural transformation of the labor force, the decline in the demand for and the employment of production workers and the increase of the nonproduction worker sector in demand and employment has not brought about a change in the total share of wage disbursements in the gross national product.

In 1968 this share was in the 53–54 percentage range just as it had been ever since World War II. We refer at this point back to Table 5-1 of this text. There it was shown that due to employers' contributions to social security and private welfare funds, total compensation of wage and salary earners had risen more than wage disbursements. However, the latter, representing the gross earnings are more truly representative of the share of labor in the G.N.P. than total compensation which also accounts for the employers' part of transfer payments.

Now within these totals which have not changed significantly there has been a redistribution of labor payments between production and nonproduction workers. This is shown in Table 11-7.

As can be seen from Table 11-7, the share of production workers' earnings in total compensation dropped from over 60 percent in 1947 to less than 50 percent in 1967. While this drop of 20 percent occurred, total industrial production rose on the basis of 57 to 59 = 100 from 65.7 per-

TABLE 11-7
COMPENSATION OF PRODUCTION AND NONPRODUCTION WORKERS
1947–1967

Year	(1) Total Compensation of Workers	(2) Total Annual Avg. Earnings of Pro- duction Workers	(3) Total Annual Avg. Earnings of Non- prod. Workers
1947	128.9	80.0	48.9
1951	180.7	109.0	71.7
1956	243.1	141.6	101.5
1961	302.6	163.2	143.4
1962	323.6	174.1	149.5
1963	341.0	181.9	151.1
1964	365.7	192.8	172.9
1965	393.9	209.1	184.8
1966	535.7	227.3	208.4
1967	469.6	239.2	230.4

SOURCE: Explanation: (1) *Economic Report of the President*, 1968 (2) Total Production Workers and Avg. Weekly Earnings of Production Workers × 52, *Manpower Report of the President*, 1968 and *Employment and Earnings*, (June 1968) respectively.   (3) Column 2 minus Column 1.

cent in 1947 to 158.1 percent in 1967. This is another perspective of the continuous increase in man-hour productivity of production workers. It also demonstrates the savings in employment cost which are associated with this development if measured against units of output. Now these savings were not translated into lower prices. They were available and were used for the ever-increasing employment of nonproduction workers.

This does not mean, of course, that demand for white-collar workers has become completely undetermined and openended. Especially the employment of clerical workers engaged in routine operations rises and falls with the level of business activity. When the volume of shares traded at the New York and American Stock Exchanges began to rise steeply in 1967 and 1968, huge backlogs in the handling of stocks and certificates developed and there was a rapid increase in the employment of white-collar workers handling this aspect of the transactions. In 1969 the average level of turnover on the stock exchanges dropped considerably and accordingly there were layoffs of office workers on a large scale. It should be noted that brokerage firms are operating in a highly competitive market and are, therefore, compelled to watch their cost structure very carefully.

Despite these fluctuations in the employment of workers in brokerage firms, it was estimated in 1969 that office employment in the downtown area of New York City would increase by 120,000 by 1972 when such gigantic projects as the new World Trade Center Towers and other structures under construction would be completed.

It is, of course, true that the rising demand for nonproduction workers especially those with higher managerial and scientific skills is inherent in the structure of an advanced technological system and its proliferating requirements for private and public services of all kinds. It is equally true that there is a certain feedback effect of nonproduction employment. It generates the need for additional managers, coordinators, researchers, supervisors and other advanced types of employment. But this does not explain how employers in the private sector can finance these increasing outlays for white-collar workers. We will now give three reasons why in the period after World War II the economy has been able to expand the nonproduction or white-collar sector of the economy without reaching those limits of cost which would make a further growth of this sector impossible.

The first reason can be found in the preceding presentation of the implied labor cost savings in the employment of production workers. As output and revenues rose, internal funds became available to employers to expand substantially their nonproduction worker employment.

The second reason is connected with the progressive corporation tax structure. Employment costs are operating costs and deductible as such. While this has not interfered basically with the marginal-utility-oriented behavior of the demand for production workers, it has diminished the urgency to calculate nonproduction worker employment at the margin. In fact under certain circumstances some payroll padding in this area may bring tax advantages.

The third reason why demand for nonproduction, especially white-collar workers has been capable of the great expansion which has occurred is to be found in the market and price structure of an advanced industrial system. A large number of firms are in a position to disregard marginal cost and marginal revenue in their factor payments and in the pricing of revenues. They can operate with a great deal of freedom in deciding on average cost and on maximum-optimum utilization of capacity and revenue. Now we have seen that within this field in which costs are averaged out, the employment cost of production workers is still fixed in terms of marginal utility. This leaves room within the average cost structure for an expansion of employment of nonproduction workers. If output per man-hour had increased and the economic system had maintained the growth rate in the first half of the 1970's which it had in the second half of the 1960's, a further increase in the demand for and the employment of highly trained workers and white-collar workers in general would be expected. The growth of the demand for nonproduction workers under these hypothetical circumstances can be seen from Table 11-8.

Actual employment in 1965 was 71.1 million. The projected employment for 1975 is 87.2 million. Of the estimated increase in employment of 16.1 million, only 5.6 million are expected in the blue-collar category. That is to say employment of nonproduction workers must rise by more than 10 million if full employment is to be maintained. This in turn *assumes* that

TABLE 11-8

ACTUAL AND PROJECTED EMPLOYMENT BY OCCUPATION GROUP
1965–1975

Occupation Group	1965 Percentage Distribution	1975 Percentage Distribution
Total Employment	100.0	100.0
Professional and Technical Workers	12.5	14.8
Managers, Officials, and Proprietors	10.3	10.4
Clerical Workers	15.7	16.9
Sales Workers	6.3	6.4
Craftsmen and Foremen	13.0	13.0
Operatives	18.8	16.9
Service Workers	12.6	13.8
Nonfarm Laborers	5.2	4.1
Farmers and Farm Laborers	5.7	3.6

SOURCE: *Manpower Report of the President* (January 1969), Table E-8.

the economic conditions which generated the effective demand for non-production workers in recent decades will continue unabated in the immediate future. It should be noted further that the greatest increase in employment is foreseen in the category of professional and technical workers. They numbered 8.9 million in 1965. For 1975 an employment of 12.9 million is projected.

In actual numbers the increase in the employment of professional and technical workers in the ten year period 1965–1975 would amount to 4 million people. This exceeds by far the projected increases in other non-production categories such as managers and officials or clerical workers. This great leap forward which is expected in the professional and technical labor force indicates the increasing share of scientists and teachers in the economy. As physical productivity continues to soar in agriculture and in industry thereby creating a super abundance on material goods, the production sector is creating such material surpluses that it becomes possible to support and to supply an ever-increasing part of the population and of the labor force in the nonproduction sector of the economy. This change from an economy of scarcity to an economy of practically unlimited production possibilities has a great impact on the supply of labor.

11-5. SUPPLY OF LABOR

The aggregate labor supply is ultimately related to the total population. For the United States a population of over 245 million is projected for the year 1980. Between 1970 and that year the population is expected to increase by more than 36 million people. The labor force itself is considered to be limited to the age group 16 and over either actually at work or seeking employment. By 1980 it is estimated that these people will amount to about 174 million, an increase of more than 24 million over

1970. This is somewhat higher than the increase of that population between 1960 and 1970, which was about 22.3 million. It is true that in the 1960's there was a drop in the birth rate, but this will not affect substantially the projections up to 1980. While the population as a whole influences the size of the labor force, what is more important is the labor-force participation rate. This is expected to rise slightly from an actual rate in 1960 of 57.4 percent to 58.3 percent. It should be noted that this increase in the participation rate applies to a much larger base and is, therefore, more significant than might appear at first sight. This rise in labor-force participation will be brought about by a substantial increase in the age group 24–34. They numbered 10.6 million in 1964 but will reach 17.6 million in 1980. Furthermore, there will be a great increase in the age group 20–24. In 1964 their number was 5.7 million. In 1980 their number will rise to over 9 million. Table 11-9 gives a summary view of the

TABLE 11-9
PERCENT DISTRIBUTION OF TOTAL LABOR FORCE, 1964–80

Age	1964	1970	1975	1980
14 years and over	100.0	100.0	100.0	100.0
14–24	20.7	23.6	24.1	23.7
25–44	41.6	38.9	39.9	42.8
45 years and over	37.7	37.5	36.0	33.5
45–64	33.7	33.8	32.5	30.1
65 years and over..................	4.0	3.7	3.5	3.4

SOURCE: *Manpower Report of the President* (March 1965), Table E-4, p. 249.

percentage changes in the age composition of the labor force from 1964 to 1980.

It will be noted that this projection of labor supply shows that the labor force will become relatively younger during the 1970's. Whereas in 1970, 37 percent of the labor force will be 45 years and over, this proportion will have dropped to 33.5 percent in 1980. On the other hand, there will be a substantial increase in the age brackets 25–44 from 38.9 percent in 1970 to 42.8 percent in 1980. There will only be an insignificant decline in the percentage of people 65 years and over still in the labor force. The increase in the group 25–44 will be exercising an increasing pressure on employment opportunities, because it is in this age that people are particularly dependent on employment income. On the other hand, the employment prospects of this group will be somewhat enhanced by the fact that by 1975 more than 70 percent of this age group will have four years of high school or additional training. This leads us to a further consideration of how labor supply can be fitted into specific types of demand for labor which is forthcoming in an advanced industrialized system.

11-6.   FITTING LABOR SUPPLY INTO THE DEMAND PATTERN

In a reversal of the famous statement attributed to J. B. Say by J. M. Keynes that "Supply creates its own demand,"[4] it can be said that demand for labor creates its own supply. This is not the same as the contention of Karl Marx that capitalism creates its own population, which is an ideologically loaded view of what actually happens on the labor market. However, the history of international migration of labor—which prior to World War I was far less restricted internationally than it became in the 1920's and 1930's—testifies to the fact that demand for labor can reach out over long distances, and that even poor transportation was no obstacle in the past to bring demand and supply of labor together. There is, therefore, a good deal of evidence for a high degree of vertical—that is, regional and inter-regional—mobility of labor. In more recent years this has also been borne out by the South-North movement of labor in Europe and by the large-scale seasonal migration, legal or illegal, of migratory workers from Mexico to California and southwestern states.

There are indications that this *vertical* labor mobility decreases somewhat with a rise in standards of living. If people are in a social condition in which literally they have nothing to lose, their willingness to take chances by seeking employment far away from home or in foreign countries is much greater than if they had built up equities in houses and had enrolled children in educational institutions in their community. More serious is the problem of the *occupational mobility* of labor. Connected with this are also specific age limits set up by employers for the hiring of new workers.

Actually, these occupational and age requirements are less rigid than they seem. They are speedily adjusted whenever labor shortages develop. During the war people in the older age brackets were considered quite employable and actually very desirable as employees. It is only when labor supply becomes more abundant that older age groups on the labor market are cut off from employment opportunities primarily on the grounds that they are less adaptable to changes in methods of work. Private pension systems also might erect obstacles toward the hiring of older employees.

Insistence on specific training and previous work experience on the part of management also becomes stronger or weaker with changes in the condition of the labor market. Whenever full employment levels give way to some measure of unemployment, hiring standards are raised. While this change offers a good deal of employment security for people with good schooling

---

[4]J. M. Keynes, *The General Theory of Employment, Interest and Money,* Chap. 3. This interpretation given to Say's law is an oversimplification of what J. B. Say said. This French economist certainly did allow for some unemployment in connection with shifts in aggregate demand and output. He held, however, that there would never be a *general* crisis of overproduction, because aggregate factor payments will always restore full employment equilibrium.

and exactly the type of training that is required, the rigidity in the demand for labor overemphasizes specialized experience and overlooks the fact that most jobs are of such nature that a rather large spectrum of applicants could very well be fitted into their requirements. Stress on specialization in the demand for labor can actually lead to layoffs if the particular job performance required of currently employed labor has to be changed in the course of further technological or organizational advances.

Actually the labor market is served best when labor supply is generally equipped through good general education to develop and to retain habits of learning and of work which will enable it to perform well under ever-changing challenges of the world of work. Effective schooling combined with on-the-job training is the best method of keeping labor supply in the shape required by the changing structure of the demand for labor. This basic condition has not been altered by the spread of automation.

Traditionally apprenticeship has been in many countries the way in which young workers were fitted into the demand structure for labor. Advanced industrialization has not diminished the role of apprenticeship in most European countries. Vocational guidance, in some cases closely connected with public employment services, is trying to keep these training programs of industry and business in line with the longer-run requirements of the labor market. This attempt involves preventing of overcrowding in currently fashionable lines of work and the counseling of young people with regard to lifetime-employment opportunities in the occupation they contemplate to assume. Against the background of these institutions of the labor market in other highly developed countries, the American record with apprenticeship is not encouraging and requires urgent improvement. Table 11-10 gives a survey of registered apprentices in some occupations for the

TABLE 11-10
REGISTERED APPRENTICES IN SELECTED OCCUPATIONS, 1966

Occupations	Active at Beginning of Year	Apprentice Actions During Year			Active At End of Year
		New Registra- tions	Comple- tions	Cancella- tions	
Construction trades	114,933	46,120	16,352	22,507	122,163
Metalworking trades	34,099	21,918	4,799	6,461	44,757
Printing trades	11,682	3,511	1,692	1,138	12,363
Total	183,955	85,031	26,511	34,964	207,511

SOURCE: *Manpower Report of the President* (April 1968), Table F-6.

year 1963. While this report does not cover all apprenticeship situations, it includes those trades in which apprenticeship is most frequent in the United States.

Table 11-10 does not cover white-collar occupations. Many large corporations have inaugurated executive trainee programs, especially for college graduates. Internships at government agencies also try to prepare college students for future careers. In these cases we note an application of apprenticeship procedures to higher rank white-collar employment in business and government. Actually, there is no substitute for on-the-job or in-service training. Simulated job situations in vocational and trade schools can never replace it. One of the great advantages of apprenticeship, trainee, and internship programs is that young people will work closely with employees of an older age and with considerable job experience. This is one way of counteracting the tendency toward segregation by age, an unwholesome characteristic of contemporary society.

While apprentice training has been very limited in scope in the United States as compared to most other advanced industrial countries, there has been a far greater emphasis in the United States on an extension of formal education to twelve years and over. Whereas in European countries the overwhelming majority of people enter the labor force as apprentices or auxiliary workers at the age of fourteen and fifteen, ever increasing emphasis was placed in this country on achieving a high school diploma. In fact in the 1950's and early 1960's such a diploma was considered a prerequisite for employment even in most blue-collar occupations. Such a certificate was treated as a prima facie evidence of employability. Increasingly dropouts were considered as outside of labor supply which incidentally meant that they were not in the labor force and by operational definition could not be unemployed. We will see in Chapter 14 of this text that in the last few years policies have been inaugurated to change the concept of employability and to extend the concept of the labor force to what has been considered hard-core cases of nonemployment especially in the age group from 16 to 20.

This slight relaxation of standards of employability has not lessened the fact that people with high school diplomas have superior chances to find employment in blue-collar or clerical and service occupations than those who lack these educational achievements. A projection of the educational attainments of the civilian labor force in 1975[5] estimates that 78.1 percent of males 25–34 years will have 4 years of high school or more whereas the next age group, 35–44 years will only have 68.5 percent of high school graduates. In the older age group 55–64, high school graduates will comprise only about half of the people in this group. In the same year almost 20 percent of the civilian labor force will have completed four or more years of college as compared to 16.1 percent of the group between 35 and 44 years.

If it is possible to generalize on the experience in the United States

---

[5]Table E-10, Manpower Report of the President, January 1969.

after World War II, then the conclusion must be reached that employment opportunities increase with educational attainments and that they become most promising when diplomas can be obtained from top educational institutions. In a way this is the response of organized society to the ability of the economic structure to employ ever-greater numbers of professional and technical workers and of specialists of all kinds. This has helped in the rapid expansion especially of higher education which has become in itself one of the most important sectors of employment in an advanced industrial society. In this way the necessity for labor supply to adjust to higher educational requirements of employment have become also a cause for the expansion of employment opportunities in all fields of education. At the same time educational institutions like business enterprises have increased to a very large extent the number of administrators, supervisors and other categories of nonproduction workers. This has created additional employment opportunities. At the same time, this raised operating cost.

To sum up: the actual development of labor supply seems to confirm the assumption made at the beginning of this section that at least in the long run, labor supply will be forthcoming in the form in which it is demanded by private and public employers. However, the question arises in what manner the labor market operates as a great clearing device to bring together demand for labor and supply of labor.

11-7. OPERATIONS AND INSTITUTIONS OF THE LABOR MARKET

It has long been assumed that wage differentials operate as a clearing device on the labor market. When demand in certain lines of work is rising and more labor is required, this is reflected in rising wages. Such an upsurge of wages will bring about a movement of additional labor supply into high wage areas. Once this is beginning to create labor shortages in lower wage industries, employers must begin to raise their wages in order to assure themselves of an adequate labor supply. This model of a labor market in which flexible wage rates bring about regional and occupational realignments of labor supply corresponding to equilibrium positions in all segments of the labor market is predicated on two assumptions: a high degree of regional and occupational labor mobility and almost perfect knowledge of the wage structure and its short run changes on the part of labor supply. We have seen that even at times when transportation and communications systems were poor, labor supply was moving often over great distances and across oceans to areas where wages and other economic opportunities were better than in places where people were presently living. Occupational mobility has been curtailed on one side by the sharp decline in demand for general, that is to say, unskilled labor. On the other side the shifting of demand for labor to higher types of employment requiring special skills and greater educational achievements have set the conditions to which people must adjust in terms of training in order to meet these employment standards. We will see in Chapter 14 that in recent years programs have been inaugurated in the United States to assist people in making up educational deficiencies thereby improving their chances to meet contemporary standards of employability. However, these factors do not provide a complete answer to the question of how the labor market is actually operating in order to bring together a job seeker and a job offer.

One of the assumptions of the labor market model outlined above, namely that there is almost a perfect knowledge of wage structures and of employment opportunity has become quite unrealistic for large segments of the labor force. It is a fact that many occupational decisions are being made in very imperfect knowledge of the choice of opportunities that is available to individuals within the labor force. As we descend on the scale of income, educational achievement and social status, we find that knowledge of employment opportunities available to a given individual becomes ever more sketchy. However, on all levels of income, knowledge of employment opportunity comes to people through a *word-of-mouth* information network. They hear from friends and relatives that the firm where they are working or where they know someone is hiring additional personnel. This type of personal information about job opportunities has always played a great role for immigrants. Often a member of a family or of a group of people ventures out into the new country. Soon afterwards he will let his friends and relatives know whether there are jobs available for them. In fact immigration of labor is highly sensitive even to the minor changes in employment conditions in the country to which people want to move in order to improve their economic opportunities. Informal word-of-mouth information is by no means restricted to the lower reaches of the labor force. It is particularly active in high level types of professional and technical as well as business employment where alumni, friends and relatives alert job seekers to employment opportunities. The same type of informal information is of great significance on the executive level. Many upper management people cannot openly appear as job seekers, that is to say, send out summaries and supply references. This would alert the executive of their present firm and this would increase friction and pressure. The only way in which they can change to another job would be through informal and cautious information. By the same token, companies in search of executive personnel will often hesitate to advertise their need in a formal manner. In recent years private employment agencies have sprung up specializing in the placement of currently employed executives who cannot go officially on the record as seeking a new job, and servicing companies looking for new managerial talent.

Some years ago a study was made of the methods used by people 16 to 21 years old to obtain a first full-time job. Table 11-11 will give the percentages of the various methods used by seekers of first full-time jobs.

TABLE 11-11
METHODS USED TO OBTAIN FIRST FULL-TIME JOBS,
FEBRUARY, 1963

Persons 16 to 21 Years Old	
	Percent
All Methods	100
Sent by School	5.7
Applied Directly	41.0
Friends or Relatives	35.1
Answered Ad	3.9
Sent by State Employment Office	5.2
Sent by Private Employment Office	3.4
Other	5.8

SOURCE: Table 22, *Manpower Report of the President* (March 1966).

It is interesting to note that for those with less than 4 years of high school the referral through friends and relatives rises to 48.6 percent whereas it drops to 26.8 percent for those with 4 years of high school. For nonwhites placement through friends and relatives is consistently higher for all subgroups than for whites. It should be noted that the share of schools, state and private employment agencies in the arrangement of first full-time jobs was very small in 1963.

Obviously informal, especially word-of-mouth systems of labor market information are highly imperfect. The connection between the job and the job seeker may be influenced by random and personal considerations. Frequently those who are not inside such a network find job opportunities often inaccessible. Furthermore, often informal job information is highly unreliable and can cause people to make wrong decisions. This is the underlying situation of one of the best known American novels, *The Grapes of Wrath* by John Steinbeck, an American Nobel prize winner. The plot is based on the fact that in the 1930's the "Oakies," whose land had been devastated by dust storms started to move to California because they had heard of jobs in the citrus plantations. When they arrived they found out that employment was highly irregular and paid only minimum wages. At best the labor market information available to these people from Oklahoma was incomplete and misleading. It should be noted that nowadays there are signs on all highways in California indicating the location of the nearest office of the public employment service of the State. With this we come to more formal institutions of clearing demand and supply on the labor market.

Notwithstanding the survival of informal information networks a large proportion of placements is handled by employment agencies. Actually there are two such systems in operation in the United States: private agencies and the Public Employment Service. Employment agencies have an important economic function. They relieve the employer of the work connected with a pre-screening of prospective employees. These agencies try to obtain complete information about the educational and occupational background of applicants. Through preliminary interviews they can gain an impression of their personality. If they have been doing business with a particular company for some time the agency will have acquired some experience with regard to the type of personnel the employer is looking for. On the other hand from the viewpoint of the job seeker, the employment agency broadens considerably the range of possible employment opportunities. It reduces the need to "pound the pavement" in an attempt to talk directly to individual employers and their representatives. It also cuts back on the still widespread practice of sending out individual summaries and requests for employment to a large number of companies or public and private agencies and institutions.

Prior to World War II private employment agencies were free to respond to orders of employers specifying the exclusion of certain types of job applicants such as nonwhites or non-Anglo-Saxons. These practices have been outlawed by State and Federal legislation and open discrimination in the form of a refusal of private employment agencies to accept registration of certain job applicants or their failure to refer them to employers could be stopped by court action. While private employment agencies are now prevented from practicing job discrimination just as was a case with public employment services from the beginning, there are wide differences in the operation and in the field of activities between private and public employment agencies.

Private agencies require a license to operate in a particular state. They can lose it if they make placements in severe violation of the obligation imposed upon them to investigate the background of applicants and to be impartial in their placement activities. For instance some years ago an employment agency lost its license because it had sent a couple, butler and cook, with a very bad criminal record to a suburban family where shortly thereafter they murdered their employers. The agency had failed completely to investigate the background and credentials of this sinister couple.

The greatest difference between private and public employment agencies is that the former requires a fee whereas the latter do not charge for their services. Private employment agencies are private businesses which are designed to produce a profit for their owners. The fees charged can range from one week's wage to one month's salary. For a good number of people this involves a certain hardship. Usually they have to wait for two weeks until their first pay is due. The fees for the employment agency are usually taken out in several installments so that it takes some time until the employee receives his full wage. In colloquial language going to a private agency especially one placing people in blue-collar or routine white-collar jobs is referred to as "buying one-self a job." Actually this is not quite fair because in many cases the agency enables people to find employment which they themselves could not obtain. But this leaves unanswered the question of what happens to people who cannot afford the fee. In principle, the Public Employment Service is available to them.

This second, public system of employment services is operated by the states but is coordinated in its procedures under the supervision of the Manpower Administration. Public Employment Services had to be set up by all states when they established state laws for the granting of unemployment compensation. This compelled all people applying for unemployment benefits to come to the Public Employment Service first. Only if these offices could not refer them immediately to a suitable job, were they declared eligible to receive unemployment compensation. However, this left out a large number of job seekers. Large groups of wage and salary workers are not covered by unemployment compensation especially if they work for very small firms. Furthermore once the benefit period, usually 26 weeks, has expired, many people will discontinue their contact with the Public Employment Service. Nevertheless Public Employment Services have become important in several areas of the labor market. In many states they supply local institutions such as hospitals with a great many of their employees. They also have become active in the placement of some workers in professional fields such as nursing and even college and university teaching. As is well known the Public Employment Service of the locality in which a convention of economists or sociologists is being held is setting up the interviewing and hiring facilities in which representatives of institutions of higher learning meet prospective new faculty members.

By and large, however, the Public Employment Service deals with special categories of labor supply. For instance in 1968 about 25 percent of all placements by State employment security agencies were carried out for job seekers under the age of 22. Another 20 percent of such placements dealt with the placement of people 65 years and over. The scope of activity of the Public Employment Service can be seen from the fact that in 1968 there were 10.6 million job applicants registered and 7.8 million placements outside of the farm sector were carried out. Despite extremely high levels of employment in 1968 with less than 4 percent unemployment prevailing throughout that year the number of job applicants with these state employment security agencies was almost twice as high as the number of nonfarm placements; it also exceeded significantly the number of job openings available to the public employment serives.

Here we encounter a basic difficulty connected with the operation of the public employment services. While people applying for unemployment compensation must register with the employment service, employers and job seekers in general have no obligation at all to use the facilities of this public agency. In fact, private employment agencies especially in the white-collar, technical and professional fields receive the bulk of the orders from private business. As far as many blue-collar occupations are concerned, such as building construction, the hiring is actually handled by unions. In industries such as the maritime industry hiring halls are being used rather than the public employment service. Actually, a great proportion of placements handled through the Public Employment Services are confined to certain types of public employment and to the lower echelon of service employment.

In recent years, however, the concept of the scope of activity has been expanded. The idea has gained hold that the Public Employment Service should become involved in Human Resources Development. This was first applied by involving these services in the manpower development and training activities especially by reaching out to disadvantaged segments of the labor force. Furthermore state employment security agencies have become involved in counselling and in the scheduling and giving of aptitude and proficiency tests. In 1968 about 2.6 million counselling interviews were held and over 2 million aptitude tests were given. The human resources concept also is leading to a greater involvement between the Public Employment Service and people on public aid programs. Generally speaking there is a tendency to end the fragmentation of public services on the labor market and to develop the Public Employment Services as the focal point for the development of employment strategies dealing with the young, with public employment and with disadvantaged groups of the labor force. Once this type of expansion has taken place the Public Employment Service will be in a better position to compete with private agencies for a greater share of the job market. The increasing scope of these projects dealing with the development of human resources rather than merely confining the function of the employment service to given labor supply such as it is is indicated in Table 11-12, covering the fiscal years 1968 and 1969. It should be noted that not all of the placements listed in that table went through the public employment service, but there is a tendency to make the Public Employment Service the main agency for these placements. While most of the programs mentioned in that table such as the Job Corps and that part of the Neighborhood Youth Corps which is represented in the table either under on-the-job training, school and summer work or community work experience will be discussed in Chapter 14 in greater detail within the context of employment policies, the involvement of the Public Employment Service in the human resources development concept has added a new dimension to the structure of the labor market which must be discussed in this section.

TABLE 11-12
INDIVIDUALS SERVED BY MANPOWER PROGRAMS,
FISCAL YEAR 1968–1969 ESTIMATES

Category and Program	1968	1969
Total	970	1,292
Structured training	492	638
On-the-job	186	281
Institutional	129	170
Job Corps	98	98
New Careers	10	13
MDTA part-time and employability training	57	63
Indian manpower activites	13	14
Work-experience programs	435	590
School and summer work	310	469
Community work experience	126	121
General manpower services and program support	44	65
Support to Concentrated Employment Program	34	50
Special Impact Program	10	15

SOURCE: *Manpower Report of the President* (April 1968), p. 194.

Indications are that the American labor market will continue to operate with a dual structure, the private employment agency sector dealing
primarily with better paying white- and blue-collar jobs and the public
employment service handling less skilled and more disadvantaged groups
of the labor force. Cutting through these two systems there will continue
the vast amount of informal labor placement through word of mouth
propaganda, friends and relatives and individual responses to "help
wanted" ads and similar methods.

11-8. THE PROBLEMS OF COMPUTERIZING
THE LABOR MARKET

It is only natural that with the rapidly increasing use of computers in
data processing and in problem solving, the question has been raised
whether computers could help to facilitate and expedite manpower
policies. In fact, in 1969 public employment agencies administering special
manpower programs began to utilize computers. The basic purpose of
this method is to match requirements of employers with labor supply
which has been made available through various training programs such
as will be discussed in greater detail in Chapter 14 of this text. At this
point in our study it is necessary to investigate further the basic assumptions and conditions which underly a computerized approach to the labor
market.

Occasionally proposals are being made to establish a national *Manpower Bank*. The main purpose of such a system would be to serve as a
nationwide clearing house in which job vacancies which cannot be filled
locally or within a state could be matched with job applicants listed in this

national automated roster of available labor supply. In fact, it is entirely
feasible to have information about the total labor force in the United
States with all the necessary data on age, sex, residence, education and
occupational experience programmed into such a data processing system
together with a total listing of jobs and employers requirements. In this
way, it would theoretically be possible to achieve a perfect matching of
labor supply and demand for labor. However, these technical possibilities
are of necessity limited by certain social and economic realities of the
structure of the labor market. Basically the labor market is free, that is to
say, individuals have choices with regard to where they want to work,
what they want to do in order to make a living and how much they want to
earn. Employers also do have a considerable margin of choice although
the civil rights laws prevent them from practicing racial discrimination.
But within these limits they retain the right to hire employees of their
own choosing. From this it follows that in a peacetime economy, the use
of computers would have to be restricted to the clearing of vacancies and
job applications on a national level which cannot be handled locally or
within the confines of a state. Furthermore, it is necessary to point out
that even the most perfect system of a manpower bank cannot create employment. It can only match actually existing employment opportunities
with people fitting into these slots of the staffing requirements of a private or public employer.

It is necessary, therefore, to make a clear distinction between *manpower policies* and *employment policies*. The former deal with the processes
of balancing the structure of employment opportunities with the distribution of skills in the labor force. At a time of rapidly changing job requirements this may lead to manpower programs designed to bridge existing
discrepancies between the mix of employment opportunities and the composition of the labor force. Employment policies are operating not so much
inside the labor market as within the macroeconomic structure. They try
to establish conditions for the maintenance of high levels of employment.
In the next two chapters we will turn our attention to these problems. In
Chapter 14 we will discuss manpower policies in some detail.

SELECTED BIBLIOGRAPHY

Bakke, E. Wight, *A Positive Labor Market Policy* (Columbus, Ohio: Charles
    Merrill Books, Inc., 1964).
Barber, M. S., and D. J. Farber. Training of Workers in American Industry—
    Report of a Nationwide Survey of Training Programs in Industry, 1962.
    U. S. Dept. of Labor, Office of Manpower, Automation and Training Re-
    search Division, Rept. No 1 (Washington, D. C.: U. S. Government Print-
    ing Office, 1964).
David, Henry. *Manpower Policies for a Democratic Society* National Manpower
    Council (New York: Columbia University Press, 1965).

Galloway, L. E. "Labor Mobility, Resource Allocation and Structural Unemployment," *American Economic Review* (September, 1963).

Greenberg, L., and E. Weinburg. "Technological Trends in 36 Major American Industries," study prepared for the President's Committee on Labor Management Policy. U. S. Bureau of Labor Statistics, Office of Productivity and Technological Developments (Washington, D. C.: U. S. Government Printing Office, 1964).

Lansing, John B. *The Geographic Mobility of Labor* (Institute for Social Research, Survey Research Center, 1963).

Meyers, Fredrich, *Training in European Enterprises* (Los Angeles, University of California Institute of Industrial Relations, 1969).

Ross, Arthur M. (ed.). *Employment Policy and the Labor Market* (Berkeley, Calif.: University of California Press, 1965).

Weiss, Leonard W. "Concentration and Labor Earnings," *American Economic Review* (March, 1966).

QUESTIONS FOR DISCUSSION

1. Classical employment theory, employing the mechanism of flexible wages, argued that involuntary unemployment could not exist for any sustained period. Of what value is this argument in a contemporary society?

2. Can wage differentials account for long-run regional and international movements on the part of the labor force?

3. State a functional relationship which will account for the magnitude of the demand for labor at any given time and show how variations in any one of these variables may be expected to change the demand for labor.

4. Contrast the employment effects of a given increase in output when U/P is greater than one with the employment effects when U/P is less than one.

5. The demand for labor is said to be more properly related to unit labor costs than merely to wage rates. Why is this so, and what are the implications of this in a period of increasing unit labor costs?

6. The fact that output in manufacturing industries has increased by sizable proportions since 1957 while employment has remained virtually constant has special implications for policy makers. What are these implications in terms of the future development of the labor market?

7. To what extent can structural changes in the demand for labor account for the fact of relatively high levels of unemployment despite the record-breaking growth of the American economy during the period 1961–65?

8. The supply of labor over the long run is most directly related to the population, but purely economic considerations can alter that supply in that they may affect the rate of labor force participation. Comment.

9. As standards of living increase, the extent of labor mobility may be affected. In what direction would this effect most likely be felt, and what are the implications of such a trend?

10. Are the use of more widespread training and apprenticeship programs a workable solution to our contemporary problems of unemployment?

11. State your opinion on computerizing the labor market.

Chapter

12

Theories of Employment

Problems of employment have claimed the attention of writers on economics from the very beginning of the modern industrial system. In the early nineteenth century there was much instability in business—great fluctuations in output, profits and employment. Under the institutions then prevailing the main burden of depressions seemed to fall on the new group of industrial workers. Their wages were not protected by longer-run contracts. Whenever business activity declined, they had to submit immediately to cuts in wages, and if the condition continued for a longer period, to widespread layoffs.

These conditions did not lead to the formulation of specific theories of employment. The problems of the labor market were seen within the context of general fluctuations of economic activity. Thus it seemed that if an adequate business-cycle theory could be formulated, it would cover the problems of employment connected with the instability of the economic system. The absence of special theories of employment as such is thereby easily explained. It is not attributable to any common opinion among classical economists to the effect that full employment always prevailed, but rather to the conviction that unemployment of more than seasonal duration increases with the decline of business and disappears with the rise of economic activities. A business-cycle theory was always intended to guide economic policies. By analyzing and highlighting certain typical causes of business crises it was hoped that policy makers would be enabled to take remedial or preventive action which would also affect levels of employment.

While the majority of economists dealt with problems of unemployment as a by-product of the cyclical behavior of the economy, there emerged also early in the nineteenth century the issue of technological unemployment. A heated controversy developed between economists who maintained that machinery was "setting workers free," or in effect committing them to unemployment and economists who argued that this was not the case. Some even went so far as to say that technological progress, instead of generating unemployment, was actually creating additional jobs. As we will see later in Chapter 13, these seemingly contradictory statements can both be true, depending on the phase of economic development for which they are being stated. We are concerned with the development of economic thought dealing with problems of employment. Unless clear distinctions are made between attempts to analyze and mitigate cyclical unemployment, and to deal with unemployment which cannot be reduced to a purely cyclical condition, our thinking on this important issue, central not only to the economics of labor but to economics in general, will not be properly focused and our conclusions and policy prescriptions will remain largely irrelevant.

12-1. CYCLE THEORIES OF UNEMPLOYMENT

When the first industrial revolution got under way the market structure resembled the perfectly competitive model of the economy much more than was later the case when technological conditions forced patterns of concentration on industry, banking, and many aspects of transportation and distribution. While a high degree of competition and a dispersal of productive activities among a large number of smaller units has many advantages and still commands the ideological preferences of many people professionally involved in economics—including "model builders"—one cannot deny that the price of having such a system is a high measure of instability.

It is hard to see how this situation could be otherwise. In such a system macroeconomic information is sketchy. Decision making must be based on short-run developments of prices and consumer demand. Under such conditions errors of business judgment could hardly be avoided. In a period of rising prices investment was stimulated by the expectation of higher profits. However, there was no way of knowing at what point such an upward trend would come to a halt and how this developing market situation was related not only to current but to future aggregate consumer demand. As a result of these conditions, a boom period was always overshooting the mark, as it were, and was inevitably followed by a difficult period of downward adjustment. It was, of course, in that phase of the cycle that unemployment developed very rapidly.

While economists throughout the nineteenth century were in full agreement about the reality of the cycle phenomenon, they differed widely on their explanations of the causes of this instability. Economists like Jean Charles de Sismondi and Johann Karl Rodbertus attributed business crises to underconsumption—more specifically, to low wages. Not only did these writers stress that wages were generally low, they pointed out that they were losing ground in various phases of a cycle. Sismondi was concerned with the practice of wage cutting in periods of depression, which he felt was aggravating the crisis and increasing unemployment. Rodbertus was more concerned with a wage lag in the upswing in which, in his opinion, productivity was bound to rise faster than labor income. In turn this would bring about a deficiency in demand because income rose at a slower pace than output.

Opposed to these underconsumption theorists were the overproduction theorists, of whom the French economist Albert Aftalion is representative. They vigorously denied even the possibility of underconsumption. In their view the crises and the resulting unemployment were due to the inevitable increase in cost of production associated with a rise in output. Eventually prices got out of line with income, and an adjustment had to take place. It should be noted that this type of cycle theory assumes the prevalence of the principle of increasing cost, which in nineteenth-century thought was considered the only operative production function.

Other economists, among them John Stuart Mill, propounded so-called psychological or "error" theories of business cycles. They emphasized that rising prices will lead to an "optimistic" error in decision making. Eventually this leads to excessively high prices, which in turn brings about a piling up of unsold goods on shelves and in storehouses. Sales are forced upon businessmen even at a loss. This sets in motion the downward phase of the cycle with its period of "pessimistic" error. People withhold purchases in the expectation of further declines in prices. This curtailment of business activity generates a great deal of unemployment. But just as in the upward-phase business activities became too high to be sustained at that level, in the downward push they shrank too much, and this very fact ultimately brought about a new turning point and the start of a new cycle.

It should be noted that the well-known entrepreneur theory of the late Professor Schumpeter is a latter-day elaboration of this type of cycle theory, with emphasis on the appearance in "clusters" of leading entrepreneurs who set in motion an upward trend. Unfortunately, according to Schumpeter, this first team is soon supplanted by second-raters. There will be overexpansion, and the inevitable downward trend with its rise of cyclical unemployment, will come to pass.

Prior to World War I a new type of business-cycle theory was developed which stressed certain aspects of the structure of money and credit. According to the theory, as the volume of business activity rises during the upswing, the demand for money and credit increases sharply. This is aggravated further by the rise in prices typical of the prosperity phase. The increase in transactions coupled with the rise in prices begins to put a severe strain on the money and credit system. Hence, banks are compelled to raise interest rates and to curtail credit lines in order to maintain the proper proportion of assets to reserves. From this viewpoint, business could not continue to rise over long periods because the very requirements of the soundness of the money and credit system would compel the banking community to put brakes on this form of momentum. In fact, from the overriding viewpoint of monetary stability, a downtrend in business and a rise in unemployment would be the price that people would have to pay to safeguard the validity of monetary institutions.

In the first two decades of this century *business cycles*, and especially the impact of monetary institutions on economic stability, were the major concern of most economists. It was felt that if a more complete knowledge of the interaction of various economic aggregates during the cycle pattern could be obtained, then business—perhaps with the assistance of government and banking authorities—could bring about a greater stability of its operations. If so, the volume of cyclical unemployment and the burden it placed on workers could also be lessened.

It is in this context that in the United States and in Europe empirical studies of the behavior of past business cycles were intensified. The German economist Arthur Spiethoff wrote a history of business crises beginning with the "Mississippi Bubble" in 1722. In the United States under the guidance of Wesley C. Mitchell impressive studies of past business cycles were started by the National Bureau of Economic Research. Historical evidence since the Civil War gathered by this research group seemed to indicate that cycles last from seven to ten years measured either from peak to peak or from trough to trough. If this was valid not only for the past but for conditions in the twentieth century, especially after 1929, then unemployment seemed to be entirely manageable because it was cyclical in nature. A better insight into "leads and lags" around turning points in upswing and downswing phases of the cycles worked out by the Bureau would be most helpful in guiding business decisions in a way to minimize fluctuations, especially by preventing the "error" aspect in cyclical behavior. Furthermore, it was understood that a system of unemployment insurance might mitigate the effects of unemployment. In this connection it is important to note, that while a general depression may last as long as four years, some workers would be unemployed sooner but also reemployed earlier than others, so that at any given time, even during a depression, the unemployment rate would not be too high.

When in the period 1937–38 a steep decline in business activities occurred in the United States and unemployment rose again to 19 percent of the labor force, doubt became widespread as to whether the cycle pattern which had characterized economic fluctuations until 1929 was still operative. A discussion arose around the concept of "economic maturity." This word was ill-chosen. What really was at stake was the rate of economic growth and its slowdown in the 1930's. The outbreak of World War II and the increasing involvement of the United States in that conflict terminated this debate before any conclusive insights could be formulated. However, many economists were of the opinion that after the end of the war a primary depression of the 1921–23 type, and a secondary postwar depression like the one that started in 1929, were to be expected. In fact, there was great apprehension about the likelihood of a return of large-scale unemployment.

These fears were not borne out by the actual development of the economy. Levels of employment remained consistently high above the rates of the 1930's. With this change in the fluctuation pattern of the economic system, cycle theories seem to have lost a good deal of relevance for the problem of unemployment. They remain important, however, because the contemporary theory of employment contains features of these cycle theories, especially those that stress monetary mechanisms. Before we turn our attention to these more recent approaches to the problems of employment and unemployment, it is necessary to go into the background of the problem of progressive technology and the demand for workers.

12-2. TECHNICAL PROGRESS AND UNEMPLOYMENT

When weavers in Lancashire and Silesia who had been engaged in the production of textiles in their cottages lost their livelihood with the establishment of textile mills, they rebelled against a development that threatened them with unemployment. Similar opposition of people engaged in cottage industries, such as rolling tobacco or manufacture of glassware in certain parts of Europe, gave evidence of the anxiety created in the early phases of the industrial revolution among groups of people who had been displaced by modern machinery.

It is obvious that the effect of technology on the rate of employment cannot be gauged by such local developments. The issue can be resolved only on the macro scale of economic analysis. Ultimately the problem is related to the rate of growth of the economic system. If technological improvements coincide with a rather small rate of economic development, the thesis that machinery creates unemployment may have validity. The possibility of this type of technological unemployment was clearly conceived by one of the main representatives of classical economics, David Ricardo.

Originally Ricardo had joined most other economists of his day in the opinion that machinery, while displacing some individual workers, did have the overall effect of increasing the volume of employment. However, in a later edition of his *Principles of Political Economy and Taxation* Ricardo reversed himself. Speaking strictly in macroeconomic terms, Ricardo visualized the possibility that as a result of technical progress the net national product could rise faster than the gross national product. Under net product he placed the final output of goods and services. He concluded "that the same cause which may increase the net revenue of the country may at the same time render the population redundant, and deteriorate the condition of the labourer."[1]

---

[1]David Ricardo, *Principles of Political Economy and Taxation*, Chapter XXXI on Machinery. In view of this rather penetrating analysis of the possibility of (involuntary) technological unemployment by a classical economist, the content of the one paragraph,

While this seemed to be a gloomy prognosis, Ricardo tried to offset it by an optimistic view of the impact of technological progress on the volume of exports. Because cost of production and prices will be lowered by machinery, sales in foreign markets might be expanded. In this way the "diminution in the progressive demand for labour" might not occur.

Actually, the nineteenth century did not experience long-run technological unemployment. But this is no argument against the Ricardian analysis. It is rather the result of the continuous secular growth of the economic system through various succeeding waves of industrialization, starting with textiles and ending with automobiles. Technological progress was generating entirely new industries. This more than compensated for the loss in labor requirements caused by the increasing use of machinery in already existing industrial enterprises.

But economists who denied that progressive technology could cause unemployment did far more than point to the historical record. They stressed that increasing use of machinery lowered unit labor cost. Under perfect competition this would assuredly translate itself into lower prices. In this way the aggregate real income had to grow in proportion to the rise in labor productivity. This development would lead to a continuous increase in aggregate demand for goods and services. Thus it could be shown that technological progress would actually increase the overall number of jobs, although it was never denied that it could also create short-run frictional unemployment.

It should be noted that this analysis is predicated on the existence of perfect competition, whose workings will always keep prices close to the least-cost level. Furthermore, this line of reasoning implies that there is no limitation to aggregate demand. If certain requirements have been satisfied, demand will shift to other, probably new goods and services. There will, however, be no increase in the rate of saving offsetting the rise in aggregate demand and spending.

Using this type of analysis economists, even in the 1930's, tried to relate unemployment to monopolistic practices. Some blamed chronic unemployment on collective bargaining, with its downward inflexibility of wages. Others pointed to pricing practices of large firms which failed to translate productivity gains into lower consumer prices. These writers overlooked the fact that the modern trend toward large-scale business organization and its counterpart, big labor unions, is in itself caused by technological progress and is as such not reversible.

It became evident around 1930 that both types of approach to problems of unemployment—its treatment strictly as a cyclical phenomenon or as a short-run effect of advancing technology—fall short of analyzing adequately

Chapter 1, of Keynes' *General Theory* has always mystified the present writer, unless he really meant to exclude Ricardo and to concentrate neoclassicists, especially Alfred Marshall.

the critical situation on the labor market. It is at this point that the "new economics" and especially Keynes' *General Theory of Employment, Money and Interest* come to the fore.

12-3. KEYNES' GENERAL THEORY OF EMPLOYMENT

Although Keynes had laid the groundwork for his *General Theory* in his earlier writings with their stress on aggregates and macroeconomic relations, beginning with his *Economic Consequences of the Peace* and climaxing in his *Treatise on Money*, it took quite some time for the contents and implications of his *General Theory* to be fully absorbed and received by most professional economists. For the last quarter of a century, however, "Keynesian Economics" has more and more dominated the thinking and teaching of economics especially in the United States. It is now clear that Keynes was a seminal thinker. That is, he gave an enormous stimulation to thought in his field, eventually creating a large school propagating and elaborating his doctrines and influencing economic and financial policies. Another seminal thinker, Karl Marx, is reported having said to a visitor late in life that he was not a Marxist. Whether Keynes would say today that he is not a Keynesian we unfortunately cannot find out, due to the early death of this great thinker.

In view of the fact that the new economics of a generation ago has become the school economics of today, it is imperative to view this whole body of thought in perspective. We must understand how it is related to preceding approaches to economics. Furthermore, we must ask whether this framework of analysis can cope with the problem of employment confronting the American economy in a period of rapid increase of the labor force and of labor productivity.

It is quite evident in many passages in the *General Theory* that Keynes regretted deeply having to depart from such neoclassical economists as Alfred Marshall and Arthur Pigou. It seems that he wanted to limit his departure from this school of economics to the minimum required to open up a new analysis of the problem of involuntary unemployment. These departures were: a return to the macroeconomic view of the system characteristic of the classical theory up to and including J. S. Mill; a challenge to Say's law by showing that there is no preestablished balance between savings and investment; finally, an emphasis on the liquidity preference of individuals and corporations which interferes to some extent with the function of the interest rate as an equalizer of saving and investment. However, Keynes, like his predecessors but unlike the original classical economists, was thinking in terms of a short-run analysis—although unlike Vilfredo Pareto he did not go so far as to make the assumption of simultaneous exchanges. It must be stressed, however, that in his restatement of the "General Theory" in Chapter 18 of his classic work he found it necessary to assert—for the benefit, perhaps, of those less enlightened readers who had not realized it from the very beginning—that his whole analysis was built around the model of a stationary system. He took as given the existing skill and quantity of labor, the quality and quantity of equipment, the existing technique, the market structure, and the consumer preferences. Of course, he was aware that in the twentieth century all these factors were changing at rates of varying speed. But he stated very clearly that for the purposes of his inquiry he was not going to take into account the effects and consequences of these changes. Instead, Keynes was setting up three independent variables: the propensity to consume, the marginal efficiency of capital, and the rate of interest. Variables depending on those independent factors he considered to be the volume of employment and the national income.

In setting up these three independent variables and the two dependent ones, Keynes was very much in the tradition of economics as it emerged about a hundred years ago almost simultaneously in England and in Austria. Scientific economics in this sense is proceeding logically from some very general assumptions, such as the desire of individuals and firms to maximize revenues and to minimize cost. It is assumed that households and firms always operate at the margin—a very precise concept which we encounter in Keynes' marginal efficiency of capital. We have found it earlier in the theory, rejected by Keynes, that the wage rate balances at all times the supply and demand of labor so that there can be no such thing as involuntary unemployment.

While Keynes demonstrated in his *General Theory of Employment, Interest and Money* that neither the wage rate nor the interest rate functioned exactly in the manner ascribed to them in neoclassical economics, his own theory is of the same category and style as that of the economists whom he felt he had to supercede with a new type of analysis. If his independent variables were really comprehensive enough to deal with the problem of employment equilibrium, they would fulfill the desire of this type of scientific economics to arrive at few, but basic, propositions. Propositions, indeed, of so general a nature that the policies derived from them would be almost universally applicable—regardless of the long-run historical, institutional, and social-psychological factors which differentiate one phase of economic development from another, and which establish structural economic differences and varying modes of economic behavior. If it is said that Keynesian economics is ambivalent with regard to market structures and problems of dynamics, then one might reply from the viewpoint of the *General Theory* that his ambivalence does not really matter, and that the propositions of the doctrine as well as their policy implications are generally valid.

Let us now turn to a consideration of the three independent variables and their role in the *General Theory*. This will enable us to understand its major parts and to assess the extent to which they are valid but also the degree to which they fail to come to grips with some of the basic factors of a greatly advanced industrialized system.

Keynes was concerned with aggregate demand. Basically this overall demand emerges in two sectors of the economy: the consumer sector and the investment sector. Actually the propensity to consume—the first of the independent variables—deals with the responses of households to changes in income. The second independent variable—the marginal efficiency of capital—is closely related to the first and third. The marginal efficiency of capital will be affected on the one hand by the rate of spending in the consumer sector and on the other by the rate of interest. The relationship of these three independent variables to employment is a simple one. The level of employment depends on the rate of spending both in the consumer and in the investment sector. Everything that tends to raise spending tends to raise employment. Conversely, whatever curtails aggregate expenditures will cause unemployment.

Propensity to Consume. Keynes observed that this propensity may remain unchanged over longer periods. This fixing of consumer habits and a stable consumption saving ratio is, according to Keynes, predicated on an unchanging level of income flow to consumers. If, however, there is an increase in the aggregate income of consumers, a change in the propensity to consume is likely to occur. The main doctrine of Keynes in this respect is that while aggregate spending certainly will rise as more income is received by households, not all of the increased income will be spent. That is, as income rises, the rate of saving will also increase. Whereas at a low average income level it might have been 5 percent of aggregate income, it may now rise to 7 percent. Keynes pays great attention to the reasons why this is so.

Unlike the classical economists who have linked the rate of saving in a very simple manner to the rate of interest, assuming that it increases as interest rates are raised and declines with a fall in interest, Keynes stresses the large number of motivations that induce the average consumer to keep some of his income, especially some increments of a higher income in form of liquid assets readily convertible into cash. Now this *liquidity preference* prevents a full conversion of increased income into increased spending. This behavior, according to Keynes, is the basic cause of unemployment. Unlike the underconsumption theorists of the past and also his contemporary J. A. Hobson, he attributed a downward trend in business and employment to a deficiency not of aggregate income but of aggregate spending.

Employment is a function of spending. If income has been increasing because of a preceding high level of output of consumer and investment goods eventually leading to full employment, this rising trend of aggregate income, according to Keynes, will cease to continue. People will save more and in the next period of production the previous high levels of output of consumer and producer goods will no longer be reached. In this analysis a causal relationship is established between the rate of saving, the rate of spending, and the rate of employment. A fall in the propensity to consume is certain to bring about a deterioration of employment. Here we find an important aspect of the new economics. As long as economists held that there was at all times an equality between the rate of saving and the rate of investment, it could be argued that investment could gain from the decisions of consumers to spend less and to save more. Inevitably savings—that is, the difference between current income and current spending—would be transformed into investment. If this was so, saving could not set in motion a downward trend in employment but rather a shift in employment from consumer goods to producer goods production.

The concept of liquidity preference introduced by Keynes points to the fact that the classical assumption of the balance between savings and investments is unrealistic. It must be underscored, however, that the Keynesian analysis involves another assumption which removes it quite a distance from the realities of the contemporary economic system. Basically Keynes is dealing with individual acts of savings carried out in the household sector. He implies that the greater part of investment funds are directly derived from individual savings. While he does not altogether overlook corporate savings,[2] he places great stress on consumer behavior with regard to changes in income.

Keynes is aware of the fact that changes in the marginal propensity to consume have a different impact according to the existing levels of employment and of economic development. This impact is measured by the "*multiplier.*" This concept deals with the effect on employment of an original increase in spending either for consumer or investment goods. The multiplier was conceived as a most important analytical tool. If, for instance, the multiplier had a value of 3 and the aggregate rate of spending was $10 billion short of full employment, then the generation of an income stream of $3.3 billion through such policies as employment in public works and incentives for investment would be sufficient to return the overall rate of spending to $10 billion.

While the multiplier concept has become an indispensable link in employment theory, the expectations with regard to the operation of the multiplier for various levels of unemployment as formulated by Keynes in Chapter 10 of his *General Theory* turned out to be the reverse of actual developments. Keynes assumed that the multiplier effect would be greatest in a period of severe unemployment and would taper off as levels of unemployment declined. This is why Keynesian economists favor public works as a prime antidote to unemployment. In fact, Keynes went out of his way to assert that "public works even of doubtful utility" would pay their way because of the multiplier effect.

Unfortunately the experience of the 1930's and the later developments in

[2] J. M. Keynes, *The General Theory of Employment, Interest and Money*, Chap. 9.

the American economy have shown that public works did not "pay their way." When unemployment is widespread the multiplier effect is very limited. This is because of the abundance of unused production capacity and labor. Inasmuch as during a depression labor productivity is allowed to decline and more workers are kept on their jobs than would be indicated by a strict marginal accounting of employment cost, a considerable expansion of output can take place without generating significantly higher aggregate income. While the propensity to consume of people employed in public works may be 100 percent, the aggregate spending will not reach to the discretionary expenditures which really stimulate economic activity. Conversely, when levels of full employment are approached the multiplier effect of additional increments of aggregate spending begins to grow rapidly. If resources and labor are already near the point of full utilization, the added income stream will sharply increase the demand for investment goods and for additional labor. This effect is one of the reasons why conditions of full employment carry with them in most cases an inflationary potential.

The foregoing is not an argument against public works as a full-employment policy. Rather is it necessary to stress the limited macroeconomic impact of such measures in periods of severe unemployment and to caution against too great a reliance on the multiplier effect when the gross national product is far below full employment levels. While Keynes places great stress on the propensity to consume, the rate of investment is also very significant in his *General Theory of Employment, Interest and Money.*

Marginal Efficiency of Capital. This concept is used by Keynes as an analytical tool to find out what determines the rate of investment, which in turn is an important element in aggregate spending and, therefore, in levels of employment. The marginal efficiency of capital can be ascertained by comparing the hoped for yield of one more unit of capital with the cost of producing this increment. Obviously if the returns on this additional unit over a period of time would be less than these costs, the investment would not be undertaken. However, this relationship between prospective yields and current costs of investment is only one aspect of the factors which according to Keynes enter into the decision-making process.

Another factor is the rate of interest. Keynes asserts that ordinarily investment will be pushed to the point where "the marginal efficiency of capital in general is equal to the market rate of interest." This relationship has very important implications. If the interest rate is high then investment will be limited, because this point of equality between prospective yields of additional units of capital and of interest-bearing assets will be reached rather soon. On the other hand, if the interest rate is low, even comparatively low prospective yields of additional capital will seem to justify new investment. It follows that the interest rate assumes a strategic role in Keynes' *General Theory.* Whereas in the classical analysis a high rate of interest was assumed to increase the rate of saving and/or investment, in the new economics of Keynes such a high rate would have the effect of limiting investment. In this way employment would be curtailed because aggregate spending for investment goods would decline.

Speaking of prospective yields, Keynes is of course aware of the fact that they cannot be ascertained with great accuracy. For the understanding of the scope and the institutional frame of reference of Keynes' *General Theory*, it is important to discuss in some detail what he has to say about the possibility of assessing future yields. This Keynes has done in his highly interesting chapter on "Long-Term Expectation." Time and again he stresses in this part of his book the great difficulties of engaging in correct forecasts for a longer period of time. He speaks of the "extreme precariousness of the basis of knowledge" in this respect. Later on he states: "Investment based on genuine long-term expectation is so difficult today as to be scarcely practicable." In fact, Keynes shows sympathy for those who try to engage in long-run forecasts, and he says that actually such people run greater risks than those who try to "guess better than the crowd."

In all frankness it must be said that this brilliantly written chapter of the *General Theory* fails to draw a sharp line between two types of expectations. The first one about which Keynes has a great deal to say has to do with the valuations and the anticipations of development on the stock exchange. The second one would be the projections and estimates which enter into the deliberations of corporation executives when they make decisions with regard to new investment. It must be noted that fluctuations on the stock market leading to purchases or sales of securities have no direct bearing on aggregate spending and on levels of employment. On the other hand, investment decisions in the business sector have a great impact on the labor market. If investment expands in a period of near full employment, the multiplier effect will also be considerable. Keynes' skepticism with regard to the possibility of long-run forecasts and expectations is inconsistent with the methods and resources of decision making in the last third of the twentieth century.

So long as the economy was operating in a close approximation to the perfectly competitive model, long-run expectations were indeed difficult to formulate. A good deal of the investment undertaken under such conditions falls into the category of risk taking. The immediate market situation may have given a stimulus to such investment decisions but it contained few cues with regard to the development over longer periods of time. The horizon of entrepreneurs was predominantly microeconomic, the macro situation was not easily discernible.

The actual economic system has moved far away from this frame of reference. A large part of aggregate investment is made by a small number of giant enterprises. Decision-making procedures in such corporations have been formalized and are based on careful research utilizing modern tools such as computers. Projections are available fifteen years ahead on such important underlying factors as population, family formation, and the labor force. Technological progress has added a great deal of "hardware" to national defense. Since World War II the government in the United States has been the largest customer of American industry. Scheduled public expenditures for procurement of products of industry may have intensified competition among very large firms for the awarding of contracts, sometimes running into several billions of dollars. But these expenditure plans are also a guide for investment decisions. These are influenced by write-off provisions of corporate income tax laws and other deductible outlays, such as company pension plans.

Most important, however, is the fact that a great deal of corporate investment is carried out through self-financing. Funds building up within the corporation are used to a large extent to increase investment. The aggregate rate of investment is therefore neither limited by nor dependent upon the rate of saving in the household sector of the economy. If all these factors are taken into account it can be seen easily that an investment decision today is not based, as Keynes assumed, on comparisons between prospective yields of additional units of capital and the market rate of interest, but on longer-term assessments of the growth potential of the market for which the firm is producing goods and services. Here we come face-to-face with an important aspect of investment. The expectation of growth leading to investment can actually generate further growth. In this sense there is a certain feedback effect of investment once the system becomes dominated by large-scale enterprises that have obtained a great deal of independence from the money market and especially from the savings of individuals.

To complete this analysis it is necessary to stress that the ability of corporations to change from external to internal financing is a side effect of the imperfectly competitive market structure of an advanced industrialized system. The prices charged to the consumer contain a markup which is large enough to secure monetary surpluses to enterprises, out of which a good deal of investment and of expansion can be paid. If there were a more perfect competition, it can be assumed that prices would be lower and that, in order to engage in new investment, corporations would have to rely far more on outside financing. Such a state of affairs might actually be more desirable, but it simply does not exist. A theory of employment with claims toward applicability in a contemporary system cannot choose a model composed of desirable, preferable, or past features of a market structure. It must incorporate into its analytical scheme those features which characterize the ongoing system rather than an idealized situation. This methodological problem is also apparent in Keynes' third variable.

The Rate of Interest. Keynes has made a great contribution to the contemporary theory of interest. However, he overrated the role that the rate of interest plays in the investment sector of the modern economic system. The gist of his argument is that if interest rates are kept low, and if credit is abundant, investment will be encouraged. Actually, interest rates were kept low in the 1930's and there was an abundance of credit. However, with the exception of the year 1937, the rate of investment remained very low. This was because of the availability of existing unused production capacity, which permitted an immediate expansion of output to meet increased demand. Just as the multiplier has low effectiveness when unemployment is widespread, a low interest rate will not stimulate investment when there is unused production capacity.

The purpose of the preceding critical analysis of Keynes' three independent variables was to bring out the fact that the economic structure which they imply has undergone profound changes. It seems that the body of thought and policy prescription known as Keynesian economics or the aggregate spending approach to full employment operates with the idea that the basic propositions of Keynes' general theory are not bound up with the implied economic model used by him. It is, therefore, necessary to state what Keynesian economics practically means today quite apart from the original frame of reference of the originator of this school of thought.

12-4. SOME FURTHER REFLECTIONS ON KEYNESIAN ECONOMICS

The main characteristic of Keynesian economics is the macroeconomic approach, emphasizing the huge aggregates of the economic system and the gross national product. The level of activity in these sectors and the interaction created by it generate aggregate spending. Employment is considered a function of spending in a very precise way. That is, employment is expected to rise with an increase in spending and to drop as aggregate expenditures decline. Hence in Keynesian economics the main emphasis is on the maintenance and, if necessary, the increase in the rate of spending. This has led to radical departures from traditional thinking, especially in the field of public finance or the government sector of the GNP.

In the United States and in many other advanced countries the government sector comprises as least 20 percent of the GNP. In this way it has become a powerful lever for the stimulation of economic activities. This is particularly true with regard to the aggregate rate of spending. If there are signs that the income stream generated in the consumer and in the investment sector is weakening, the public sector can be used to counteract this trend by a corresponding rise of its share in the gross national product. The flow of payments going out from government can be increased by additional procurement from industry, by public works, by larger appropriations for public housing and road building, by additional outlays for resource development—especially water—and by an expansion of programs operating in the poverty sector of the economy.

The main point is that the funds for this increased activity must not be taken away from the consumer and the investment sector. They must be injected additionally into the aggregate income stream. For this reason, deficit financing is one of the most important aspects of Keynesian economics. While most economists prior to Keynes viewed deficit financing with alarm and felt that at least in the short run some additional unemployment might be preferable to such dangerous financial tactics that might jeopardize the soundness of money, most economists today have accepted deficit financing as one of the main *fiscal* weapons against unemployment. Lowering interest rates and easing credit are the main *monetary* techniques suggested by Keynes and his followers.

Keynesian economics does not confine its policy prescriptions to the public sector. Even if large-scale additional public expenditures, as described in the preceding paragraph are not contemplated, additional aggregate spending might be generated in the consumer and in the investment sector through tax cuts. Again, if this unbalances public budgets, it will be viewed with equanimity. A lessening of the tax burden on consumers is expected to increase the aggregate rate of spending in that sector. Similarly, cuts in the corporate income tax, perhaps combined with a liberalizing of write-off provisions, are designed to raise the rate of investment to a higher level. It is argued that the additional income stream generated by this tax relief will actually offset a lowering of government revenues because of the general increase in income. In this way it is felt that government has a number of instruments in hand which can be used separately or jointly to assure a level of employment consistent with the full-employment goals of contemporary industrialized society.

To this "spending approach" to full employment no problem of contemporary economics seems to present major difficulties, even in relation to automation. Professor Paul A. Samuelson in the eighth edition of his celebrated and much translated *Economics*[3] gives a careful analysis of technological unemployment. Very significantly this problem is treated in Chapter 18, which gives a "Synthesis of Monetary Analysis and Income Analysis." Here Samuelson deplores the "backward looking" concept of technological unemployment. While the impact of technology was completely outside the intent and scope of Keynes' *General Theory*, Keynesian economics are nevertheless brought in by Samuelson to deal with automation. It is all very simple. True enough, workers will be displaced by automation. But instead of merely deploring this result of technological progress we are asked to consider the following question: "Regardless of why those men lost their jobs, why aren't there enough *new* jobs for them? What fiscal and monetary policies are needed to create the new dollar purchasing power necessary for them to be hired anew?"

[3]P. A. Samuelson, *Economics*, 8th ed. (New York: McGraw-Hill Book Company, 1970). It was announced in 1965 that this standard text was being translated into Russian.

Professor Samuelson proceeds to supply us with the answer in terms of the aggregate spending approach. The analysis is bolstered by graphical demonstrations of the workings of these policies. It is assumed that labor-saving inventions raise productivity 30 percent. This in turn will generate large-scale unemployment. But unemployment can be warded off by an expansionary monetary policy, increasing income at a rate sufficiently large to create additional demand in such a volume that the workers displaced by automation will find new jobs. It must be assumed that this monetary remedy can be repeated time and again whenever a new wave of technological progress rises. By implication it must also be assumed that an even stronger dose of income injection would take care of the situation if automation—that is, a sharp drop in labor requirements per output—coincides with a substantial increase in the labor force. We are told that such considerations, which might even lead to the concept of "structural unemployment" are completely out of line with the new economics. Actually, we find in these teachings a new type of "Say's law." Whereas Say did maintain that in the long run the factor payments supplied the income for the full employment of the factors, including labor, Keynesian economics maintains that additional aggregate spending will guarantee full employment at all times, no matter what changes might occur in the structure of the economy.

This widely accepted Keynesian approach is based on very simple assumptions. Samuelson in his analysis of the effects of automation implies that there is a linear relationship between the rate of spending and the rate of employment. Furthermore, it extends the accounting concept that all GNP expenditures are factor payments to an analysis of the relation between aggregate spending as accounted for in the GNP and employment. Thus it is said that whenever spending increases, employment increases, and if spending increases fast enough and high enough there cannot be any unemployment other than seasonal and frictional.

Propositions of such magnitude and significance require a critical reappraisal. If we want to become thoroughly convinced of the practicability of the Keynesian approach in the last third of the twentieth century, we cannot be content to accept without reexamination propositions that emerged in the first third of this fast-moving period. Accordingly we must also examine the problems of full employment outside the context of Keynesian economics. The new economics of Keynes and his followers operate in a macroframework. It deals in aggregates, their interrelations and the impact of changes such as the rate of interest, levels of spending and of savings. But the fundamental data of the system, such as man-power requirements and the structure of demand for labor and of the labor force are considered as given. There is no consideration of structural transformations. All this leads to the conclusion that this type of employment theory is macrostatic. We have seen however that this does not come to grips with the problems of accelerated change and growth of economic systems in the last third of the twentieth century. They must be analyzed within the framework of a macrodynamic analysis. We will now proceed to outline this approach.

SELECTED BIBLIOGRAPHY

Hobson, John A. *The Economics of Unemployment* (London: George Allen & Unwin, Ltd., 1929).

Keynes, John M. *The General Theory of Employment, Interest and Money* (New York: Harcourt, Brace and World, Inc., 1965).

Leijonhyfvud, Axel. *On Keynesian Economics and the Economics of Keynes: A Study in Monetary Theory* (New York: Oxford University Press, 1968).

Lekachman, Robert, ed. *Keyne's General Theory: Reports of Three Decades* (New York: St. Martin's Press, 1964).

Murad, Anatol. *What Keynes Means* (New York Bookman Associates, 1962).

Pigou, A. C. *The Theory of Unemployment* (London: Macmillan & Company, Ltd., 1933).

————. *Employment and Equilibrium* (London: Macmillan & Company, Ltd., 1949).

QUESTIONS FOR DISCUSSION

1. Discuss the pre-Keynesian business-cycle theories from the point of view of their role in the development of a theory of employment.

2. What role did Wesley C. Mitchell and the N.B.E.R. have in the development of a more complete understanding of business cycles, and of what could be done to eliminate them or reduce their impact?

3. What were Ricardo's basic views on the question of technological unemployment?

4. In our contemporary society, what is your view concerning the impact of technological unemployment resulting from automation?

5. What is the great contribution to modern economics which J. M. Keynes made in his celebrated *General Theory*?

6. While the gist of the *General Theory* can be explained in terms of a relatively small number of technical relationships, much of what Keynes said was related to intangible concepts such as expectations and consumer-business psychology. Is this a realistic approach, and do such considerations add to the value of the *General Theory*?

7. Evaluate the traditional "spending approach" to full employment in our present day system.

8. In light of your answer to the above question, can increased government spending and tax adjustments, (Keynes' principal policy recommendations) be expected to maintain at least tolerable levels of employment despite the dynamic nature of our economic institutions?

Chapter

13

A Macrodynamic Analysis
of Employment

In our study of contemporary problems of employment and unemployment in Chapter 10 we saw that in the 1930's unemployment remained at least three times as high as it was in the first half of the 1960's, when it averaged roughy 5 percent of the labor force. These high levels of unemployment which continued even at the peak of prosperity in 1937 seemed to indicate that some structural changes of the economy were in progress, interfering with the assumed ability of the market system to eliminate cyclical unemployment in the course of the business upturn. In those days unemployment that could not be absorbed even at the peak of business activities was called "structural unemployment." The concept of "chronic unemployment" was also used.

In more recent years, when actual conditions were much closer to full employment, the concept of structural unemployment has undergone a certain change. Now it is applied to a situation in which certain segments of the labor supply remain unemployed because they do not fit into the highly differentiated and upgraded job structure. However, we have already seen in Chapter 10 that the projected growth of the American labor force until 1975 creates not only qualitative problems of fitting segments of labor supply into an upgraded system of employment but also a quantitative challenge to the goal of full employment due to the rapid rise in the number of new workers.

Moreover, we have noted in Chapter 12 that Keynesian economics proposes to deal with the problem of unemployment, no matter what its cause may be, by stepping up the rate of spending. From this point of view structural unemployment is a "false problem." One is reminded of a similar treatment given to "involuntary unemployment." Neoclassical economists simply dismissed this problem, it did not fit into the framework of their system. True, structural unemployment does not fit into the framework of Keynesian economics. However, it does exist as a very real problem in advanced industrialized systems. In Western Europe it has not come to the fore due to war-induced labor shortages, a general stepping up of consumer and investment spending, and a catching up with material standards already achieved in the United States. In this country, however, structural unemployment is a problem that has to be faced. It can be pinned down only with the analytical tools of macrodynamics. This body of theory deals with longer-run changes of the economic system. In the course of these dynamic trends significant changes occur in the demand for labor and in the relation between total aggregate income and levels of employment. Unless these facts are brought into the framework of research and theory, economics will not be able to come to grips with the challenge posited by structural unemployment. The fact that in the United States full employment levels were reached in terms of the 4 percent criterion in 1966, does not relieve us of the need to inquire into the conditions which in a highly advanced industrialized country must prevail to maintain this equilibrium on the labor market. The analysis carried out in subsequent sections of this chapter will show that full employment in such an advanced system is predicated on rates of growth, which far exceed what had been considered sufficient only a few years ago; and that a mere stepping up of aggregate spending is running into diminishing responses as far as employment is concerned.

13-1. BASIC ASPECTS OF MACRODYNAMICS

The new economics of the first part of this century restored aggregate, macroeconomic analysis to its full significance. A major achievement of this newly awakened interest in the system as a whole and in its sectors was the development of the concept of the gross national product. It enabled government agencies in many parts of the world to start publishing regularly GNP series and detailed gross national product accounts. It is hard to see how professional economics could be practiced today without this basic type of information; the contemporary economist finds it difficult to visualize how his predecessors in earlier generations could do without it.

Furthermore the tracing back of these series to 1929 in the United States has made it possible to analyze with greater precision than ever before the development of the system, the rate of growth, and the interaction between the various sectors of the economy. But macroeconomics becomes macrodynamics only when an attempt is being made to establish a systematic set of concepts dealing with the impact of long-run changes on various sectors of the economy and on the system as a whole. In other words, the factors which Keynes considered as "given" [1] must be examined in their

---

[1] See Sec. 12-3.

various processes of change, and the impact this has on their relation to each other, on the various sectors of the economy, and last but not least on the labor market. In macrodynamics such profound changes as the size of the labor force, the change in unit labor requirements, and the impact of new inventions, products, and services must be brought into economic analysis. This leads to a determination of an equilibrium growth rate which is the expression of the annual entry of new workers into the labor force and of the rise in productivity of labor, measured in output per man-hour. This is also rising each year. In the 1950's there was vast agreement among economists that these variables—growing labor force and productivity—established the need for the economy to grow by about 3.4 percent per annum. In the 1960's the same variables seemed to require an annual growth rate of about 4.3 percent.

Figure 13-1, taken from the Economic Report of the President, Janu-

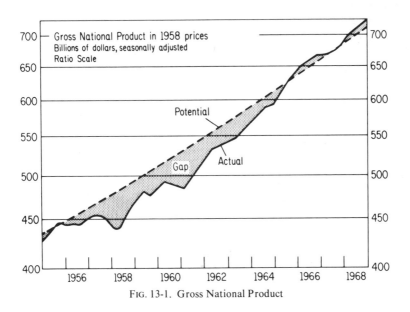

FIG. 13-1. Gross National Product

ary 1969, shows that up to 1965 the actual development of the gross national product fell short of the full employment equilibrium path represented in that figure by the dotted lines. It is highly significant that in 1966, after the vast escalation of the military effort in Viet Nam the actual GNP was going slightly beyond the dynamic equilibrium path. When the two lines intersected, unemployment fell below 4 percent so that a condition of full employment prevailed in the United States. In the years preceding 1965 there was a sometimes considerable gap between the equilibrium growth potential of the American economy and its actual performance thereby generating, especially in 1957 and 1961 unemployment rates close to 7 percent of the labor force. One problem of employment theory and policy is to provide analytical tools and policy prescriptions to avoid a recurrence of such a gap once a shift in national resource allocation from defense to nondefense projects is decided upon. This does not envisage a complete cessation of defense expenditures but their returns to levels of the 1950's. In order to clarify the structures underlying these issues it is necessary to state employment theory and policy within the framework of a macrodynamic theory.

Macrodynamics is concerned with rates of change. Dynamic equilibrium may be said to prevail whenever the various rates of change interact in such a way that the system maintains a reasonable condition of full employment as it moves into a higher level of activity brought about by additions to the labor force and to the productivity of labor. These two variables have played an important role in macrodynamic theory. We present first the basic model worked out by R. F. Harrod[2] because it has become fundamental in contemporary macrodynamic theory.

Using G to indicate a growth in production over the preceding period and C to represent an increase in capital, Harrod sets up the following statement:

$$GC = s$$

where s is the fraction of the income saved. To accommodate either a Keynesian situation whereby savings increase as income rises, or a more traditional view linking savings to the rate of interest, Harrod confines himself to stating that s is the *fraction* of the income saved. If we think of this basic dynamic theorem as representing a time series, then we have here in simple terms a definitional equation of a continuously expanding economic system. Since the base GC is larger in each subsequent period, generating a higher addition to income, s also has to increase. In the next round this increase leads to a further rise in GC, and so on.

It is necessary now to relate this simple statement of a dynamic system to actual growth factors. Naturally the national income Y is bound to increase as a result of the continuous increase in capital. But this does not yet answer the question of the relation between this general growth model to the behavior of growth factors. Unlike the aggregate-spending approach discussed in the preceding chapter, the macrodynamic analysis of unemployment must try to relate in a most specific way processes of economic growth to the structure of the labor market, in relation to both demand for labor and supply of labor.

Harrod takes into account two growth factors: the increase in the labor force and the increase in productivity. Domar has contributed the con-

---

[2] R. F. Harrod, *Towards a Dynamic Economics* (London: Macmillan, 1952).

cept of the capital output ratio to this analysis so that very often reference is made to the "Harrod-Domar model." We will see later in this chapter how this can be used to make projections of employment and unemployment. We will also observe that the concept of growth required for the maintenance of full employment implied in this model is no longer adequate to deal with the dynamic problems of the American economy. But in order to understand why this is the case, it is necessary to go into a further discussion of Harrod's concepts of growth.

13-2. CONCEPTS OF ECONOMIC GROWTH

In the spending approach to full employment, emphasis is placed on an increase in aggregate expenditures large enough to eliminate unemployment. These expenditures, of course, will bring about an increase in Y. In macrodynamic analysis an attempt is made to relate in a most specific way the growth factors to the gross national product. A rising labor force and increased productivity bring about proportionate growth of the economic system if adequate managerial know-how and monetary institutions are available.

If the rate of growth of the national income corresponds exactly to the rate required by the dynamics of population and of productivity, Harrod speaks of a natural rate of growth n. It is now significant that Harrod does not assume that business decisions leading to an increase in C will coincide with this natural growth rate. He establishes a second concept of growth, the warranted rate, or increase in investment which seems to be the optimal rate from the viewpoint of maximizing the profits of enterprises. Harrod indicates that here the possibility of an underemployment equilibrium can develop. The implication is that the rate of investment considered satisfactory by the decision makers in the private sector may be insufficient from the viewpoint of a dynamic equilibrium on the labor market. There is also the possibility under certain circumstances for the warranted rate of growth to exceed the natural rate. This excess could occur in the most hectic phases of a business boom. Actually this did happen in Europe in the early 1960's, forcing governments to adopt restrictions on investment in order, as it was said, to "take the heat out of the boom."

The assumption of Harrod that there is usually a divergence between natural and warranted growth has particular validity for an economic structure in which decision making has been diffused in many sectors in large enterprises accounting for a major share in output, sales, and employment of the whole industry. For these firms, break-even points are very low. Satisfactory profits can be obtained even if actual production is far from the output potential of existing productive capacity.

In order to refine the concepts of growth in macrodynamics it is necessary to distinguish between various structures of growth more precisely than was done by Harrod. The structure of growth, without which there cannot be any increase in employment, varies with the type of competition prevailing in a given market. Obviously, growth structures differ widely for the cases of centralized planning of growth targets as in the Soviet Union or of decentralized planning on the micro scale even if that happens to be a very large one in the case of big enterprise.[3]

In a market characterized by small or medium-sized enterprises with a limited public sector and little macroeconomic information, businesses can survive only if they can adjust themselves continuously to new least-cost combinations made possible by the advance of technology. It is in this way that increased labor productivity asserts itself. The rate of interest and profit expectations plays a great role in that market structure. In fact, the Keynesian analysis, although static in its frame of reference, applies to what actually happens in the dynamics of growth of a more or less perfectly competitive system. Under such conditions there is a large decentralization of decision making in the investment sector. Ideally, all these innumerable decisions are made entirely independent of each other. Nobody talks about growth in this setting, but everybody is doing something about it. What results is a process of *"spontaneous growth."* In the short run this may result in plus or minus departures from *n*, but in the longer run the spontaneous growth pattern will be close to the natural growth rate.

As long as such a system is operating in a social environment in which growth factors dominate it will respond in a free, flexible manner to the stimuli they give to the rate of investment and thereby the increase in the national income. In this macrodynamic prospective, changes in investment are triggered not so much by changes in the interest rate but by profit expectations that are actually expectations of economic growth—of the ability to sell more in the future than in the past and the resulting decision to produce more than before. Inasmuch as in a perfectly competitive system production at any given time is always pushed to the limits of capacity, additional investment is the inevitable outcome of these profit and/or growth expectations. Small and medium-sized enterprises will be able to stay in business only if they can adapt to these general dynamic trends.

In our discussion of the concept of the marginal efficiency of capital[4] it was observed that the actual economic system with which a theory of employment has to deal does not correspond to the model of a perfectly competitive market. This fact has great implications for the structure of economic growth. In a system like that of the United States in the later decades of the twentieth century decision making involving large propor-

---

[3] A fuller discussion has been presented by the author in his *"Economic System Analysis: Concepts and Perspectives* (New York: Fordham University Press, 1960).

[4] See Sec. 12-3.

tions of total investment is concentrated with comparatively few firms. Furthermore, decisions with regard to expenditures made for purposes of procurement in the public sector have great influence on the general level of economic activity and on the national income itself. We have seen also that in order to obtain the funds necessary for investment, corporations look to an internal accumulation of profits after taxes more than to external sources. This removes much of the decision-making processes out of the context of the money market. The role of the interest rate in investment decisions is deemphasized.

A far more immediate confrontation takes place with the macrodynamic condition of the system—that is with its prospects of real growth in terms of potential consumers and in terms of output potentials and future unit labor cost. Investment decisions are no longer forced upon enterprises by short-run fluctuations on the market but by an assessment of long-run growth potentials. Budgets are set up for investment expenditures extending over several years. Whereas under a perfectly competitive market structure businesses have to adapt themselves to ongoing changes of the growth factors, the more concentrated pattern of decision making in an imperfectly competitive market leads to long-range, autonomous investment schedules. The time framework of these decisions is widened. They not only take into account the immediate situation but also projections of economic development based on estimates of rates of growth of the economic system.

Nor are these decisions confined to the private sector. Government programs subsidizing such types of investment as low-rent housing or highway construction are a response either to pressures of growth factors already in operation or an anticipation of the expanding exigencies of the years ahead. Furthermore, the public commitment to maintain maximum levels of employment will contribute toward this type of investment. With these structural changes in the private and public sectors the processes of growth themselves become subject to deliberate decision making. The pattern of growth that emerges is autonomous and conscious, rather than the conditioned-reflex type of business behavior linked to perfect competition and leading to spontaneous growth.

Deliberate expansion is the type of growth which characterizes the dynamics of advanced industrialized systems. It takes different forms. In the United States with its precarious situation on the labor market and the many pockets of poverty, the goal of full employment is continuously kept in mind and influences the interplay between investment and spending decisions in the private and in the public sectors. Since 1946 France has been operating under four-year plans. Goals for the buildup of productive capacity in basic industries, for housing and for other resources are being formulated. Within this overall plan, investment decisions of private and public economic institutions are falling in line—without, however, requiring formal centralized planning.

The distinction made here between spontaneous growth and deliberate expansion has great significance for a theory of employment. If we think of economic development only in terms of the first type of growth structure, then the theoretical effort will focus on ways how to trigger a new leap forward through such mechanisms as the rate of interest, changes in money supply, and similar devices—including tax cuts. If we have the deliberate expansion structure in mind, the horizon widens. Without discarding the instrumentalities of Keynesian economics, greater stress is placed on concrete, tangible goals of development to which expenditures and additional aggregate spending are to be directed in the public and in the private sector of the economy. These include problems of the aggregate income of those in the labor force and those outside, ways of raising the earning potential of low-income segments in the labor force, and programs for a continuous improvement in the urban environment and natural resources of an advanced industrialized society beset by the socioeconomic problems created by the "megalopolis." In order to bring out the macrodynamic problems of employment in our rapidly changing economic structure, we now present an analysis of the development of the labor market based on the work of Harrod, Domar, and others, including the present author.[5]

13-3. THE HARROD-DOMAR MODEL AND RECENT EXPERIENCE

We have shown above that Harrod's concept of natural growth makes allowance for the annual growth of the labor force and annual increase in labor productivity. The census data in most countries today permit a projection of the increase in the labor force over at least half a generation. This arises from the fact that children born at the time a census was taken will enter the labor force at the earliest sixteen years thence. If we take into account experience rates of withdrawal from the labor force due to retirement, death, marriage, and similar causes, an estimate of the annual net increase in the labor force can be made. Table 13-1 demonstrates the very different outlook with regard to labor force increases until 1970 in some leading countries. In absolute numbers this means that in the United States more than 7 million people were added to the labor force in a five-year period. On the other extreme, the labor force of the Federal Republic of Germany will have declined by 400,000 by 1970. Between 1970 and 1975

---

[5]Typical of this approach is the demonstration given by the author in his text in *Fundamentals of Labor Economics,* 2d ed. (New York: Fordham University Press, 1952), pp. 169ff.

TABLE 13-1
GROWTH IN THE LABOR FORCE 1950–70

Country	Average Annual Percent Changes			
	1950–55	1955–60	1960–64	Forecasts, 1965–70
United States	+1.2	+1.2	+1.3	+1.7
Japan..............	+3.7	+1.5	+1.1	+1.4
France............	+0.2	+0.02	+1.1	+0.7
Italy..............	+1.3	+1.2	−1.0	+0.3
Britain............	+0.8	+0.4	+0.8	+0.2
Germany	+2.0	+1.1	+0.2	−0.3

SOURCE: *New York Herald Tribune*, August 16, 1965.

the rate of growth of the labor force in the United States will continue at the 1.7 percent rate each year. It should be noted, however, that a certain downward revision of the labor force estimate for 1975 has taken place. Whereas at one time it was calculated to rise as high as 94.8 million, the 1965 *Manpower Report* projects the labor force for 1975 to be 93.6 million. Obviously a statistical revision of this type will make it easier to report approximations of full employment.

The second variable used by Harrod is productivity. The time has long since passed when it could be asserted with a straight face that productivity measurements are, if not impossible, highly unreliable.[6]

Actually output per man-hour and its reciprocal, unit labor requirements, are known to management as well as unit labor costs. They can also be ascertained approximately with the help of such data as indexes of agricultural, durable and nondurable goods output, and indexes of man-hours. In this way increases in productivity can be estimated with a good degree of confidence. Table 13-2 summarizes the findings of the Bureau of Labor Statistics.[7] The most striking increase in productivity as indicated in output per man-hour has taken place in agriculture. In this sector, productivity tripled in a fifteen-year period. It was 34.4 percent higher in 1964 than in the base period 1957–59. It should be noted that the agricultural labor force numbered 8.3 million in 1947 but shrank to 4.8 million in 1964. Total farm output rose at the same time (taking 1957–59 = 100) from an index of 81 in 1947 to 111 in 1964. Productivity in agriculture has risen much faster than output per man-hour in the industrial and the nonmanufacturing sector of the economy. It is in this sense that we

[6]An establishment study of a large steel company in Europe carried out in 1954 by the author of this text yielded a high degree of consistency between the microdata on labor productivity and published industry data on output per man-hour. See also *Journal of Economic Abstracts*, vol. 1, pp. 245ff.

[7]Bureau of Labor Statistics, "Trends in Output per Man-Hour in the Private Economy," Bulletin No. 1249.

TABLE 13-2
INDEX OF OUTPUT PER MAN-HOUR
(1957–59 = 100)

Year	Total Private	Farm	Nonfarm Industries		
			Total	Manufacturing	Non-manufacturing
1948	72.0	58.0	76.5	76.4	76.3
1949	74.2	56.5	79.5	79.3	79.6
1950	80.3	64.4	84.4	85.0	84.1
1951	82.7	64.7	86.3	86.9	85.6
1952	84.3	70.3	87.0	87.3	86.7
1953	87.8	79.6	89.6	90.2	88.6
1954	89.9	83.7	91.6	91.8	91.5
1955	93.9	84.4	95.7	97.2	94.7
1956	94.1	88.0	95.2	96.2	94.3
1957	96.9	93.3	97.2	98.2	96.7
1958	99.8	103.0	99.7	98.1	100.6
1959	103.4	104.8	103.1	103.7	102.9
1960	105.0	110.7	104.4	105.5	103.9
1961	108.6	119.4	107.4	107.9	107.4
1962	113.8	122.2	112.3	114.3	111.5
1963	117.9	133.1	115.7	118.9	114.3
1964	132.5	135.5	120.0	124.7	118.0
1965	126.6	148.1	123.6	129.8	120.5
1966	131.4	152.9	127.7	131.6	125.4
1967	133.5	171.7	129.0	132.5	127.1
1968	137.9	172.1	133.4	136.2	131.9

SOURCE: *Economic Report of the President* (January 1969), Table B-34.

speak of today's agricultural revolution, in which the United States is far ahead compared with other countries. Although increases in productivity in nonagricultural sectors are less striking, they are more significant because more people are involved. Output in manufacturing per man-hour rose by 30 index points since 1958. Total industrial production in 1968 was at 133.4 percent of the base period, whereas actual production in 1957 had been 98.2 percent. In 1957 total employment in manufacturing was 17.2 million. About the same level of employment was reached again in 1964 but at that time as can be seen in Table 13-2 output per man-hour had risen by 25 percent and the index of industrial production in manufacturing was 33 percent higher than it had been in 1957. Now between 1964 and 1968 output in manufacturing rose from 133.1 index points, based on 1957 to 1959 to 166.8. That is to say in these four years output in manufacturing almost doubled the rate of growth of the eight years prior to 1964, and increased by about 25 percent. Manufacturing employment also rose from 17.3 million in 1964 to 19.7 million in 1968. That means that a 25 percent increase in output was handled by an increase of employment of 15 percent.

This brief quantitative analysis shows the great impact that increases in output per man-hour, the second variable in the Harrod-Domar Model has on the employment of production workers. It must be understood, however, that the series shown in Table 13-2 are based on total employment, that is to say, they also include the nonproduction workers whose productivity gains are far less than those of production workers. In Sec. 13-4 we will take the transformation of the labor force into account. It must be worked into a macrodynamic concept of the rate of growth required for the maintenance of full employment as the labor force and productivity are continuing to rise year after year.

Using the revised labor-force projection for 1975 made by the Bureau of Labor Statistics and productivity data, the natural growth rate of the American economy was established as 4.2 percent per annum in that study. The actual growth rate for the period 1957–60 had been averaging only 2.5 percent per annum. Hence there was an accumulated growth lag when the protracted recovery period set in early in 1961. The spectacular jump of the GNP in the period 1961–62 of more than 6 percent and the above average rise in the GNP in the years 1963–64 were not sufficient to overcome the effects of the retardation in growth of the years between 1957 and 1961. Using 1964 dollars, the GNP ought to have reached a level of $658 billion in 1964 if the growth pattern had been according to the Harrod model. Actually this rate of GNP was reached only one year later—in the middle of 1965. This condition explains why for all years after 1961, despite what seemed to be a spectacular recovery of the American economy, unemployment remained somewhat higher than the 4 percent full-employment criterion with which we are operating in this text. Unemployment was substantially higher than the 4 percent concept employed by many economists, especially in government. No wonder that the aforementioned study projecting trends to 1975 pointed to the possibility of a doubling of the unemployment rate by that time.

This macrodynamic analysis shows clearly that the use of concepts derived from cycle theory, especially the terms "recession" and "recovery" have lost a good deal of their meaning. The actual condition of the economy of an advanced, industrialized country undergoing continuous structural changes, must be plotted against an equilibrium-growth path. Comparisons with past levels of activity while significant fail to reveal the real state of affairs.

Completely misleading, however, are attempts to set up growth models containing, for example, a constant growth factor *a* and other factors denoting increases in output *e* if these abstract numbers are then filled in, with historical data going back to the earlier part of this century yet assuming a continuation of this trend in the future. This kind of unrealistic assumption can lead to serious understatement of the equilibrium growth rate.[8]

Up to the early 1960's the Harrod model served fairly well as a measur-

---

[8]Paul E. Smith, "An Econometric Growth Model," *American Economic Review* (September 1963) projects the GNP for 1964 to $499.2 billion in 1954 dollars, whereas actually it was $515.7 billion. The error increases as we approach 1975 in the projection.

ing rod for equilibrium growth and it could be assumed that if the GNP in constant dollars increased at the "natural" rate, full employment could be maintained while the labor force and productivity continued to rise. In the next two sections we will show that structural changes in the American economy have created a new situation. In order to keep unemployment at the 4 percent level and to reduce large pockets of structural unemployment, the GNP now must be kept growing at rates exceeding the Harrod-Domar precepts.

13-4. SPENDING AND EMPLOYMENT

Keynesian economics is concerned with that rate of aggregate spending which it assumes is necessary to keep the economy at a full employment level. It does not spell out in detail what this rate must be. Macrodynamics operating with growth factors comes much closer to pinpointing the required rate of spending by relating it to real structural changes in the economy. In both approaches it is assumed that a fairly simple relationship exists between spending and employment. That is, whenever spending is increased, an increase in employment is to be expected. This was generally true before World War II as shown in Table 13-3. The development of the American economy has demonstrated that in recent years levels of employment have responded at an ever-decreasing rate to higher levels of spending. In fact, a stage seems to have been reached where the law of diminishing returns, which played such an important role in the economics of the past, is re-asserting itself. This time, however, the relationship is not occurring on the input-output scale but on the ratio between increases in spending and increases in employment. Until 1939 employment-spending ratios were close to the 1:1 ratio. This changed radically after 1947. These trends are shown in Tables 13-4 and 13.5.[9]

TABLE 13-3
EMPLOYMENT-SPENDING RATIO, 1929–39
(in 1958 dollars)

Year	GNP	Index	Employment	Index	E/S	S/E
1929	203.6	100.0	47,890	100.0	1.000	1.000
1930	183.5	90.1	45,740	95.5	1.059	.862
1931	169.3	83.1	42,660	89.1	1.072	.932
1932	144.2	70.8	39,190	81.8	1.155	.865
1933	141.5	69.4	39,000	81.5	1.174	.851
1934	154.3	75.7	41,550	85.9	1.134	.881
1935	169.5	83.2	42,530	88.8	1.067	.937
1936	193.0	94.7	44,710	93.4	.986	1.014
1937	203.2	99.8	46,620	97.3	.974	1.026
1938	192.9	94.7	44,560	93.0	.982	1.018
1939	209.4	102.8	46,120	96.3	.936	1.068

[9]"Aggregate Spending and Employment," Senior Research Project No. 7, Fordham College, Fall Term, 1964.

TABLE 13-4
EMPLOYMENT-SPENDING RATIO, 1947–57
(in 1958 dollars)

Year	GNP	Index	Employment	Index	E/S	S/E
1947	309.0	100.0	58,630	100.0	1.000	1.000
1948	323.7	104.4	59,800	101.9	.976	1.024
1949	324.7	104.5	59,266	101.0	.966	1.035
1950	355.3	114.6	60,570	103.3	.901	1.109
1951	383.4	123.7	63,062	107.5	.869	1.150
1952	395.1	127.4	63,848	108.8	.854	1.170
1953	412.8	133.2	64,728	110.4	.828	1.207
1954	407.0	131.3	63,460	105.9	.806	1.240
1955	438.0	141.3	65,220	111.2	.786	1.272
1956	446.1	143.9	66,659	113.6	.789	1.267
1957	452.5	146.0	66,871	114.0	.780	1.282

Although the period 1929–39 shows employment-spending ratios and their reciprocal, spending-employment ratios, close to unity, it is interesting to note that between 1929 and 1933 the GNP dropped to a far greater extent than employment. On the other hand, between 1936 and 1939 the GNP rose at a faster rate than the levels of employment. Although the GNP in constant dollars was 4.2 percent higher in 1939 than in 1929, employment failed to return to the level of that year. Nevertheless the relation between changes in employment and changes in spending as they operated in the 1930's justified the assumption that generally a linear functional relationship exists between spending and employment. This lent substance to the aggregate-spending approach to employment which is still so widely used in our times. While the rate of spending is of great significance for the level of employment, it is, however, necessary to examine the employment spending ratios of the more recent past. This study will bring out the problems we have to face in formulating policies for full employment in the late 1960's and in the 1970's.

During the period 1947–57, shown in Table 13-4, there were slight drops in employment in 1949 and in 1952 and 1954. However, these declines do not compare in severity to the decline in employment shown in the previous table. Only once was there a decline in the GNP—in the period 1953–54. This decline also led to substantial drop in employment by 1.2 million wage and salary earners. What is of overriding importance, however, is the fact that the gross national product in constant dollars rose by 46.1 percent in this ten-year period, whereas employment rose only by 14.2 percent.

The employment-spending ratios 1947–57 show that there was a continuous drop to less than unity. Additional doses of spending did bring about less than proportionate increases in employment. The last column of Table 13–4 represents the spending-employment ratio, which rose far above unity, going from 1.000 in 1947 to 1.279 in 1957. In the period 1947 to 1948 an increase of $13 billion in the GNP in 1963 dollars resulted in an increase of employment of 1.1 million. In 1952–53 an increase in the GNP of 19.3 billion brought about an increase in employment of less than one million wage and salary earners. We see from this analysis that the pattern of relations between employment and spending began to change radically after World War II, as compared to what there had been at the time when Keynesian economics, with its undifferentiated emphasis on aggregate spending, had gained ascendancy. The year 1957 is regarded by many as a good year in which acceptable levels of full employment prevailed in the United States. There was a sharp drop in employment in 1958, primarily in manufacturing. Since then employment did rise but, as shown in Table 13-5,

TABLE 13-5
EMPLOYMENT-SPENDING RATIO, 1957–67
(in 1958 dollars)

Year	GNP	Index	Employment	Index	E/S	S/E
1957	452.5	100.0	66,871	100.0	1.000	1.000
1958	447.3	98.9	65,672	98.2	.992	1.007
1959	475.9	105.2	67,182	100.4	.954	1.047
1960	487.7	107.8	68,292	102.1	.947	1.055
1961	497.2	109.9	68,318	102.1	.929	1.076
1962	529.8	117.1	69,530	103.9	.887	1.127
1963	551.0	121.8	70,500	105.4	.865	1.155
1964	581.1	128.4	72,044	107.7	.838	1.192
1965	616.7	136.2	73,818	110.3	.809	1.234
1966	652.6	144.2	76,018	113.6	.787	1.269
1967	669.2	147.8	77,818	116.3	.786	1.270

more and more spending in constant dollars is required to bring about an increase in employment.

The years after 1961 have been characterized by high annual rates of growth in aggregate spending. They were above the natural growth rate indicated by the Harrod model. Nevertheless, they barely sufficed to absorb the increase in the labor force. They did not push down levels of unemployment to a point at which pockets of persistent joblessness or poverty could have been reduced to a large degree. To clarify these relations further, sectional studies of the relations between aggregate expenditures and employment were carried out in the research project mentioned in footnote 9.

Using data from the *Survey of Current Business* released by the Department of Commerce and of *Employment and Earnings*, and issued by the Department of Labor, it is possible to analyze the relation between personal consumption expenditures for specific times and employment in the industries producing these items.

Between 1957 and 1963 consumer expenditures for new and used cars rose by 18 percent. Employment dropped by 4.5 percent;[10] aggregate spend-

---

[10] The source of this data is the Senior Research Project No. 7 cited in footnote 9.

ing for radio and television receivers rose during that period by 31.7 percent but employment was down by 3.2 percent. Consumer expenditures for toys and sporting supplies rose by almost 30 percent during that period but employment dropped by 10 percent. Even if we consider that a certain proportion of toys, radios, and automobiles are imported from abroad, the discrepancy between increases in spending and in employment remains striking. Consumer expenditures for clothing rose by more than 10 percent between 1957 and 1963, while employment dropped by 7 percent. Almost similar ratios can be found in cleaning, dyeing, and laundering.

We see that increases in aggregate spending in general and in particular sectors are not necessarily accompanied by increases in employment. On the contrary, a rise in demand and output may actually coincide with a decrease in employment, or at best a less-than-proportionate rise in the number of wage and salary earners. Using the conventional aggregate-spending approach to employment it seems that the ratios shown in the preceding three tables strongly indicate that the increase in expenditures was too small and that the spending-employment ratio, shown as the last column of these tables, could yield a clue as to the extent to which aggregate spending should have been increased above its actual rise in the period between 1957 and 1963. If we take into account the actual development since 1947, we are led to the conclusion that the rate of growth of the GNP itself must be increasing each year in order to maintain full employment. The growth rate changes from a linear to an exponential function as is implied in Harrod's basic dynamic theorem as explained in Sec. 13-3.

Annual increases in productivity which are one of the variables of the Harrod theorem reflect over the long run changes in the composition of the labor force especially the ratio between production and nonproduction workers. Table 13-6 will show the development.

Table 13-6 shows the steady shift away from production workers to white-collar employment. Most dramatic is the steady decline in farm

TABLE 13-6
TRANSFORMATION OF THE LABOR FORCE 1958–1967

Year	Total Employment	White-collar	Blue-collar	Service Workers	Farm Workers
1958	100.0	42.6	37.1	11.9	8.5
1959	100.0	42.7	37.1	11.9	8.2
1960	100.0	43.4	36.6	12.2	7.8
1961	100.0	43.9	36.0	12.6	7.5
1962	100.0	44.4	36.1	12.6	7.0
1963	100.0	44.2	36.6	12.8	6.5
1964	100.0	44.5	36.5	12.8	6.1
1965	100.0	44.8	36.9	12.6	5.7
1966	100.0	45.4	37.0	12.6	5.0
1967	100.0	46.0	36.7	12.5	4.8

SOURCE: *Manpower Report of the President* (April 1968), Table A-9.

employment relative to all the other categories of work. While the share of service workers increased from 11.9 to 12.5 percent in the period 1958 to 1967, white-collar workers, subdivided into professional and technical, managers, officials and proprietors, clerical workers and sales workers increased their share from 42.6 percent of the employed persons to 46.0 percent. Within the subdivisions enumerated above, the growth was concentrated in the groups of professional and technical employees and of clerical workers whereas there was a slight decline in the share of managers and sales workers in total white collar employment. In absolute numbers we find that white-collar employment increased in this period by 7.4 million whereas blue-collar employment increased only by 3.8 million. It should be noted that a substantial proportion of this rise was concentrated in the period from 1964 to 1967 and is associated with the stepping up of defense expenditures.

Now these transformations and realignments within the structure of the labor force do have an influence on the determination of the growth rate of the system necessary to maintain full employment as the labor force and the productivity of workers is rising year after year. As the transformation of the labor force shown in Table 13-6 continues and as the shift from blue-collar to white-collar employment becomes ever more pronounced, it is necessary to ascertain the differentials in productivity increases as they are occurring in the blue-collar and in the white-collar sector of the economy. Table 13-7 shows that as the G.N.P. has risen by 47.8 percent be-

TABLE 13-7
INDEXES OF G.N.P. BLUE-COLLAR AND WHITE-COLLAR
EMPLOYMENT BASED ON 1957 = 100

Year	G.N.P.	Total Employment	Blue-collar	White-collar
1957	100.0	100.0	100.0	100.0
1958	98.9	98.2	93.8	101.4 (!)
1959	105.2	100.4	96.5	104.2
1960	107.8	102.1	96.7	107.8
1961	109.9	103.9	95.2	109.1
1962	117.1	104.3	96.6	112.0
1963	121.8	105.4	99.6	113.2
1964	128.4	107.7	101.4	116.6
1965	136.2	110.3	105.5	120.4
1966	144.2	113.6	108.3	125.0
1967	147.8	116.3	109.5	129.4

SOURCE: Derived from various tables of *The Manpower Report of the President* (1968), and *Economic Report of the President* (1968).

tween 1957 and 1967, total employment increased only by 16.3 percent. This indicates a substantial rise in productivity for the labor force as a whole of roughly 3 percent per annum. However, a separate study of blue- and of white-collar employment shows that the latter rose much faster than the former. This means that within an aggregate macroeconomic rise in productivity, there are vast differentials between the blue-collar and the white-collar sector.

It is apparent that a breakdown of spending-employment ratios for blue-collar and for white-collar workers must show a far steeper rise for production workers than for nonproduction workers. This will be shown in Table 13-8.

TABLE 13-8
SPENDING EMPLOYMENT RATIOS, TOTAL, BLUE-COLLAR AND WHITE-COLLAR
1957–1967 (In current dollars)

Year	Total Employment S/E	Blue-collar S/E	White-collar S/E
1957	1.000	1.000	1.000
1958	1.025	1.081	1.000
1959	1.087	1.135	1.051
1960	1.112	1.179	1.058
1961	1.149	1.314	1.133
1962	1.219	1.303	1.181
1963	1.265	1.423	1.237
1964	1.334	1.469	1.278
1965	1.397	1.555	1.348
1966	1.481	1.624	1.374
1967	1.534	1.757	1.447

SOURCE: See Table 13-7.

Table 13-8 shows clearly that the equilibrium growth rate of the system as a whole cannot be determined merely by increases in productivity of blue-collar workers. Projections based on production worker productivity alone would lead to an overstatement of the growth requirements of the economy. In such projections it is necessary to consider the blue- to white-collar shift which is likely to occur in the period for which the projection is being made. It is estimated that by 1975 only 32.3 percent of employment will be in the goods-producing industries outside of agriculture and 67.7 percent will be in service-producing industries. Now we can see from Table 13-8 that in order to increase employment in the nonproduction sector a much lower rise in spending is required than in the blue-collar sector. It follows that the macroeconomic growth rate must be a reflection of the steadily increasing gap between the blue-collar and the white-collar spending employment ratios. A projection of these ratios, shown in Table 13-8, to 1975, shows that in that year on the basis of 1957 equal to 1.000 the white-collar S-E ratio would be 2.060 and the blue-collar S-E ratio would be 2.603.[11] Obviously if the blue-collar S-E ratio would be applied to the economy as a whole the projected G.N.P. for 1975 even in constant dollars,

[11]Based on Senior Research Project No. 11, Fordham University, Fall 1968.

allowing merely for a noninflationary price increase of 2 percent per annum would be vastly overstated; by the same token the white-collar spending employment ratio as such would lead to an understatement even while the white-collar sector is continuing to expand.

It is necessary, therefore, to deflate the blue-collar spending employment ratio by a factor representing the slower growth of the white-collar ratio on the one side and the projected increase in white-collar employment on the other.

Such a refinement of the variable factor "productivity" in the Harrod formula enables us to make a projection for the growth rate required for full employment which takes into account the clearly forseeable labor force transformation. Using this method the G.N.P. in 1975 would be in excess of 1.3 trillion dollars in terms of the purchasing power of 1968.

This means that the annual growth rate would have to be more than 7 percent in real terms in order to satisfy the spending employment ratios of the blue-collar and of the white-collar sector of the economy. Although there will be no further "labor force explosion" in the 1970's, the continuous increase in productivity and realignment of the labor force forces the economy into this dynamic growth structure.

13-5. ASPECTS AND IMPLICATIONS OF ACCELERATED GROWTH

We have seen in the preceding sections of this chapter that contemporary employment theory must not be placed only into a macroeconomic context, it must operate within the framework of macrodynamics. Maintenance of full employment requires a continuous rise in aggregate spending. The analysis carried out in Sections 13-3 and 13-4 enables us to spell out what growth rates must prevail in order to assure a continued operation of the economy at levels of full employment.

Let us return for a moment to Figure 13-1. There we saw that in the first years of the 1960's the American economy was growing but not at the rate which was required to assure a 96 percent rate of employment. If this less than equilibrium growth rate would have continued for the rest of the decade, there would have been a further increase in unemployment. Actually between 1966 and 1969 the American economy has operated on the equilibrium growth path and unemployment dropped to less than 4 percent of the labor force. Now it is necessary to realize that this performance was not the result of a deliberate policy designed to place the American economy on the full employment growth path. It was brought about by a "random" or—to use a Schumpeterian concept—exogenous factor which pushed the American economy on this line. Vastly increased spending for national defense, on top of the long run growth factors accounts largely for the prevalence of full employment in the late 1960's. It is necessary to see this clearly and to consider in a more general way the implications for economic theory and policy which can be gathered from this type of economic development. Over the years manpower reports of the President have given valuable information on the impact of the defense expenditures on employment and investment. Even prior to the stepping-up of the war in Vietnam in 1965 the employment resulting from government purchases of goods and services in private industry was of considerable proportion. Generally employment in private industry resulting from federal purchase of goods and services was way over 3 million workers a year from 1962 to 1966. Total employment military and civilian originating with the Federal Government rose from 5.1 million in 1962 to 6.2 million in 1969. Whereas the Armed Forces had been kept at an almost constant level of 2.7 million men in the early 1960's, in 1969 the Armed Forces were 800,000 men larger than in the preceding year. Inasmuch as the military is part of the labor force every increase in the Armed Forces is bringing about a corresponding decrease in the labor force of the civilian sector or at least it reduces the increase in the civilian labor force and therefore levels of unemployment.

The full effects of the increase in outlays for the Vietnamese war became felt in 1967. In that year, in the words of the Manpower Report of the President, April 1968,

" . . . . . the increase in private employment generated by Federal expenditures was a half million larger than in the previous year. It accounted for almost three-fifths of the new jobs in the private nonfarm sector as compared with 1 out of 8 in 1966. The sharp rise in federally generated private employment was due primarily to the expansion of defense spending." [12]

It should be noted that we are dealing here only with an increase in employment in the private sector of the economy, operated by private corporations which is directly related to an increase in defense spending. It is clear then that the rise of total civilian employment in the United States to the 96 percent or full employment level is closely associated with the expanding scope of defense expenditures. Table 13-9 shows five defense related

TABLE 13-9
EMPLOYMENT IN FIVE DEFENSE-RELATED INDUSTRIES, 1965–1966
(Numbered in Thousands)

Industry	1965	1966	Change, 1965–66	
			Number	Percent
Total...................	1,731.7	2,022.7	291.0	16.8
Aircraft and parts.....................	625.2	756.0	130.8	20.9
Communication equipment	416.8	464.9	48.1	11.5
Electronic components and accessories .	304.9	374.3	69.4	22.8
Ordnance and accessories	226.0	255.7	29.7	13.1
Ship and boat building and repairing ...	158.8	171.8	13.0	8.2

SOURCE: *Manpower Report of the President* (April 1967), Table 7.

[12]Manpower Report, 1968, p. 161.

industries in which more than half of the employees are directly engaged in defense production. In 1966 overall defense generated employment in these industries had risen by 16.8 percent. Department of Defense generated employment continued to rise sharply through 1968. Private employment created by defense spending reached a high of 3.574 million people in 1968. This represented an increase of 1.452 million employees in defense production of the private sector over 1965. In 1969 this type of employment began to drop slightly. Altogether "DOD" generated employment amounted to 6.1 percent of total employment in the private sector, in actual numbers, 3.574 million. The share of defense employment in manufacturing was 12.1 percent in 1968. That is to say that of the 19.5 million employees in private manufacturing 2.3 million were engaged in defense production. If we go back to 1965 when total employment in manufacturing was 17.6 million, we find that half of the increase in manufacturing employment between 1965 and 1968 was defense generated.[13]

Generally speaking this type of employment increases the proportion of professional, technical and highly skilled employees relative to total employment. This means that the income of wage and salary earners is pushed up in the aggregate because of the large number of high wage and salary earners in defense related private employment. This structure is bringing about a particularly high multiplier effect. Its impact is particularly high as the economy is changing from less than full employment to full employment. Once this condition has been reached, the multiplier effect is bound to exercise increasing pressure on prices especially if aggregate public spending continues to rise as was the case in the United States in 1966 and 1967. Table 13-10 will show the increase in private spending in the

TABLE 13-10
INCREASES IN PUBLIC AND PRIVATE SPENDING AND THE MULTIPLIER
1962–1965

Year	Increase, Public	Increase, Private	Multiplier (Δ Private) / (Δ Public)
1962	9.5	30.7	3.23
1963	5.4	24.8	4.59
1964	6.2	35.7	4.79
1965	7.7	43.8	5.68

SOURCE: *Senior Research Project No. 11*, Fordham University (Fall 1968).

U.S.A. in the years 1962 to 1965 as it relates to increases in public spending. The multiplier is shown as a ratio of the increase of private spending over the increase in public spending.

[13]Richard P. Oliver, "Increase In Defense-Related Employment During Viet Nam buildup,"Table 1, Monthly Labor Review, February 1970.

The preceding analysis has given some quantitative support for a well known thesis, which is at the same time a truism and a platitude, namely that large-scale spending by government for highly complex and extremely expensive defense equipment is one way in which full employment can be achieved and maintained as long as this type of spending continues. In fact the high cost of maintaining a credible defense posture and of waging "limited" wars is closely related to the permanent technological revolution of our times. The development of new weapons systems requires a long preliminary period consumed by research and development activities and the production of prototypes. In this way it can happen that when large scale production of these new devices is finally underway, novel developments are beginning to render these defense products already obsolete. One of the underlying reasons of the widespread uneasiness in modern post-industrial society is the danger that technology establishes a dynamism of its own which becomes almost an autonomous system imposing itself on basic, nontechnical policy decisions.

But while society is struggling to maintain itself on top of technological changes, controlling them rather than be controlled by them, another cause for social concern surfaced again as a beginning was made in 1969 to curtail defense expenditures to a certain extent. The plans referred to here have nothing to do with radical disarmament. They merely indicate a slight descent from a high peak. But government experts estimated that defense spending cuts totaling $1.4 billion would cut about 212,000 jobs from the payrolls of private industry. Furthermore reductions in military spending would reduce the armed services by 220,000 men and lead to the layoff of 68,000 civilian employees of the Defense Department. By and large this cut in defense spending would lead to job reductions in the public and private sector of about 500,000 people.

This estimated decline in employment in the defense sector illustrates clearly that actual increases or cuts in spending programs in the public or in the private sector rather than generalized fiscal and monetary policies translate themselves into increases or decreases in employment. The fact has to be faced that there is no recent experience in the United States with full employment in a situation in which the share of military spending in the GNP would be far less than it has been since the 1940's.

It is true that other advanced industrial countries such as Japan and West Germany as well as most other European countries succeeded in achieving and maintaining full employment without the large share of military spending in the G.N.P. characteristic of the United States. But before the argument can be accepted uncritically that this demonstrates that technologically advanced countries can maintain a forward momentum of full employment, it is necessary to stress some differences. The first one is to be found in the population variable of the Harrod theorem. The natural increase in the labor force in these countries is far less than it is in the United States. In fact, in most of these nations in Europe acute labor shortages prevail. There was a condition of over-employment with vacancies exceeding job applicants, so that these countries had to rely on foreign workers to satisfy their demand for labor. The very fact that the United States was far ahead of other countries in the rate of industrialization and especially in mass production for the consumer sector created in many other countries the desire to catch up with these advanced American standards or at least narrow the gap. This attitude of mobilism, contrasting favorably with the stagnation psychology of the period between the two world wars, placed emphasis on domestic investment and gave a powerful impetus to economic growth. Last but not least, for the first fifteen years of the period after World War II in most of these nations huge outlays were necessary to repair the damage to residential and industrial buildings caused by World War II, to reestablish roads and transportation facilities and make other investments in social overhead capital.

These considerations reinforce the opinion stated above that the real test of employment theories and policies lies ahead. We have had full employment here and abroad within an historical and economic setting that differs in many important aspects from the model of a modern market economy. The question remains unanswered in terms of actual experience, whether the rate of growth required for the maintenance of full employment outlined in the preceding sections of this chapter can be maintained once defense spending has been curtailed. After World War II when the Armed Forces and defense spending were cut drastically, there was a mushrooming of delayed consumer demand which replaced within the framework of aggregate spending the cut in defense expenditures. During World War II the real income of wage and salary earners increased especially through overtime earnings because prices were kept more or less under control. There was a great backlog of demand for automobiles, household appliances, and new residential housing. During the war years the rate of savings rose sharply and for this reason there were sufficient funds available in the household sector to sustain an upsurge in consumer spending.

Up to 1968 income of wage and salary earners was maintained although consumer prices began to rise sharply. On the other hand due to the policy of "guns and butter" consumer spending went on unabated. Only in 1969–1970 was there a slight decline in the purchasing power of wage and salary earners. The previous high rate of spending in the consumer sector makes a cutback in defense expenditures more difficult to absorb than was the case after World War II.

However, we have seen that the rate of change in the labor force in productivity, plus the effect of the labor force transformation requires an annual rate of growth of the American economy by about 7 percent. This goal cannot be achieved merely by reliance on the fiscal and monetary policies suggested by the conventional Keynesian prescriptions. What is necessary is a change in emphasis. Economic growth must be seen from now on in real terms, in a bundle of public and private investment projects which will lead to the required increase in the monetary G.N.P. This line of thought will be pursued further in the next section.

13-6. FULL PRODUCTION POTENTIAL AND FULL EMPLOYMENT

The employment policies discussed so far require an increase in spending above and beyond the level of 4.2 percent indicated by the Harrod-Domar model. This applies also to the structural approach, because obviously projects such as those falling under the Economic Opportunity Act of 1964 or the manpower retraining legislation of 1962 require additional money outlays. One of the main differences between these aggregate-spending and the structural-employment policies is that the structural technique channels spending into particular sectors of the labor market and labor force, whereas the aggregate-spending approach relies more heavily on the macroeconomic effects in general of additional amounts of spending. In all these policies it is assumed that output and employment are functions of levels of spending. We have seen, however, that in carrying out employment policies based on these assumptions we run into frustrations in relation to the aggregate spending approach, and into foreseeable limitations of the structural policies.

In the aggregate-spending approach, the relation of aggregate spending or income Y to outlays for consumer C, investment I, and government spending G, is such that $Y = C + I + G$. If we follow through this relationship over a period of time t and identify the aggregate product which has been forthcoming in the form of demand in the C, I, and G sectors as aggregate output O, we can then write

$$Y_t = f\,O_t$$

Just as the level of output is related to aggregate spending, the level of employment is related to aggregate output. If we write full employment as E, then there must be a level of output which will require the full utilization of the labor force. Writing this level of output as O , we then see that

$$E = f\,O_{te}$$

There must then be a level of Y which brings about an aggregate output which in turn would employ the labor force fully. Bearing this in mind, we can now write the relationship betwen full employment spending and the rate of employment as

$$E = f\,Y_{te}$$

However, at this point we must remember that these functional relationships exist only so long as the spending-employment ratio and its reciprocal, the employment-spending ratio, are equal to one or are oscillating around this unity level, departing from it positively or negatively only for short periods of time. But in an advanced industrialized system the linear growth rate no longer achieves a dynamic full-employment equilibrium as the system moves to ever-higher levels of labor productivity. Theoretically the rate of growth becomes exponential—that is, it slopes upward toward the left.

Such an exponential growth rate could in theory be brought about by wage structures providing for annual increases and thereby pushing up C very rapidly; by monetary measures increasing substantially I and, should these devices still be insufficient, by increasing public spending, perhaps to a degree that the G sector assumes a larger proportion within the structure of aggregate spending. Positively, this assumes a market structure in which, once additional streams of spending have been injected, automatic responses occur in terms of additional employment. Negatively it assumes that there are no leakages from aggregate income into areas of the economic structure which are only remotely connected with current levels of employment. In other words, the approach to full employment through the concept of a full-employment aggregate income, even such an income conceived as growing exponentially, seems to become a decreasingly useful tool for the formulation of full-employment goals and policies. A more adequate approach would be to reverse the procedure and to develop full-output goals requiring full utilization of the labor force and then derive levels of adequate full-employment spending from these output targets.

The approach to full employment through a determination of aggregate output[14] rather than aggregate spending does not, of course, require centralized decision making but the promulgation of goals of growth and progress in the private and public sectors of the economy which could be easily reconciled and coordinated by cooperation of government, business, and labor.

In this approach to full employment, large-scale schemes for urban renewal, public housing, and construction of educational facilities and roads could be geared not only to the long-range needs they are designed to meet but also to the requirements of full employment. This method could also be applied if and when substantial cuts in defense procurement take place. As we have seen earlier, this should not lead to a drop in public spending but to a shift in expenditures to meet the always pressing needs on the state and the local level of government. Using the output rather than the spending model of full employment would make it easier to fit into these policies the types

---

[14]See the author's study outlined in *Journal of Economic Abstracts*, vol. 1, p. 245 and the emphasis on the continuous acceleration of growth in Erich Schneider, *Einfuhrung in die Wirtschaftstheorie*, III, vol. 7, Tubingen (1962), p. 239.

of projects now carried out under the Economic Opportunity Act. They could be more closely related to wider perspectives of a real growth of the economy, thereby losing their "dead-end character," which cannot be permitted to continue for too long without causing additional psychological harm to disadvantaged segments of the labor force. The new stress on the elimination of water and air pollution fits into the approach outlined here.

Stressing the full-employment potential of our productive capacity cannot be limited to the abundant and ever-increasing material resources of the economy. A revision of current concepts of employability is also required. While the advanced nature of modern systems of production and business and administration require far higher educational achievements than were demanded earlier in the century, the tendency towards a mechanical equating of educational levels and employability is also fraught with dangers. On the one hand it creates a pool of prima facie "rejects" which may actually have a good employment potential. On the other hand it may also lead to a progressive devaluation of diplomas and degrees earned with such considerable effort by those receiving them. Employment policies, while forced to operate with huge aggregates of spending and, as is being proposed here, of output as well, must also reach down to individuals. Somehow a way must be found to utilize not only the immediately apparent abilities of people in the labor force but to trace and develop potentials often hidden below the surface of people considered to be somewhat of less than average achievement. We will see in Chapter 14 that in recent years there has been a turning point in attitudes of employers towards employability. This has considerably broadened the areas in which employment policies can operate. We will now turn to a consideration of the various methods currently used to assure that the American economy remains on the full employment growth path.

SELECTED BIBLIOGRAPHY

Baerwald, Friedrich. *Economic System Analysis* (New York: Fordham University Press, 1960).

Baumol, Will J. *Economic Dynamics* (New York: The Macmillan Company, 1958).

Gilpatrick, Eleanor G. *Structural Unemployment and Aggregate Demand* (Baltimore: The Johns Hopkins Press, 1966).

Harrod, Roy F. *An Essay in Dynamic Theory* (Toronto: The Macmillan Company, Ltd., 1952).

Hicks, John. *Capital and Growth* (New York & Oxford: Oxford University Press, Inc., 1966).

Kurihara, Kenneth K. (ed.). *Post-Keynesan Economics* (London: George Allen & Unwin, Ltd., 1959).

Roll, Sir Eric. *The World After Keynes: An Examination of Economic Order* (New York: Frederich A. Praeyer, 1968).

Stieber, Jack, ed. *Employment Problems of Automation and Advanced Technology* (New York: John Wiley & Sons, 1967).

QUESTIONS FOR DISCUSSION

1. What is the essence of macrodynamics as applied to economics?

2. State the principal ideas contained in the macrodynamic model forwarded by R. F. Harrod in 1939.

3. What contribution to the model was made by Domar?

4. In a study of macrodynamics, why is it especially important to consider key economic institutions and their relation to the model itself (i. e., market structure and role of government)?

5. What is "deliberate expansion" and how does it contrast with "spontaneous growth"?

6. Macrodynamic analysis shows that the use of concepts derived from cycle theory, especially the terms recession and recovery, have lost a good deal of their meaning. Comment.

7. Compare the relation between spending and employment that existed in the period prior to World War II with that of the postwar period.

8. What special implications can be drawn from the comparison made in the above question?

9. The fact that aggregate personal income includes a relatively large amount of nonfactor payments may have important implications for our attempts to more precisely formulate relationships between employment and spending. Why is this so?

10. To maintain full employment over the next decade, an accelerated or exponential rate of growth may well be required. Present a detailed statement of the reasons for this view.

Chapter

14

Economic Goals and Methods of Employment Policies

The professional economist writing in the second half of the twentieth century will do well to assume that full employment will remain a social goal with paramount priority in advanced industrial societies. Furthermore, developing countries are characterized by the desire of increasing numbers of people to move from remote villages in the subsistence sector of the economy into urban and industrial centers where they hope to become wage earners. The great production possibilities of highly industrialized areas in which labor requirements and employment do not keep pace with actual and potential growth in output have not diminished the aggregate demand for employment but rather have tended to increase it. This is because the great material wealth that is continuously being produced and advertised stimulates consumer demand and expectations, thereby necessitating a steady increase in household income. These attitudes and needs in turn increase the number of family members who are actually employed or looking for jobs. Rising educational requirements for better-compensated jobs raises family expenditure further, again augmenting the need for additional employment and income.

The increase in leisure time has not diminished the total demand for remunerative employment. On the contrary, since leisure-time activities require such high-cost items as boats, advanced hi-fi equipment, and extensive travel, the need to increase earnings of household members during the five-day week becomes more urgent. Actually we are facing here an important aspect of the aggregate-employment problem: multiple jobholding. This phenomenon has two different causes. In many instances it may implement an inadequate income derived from the main occupation while in others it may be attributable to the desire to raise the joint income of the household to higher levels. It was estimated that in May 1964, 3.135 million wage and salary workers, or 5.3 percent of this group employed in nonagricultural industries, were persons with two jobs or more.[1]

A diminution of the aggregate demand for employment is not a characteristic of an affluent society. While the pressures will continue for a shortening of the work week and for an expansion of "extended vacations," the overall demand for remunerative work will remain at least as high a rate as it is today. This forecast assumes that the problems connected with the maintenance of full employment must be solved, in the foreseeable future as in the immediate past, in a social setting in which people are expected to exert most of their energies as productive members of the labor force. Although the time available for leisure is expected to increase even further, its enjoyment is considered a reward for intensive economic efforts and contributions for profitable business operation. Thus the goal of full employment remains in force, but it is necessary to differentiate within this broad objective between various aspects of unemployment and their different responses to employment policies.

The aggregate-spending approach to employment fails to make such a differentiation. It transfers to the labor force and to the labor market techniques of analytical aggregation which are far less appropriate to these sectors of the economy than they are to the flow of income and funds. This condition brings out again the fact that employment policies must be supplemented by manpower policies. Both belong together but they are not the same.

The macroeconomic, aggregate spending approach flowing from conventional Keynesian economics, can be compared to a remote control system. The fiscal and monetary policies which are intended either to raise spending levels to full employment or to restrain a further increase to avoid runaway inflation assume that these steering devices are sufficient to bring about required rates of spending in the consumer, investment, and government sectors and that there will be a corresponding response of the rate of employment. One reason why these employment policies have found such wide approval among economists is that they avoid dealing with basic structural conditions of the system, such as the degree of concentration in industry and finance, the impact of technology on the structural transformation of the labor force, the impediments to overcoming persistent unemployment for segments of the labor force having been exposed over a long period to economic and educational discrimination. Macroeconomic employment policies are entirely neutral vis-à-vis such conditions which indeed are not strictly economic in nature but social and institutional.

Manpower policies attack in a more direct way conditions of unem-

[1]See Harvey R. Hamel and Forrest A. Hogan, "Multiple Jobholders in May, 1964," *Monthly Labor Review* (March 1965), p. 266.

ployment. Within the framework established by a required aggregate rate of spending they address themselves to specific segments of the labor force, especially to pockets of unemployment caused by industrial shifts, occupational changes and effects of a disadvantaged condition among certain minority groups.

Employment policies can be effective in the new kind of *Cyclical unemployment* characterized by the type of shorter run *recessions* as they have occurred in the Western World since World War II. *Hard-core unemployment* whether it be persistent unemployment of workers with previous experience or structural unemployment of people requiring additional education or training to make them fit into contemporary labor requirements must be met by manpower policies. In view of the recent stress on manpower policies which is most welcome, it is necessary to emphasize that they are not a replacement of employment policies but must go hand in hand with them.

We have seen in Chapter 13 that conventional employment policies are still predicated on the asumption, no longer justified by actual employment-spending ratios, that an increase in spending will bring about a proportionate increase in employment and vice versa. In fact maintenance of full employment requires ever greater doses of spending as the system becomes more industrial and is using advanced technological systems in agriculture, industry and in business operations. For this reason the impact of spending differs widely according to the rate of unemployment. As long as unemployment has a critical level, under contemporary conditions beginning with a 6 percent plus rate, the "remote control" employment policies may be rather ineffective. They also become inoperative once full employment has been reached which again under the structure of an advanced economy leads to inflationary pressures which cannot be held down merely by the steering devices of conventional monetary and fiscal employment policies. This will be shown in detail in the next section.

14-1. THE FULL-EMPLOYMENT VERSUS INFLATION ISSUE

In Keynes' *General Theory* there is the implication that full employment has a built-in tendency to vanish once it has been achieved because people start saving more and spending less than they did while the economy was moving up to this equilibrium level. His policy recommendations, especially with regard to low interest rates and easy money policies, as well as his advocacy of deficit spending by government in periods of declining employment, were designed to maintain aggregate spending on a level commensurate with full employment. In the context of the early 1930's when the *General Theory* was being formulated and when commodity and consumer prices as well as money wages had declined sharply from their 1929 levels,

TABLE 14-1
PRICES, WAGES, AND EMPLOYMENT, 1929–33

Year	All Commodities	Consumer Prices (1957–59 = 100)	Weekly Earnings in Manufacturing	Unemployment (thousands)
1929	52.1	59.7	$24.76	1,550
1930	47.3	58.2	23.00	4,340
1931	39.9	53.0	20.64	8,020
1932	35.6	47.6	16.89	12,060
1933	36.1	45.1	16.65	12,830

SOURCE: *Economic Report of the President* (January 1965), Tables B-43, B-45, B-29, and B-21.

the purpose of these policies was to counteract deflation and the contraction of business activity and employment it inevitably brings about.

To demonstrate the seriousness of the decline in prices, the development between the years 1929 and 1933 is shown in Table 14-1.

In 1964 prices the GNP declined from $217.8 billion in 1929 to $153 billion in 1933. Within this setting, the great stress placed on Keynesian economics appears in its full original significance. The years from 1933 to 1940 supply further insights into the relations between levels of employment, aggregate spending, and prices. In the fiscal year 1930 there was a budget surplus of $738 million in the Federal treasury. After that deficit spending gained great momentum. Starting with less than $500 million in fiscal 1931, it rose to more than $4.4 billion in fiscal 1936. In that year more than half of the expenditures of the Federal government were financed by public borrowing. Within the short period between 1931 and 1935 the public debt of the Federal government doubled. In the same period there was a substantial decline in unemployment. It dropped from 24.9 percent of the civilian labor force in 1933 to 20.1 percent in 1935 and 16.9 percent in 1936. While the unemployment rate for 1933 looks suspiciously high and may, due to the imperfections in statistical reporting at that time, contain duplications, there is no doubt that substantial improvements were made in employment during that period. But in 1936 the GNP in constant prices was still below that of 1929. The rate of unemployment which persisted would be termed catastrophic were it ever to return.

There is no doubt, however, that the substantial injection of funds into the money flow brought about by public borrowing did put a halt to the dangerous deflationary downward glide of the early 1930's and helped to raise the economic system from the lowest depths of the Great Depression. On the other hand, the doubling of the public debt, the unprecedented stepping-up of deficit spending, and the vast expansion of government subsidies to farming and shipping had hardly any impact at all on the price level. In fact, consumer prices between 1933 and 1936 rose by less than one index point per annum.

A general conclusion can be drawn from these experiences of the 1930's.

The application of the spending approach to full employment does not bring about inflationary price rises so long as full employment levels have not yet been reached. It follows that the choice between policies designed to raise levels of employment and policies oriented towards maintaining of price stability and an unchanging value of money does not have to be made whenever the condition of unemployment is serious.

This neutrality of increased aggregate spending with regard to price levels ceases to function when full employment has been reached. From that point on, additional injections into the money flow raising aggregate spending may set in motion steep price rises. Only substantial price rises telescoped into short periods should be classified   as inflationary. It seems evident, then, that an employment policy stressing the aggregate-demand-and-expenditure approach cannot be the cause of inflation so long as it has not reached its goal.

One of the reasons why even dramatic increases in aggregate spending do not bring about significant price increases prior to the point of full employment is that, in modern industry, there is a cyclical behavior of labor productivity. When output is low, productivity of labor in terms of output per man-hour and per worker is also far below maximum. This condition leads to the paradox that unit labor costs are high when output is low and decline sharply when output rises. Injection of additional funds into the aggregate income flow leading to increases in employment inevitably bring about an increase in labor productivity primarily of blue-collar production workers. Only when existing resources are already fully utilized, and when additional output requires the reopening of obsolescent production units and the hiring of marginal or inexperienced workers, is there a decline in labor productivity as a result of additional spending. Such conditions are characteristic of a full war economy and also of a labor market in rapid structural transformation into a predominantly white-collar economy. Under such conditions the inflation potentials rise rapidly. This increases aggregate unit labor cost because the high productivity sector is contracting. In this country the relationship between output and productivity sector is contracting. In this country the relationship between output and productivity can be seen in Table 14-2.

In order to evaluate correctly the series shown in Table 14-2 it is necessary to relate increases in output to increases in capacity. Both increase at about the same rate. This explains why there was no significant change in the rate of utilization of capacity in manufacturing although output increased by about 30 percent between 1957 and 1964. It must be inferred from these trends that more and more efficient equipment was put into use as capacity was being expanded, thereby lifting labor productivity to higher levels. The trend in output per man-hour confirms the view that in a "blue-collar" system labor productivity increases as output reaches higher levels. In the period 1957–58 labor productivity increased by only

TABLE 14-2
INCREASE IN MANUFACTURING CAPACITY, OUTPUT, AND PRODUCTIVITY,
1957–64
(1957–59 = 100)

Period	Capacity	Output	Utilization Rate	Productivity*
1957	119	101	85	98.0
1958	122	93	76	98.8
1959	125	106	84	103.2
1960	131	109	83	104.1
1961	134	110	82	106.1
1962	139	119	85	111.1
1963	145	125	86	113.2
1964	152	133	87	116.1

*Labor-force basis.
SOURCE: *Economic Report of the President* (January 1965), Tables B-32 and B-35.

1.2 percent, whereas in the period 1963–64 it rose by 3.5 percent. These basic relationships must be considered in any assessment of the danger of inflation assumed to be inherent in a rapid stepping-up of spending and of output as such. A more differentiated analysis must be made.

The argument presented here has been confirmed by price developments in the United States after 1965. In that year full employment in terms of 96 percent employment of the labor force had been achieved. However, total public expenditures continued to rise steeply. National defense expenditures alone rose from $50.1 billion in 1965 to $79.3 billion in 1969. After the peak of defense spending in that year, a cut of about $4 billion was proposed by the Nixon administration. The increase in total public spending after 1965 was not confined to national defense. There were also very sharp rises in state and local spending from $63.5 billion in 1965 to $97.1 billion in 1968. As a result the G.N.P. continued its accelerated growth in current dollars. However, in 1969 the growth of the G.N.P. in constant (1958) dollars began to slow down considerably. From the first to the fourth quarter of that year it rose only from $723.1 billion to $729.8 billion. As we have seen in Chapter 13 already this minute increase simply is not enough to maintain full employment. As a result unemployment rose steadily. In January 1969 total unemployment was 3.4 percent of all civilian workers. In January 1970 it was 3.9 percent but in April of that year it had risen sharply to 4.8 percent. That indicated that the period of full employment which had begun in 1965 with the Vietnam buildup was over for the time being.

When prices began to rise steeply after 1965, economists relying on the Phillips analysis began to talk about trading off some unemployment against price stabilization. However, throughout 1969 unemployment and prices rose simultaneously demonstrating thereby that at least in the short run the Phillips theorem is inoperative. We know that unemployment is twice as high among new workers and among nonwhites, so that even a slight average rise in unemployment can aggravate local tensions in disadvantaged areas.

One reason for this failure of the American economy to respond elastically to changes in employment or in prices are the ongoing structural changes in the labor force. The transition from a blue-collar to a white-collar economy tends to offset gains in productivity achieved in the goods producing sector and is steadily increasing employment costs in the non-production part of the economy. Increases in total employment costs brought about by higher social security taxes and allocations to private pension funds are shifted to the consumer and add to the upward pressures on prices. All this tends to decrease the employment effects of additional spending in a manner not sufficiently taken into consideration in the conventional employment theory.

In most macrodynamic models used to make growth and full employment projections, productivity is ultimately treated as an average, homogeneous unit. However, the rapid advance of technology on the one hand and the resulting relative decline of the labor force engaged in production has placed a downward pull on overall productivity gains. Inasmuch as production worker wages are geared to productivity and set the pattern of the compensation of nonproduction workers, it is inevitable that unit labor costs for wage and salary workers as a whole have started to rise whereas they still remain stable as far as the compensation of production workers is concerned.

Chart 11, of the Manpower Report of the President, January 1969, illustrates the development discussed in the preceeding paragraph. In the long period 1947 to 1961 productivity gains in durable and nondurable goods manufacturing only achieved medium annual gains in the range of 2.5–3.4 percent a year. From 1961 to 1967 productivity gains per annum were classified as "very high" in manufacturing exceeding 4 percent per year. Similar high values were achieved in transportation, mining, and agriculture. On the other hand, productivity gains in trade, services and finance are represented for the same period 1961 to 1967 as "low" meaning less than 2.5 percent per annum. During that period, employment in these nonproduction categories of wage and salary workers rose from 21.6 million in 1961 to 28.0 million. Furthermore, employment by state and local governments rose by 3 million. Total employment rose by 13.8 million. It follows that almost 80 percent of the increase in employment in the 1960's occurred in the nonproduction sectors of the economy. It is no wonder that in the 1960's the long run stability of unit labor costs which was stressed in our presentation Wage Theories especially of the productivity wage theorem in Sec. 5-6 has undergone modifications. They are caused by two factors: the continuous sharp rise of productivity of production workers and the application of wage increases justified by these advances to wage and salary workers operating in the ever increasing low productivity sector of the American economy. This is not stated in advocacy of a curtailment of wage increases for nonproduction workers but merely to stress that employment policies from now on must take into account the structural transformation of the labor force and its impact on unit labor costs. Just how decisive these changes are will be shown in Table 14-3.

TABLE 14-3

ANNUAL AVERAGE PERCENT CHANGES OF OUTPUT PER MAN-HOUR, HOURLY COMPENSATION, AND UNIT LABOR COSTS

Period	Output	Man-hours	Output per Man-hour	Compensation Per Man-hour	Real Compensation Per Man-hour	Unit Labor Costs
Total Private Economy						
1947–68	3.8	0.6	3.2	5.0	3.2	1.7
1957–68	4.6	1.1	3.4	4.8	3.0	1.3
1961–65	5.7	1.7	3.9	4.4	3.1	0.5
1965–68	4.1	1.4	2.8	6.8	3.4	3.9
1966–67	2.0	0.4	1.6	6.1	3.2	4.4
1967–68	4.9	1.6	3.3	7.5	3.1	4.0

SOURCE: *Monthly Labor Review* (June 1969), Table 1, p. 12.

It should be noted that Table 14-3 takes in the total private economy including agriculture where productivity gains are highest while employment continues to drop sharply. As a result output per man-hour is far higher in the farm than in the nonfarm sector as far as annual increases are concerned. Table 14-3 shows, however, that in the economy as a whole not withstanding the deviation from the trend in 1966–1967 there continues to be a remarkable consistency between changes in output per man-hour and real as distinct from current dollar compensation per man-hour.

In 1965 a study of output per man-hour was published in which developments for production workers and nonproduction workers were shown separately. Table 14-4, covering the period from 1957 to 1964 shows that with the onset of the long recovery period in 1961 output per man-hour of production workers began to grow more rapidly than that of nonproduction workers.

The preceding discussion has clearly shown that it is not advisable to speak of the relation between employment and prices in global terms. A certain degree of "disaggregation" is necessary in order to pinpoint the trouble areas.

Unit labor cost of production workers has remained virtually unchanged in the period 1957–64. Inasmuch as wage increases for these workers were matched by productivity increases and a substantial rise in output, the effect of these higher wages on unit prices was neutral. This is not true of the non-

TABLE 14-4
INDEXES OF OUTPUT PER MAN-HOUR IN MANUFACTURING
FOR PRODUCTION AND NONPRODUCTION WORKERS,
1957–64
(1957–59 = 100)

Year	Output per Man-hour of Employees	Production Workers	Nonproduction Workers
1957	97.7	96.5	101.6
1958	99.1	100.3	95.4
1959	103.3	103.4	102.8
1960	103.8	105.0	100.1
1961	106.7	109.1	99.9
1962	112.6	114.3	107.5
1963	115.3	117.3	109.2
1964	119.6	121.3	114.5

SOURCE: Jerome A. Mark and Elizabeth Kahn, "Recent Unit Cost Trends in U.S. Manufacturing," *Monthly Labor Review* (September, 1965).

production workers. As we have shown in Table 14-4, they lagged substantially behind the rise in output per man-hour of production workers. For this reason their unit labor cost rose to 109.6 percent in 1964 of the 1957–59 basis. Actually the concept of inflation should be connected not with a wage-push but with a salary-push. Undeniably the fact that unit labor cost of nonproduction workers has increased substantially explains part of the reasons why employment-cost outlays have risen. We can then focus our analysis of the relation between levels of employment and levels of prices on two areas—the increase in total employment cost imposed by such legislation as the Social Security Amendment of 1967, and the increase of the nonproduction workers employed throughout the economy whose productivity is increasing at a much slower rate than that of production workers.

Inasmuch as the two areas singled out in the preceding paragraph are likely to continue their upward pressure on prices, we have to decide whether these higher prices are preferable to higher levels of unemployment. Undoubtedly unit labor cost of nonproduction workers could be brought down by introducing a more marginal behavior in the hiring practices of this vast segment of the labor force. On the other hand, it is precisely the expansionary power which seems to be a built-in feature of office and managerial employment that has made up for the actual or implied loss in the production-worker sector of employment opportunities.

To sum up the main argument based on the line of thought developed in Part III of this text, we see on the one hand that spending is not inflationary up to a full-employment level; on the other hand, we discover that even additional doses of spending have a tendency to fall short of the goal of maintaining or reestablishing a dynamic employment equilibrium in a highly advanced industrialized system. To recognize this macrodynamic structure is the prerequisite for the formulation of effective employment policies. These must be predicated on a clear distinction between various types of unemployment. The categories of cyclical, persistent, and structural unemployment established in our analysis in Chapter 10 have different types of responses to the aggregate-spending approach to full employment. Actually it will be necessary to develop a three-pronged approach to unemployment and to the goal of full employment. We will see that cyclical unemployment is more likely to yield to the aggregate-spending approach suggested by contemporary economics. Other techniques have to be devised to deal with persistent and structural unemployment. The Economic Opportunity Act of 1964 is characteristic of still another approach to socially disturbing pockets of unemployment remaining even at periods of generally high levels of employment. Employment policies emerging to cope with this situation which are more socially oriented than strictly economic will be discussed in Sec. 14-5.

14-2. DEALING WITH CYCLICAL UNEMPLOYMENT

We have seen that the contemporary economic system has achieved a far greater degree of stability than was characteristic of the earlier eras of capitalism. Nevertheless, it must be assumed that downward turns will occur in the future as they have in the past. The 1957–58 recession did bring about substantial declines in employment in durable-goods manufacturing and contract construction. Had there not been some slight increases in employment in trade, finance, and services, the overall situation of the labor market would have been even more unfavorable, and the unemployment rate would have been higher than the actual 6.8 percent in 1958. We must also understand that the slowing down of the growth rate of the economy, even if it does not lead to the actual decline in employment (as we have been illustrating by the example of the 1957–58 period), could rapidly lead to an increase in unemployment. In fact, it would be well to expand the cycle concept to fluctuations in the growth rate itself. From this viewpoint, countercyclical policies would have to be initiated or continued even in periods of rising activity in order to bring growth rates at least up to the level indicated by the behavior of the two variables: the annual increase in the labor force and the annual increase in productivity. We have seen in Sec. 13-6 that the most recent experience suggests that actual growth rates must be even greater. However, so far as cyclical unemployment is concerned, a return to a rate of growth commensurate with the increase in the two variables mentioned above is likely to eliminate it.

To achieve such a goal the techniques of Keynesian economics seem to be most suitable. As we have seen, they suggest to policy makers that if a choice presents itself between balanced budgets and a considerable level of unemployment on the one hand, and, on the other, deficit spending and a reduction of unemployment to between 4 and 5 percent of the labor force, the latter alternative must be chosen. It is in this context that the cut in individual and corporate income taxes was carried out in the early 1960's, although the Federal budget was not balanced at that time. These tax cuts were advocated and enacted on the ground that they would increase disposable consumer income, stimulate aggregate spending for consumer and investment goods, and thereby increase employment. It was further argued that the losses to the Treasury implied in a reduction of tax rates would be offset by an increase in the GNP and especially in the national income brought about by the additional spending following a tax cut.

The performance of the American economy in 1965, after these tax reductions had become fully effective, seems to validate the assumptions based on these employment policies. Obviously income-tax cuts cannot be repeated too often. Government in our time is inescapably big. Even if Federal spending could be either stabilized or actually reduced by effective international limitations in armament, there would not be a noticeable overall decline in public spending. Local and state governments are exposed to the pressures of population, and to the problems of accelerating urbanization. It must be expected, therefore, that in the long run there will neither be an absolute nor a relative decline of total public spending on all three levels of government combined. The best that can be hoped is that the share of the public sector in the GNP will remain the same—in other words, it will not rise faster on a year-to-year basis than the GNP itself. It is obvious then that the tax burden will remain high and that the agreeable device of lowering it somewhat in order to give more spending power to consumers and to business cannot be used time and again. For this reason other well-known methods of dealing with cyclical unemployment must not be overlooked.

To a certain extent public spending, especially in the form of deficit spending, can be timed so that it reaches a peak when business activities are low and is curtailed or held back altogether when full employment is approached. For instance, the rate of construction of low-rent housing could be accelerated during a downturn and stretched out over longer periods when labor and capital resources approach full utilization. The same flexibility could be obtained in highway and other public construction. Furthermore, the financing of this type of construction should never be made through appropriations in the yearly expenditure budgets, but rather through the selling of bonds on the capital market.

The effectiveness of such countercyclical spending can be impeded by rigid rules of fiscal administration. For this reason appropriations for low-rent housing, urban renewal, and improvement in transportation and road-building should be made on a three-to five-year basis. This could be done by establishing normal annual rates of spending but empowering the government agencies charged with administering these programs to make flexible adjustments to changing conditions on the labor market by increasing or decreasing the rate of spending within the overall three to five-year time framework—by either accelerating or slowing down the start of new projects.

These actions of government, designed to speed up the elimination of cyclical unemployment, will have to be supported by well-known monetary policies, such as a lowering or raising of interest rates and open-market operations in a countercyclical fashion. The experience of the first five years of the 1960's has shown that the type of employment policy outlined in this section has a good chance of succeeding. However, during that period there remained a hard core of persistent unemployment, as shown in Table 10-2. We must turn our attention again to the problem of unemployment.

14-3. MITIGATING PERSISTENT UNEMPLOYMENT

As the overall rate of unemployment dropped from 6.7 percent of the civilian labor force in 1961 to less than 5 percent in 1965, persistent unemployment remained substantially higher than it had been in 1957, the last year of full employment. In that year 10.9 percent of the unemployed had been unemployed between 15 and 26 weeks, and only 8.1 percent 27 weeks and over. As the GNP reached unprecedented growth rates after 1961, persistent unemployment remained substantially higher than it had been before. In 1961 it reached 31.9 percent of the unemployed, but in 1964 it still was 25.1 percent. It can be assumed that this decline represents the impact of the cyclical upswing since 1961. But this cycle merely helped to outline more clearly the hard core of persistent unemployment.

In dealing with this aspect of unemployment, certain institutional and administrative structures have to be taken into account. We have described in Sec. 10-5 the methods used for counting the unemployed. While the use of a very large sample may be the best available way to assess the extent of unemployment in the aggregate, clearly we cannot come very close to analyzing particular types of unemployment such as persistent unemployment in this way. So long as people without a job have to present themselves regularly to the Public Employment Services in order to obtain their unemployment benefits, they are subject, as it were, to a nose count, and we can be quite certain as to their numbers, occupational grouping, and duration of unemployment. But the coverage of unemployment compensation laws is far from comprehensive. In many states employees of very small firms as well as agricultural and domestic workers were left out in the 1960's. This means they are not eligible for unemployment compensation and therefore were unlikely to come in touch with employment services. Furthermore, a considerable number of employees, especially in the service industries, continuously alternate between short periods of employment and joblessness in a way that keeps them from ever accumulating sufficient periods of covered employment to qualify for unemployment benefits. These people may of course turn up in the carefully selected 52,500 sample interviewed each month, but because of the character of this type of marginal employment some doubts may be permitted as to the use of information obtained in the interviews. The development of workable concepts of these groups might be vitiated if they turn out to be persistently unemployed after losing their rather tenuous hold on employment opportunities.

But even those groups of the unemployed who, prior to losing their jobs, worked steadily and were covered by unemployment compensation are requested to appear in the offices of the employment service only if their benefit period has not been exhausted. For this reason the first category of the persistently unemployed—those out of work between 15 and 26 weeks—seems to be a definitely ascertainable figure. It is quite different for those who have exhausted their unemployment compensation benefit period. They are under no obligation to continue reporting to the public placement services.

One way of dealing with this type of hard-core unemployment would be to find arrangements whereby those jobless who have no further claims on unemployment could keep in touch with employment agencies. We might achieve this objective by stressing the significance of an intensive terminal interview with a placement officer of the public employment services during the last week for which unemployment compensation is due. This would help to determine a number of things. In the first place, a judgment could be made whether the jobless can be considered being a member of the labor force in terms of general employability. Secondly, attempts could be made to find out what the longer-run outlook for employment opportunities are in which the long-term unemployed has occupational experience. Last but not least, the question of retraining ought to be actively considered. We have seen in Sec. 10-6 that in the initial stages of the operation of the Manpower Development and Training Act a considerable proportion of the unemployed enrolled in the retraining projects had been unemployed only for a short period of time. The program under M.D.T.A. provides for institutional and on-the-job training. Over the years there has been a wide discrepancy between enrollment and completion of training. In the fiscal year 1968 there were 265,000 enrollments and 145,000 completions. Since similar ratios also prevailed in preceding fiscal years this must be considered one of the characteristics of the program. On the other hand a vast proportion of those who completed the training obtained posttraining employment. Of the 145,000 trainees who completed their institutional or on-the-job training in fiscal 1968, 114.5 thousand obtained regular employment.

Persistent unemployment is often connected with areas in which certain industrial activities such as mining have come to an end—for example in parts of West Virginia, Pennsylvania, and other states in the Appalachia Region. Redevelopment of such labor markets through establishment of new industries and better transportation facilities can assist substantially in attacking regional hard-core unemployment by fitting retraining programs in with redevelopment projects. The Area Redevelopment Act of 1961 is designed to bring about structural improvements and new employment opportunities to labor markets in which persistent unemployment is high.

14-4. POLICIES WITH REGARD TO STRUCTURAL UNEMPLOYMENT

Throughout this text it has been stressed that the American labor market will remain under heavy pressure, at least until 1980, because of the large numbers of new workers which will be added to the labor supply each year. Wage and salary workers in nonagricultural occupations numbered 58.2 million in 1964; in 1970 they were expected to grow to 67.7 million.[2] As a result of the ever-increasing productivity of labor, the rise in employment in the goods-producing industries will occur at a comparatively slow rate. From a level of 21 million in 1964 it will at best move to about 24 million in 1970. But this means that if full employment is to continue in the 1970's more than a million additional workers will have to be absorbed annually in service producing industries such as trade, finance, transportation, services, and government.

A failure of the labor market to absorb these new workers could lead to a rapid accumulation of unemployment, even if an actual downturn of economic activities such as occurred in 1969–1970 could be reversed. Even a slowdown in the growth rate would translate itself almost immediately into higher rates of unemployment. This type of unemployment would be structural and would have the highest incidence among the youngest age groups of the labor force—those between 16 and 24 years. Without doubt a slowdown in growth rates would also bring about a steep rise in persistent unemployment. Table 14-5 shows that over the long run, even in periods of rapid growth, the ratio of inexperienced workers among the unemployed has been rising steadily.

As can be seen from Table 14-5, there has been a sharp decline in the ratio of experienced wage and salary workers among the unemployed since shortly after World War II. As unemployment rates dropped from a high of 6.8 percent in 1961 to 5 percent in 1964, the ratio of experienced wage earners among the unemployed dropped from 84.9 to 81.4 percent. This sharp decline in unemployed with work experience in a comparatively short period of time highlights the significance of structural unemployment, especially among young workers. Projections for the number of laborers employed in 1975 indicate that their share in the occupational structure will decline from 5.5 percent in 1960 to 4.3 percent in 1975. Farm employment

[2]*Manpower Report of the President* (March 1964), Table E-6.

TABLE 14-5
INEXPERIENCED AND EXPERIENCED WORKERS AMONG
THE UNEMPLOYED, 1948–67
(percent distribution)

Year	Total Unemployed*	Experienced	Inexperienced
1948	100.0	87.7	12.3
1949	100.0	89.6	10.4
1950	100.0	89.1	10.9
1951	100.0	87.8	12.2
1952	100.0	87.7	12.3
1953	100.0	88.6	11.4
1954	100.0	89.8	10.2
1955	100.0	88.0	12.0
1956	100.0	85.8	14.2
1957	100.0	87.2	12.8
1958	100.0	87.8	12.2
1959	100.0	85.6	14.4
1960	100.0	85.3	14.7
1961	100.0	84.9	15.1
1962	100.0	83.9	16.1
1963	100.0	82.5	17.5
1964	100.0	81.4	18.6
1965	100.0	79.0	21.0
1966	100.0	81.0	19.0
1967	100.0	83.6	14.4

*Also includes the self-employed, unpaid family workers, and those with no previous work experience, not shown separately.
SOURCE: *Manpower Report of the President* (April 1968), Table A-15.

which had a share of 8.1 percent in 1960 is expected to drop to 4.5 percent in 1975. The share of operatives and kindred workers is assumed to decline from 18 percent in 1960 to 16.3 percent in 1975, whereas that of craftsmen is expected to remain exactly the same, namely 12.8 percent.[3]

The pattern emerging from these trends is the simultaneous existence of full employment and of structural unemployment. High levels of employment, up to 98 percent of white males age of 25–44 can exist simultaneously with considerable proportions of unemployment of nonwhite groups of the same age bracket, of males and females age 16–24 and with people 45 years and older. Structural unemployment of this type seems to be compatible with high levels of industrial activity and a rapidly rising gross national product. There seems to be a danger that even a further growth of the gross national product will not reduce it substantially. This is the setting in which the employment projects of the Economic Opportunity Act of 1964 have been conceived. They fall completely outside employment policies along conventional Keynesian lines and have developed rapidly since 1964. Actually a war against hard core unemployment has been started which is waged as it were on two fronts: employment projects set up by the government under the Economic Opportunity Act, and the opening up of addi-

[3]*Manpower Report of the President* (March 1965), Table E-5.

tional job opportunities in the business sector by the National Alliance of Businessmen.

14-5. POLICIES TO REDUCE HARD CORE UNEMPLOYMENT

One of the major problems of structural unemployment is the accumulation within the labor force of considerable groups of people without work experience or with such limited general educational background that they appear to be unsuited for the more exacting labor requirements of our advanced industrialized society. Despite the accelerated growth of the American economy in the period 1965 to 1969, unemployment among juveniles, white and nonwhite remained very high. For all groups together the unemployment rate for 16–19 years old was 14.8 percent in 1965 and dropped to 12.7 percent in 1968. At that time average unemployment among the young did not make any dent in the ratio of nonwhite to white unemployment. While it was 2:1 in 1965 in favor of the white unemployed, the ratio was even somewhat more unfavorable for the nonwhite unemployed in 1968.

While the problem of hard core unemployment among the young remains serious it is necessary to keep in mind that unemployment for all categories of the labor force, white and nonwhite, male and female, drops sharply once these people are 20 years or over.

If economics were conceived as existing and operating in a social vacuum, it might be assumed that the type of unemployment still existing in 1965 when in the latter part of the year it dropped below a national average of 5 percent of the civilian labor force could be tolerated and handled with established devices including relief systems. But as we have stressed at the very beginning, labor is two-dimensional, representing both a factor of production and at the same time an individual with individual needs and aspirations. For this reason the type of hard core unemployment covered by the general concept "structural" must find a response in terms of social and economic action. The Economic Opportunity Act of 1964 was at least a partial answer to this requirement.

This legislation had set up a number of employment programs designed specifically to reduce unemployment among young people. Inasmuch as this legislation was inaugurated at a time when on the macroeconomic scale full-employment levels were already in sight, it would be wrong to label this legislation part of a full-employment policy. Instead it is characterized here as a subsidiary employment policy designed not really to increase output even further, but rather to establish worklike situations for people who seem to be unable to fit into the existing job structure. Unlike the work projects of the 1930's, no sanguine expectations with regard to a multiplier effect have been voiced. This restraint seems to be eminently justifiable in view of the fact that even in the 1930's the large outlays for public works did not seem to provide a sufficient lift to the economy in terms of the multiplier to even approximate levels of full employment.

The three main projects dealing with young people under the Economic Opportunity Act are The Job Corps, The Neighborhood Youth Corps, and The Work-Study Program. By far the largest number of young people are in The Neighborhood Youth Corps. Compared to that the Job Corps was on a small scale, having enlisted only slightly more than 17,000 young men in 1965.

The enrollment in the Neighborhood Youth Corps has been consistently high as can be seen in Table 14-6.

TABLE 14-6
ENROLLMENT IN NEIGHBORHOOD YOUTH CORPS
FISCAL YEARS
1966–1968

	1966	1967	1968
Enrollment Opportunities			
Total	527.7	512.7	537.7
In School.	188.8	139.0	135.0
Out of School	98.6	79.3	62.7
Summer	240.3	294.3	339.1

SOURCE: Table F-1, *Manpower Report of the President* (January 1969).

The Neighborhood Youth Corps—N.Y.C.—is by far the largest of the projects set up under the Economic Opportunity Act of 1964. Table 14-6 shows that it comprises a variety of programs. The common denominator of these schemes is to make it possible for disadvantaged young people to complete their education or if they have dropped out of school, to motivate them so that they will resume their education. Failing this, young people will be readied to accept jobs in the competitive labor market. The first of these programs is *the in-school program.* Students enrolled in this plan can be employed up to fifteen hours a week for a pay of $1.25 per hour. One of the main purposes of this N.Y.C. plan is to enable students to purchase clothing and cover other incidental expenses so that they can continue to attend school. In the out-of-school program, work can be supplied up to 40 hours per week for which again $1.25 per hour can be paid. It is, however, significant that within this 40 hour framework, compensated time can be allocated for such supportive services supplied by N.Y.C. as the remedial education, counselling and medical assistance.

The third program of N.Y.C. concerns summer employment. Again one of the main purposes of the summer program is to keep in touch with teen-agers, employ them in such tasks as beautification projects, maintenance of parks and recreation facilities and even of school buildings. Also great care is taken to see to it that the enrollees in the summer program return to school.

The Neighborhood Youth Corps is without precedent. To a certain extent it signifies a failure of the public school system in many deprived neighborhoods. Many graduates of these schools are several years behind in their reading skills. While it is necessary to provide remedial education within the framework of the out-of-school program of the N.Y.C. it must also be realized that this fact alone hints at the waste which is somehow connected with educational techniques and procedures in these sections of the school system. Compulsory elementary education spread throughout the Western world when early in the 19th century the growing industrial and commercial sectors of the economy required a literate labor force. It seems that late in the 20th century this role of public education which is, of course, not the only one for which it was established, is not being achieved for a significant minority of students thereby depriving them of equal opportunities on the job market. The economist must emphasize, however, that the proper and rational allocation of manpower will place the task of preparing young people for the participation in productive activities into the school system. He will consider the use of special employment projects for the purpose of remedial education as a costly program which can be accepted only on a temporary basis until such time that certain segments of the public school system have developed new and more effective methods of conveying adequate reading and other skills to all of their students.

As can be seen from Table 14-6 enrollment in the in-school and out-of-school programs was highest in 1966 but declined in subsequent years. By contrast the summer program showed a substantial increase until 1968 but was curtailed for the 1969 and 70 seasons. Although projects coming under N.Y.C. have early come under criticism and investigation for fiscal malpractices, the Office of Economic Opportunity—O.E.O.—while reorganized in 1969 is continuing.

The need for the maintenance of such a program can be clearly shown by a study of the economic background and the size of the families of the enrollees in the Youth Corps as well as their racial composition. This will be shown in Table 14-7.

The information gathered from Table 14-7 demonstrates in a way the social cost of poverty. We see that the vast majority of enrollees in N.Y.C. come from families in the poverty sector of the economy. Only 6.8 percent came from families with an annual income of $5,000 and over. We also gain an insight into the close association between low family income and the size of the family. More than 50 percent of the participants in the Neighborhood Youth Corps came from families comprising more than 5 persons. While the proportion of whites among the enrollees are in a majority, Negroes, as expected are represented among the enrollees to a far larger proportion than is indicated by their share of the total popula-

TABLE 14-7
CHARACTERISTICS OF YOUTH ENROLLED IN NEIGHBORHOOD YOUTH CORPS
SEPTEMBER 1967–AUGUST 1968

Race
White. 53.9
Negro 42.1
American Indian 2.6
Oriental. 4
Other 1.0

Years of School Completed
6 years or less 9
7 years 2.6
8 years 9.8
9 years 21.6
10 years 34.0
11 years 29.9
12 years 1.1

Estimated Annual Family Income
Below $1,000 2
$1,000–$1,999 . . . . 30.6
$2,000–$2,999 . . . . 27.4
$3,000–$3,999 . . . . 22.8
$4,000–$4,999 . . . . 12.1
$5,000 and over 6.8

Number of Persons in family
1 person 8
2 persons 3.4
3 persons 7.5
4 persons 10.9
5 persons 13.4
6 persons 13.6
7 persons 12.6
8 persons and over 37.9

SOURCE: Table F-8, *Manpower Report of the President* (January 1969).

tion. This social profile of the N.Y.C. reinforces the objections raised throughout this text against classifying the enrollees as "employed." Actually the main purpose of this campaign within the overall war against poverty is to prepare the participants for an entry into the job market and to improve their employment potential. But this shows clearly that N.Y.C. is not so much an employment program but an attempt to reduce structural unemployment of inadequately educated and trained people in the future. It should also not be overlooked that one of the intended side effects of N.Y.C. is not so much economic as social and political. It was hoped that this involvement of teen-agers in various programs of activity and remedial education would demonstrate to them that there is great concern for them and that they should not feel abandoned by modern industrialized society.

The Job Corps has been kept very small within the framework of the Economic Opportunity Act. In June 1968 only 33,013 people were enrolled in it, of whom 71 percent were male and 29 percent were female. In contrast to N.Y.C., Negroes were in a majority, amounting to 59 percent of the enrollees. Here again we find great stress being placed on remedial education. The need for this can be seen all too clearly from Table 14-8.

TABLE 14-8

EDUCATIONAL PROFILE OF JOB CORPS ENROLLEES, JUNE 1968.

Years of School Completed		Reading Level	Mathematics Level
Per cent	100	100	100
6 years or less.	7		
7 years	10		
8 years	21		
9 years	25		
10 years	18		
11 years	8		
12 years	12		
1st grade		6	
2nd grade		10	
3rd grade		13	
4th grade		20	
5th grade		18	
6th grade		16	
7th grade		9	
8th grade		4	
9th grade and over		5	
1st grade			3
2nd grade			11
3rd grade			10
4th grade			17
5th grade			24
6th grade			20
7th grade			10
8th grade			4
9th grade and over			3

SOURCE: Table F-15, *Manpower Report of the President* (January 1969).

While the total number of participants in the Job Corps has been kept small, the educational profile revealed in Table 14-8 is a graphic illustration of the problems of employability resulting from the inadequacy of the type of elementary school instruction received by typical enrollees in the Job Corps. Although 63 percent of the enrollees had completed from 9 to 12 years of school, a full 65 percent of the enrollees did have cumulatively only a sixth grade reading level. It should be noted that a sixth grade reading level is a minimum requirement for acceptance in the Armed Services of the United States.

As originally conceived, the Job Corps was quite similar to the Civilian Conservation Corps—C.C.C.—of the 1930's in that it took young people out of their urban environment and placed them into camps, often deactivated Army barracks in the countryside. There was, however, one great difference: whereas the old Corps was available only to boys, the Job Corps also developed programs for girls. The C.C.C. was well-financed from the beginning and in 1934 it already reached an enrollment of 330,000 young men. For a number of reasons the Job Corps of the 1960's was far less popular. Inevitable incidents in various camps were widely recorded and criticized. In 1969, disregarding opposition, many camps were closed and the activities were relocated into deprived urban centers, concentrating on preparation for jobs. One reason why the Job Corps did not develop as successfully as had the old Civilian Conservation Corps is, of course, found in the fact that it had to compete to a certain extent with the Neighborhood Youth Corps. But it would be futile to deny that a changing social climate with increased racial tensions also contributed to the very limited scope of the Job Corps in the 1960's.

When the Economic Opportunity Act was passed in 1964 most enterprises still insisted that job applicants had at least a high school education. Failure to stay in school for the time required to receive a high school diploma was equated with unemployability. In view of the fact that the numbers of school dropouts kept increasing, a potentially dangerous situation seemed to be in the making. Within a few years, it was feared, a sizable number of young people concentrated in urban slums would accumulate without hope of ever getting regular employment. We have seen already that this is one of the reasons why the antipoverty projects place such emphasis on remedial educational activities. But soon after the inauguration of these programs, a change of attitude of private business could be noted. Partly under the pressure of Federal agencies, partly due to the favorable financial situation, many leading enterprises began to recognize that they have a social obligation to try to reduce hard core unemployment by giving so-called "unemployables" an opportunity to make up for educational deficiencies while undergoing on-the-job training. The Manpower Administration of the Labor Department has made available in the fiscal year 1969, $200 million to finance in part a program called *Job Opportunities in the Business Sector (JOBS)*. The projects are carried out in cooperation with the *National Alliance of Business Men*. As a result many banks and insurance companies have undertaken on-the-job training programs of young people who even a few years before would not have been considered as good or even minimal employment risks. Although a considerable proportion of these trainees did have some work experience, it usually was of a type that indicated that actually they were unemployable. However, a large proportion of the trainees responded well to the combined training and remedial education program. Most important upon completion of the training 68 percent of the trainees remained with the company which has undertaken the program. A recruitment goal of over

600,000 trainees had been established for the year 1971 but the slump in 1970 curtailed the program.

Concepts of employability have also been broadened in many manufacturing industries. Early in the 1960's job applicants who had trouble filling out simple application forms for factory jobs were not processed further. They were considered unemployable. In 1967 the automobile companies in the Detroit area started recruitment drives in the poorer sections of town where the nonwhite unemployment rate was very high. But now applicants were assisted in filling out the necessary blanks and a considerable number of hard core unemployed were actually taken on. This example was followed by many other companies in the manufacturing industry.

While this broadening of the concept of employability must be considered a breakthrough if compared with the more rigid employment practices of the recent past, the fact cannot be overlooked that this liberalization coincided with a period of full employment. Especially banks and insurance companies found that the traditional supply of low echelon office workers was running low and that those with a high school diploma or some training beyond that level were able to find employment in departments operating computers. At least in part the willingness of private business to give so-called unemployables a job opportunity is connected with this developing shortage of labor supply in the lower ranges of the occupational structure on the labor market. This being so the question can very well be raised whether the subsidy by business to finance the training cost above and beyond wages paid by business to the trainees is really justified. In many other countries apprenticeship training has traditionally and is presently being carried out on a vast scale by private business without any subsidies coming from government agencies. Cost arising from this type of on-the-job training has always been considered as an inevitable expense connected with conducting business. It is true that in other countries apprenticeship training does not have to concern itself with "remedial courses" in such areas as reading and arithmetic because in many countries it can be assumed safely that graduates of elementary schools offering eight or nine years of primary education have mastered these skills. It should also be stressed that apprenticeships as discussed here are not identified with "on-the-job-training." The latter usually enables a trainee only to carry out a specific operation. Unlike training programs for junior executives which are far more varied, it at best enables people to function in a one-track situation.

It must be realized, however, that these breakthroughs in manpower policies occurred at a time when unemployment dropped below 4 percent in connection with the step-up of production in consequence of the Vietnamese War. Once the attempts to "wind down" that conflict became noticeable on the labor market and the unemployment rate rose sharply in the first three months of 1970, indications multiplied that employers planned to cut back the number of trainees which had been taken in by them in recent years. There were forecasts that unemployment among the young would begin to rise and that employment opportunities available to new entrants into the labor market would be curtailed further by the assignment of experienced workers to lower classified jobs in order to retain them in employment. These developments made it clear that the measures to increase youth employment taken in the 1960's were of a "stopgap type" and did not really provide for long-run solutions. This has to be borne in mind as we study in the next section the message on manpower training of President Nixon of August 12, 1969.

14-6. TOWARDS A UNIFIED MANPOWER TRAINING POLICY

In the preceding sections we have surveyed the major programs which have been inaugurated in the nineteen sixties to deal with structural unemployment and to reduce hard core unemployment. One result of the initiation of these various policies through separate laws such as the Manpower Development and Training Act and the Economic Opportunity Act was the growth of complex and confused agencies each dealing with bits and pieces of manpower policies without common guidelines and coordination. This confused structure also made it difficult for individuals desiring to get into training programs to find out where to go and to obtain information about all the available options. One example of the random way in which trainees were selected was offered by the New York Police Department which occasionally set up recruiting centers at busy subway stations and even on the corner of Wall Street and Broadway in the heart of the financial district.

The message of President Nixon mentioned above proposed to merge ultimately the various training and placement efforts into one manpower development program to be administered by the Department of Labor. This is a tremendous step forward. It would have been much better to establish a unified administrative framework for these employment policies at the time when they were initiated. When the Administration ordered a change in the "Concentrated Employment Program" (CEP) that had been funded jointly by the Office of Economic Opportunity and the Department of Labor and administered by local community agencies, transferring it to state employment agencies, great opposition arose against this change. Ultimately the Public Employment Service must become the one agency responsible for the administration of all employment policies.

It is obvious that these public employment services can handle the administration of specific manpower development programs only if they succeed in penetrating also the general labor market to a larger extent than they have been able up to now. We have seen in Sec. 11-6 that labor placements in this country have a dual structure and that the public employment service has so far not succeeded in penetrating to its core where the bulk of white-collar and high wage blue-collar hiring is being carried out. The consolidation of the manpower training programs should not be permitted to develop into a further fragmentation of the institutions on the American labor market. It is true that the merging of the various training programs is intended to eliminate one type of such fragmentation but unless the training programs are geared to transfer eventually the trainees to the mainstream of American labor supply, there is great danger that the consolidation of the various projects in one administration will be organizational rather than social and economic in real terms.

It must be borne in mind that even the best of these programs cannot generate employment. On the contrary, they presuppose the continuation of very high levels of full employment with a constantly increasing demand for adequately trained labor. The avoidance of unemployment remains, therefore, the overall objective of an employment policy. We will now offer some concluding thoughts on this problem.

We have seen that the tremendous increase in aggregate public spending for defense and in the sector of state and local governments in the mid-sixties had pushed employment to the 96 percent level. However, towards the end of the 1960's resistance increased in Congress and in the country against the continuous rise of expenditures for national defense. After the "quantum jump" in employment in state and local governments which occurred after 1965, some flattening out of this rising trend also became discernible. This is to say that the two main additional injections into aggregate spending are bound to lose some of their strength in the 1970's. A first indication was seen already in the increase of the unemployment rate which set in in the second half of 1969. We have seen, however, in Chapter 13 that unless aggregate spending continues to grow, unemployment is bound to increase. The problem before us is how we can assure a continuation of economic growth even after social and political priorities have shifted from the predominance of war and defense to domestic programs of renewal and sustained progress. We will discuss this now at least in outline form.

14-7. PERSPECTIVES FOR EMPLOYMENT AND MANPOWER POLICIES

We have stressed in Sec. 11-8 that it is necessary to distinguish clearly between manpower and employment policies. Actually the two approaches must go hand in hand especially when it comes to the problem of reducing hard core unemployment and to prevent the buildup of chronic unemployment. The danger of such a development cannot be discounted as military spending and the size of the armed forces are being reduced somewhat from their peak in the late 1960's. Now the main burden of our discussion in this Part II of this text has shown that full employment cannot be engineered or programmed merely by a manipulation of aggregate spending through monetary and fiscal policies. Ultimately levels of employment must be linked to output targets in the private and public sector spelled out in real terms. As we have seen in Chapter 13 this can be done by a "reversal" of the employment equation writing on the left-hand side total output and on the right-hand side the national income which can be derived from full utilization of the labor force. This technique can be used for the setting up of output and employment budgets. They would be indicative of the levels of the G.N.P. which must be achieved if we are to maintain reasonably high levels of full employment while also liquidating a good deal of hard-core unemployment as it prevailed in the United States even after the national unemployment rate dropped below 4 percent. A good illustration for this type of program which may be developed within this frame of reference, we refer to some of the suggestions contained in the Report of the National Advisory Commission on Civil Disorders, dated March 1, 1968. Among the projects advocated there for a three year period were:

(1) creating one million new jobs in the public sector in three years.
(2) creating one million additional jobs in the public and private sectors in three years.

Among the programs mentioned under No. 2 would be improvement of rundown neighborhoods, employment in community service offices of the police department. Other socially useful public services may be created in additions to hospital staff or services at home to old people and similar type of services for which there is an unmet need in the affluent society.

The Advisory Commission also proposes an expansion of employment in the private sector through the buildup of training programs already discussed in the preceeding section of this chapter. In addition to these proposals which are designed primarily to reduce hardcore unemployment to its inherent irreducible minimum, the Advisory Committee proposed a major stepping up of building construction activities. They proposed a plan to build 600,000 low and moderate housing units immediately and then plan to add 6 million such units over the following five years. This sounds like a tall order, but it is precisely this type of program which ought to be substituted for that part of defense spending which is in the process of being eliminated in the public sector of aggregate spending.

It would be hard to sustain the argument that such vast projects are beyond the means or the ability of the United States. The question arises whether the high degree of scientific competence, team work and technical precision which led to the success of the Apollo 11 project could not be duplicated when the objective is not concerned with the solution of technical problems but with the solution of such special problems as the maintenance of full employment and the reduction to a minimum of hard core unemployment. While there are basic differences between purely technical difficulties which have to be overcome to achieve a certain goal such as manned space explorations and the complex human and sociological effects underlying social-economic situations, it would be a defeatist attitude to assume that this high level of cooperation could not be effective in our social world.

SELECTED BIBLIOGRAPHY

Delehanty, John A., ed. *Manpower Problems and Policies* (Scranton Pa.: International Textbook Co., 1969).

Hansen, Alvin H. *Economic Issues of the 1969's* (New York: McGraw-Hill Book Company, 1963).

Harris, Seymour E. *Economics of the Kennedy Years* (New York: Harper & Row, Publishers, 1965).

Mangum, Garth L. *The Emergence of Manpower Policy* (New York: Holt, Rinehart and Winston, Inc., 1969).

Okun, Arthur M., ed. *The Battle Against Unemployment* (New York: W. W. Norton & Co., Inc., 1964).

Pearl, Arthur, and Frank Riessman. *New Careers for the Poor: The Non-Professional in Human Service* (New York: The Free Press, 1966).

QUESTIONS FOR DISCUSSION

1. During an economic expansion or a period of sustained growth, there are important factors evident in highly industrialized nations which tend to offset or at least reduce the threat of inflation until full employment has been reached. What are these factors and how do they manifest themselves?

2. The techniques of Keynesian economics seem well suited to the problems of cyclical unemployment. For what reasons may the above statement be made?

3. In what ways could government attempts at dealing with cyclical unemployment be made more efficient?

4. Since traditional Keynesian economics does not seem capable of eliminating the problem of persistent unemployment, what specific policies (public and private) seem best suited to this difficult task?

5. To what extent do you feel that the major legislation of the 1960's which has been directed at the problem of persistent unemployment will be successful in the longer run? (i.e., The Area Redevelopment Act, The Manpower Development and Training Act, and the Economic Opportunity Act.)

6. The structural-unemployment thesis seems to require a unique approach to finding a workable solution to this problem. To what extent (economically, socially, and psychologically) do you feel that training and retraining programs offer such an approach?

7. What would be your reaction to a contemporary economist who would maintain that ultimately the solution to unemployment in general can be found in the spending approach?

8. Economics deals with the proper allocation of scarce resources. Can a three-pronged attack on unemployment such as suggested in this chapter provide for a more efficient and complete realization of this objective?

9. Is the approach to full employment through a determination of aggregate output rather than aggregate spending a workable one?

10. Give a summary statement of the features of a macrodynamic approach to full employment and point out the important features that such an approach has for a highly industrialized nation such as the United States.

COLLECTIVE BARGAINING

Wage determination in an organized labor market has already been analyzed in Part II. We must now turn our attention to the developments and institutions that bring about an organized labor market in many important sectors of the economic system. Collective bargaining procedures occur in an intricate social setting in which historical, legal, personal, and psychological factors are operating, often at cross purposes. In order to clarify these complexities the institutional setting and the nature and scope of collective bargaining will be examined. Special attention will be given to the perplexing problems of labor relations in the public sector. Day to day industrial relations will be studied within the overall framework of the union contract as the shop constitution. International comparison of labor relations conclude this point.

Institutional Setting for Collective Bargaining

THE INSTITUTIONAL SETTING OF COLLECTIVE BARGAINING

So far in our study of labor, we found it necessary to place the problems of wages and of employment into a macroeconomic framework. There is no way of analyzing and understanding the issues arising in these areas without taking into account the dynamics of the economic conditions which shape in specific ways wage structures and levels of employment. We must remember moreover that labor is two dimensional. On the one side it must be viewed as a factor of production. On the other it must be analyzed as an organized group in contest at all times with others for a share in the national income. To the purely economic there are added the social dynamics of group interaction as they occur in industrial relations. In classical and neoclassical economics "labor" was not seen in this context. It was rather viewed as a mass of individual increments of the factor labor governed only by the invisible hand of forces establishing parameters for the demand for workers and wage rates. As we have seen in Chapter 6, it was assumed that these forces would establish clearly determined wage rates and levels of employment given specific shapes of the demand curve for and a supply curve of labor. When collective bargaining asserted itself, neoclassical economists considered it as an intrusion into the free labor market. Unions were viewed as outsiders on the factor market causing distortions of the operations of the forces tending to insure equilibrium in the distribution of income shares of employment.

The time has long passed when collective bargaining and its results can be analyzed as "deviations" from a pure equilibrium state of an unorganized labor market. They are part and parcel of the contemporary economic structure. Attempts to restate the conditions of equilibrium in an advanced industrialized society must, therefore, allow for the dynamics of collective bargaining. In this chapter we will deal with the institutional setting which has evolved in the United States to promote and to protect collective bargaining. The history of American labor contains the clear lesson, that the structuring of relations between management and labor and the final acceptance of collective bargaining is the end product of turbulent developments. Legislation was necessary to establish a workable framework for collective bargaining. A clear indication of what the absence of established voluntary or legal procedures of collective bargaining implies could be gathered in the late 1960's when Cesar Chavez began to organize agricultural workers in the western part of the United States. Since these workers are specifically exempted from coverage by the American labor relations laws, this new organization lacked legal standing in its attempts to get employers to agree to bargain collectively. Only in 1970 was Chavez successful in signing contracts with some grape growers providing for improved pay.

The experience of advanced industrial countries shows that the practice of collective bargaining does not necessarily presuppose a prior legal framework. For instance in Sweden a voluntary master agreement between national groups of management and of labor was reached in which both parties obligated themselves to recognize their member organization as collective bargaining representatives. When in the 1930's a spread of the practice of collective bargaining, especially into the mass production industries was considered desirable in the United States, the practice could not be set up through voluntary agreements between labor and management groups because many influential employers continued to oppose recognition of trade unions for the purpose of negotiating with them on conditions of pay and work. As a result the question was settled by law through the National Labor Relations Act of 1935 which was subsequently expanded through the Taft-Hartley Act of 1947. We will have to concentrate on the institutional setting of collective bargaining established by this legislation. American labor relations legislation cannot be understood without a study of conditions as they prevailed in the vastly unorganized labor market of the 19th and early 20th centuries in this country.

15-1. INDUSTRIAL CONFLICT AS A CLASH BETWEEN TWO SETS OF RIGHTS

In order to have any type of collective bargaining at all there must be legal equality between all members of a society. Obviously as long as some groups of labor, for instance from rural areas, can be commandeered for road and canal building and similar projects, compensation if any will be given by *unilateral acts* of the authorities. Similar conditions were characteristic of feudal estates and guilds operating under strict regulations.

The French Revolution did away with such inequalities in Europe. The enactment of the Bill of Rights in 1791 conferred to Americans all the rights essential to the formation of trade unions such as the rights of free speech and free assembly. This repealed for the United States the English conspiracy laws prohibiting combinations of labor. Originally enacted in 1349 they still were in force at the time the Bill of Rights was accepted. They were not repealed in Britain until 1825.

But soon the workers found out what in the 20th century the descendants of slaves also experienced: *The granting of equal rights does not of itself establish de facto equality* in the real world of the labor market or in business, education, professions or government. The labor movement can be viewed in its initial stages as an embodiment of a long drawn out struggle to transform purely legal or theoretical equality into real and operational equality.

The mere establishment of legal equality between employers and workers, the formal conversion of traditional employment situations into contractual relationships establishing wage rates which assumedly were freely agreed upon, did not eliminate the great gulf separating people into two distinct groups: the property owners and those without property. In the early stages of industrialization personal ownership and management coincided to a much larger degree than is the case in our contemporary, post-industrial society. Proprietorship conveyed social status and prestige. Lack of property meant powerlessness. In spite of legal equality between employers and workers, the latter approached an employment relationship with rare exceptions from a position of weakness. Since a great deal of the demand for labor that was forthcoming was for the unskilled or semiskilled category, employers as a rule were assured of an ample labor supply even if occasionally individual workers turned down a job because the wage offer was too low. The elimination of ancient privileges and the establishment of an institutional framework of the labor market characterized by freedom of contract and freedom of movement between localities and countries and between occupations and employments did not equalize the relative bargaining positions of employers and of individual workers in the determination of the conditions of pay and work. Usually management could "negotiate" from a position of strength.

Unions are an organizational device of labor to overcome the inherent weakness of individual workers in their dealings with employers by combining into units of aggregate labor which will be made available only if certain demands of labor have been met. It is easy to see then why for such long periods of the history of modern industry, management resisted organized labor and tried to avoid as long as possible entering into collective bargaining agreements with unions.

It is misleading to view labor relations up to the 1930's under the viewpoint of labor's fight for the "right to organize." This right already existed. What was at stake was the ability to exercise this right vis-a-vis management. The framework of all the conflicts between labor and management was established by the fact that management invoked *property rights* to frustrate collective bargaining, whereas labor based its demand for recognition on such *civil rights* as free speech and free assembly.

Property rights were interpreted as entitling the owner of an enterprise to determine, without interference by either legislation or "outsiders," who should be employed on his premises, who should be permitted to enter, and under what conditions employment could either be continued or terminated. There was nothing on the statute books to prevent an employer from setting up a rule whereby workers who were members of a labor organization or who had shown interest in joining such a group could not remain in his employ. Property rights would also be referred to whenever an employer refused to have any dealings with a union representative. He could refuse to bargain with them on the simple ground that no contractual relationships existed between him and the person trying to represent his employees.

The exercise of these property rights proved to be a powerful weapon in labor-management conflicts. Using their rights to discharge active union workers, to forbid entry of union representatives, and even to ask local magistrates for an injunction prohibiting organizational activities of unionists in the area, many employers were able to frustrate union attempts to set up collective bargaining. These old-time "labor injunctions" were deeply resented by organized labor. Although they were abolished by the Norris-LaGuardia Act of 1932 and never revived, the memory of this practice was still vivid enough to cause protests against the altogether different type of injunction provided under certain conditions by the Taft-Hartley Act of 1947.

Management interpreted property rights as empowering it to establish, in a unilateral way, such labor conditions as the "nonunion shop," barring from employment all workers who were members of unions or who had shown active interest in getting them organized. Employers felt that they had a right to enforce their antiunion employment practices by checking on the attitude of workers. For this purpose the "Yellow Dog Contract" was conceived, in which a worker promised not to join a union—a pledge implying that he was subject to automatic discharge if he violated this agreement. Like the old-style labor injunction, this employment practice was outlawed by Congress in 1932. But because management did no legal wrong in maintaining nonunion shops, employing labor spies, or blacklisting workers who were suspected of unionism, organized labor had no legal means at its disposal to counteract such methods.

The main weapon of labor in opposing the nonunion shop and other discriminatory antilabor practices was the strike. Inasmuch as workers had achieved equality before the law, they were free, either individually or collectively, to refuse to work for conditions which they felt were unfair and burdensome. In trying to enforce the demands of labor by strike, unions were utilizing the rights of freedom of contract, of movement, of speech, and assembly inherent in equal-citizenship status. It is clear, then, that the conflicts between management and labor up to the 1930's in the United States were caused by the clash of two sets of rights conveyed to the citizens in this democratic setting. There was no legal definition of the way in which the property rights of management and the right to form associations of labor, could be reconciled. Lacking such legislation, labor-management relations actually occurred in an uncharted area in which ultimately a power equilibrium would establish itself.

In this legally undefined situation of conflicting rights of management and of labor unions were able to make progress only slowly. Highly skilled workers such as printers, facing an industry characterized by many small plants, were able to achieve union wage scales as early as the middle of the nineteenth century in some of the largest cities of this country. Eventually building contractors operating small enterprises had to come to terms with craft unions because of the relative strength of the latter on their particular labor market. Union organization also gained considerable strength in the garment industry, which is still characterized by a large number of small-scale employers. In the same way organized labor achieved an early ascendancy in the entertainment field. But in attempting to represent the vast majority of production workers collective-bargaining drives ran into powerful resistance by large-scale mass production industries.

The inherent conflict between property rights and rights of labor to organize required a resolution through legislation. The National Labor Relations Act of 1935 also known as the Wagner Act introduced certain restrictions on the exercise of property rights by management. This first comprehensive labor relations law intended to correct "the inequality of bargaining power between employees who do not possess full freedom of association or actual liberty of contract" (Sec. 1, Par. 2). The method selected to achieve de facto equality was certainly rather one-sided although this was understandable in the light of the preceding decades of antiunion employment policies. In this first version of Federal labor-relations legislation it was assumed that only management could be wrong. As a result, the law of 1935 contains merely a catalogue of "unfair labor practices for an employer." According to Sec. 8, which also reappears in the Management-Labor Relations Act of 1947, also known as Taft-Hartley Act, employers are prohibited from interfering, restraining, or coercing employees in the exercise of their "right to self-organization, to form, join, or assist labor organizations, to bargain collectively through representatives of their own choosing, and to engage in concerted activities for the purpose of collective bargaining or other mutual aid or protection" (Sec. 7). This restriction of the property rights, including the unrestrained right to hire and fire, also rules out the company union, an organization of employees set up with the assistance of management and dominated by it. Finally, a refusal of employers to bargain collectively with representatives of their employees is also considered an unfair labor practice. (In Sec. 15–2 of this text there is a more detailed discussion of the issues that have arisen in the area of unfair practices of employers.)

While the Wagner Act confined itself to curtailing the rights of employers with regard to union members and relations to organized labor, it became evident, especially after World War II, that a certain curtailment on the activities of organized labor was also necessary. This applied specifically to the then prevailing "jurisdictional strikes" which were interruptions of work not because of a dispute with management over wages and conditions of employment but due to intramural conflicts of rival labor organizations, very often two craft unions, each claiming the right to perform certain jobs. This type of labor unrest, the frequency of strikes immediately after World War II, and a general swing of the pendulum somewhat to the right brought about an insertion of a catalogue of "unfair labor practices for a labor organization" into the legislation of 1947. These provisions bar a union from calling an "organizational strike" in order to compel an employer to start collective bargaining. They outlaw secondary boycotts, jurisdictional strikes, and attempts at "featherbedding," that is, forcing an employer to hire, or to keep in his employ, more people than management deems necessary. Problems connected with this list of unfair union practices are explored in Sec. 15–3.

15-2. LIMITATIONS ON MANAGEMENT IN INDUSTRIAL RELATIONS

The general principle underlying the concept of unfair practices of management in that there should be no interference with the right of workers to organize. There must be a complete absence of restraint or coercion. Under the rules of the Wagner Act of 1935 this restriction on management was given a very strict interpretation. The National Labor Relations Board ruled that representatives of management had to abstain almost completely from any verbal and written statements that might take a position on ongoing organizational drives and union activity. Some interpretations of the noninterference principle went so far as to state that management could not even point out the fact that union leaders involved in organizational or bargaining activities had been proven to be under the influence of underworld or subversive elements. Distribution of handbills at factory gates stating the management view on unionization of employees was also considered an unfair labor practice of the employer.

While it is easy to understand the strictness of the interpretation of the noninterference principle in the light of industrial-relations patterns preceding the legislation of the 1930's, there is no doubt that this legislation amounted to a rather drastic curtailment of the freedom of speech privilege of management. The Taft-Hartley Act restored a better balance in this respect. Today management is free to express views, arguments, or opinions about unionization and particular unions, subject only to one important limitation. Such opinions of employers and the way which they are disseminated must not contain any threat of economic or personal reprisals in the event that workers decide to disregard the views of management, nor can they promise any benefits as a reward for a compliance by workers with the wishes of management concerning the question of collective bargaining.

According to this legal framework an employer might very well say that in his opinion unionization or the joining up of employees with a particular union would be unnecessary or a mistake. However, he cannot go so far as to say that, if workers go ahead with unionization, he might become "fed up with the whole business" and close down the enterprise. Such a remark would clearly be a threat of an economic sanction and without doubt an unfair labor practice of management. The point is that no law exists whereby a person can be compelled to stay in business if, for whatever reason, he desires to get out. But threatening to do so as a response to the desire of workers to affiliate with a union and to start collective bargaining would be considered an illegal interference with the right of labor to organize as guaranteed in industrial-relations legislation.

On occasion employers have threatened to move their operation to another part of the country should a majority of the employees vote to be represented by a union. Such plant removals might be comparatively simple in industries operating with a minimum of fixed equipment. Again, if such a move is mentioned in the context of organizational or bargaining activities, it can be construed as a threat and an interference with the rights of employees. Actually in a number of cases the National Labor Relations Board ordered a return of enterprises to their original locations because the evidence before it had shown clearly that the removal of the business had been motivated exclusively by the determination of management to avoid dealing with organized labor. As in the previously discussed case of a closing down of a business, it must be stated that enterprises have the right to change their location if this seems to be warranted by such considerations as better transportation facilities, proximity to raw materials or markets, or even lower employment costs. But such moves must clearly be made for rational economic reasons and completely outside the context of an industrial relations situation.

The law not only bans threats of economic disadvantages if workers exercise their right to organize, but also forbids the promise of benefits as a reward for abstaining from unionization. Thus it would be an unfair labor practice of management to raise wages and make other inducements to demonstrate to employees that they really don't "need" collective bargaining. Although collective bargaining is primarily concerned with higher wages, the right of labor to organize exists as such and cannot be challenged by management through the promise of bonuses if employees abstain from exercising their right to organize.

Antiunion attitudes can also be reflected in managerial policies dealing with individual employees. For this reason discriminatory hiring or promotion policies through which nonunion workers receive preferment as a reward are an unfair labor practice. Such practices are possible only in firms that have not signed a union-shop clause and where, therefore, a considerable number of employees may not be members of the union. The burden of proof for all charges of discriminatory personnel policies is with the complainant. It must be clearly established that hiring or advancement policies of an employer show a pattern of discrimination. The same would be true of discharges. It would have to be shown that the termination of employment was directly attributable to union activities and not to other causes.

Organizational activities of labor are strengthened further by the protection of employees against discharges or other discrimination because they have filed charges of unfair labor practices against management or have testified to this effect before the National Labor Relations Board.

Summing up, it can be stated that the law provides a good number of safeguards for the exercise of the right of labor to organize. All complaints against management for having engaged in unfair labor practices must be filed first with the competent regional Labor Relations Board. A trial examiner will be appointed by the board which will conduct formal hearings if his original attempt to arrange a settlement of the dispute directly has failed. The trial examiner will hear witnesses and can also order that relevant records of the company be submitted to him. In the early days of the Wagner Act, trial examiners often interpreted their role to include giving advice and guidance to workers about the type of complaint that could be formulated under the circumstances of the dispute. This less than completely impartial role is no longer admissible today. The change in practice and procedures corresponds to the "coming of age" of organized labor and to the more balanced approach represented by the Taft-Hartley Act. After completion of the hearing, the trial examiner submits a report to the regional Labor Relations Board containing his findings of fact and his recommendations as to the disposition of the case. The board can act accordingly; it can also reject the proposal of the examiner, order additional hearings, and ask for a consideration of legal points overlooked or handled differently by the examiner in the first round of the case. Decisions of the regional boards can be appealed to the National Labor Relations Board.

The usual form of order issued by the National Labor Relations Board is of the "cease and desist" type, enjoining the accused party to stop engaging in unfair practices. If there has been a discriminatory discharge of employees, for example, in connection with legitimate activities during a strike, the Board can order a reinstatement. Orders of the Board can be made enforceable by the Federal courts. Noncompliance would place the violating party in contempt of court and make it subject to fines and even a jail sentence.

Taking all this into account, it is hard to see why labor unions cannot succeed in extending their membership and their organization into areas with a low degree of unionization, or drive for the inclusion in their ranks of hitherto weakly organized categories of wage and salary workers. So far as interstate commerce is concerned, which is subject to the Management-Labor Relations Act, management cannot legitimately engage in activities that would make unionization difficult or impossible. It can be challenged and charged with unfair labor practices before regional Labor Relations Boards wherever such practices take place.

So far we have considered only unfair labor practices of management. We have already seen in the preceding section that the original assumption of the Wagner Act that in industrial relations only management could engage in unfair practices could not be maintained over longer periods of time. After all, industrial relations are bi-lateral and it is only natural that violations of the principle of fairness in the conduct of collective relations can occur on either side. Unfair labor practices of management, as we have seen, deal with actions which could effectively impede the self-organization of labor, the right to organize and to engage in collective bargaining. The restraints on labor are in forms of prohibitions of certain practices in connection with labor disputes.

15-3. RESTRICTIONS ON LABOR IN INDUSTRIAL CONFLICTS

Especially in the period immediately after World War II *jurisdictional strikes* were quite frequent. Usually they involved craft unions and centered around the question of what particular job should be awarded for instance to plumbers rather than to electricians or to a union of stage setters rather than to carpenters. It is characteristic of this type of conflict that no disputes exist between management and labor. What is at stake is a struggle between two groups of organized labor both claiming to be eligible to perform certain types of work. Occasionally such jurisdictional strikes led to a considerable interruption of production. This type of labor dispute is now considered an unfair labor practice by a labor organization. It should be noted, however, that in a number of state labor relations laws, for example in New York, such union practices are not banned altogether because these laws did not incorporate the corresponding sections of the Taft Hartley Act into their statutes which govern intrastate labor relations. For this reason there are occasional interruptions of activities especially building construction due to such disputes between craft unions.

There is also a ban on *organizational strikes*. Unions cannot call out on strike employees with the intent of forcing management to agree to union recognition and collective bargaining. Such strike action would actually be an attempt to bypass the orderly procedures which have been set up by the law to obtain certification of a labor organization as exclusive bargaining representatives, as they will be discussed in further detail throughout Chapter 16. The ban on organizational strikes does not extend to a complete prohibition of *organizational picketing*. This type of picketing, however, is excluded when the employer has already recognized another labor union. That means this covers cases in which the underlying reason for the conflict is a jurisdictional dispute or at least the attempt of one union to displace another one from the collective labor relationship with management. This type of picketing can also not be conducted by a labor organization within twelve months after it had lost out in a union election.

One of the most difficult issues raised by the Taft-Hartley Act is the *"secondary boycott,"* another unfair union practice. In actual cases the determination of whether or not the facts of the situation constitute a secondary boycott may be quite difficult. The guiding principle is that such actions as a walkout and the setting up of picket lines at the plant where the striking workers are employed are an exercise of the right of labor to organize and would be a legal *"primary boycott"* subject only to police rules to safeguard traffic and public safety in general. Furthermore, managerial employees must be given access to strike-bound premises. However, an interruption of work or picketing of plants of an employer not involved in the dispute constitutes a secondary boycott and thus is considered illegal.

To illustrate this general principle, the rulings of the National Labor Relations Board and of the Supreme Court of the United States concerning subcontractors can be mentioned. Picketing by a construction workers' union against one of the number of employers engaged in a huge construction project has been limited by the NLRB to the gates of the construction site leading directly to this particular sector of the project. It ordered the withdrawal of pickets from other gates through which employees not involved in the dispute but working for subcontractors were entering the premises. Picketing the first-mentioned gates would be a case of a legitimate primary boycott, but throwing a picket line around the other entrances—or for that matter in front of the plants of subcontractors—constitutes a secondary boycott and is considered an unfair labor practice by unions.

No collective action can be taken by labor to force management to accept a *closed shop*. Prior to the Taft Hartley Act this system was widespread especially in craft unions. It stipulated that management could only hire employees who already were members of the union. Further problems connected with hiring practices, especially the union shop, requiring new employees to enter the union with which management holds a collective contract will be discussed in Chapter 16.

Labor organizations are also forbidden to call strikes in order to force management to employ or to hire more people than are required in the judgment of the business executives. In our period of rapid changes in the technical structure of production systems the handling of the resulting problems of employment, especially permanent lay-offs becomes one of the most difficult issues in management-labor relations. Many demands of labor, for instance, for a shortening of the work week are in reality related to the issue of how many people, especially union members, will remain in their jobs after modernization programs have been carried out or automation has been introduced in various lines of production. Sometimes union resistance is prematurely or wrongly presented by management as the illegal practice of "featherbedding." In order to gain a wider perspective this complex problem will be discussed in greater detail in the next section.

15-4. "FEATHERBEDDING" AND AUTOMATION

The years prior to the passage of the Taft-Hartley Act of 1947 had witnessed the beginning of what only some years later became known as automation. Radio stations to an increasing degree relied on "canned music" and sought to dispense with "live musicians." Already the "talkies" had substantially reduced employment of musicians in movie theaters. Now the process of labor displacement was spreading to the broadcasting industry. The American Federation of Musicians tried to save the jobs of many of its members by requiring radio stations to pay for "stand-in orchestras." Clearly this was a demand of the union for the retention of more employees than were considered necessary by management. These and other instances led to the insertion into the Taft-Hartley Act of the ban on featherbedding.

Since then automation has become one of the major issues in labor-management relations, although sometimes it does not come to the surface in the official definition of issues to be negotiated. But many demands of labor and corresponding concessions of management are actually designed to deal with the problem of the impact of automation on levels of employment. These problems are an extremely difficult topic for collective bargaining, and the question may well be raised whether the far-reaching consequences of automation are a proper subject for negotiation within the framework of traditional labor-management disputes.

This difficulty has been demonstrated rather clearly in the case of railroad firemen. Since these employees are represented by a Brotherhood, to ask them to consent to eliminating virtually all the jobs of firemen in freight and yard service was tantamount to demanding that the labor organization terminate its very existence. While the railroads did have an excellent case in insisting that this cutback was a necessary result of the introduction of the oil-burning diesel locomotive, it became apparent that this life-and-death issue could not be settled even by the more elaborate conciliation and arbitration procedures of the Railway Labor Act. As will be shown in Sec. 15-7, Congress in 1963 had to set up an arbitration board. This board eventually ruled that 90 percent of the firemen jobs had to be abolished.

This ruling became binding upon the two parties and affected 40,000 workers. The board however, did not permit the immediate layoff of all these employees. The method outlined by the board can be considered one of the more important models for dealing with the problem of automation. It is the phasing-out system. This system provides for a gradual attrition and final disappearance of the group of workers affected by automation. In other words, jobs will be left vacant if employees die, quit, retire, or are dismissed for cause. Employees in this category must also accept comparable jobs offered to them by their employers. In case they refuse other comparable employment, they can be discharged.

Admittedly this phasing out may extend over a number of years. Hence the initial cost of employment saved may amount to very little. In the long run, of course, the savings will be substantial.

This type of approach to the impact of automation therefore spread both the advantages to management and the disadvantages to labor over a longer period of time, making the latter more tolerable and sheltering those immediately affected against the loss of their livelihood. The phasing-out method suggests itself primarily wherever the question of complete elimination of jobs arises. When the issue can be broadened by considering the effects of automation on the total number of employees of an enterprise rather than on one occupational subgroup, other solutions can be found. In such cases collective bargaining has proved to be a technique capable of solving these difficult problems.

The primary method employed is early retirement. The contracts negotiated in the automotive industry in 1964 can serve as an example. Early retirement is the device selected to bring about an attrition in the number of employees. In order to create an incentive for employees to retire before they reach the age of 65, workers can now claim their pension at a some-what reduced monthly rate if they have served with the company for 30 years and have reached age 55. If they retire at age 60 with the same minimum years of service, they can obtain a total retirement pay of $400 a month until they are 65. At that time they will receive their full social security benefits plus a company pension. However, these two monthly retirement payments will be somewhat less than the $400 in pensions that retired workers can receive between age 60–65.

Similar arrangements were introduced in the steel industry in 1965 and in some localities in the brewing industry. The Teamsters also have an incentive plan for early retirement. Under this scheme a substantial lump sum can be paid out that enables the retired teamster to move to a lower-cost area of the country, make a substantial down payment on a home, or start a small business. This arrangement would enable retired persons to live in comparative confort once they become eligible for old-age benefits.

Negotiating for incentives for early retirement is, of course, not a violation of the ban on "featherbedding." Even where automation threatens to abolish certain types of employment completely, attempts of unions to resist this development or to insist on phasing-out method should not be called featherbedding as construed by the Taft-Hartley Act. The indiscriminate use of this word in the complicated and far-reaching problems created by automation does not promote rational solutions.

15-5. THE IMPACT OF THE LEGAL FRAMEWORK OF INDUSTRIAL RELATIONS

At this point of our study of the American labor relations system it is well to pause and to establish clearly what current legislation does and does not do in this vital area of the contemporary economic structure. The main achievement of the legislation of the last forty years has been to transform the unstable, conflict-prone relationship between employers and employees into a more orderly system of resolving conflicts. It is well to realize that this legislation does not eliminate disputes and conflicts between management and labor as such. But it defines in specific ways certain actions which cannot be undertaken by management and certain activities which cannot be engaged in by labor in the course of their continuous confrontations. To that extent the spelling out by legislation of the institutional setting for collective bargaining has increased to some extent the stability of the labor relations system. It has made the timing of conflicts more predictable. Most important it has established a condition closer to equilibrium in the bargaining position of management and of labor. In so doing it has stopped the old practices of management which in the earlier phases of the industrial system curtailed so severely the growth of trade unionism. But in encouraging the self-organization of labor and the practice of collective bargaining, the law also created situations in which the regulated conflict between labor and management becomes more difficult to solve in many instances than in the old unregulated condition of the labor market.

The labor relations which have been regulated in some detail by recent legislation deal more with the preconditions of collective bargaining than with the processes of collective bargaining itself. But it is in the latter area that new issues are arising which require an intensive analysis. Before we address ourselves to these problems in Chapter 16 it is necessary to study the current legal devices dealing with collective bargaining. As late as 1966 Professor A. M. Ross, at that time U.S. Commissioner of Labor Statistics reported that most violations of the duty to bargain collectively were "bottomed upon a rejection of the principles of collective bargaining." A breakdown of types of violations of the duty to engage in collective bargaining showed that 51 percent of the cases represented attempts to bypass the union and to deal directly with employees; 35 percent of the cases were concerned with "bad faith" bargaining; 32 percent of the violations were based on a failure by management to recognize a majority union. In order to gain a proper perspective, it must be stressed that violations of the good faith bargaining provisions of the Taft Hartley Act were found predominantly in smaller firms. After an initial resistance in the years immediately following the adoption of the Wagner Act in 1935, major firms in most industries have accommodated themselves to the practice of collective bargaining. While often they engaged in hard bargaining, opposing vigorously specific demands of labor, for the last 30 years resistance to collective bargaining with production workers has vanished in large industrial enterprises. The story is, of course, very different when it comes to such white collar businesses as finance and insurance but in these instances the willingness of employees to press consistently and energetically for unionization and collective bargaining is rather weak.

It must be borne in mind that management-labor relations legislation has been fairly effective in bringing the two parties to the "bargaining table" but as we will see presently what happens afterwards, once negotiations have started is often outside the scope of the provisions of this legislation.

15-6. MEDIATION AND CONCILIATION OF INDUSTRIAL DISPUTES

While the Taft Hartley Act imposes on most parties the duty of good faith collective bargaining there is little that can be done under present legislation if one or both parties are willing to endure a long strike rather than to achieve a compromise. Early rulings of the National Relations Board established the principle that the parties in order to live up to the requirements of bargaining in good faith must discuss all issues subject to negotiation seriously. This would be more than going through the motions of an exchange of proposals and their immediate rejection. Attempts must be made at clarification and at finding a common ground on which an agreement could be built. Good faith in collective bargaining also imposes an obligation on the negotiators to present all the requests or demands at the beginning of the bargaining period. Only in this way will it be possible to locate areas where compromises seem to be possible and to reconcile in general the opposing positions.

It seems that these guidelines for collective bargaining are sometimes neglected by both parties. But if neither party files a complaint, there is no possibility of intervention by the National Labor Relations Board. When the outstanding labor-relations expert George W. Taylor was appointed as a fact-finder in the steel strike of 1959, he stated publicly that he had had a very difficult time in pinning down the issues. This statement was made a long time after collective bargaining negotiations had been conducted, had failed, and the walkout had started. In the newspaper strike in New York in 1965 a thorny issue was involved in the demands of the newspaper guild for a better company pension system. It became apparent that the strike had been called prior to a full exploration of the financial and other implications of the retirement pay scheme demanded by the union. While the presses stood still, management and labor called in their respective experts in order to study what was really involved in this pension plan. While strikes remain the ultimate weapon of labor it cannot be said that everything possible is being done for their prevention if, after the union has struck, it becomes clear that the bargaining preceding that walkout had not covered all issues completely.

A greater insistence on collective bargaining in good faith as originally conceived in American industrial-relations legislation could contribute towards the prevention of strikes called as a result of incomplete or faulty communications between labor and management in the bargaining that preceded the walkout. This would not interfere with the right to strike which has been reaffirmed by the Taft-Hartley Act of 1947 but it would protect the public against the unwelcome general effect of an involuntary or even a deliberate breakdown of communications between the parties obligated to engage in collective bargaining.

Traditionally, American labor unions have operated on the "no contract, no work" principle. Prior to the legislation of 1947, this often led to the calling of a strike the moment the existing contract had come to an end, without benefit of prior extended collective bargaining. A glance at the figures of man-days lost in Table 16-1 is an indication of the extent of this practice. In this respect the Taft-Hartley Act has brought important innovations and improvements. It is now required that 60 days prior to the expiration of a contract, both parties must notify each other regarding proposed changes in the conditions of work and pay. This sets collective bargaining in motion. Parties cannot, as it were, come forward with demands at the very last moment. Actually, in many cases, unofficial moves are made by the partners of the collective relationship sometime prior to the 60-day period. If 30 days before the expiration of the contract no new agreement is in sight, then the Federal Mediation and Conciliation Service can enter the negotiations if it feels that a deadlock leading to a strike would have wider repercussions throughout the economy. Unlike the Conciliation Service which existed in the United States Department of Labor prior to the law of 1947, the Federal agency established by that legislation does not have to wait for a request of the parties involved to come into the dispute and to try to settle it.

This injection of the Federal Mediation and Conciliation Service does not interfere with the prevailing concept of "free collective bargaining," which implies that a labor contract is achieved by the parties themselves rather than imposed by a government agency through "compulsory arbitration." Essentially, this service makes itself available to the parties in order to help them come to a voluntary agreement among themselves. Historically, conciliation in labor disputes has meant that the neutral person acting as a conciliator helps the parties to define their positions more clearly and facilitates an agreement by clearing up misconceptions with regard to the issues and misunderstandings between the two parties. Mediation goes beyond conciliation because it provides for the possibility of presenting the parties with a compromise proposal. While such a suggestion can be either accepted, rejected, or simply ignored, the more affirmative view is that such a plan might be the basis for an actual agreement among the contesting parties themselves. If the activities of the Federal Mediation and Conciliation Service do not succeed prior to the expiration of the original 60-day period, and if the parties cannot consent to a postponement of unilateral actions such as a strike or a lockout, then a walkout can start after the old contract has lapsed. There is no doubt that the legal obligation to start collective bargaining prior to the expiration of a contract has averted many strikes which would have been called otherwise.

The 60-day notice requirement with regard to desired changes in contracts to be negotiated and the mediation and conciliation procedures outlined above have cushioned the effects of the right of labor to strike and of management to lock out employees. The effectiveness of these delaying devices and of the methods of bringing parties to the point of signing a new labor contract without resorting to a strike depends very much on the general social climate. This climate is often impaired by the way industrial conflicts are treated in the daily press. There is a great emphasis on externals, such as picketing, but frequently the public at large is not fully informed of the issues and of the developments leading to the dispute. While the conduct of good labor relations is primarily an obligation of those who are immediately concerned, a greater awareness in the public mind of the key issues in industrial disputes would create additional motives for a more successful use of the mediation and conciliation procedures provided by law.

Arbitration as distinct from the mediation and conciliation system of the Taft-Hartley Act is not based on law but on a contract between the two parties to submit certain issues to an arbitrator. Usually only problems arising out of an existing contract—for example differences between the two parties with regard to the application of the seniority principle in a particular case—are submitted to arbitration. This type of arbitration is called voluntary because it can come into operation only if both parties have freely agreed to write an arbitration clause into their contract. Such voluntary agreements never deal with the problem of negotiating and signing a new contract. If negotiations fail, a strike can be called.

Although strikes are legal as a weapon for obtaining certain desired objectives in a new contract being negotiated, strikes called during a period covered by a contract are a breach of such an agreement and in this sense are illegal. For a national union to call a strike in violation of a running contract has become almost inconceivable. However, occasionally "wildcat strikes" are called by local union officials, sometimes perhaps in order to force the hand of the higher union leadership. Such strikes are, of course, a violation of the collective agreement and workers can be enjoined by the National Labor Relations Board or a court to return to work immediately. A strike is also illegal if conducted for the purpose of obtaining union recognition or a closed-shop agreement, or of forcing management to employ more people than it deems necessary for the conduct of its business. However, a dispute with management with regard to layoffs as a result of the introduction of automation does not constitute an illegal strike.

Voluntary arbitration has been discussed above. The Labor Relations Laws of the United States do not recognize the system of compulsory arbitration except under circumstances to be explained in the next section. Under compulsory arbitration a board or an individual will work out the terms of employment for a firm or for an industry and will have the power to enforce compliance. Wherever such arrangements exist in other countries, strikes are outlawed—for example, in Italy under the Fascist regime or today in countries retaining more or less a one party structure of government. However, this enforced "industrial peace" is a most doubtful way of settling issues in management-labor relations. In the long run the operation of compulsory arbitration would lead to centralized control not only over wages but over prices. It is not feasible to fix the former without also determining the latter. For this reason compulsory arbitration of labor disputes has so far not found serious advocates in the United States despite considerable concern about the frequency of strikes or strike threats in important sectors of the economic system. Even in a national emergency, compulsory arbitration is only a last resort, and one that is hardly ever used.

15-7. STRIKES THREATENING NATIONAL EMERGENCIES

The spectre of strikes paralyzing large sections of the economy has haunted legislators ever since the emergence of modern industry with its high degree of interdependence. In 1926 a general strike was called by the Trade Union Congress (TUC) in England in support of a conflict between mine workers and mine operators. For a while this strike was effective and for all practical purposes it closed down all economic activities. Eventually the strike was called off and legislation, no longer in effect today, was passed in Great Britian outlawing this type of a general walkout called by a national labor federation. Such a "sympathy strike" is also outlawed in the United States because it falls under the concept of a "secondary boycott." Here we are concerned with the methods devised in the Taft-Hartley Act to ward off or at least postpone grave economic dislocation resulting from strikes in industries upon which many other producers and businesses depend.

It must be stressed that whatever action is taken in these strike situations depends on the judgment of the President of the United States. The wording of Sec. 206 of the Management-Labor Relations Act would make it possible for the President to step into a potentially dangerous situation even before a strike has started in a vital industry. Whether or not this is done depends to some extent on the general political philosophy of the President and his advisors. Although the steel strike of 1959 had been anticipated long before its start, the President waited for a considerable period after the outbreak of the strike before setting the National Emergency Machinery of the Taft-Hartley Act in motion. This of course, is consistent with the doctrine that government should intervene as little as possible in economic processes.

The first step in the approach to strikes threatening a national emergency is the appointment by the President of a Board of Inquiry. This group has a fact-finding mission, exploring the issues and clarifying the positions of the parties locked in the labor dispute. If the President finds that the facts reported by this board warrant further action, he can ask the Attorney General to obtain an injunction by a Federal District Court enjoining the strike or the lockout to be discontinued for a 60-day period and to order labor and management to resume production under the old conditions of work. If during this "cooling-off" period no new contract is negotiated, the National Labor Relations Board can schedule within a 15-day period a referendum among the employees involved in the strike in which they must indicate in a secret ballot whether they are willing to accept the last offer of management or want to resume the walkout. Within five days of the referendum, the NLRB must certify the results.

In the fall of 1968 the International Longshoremen's Association was enjoined to resume work under the National Emergency Provisions on the Eastern Seaboard and Gulf Ports of the United States. They complied. During this period of enforced resumption of work, negotiations between labor and management continued. The stickiest issue was "containerization" that is to say, the transfer of large cargoes inside a container from tractor or train to a merchant vessel. Obviously this involves a good deal of labor saving. Now at the end of the 80-day period, no agreement had been reached and consequently the strike was resumed in December of 1968. There was nothing in the law preventing such action on the part of labor short of a special act of Congress. But the Federal Legislature was in recess: a new President had been elected and was not slated to assume his office until January 20, 1969. The strike continued for many weeks. Different settlements had to be worked out for the various ports. In the port of New York an agreement was reached in January providing for some work of longshoremen on containers such as unpacking and repacking some of the containerized merchandise. But the local union leadership postponed putting this local settlement to an acceptance or rejection vote of the members until such time as agreements had been reached in all other strike bound ports. At the request of management the Federal Court enjoined the local union to submit the agreement to a vote. The union complied and work was resumed in New York while strikes continued in other cities.

Early in 1970 it became clear that the cooling off periods provided in the Railway Labor Act of 1926 and in the Taft-Hartley Act of 1947 were insufficient to resolve long drawn out conflicts in cases in which one or the other parties to the dispute was willing and apparently able to hold out indefinitely. The machinery of the Railway Labor Act proved inadequate to convince one of the shop craft unions in the railroad industry, the lathe metal workers comprising about 6,000 members, to agree to a settlement to which the other shop craft unions had consented. Their main objection was to work rules which they interpreted as empowering railroads to employ workers belonging to other craft unions in jobs that the lathe metal workers considered to be under their own exclusive jurisdiction. In this case Congress had to rush through legislation imposing the last arbitration proposal which had been criticized so strongly by one of the four shop craft unions involved in the protracted procedings within the scope of the Railway Labor Act.

Obviously such an enforced settlement by ad hoc legislation of Congress is one of the least desirable methods of ending intractable labor disputes. All in all by early 1970 the emergency machinery had been invoked 29 times. Only in two cases, both in the transportation field, was Congress compelled to pass binding arbitration legislation. But in these two cases the imposed settlement was limited in time and as far as the shop craft unions were concerned in the railroad industry that time had run out early in 1970. As a stop gap measure, court injunctions postponed a strike but they also had time limitations. To avoid such occurrences in the future, President Nixon proposed legislation providing for the setting up of a neutral panel of three to evaluate the final offers as they had emerged in intractable collective bargaining situations. Provisions were proposed for some final bargaining under the auspices of the panel. But if this fails the panel could select one of the two last offers, either that of management or of labor to impose it as the new settlement.

These new developments while necessary as a result of the deadlocks discussed here do not obviate the view expressed in Sec. 15-6 that compulsory arbitration if introduced on a wide scale would have far reaching effects leading in the long run to a controlled economy in which not only wages but prices would have to be fixed. The new proposals of binding arbitration in important conflicts should be rigidly limited to such exceptional cases.

15-8. MORE ON STRIKES, THEIR IMPACT AND MEASUREMENT

Strikes represent usually the maximum pressure which is used by labor against management in order to obtain goals relating to compensation and to working conditions. Occasionally management uses the *lockout* as a counter measure especially if a walkout is directed only against some firms of an industry. If other companies shut down and thus interrupt operations they intend to weaken all organized labor in the industry not only those workers who started a strike against selected enterprises. In actual conflict situations the question often becomes controversial whether a particular work stoppage is a strike or a lockout. In their competition for public support parties frequently try to convey the impression that the other side is guilty of having brought about the interruption of work. Labor will insist that there is a lockout caused by management. Employers will deny this and stress the fact that it is a strike initiated by the union. Sometimes both parties resort to newspaper advertising in order to convince the public of the justness of their particular position. One of the less ingenious advertisements was placed in many newspapers by the steel industry during the long strike of 1959. In these advertisements a Russian steel worker called Ivan was depicted with the Kremlin as a background. Figures were given for the extremely low wages earned by Russian steel workers especially in comparison to the hourly wage rates in the American steel industry. No mention was made that American steel workers have the highest productivity of all such workers throughout the world whereas the Communists themselves would not deny that productivity in the Soviet Union while improving leaves very much to be desired. This argument of the steel industry was senseless also in a more general way. To counter wage demands of an American union with references to conditions of pay and work of countries which have not achieved the level of economic development existing in the United States was indeed curious. This example is given here to demonstrate that in actual industrial conflict situations there is often on both sides a complete loss of perspective. Furthermore the settlement of conflicts is often eased or made more difficult by personal considerations and problems of the negotiators. In many areas of collective bargaining negotiating teams of management and of labor have become acquainted with each other over a series of encounters during bargaining periods. Often they have been able to reach some sort of a personal equation between themselves which facilitates the negotiations before and even during a strike. But personal factors occasionally add to the difficulties inherent in conflicting bargaining goals of the parties to the labor relationship. Union leaders sensing opposition in their own organization and aware of the formation of rival factions or contenders for their position may be reluctant to make concessions and will engage in particularly hard bargaining. One of the underlying factors in the strike of transit workers in New York City in 1965–1966 was the fact that a new mayor belonging to a different party had been elected. The old union leader of the transit workers, part of the old local power structure was quite disturbed at the thought of having to deal with a team of negotiators with whom he was not familiar. There were other factors in that situation which will be taken up in Chapter 17 where we will deal with industrial relations in the public sector. It is important, however, to stress these personal, subjective factors in negotiations and strikes. They complicate attempts currently made to use such analytical devices as modern *game theory* in the forecasting of the course and outcome of industrial disputes.

SELECTED BIBLIOGRAPHY

Chamberlin, Edward H., Philip D. Bradley, Gerard D. Reilly, and Roscoe Pound. *Labor Unions and Public Policy* (Washington, D. C.: American Enterprise Institute for Public Research, 1958).

Cole, David L. *The Quest for Industrial Peace* (New York: McGraw-Hill Book Company, 1963).

Healy, James J. (ed.) *Creative Collective Bargaining* (Englewood Cliffs, N.J.: Prentice-Hall, Inc., 1965).

Rees, Albert. *The Economics of Trade Unions* (Chicago, Ill.: University of Chicago Press, 1964).

Willington, Harry H. *Labor and the Legal Process* (New Haven: Yale University Press, 1968).

QUESTIONS FOR DISCUSSION

1. Industrial relations can be viewed as involving a conflict between rights peculiar to management and rights peculiar to labor, neither of which seemed re-

concilable with the other. What are those respective rights and how do they fit into a system of collective bargaining?

2. Significant legislation in 1932 and 1935 considerably enhanced the position of American organized labor. In what form did this legislation appear and what were the principal characteristics of these laws?

3. Discuss the way in which labor legislation is limiting managerial rights in dealing with organized labor and employees belonging to trade unions.

4. Explain the reasons why after World War II certain restrictions on union practices were enacted. Describe the major changes brought about in this area by the Taft-Hartley Act of 1947.

5. "Featherbedding" has been outlawed. Discuss this practice and refer to underlying issues reaching into this problem.

6. Discuss the role of mediation and conciliation in labor disputes.

7. Give an analysis and evaluation of the "national emergency" provisions of the Taft-Hartley Act.

16

Nature and Scope of Collective Bargaining

Although collective bargaining has been practiced in many industrial countries for half a century, developments in the later part of the 1960's have shown that the customary ways and laws dealing with labor relations have become more and more inadequate to deal with new types of conflicts in this area. Even in Great Britain with its long established acceptance of trade unionism the Labor Government released early in 1969 a white paper in which cooling-off periods, especially in wildcat strikes were proposed as well as mandatory membership voting prior to the calling of the strike. However in view of union protests no formal legislation to this effect was enacted and attempts were made to remedy these conditions by voluntary arrangements. In the United States it had been widely assumed that the labor relations legislation of the 1930's and 1940's which was primarily designed to encourage collective bargaining had established a framework within which industrial relations would proceed smoothly on a basis of equality of bargaining power between organized labor and management. However, in the 1960's difficult conflict situations between labor and management arose in the public sector of the economy which up to that time had been virtually exempted in federal labor relations legislation and only inadequately dealt with on the level of state government. Nor were these difficulties in public labor relations confined to the United States. The great labor crisis which erupted in France in the spring of 1968 was aggravated by the fact that in France, as in some other European countries, the public sector reaches into such areas as mining and automobile manufacturing, so that wage settlements in the industrial sector operated by government involve immediately the top political leaders. Eventually an agreement sets the pattern for labor contracts in private industry. In the private sector of all advanced countries even with a considerable tradition in collective bargaining the structural changes in the economy, in the labor force and in the size of enterprise have changed substantially the economic and institutional assumptions relating to collective bargaining. It has become apparent that the challenges of contemporary industrial relations cannot be met by theoretical patchwork devices. It is necessary to go back to the fundamentals in order to rid current concepts and practices of many of the ambiguities and confusions which have accumulated and are threatening to make the existing system obsolete and endanger the gains made over the recent decades by organized labor.

16-1. THE CONCEPT OF COLLECTIVE BARGAINING

American labor relations legislation, as embodied in the Taft-Hartley Law of 1947 establishes rules and procedures only for the private sector of the economy. In Title 1 Section 2 Paragraph 2, the law specifically states that the term "employer . . . shall not include the United States or any wholly owned government corporation." This exempted the Federal Government from the obligation to bargain collectively with representatives of government employees. The determination of public labor relations including pay scales and other conditions of employment was considered the duty of the legislature with details worked out by the executive branch of the government. Pay raises and other changes require acts of Congress or of state and local legislative bodies. Public employees do not have the right to strike that is granted to wage and salary workers in the private sector as is so clearly indicated in Title 1, Section 13 of the Taft-Hartley law. There it is stated: "Nothing in this Act, except as specifically provided for herein, shall be construed so as either to interfere with or impede or diminish in any way the right to strike, or to affect the limitations or qualifications on that right." This clear legal situation failed to prevent the walk-out of postal workers in March 1970 and the "sick-in" of air-controllers. We will analyze labor relations in the public sector in some detail in Chapter 17.

Labor unions are seen correctly as "self organizations" of workers for the purpose of exercising jointly economic pressures on management which could not be employed by workers individually or even by small unstructured groups of employees. In this way organized labor can meet the pressures upon wages and working conditions traditionally used by management in an unorganized labor market by generating counter pressures. In this context the collective withholding of labor, that is to say, a strike, is seen as the ultimate weapon of labor. Historically this right to strike was a by-product of the establishment of legal equality and the conferring of citizenship rights to all regardless of their social origin and status. In this institutional setting people were legally free either to work or to refuse to do so if conditions of pay and other considerations seemed unacceptable. Since the right of labor to organize and to exercise joint economic power up to the calling of a strike seemed to be rooted ultimately in the concept of a democratic society, it was widely assumed that collective bargaining and the right to strike were inextricably joined together. Consequently it seemed that wherever the right to strike is challenged or denied as it is in the public sector, collective bargaining would become meaningless and inoperative. In fact occasionally the right to strike was worked into the concept of collective bargaining itself. As long as the public sectors employed comparatively few people and were quiescent this linkage between collective bargaining as a procedure in industrial relations and the right to strike did not create basic problems. However, with the rapid increase in the number of government employees, especially on the state and local level, a new situation came into being. State laws began to confer upon public employees on one side the right to organize while on the other side maintaining a ban on strikes of public employees. It should be realized that this was a departure from the prevailing concepts of collective bargaining. The need therefore arises to arive at an understanding of collective bargaining without identifying the concept and the procedure with the right to strike. Such an approach does not challenge the right of workers to withhold collectively their labor in the market sector of the economy. But in view of the fact that everywhere in the world the public sector is increasing, it becomes necessary to separate conceptually collective bargaining and the right to strike.

Generically collective bargaining is a procedure through which representatives of management and of wage and salary earners arrive at a formal agreement establishing general standards of pay, of fringe benefits and of working conditions. A closer investigation of the various terms of this definition will enable us to outline more clearly the structural and institutional implications of collective bargaining.

Standards agreed upon in collective bargaining mean that all employees will benefit equally from the terms of the contract. There cannot be individual differences in basic pay rates between workers falling under identical job classifications. Private deals between labor representatives and management whereby certain groups of workers would not necessarily have to receive the contractual pay, so-called "sweetheart contracts" are a most serious violation of the principles of collective bargaining. Victims of such practices in the 1950's were especially immigrant workers in low wage industries in metropolitan areas of the United States. While such practices, as it were an exploitation of labor by labor organizations of doubtful standing, were not widespread, they illustrate precisely what is not permitted once uniform standards of pay have been established through an agreement between labor and management. It is equally wrong when in times of over-employment, workers with scarce skills are promised or given pay exceeding the contractual wage rate, provided that this leads to a differentiation in earnings between workers doing substantially the same kind of work. While this malpractice is not widely spread in the United States, it has plagued some European countries in their periods of over-employment after World War II

Generally speaking the standards established in collective agreements eliminate favoritism or the exploitation of particularly weak segments of labor, especially newcomers or immigrants.

Representatives rather than individual managers or wage earners are involved in collective bargaining. In a way then this type of negotiation is the opposite of individual bargaining or deals. Practically in most cases where there is no collective bargaining, conditions of pay and employment are only in a formal sense consensual or bilateral. In reality there is often a unilateral imposition of terms of employment by management on labor.

Wherever there are representatives there must exist a structure for their selection. This means that in order to have collective bargaining at all, management and labor must assume structures which make the selection and the work of bargaining representatives possible. Here a number of issues and problems arise which must be considered separately for management and for labor.

As far as *management* is concerned the old-time personnel department, taking care of hiring and discharges and of pay-scales, has expanded into more elaborate units which often are called "industrial relations" departments. These units have a two-fold assignment. First of all it is their duty to provide on a day-to-day basis for good labor relations, that is to say, for cooperation with employees or their representatives on complaints and grievances on lay-offs and discharges, promotions, and other matters to be judged on the basis of existing agreements. Secondly, top members of such a department have to lay the ground work for the negotiation of new contracts, devise a strategy for forthcoming collective bargaining sessions and act as representatives in the negotiations of a new contract. In industries in which the size of firms is fairly large, industrial relations departments will be highly structured and will be geared to negotiate contracts between their company and organized labor. In some cases for instance, in the automobile industry, locals comprising only workers of one particular firm or department of such a corporation have been set up by the national union. This structure implies a system of *company-wide* collective bargaining. Actually in industries dominated by a few very large firms the company-wide bargaining of one particular corporation with organized labor is understood by all management and labor concerns as establishing the pattern to be adopted eventually throughout the industry. While this does not preclude minor individual variations to be adopted in individual firms after the master contract has been negotiated, the basic issues will have been settled by negotiations which while formally company-wide actually are carried out with *industry-wide* implications.

When the size of firms is smaller and the number of employers larger, official industry-wide bargaining will take place. For instance, the negotiations dealing with contracts for longshoremen are carried out between the International Longshoremen's Association (ILA) and the Association of Shipowners. Similar patterns of collective bargaining have traditionally been used in the bituminous coal industry and in the garment industry. However, in all cases management groupings for the purpose of collective bargaining must remain loose in order to stay clear of the anti-trust provisions of the Sherman Act.

Collective bargaining can, therefore, be going on either within the scope of an individual firm or within the framework of an industrial, regional or national grouping of companies. From the viewpoint of organized labor, company-wide collective bargaining has obvious advantages. If competitors of a firm engaged in bargaining and subsequently in a strike, are themselves not affected by this conflict situation they might gain a competitive advantage. The fear of losing its share of the market can develop into a powerful pressure on the firm involved in company-wide bargaining either to make substantial concessions to avert a strike or to end it if it has already started. However the union tactic of negotiating and eventually striking only with regard to one or a selected few firms in a particular industry or locality does not always succeed. On various occasions craft unions in the newspaper industry in New York City such as the Typographical Workers or the Newspaper Guild tried to limit their actions to two papers. However, other papers, members of the newspaper association, closed down their operation in a demonstration of solidarity with these strike-bound publishing enterprises. But *single-firm* collective bargaining while advantageous from the viewpoint of trade unions is not feasible in industries characterized by a large number of separate business establishments. In this case the procedure will of necessity assume the characteristics of *multi-firm* bargaining. As we have already seen this does not preclude the emergence of one or two firms as spokesmen or de facto representatives of the whole employer group.

While the self-interest of management points to multi-firm procedures and that of organized labor to single-firm collective bargaining, suggestions were occasionally made in the 1950's by employers' organizations to break up national or international unions and permit labor organization only on a local or district level without tie-ins with other unions. Such a fragmentation of labor organizations would weaken unions and deprive them of financial support of larger combinations of labor in their struggle with management. It would presumably outlaw the accumulation of strike funds and the transfer of money from one union to another. Occasionally

there were outright demands for a repeal of that section of the Clayton Act
exempting unions from anti-trust legislation. These attempts of a partial
disestablishment of organized labor never came to the point of legislative
action. They have now merely historical interest and are being recalled
here in order to clarify basic structures of collective bargaining. We now
turn from analysis of managerial structures to a study of the institutional
requirements for collective bargaining on the part of organized labor.

In order to prepare effectively for collective bargaining and to participate in this procedure with success, labor must have a formal *union
structure*. This implies a clear determination of the question of what union
is to represent the employees and who has the power to negotiate with
management. As we will see shortly American collective bargaining does
not allow for *multi-unionism* in the sense that more than one union can
claim to represent groups of employees belonging to the same occupational
grouping. This is a pattern of collective bargaining well known and usually
practiced in Europe. While only one union can represent the employees in
dealings with management in this country, there is the possibility of *coalition bargaining*. In such a case unions of different crafts dealing with management try to coordinate their strategy and demands so that settlements
can be achieved faster than in completely isolated and separated negotiations of single unions.

16-2. DESIGNATION OF BARGAINING REPRESENTATIVES

As far as American labor management legislation is concerned, the
question seems to be settled once and for all in favor of a single union
concept of collective bargaining. Title 1, Section 9 of the Taft-Hartley
Act states clearly that "representatives designated or selected for the
purposes of collective bargaining by the majority of the employees in a unit
appropriate for such purposes, shall be the exclusive representatives of all
the employees. It is clear then that the law insists on the *majority principle*
to which is added the *exclusivity principle* in order to establish representatives for collective bargaining. Since this legal requirement of single union
collective bargaining is characteristic primarily of American labor relations legislation and is unknown in many other advanced industrial countries, it is necessary to examine in greater detail the underlying reasons for
this arrangement.

Collective bargaining as defined at the beginning of this section does
not necessarily require prior legislation in order to become effective. As a
matter of fact in the United States craft unions in the printing trade, in
building construction, and in the railroad industry had developed practices of collective bargaining long before the original Wagner Act became
law in 1935. In some European countries, for instance in Sweden and in
Germany, collective bargaining was instituted after World War I in "sum-

mit meetings" of top representatives of industry and of labor organizations. In a similar but more diffuse fashion collective bargaining developed in the private sector in Great Britain. In the United States, however, large scale industry was opposed to the recognition of unions and, therefore, to negotiating with representatives of labor. This opposition continued even in the early part of the 1930's in the United States. If we consider these managerial attitudes we understand why in this country legislation was necessary to define the conditions under which collective bargaining had to be accepted by employers. In sharp contrast to voluntary master agreements between industry and labor organizations mutually recognizing each other and their members as partners in collective bargaining once and for all either on a national or regional level, American labor legislation in principle makes collective bargaining contingent on the designation of representatives by a majority vote of employees in a bargaining unit. Such a unit is not necessarily identical with the firm of the employer. The decisive criterion for the setting up of such a unit is the community of interest among the employees. In this way, if office workers want to organize, they may be considered as constituting a separate bargaining unit distinct from that of production workers of the same employer.

The main difference between collective bargaining based on voluntary mutual recognition of employers and employees' organizations and the American method of recognition as a matter of law is that the latter is contingent on the maintenance of a majority of employees by the union. The right to represent employees for the purpose of collective bargaining can be lost by attrition of the numbers of union supporters or by the emergence of a rival union which in a new election may be able to command a majority vote of the employees in the bargaining unit. Here the exclusivity principle asserts itself. Later in this chapter we will discuss the effect of the majority principle on union security, that is to say the systems which have been developed to shield a particular union against the loss of bargaining rights. In our present discussion of the concept of collective bargaining it is necessary to elaborate further the implications of the exclusivity principle. It means that in current American usage allowance is being made only for single union bargaining. While this is a comparatively smooth procedure in the case of industrial unions representing workers of various occupational achievements and levels, difficulties arise very frequently when it comes to collective bargaining with craft unions each representing workers with specialized skills. In application of the American concept of collective bargaining, negotiations must be carried out separately with each of the craft unions involved in work for an employer, for instance in contract construction in the railroad industry and the printing trades. On the one side, the single union principle forces management and labor to split up the whole bargaining process for one company or a group of companies into separate negotiations which very often have a tendency to get out of line with each other unless true coalition bargaining is being practiced. On the other hand every single craft union has, as it were, a veto on the over-all settlement by holding out for additional demands and special settlements.

Recently the idea has been proposed to develop in such cases a system of "multi-union" groupings for the purpose of bargaining collectively with employers. This type of coalition bargaining is entirely feasible within the current legal framework of labor relations legislation. It would not abrogate the system of single-union bargaining but would lead to processes of simultaneous or at least structually coordinated methods in collective negotiations. Such improvements in the techniques of collective bargaining would contribute to a shortening of labor disputes especially in the area of craft unionism where employers have to deal with a number of unions.

An issue closely related with single and separate bargaining procedures is the coordination of *contract termination dates*. This is also important in industrial unionism. In the latter case, for instance with regard to the Teamsters dealing with a very large number of employers all over the country, a uniform contract termination date is of great advantage to organized labor. In this particular instance it would open up the possibility to shut down all trucking operations simultaneously and thereby exert maximum pressure not only on management but on the country at large. It is easy to see why management has resisted such uniform terminal dates for union contracts in this type of situation. In collective bargaining with a number of craft unions a uniform contract termination data seems more advisable. In the past, time differences in expiration dates were sometimes an added cause for the sharpness and the duration of conflicts and impasses in collective bargaining. If one craft union having an earlier date of expiration of a current contract would become involved in collective bargaining with the employer some time before the agreements with other unions ran out, the impression could easily be created that this particular union was trying to assume leadership in the total situation and relegating other unions to the role of adopting the patterns of the settlement made ahead of the others.

In this section we have dealt with the concept of collective bargaining and with basic configurations in the structure of negotiations between management and organized labor. To some extent these fundamental patterns are inherent in the very idea of collective bargaining; to a great degree, however, they are wound up with the particular way in which collective bargaining has been translated into labor management legislation in the United States. In the next sections of this chapter we will deal with problems and strategies resulting from the adoption of these legal concepts and methods.

16-3. THE PROBLEM OF UNION SECURITY

We have stressed that the American system of collective bargaining is not based on voluntary acceptance of this procedure by management and labor organizations. To clarify the impact of this situation, the fact may be stressed that employers can refuse to bargain collectively with labor representatives if a union fails to achieve the majority vote in a shop election and, therefore, cannot be issued a certification by the National Relations Board that it is representing the employees. Even if the union would miss achieving this majority by a narrow margin, the certification must be withheld and the employer cannot be compelled to deal with the union. Furthermore, even a majority vote, instituting the union as the collective bargaining representative does not settle this issue once and for all. The principle of single union bargaining does not guarantee to a particular labor organization that it will forever be the exclusive bargaining agent. If in a new election the employees shift their allegiance, the union having negotiated a contract may be replaced by a rival group. Occasionally attempts have been made to do just that but the displacement of a union by another may meet with formidable obstacles.

The case of the International Longshoremen's Association (ILA) can serve as an illustration. For a considerable time the leadership of that union had been under attack. At one time in the 1950's the union had been forced to withdraw from the AFL-CIO. It was asserted that in a secret ballot the rank and file would vote for affiliation with another labor organization if they had an opportunity to do so. Actually, the AFL-CIO started to organize a rival dockworkers' union. The National Labor Relations Board scheduled elections. When the votes were counted, however, the ILA again emerged as the representative of the employees and retained its certification. Eventually this union rejoined the AFL-CIO.

It is only natural that given this built-in uncertainty of the status of a union in collective bargaining that organized labor has tried to develop devices protecting it against this uncertainty. This is the meaning and function of the *union shop*. Such an arrangement is embodied in a clause of a collective contract in which the employer pledges himself to make it a condition of employment for all newly hired employees to join the union with which management has signed a collective labor contract. In view of the sometimes deliberately created confusion about the scope of such a union shop clause, it is necessary to analyze it in some detail.

Under such an agreement with the union the employer remains entirely free to put on the payroll whomever he deems advisable or necessary to hire. The union has no right to interfere with management in the selection of new personnel. However, management must enforce its commitment under the union shop clause to see to it that the new worker joins the union. Very frequently this arrangement is reinforced by the *check-off* of union dues. Management agrees to withhold the union dues from the gross earnings of the workers and turn the amount over to the union. It is obvious that this system offers great advantages to labor organizations, because it frees them from the laborious business of collecting dues from individual members. In fact, this method of financing unions was considered so favorable for them that an attempt was made in the Taft-Hartley Act of 1947 to put some obstacles in its way by requiring a written consent of each employee to having its union dues withheld by the employer. Since all that was required of the employee was a signature on a form, this innovation did not have any adverse effect on the operation of the check-off system. The check-off system is so convenient for unions that one of the penalties in state laws dealing with organizations of public employees provides for a suspension of dues collected by the employing agency, if the union has violated the strike ban.

The pro's and con's of the union shop which in the 1950's had become somewhat controversial cannot be discussed out of context with the legal system of union recognition. This shop clause protects the union against loss of membership for the duration of the contract and establishes it as the bargaining agent for negotiations concerning its renewal. This does not mean, according to the law, that employees in a union shop must forever remain captives of the labor organization holding the contract. In fact, the law opens up the possibility to initiate a *decertification* action. New elections for bargaining representatives must be scheduled when 30 percent of the employees in a bargaining unit request it. If, in the subsequent election, more than 50 percent of the employees vote for another union, that labor organization will obtain certification. It is, of course, also possible that the vote shows that there is no majority for any bargaining representative. In such a case the employer would no longer be compelled to live up to the requirement of having to bargain in good faith with any representatives of the employees.

There have been hardly any cases in which the decertification procedure has been invoked. The union shop clause has contributed towards stability in labor relations by practically settling if not once and for all then at least for the longer run the question of union representation. To label the union shop as a form of "compulsory unionism" is completely unjustified. In the complex system of the modern industrial state there are other requirements which are made a condition of employment especially in large companies. In many cases it is a condition of employment that employees participate in group life insurance and in group hospital and health insurance. Under certain conditions employees will also be compelled to make contributions to pension plans set up by private corporations and nonprofit institutions. The fact has to be accepted that in the contemporary world a certain amount of private or public collectivism has become inevitable in social and economic arrangements.

In spite of these considerations the opposition to the union shop was strong enough to lead to the adoption of a "sleeper" clause Title 1, Section 14, Paragraph (b) in the Taft-Hartley Act of 1947. This clause which slipped by almost unnoticed empowered the states to enact legislation prohibiting the union shop system. As a result a number of states enacted legislation, popularly known under the flamboyant and completely misleading title of *"Right To Work Laws"* voiding union shop clauses in their jurisdiction. The expectation of at least some of the advocates of this type of law that this would lead to a substantial weakening of already established organized labor and of collective bargaining were not fulfilled. A number of studies conducted to ascertain the effects of these laws could not show that there had been significant changes in the situation. The maintenance of a status quo in industrial relations despite right to work laws was bolstered by the legal device of the *"Agency Fee"* system. This scheme deserves close attention because one of its underlying principles deals with one of the most basic issues of organized labor, the concept of *solidarity* of workers and the resulting obligation to support collective efforts through joining unions or in other ways. The agency fee system entitles the union to fees in lieu of dues of nonunion members of a bargaining unit. In this way the union is assured of a steady flow of income although the union shop clause is in these cases inoperative so that a considerable proportion of employees in a bargaining unit may not become members of the union. This system has been upheld by the courts and the principle which has been used for the validation of the agency fee is very basic.

The union is seen in these arguments as representing not only its members but all employees which will be covered by a collective labor contract. Inasmuch as the union is bargaining for wages and other benefits for all workers, it can very well be considered as an agent for the nonmembers. It follows that the latter can be charged a fee to the union because it has acted in their behalf. Obviously this concept of the union acting as an agent for nonunion members does not sit too well with labor organizers who have the understandable objective of signing up the largest number of employees as members of a local. There is no doubt that this system strengthens a widespread feeling among union workers that those who stay outside a local are actually taking a free ride benefiting from the struggles of organized labor without really contributing to it. The agency fee, of course, takes care of the financial aspects of the free ride argument. But it is important to stress that unionism is more than a purely financial or for that matter material arrangement. At its best it requires membership participation in decision making and involvement not only in the carrying out of certain union tactics such as picketing but also in the design of larger strategies. Wide spread nonmembership in unions is contrary to contemporary trends of activating people in spheres of their immediate interests in local and in occupational and educational concerns. While the union shop clause is a response to the legal system of union recognition in the United States, the *closed shop*, outlawed in all interstate types of industries and businesses in the Taft-Hartley Act is subject to most of the criticism which, as we have seen, has been wrongly addressed to the union shop.

The closed shop has survived as a reality in many intrastate activities, for instance in a large segment of contract construction. Under this arrangement management agrees to employ only workers who are already members of a union. Union membership becomes, therefore, a pre-condition of employment. Workers who desire to enter the job market covered by such arrangements must first overcome the hurdle of acquiring union membership. This may be easy for sons or relatives of union members and very hard for others especially if they belong to minority groups. The persistence of legal or de facto closed shop situations can also be explained by the advantages this system offers especially to smaller firms. Under the closed shop system the union becomes for all practical purposes the hiring agent. When workers are needed, the employer will call up the union and they will send available workers to him. Inasmuch as this system is tied in with craft unionism, management is entitled to expect that qualified workers will report.

The main justification for the outlawing of the closed shop is that it interferes with the rights of management and of individual workers to get together through the workings of a free labor market. While it is convenient for certain types of employers, it does place unwanted limitations on the basic managerial right to hire whomever they want to put on their payroll. It also interferes with the free mobility of labor. Such barriers to free mobility of labor could consist of high initiation fees, unduly difficult qualifying examinations and special levies imposed on workers coming from other areas. In recent years there has been an easing of these standards but this does not eliminate the objections to the closed shop.

Hiring halls have been affected by the outlawing of the closed shop. Considered in themselves hiring halls are a great aid in the rational allocation of labor to employers whose manpower requirements are fluctuating often on a day-to-day basis. The absence of such a hall for longshoremen in the port of New York in the old days had forced those who were seeking employment on the docks to "shape up" in the morning in front of a particular pier so that they could be hired by the so-called "straw bosses." If they were not selected they had lost their chance to work that day because the shape-up took place simultaneously at all hiring points. A hiring hall provides for a centralization of all calls for workers coming in at a stated time. However, under the rule of the closed shop workers had to show their union card in order to gain admittance to the hiring hall. With the outlawing of the closed shop, hiring halls, for instance in the maritime union, must admit all job seekers. This has at least theoretically widened the employment opportunity beyond the ranks of union members.

The institutions such as the union shop, which have been discussed in this section, are related intimately to the legal framework which has been set up in the United States to establish collective bargaining. They do not derive from the concept and nature of collective bargaining itself but from the unique way in which they have been applied in this country. We must now turn our attention to a problem which underlies all collective bargaining systems: the collective withholding of labor, that is to say, the strike. As we have seen this is widely considered the ultimate weapon of labor. It is precisely in this area that late in the twentieth century new problems have arisen which require a reexamination of the assumptions and the realities of the economic structure underlying industrial conflicts.

16-4. LABOR AND MANAGEMENT STRATEGIES IN COLLECTIVE BARGAINING

It is part of an orderly bargaining procedure for the parties involved to prepare some time before the start of negotiations their own positions with regard to the minimum and maximum goals they visualize as acceptable or desirable as a result of the forthcoming bargaining period. In fact to enter negotiations without any preparation or concept of what is to be talked about would be incompatible with the concept of good faith bargaining. There is a basic distinction between tactics and strategy which applies to many types of social relations and most assuredly to collective bargaining. Tactics refer to immediate "battlefield" or conflict situations. For instance the first demand or offer concerning new wage scales may be so formulated as to enable either party to retreat from its maximum position and eventually arrive at a settlement within the range of the respective minimum-maximum bargaining goals. Tactics can also be influenced by external factors such as internal personnel tensions within union or industrial relations department of employers. Often they are also conditioned by the need of a negotiator to "go on record" with certain demands in order to facilitate ratification by proving that he has done everything possible to fight for particular objectives. Complete rigidity or "take it or leave tactics" are incompatible with good faith collective bargaining. One of the preconditions for such flexibility is the ability of both parties but especially of the employer to rearrange conditions in a manner to incorporate the results of collective bargaining into the organizational structure.

To illustrate, a union confronted with the demand of employers to consent to a cut-down in the size of the work gangs must be able to obtain concessions with regard to the phasing out of workers no longer needed. Employers granting substantial wage increases must be given the opportunity to rearrange their production system so as to minimize increases in unit labor cost. It can be noted already at this point that the space that both bodies can maneuver varies considerably from one case to another. Obviously an industry which is producing defense materials on a cost plus basis has greater flexibility than companies which are operating in very competitive situations. On the other hand, public authorities such as transit or school systems which become increasingly involved in collective bargaining do not really control their revenues and therefore often initially are compelled to assume a posture of inflexibility until such time that legislative bodies or state and local governments promise necessary funds to honor the new agreement. For instance in the protracted negotiations between the union and the Transit Authority of New York, the latter made a money proposal only on the very day on which the contract expired, December 31, 1969. Once this suggestion was made a settlement was reached in short order and almost immediately the fares were raised by 50 percent. In a "miraculous" way the new 30-cent tokens made a rapid appearance. Apparently they had been ordered months ahead of time thereby creating the question whether the typical "cliff-hanger" negotiations affecting the daily lives of millions in the New York metropolitan area were genuine rather than a psycho-drama enacted for the benefit of naive onlookers.

Although the newspaper industry is private, the publishers of New York newspapers came up with their first money offer also on the day the old contract expired in 1969. This was promptly rejected by the craft unions but negotiations continued and papers were published as it were on a day to day basis. Obviously such tactics are impairing the effectiveness and the credibility of collective bargaining. They are hardly compatible with the simple concept of good faith bargaining embodied in the law.

Strategy deals with long range goals. It has been a union strategy in the United States after World War II to lay the ground work for important advances in working conditions during a negotiation period prior to the one in which they really intend to push very hard for such new contract features. For instance during the negotiations of 1952 the United Steel Workers put into the "negotiating basket" a demand for a guaranteed annual wage. However, that year they did not try really hard to have it accepted by management. The request was then picked up by the automobile workers and led to the insertion of supplementary unemployment benefits into the 1955 agreement. A similar clause was then also written in steel contracts and in agreements in the rubber industry. In 1969 the president of the steel workers union came out in favor of a four-day work week. Inasmuch as a labor contract just had been concluded that year the demand for a 32-hour week was clearly of long range, strategic significance.

For a considerable period of time management tactics in collective bargaining were still influenced by the spirit of the period prior to the enactment of labor relations laws in which collective bargaining was resisted and considered a restriction on the freedom of enterprise. Without determined efforts of organized labor, management would not have conceded the elaboration of the wage structure through such fringe benefits as vacations and company pensions. However, the new generation of management has dropped many of the old psychological reservations to collective bargaining and accepted it as an inescapable aspect of modern business operations. One particular strategy of management has gained wide attention and also criticism. It is known as the management strategy of "Boulwarism" called after Mr. L. R. Boulware[1] who after World War II was given charge of employee relations at the General Electric Company.

Essentially this management strategy operated in the following way. After the unions had made their demands, management would come forward with its own "firm, fair offer" and would indicate that this proposal was final and would not be altered throughout the further negotiations. Furthermore, the company engaged in an active marketing of this package going so far as to try to sell its proposal to individual employees by communicating with them directly.

This tactic was attacked by the union as a violation of the "good faith" bargaining requirement of the National Labor Relations Act on October 28, 1969. The United States Court of Appeals in New York ruling on a complaint which originated in the 1960 negotiations with the General Electric Company that a "take it or leave it" tactic of management, allowing for no flexibility or give and take in the actual bargaining was a violation of the good faith mandate of the labor relations law.

It should be noted, however, that this decision was based only on the company attitude that its first offer was also its last. That amounted practically to the assertion that the proposed management package was not negotiable. The decision, however, did not rule out other aspects of so-called "Boulwarism." The decision stated:

> We do not today hold that an employer may not communicate with his employees during negotiations. Nor are we deciding that the 'best-offer-first' bargaining technique is forbidden. Moreover, we do not require an employer to engage in 'auction bargaining,' or, as the dissent seems to suggest, compel him to make concessions, 'minor' or otherwise.

We have seen already in Sec. 15-6 of this text that the National Labor Relations Law merely establishes the setting for collective bargaining. It does not provide solutions for the case that ultimately industrial conflicts

[1]H. R. Northrup, "Boulwarism," University of Michigan Press, 1964.

remain unresolved even after protracted mediation and conciliation procedures even the invocation of the national emergency clauses. For this reason management should not be discouraged from making comprehensive
proposals of its own in the cause of collective bargaining sessions. While
both parties must remain flexible, an attitude of management, that it is only
up to labor to make proposals and to management to either reject them
totally or in part and aim at a compromise without making offers of its
own, is not conducive to constructive and creative collective bargaining.

16-5. THE CHANGING ASPECTS OF STRIKES. PROBLEMS OF CONTRACT REJECTION

Even at a time when organizations of labor were far weaker than they
are today, strikes occurred. In those days they were often terminated by
the invocation of the intervention by state militia, company police, or as
happened in the strike against the Baltimore and Ohio Railroad in 1877,
of Federal troops. While most strikes were called in order to exercise
pressure on employers for the granting of higher pay and better working
conditions, sometimes strikes of all workers in a particular area were called
in support of a union involved in a specific labor dispute. One example of
such a *general strike* occurred in England in 1926 when the Trade Union
Congress (TUC) called a nation-wide strike in support of the walk-out of
the coal miners. The general strike is only apparently the strongest weapon
that labor can employ. If it is carried to the point where very great incon-
veniences to the public occur through the cessation of essential services
to the community, public opinion is likely to turn against these strikers. In
Great Britain the strike of 1926 led to legislation outlawing such national
and general walk-outs. While these laws were repealed after World War II
national labor federations everywhere have been quite reluctant to call for
a general strike for an indefinite period of time. Instead in European countries, for instance Italy and France, general strikes or strikes of railroad
workers or other employees providing essential services have been called
frequently but for limited periods, such as twenty-four or forty-eight hours.
This use of a strike weapon is often linked with attempts to cause governments to change official wage policies. Their frequency is related to the size
of the publicly controlled sectors of the economy. In the mixed economies
of Western Europe with the government involved in the railroads, the
mining industry, in communication media, in the setting of wage standards
even in the private sector, such short term strikes sometimes repeated at
short intervals are designed to influence government rather than to gain
concessions from particular employers or private industry.

In the spring of 1968, student unrest in France eventually led to a general strike which however the union leadership declared most reluctantly
and primarily for the purpose of gaining control of spontaneous actions

which had been started by workers in many industrial plants, for instance the state-owned automobile plant, the Regie Renault. As in England more than forty years earlier the public reaction to this general strike was most unfavorable as was clearly evident in the vast government majority which was returned in the June 1968 elections in France. Actually general strikes are not an ultimate economic weapon; they are political in nature even if the issues are predominately economic at the outset.

While general strikes are infrequent even in Europe, they virtually never have occurred in the United States. They certainly would come under the ban on secondary boycotts contained on the Taft-Hartley Act. On a more basic level the absence of general strikes in the United States is connected with the much larger extent of the private sector of the economy. This enables organized labor to use the strike as a weapon against private industries which elsewhere are in the public domain such as transportation and communication. However, the American economy although it has this much wider private sector has undergone vast structural changes which have left their impact on the pre-conditions, methods and implications of strikes as the ultimate weapon in management-labor contracts.

R. J. Hicks in his *Theory of Wages*[2] has offered a graphical analysis of the forces which operate in a strike situation on the side of management and of labor. The main element is *time*. As a strike continues over a longer period the willingness of labor to insist on higher wages will decline. On the other hand the resistance of employers to the demand of labor will also weaken somewhat as time progresses. The impact of the time factor is that labor which started out with high demands is willing to settle for less than originally proposed whereas management will acquiesce to the higher wage rate than they were originally willing to concede. If wage rates are marked off on the vertical axis and time units on the horizontal, the curve of labor's resistance to wage offers will slope downward to the right whereas management's concession curve will run upward to the left. The point of intersection between the two curves would indicate how much time it would take to settle the dispute and at what wage rate a new agreement could be achieved. While this graphical analysis has value for the demonstration of the basic pulls which operate in time on management and on labor, the predictive significance of such a graph declines as the field in which a firm and organized labor is operating becomes less and less perfectly competitive as far as the structure of the industry or business is concerned and as labor itself becomes more autonomous and is able to isolate its organization from short-run fluctuations on the labor market.

The course of a strike is entirely different in the situation where management has to operate under more or less perfectly competitive conditions

[2]Second edition (New York: St. Martin's Press, Inc., 1963).

than under imperfect competition which is usually associated with large-scale enterprises which are using technologically sophisticated production systems, have scientific management and have great leeway in their pricing policies. Under perfect competition a firm must price its products close to cost of production. If the markup is too high, competing firms will capture a greater slice of the market. Under such circumstances the ability of a firm to accumulate considerable internal resources for the financing of investment in improved production equipment or for the strengthening of working capital are limited. Under such circumstances long run planning is limited in scope and the firm is dependent on fluctuating market conditions. The time factor begins to operate immediately upon the start of a strike and will exert ever increasing pressure on the firm, making it more ready to agree at least partially to the demands of labor. In a similar fashion this same factor will force organized workers to lower their original demands and come to terms with the employer whenever labor is only weakly organized and is operating in a labor surplus economy. In this more or less perfectly competitive situation, the pulls emanating from the market itself would in a comparatively short period of time establish a new balance between management and labor and a compromise settlement would result. One of the difficulties in contemporary industrial relations and in policy suggestions for their improvement can be found in the fact that this economic model of the strike has not been readjusted to the actualities of the contemporary highly concentrated and industralized market structure. We will now investigate separately for management and for labor the positions which they hold in an industrial conflict developing within the setting of an imperfectly competitive economic system.

One of the main effects of monopolistic or imperfectly competitive situations is the acquisition of greater strengths and stability of the *management* of firms operating in such a setting. Pricing becomes more autonomous and profit margins can be planned. Vast internal resources can be built up. In this manner reliance on the capital market declines. This condition is shown clearly in the ability of large industrial firms to discount a strike and a long interruption in production by building up huge *inventories*. Obviously such a policy is tieing up considerable working capital. But modern enterprises are in a position to do so to a vast extent. This stockpiling of merchandise long before the termination of a current contract is facilitated by the advanced technology of modern production systems and the continuous addition to productive capacity. Part of this capacity is designed as a reserve or standby facility which can be put into operation at peak periods of business or in preparation for a long drawn out industrial conflict. A new type of cyclical behavior has evolved in key industries such as steel and automobiles. In order to keep customers and dealers supplied even during a strike of long duration, periods of steep increases of production precede the time scheduled for negotiations and a possible shut-down of operations. If, as has happened frequently, the anticipated strike did not materialize, there will be a considerable drop in output levels. In 1968 the steel industry went through a short run cycle. On the basis of 1957–59–100, output rose from 132.2 percent in January 1968 to a peak of 148.4 percent in June of that year. It dropped to a low of 107.3 percent in September 1968 because the strike which had been anticipated earlier was averted through a new collective agreement. Whereas in the first half of 1968 output was way above the average of the preceding year, in the latter part of that same period it dropped far below that level. Similar trends could be observed on various occasions in the automobile industry.

These examples demonstrate the changes which have been brought about on the operation of the time factor as far as large-scale management is concerned. Through advance planning and stockpiling the time when economic pressures begin to operate on management through the interruption of production can be pushed back for a considerable period. Ultimately of course these pressures will reassert themselves. Late in 1959 when the steel strike of that year had already lasted more than two months and no settlement seemed in sight, large customers of the industry who had exhausted their steel supplies, began to exercise pressure on the industry to come to terms with the unions. But there is no doubt that the great strength that large companies have acquired can be a contributing factor to the long duration of an industrial conflict.

Another element in the strengthening of management is the structural change in employment categories especially the upgrading of employees to the managerial or executive level. Labor relations legislation guarantees the right to strike only to wage and salary earners who come under the classification of "employees." Already the foreman is taken out of this group because he is considered the intermediary link between management and labor. All executive and managerial personnel is excluded from collective bargaining. Now in recent years there has been a very great increase in the proportion of executive and managerial employees in large companies. This has often led to situations in which essential services for instance in electric power companies could be maintained during a strike by the staffing of essential jobs by "managerial" employees. This practice is being enforced by rulings of the Labor Relations Board whereby picket lines are not permitted to prevent executive personnel from entering the premises of a strike-bound company. Whereas strike breakers can be effectively prevented by picket lines from entering plants, organized labor cannot hinder management from trying to maintain operations at least partially. It is obvious that these rather novel uses of managerial personnel in certain industries suitable for such practices has modified the time element in industrial disputes in favor of management. However, these new developments have not given a one-sided advantage to management.

Organized labor has also been benefiting from recent changes in the structure of the labor market and the considerable upgrading of labor force from less skilled to higher skilled occupational classifications.

We have seen that modern industrial management is in a position to protect itself for a much longer period of time than has been the case in earlier periods against the time pressures which become operative in a strike situation. But labor is also benefiting from these managerial tactics. The stepping up of production for the purpose of supplying major customers and of stockpiling products prior to an anticipated work stoppage usually leads to overtime. In the pre-strike period of April 1968 average weekly hours in the steel industry rose to 43.9, that is to say they were 10 percent above the normal forty hour work week. Compensation for this overtime increased earnings of workers by at least 15 percent. Throughout the first half of 1968 actual working hours were significantly in excess of the normal work week for which only straight time pay was due to the workers. It follows that workers enter into a strike in such industries with a small "nest egg" earned as overtime pay in the period preceding the strike. Just as production drops sharply if a strike is averted, working hours also decline substantially. In August 1968 there were fully 5½ hours less than in April of that year. By October 1968 average weekly hours in the steel industry were still 38.5.

The position of labor is strengthened further at the outset of a strike because very often wages for the last one or two weeks would have to be paid. In many cases individual workers can also claim vacation pay and other such benefits at the time of the beginning of the labor dispute. In most states workers who are on strike are not eligible for unemployment compensation. However, in some states, for instance in New York State, workers can become eligible for such benefits seven weeks after the start of the work stoppage. The denial of unemployment compensation to workers on strike is based on the sound principle that this type of social insurance benefit should be reserved for workers who have lost their employment for reasons completely beyond their control, especially through layoffs in periods of declining business or a termination of jobs in connection with modernization and automation. In fact the possibility of obtaining unemployment compensation after a certain number of weeks as is the case in New York, is bound to make settlements of labor disputes even more difficult than they are considered in themselves.

While social insurance ought to be excluded completely from any participation in industrial disputes, unions are, of course, entirely free to commit themselves to the payment of *strike benefits.* Just as management is free to undertake precautionary measures such as the stepping up of production in anticipation of a labor dispute, organized labor is equally free to bolster its strength by accumulating strike funds or even levying "war chests." In American unionism the practice of paying strike benefits is of comparatively recent date. Even before World War II such benefits were guaranteed to members in many European trade unions. This commitment to strike benefits worked very often as a brake on the willingness of union leaders to initiate strike action. With the sharp rise in the compensation of workers and the organizational strengthening of unions, especially through the check-off system, the promise of payments to strikers does not seem to have interfered with the willingness of union leaders to have a strike vote taken whenever collective negotiations are deadlocked and the termination of the old contract is near at hand. Furthermore there is no legal bar for one union to come to the financial assistance of another whenever there is danger that funds set aside for strike benefits are running out in the union engaged in a labor contract.

We see, therefore, that organized labor has been able to develop strength which to some extent is able to offset the ability of modern management to postpone for a considerable period of time the attrition inherent in the time factor in the forces operative in industrial conflict.

Under the free competitive model of industrial disputes, it was correctly assumed that union strategy would try to time strikes to occur at peaks of business activity when business was most anxious to continue production without interruption and to avoid strikes in periods of depression with the higher levels of unemployment. It should be noted that this concept of a union strategy assumes that there are no fixed dates of contract termination so that organized labor could pick a date for new demands and an eventual strike which seems to be most favorable. However, the fixing of termination dates of union contracts is forcing as it were the hand of management and of labor. The law provides for a start of formal negotiations sixty days prior to the expiration of the current collective agreement. There have been instances when unions would have been willing to renew with minor modifications an existing contract, for example in the steel industry in 1959. Management was intent on obtaining a repeal of certain contract features, especially on local working conditions and a strike ensued. Even under the actual conditions of imperfect competition it would seem feasible at least theoretically for labor and management to take into account changing market situations and to arrive at a simple renewal or renegotiation of a current contract without significant changes. But this rarely occurs and usually a new contract is also a somewhat improved collective agreement. While this corresponds basically to the progressive nature of the system, especially the fact and the requirement of continued growth, this economic setting contributes in many cases to the difficulties in finding a common ground for compromise in collective bargaining. This tendency is reinforced by still another aspect of the strength of labor, especially as far as skilled workers are concerned.

In the prosperous period of full employment after World War II, many workers discovered that it was possible for them to be on strike and work at the same time. Of course this could never be with regards to the same employer. Occasionally, however, the dividing line was very thin. For instance in a newspaper delivery strike in New York, which was directed only against the daily papers, the delivery men continued to work providing news dealers with all other publications especially magazines and also out-of-town newspapers. It was obvious that they were not under immediate pressure to come to terms with management. In larger metropolitan areas a strike against contractors in one city makes it possible for skilled workers to commute to other municipalities and work on construction projects in these nearby areas. Such substitute employment may not be available in "one industry towns" or generally for less skilled labor. It is, however, necessary to realize that especially in times of full employment a work stoppage does not necessarily mean that workers involved in industrial dispute are thereby completely deprived of a livelihood.

This increased strength of organized labor and the possibility of obtaining temporary employment elsewhere which is available to a significant group of strikers has led to a comparatively novel complication in collective bargaining processes. Of seventy-three national union constitutions, fifty-seven provide for the involvement of local unions in negotiations and in ratification of negotiated settlements. In twenty-four cases an explicit *vote of ratification* is required by the union constitution.[3] In recent years cases have been multiplied in which a union contract which had been agreed upon often in laborious negotiations by duly designated labor representatives and by management were rejected in votes taken at membership meetings.

Perhaps the most spectacular *contract rejection* occurred in 1966 in the case of The International Association of Machinists and Aerospace Workers. These highly paid employees formulated demands for higher wages and fringe benefits and set a strike deadline for April 23 of that year. They rejected an offer of the National Mediation Board to arbitrate the dispute. In view of the economic significance of air transportation, the President of the United States established a special board to investigate the situation and to make recommendations. Union representatives rejected this proposal and now the negotiations were taken over by the Secretary of Labor, Willard Wirtz. Nevertheless the union called a strike beginning on July 8,

---

[3]Herbert J. Lahne: "Union Contract Ratification Procedures," *Monthly Labor Review* (May 1968).

1966. Negotiations continued during the walkout and an agreement was reached between the union negotiators and the airlines which was deemed so important that its terms were announced by President Johnson in the White House. At that point the full prestige of the federal government had become involved. Nevertheless the membership voted down this negotiated contract primarily because additional fringe benefits were to be postponed until 1967. The strike continued. It was finally settled on August 16 after management had made additional concessions which amounted to a 6 percent rise in wages and benefits and especially an earlier effective date for the fringes. This dispute occurred at a time when the Federal government tried to adhere to wage guide lines limiting increases to 3.2 percent.

It was not until some time later, that these guide lines were dropped. New contracts failed to give evidence of compliance by management and by labor. Actually the limitation of wage increases to productivity gains which was characteristic of these Federal standards is no longer consistent with the new structure of the American economy, as we have already seen in Chapter 11 of this text.

Contract rejection is sometimes also linked to internal stresses within the union and to failures of union negotiators to communicate with rank and file members who ultimately have to vote for acceptance of the new contract. There have been cases when locals rejected contracts at the instigation of opponents of current labor leaders and as a tactic in internal union struggles rather than because of a disagreement on the terms of the contract itself. Failure to interpret new provisions of a settlement led to contract rejections of an agreement negotiated between the New York Shipping Association and the International Longshoremen's Association. The issue revolved on the reduction of a work gang which actually had been under negotiations for years. The union leadership presented the agreement as "the best ever." Nevertheless rank-and-file members, fearing the loss of some jobs, turned it down in New York and Baltimore. Union officials appeared before these locals and cleared up "misunderstandings." As a result the New York and Baltimore locals reversed themselves and the contract went into effect.

Contract rejection also played a role in the strike against a new New York afternoon newspaper which was set to publish its first issue on April 25, 1966. A strike was called against the publishers even before the first issue could appear. For months, difficult negotiations were conducted with severence pay for employees not to be taken over by the new publication and the observation of strict seniority in layoffs the main issue. Eventually an agreement was reached but the printing pressmen refused to go along for a considerable period of time. This rejection set in motion developments which forced the new paper to cease publication after a few months because during the strike potential advertisers withdrew in great numbers thereby depriving the publication of revenues necessary for its economic survival.

16-6. A REAPPRAISAL OF COLLECTIVE BARGAINING CONCEPTS

We have seen in the preceding section that the ultimate weapon of labor, the strike, considered by most as inseparable from collective bargaining itself, has undergone great modifications as the structure of the economy and of organized labor underwent significant changes. In order to have any predictive value at all, the Hicksian analysis of the prospective duration of the strike and the compromise wage level must be extended to include such strategies of management as stockpiling or staffing of operations with executive personnel. It must also take into account the increased number of options which are available to strikers, especially in craft unions, to avail themselves of alternative employment opportunities for the duration of the work stoppage and more generally the ability of the union to strengthen employees' resistance through strike benefits. Furthermore this type of analysis must also take note of the fact that the simultaneous strengthening of management and of labor has led to many situations in which what appear to the outsider as minor issues such as the effective date of certain fringe benefits can hold up the conclusion of a settlement and prolong a strike. Whereas it could be assumed formerly that industrial conflicts carried out under a setting of more or less perfect competition would very soon come under the influence of competing firms and competing units of labor, thereby forcing the parties into an early settlement, the pattern of imperfect competition shaping management and labor today has a tendency to raise side issues to major obstacles in a settlement and to prolong the duration of strikes.

In collective bargaining in the private sector questions of cost involved in wage settlements and their impact on revenues and profits are at stake. Management must arrive at decisions which will have a considerable impact on its pricing policies and expectations of future profits. But especially large corporations operating under conditions of oligopoly or imperfect competition have a number of options with regard to the incidence of the burden arising from wage concessions. A part of the additional money outlays may be offset by labor savings in the employment of production workers; another part may be shifted to the ultimate consumers. At any rate in the private sector the parties involved in collective bargaining are also more or less in control of their own financial status. They do not depend on outside agencies for the financing of their operations. There may be a number of unknown factors in the situation. But basically the settlement will be reached at one or another point of the zone of indeterminacy which was shown in Figure 6-2 of this text.

We have seen in the first section of this chapter that frequently collective bargaining is assumed to require the recognition of the right to strike on the part of employees. Furthermore, we have stressed that the structure of strikes has been changing as the economy itself moved from perfect competition to concentration, large-scale business and monopolistic structures. This change in the underlying conditions of the strike as the ultimate weapon of labor suggests strongly that a clearer distinction has to be made between collective bargaining on the one side and strikes on the other.

Collective bargaining is a formal procedure through which both parties to a union contract can communicate their demands for changes and strive to strengthen the bilateral and equal nature of the management labor relationship. Hence the normal product of collective bargaining is a new contract. As innumerable instances show, a new agreement rather than a strike is the outcome of collective negotiations.

There is no denying of the fact that at least in the private sector of a pluralistic society the strike remains this last resort of labor. But this does not mean that more effective procedures than are in existence today could not be devised to increase the probability of averting a strike.

When labor relations legislation was initiated in the United States in the 1930's it was widely assumed that public policy with regard to collective bargaining has achieved its objectives once the practice has been firmly established either by custom or both and the two partners involved in the negotiations of union contracts have achieved near equality. Beyond this, laissez faire has largely prevailed with regard to collective bargaining. True enough the law now requires the parties to start negotiating sixty days prior to the expiration of a contract. The Mediation and Conciliation Service can enter these negotiations thirty days before the ending of the current contract. Under the Railway Labor Act and under the National Emergency provisions of the Taft-Hartley Act *"cooling-off periods"* or court orders enjoining strikers to return to work for a limited period of time can be issued. But ultimately the terms of a new settlement are up to the parties involved in the dispute. Compulsory arbitration by an ad hoc board as outlined in Sec. 15-8 should not become a general method to escape from the frustrations and procrastinations of collective bargaining procedures.

Genuine compulsory arbitration would undermine collective bargaining completely. Voluntary agreements would become virtually impossible because one or the other party or even both would hold out for a binding arbitration award in the hope of getting from such a board more than they can obtain through mutual agreement. Actually imposing of wage scales through compulsory arbitration amounts to a fixing of wages by government. If wages were to be established in this manner, prices would have to be included in this controlled system. One of the great errors in wage policies was made in the United States after World War II when wage ceilings and controls were removed while the government tried in vain to retain some price controls. The control of wages and of prices is interdependent. It is impossible to decontrol one while leaving the other subject to restraints and regulations.

The fact that the extreme solution which would be embodied in compulsory arbitration is not feasible and has to be rejected, does not imply however that the only alternative is the opposite extreme, the now-prevailing attitudes towards collective bargaining, namely a hands-off attitude barring national emergency situations. Mediation and conciliation procedures are quite effective in a large number of bargaining situations. It is only natural that successful efforts gain less public attention than failures of these procedures to help writing a new contract prior to the expiration of the old one. Such a breakdown in bargaining is usually associated with conditions in which management and labor are both bargaining from positions of strength. Naturally this is the case in most key industries where protracted work stoppages will have a noticeable impact on overall economic conditions and levels of activity. The question arises whether bargaining procedures and methods can be developed which fall short of compulsory arbitration but are also going beyond the very limited power of public authorities legally committed to often ineffectual attempts to influence collective bargaining and to avoid strikes.

As we have seen in Part 11 of this text wage structures, especially fringe benefits have become quite elaborate and often complex. It is natural that management when confronted with demands for substantial improvements in pension systems would like to get full appraisals of the actuarial and financial implications of such vast schemes operating in a long-run frame of time. Experience has shown that if such negotiations are compressed within the currently prescribed sixty-day period, they can often not be concluded successfully prior to the reaching of the deadline. However a substantial extension of the sixty-day period is hardly compatible with the currently normal two-year contracts. Only in exceptional cases such as the 1950 contract in the automobile industry do we encounter a five-year duration provided for a collective agreement. In that case labor and management began to move more than one year prior to expiration to lay the ground work for the formulation of their respective positions. Already in 1953 United Automobile Workers came forward with a demand for a Guaranteed Annual Wage. Management made counter proposals and there was a considerable amount of public debate. Nevertheless in the first months of 1965 there was a widespread impression that a strike could not be avoided. Automobile production reached an all time high, there was stockpiling and labor also prepared itself for a long strike. Due in part to the early start of public and private discussions when the expiration date of the five-year contract was at hand, a new collective aggreement had been negotiated and the widely anticipated strike never occurred. While there have been no five-year contracts in recent years, the change in the structure of collective bargaining suggests very strongly a general adoption of three-year contracts such as the agreement achieved without a strike in the steel industry in 1968 and running into 1971. If this format could be accepted more generally, it would be possible through amendment of the Taft-Hartley Act to lengthen the current sixty-day period prior to the expiration of the contract at which point parties now are under an obligation to start exchanging their proposals for changes to, for instance, one hundred twenty days. This would leave more time for a thorough exploration of the effects of all issues which rise in the negotiations. Whereas the current 60-day period all too frequently leads to "crisis bargaining" in order to beat a deadline, the longer negotiation period, if used properly, would remove a good deal of such time pressures and lend itself to a more rational approach to the settling of outstanding issues. This, however, requires a return to concepts of "good faith collective bargaining" as evolved originally after the enactment of the National Relations Act of 1935. Section 8a of The Wagner Act stated that it is an unfair labor practice "to refuse to bargain collectively with representatives of his employees." The Taft-Hartley Act has retained this position. While there is nothing in the law which would compel the parties to reach an agreement, it is clear that the law as interpreted by the Labor Relations Board and the courts requires serious negotiations. This in turn makes it mandatory on the parties to lay on the bargaining table all their demands at the beginning of the negotiation period so that there is enough leeway for the give and take which is essential to genuine bargaining.

Unfortunately the "bargaining table" just mentioned is in many negotiations more a figure of speech than of reality. Once a deadlock seems to have developed and the conciliation and mediation service has moved in, the parties in many cases meet separately and talk to mediators. Only after the clarification of all the issues has been achieved and communicated to the other side assembled in other rooms by way of back and forth messages will there be a final meeting around the table. Perhaps this procedure has become inevitable as a result of the growing complexity and number of items which have become subject to collective bargaining, but if that is so, then the procedural system should be adjusted to deal more efficiently with these new conditions. We will discuss in this context the use of *computers* in collective bargaining and the role of *yardsticks* in wage determination through union-management negotiations.

We have already mentioned the fact that the sixty-day period required by law for the opening of contract talks has proved to be too short in many instances. Actually management and labor have begun to use *computers* in devising their respective strategies and to "cost out" the various packages which are offered by both sides. The greatest assistance to collective bargaining can be rendered by computers in the examination by one side of the significance of the proposals of the other. But obviously there are limitations to this method which are inherent in data processing itself. The opposite side does not really have at its disposal the data which have been fed into the computer by the original proponents of a package. It must always be borne in mind that solutions or conclusions supplied by computers are dependent on the information which has been taped into them. Other data for instance those which are relevant for the other party in collective bargaining would, of course, yield entirely different results.

While computers even under present conditions can be helpful for the internal clarification of cost structures and implications of proposals for both sides involved in collective bargaining and in this way can help to speed up proceedings, they can be of use in the resolution of impasses only if there is a prior verbal and conceptual agreement between the two parties about the frame of reference within which a resolution of the conflict is to be sought. Unless such a consensus can be achieved, the use of computers on both sides of the proverbial bargaining table can also lead to a hardening of positions and, therefore, can threaten the process of collective bargaining itself. The growing possibility of using computers in bolstering up positions taken in collective bargaining makes it imperative to analyze the role of guidelines or yardsticks to be observed by both parties in negotiating a union contract.

16-7. THE ROLE OF GUIDEPOSTS

We have shown in the preceding section that compulsory or binding arbitration is not compatible with the systematic structure of the private sector of the American economy. It also became clear in the course of our discussion that the other extreme, a laissez-faire attitude modified only by emergency provisions of doubtful value can lead to many impasses and deadlocks in collective bargaining which can do great harm to communities or even to the country at large. The question arises whether there is a middle way between compulsory arbitration and the present largely unchartered field in which many negotiations seemed to end up seemingly without a way out. An attempt was made in 1962 by the Council of Economic Advisers to establish wage-price guideposts which were to be observed in collective bargaining. There was, of course, no way for government agencies to compel parties to adopt these yardsticks. But for about four years efforts were made to convince management and labor that they ought to comply with the basic concepts incorporated in these guideposts. Actually it was not so much the intention of the Council of Advisers to break impasses in collective bargaining as to assure price stability. It was assumed that any wage settlement which would exceed increases in labor productivity would be inflationary in character. Hence it was suggested that negotiated wage settlements should as a rule not be higher than the average national increase in output per man-hour. If there would have been widespread compliance with these guideposts this would have contributed to the settlement of many collective bargaining impasses. But on occasion government agencies themselves disregarded these guideposts as we have seen in Sec. 16-4 when the contract rejection in 1966 by the machinists was reviewed. At that time the guideposts tried to limit wage increases to 3.2 percent per annum whereas actually with the active assistance of the Secretary of Labor a final settlement providing for a 6 percent increase was reached. The steel contract of 1968 which was concluded without a prior strike provided for similar rates of increase. By that time, however, the guideposts had gone by the board and the opinion spread that it probably had been a mistake from the beginning to try to get management and labor to observe voluntarily the limitations implied in these yardsticks. But such a conclusion seems to be premature. If it were to be accepted generally, collective bargaining would be condemned to continue on its unsteady and unstable course between the poles of binding arbitration and unregulated power conflicts.

There is no doubt that the guideposts of 1962 with their inflexible limitations to a 3½ percent range of wage increases were unrealistic because they were based on outdated assumptions with regard to the operation of the American economy. But the fact that the guidelines which were in effect in the 1960's did not achieve the desired impact on wage settlements in collective bargaining does not militate against the idea of having yardsticks setting up ranges within which management and labor should agree voluntarily to find the specific level of wage changes meeting their special requirements. In a democracy it is possible to marshall social forces in the direction of voluntary compliance with policy goals. This, however, requires that these policies are realistic and can, therefore, claim general assent. The guideposts of 1962 did not meet these requirements. They overlooked the fact that in the advanced industrial society of the United States there are other factors than productivity which enter into the problem of dynamic equilibrium as we have seen in Chapter 13 of this text. Furthermore they did not take into account the impact of the structural transformation of the labor force, especially the seeming openendedness of the demand for white-collar workers in a defense stimulated economy which adds to total employment cost quite independent of considerations of productivity which become very vague and ill-defined once we leave the blue-collar sector.

The problem then is not the discarding of guidelines but their reformulation in a macrodynamic context. The old guidelines were bound to fail because they were based on simplistic ideas of the relations between wages and prices. New guidelines would have to develop models of wage structures in which the transformation of the labor force, the increase of the man-hour productivity of blue-collar workers and the growth requirements of the system at points of full employment would be taken into account. It is precisely at this point that computers could play an important role. Guideposts for collective bargaining resulting from this type of macrodynamics data processing could supply parties to collective bargaining and mediators with general and specific information about the margins within which settlements could still be considered compatible with the requirements of a balanced growth of the system. It should not be beyond the capability of government and of the academic community and of the public at large to propose forcefully to labor and management that anarchic procedures in collective bargaining are incompatible with the progressive nature of an industrialized society. What compulsory arbitration can never do, an acceptance of valid guideposts can.

SELECTED BIBLIOGRAPHY

Farmer, G. *Management Rights and Union Bargaining Power* (New York: Industrial Relation Counselors, Inc., 1965).

Peck, Sidney G. *The Rank and File Leader* (New Haven: Yale University Press, 1963).

Prasow, Paul and Peters, Edward. *Arbitration and Collective Bargaining* (New York: McGraw-Hill Book Co., 1970).

Stone, Morris. *Labor Grievances and Decisions* (New York: Harper & Row Publishers, 1964).

QUESTIONS FOR DISCUSSION

1. Discuss the structural prerequisites for collective bargaining, especially the problems of multi-unionism and coalition bargaining.

2. Explain the reasons for the American system of designating bargaining representatives. What is meant by union security?

3. Evaluate Boulwarism in the light of good faith bargaining.

4. Explain the frequency of contract rejections.

5. In what ways can guideposts and computers contribute to collective bargaining?

Chapter

17

Labor Relations in the
Public Sector

When the need arose in the 1930's for Congress to enact legislation to encourage the practice of collective bargaining the law was specifically limited to the private sector of the economy. In Section 2, "Definitions" of the Labor Management Relations Act it is stated that the terms "employer" shall not include the United States or any wholly owned Government corporation or any Federal Reserve Bank or any State. . . ." This was understood at that time to mean that public agencies, unlike private employers, did not have to recognize representatives of public employees, did not have to bargain collectively with them and could conduct their relations with their own workers whether in civil service or otherwise employed in the customary manner of unilateral determination of wages and other conditions of work by legislative bodies.

The Taft-Hartley Act in Section 305 specifically confirmed the illegality of a strike against the Federal government. It threatened individuals participating in a walkout with immediate discharge, loss of his civil service status and a ban on re-employment by the government for three years. Long before the passage of this legislation executive orders prohibited federal employees even from "lobbying." One such Order of 1906 specifically forbade associations of employees "to solicit an increase of pay or to influence or to attempt to influence in their own interest any other legislation. . . . " As we will see later in this chapter this went much farther than European practices.

On the federal level these laws and administrative measures had been effective until early in 1970 when wildcat strikes of postal employees erupted in key metropolitan areas. At the same time air controllers demanding better working conditions staged a "sick-in" forcing the Civil Aeronautics Administration to curtail air traffic. Congressional action to raise wages by 6 percent rectroactively ended the illegal walkout of the postal workers. Court orders forced the air controllers back to work.

As we will see in some detail in Sec. 17-3, the ban on strikes of public employees contained in the Taft-Hartley Act has been incorporated in a number of state laws. The most famous case of a strike against a city government, the Boston Police strike of 1919 during which the governor of the state, Calvin Coolidge, called out the national guard, remained an isolated occurrence. Fifty years later, the national guard was called out in a city in Iowa because the local firemen had gone on strike. The police could not handle all the fires and so the state militia had to come to their assistance. In the same year hospital workers in a city in South Carolina walked out in order to push their demands for collective bargaining of employees in public institutions. Although this strike found widespread national attention and support, the government of the state refused to meet with the representatives of the hospital workers because the state law did not permit them to organize.

In 1967, 181 work stoppages occurred in the public sector. Although in a number of states, laws providing for stiff penalties against public employees going on strike were enforced, it became evident that these legal sanctions were largely ineffective and did not actually prevent often protracted strikes of public employees.

The increasing incidence of strikes in the public sector and especially their often disastrous impact on communities and metropolitan regions shows clearly that the assumption can no longer be taken for granted that strikes in the public sector are unthinkable merely because they are forbidden. It has, therefore, become necessary to study in greater detail the changing role of public employment in the econmy, the problems involved in granting to public employees on the one side the right to organize but continuing on the other side the ban on strikes. In this connection it becomes necessary to investigate recent experiences with state laws and the degree to which their enforcement has been effective. Finally, suggestions for a better structuring of management labor relations in the public sector must be considered.

17-1. EXTENT AND NATURE OF PUBLIC EMPLOYMENT

In 1929 public employment in federal, state and local government agencies amounted only to 10 percent of all wage and salary workers. In 1969 the share of public employment in this group had risen to about 18 percent. Whereas in the 1930's and 1940's the number of employees in the Federal government rose very sharply, since 1960 total civilian employment on the federal level remained almost frozen. On the other hand employment in state and local government rose from just over 6 million in 1960 to almost 9.5 million in 1969. In fact this area of public employment provided the greatest increase of all categories of employment of wage and salary workers. It exceeded by far increases of employment in manufacturing, contract construction and services to name only these groups. It is easy to see why there has been such a rapid expansion of public employment in state and especially in local government. The effects of urbanization and the concentration of more and more people in metropolitan areas has raised the demand for public services of all kinds very rapidly. This has increased the general significance of public employment and the dependence of complex communities on the continued functioning of public services. The greater urban conglomerations become, the more are they vulnerable. Even a short interruption in public services such as transportation or sanitation is bound to create very serious disruptions of normal activities. Herein lies one of the main differences between private and public employment. Even large and protracted strikes in the private sector such as have occurred in the automobile, steel, and electric industries have less generally damaging effects than work stoppages of public employees responsible for the maintenance of vital services in the community.

Traditionally this community aspect of public employment has been dealt with by the establishment of systems of compensation and working conditions which differed widely from those in the private sector. While wage scales were modest, job security and retirement pay were considerably better than was the case in the private sector of the economy at least until the period after World War II. For the first 100 years of its existence the United States did not have a formal civil service system. However, under Secretary of the Interior Carl Schurz who served under the administration of President Hayes (1877–1881) the beginnings were made in the development of civil service concepts of public employment. Up to that time the "spoils system" was widely used even on the federal level. The idea was that the Chief Executive should be served in the various offices of government by people who were his political followers and, therefore, most likely to carry out their function according to his policies.

The introduction of civil service principles in public employment brought about basic changes for the overwhelming majority of public employees. Increasingly their employment and promotion was predicated on the passing of tests and examinations. To a vast measure the spoils system was superseded by the merit system which created a presumption that those who qualified in these examinations did have the necessary skills to carry out their assignments. In 1969 postmasters who had been political appointees were also taken into the merit system, thereby reducing the number of noncivil service employees to a minimum. This group is now limited to policy making assignments in the highest echelons of the executive branch of the federal government. Actually the overwhelming majority of civil service employees continues to function regardless of changes in the Presidency. In this way the American civil service now resembles the older European systems of public employment.

Nevertheless, in the market or private sector oriented economy of the United States with its ideological emphasis on self-reliance, economic independence and ascendency on the income ladder through the workings of competitive processes, public employment does not have the high regard that it has won in countries where public service systems can look back on a longer tradition. In these countries public employment has always been operating on a service principle. People were attracted to public employment within this tradition not because it provided a shelter from the competitive struggles of the market place but because it carried with it the psychic rewards of service and public esteem. Another difference between the United States and European civil service structures is that whereas in the United States the lower and middle echelons of government employees were brought into the merit system first leaving out the higher posts, the development was exactly in the opposite direction in Europe where executives in government departments below the top level of Ministers or as they are called in this country, Secretaries, were put into formal civil service employment first. Generally these public servants are taken from the group of young men who have completed their legal training at a university, or are graduates of specialized schools for high level administrators. Eventually public employment with tenure and pension rights was extended to middle and lower categories of government workers.

In more recent years, however, there have been developments which show the continuation of significant differences between the American and the European civil service system. While in the United States more and more people working for the government are brought into the civil service system, the trend in Europe has been to convert many routine operations in government agencies from civil service into simple employment contracts comparable to those in the private sector, but maintaining rigidly the training requirements for the higher categories which remain under civil service. There is another historical difference between European and American systems of civil service which as we will see later in this chapter has great practical significance for the shape of management-labor relations in public employment.

European civil service systems pre-date on the Continent the rise of representative government. In fact they are a creation of the absolute monarchies of the 17th and 18th centuries which laid the basic structure of modern government in this area. The underlying concept of labor relations between the state and its public servants was that of *paternalism.* This, of course, put all the power into the hands of the employer, that is to say, ultimately the king and more immediately the various department heads of government. But on the other hand the concept of paternalism was also interpreted as creating the obligation upon the state to be responsible for the material well being of the public employees. While, as we have seen, this did not involve high remunerations even for top level executives it was interpreted as obligating the state to provide a permanent, lifetime income for the employee and a widow's pension. Furthermore while the salaries were modest they were defined in the context of a class society in which people belonging to various groups were entitled to a standard of living consistent with their background and training. Even today the concept is accepted that the government has an obligation to guarantee to civil service employees this lifetime income and to come to his financial assistance in incidental costs of catastrophic illnesses not covered by compulsory or voluntary health insurance. This paternalistic approach has been carried over in Europe into the age of democracy. Hence it is considered an obligation of the legislature to provide salary scales and make appropriations sufficient to maintain patterns of compensation which will enable public employees at all times to preserve a standard of living in keeping with their status in society.

Before we turn our attention to labor relations in the public sector in the United States, it is advisable to discuss briefly the more recent development of these relations in Europe. With the growth of numbers of employees in government agencies outside of a formal civil service status, unions of public employees have been formed and for a considerable period of time collective bargaining procedures have been used to establish conditions of compensation and of work. With the spread of collective bargaining in the public sector, the question arose in European countries as it has recently in the United States whether public employees have the right to strike. In France a law enacted in 1963 has given this right to civil servants if they have given at least five-days' notice prior to the strike. The unions must also indicate whether this is to be a limited walkout or whether the strike is called for an indefinite period of time. In Sweden civil servants are also explicitly given the right to strike. In Germany government and public employees unions proceed on the assumption that, as in the United States, public employees do not have the right to strike. This has not precluded occasional "job actions" for instance by postal employees. They remain on their jobs but carry out a slow-down by observing all rules and regulations.

It should be noted, however, that unlimited strikes have rarely been called by public employees in Europe with the exception of the "events of May 1968" in France. Frequently there have been 24-hour strikes to exercise pressure on the government in matters of public compensation.

While the practice of collective bargaining with public employees has spread in Europe, it is also important to consider the impact of old established associations of civil servants. These rather powerful groups are dedicated to the promotion of the material and other rights of government employees. They frequently formulate demands for major improvements. But these associations do not address themselves so much to the government as to the legislatures. The best parallel to these groups in this country could perhaps be found in such professional organizations as the American Medical Association (AMA) or the American Association of University Professors (AAUP). To be quite frank about it—these associations present in many countries a powerful lobby which like other pressure groups are making their influence felt in the halls of parliaments. After all, with the steady increase in the numbers of public employees, such associations present significant blocs of voters, and political parties especially in election years will think twice before they vote against increases in the pay scales of civil service workers.

17-2. LABOR RELATIONS IN THE UNITED STATES FEDERAL GOVERNMENT

The concept of civil service in the United States developed in a social environment somewhat different from that of Europe. Originally the rights of civil service employees were rather restricted. There was even doubt whether public employees had a right to form associations to promote their interests. In 1912 the *Lloyd-La Follette Act* was passed. It specifically permitted civil service employees to join associations provided that these groups did not impose on their members the duty to participate in strikes against the United States. This right of free assembly and association of people working for the government did, however, not imply that there was to be collective bargaining between representatives of government employees and agencies of the government. Like all other citizens, government workers had the right to petition Congress but again this did not mean that they could combine for the purpose of entering into collective relations with the government.

This legislation gave greater job security to civil service employees. If an agency planned the removal of a public employee "to promote the efficiency of the service," it could do so only by initiating formal procedures before the Civil Service Commission.

Up to the 1960's the controlling concept of labor relations in the public sector of the United States was that of "sovereignty." People working for the government were subject to it as far as conditions of pay and employment were concerned precisely because they were rendering a public service. While the originators in modern times of the civil service in Europe were also "sovereigns" they embodied this quality in person and hence as we have seen already a system of benevolent paternalism permeated civil service conditions. In the more austere setting of the American Republic the sovereignty aspect of the relationship was and is more impersonal. The idea that the sovereign employer, acting through the legislature, has a traditional obligation of maintaining an economic status of public employees commensurate with their social standing is stronger in Europe than it has been in the past in the United States. It is true that after World War II public employees in some European countries were easy targets for attempts of government to bring about a general freeze in wages in connection with anti-inflationary policies. But these attempts to interfere with traditional differentials and income relationships between public and private pay scales, to keep the former down while seeing the latter rise have been successful only in the short run. The great unrest which rose to the surface on various occasions in the late 1960's in France and Italy is evidence that the tradition of providing adequate and secure incomes for public employees is stronger than the attempt to make public pay scales a model for a general policy of wage restraints.

All civil service systems have in common that the funds necessary for compensation of public employees must be raised by taxes levied on the public and specifically appropriated in annual budgets by the legislature. We have seen in the preceding section that in some European countries members of Parliament are quite responsive to pressures exercised by associations of the type which the Lloyd-La Follette Act specifically permitted civil service employees to join. However, recently, beginning in the administration of John F. Kennedy, significant changes have been introduced for federal employees. The main result of these innovations is the introduction of a higher degree of bilateralism in public labor relations.

On January 17, 1962 President Kennedy signed Executive Order 10,988. While as we have seen public employees had been granted the right to belong to associations as defined by the law of 1912, the Executive Order of 1962 provided for a recognition of such an organization by federal agencies if it had been designated by a majority of the employees. In Section 2 of this Order it is stated that the primary purpose of such an organization must be "the improvement of working conditions among federal employees." However, recognition cannot be extended to any union which asserts the right to strike against the U. S. government. This has given rise to the question whether public agencies can require of new employees a statement that they do not *assert* the right to strike. A similar provision is contained in the Taylor Act of New York State which will be discussed in greater detail in Sec. 17-4. The constitutionality of this provision was challenged by the President of the City Welfare Department Local in New York City. A ruling of the State Supreme Court in Rogoff vs. Anderson of November 1968, concurred with the view that a mere assertion of the right to strike would come under the protection of the First Amendment. This ruling, however, does not imply that a ban on strikes by public employees is unconstitutional.

The main purpose of this executive order was to open up a direct channel of communications between organized public employees and the government. Obviously pay schedules and promotion systems fall under the concept of improvement of working conditions. They are, therefore, a legitimate topic of discussion in informal or formal contacts with the government. However, the great similarity of the sections of this Executive Order dealing with recognition of employee representatives with corresponding passages of the Taft-Hartley Act must not lead to the conclusion that this order introduced collective bargaining into the public sector comparable to these procedures in the private economy. While the adequacy of wage scales can be discussed, the agency is specifically empowered to omit its budget from the topics under consideration. This is a reflection on the fact, stressed above, that it is not the agency but Congress that disposes the funds necessary for the operation of this public and private labor relations. A private company is more or less in control of its revenues and expenditures. A public agency depends on budgetary appropriations therefore literally speaking, it has nothing to bargain with.

The ban on strikes which was clearly upheld by the Executive Order outlined in this section was also reflected in the constitutions of public employee unions. A survey published in the *Monthly Labor Review*, March 1969[1] showed that out of 16 such unions on the federal level, 7 have a specific no-strike pledge in their constitution. However, The National Postal Union which used to have a no-strike clause dropped it recently. The same was done by the United Federation of Postal Clerks. On the state and local level, the American Federation of Teachers and the State, County and Municipal Employees Union adopted statements supporing work stoppages under certain circumstances.

It should be noted that such resolutions or changes in the union constitutions of public employees have no effect on the validity of the ban on strikes which is embodied on the federal level in the Taft-Hartley Law and as we will see in the next section in a significant number of state laws.

There is no doubt that the executive order discussed here has improved the climate of labor relations in the federal government. This favorable development has been reinforced by the establishment of a formalized grievance procedure in federal agencies. Adverse actions by such an agency against a civil service employee can be appealed, the aggrieved employee has to be heard and must be protected against intimidation. Furthermore a council may assist the complaining employee. These grievance procedures do not apply, however, to such maximum security agencies as for instance the CIA, the FBI and the Atomic Energy Commission.

The overall effect of these recent innovations in federal labor relations

[1]Anne M. Ross: "Public Employee Unions and the Right to Strike."

has been a certain mitigation of the traditional stern sovereignty stance of the Federal government. There is more communication, requests and complaints of civil service employees can be properly channelled to appropriate agencies, there is no longer the assumption that all the rights are with the employer and all the duties with the employees. Furthermore, in recent years votes of Congress to raise civil service pay scales were automatically applied to the remuneration of members of Congress. This linkage assures greater speed in adjusting civil service pay schedules to changing economic conditions.

But these innovations have left unchanged the absolute ban on strikes for federal employees. We have seen that the granting of the right of public employees to form associations and to file complaints does not lead to genuine collective bargaining with the Federal government. Hence it cannot be said that federal statutes have created a dichotomy between the right to organize and to bargain collectively and the right to strike. Actually the right to organize of federal employees does not lead to collective bargaining as it is known in the private sector. However the counterpart to the strike ban of public employees is a permanent public commitment of the legislature to deal fairly with all federal workers and to adjust their pay to changing conditions without delay. The wildcat strike of postal workers in 1970, while illegal, was brought about in part by delays in the increase of pay due to an attempt of the Administration to link this raise to a proposed reorganization of the Post Office. When it became apparent that this linkage was unfair to the employees, the pay raise was voted on separately. We now turn our attention to labor relations on the state and local level where as we have seen conflicts and strikes have become rather frequent.

17-3. PUBLIC EMPLOYMENT IN STATE LEGISLATION

The principle contained in Section 305 of the Taft-Hartley Act was incorporated into many state laws. In a considerable number of states, for instance, Connecticut, Massachusetts, and Wisconsin, strikes of public employees are specifically prohibited, without, however, attaching specific sanctions against civil service employees disregarding the state law and going on strike.[2] In such cases state agencies that would be closed down by an illegal strike can appeal to state courts, asking for an injunction requiring strikers to resume their work. Those not obeying would be in contempt of court and subject to the penalties and sanctions connected with these violations of court orders. In other states such as Michigan sanctions against employees of the government violating the strike ban, such as dis-

[2]Joseph P. Goldberg, "Labor-Management Laws in Public Service," *Monthly Labor Review*, June 1968.

missals are specifically declared to be subject to court review. A whole catalog of sanctions has been provided in the legislation of New York State. Public labor relations in that state will be taken up in a case study in the next section.

Most state laws deal with the recognition of employee representatives by government agencies. In many cases agencies have been set up to rule on representation questions. Following the method used in the Taft-Hartley Act and in the Executive Order of 1962, discussed in the preceding section, the principle of exclusive representation is being applied in the designation of bargaining representatives. The state laws also established obligations of state agencies to deal with representatives of employees. There are, however, significant differences in the language used. In California and Minnesota the law requires agencies to "meet and confer" with representatives. In other states such as Oregon and Wisconsin "bargaining" is mandatory. Inasmuch as in all states strikes of public employees are not permitted, the "meet and confer" phraseology seems to be more to the point and less misleading than the term "bargaining."

Because state legislation has imposed on government a duty to negotiate with public employee representatives while maintaining a ban on strikes, it was clearly foreseen by many state law makers that provisions would have to be made for mediation and factfinding by state laws and the settling of impasses. Nowhere, however, has state law empowered a mediation board to issue a binding ruling settling the dispute. All these laws have shied away from introducing compulsory arbitration. If agreements cannot be reached, some state laws, for instance Michigan and Minnesota, specifically provide for nonbinding recommendations by state boards. Two states, Rhode Island and Vermont, emphasize efforts to obtain a voluntary arbitration agreement between the employee representatives and state agencies. The latter system is preferable to nonbinding recommendations by mediation and factfinding boards of the state. Even if a great deal of detachment and independence can be presumed to prevail in nonbinding arbitration proposals of a state board, the basic fact cannot be overlooked that the state, embodied in such mediation and factfinding boards, even if they contain outside members, is ultimately judging its own case. A voluntary agreement to abide by arbitration of a board consisting of members not connected with state and local government seems to be preferable.

Another difficulty in these negotiations no matter whether they are called bargaining or conferences is that the state agency often feels that it can make no concessions because it has no control over revenue. Thus an impasse is often reached early in these negotiations. "Crisis bargaining" sets in as deadlines expire. Often funds are made available by state governments or public authorities in the last minute, making it possible for the parties to resolve the contested issues. But as we will see in the next section if the *deus ex machina* does not appear on cue, this is triggering serious troubles in public labor relations.

17-4. A CASE STUDY OF PUBLIC LABOR RELATIONS: NEW YORK STATE

Within a comparatively short period of two decades the State of New York has had three major legislative attempts to settle labor relations of state and local employees. The *Condon-Wadlin Act* of 1947 followed largely the pattern which can be found in Section 305 of the Taft-Hartley Law and which was outlined in the preceding section of this chapter. However, to a certain extent it even went further than the federal law. It stipulated that should an employee who had gone on strike be reemployed his compensation was to be frozen on the level established prior to the walkout for a period of three years. Furthermore it terminated the civil service status of striking employees and if they were reemployed after the conclusion of an illegal strike, he would be placed on a probationary status for five years.

Obviously this legislation operated on the principle of *deterrence*, well known also to theorists and practitioners of criminal law. But as in the latter area, the principle seemed to be vastly ineffective. This was clearly demonstrated in 1966. The transit workers in New York City had gone on strike, creating a great deal of inconvenience and disruption of regular activities in the New York metropolitan area. That the strike was a prima facie violation of the Condon-Wadlin Act was acknowledged even by the strike leaders. Once the conflict had been resolved and the transit workers had gone back to work they would in theory have been subject to the sanctions provided by the state law. However, the law designed to deter civil service employees from striking and which had failed in this, its primary purpose, collapsed also in all other respects. The transit workers, far from being frozen in their wages for three years, obtained substantial increases in pay. Furthermore there was no suspension of their civil service status. Now in order to make this noncompliance with an existing law by the authorities concerned legal, it was necessary for the legislature to adopt a specific exemption ruling for the workers who had participated in this unlawful strike. In fact, the only time the Condon-Wadlin Act was enforced according to the letter of the law was in the case of a few tugboat workers. They had gone on strike and were penalized by dismissal and loss of civil service status. Now a law whose enforcement provisions are suspended when a strong organization like the Transit Workers Union can exercise enough pressure to this effect, whereas it is applied to a few strikers not backed up by a large labor organization, is worse than no legislation at all. The experience with the Condon-Wadlin Act clearly shows that it was "a paper tiger" and of no help in preventing strikes of large groups of public workers. The ineffectiveness of this law became generally acknowledged. The desire to create a better law led to the New York State "Public Employees' Fair Employment Act" (PEFEA), also known as the Taylor Act, named after the well-known arbitrator and Professor at the University of Pennsylvania.

In sharp contrast to the New York State law it replaced, the Taylor Act places great emphasis on the right of public employees to form and participate in "employee organizations of their own choosing." (Section 202). Not only this, the law specifically makes it mandatory on the public employer to "negotiate collectively" (Section 204.2).

On the other hand, the Taylor Act states, "No public employee or employee organization shall engage in a strike, and no employee or organization shall cause, instigate, encourage or condone a strike" (Section 210.1). The New York State Taylor Act, therefore, presents an attempt to have it as it were both ways in public labor relations: a duty to bargain collectively and a ban on strikes. In order to bridge this chasm, the Taylor Act has made some determined efforts. Detailed provisions have been made to deal with *impasses* developing in the course of collective negotiations between the public employer and employee organizations. Such an impasse is considered as prevailing, if the parties have failed to come to an agreement at least sixty days prior to the day at which the government agency must submit its budget. The parallel between this provision and the similar time period in the Taft-Hartley Act is interesting. It is, however, also highly informative to outline the differences. As we have seen in Sec. 15-6, if mediation and conciliation have failed, a strike becomes legal in the private sector of the economy. Since it has been declared illegal in the Taylor Act, this law has established an impasse resolution machinery which provides for a number of subsequent stages. In order to help the parties to come to an agreement once the impasse has set in, a *mediator* taken from a panel listed by the *Public Employment Relations Board* can be appointed by this agency. If his efforts fail, a *fact finding board* of not more than three members can be sent in. This board has the right to make public its recommendations for the settlement of the dispute. If the parties still fail to agree, the fact finding board must submit its proposals at least fifteen days prior to the budget date to the chief executive of the government agency and simultaneously to the employee union. Furthermore, the Public Employment Relations Board can intervene directly, can make recommendations but is not empowered to create an additional fact finding board.

Now if mediation, fact finding and intervention of the Board do not succeed, the competent government officer must submit the recommendations and the findings to the legislature together with his own proposals to settle the dispute. Clearly it is then up to the legislature to reach a final decision. It can for instance increase pay scales, obligating itself thereby to vote the necessary appropriations, or it can totally reject whatever propositions for an improvement of pay and working conditions of public employees have been advanced during the impasse procedures. No matter what the outcome of the deliberations of the legislative body is, the absolute ban on strikes remains. It should be noted at this point that in New York City a special Office of Collective Bargaining has been established. It is supposed to operate along the same lines as described above.

The Taylor Law has proved to be quite effective in smaller units of local government. Actually in 1968, 229 bargaining impasses were settled according to the procedures of the law.

One of the main criticisms which have been leveled against the Condon-Wadlin Act was that its *penalties* were so drastic that there was great hesitation to go through with its enforcement. The Taylor Act of 1967 accordingly mitigated substantially the sanctions against employees violating the no-strike provisions of the law. Now the penalties mentioned dismissal only as the last and most serious action which can be taken. Striking public employees, however, can get off with a simple reprimand. More serious measures are suspension, fine or demotion. The act also provides for sanctions against public employee unions conducting a strike. In the law of 1967 such labor organizations could be deprived for a period of 18 months of the use of the check-off system of collecting union dues. They could also be fined $10,000 a day for each day of the duration of the illegal strike. Furthermore, union officials disregarding orders not to call a strike are subject to imprisonment up to thirty days.

While the provision of the law of 1967 concerning the jailing of union leaders was enforced during the strikes of sanitation workers and teachers in 1968, providing great publicity and an image of self-sacrifice to these leaders, it became clear that the Taylor Act could not prevent major confrontations and strikes in the public employment sector of New York State. Less than two years after its enactment, the penalty provisions of the Taylor Act were "beefed up" again. While there was no return to the severity of the Condon-Wadlin Act, check-off privileges can now be taken away from the striking union for an indefinite period; the limitation on fines to be imposed on unions for each day of a strike has been removed and courts now can impose financial sanctions exceeding $10,000 a day. Most important, employees following the strike call of their leaders can be docked for two days' pay for each day they absent themselves from work as participators in the strike.

It would be wrong to say that with the stiffening of the penalties against violators of the no-strike provisions of the Taylor Act a full cycle has been completed. The amended law still falls short of the severity of the Condon-Wadlin Act in important respects. While it imposes stricter economic sanctions on public employees engaging in a strike, it does not call for the automatic dismissal and loss of civil service rights. Furthermore, the impasse procedures remain intact. The main reason the Taylor Act of 1967 failed was not in the mildness of its penalties. It is to be found in the fact that when powerful unions with a large number of members became involved in a dispute, the impasse procedures ceased to be effective. In fact, one of the most important effects of the law of 1967 with its emphasis on employee representation, their recognition by public employers and the duty to bargain collectively has been a doubling of membership in unions of civil service workers in the State of New York.

This development requires a futher interpretation in order to understand the progress and the problems which have been created by these developments.

As was stressed in Sec. 17-2, recent developments of public employment relations on the federal level have brought about a much better system of two-way communications between the public employer and civil service workers. The same effect has without doubt been achieved in New York State. The rapid growth of civil service employees organizations is proof that the whole climate of the public employment relationship has improved and that individual employees now find that joining such a union may increase their chances of obtaining greater betterment in their conditions of pay and work.

However, the emergence of strong civil service unions in a labor relations field in which there are bars to collective bargaining has accentuated the difficulty created by the fact that the law encourages collective bargaining but forbids strikes. Leaders of public employee unions, imbued with the traditions and spirit of the American Labor Movement find it hard to operate in a setting in which there is a ban on the use of the ultimate weapon of labor. They have tended to break the law of the state rather than to depart from the patterns of collective bargaining familiar in the private sector. It is time, however, to realize that in many conflict situations and impasses in public labor relations, there are underlying factors and conditions which cannot be dealt with by traditional union tactics.

The teachers' strike in New York City in 1967, called in defiance of the just enacted Taylor Law, could perhaps be brought under the concept of a management-labor dispute of the conventional type as far as the demand of the union was concerned, to cut down on the size of classes. Other requests dealing with the conferral of greater disciplinary power on teachers, no matter how justified they may have been, are already doubtful as an agenda for collective bargaining. The long teachers' strike in New York City in 1968 was a strike in name only. No issues of compensation or work load were at stake. Actually the work stoppage was a syndrome of deep rooted community conflicts and disagreements on organizational and educational policies. These issues, however, can not be resolved by collective bargaining. It is incumbent on state and local governments and their legislative bodies to come up with solutions. The teachers' strike in New York City in 1968 was not a strike in the tradition of American unions; it was far closer to concerted political action, such as occur frequently in European countries with the difference, however, that abroad these "strikes" are usually only called for twenty-four hours. A recent example of such a general strike happened on March 11, 1969 in France. It is significant that on that occasion civil service workers obeyed the twenty-four strike call to a greater degree than did workers in the private sector. Inasmuch as the duration of the strike was rigidly limited, its effects on the community were far less disrupting than the strikes of public employees which did take place in major American cities in recent years.

The partial failure of the New York State laws of 1967 and 1969 leads to some further consideration in search of solutions for these difficult problems.

17-5. FURTHER CONSIDERATIONS ON PUBLIC LABOR RELATIONS

We have seen in the beginning of this chapter that the public sector of employment has increased substantially and that it is likely to continue to grow in the forseeable future. Attempts on the Federal, state and local levels of government to replace the traditional sovereignty principle with a more bilateral type of relations between public employers and public employees are a step forward. However, the dichotomy created by granting recognition to employees' representatives while maintaining the ban on strikes remains unresolved.

Among these suggestions which have been advanced to overcome this difficulty is a *cooling-off* period similar to the one applying to national emergency strikes but this is not applicable to public employment. As we have seen in Sec. 15-6, the imposition of such a temporary back-to-work order does not necessarily lead to ultimate settlement of a labor dispute. Furthermore a cooling-off period assumes that fundamentally public employees do have the right to strike. Such an assumption, however, is unacceptable given the nature of public service.

Actually public labor relations are still in the process of evolution. What is necessary is to carry out this development to its logical end. This has not been done so far. While government agencies increasingly deal with representatives of public employees, the legislatures retain their sovereignty as far as wage scales and budgetary appropriations are concerned. This is clearly illustrated in the Executive Order 10988 which was discussed in Sec. 17-2.

The way out of the present dilemma in public employee relationships must be found on the legislative level. There ought to be a binding declaration stating that public employees are entitled to adequate pay commensurate with their education and responsibilities. In view of the greater job security and better retirement pay this does not necessarily mean that the compensation of civil service workers must be equal to that of employees in the private sector. However, such a declaration could very well contain general guideposts assuring government employees increases in compensation commensurate with the increase in earnings in the private sector. That is to say that in a rapidly growing economy with a continuously rising personal income, governments would become committed to maintain public pay scales on a level that would keep them in line with the general trends in the economy and in personal income. If the question would be raised how the legislative branch could implement such a proposal the answer would be that it has been done for decades in the farm sector with the *parity* formula. This is not to say that the technical makeup of such a guidepost for public pay scales should be similar to that now ancient statistical device. Actually the adoption of such a resolution would match on the part of the public employer the commitment that civil service employees make in pledging themselves not to strike. This promise would be balanced by the commitment of the legislature to guarantee to civil service employees not only steady employment but an income which will at all times be in line with the growth of the economy and of the income structure in the private sector. If this be "benovolent paternalism" this may be the ideological price we have to pay for stable and good public employment relationships.

SELECTED BIBLIOGRAPHY

Cullen, Donald E. *National Emergency Strikes.* (Ithaca, N.Y.: Cornell University, 1968).

Hanslowe, Kurt L. *The Emerging Law of Labor Relations in Public Employment.* (Ithaca, N.Y.: Cornell University, 1967).

Levin, Edward. New York State Public Employment Labor Relations. (New York State School of Industrial and Labor Relations, Cornell University, April 1968).

Nigro, Felix A., *Management-Employee Relations in the Public Service* (Chicago: Public Personnel Association, 1968).

Oberer, Walter E.; Hanslowe, Kurt L.; Doherty, Robert E.; The Taylor Act Bulletin 59, New York State School of Industrial and Labor Relations at Cornell.

Ocheltree, Keith, *Government Labor Relations in Transition* (Chicago: Public Personnel Association, 1968).

Tracy, Estelle R. Ed. *Arbitration Cases in Public Employment* (American Arbitration Association, 1909).

Warner, Kenneth O., *Collective Bargaining in the Public Service: Theory and Practice* (Chicago: Public Personnel Association, 1968).

Warner, Kenneth O., Ed., *Developments in Public Employee Relations: Legislative, Judicial, Administrative* (Chicago: Public Personnel Association, 1968).

Woodworth, Robert T. and Peterson, Richard B. *Collective Negotiation for Public and Professional Employees* (Chicago: Scott, Foresman and Co., 1969).

QUESTIONS FOR DISCUSSION

1. Discuss recent trends in public employment and compare American and European patterns of civil service.

2. In recent years bargaining rights have been conferred on public employee representatives. Evaluate this trend in terms of the differences between public agencies and private enterprises.

3. In view of the dichotomy between collective bargaining and the ban on strikes what solutions would you suggest?

4. What conclusions would you draw from the experience of New York State with the Taylor Act of 1967 and its revision in 1969?

Chapter

18

The Shop Constitution

In our study of labor economics there have already been many occasions for stressing that in modern labor-management relations more is at stake than rates of pay. While pay rates are included in collective contracts, labor agreements today embrace much wider areas. The nonwage aspects of collective contracts can be considered a "shop constitution" that establishes patterns of dealing with such important questions as discharges, grievances, and arbitration. As a result of the American system of designating representatives of labor for collective bargaining, many contracts contain a *recognition clause* in which the designated union is specifically confirmed as having exclusive collective bargaining rights. In some cases the first section of an agreement contains a statement of purposes and policies of a general nature on which the two parties have agreed. Since 1947 the following statement has been embodied in agreements between the United States Steel Corporation and the United Steelworkers of America:

> The Company and the Union encourage the highest possible degree of friendly, cooperative relationships between their respective representatives at all levels and with and between all employees. The officers of the Company and the Union realize that this goal depends on more than words in a labor agreement, that it depends primarily on attitudes between people in their respective organizations and at all levels of responsibility. They believe that proper attitudes must be based on full understanding of and regard for the respective rights and responsibilities of both the Company and the Union. They believe also that proper attitudes are of major importance in the plants where day-to-day operations and administration of this Agreement demand fairness and understanding. They believe that these attitudes can be encouraged best when it is made clear that Company and Union officials, whose duties involve negotiation of this Agreement, are not antiunion or anticompany but are sincerely concerned with the best interests and well-being of the business and all employees.

In the agreement of January 1960, concluded after the long steel strike of 1959, a paragraph was added to the passage reproduced above in which notice was taken of the fact that the goals established in that paragraph had only been partially achieved. Both parties pledged themselves anew to live up to those high standards of the contract and to meet from time to time to appraise the way in which this agreement was being administered. In view of the emphasis on the growing need for continuous negotiations, it is interesting to observe that the opening statements of the steel agreement of 1960 differentiate sharply between continuous negotiation and occasional contacts among representatives of labor and management to discuss the actual working out of various clauses of the collective agreement. Continuous negotiations are specifically ruled out.

In addition to these very general clauses of the steel contract, which are actually in the nature of a preamble, there is an enumeration of the responsibilities of the parties. Labor recognizes that "there shall be no intimidation or coercion of employees into joining the union or continuing their membership." On the other hand, management promises that "there shall be no interference with the right of employees to become or continue members of the union." Furthermore, it is specifically stated that there shall be "no discrimination, restraint, or coercion against any employees because of membership in the union."

It should be noted that the promises of labor and management respectively refer to lines of action which are unfair practices of management and of labor according to the Taft-Hartley Act. In substance, therefore, these passages of the contract merely state that the parties are willing to obey the law. To that extent these pledges add nothing to the obligations which are already incumbent on the parties concluding a collective agreement.

18-1. THE MANAGERIAL PREROGATIVES

The obligation to bargain collectively in good faith with unions certified as exclusive bargaining agents is a limitation on the absolute freedom claimed by property owners prior to the enactment of management-labor relations legislation. In view of this fact, many labor agreements contain a brief clause outlining the area which remains under the exclusive domain of management. In the aforementioned steel contract of 1960 this clause reads as follows:

> The Company retains the exclusive rights to manage the business and plants and to direct the working forces. The Company, in the exercise of its rights, shall observe the provisions of this Agreement.
> The rights to manage the business and plants and to direct the working forces include the right to hire, suspend or discharge for proper cause, or transfer, and the right to relieve employees from duty because of lack of work or for other legitimate reasons.

A study of the U.S. Department of Labor of management rights provisions showed that the practice of inserting such clauses has become

TABLE 18-1

MANAGEMENT RIGHTS PROVISIONS IN TYPICAL UNION CONTRACTS

Type of Employer Bargaining Unit	Total Studied		Total with Formal Managements Rights	
	Agreements	Workers (in thousands)	Agreements	Workers (in thousands)
Total	1,773	7,447.0	860	3,501.5
Single employer .	1,098	4,229.1	769	3,124.8
Multiemployer ..	675	3,217.9	91	376.7

SOURCE: U. S. Dept. of Labor, Bulletin No. 1425-5 (April 1966): *Management Rights and Union-Management Cooperation.*

rather widespread. As is shown in Table 18-1, 1773 agreements were studied and almost half of these contracts did have management prerogative clauses.

The exclusive right to manage the business covers all the basic decisions with regard to the increase in production facilities or a shutdown of certain plants or departments. It also leaves to management the exclusive right to decide on the introduction of advanced mechanized or automated equipment, on the types of products to be manufactured and, if need be, on discontinuing certain lines of business. Some of these decisions especially with regard to the introduction of labor saving machinery are bound to affect labor in the long run. A strict legalistic interpretation of a management prerogative clause could lead to the conclusion that there is no obligation for the executives of the enterprise to alert employees and their representatives of the impending changes and to discuss with them the problems bound to arise from the application of such innovations.

It would be, however, a poor labor relations policy to insist rigidly on the legal rights of management to determine these matters unilaterally. Even if no formal provisions have been made in a union contract to inform employees of plans to improve production systems it is prudent to consult with labor on these matters, especially if lay-offs will result in the long run. The desirability of cooperating with unions in the preparation and the adjustments necessary in technological changes of production systems has been recognized in a number of agreements. A typical provision in a multi-employer-union contract between Clothing Manufacturers Association and the Clothing Workers (AFL–CIO) has the following wording, pledging the union to

cooperate in the installation of methods and technological improvements and suggest other improvements where possible, it being understood that the company will make such installations after advising the union, and will cooperate in placing any employees whose jobs are eliminated through such methods or technological improvements.[1]

[1]See U.S. Dept. of Labor Bulletin No. 1425-5, page 35.

It is clear from formulation of this clause that management does not undertake a hard and fast obligation to protect the jobs of employees eliminated through technological change. The main emphasis of such provisions is that there must be communication and if possible agreements between management and labor on the handling of the impact of technological improvements on employees. We have seen in Chapter 9 that some fringe benefits such as extended vacations and severance pay are also means to mitigate the impact of labor displacements by innovations in production systems.

The managerial prerogative is effective without any restraints if layoffs are not due to automation but to a decline in orders leading to a "lack of work." In such case management can proceed with layoffs and will not be challenged in the exercise of this right by the union. However, the order in which workers are to be laid off and rehired is a subject for negotiations between labor and management, as discussed in the next section.

18-2. SENIORITY

Prior to the enactment of a shop constitution through collective bargaining, management had the right to exercise its power of hiring and firing in an entirely arbitrary manner. Considerations such as length of service did not have to enter into personnel policies and employment practices. Seniority clauses in collective contracts have removed a great deal of the uncertainty and insecurity connected with the old unregulated system of taking on or discharging workers. As we have seen in the management clause quoted in Sec. 18-1, management has the right to discharge for proper cause—intoxication, tardiness, or other behavior contrary to the work rules. But when it comes to layoffs for economic reasons, the seniority system has to be observed. This system has often been condensed in the well-known phrase: "last hired, first fired," and vice versa. The latter fact is important, because the seniority system applies also to the order of recall.

The seniority system applies also to the determination of the order of promotion of equally qualified workers. The charge that such a system would punish the efficient and protect the inefficient workers is not valid. In fact, in many contracts promotions are to be based primarily on the ability to perform the work. This means that if two workers are considered for promotion, the one with the somewhat longer service can claim to be upgraded into this higher job only if his ability to do this type of work cannot be questioned. If he lacks this ability while the other worker with a shorter period of service possesses it, this latter can be promoted, and any complaints against this action cannot be based wholly on a length-of-service argument. The same is true when a simple recall is at stake.

Seniority has extremely far-reaching effects on the contractual rights of employees. This is particularly true of the length of vacations which can be claimed. Contracts often give employees a fourth week of vacation after twenty years of continuous service. In enterprises where shift differentials are being paid, workers often have priority in the selection of the shift if they have higher seniority than others.

The impact of seniority is also very considerable in settling the problems of staffing new plants. In order to provide a nucleus of experienced workers, management may induce employees to transfer to this new operation by guaranteeing him the retention of his seniority status. However, such practices are not customary when a department is being closed down and workers with high seniority in their former shop are transferred to a division which will be continued. The transferred workers will be placed at the bottom of the seniority list in the new department in order to protect the rights of long-time employees who had started to work in that unit long before the transfer occurred.

Generally speaking the principle of seniority has led in many agreements to the granting of transfer rights to old employees into new units or into divisions which are being relocated. This means that new workers can be recruited only after those who claim transfer rights have filled some of the positions in the new plant.

It is clear that a proper handling of the seniority system can prevent its deterioration to a device in which mere inconspicuous survival in service is rewarded while exceptional performance does not find proper recognition. The seniority system is generally a great improvement over the arbitrariness of former hiring practices, but the danger of a mechanical application of this employment policy should not be underrated. While a consideration of work performance is an important point, promotion of workers with shorter service before those with longer service is quite certain to create complaints and lengthy disputes. Management must be willing to take this chance and to establish relations with labor that enable the union to go along with sound personnel policies. But problems of seniority are usually controversial, and very often the grievance procedures will be invoked to settle disputes arising in this area of personnel management.

18-3. GRIEVANCE PROCEDURES

Collective labor agreements have elaborated grievance procedures to a great extent. In the steel contract of 1960 no less than four steps are outlined in great detail. Prior to filing a grievance, the condition giving rise to it must be discussed in an informal way between the employee and his foreman. In this preliminary stage the request is called a "complaint." Attempts must be made to settle the issue at this complaint level. In this way minor problems can be settled informally. Furthermore, since settlements of certain issues achieved in formal grievance proceedings will be made known, like issues can be disposed of at the complaint level. A grievance is then defined as a complaint which could not be settled by discussions be-between the employee and his foreman. In day to day industrial relations on the department level, the *shop steward* plays a significant role. He is an employee and has a definite work assignment. On the other hand he is appointed by the union to see to it that all the provisions of the contract are carried out in a given sector of the enterprise. Workers who have a complaint will usually come to the shop steward first and the latter will discuss the problem with the foreman. While the foreman is often defined as the link between management and employees, the shop steward can be regarded as the link between workers and the union on the one side and the foreman and therefore, management on the other. Good relations be-tween the foreman and the shop steward can keep many issues on the com-plaint level, preventing the use of more formal grievance proceedings.

In order to process a grievance, union grievance committees must be set up in each plant. Actually, the disposition of grievances on ever higher levels occurs in an exchange of views between managerial officials and the committee. The first step would involve such a "dialogue" between the com-mittee and the foreman who has turned down the original complaint, causing it to be converted into a formal grievance. Of course if the union grievance committee agrees with the foreman, the procedure stops then and there. On the other hand, if the committee sides with the employee while the fore-man upholds his original negative decision, step two will be initiated by an appeal against the decision of the foreman. In this second step the inter-change of opinions will be between the committee and the department superintendent. If this phase again is unproductive of an adjustment, the third step will involve the general superintendent of the plant. If this is again futile, then the fourth step can be taken. This projects the grievance from the plant level to the management level of the company on the one side and to the international union on the other side of the table. Step four pro-vides for exhaustive investigations and a series of meetings. If either party comes to the conclusion that no settlement can be achieved through addi-tional meetings on this fourth level, it can, within 30 days after having re-ceived the minutes of the last meeting, file a request that the case be sub-mitted to arbitration.

Very often grievances arise because a written contract contains am-biguous language or a company policy is not spelled out clearly. To illus-trate the latter point: an employee was dismissed because she had married another employee of the same firm. The company was of the opinion that it had made it clear that such an action would bring about the dis-missal of one of the employees involved. The employee based her grievance on the assertion that this company policy had not been spelled out. Different interpretations of the contractual obligation of the employer for holiday pay can lead to grievances. In one company the question arose whether employees can claim this pay if they worked only half a day on the Wednesday preceding Thanksgiving Day although the company had scheduled an eight-hour work day. Overtime assignments are a frequent cause of grievances. Overtime is often treated as an opportunity for employees to increase their total earnings. Hence, questions arise with regard to the distribution of overtime according to seniority, according to the job classification of employees, and similar aspects of the contract where the administration of the clause permits a certain amount of discretion to the employer. Obviously not every contingency can be covered by a contract. It is, therefore, inevitable that grievances arise. It is better to resolve these issues through grievance procedures rather than to overload contract clauses with too many details.

Although the grievance procedure is geared primarily to the processing of grievances of employees, it can also be used by the company and by the union in order to air differences and resolve difficulties. While this elaborate structure provides ample opportunities to discuss and to settle the grievance at ever higher levels, both parties can agree to waive some of the steps and submit the case to arbitration directly. Such a waiver would usually be made only when it becomes apparent almost immediately that no settlement acceptable to both parties can be achieved in the four steps of the procedure and that ultimately the question must be arbitrated.

18-4. ARBITRATION

We have seen in our discussion of industrial conflicts and their settlements in Chapter 16 that the labor-management-relations legislation does not provide for regular arbitration procedures that could issue decisions binding on those parties. This type of arbitration can therefore be instituted only through a contractual agreement between the two parties to a labor contract. Such arbitration clauses usually make it incumbent on the parties to agree on a chairman who then will be responsible for the decisions made by the board. In many cases the parties turn to the Arbitration Association, a private organization dedicated to settling commercial and industrial disputes outside the regular courts. This association maintains a panel of qualified arbitrators from which the parties may select one or more members. The awards made in such proceedings are binding on the parties who have signed an arbitration agreement. The advantage of arbitration is that these procedures are more flexible than those which must be adopted by the courts. Furthermore, hearings can be scheduled at short notice and litigation will not be pending over a long period of time.

Arbitration clauses can be found in many union contracts. In 1966 the

Bureau of Labor Statistics issued a study of 1717 contracts.[2] Of these 1,466 contained arbitration clauses. Only in 349 contracts was it stated specifically that there could be no work stoppages in connection with problems under arbitration. Actually such no-strike clauses are not necessary. A strike which is called while an existing contract has not yet expired is clearly illegal. It would not become legitimate even if grievances were not specifically excluded as a cause for a work stoppage. In only 2 percent of the contract studied by the BLS was arbitration extended to disputes over a new contract. It should, however, be stressed that one way to prevent strikes is precisely a wider use of voluntary arbitration for the writing of a new labor agreement. This is in fact far preferable to ad hoc compulsory arbitration which is the ultimate resort in the national emergency provisions of the Taft-Hartley Act.

The arbitration board can deal with the interpretation of the labor contract and also with problems arising out of local working conditions. However, the competence of the board ends with the labor agreement. For this reason arbitration clauses have to be inserted into subsequent contracts.

18-5. DISCHARGES

An important aspect of a collective contract as a shop constitution is the protection of employees against arbitrary discharges or suspensions. In fact it is stated in Section 8 of the steel agreement of 1960: "an employee shall not be peremptorily discharged." While the right to discharge an employee for proper cause remains a managerial prerogative, the exercise of this right is subject to specific procedures which actually are quite similar to those already described in Sec. 18-4. It also means that ultimately such discharge cases or a suspension can be adjudicated by the board of arbitration.

Obviously discharge cases are often highly controversial and wind up in arbitration, if there are such clauses in a union contract. There can be doubt, for instance, whether an employee who refuses a transfer to another shift although such a measure was deemed essential by management, ended his employment by "self-termination" or whether the employment was ended by management. Absenteeism can also become highly controversial, especially if it is in connection with illnesses and injuries.

Usually shop stewards have some additional protection. Their discharge for cause is, however, possible. These workers are regular employees with work assignments. If they leave work without permission or fail to return to it after completion of a conference with the foreman they can be dismissed. It is clear, however, that the rights and duties of a shop steward

[2]U.S. Bureau of Labor Statistics, Bulletin No. 1425-6 (June 1966).

cover a sensitive point in industrial relations and that it is best to exercise circumspection in the treatment of shop stewards.

Grievance procedures in complaint and discharge cases vary with the structure of the enterprise. If an employer operates a number of plants in different localities or if one plant is broken up into a number of departments, grievance procedures will, in most cases, contain all the steps outlined here. In smaller plants and enterprises the proceedings will be telescoped into fewer steps. Shop stewards will take the place of the union committees described above.

18-6. THE IMPACT OF THE SHOP CONSTITUTION

Early descriptions of employment conditions in modern industry stressed the high degree of helplessness and insecurity of workers. While in theory on equal terms with employers as far as their civil rights were concerned, they had no protection against unilateral actions of management with regard to the setting of pay scales, hours of work, conditions of employment, layoffs, and discharges. It is against this background of early industrialism that Karl Marx developed his exploitation theories, decrying the alienation that befell workers involved in this type of a shop situation.

One of the important results of collective bargaining is the heightened sense of security it gives to workers who have selected representatives to negotiate collective contracts. They feel that they are being protected against arbitrary exercise of managerial prerogatives. Grievance procedures can be used as an outlet for ventilating frustrations and disappointments of individual workers. In this way industrial workers covered by such agreements, or nonorganized workers employed by enlightened management, can more easily identify with and feel part of a large functioning organism than was possible under more primitive forms of industrial relations. Throughout the process of elaboration and maturing of these relations, organized labor in the United States has insisted on maintaining a clear line of separation between labor and management. While always seeking more pay and better fringe benefits as well as greater latitude in the area of shop constitutions, American labor has never demanded a share in management itself. In order to gain a wider perspective on the problems involved here we now turn to a comparative study of labor relations.

SELECTED BIBLIOGRAPHY

Keller, Leonard A. *The Management Function: A Positive Approach to Labor Relations* (Washington, D. C.: Washington Bureau of National Affairs, 1963).

McLaughlin, Richard P. "Custom and Past Practice in Labor Arbitration," *Arbitration Journal* (1963).

U.S. Dept. of Labor. "Arbitration Procedures" (Bulletin number 1425–6). W. Willard Wirtz, Secretary, Bureau of Labor Statistics.

U.S. Dept. of Labor. "Grievance Procedures" (Bulletin number 1425–1). Willard Wirtz, Secretary, Bureau of Labor Statistics.

U.S. Dept. of Labor, "Management Right and Union Management Cooperation" Bulletin Number 1425–5. W. Willard Wirtz, Secretary, Bureau of Labor Statistics.

Zitron, Celia Lewis, *The New York City Teachers Union 1916–64: A Story of Education and Social Commitment* (New York, Humanities Press, 1969).

QUESTIONS FOR DISCUSSION

1. What is a "shop constitution," and what are some important features of a contemporary version of such a constitution?

2. A properly functioning collective-bargaining system must be aware of the fact that management has certain basic prerogatives which are not the subject of bargaining as such. What are several key examples of such prerogatives, and why are these matters reserved to the decisions of management alone?

3. How does the issue of "seniority" fit into the realm of collective bargaining?

4. It is entirely possible that the existence of seniority provisions can provide for some degree of inefficiency in the handling of job opportunities. Why is this so, and does this possibility limit the effectiveness of management decisions in this respect?

5. How do "grievance committees" function in our contemporary industrial system?

6. On balance, what has been the impact of the shop constitution in terms of labor-management relations, and what has been its effect in terms of the creation of a more stable climate within which labor and management may prosper together?

19

Comparative Labor Relations Systems

Labor organizations everywhere reflect the general social, political, and legal structures of the countries in which they developed and operate. During our first glimpse of organized labor in the United States in Chapter 3 it was stressed that American trade unions have certain unique features—such as relative aloofness from partisan politics—that have clearly distinguished them from labor organizations of other countries—even countries with similar basic economic institutions. Since patterns of unionism are flexible or at least fluid rather than rigid, a full understanding of the many issue of labor economics requires a wider horizon than that of a single nation or country. Furthermore, since the latter part of the nineteenth century national federations of labor have maintained liason with similar groups in other countries. While organized labor in the United States held itself more or less aloof from such organizations prior to World War II, it plunged wholeheartedly into international labor politics and organizations in the late 1940's.

19-1. INTERNATIONAL LABOR ORGANIZATIONS

The Communist Manifesto issued early in 1849 and subsequent writings of Karl Marx and his lifelong associate Friedrich Engels stressed the international solidarity of the working class. The great social convulsion which according to them was expected to bring about the transition from capitalism to socialism was conceived as an international cataclysm erupting simultaneously in a number of economically advanced countries. It was consistent with this line of thought that the First International, an association of workers organizations in a number of countries, was founded under the auspices of Marx and Engels as early as 1864. It did not last very long. Torn by controversies over the tactics employed by the uprising of the Commune in Paris early in 1871, this first international labor organization was disbanded in 1872. About that time industrial development accelerated in most Western and Central European countries and with it socialistic parties and trade unions strongly influenced by them 'did experience considerable growth. In 1889 the Second International was founded. It was primarily an organization comprising socialistic parties in a large number of countries. In order to combine labor unions in a more specific way on the international level, an International Trade Union Secretariat was established in 1903 with headquarters in Berlin.

Developments before and during World War I put these international labor structures under a severe strain. For about a decade prior to 1914, European countries stepped up their armament expenditures to a considerable degree. This armament race indicated to a large number of observers that Europe was headed toward a general war. However, at least on the verbal level, internationalism was strong in the organizations cooperating in the Second International and in the International Trade Union Secretariat. In 1912 the Second International held a convention in Basel, Switzerland, in which resolutions were adopted voicing the opposition of socialist groups to the heavy armament expenditures and indicating that these parties would not support the war efforts of their respective governments.

The outbreak of World War I showed clearly that nationalism was stronger than the international solidarity of the working class. Vast majorities of socialist parties everywhere approved of the war policies of their governments. As the war continued, informal contacts between socialist parties were maintained in neutral countries. Their efforts to bring about a peace on a more or less status quo basis failed, however. At the end of World War I an open break occurred between moderate Socialists who were trying to work toward socialism while observing the rules of the game of a pluralistic democracy and the Bolshevists, led by Lenin, who advocated the violent overthrow of the government and the establishment for a long transition period of a "dictatorship of the proletariat." The Communists, who had no entirely separate organization of their own before the war, now organized political parties and achieved complete control over Russia. Soon they started a Third International.

Between the two world wars moderate Socialists and Communists waged a fratricidal struggle on the national and international level. Although the Second International had been greatly weakened through the de facto breakdown of the international solidarity of the working class, it struggled to survive under continuous attack by the forces of the Third International. However, the great National Federations of Labor such as the Trade Union Congress in Britain (TUC) and the Confédération Générale du Travail (CGT) and similar groups in Central European countries were kept under firm control by non-Communist labor leaders. Organized labor made giant steps forward during and after World War I in many European countries, but it received great setbacks in the 1920's in Facist Italy and in the 1930's under National Socialism in Germany. The Italian Labor Unions were dissolved by Mussolini and in their place "syndicates" were set up in close organizational affiliation with the Facist party. In Germany the trade unions were disbanded by Hitler and replaced by a "labor front." In these countries collective bargaining, which had made such headway in the 1920's, was completely abolished. Strikes were forbidden and wages were for all practical purposes frozen or fixed by the government.

However, in Italy and in Germany trade-union tradition remained so strong that labor organizations of the accepted democratic type were among the first to emerge after the end of the totalitarian episodes in these countries. At the same time the American labor movement showed greatly increased interest in the strengthening of democratic, non-Communist trade unions in the Western world. This involvement became particularly urgent because in France and in Italy the old labor federations came under the control of Communists at that time. One reason for this capture was the role played by the Communist underground in World War II resistance movements in which members of the old unions also had been active.

As a result of this infiltration by Communists in the older union organization, non-Communist unions were established in Italy and in France. In the former country the federation had the name Free Italian Confederation of Workers [Libera Confederazione Generale Italiana dei Lavoratori (LCGIL)].The structure of unions emerging in France was somewhat different. In that country as in Belgium, Holland, and Germany, Christian trade unions had begun to be active at the turn of the century. Although they were numerically much weaker than the large labor organizations closely affiliated with the Socialist party, they did exercise considerable influence through their ability to elect a good number of their leaders to the legislatures of their respective countries. In Germany the Christian trade unions were supressed by Hitler, together with the other labor organizations.

In France the non-Communistic workers are now organized into great federations, the Force Ouvrière (FO) and the Confédération Francaise des Travailleurs Democratiques (CFTD). In the Federal Republic of Germany an agreement was reached between representatives of the old Socialist and Christian labor groups to establish a neutral, "business unionism" type of labor federation. Recent attempts at reviving Christian unions in that part of Germany failed. But this type of unionism also gained considerable strength after World War II in Belgium and Holland.

The American union leadership felt that it was its duty to help European workers and those in developing countries to strengthen their labor organizations and, occasionally show them how to get started. Labor unions claiming suprisingly high membership figures sprang up in many newly established African nations. In 1961 a Pan African Federation of Labor was founded. Claims of extremely large memberships are also made by most unions in Latin America. Like the African unions they also have a regional organization, the Organización Regional Interamericana de Trabajordores (ORIT).

Toward the end of World War II the Third International was officially disbanded by Stalin, but this was obviously a tactical move. Shortly after the end of hostilities a Communist-dominated World Federation of Trade Unions (WFTU) made its appearance on the international labor scene. For a short while the CIO, which at that time had not yet reaffiliated with the AFL, considered joining that international group. Soon, however, this decision was rescinded.

In the meantime, work went forward toward the establishment of an international organization of non-Communist unions. This led to the establishment of the International Confederation of Free Trade Unions (ICFTU). The WFTU has been hurt by the Russian-Chinese conflict, but representatives of Russian and Chinese labor organizations attended the international convention held in Poland in 1965. According to the statutes of the ICFTU, international conventions of this organization have to be held every three years. The headquarters of this group are in Brussels which also houses the administration of the European Common Market. It can be expected that European trade unions in that region will intensify their cooperation as this vast industrial and trading area progresses toward economic integration. The close cooperation of American organized labor with unions in other parts of the Western world has tended to increase American influence on the patterns of industrial relations in other advanced industrialized countries. Nevertheless, significant differences persist, as will be shown later in this chapter.

International labor organizations do not exist only as federations of national unions. The Peace Treaty of Versailles of 1919 established the International Labor Office (ILO). This international agency operated within the framework of the League of Nations. It is now affiliated with the United Nations but still is located in Switzerland because a special building was erected in Geneva prior to World War II. In 1969 the 50th anniversary of the ILO was celebrated. World leaders, among them Pope Pius VI, addressed the commemorative assembly. From the very beginning a tripartite structure was devised for the ILO. Each participating country would send four delegates to the organization—one representing employers, one labor, and two representing government. This created difficulties in countries where either some or all industries are socialized, and where labor unions have an altogether different character from those organizations that are clearly the opposite of management. This issue of seating delegates from one-party countries such as the Soviet

Union has not found a final solution. However, it did not keep the Soviet Union from rejoining the ILO in 1954.

The ILO has done valuable work in the areas of research and the elaboration of standard labor codes which can serve as models for labor legislation in a particular country. This organization publishes the *International Labor Review*, an important source of labor information. In addition to comprehensive statistical series it contains important monographic studies.

19-2. LABOR LEGISLATION AND COLLECTIVE LABOR AGREEMENTS

Throughout our study of labor economics we have seen that collective contracts concluded in the United States have developed elaborate wage structures, fringe benefits, and those aspects of industrial relations referred to as a "shop constitution." In a comparative study of industrial relations systems we find that in many countries, especially in Western Europe, such matters as fringe benefits or grievance procedures, including seniority, are handled by labor legislation rather than by the processes of collective bargaining.

These differences between American and Western European approaches to industrial relations are grounded in deeply rooted divergent attitudes toward the role of government itself. Conforming to a tradition of government regulation and intervention rather than group initiative and stressing reforms from "above," many Europeans tried to solve social problems through legislation rather than through the gradual elaboration of voluntary agreements between organized labor and management. An additional factor contributing toward the political method of establishing industrial-relation patterns is the fact that European trade unions are more closely linked to large political parties than is the case in the United States. In this way organized labor has been able to influence labor legislation to a far greater degree than has been possible in this country. The Taft-Hartley Act of 1947, vetoed by President Truman but passed over his veto by Congress, was opposed by organized labor. But all its expressions of disapproval were disregarded by the majority in both houses of Congress. In 1965, the repeal of Sec. 14-b of this law was not acted upon by Congress, although organized labor had given top priority to efforts to eliminate this section from the Taft-Hartley Act.

It would be beyond the scope of this chapter to analyze on a country-by-country basis what has been done in way of fringe benefits by legislation rather than by collective bargaining. France led the way prior to World War II in introducing legislation to cover the system of paid vacations. About the same time a similar practice was introduced in Germany. Throughout Western Europe legislation of this type has been adopted. It imposes an obligation on employers to grant these vacations whether or not they are covered by collective agreements. In France paid vacations extend for at least three weeks. There in the 1950's, it was customary for major industries to shut down simultaneously in August of each year in observation of the paid-vacation law. Recently a more sensible system of staggering these vacations has been attempted in that country.

Seniority is an important aspect of collective labor agreements in the United States. In other countries, for example Germany, legislation has been in existence since before World War II, giving considerable protection to older employees against short-notice dismissals. Again, these rules have to be observed by all employers. While the German law is basically an embodiment of the seniority rule in layoffs and recalls, it is somewhat more comprehensive and flexible than the seniority clauses in American labor contracts. Consideration of the family status of workers also enters into the handling of individual cases, and a general hardship clause is in effect. For instance, a bachelor with a longer period of service will be laid off earlier than a more recently hired worker who may be the head of a large family.

The United States is one of the few countries in which family allowances as supplementary payments to workers with children are unknown. In France very liberal family-allowance systems were enacted after World War I to encourage larger families. They also provide for extensive maternity leaves with pay for working women. Population statistics seem to indicate that the purpose of this legislation has been achieved. The system is financed by contributions of employers or self-employed people and is all-comprehensive. A family-allowance system was also created in England after World War II. It is financed out of general taxation, and every family with more than one child is eligible regardless of income. Bonuses are also paid to large families in the Soviet Union and other Socialist countries.

These examples may suffice to show that in many other advanced industrial countries certain topics which are on the agenda of collective bargaining sessions in the United States fall outside these procedures, because they have been settled by laws binding on management and labor alike. Changes in such laws are discussed in these countries on the political level—for example, in Parliament—but not at the bargaining table. After World War I legislation also got under way to set up many of the provisions of a shop constitution.

19-3. SHOP COUNCILS IN GERMANY AND ITALY

The collapse of traditional government in Germany at the end of World War I occurred exactly one year after the successful Communist revolution in Russia. While the vast majority of political parties, including the Social Democratic Party, were calling for a Convention to draft a democratic constitution, the newly emerging Communists were opposed to this democratic method and demanded a comprehensive system of Councils elected only by workers and agricultural laborers. A Central Council was to be given dictatorial powers. The moderate parties won out in the election for a constitutional Convention and the Weimar Constitution was speedily enacted setting up a parliamentary democracy but providing for popular election of a President. However, it contained, by way of a compromise with the more radical elements, an Article 165 in which a second system of representation along economic groupings and functions was outlined, and legislation implementing this principle was scheduled. While the overall Council system was never put into effect, the Shop Council Law was enacted in 1920. After its abolition during the Hitler regime it was speedily revived by the Allied military government after World War II and it is still in effect at the present time.

Basically this law established a grievance procedure such as is found with considerable elaboration in many collective labor contracts in the United States. The shop council is elected by the employees. Candidates are fellow employees and, in most cases, are members of the union which holds a contract with the company. Sometimes the composition of the shop council reflected the relative strength of more or less Socialist and of Christian or neutral labor organizations. The shop council elects a president. In very large companies this representative of the employee will, with the consent of management, devote himself full time to the business of the shop council. He remains, however, on the company payroll. The law provides special protection against dismissal—actually almost a state of tenure—for the president of the shop council.

The main function of the shop council is to participate in discharges and in the settlement of grievances. If an employee is to be dismissed for cause, the company must explain the reasons to the shop council. In case the shop council refuses to go along with the discharge, the company must go to a special Labor Court in order to obtain a declaratory judgment concerning the justification of the dismissal.

The shop council has no right to interfere in any way with strictly managerial decisions. According to legislation enacted after World War II, management has, however, the obligation to keep the representatives of employees in the shop informed of important pending decisions, such as large-scale layoffs and organizational changes. The shop council has become a fixture of the industrial structure in Germany. For instance, in the extensive obituary notices customary in the German press when a corporation executive dies, the public announcement is issued jointly by the chairman of the supervisory board and the chairman of the shop council. Another indication of the strong influence and participation of the shop council in Germany is the fact that any research project dealing on an establishment basis with industrial relations or purely economic issues such as productivity must be cleared with the shop council if it is to succeed—even if top management has already given the go-ahead signal.[1]

A system similar to the German shop councils has existed since World War II in Italy. Due to the presence in that country of two national labor federations, the outcome of shop elections has occasionally been an indication of shifts of power between Communist and non-Communist labor organizations. Some caution is, however, indicated because quite frequently workers would vote for a "radical" shop council member while giving their political preference to a moderate member of Parliament.

The shop-council system has maintained a very sharp distinction between management and labor. Although management must clear a considerable number of decisions with the shop council especially in the area of personnel administration, the shop council has no right to participate in the decision-making process itself. This power has been obtained by workers in the Federal Republic of Germany through two laws enacted by Parliament after World War II. The first one is the system of codetermination in the German mining and steel industry of 1951, and the second deals with the shop constitution in all other industries and was enacted in 1952.

19-4. CODETERMINATION AS AN INDUSTRIAL RELATIONS SYSTEM

Codetermination exists only in the German mining and steel industries. Its main feature is the requirement that one of the corporation officials entitled to membership in the executive committee must be a "Labor Director." As a director of the executive committee he is entitled to receive all internal information necessary for decision making. Although primarily concerned with industrial relations in the plant, he is a full-fledged member, with equal rights, of the top-management team. In order to understand this structure it is necessary to point to a difference in the corporation laws of the United States and those of Germany. In Germany the stockholders elect a "Supervisory Board." This board in turn appoints the top executives. The codetermination law of 1951 fixed the membership in the supervisory board at eleven and stipulated that five members should represent management—such as banks or other industrial enterprises, whereas the other five members voted on by the stockholders should come from the ranks of employees. That group can consist in part of wage or

---

[1]The author of this text did run into some trouble in a textile plant in Northern Germany while directing students in a certain field study in 1962. The project had been approved by management and the shop council. However, the selection of a random sample of employees, every sixth in the file, was made while no representative of the shop council was present. This created totally unwarranted suspicions that management had "pinpointed" certain employees for questioning. It was necessary to reestablish good feelings before the project could be successfully completed.

salary workers and in part of full-time union officials. The management and labor factious of the Supervisory Board must select a "neutral" chairman who may be a high government official or a university professor. As already indicated, this board appoints the top executives of the corporation, among them the Labor Director. The latter will, in many cases, have some background in organized labor, but not necessarily. In fact quite a number of Labor Directors have been selected who have never been officially identified with trade unions.

It is easy to understand that rank-and-file employees have tended to look upon the Labor Director as "our man." According to the intent of the law he is, however, a member of management and must have the best interests of the company at heart. Actually one of the main functions of the Labor Director is to serve as a "channel of communication." This function has proved to be of great importance especially in the mining industry, which has undergone, in Germany as in the United States, considerable structural changes. Many operations had to be shut down and there was a drastic reduction in employment of miners. Actually, surplus coal was permitted at times to accumulate in huge mounds, and government subsidies were employed to maintain certain output levels. The task of the labor director in these difficult adjustments was facilitated by the general condition of overemployment in Germany, which enabled many of the younger miners who had been displaced to undergo successful retraining, especially for jobs in automobile-assembly plants. The Codetermination Law was enacted at a time when there still was a coal shortage in Europe, and when it was deemed necessary to improve the morale of workers in the strategic coal-mining and steel industries. Furthermore, the law was also designed to ward off demands for a nationalization of the mining industry which had been taken over by the governments in Great Britain and in France after World War II.

The Shop Constitution Law of 1952 applies primarily to the manufacturing industries in the Federal Republic of Germany. It does not go as far as the codetermination system. There is no Labor Director as part of the top management of the corporation. However, the Supervisory Board is similarly constructed as in those enterprises covered by the Codetermination Law. It is also stipulated that this board must meet four times a year. Labor members therefore have ample opportunity to express their views and exercise influence on broad lines of company policy.

The West German Labor Relations laws discussed in this section have not superseded the Shop Council Law. These councils continue to function and are primarily concerned with grievance procedures.

Codetermination has come under attack by American trade union leaders who feel that this system abolishes the sharp line of distinction between management and labor. At a congress of the ICFTU held in Milan,

Italy, that international labor organization also went on record as being opposed to codetermination. While, for a considerable period of time the issue of codetermination was quiescent in Germany, in the mid-1960's it became a subject of renewed controversy. After the successful adjustment of the mining industry to novel conditions of production and competitions with other fuels, management circles began to urge a repeal of the law. On the other hand, organized labor demanded its extension to industry-wide bodies setting up guidelines for policies to be followed by companies belonging to these sectors of the economy. There were strong indications that the ideas orginally embodied in Article 165 of the Weimar Constitution, demanding "a second system of representation along economic groupings," have not died out.[2] Actually, an economic council system is in operation in Holland which is called in to advise on industrial policies.

One would have been entitled to assume that the long tradition of trade unionism in Germany, the Shop Council System and codetermination would have established excellent communications between labor and management on one side and between union leadership and the rank and file members on the other. However, this orderly and differentiated industrial relations system became suddenly unstuck in the summer of 1969. By that time the West German economy had recovered from its mild recession of 1966. Industrial output, experts, employment and profits reached new peaks. On the other hand unions in the metals and in the mining industries, still under the impression of the recent recession had signed agreements in 1967 embodying only moderate wage increases. These contracts were still in force when this new wave of prosperity spread throughout the economic structure leading to great distortions between profits and wages. In major steel plants workers became extremely dissatisfied and eventually a series of wildcat strikes started in steel plants and in mines. Workers became highly critical of the alleged inactivity of shop councils and of union leaders. Especially the latter felt that they could do nothing as long as the current contracts were in force. They refrained from demanding a consent of management for immediate renegotiations of wage clauses. But something unprecedented happened. Management granted an immediate wage increase. The unauthorized walkout of metal workers and coal miners in the German industrial district was successful and work was resumed.

[2]The idea of separating economic from political issues in the constitutional setup of a country goes back to the teachings of Saint-Simon (1760-1825), which were assiduously propagated by his many disciples in the first half of the nineteenth century. These ideas influenced also Marx and Engels in the development of their concept of the State as a "superstructure." After World War I these ideas were again advocated in Europe, supported by a well-financed publicity campaign headed by Rudolph Steiner, the leader of a theosophic movement with headquarters in Switzerland.

It should be obvious that rewarding a wildcat strike with wage concessions is utterly disruptive of an orderly system of industrial relations. It is up to the officialdom of organized labor in unions and shop councils in Germany to become more flexible and prevent in the future the repetition of such a runaway situation.

19-5. INDUSTRIAL RELATIONS IN GREAT BRITAIN

Up to the middle of the 19th century Great Britain was the leading manufacturing country of the world. It is, therefore, understandable that trade unionism was able over a long period of time to build up strong traditions and organizations. Actually up to the early part of the 19th century formal trade union organizations could not become effective. The Combination Acts of 1799 and 1800 merely reaffirmed earlier prohibitions. Nevertheless workers in many crafts were able to form loose associations in the 18th century. The year 1825 was a turning point in British labor history. The Combination Acts were repealed and now the formation of labor unions for the purpose of collective bargaining became legal. The development which ensued from this voiding of anti-union legislation was similar to what was going to happen in the United States about thirty years later when the Knights of Labor suddenly burst on the scene only to disintegrate a short time later. In 1834 the Grand National Consolidated Trade Union was established. Robert Owen, the early pre-Marxian socialist whose lasting contribution was to be the founding of the first cooperative in Rochdale, England, in 1847, became its first president. However a series of unsuccessful strikes in the late 1830's broke the backbone of this first large-scale labor organization in Britain. As in the United States unionization first became effective on the smaller scale of craft unionism. In the 1870's trade union acts were passed which facilitated the consolidation and expansion of union activities. Anticipating much later American legislation of the Clayton Act, British unions were exempted from laws prohibiting activities in restraint of trade. Furthermore they were given the right to incorporate so that they could accumulate funds in the name of their organization. Eventually British labor organizations added some unions to their organization which comprised large numbers of semi- and unskilled workers. The Transport and General Workers Union had reached a membership of 1.2 million after World War II. Much earlier than in this country unions of employees of municipalities and of postal and other civil workers were enlisting a large number of employees in the public sector.

Now the most important aspect of British unionism is that it was able to get employers into collective bargaining procedures without the benefit of the type of legislation which proved to be necessary in the United States in the 1930's. Long before that a significant number of unions had succeeded in signing collective agreements with employers' associations. But unlike the development in Germany and in Sweden where master agreements between national business organizations and unions were concluded recognizing each other as agents for collective bargaining, such agreements in Britain were more of a regional nature. However as a result of the nationalization of the coal mining industry a national conciliation scheme was adopted in this area.

The result of these gradual and pragmatic settlements has been that collective bargaining could proceed without the legal structure which was adopted in the United States in the 1930's. This voluntary character of collective bargaining in Britain certainly has advantages. It has eliminated to a great extent the inherent problem of union insecurity which underlies many issues of labor relations in the United States. On the other hand British unions had succeeded in many instances in having agreements with management which are very similar to the American union shop. Up to recently the absence of elaborate management-labor relations legislation in Great Britain had not led to serious problems. However in the 1960's jurisdictional strikes became rather frequent. Furthermore occasionally strikes were called while a labor contract was still in force. These "wild cat" strikes threatened serious economic consequences for Great Britain because they endangered vital exports industries. For this reason the Labor Government contemplated in 1969 the introduction of legislation banning jurisdictional and wildcat strikes. These moves were strongly opposed by the Trade Union Congress, the Federation of British Unions. Already earlier, in 1968, the TUC had opposed wage freeze and other economic measures of the labor government headed by Harold Wilson which were designed to balance exports and imports. This was to be achieved by making British products more competitive through wage restraints leading to lower prices. At the same time these measures were designed to curtail aggregate income increases thereby putting a damper on imports. From the very beginning, the Wilson government had strived to encourage the rapid increase in labor productivity. In this area also it did not find an enthusiastic support of organized labor. Eventually Prime Minister Harold Wilson was dissuaded from insisting on legislation outlawing jurisdictional and wildcat strikes. In return he received a pledge of union leaders to suppress these abuses. However even during 1969 there were some breaches of these promises.

The development of the 1960's in Great Britain has shown that the traditional close cooperation between organized labor and the Labor Party, which also has led to the appointment of many union leaders to Cabinet posts has come under considerable strain once the political branch of the labor movement, the labor party, had to assume wide responsibility for government policies.

One of the difficulties encountered by the labor government in pushing for higher productivity is the lingering fear of union leaders and members that further mechanization and automation would reduce the number of jobs. Especially the old generation of union leaders has not forgotten the long drawn out depression of the inter-war period.

Britain is a country where traditions are strong and organized labor in England has succeeded admirably in becoming part of this traditional structure in the course of the last one hundred years. It has succeeded in giving a strong sense of social identification to the working class and to wage and salary workers in general. This is an important achievement in a country where social classes and their distinctive characteristics survive as a psychological fact even as in terms of pure economics there is a leveling down of class differences.

19-6. INDUSTRIAL RELATIONS IN FRANCE

Although the German Federal Republic and France have been associated now in a Common Market together with Italy and the low countries of Holland, Belgium, and Luxemburg for a considerable period of time, great divergencies continue in the area of industrial relations. As we have seen in Sec. 19-3, the year 1920 brought basic changes in industrial relations through the Shop Council Law, the extension of collective bargaining and other measures which integrated labor into the social structure to a considerable degree in Germany. When Hitler took over and disbanded the unions and replaced the Shop Council Law with a so-called leadership system, the "labor front" was created. This was a clear indication that even a totalitarian regime operating in a modern industrialized society must create the image of some concern for labor. Now in France it took until 1936, the year of the short lived "popular front" government to enact some reforms in industrial relations. At that time two institutions were established in large scale industrial enterprises: the Delegate of the Personnel and the Enterprise Committee. The Delegate has the obligation to present individual complaints and grievances to management. This procedure is less structured and less effective than the various stages through which grievances can go in American enterprises operating with a union contract. The Enterprise Committee has a certain right to obtain general information from management but it is a far cry from a Shop Council of the German type.

By the late 1960's these innovations of thirty years ago were considered quite inadequate. In the meantime the French industrial system had undergone major changes. While still way behind other Western industrial countries in the rate of industrialization, modernization and organization had progressed substantially after World War II. At the same time, however, at least on a psychological level, class distinctions and tensions continued. It is perhaps significant that the French word for employer or "boss" is "patron." The Employer's Association is known as the "patronat." This term conveys the more authoritative and personal aspects that French management has retained up to recently. On the other hand unions also have preserved more of a "class struggle" pattern than is the case especially with Anglo-Saxon unions.

Another difference is predicated on the fact that French economic policy under the Fourth and Fifth Republics have been more interventionist than those of many other Western countries. A considerable part of industrial workers, for instance in mining, in transportation and in the largest automobile manufacturing combine in France are working in the nationalized sector of the economy. Even in the private sector wage scales are related to a minimum wage which in turn is subject to government regulations. As a result of this structure, the most important phase of contract negotiations consists of bargaining not between labor and management but between the top union leadership and the government. This was clearly evident during the crisis of May 1968. Once a basic agreement had been reached on the government level collective contracts and wage scales fell in line. It can be expected that industrial relations in France will retain some of their unique characteristics which are a product of history and of the traditions of strong centralized government and of interventionism on one side and greater identity between owners and managers on the other.

19-7. INDUSTRIAL RELATIONS IN THE SOVIET UNION

In Sec. 19-1 mention was made of trade unions in Communist countries. At this point we will discuss the structures of unions in the U.S.S.R., which are a prototype of similar organizations in other Communist countries. Despite the ideological split between Moscow and Peiping the basic structure of party and government is identical in all Communist countries: the Communist party has the monopoly of political power even where it does not operate under this name, as for example in Poland or East Germany. The party is the sole policy-making body and the "state" is conceived merely as an administrative structure which has to implement and carry out the party line. All these countries operate on the theory that "exploitation" of labor has been eliminated because private ownership of production facilities has been transferred to social ownership. This theory has great bearing on the way in which labor organizations are viewed under Communism. Inasmuch as "society" or "the state" owns all means of production, the workers and especially the aggregate of people employed in industry, trade, and commerce are the ultimate owners of the installations and offices where they work. Seen from this angle, strikes become meaningless because no one can strike against himself. Communists insist on this interpretation and deny that strikes have been forbidden. They say merely that they have become inconceivable.

Actually, trade unions in the Soviet Union are compulsory for all persons employed in industry. They are of the industrial rather than the craft union type and, of course, levy dues. Membership in these unions does by no means establish individuals as members of the Communist Party. Admission procedures to that "elite" are rigid and require a number of steps before a "candidate" becomes a full-fledged member of the party. Naturally all important positions in the trade union are manned by reliable party members.

There is no collective bargaining in the Soviet Union in any meaningful sense of the word. Labor, however, has a voice in the top planning agencies which have to determine annually (or more recently, on a somewhat longer basis) how much shall be allocated for the national "wage fund." Out of this immense pot appropriations are made to the ministries set up to supervise the various industries under their jurisdiction. From this level allocations of a global wage fund flow to the actual enterprises. It is at that point that unions in the Soviet Union can exercise some influence. While the director of a Soviet enterprise has very great managerial power, local unions participate in the allocation of the enterprise wage fund to the various categories of workers. They can argue in favor of setting up somewhat higher occupational classifications, provided such a system does not exceed the overall allocation. Furthermore, they can take up individual grievances with regard to the compensation of workers.

Since these unions operate in an economic system in which workers, in theory, share the ownership of the means of production with the Russian people as a whole, unions are not conceived as the opposite of management but as organizations in the service of society. This attitude is evident in the area of production norms. Traditionally, unions in Western countries have been attempting to curtail excessive "speedups." Actually, they have been successful in many areas in putting unofficial ceilings on work performance. In the Soviet Union, labor unions, at the request of the Communist party, have been in the forefront of concerted drives to speed up productivity and to encourage workers to participate in intra- or interplant competitions for higher output. Since unions have virtually no influence on the establishment of aggregate wage funds; they were also powerless when, in the late 1950's, the income of labor lagged far behind productivity gains. When, however, in the early 1960's the rate of growth of the Soviet economy slowed down considerably, the Soviet leaders announced that from that point on wages should be more closely pegged to rising levels of productivity.

Since Soviet labor unions have very limited scope along conventional lines unlike organized labor elsewhere, they have been given a very important administrative function—they are in charge of the Social Security system, especially the handling of retirement pensions.

On the operating level of the economy, management and labor remain completely separate in most Communist countries. However, this is not the case in Yugoslavia, where Workers' Councils have been set up. Production plans and wage and price schedules are submitted to these councils. The actual management of the enterprise is carried out by a board selected from members of the Workers' Council. The salaries of the director and other executives are set up by this body.

The Yugoslav system goes much further in the direction of "industrial democracy" than the German system of codetermination and shop constitutions. It must be remembered, however, that Yugoslavia cannot be compared in terms of industrialization with either the Soviet Union or Germany. Yet there is no denying the fact that everywhere highly industrialized countries, regardless of forms of industrial ownership, are compelled by force of circumstances to improve communication between management and labor. While this need does not necessarily lead to constitutional plant government, it helps overcome earlier misconceptions that workers as individuals are of necessity involved in industrial situations which they know little about, and in which they are powerless against arbitrary shop policies.

19-8. SOME OBSERVATIONS ABOUT UNIONS AND CONTINUED SOCIAL PROGRESS

The brief historical survey of the growth of unionism in the international sphere and in the United States as well as in some other leading industrial countries has shown that in the last one hundred years organized labor has succeeded in bringing about vast improvements in the total economic and life situation of workers. While unions nowhere had a monopoly on the promotion and in the fight for social reforms and progressive legislation, there is no doubt that their presence and pressure was indispensable for the progress of labor which has been chartered and analyzed in this text. But the very success of unionism has created the need for an ever renewed examination of the role of unionism in the larger context of a highly organized industrial society in which especially in the United States new problems, including new aspects of poverty, are challenging society. Unionism, of course, never played a significant role in the Marxist anticipation of the way in which capitalism would transform itself through ever more severe crises into socialism. As a matter of fact unions would have been unable to achieve the concessions from management they were able to obtain over the years if the capitalistic system had been actually in the state of crisis to which it was headed "inevitably" according to the "scientific" analysis of historical materialism. From the viewpoint of orthodox Marxists, unions were always somehow suspect because as a practical necessity they had to bargain for better working conditions within the context of the capitalistic system rather than to wait for its collapse. The current trend, especially among younger writers, to accuse unions as being conservative and part of the establishment, is novel only in its terminology not in its substance.

In recent years adherents of the method of Historical Materialism (Histomat) of analyzing social trends have run into considerable difficulties because largely due to the successful activities of organized labor over the last one hundred years a considerable proportion of the working class has moved into the lower ranges of the middle income groups and has experienced vast improvement in their manner of living. This does not fit into the world view of Histomat according to which the working class is still in the forefront of the progressive movements pointing to a classless society. Actually the working class especially in the Western world has found its niche in a social structure which, while no longer the class society of early capitalism is even in the Soviet Union very far away from the egalitarian utopia of pure Communism. As a result the working class and with it its organized and economically effective branch, the union movement, is no longer considered an element in the "historical dialectics" underlying social change and the inevitable progression from capitalism to socialism and/or Communism.

One would assume that such a contradiction between actual social development and the theoretical model presented by Histomat would lead even Marxist scholars to a revision of their basic frame of reference. But some influential writers of this group, for instance, Herbert Marcuse,[3] rather than modifying their life-long commitment to the dialectical method of historical and social analysis have tried to shift the center of the real historical dialectical process of change from labor, especially organized labor, to students, intellectuals in general, and those groups often outside the labor force who have not made an identification with the existing social structure or have often feelings of rejection and nonacceptance. Actually it is not necessary to adopt the rigid, ironclad analytical method of historical materialism to understand that even the most successful economic system will in the course of time give rise to criticism and to drives for a change. But it is only natural that in an increasingly industrial society in which partly due to the great efforts of organized labor the vast majority of wage and salary earners have found their place, trade unions are most unlikely to participate in movements advocating the restructuring of the social order and a transvaluation of social priorities. This does not

---

[3]*One Dimensional Man*, Beacon Press, Boston, 1964.

diminish the great social role that organized labor continues to play. But it will continue to do so as part of the operating system rather than in fundamental opposition to it.

SELECTED BIBLIOGRAPHY

Broderson, Arvid. *Soviet Worker: Labor and Government in the USSR* (New York: Random House, Inc., 1964).

Dunlop, John T. *Industrial Relations Systems* (New York: Holt, Rinehart & Winston, Inc., 1964).

Forsythe, E. J. "Collective Bargaining in Western Europe" *Labor Law Journal* (November, 1963).

Galenson, Walter. *Trade Union Democracy in Western Europe* (Berkley, Calif.: University of California Press, 1959).

Johnston, T. L. *Collective Bargaining in Sweden* (Cambridge, Mass.: Harvard University Press, 1962).

Matthews, P. W. and Ford, G. W. (ed.) *Australian Trade Unions* (Melbourne, Australia,: Sun Books Pty, Ltd., 1968).

Raffaele, Joseph A. *Labor Leadership in Italy and Denmark* (Madison, Wis.: University of Wisconsin Press, 1962).

QUESTIONS FOR DISCUSSION

1. Trace the development of international unions, noting especially the factors both economic and political, which had extraordinary effects on the development.

2. What is the International Labor Organization and what are its principal functions?

3. Discuss some of the more important differences in terms of employment and collective bargaining as they exist in the United States and Europe.

4. What factors, economic and noneconomic, do you feel account for these differences cited in the above answer?

5. The German Shop Council is a unique institution. Characterize the nature, duties and jurisdiction of this type of organization.

6. With respect to systems of labor-management relations, what is codetermination and how does it function?

7. Do these features to the system of codetermination offer advantages over the labor relations systems which we find in the United States?

8. Characterize labor relations under a Socialistic or Communistic System, and point to the important differences between such relations and those in the industrialized nations of the West.

9. It has often been said that Russian economists are faced with the same basic problems as are American economists, and that the differences are only in the manner in which these problems are attacked. Does this comparison hold in the case of labor relations?

Part

V

SOCIAL SECURITY

In order to understand the issues in Social Security and the attitudes toward some of its features and developments, it is necessary to view them in an historical perspective. The vast growth of Social Security systems requires a detailed analysis of their impact on the flow of income and on the national income as a whole. Old Age, Survivors, and Disability Insurance, Unemployment Insurance, and Medicare are examined in detail. Finally, the "Welfare State" is analyzed and evaluated.

From the Poor Laws to Social Security

Throughout this study we have been able to discern many indicators of the great improvement made in the past hundred years in the income and working conditions of wage and salary earners. A considerable proportion of the vast majority of people participating in the labor force has achieved a middle-class status. Although many problems of employment remain, there is greater concern about them now than at the beginning of the century. Collective bargaining has extended the wage contract to include provisions for retirement, group health and life insurance, and the establishment of some form of shop constitution.

There is, of course, another side to the coin. Modern industrialized society has created a great dependency on the steady flow of income derived mainly from two sources—current employment, or cash benefits derived as a result of coverage in social-insurance schemes. Social Security income has, therefore, become one of the cornerstones of contemporary society. No study of the total economic situation of wage and salary workers would be complete without a careful analysis of the economic consequences of social security and of its operations.

Social security legislation came to the United States almost a generation after it had been adopted in Great Britain and in many European countries. Therefore it is quite remarkable how quickly it has been accepted here as an inescapable fact of modern industrial life. Nevertheless, Social Security entails a number of unresolved emotional and social issues which are epitomized by the concept of the "Welfare State." In this chapter we deal with these questions from an historical point of view, showing the comparative novelty of social insurance as compared to older methods of dealing with problems of poverty and loss of income. Once we have completed our study of the American social security system we will be able to assess more properly the real meaning of the welfare state in the last third of the twentieth century.

20-1. TRADITIONAL APPROACHES TO POVERTY AND THE ENGLISH POOR LAWS

Traditional society almost everywhere in the world is characterized by strong family ties, often extending to a much wider degree of kinship than in the modern American "one-generation" or nuclear family. In rural areas such extended families also provide a minimum amount of social security because family members are permitted to share scarce resources and primitive facilities. This is particularly true of the care even of distantly related descendants of common ancestors. We must take into account that life expectancy is low and infant mortality high in these circumstances, and comparatively few people reach a really old age. Traditional societies are also characterized by their tolerance of large-scale begging in public places. During the Middle Ages monasteries did provide shelter for migratory poor for a limited period of time. As prosperity increased and merchants acquired greater wealth, foundations were established in the Middle Ages—for example, in cities in Northern Italy and in the Low Countries—for the construction and operation of hospitals in which elderly persons could also be cared for. Orphanages also were set up in that period. Generally speaking, the Church as the paramount charitable institution in the Middle Ages was the ultimate recourse of the destitute. A proportion of the considerable revenues of bishoprics, monasteries, and parishes from their extensive land holdings had to be set aside in order to carry this relief burden.

While a fairly high degree of prosperity was achieved toward the end of the Middle Ages, increasing social pressures were felt on the countryside and in the cities. By the middle of the fourteenth century, Europe had reached its "frontier." All land had been awarded to owners holding titles and there was no room left for the type of pioneer farming which had been characteristic of earlier centuries and had enabled people to improve their economic situation by opening up new land and settling in new towns.

The bloody Peasants' War in Germany in 1524–25 was a clear indication of the economic deterioration of the status of peasants and their opposition to the encroachments of the big feudal land owners. The farmers were defeated and their situation grew worse. About the same time big landlords began to improve their situation in Great Britain. They turned to "commercial farming" by raising huge herds of sheep and selling the wool to the merchants and manufacturers in Flanders and in England itself. To carry out these operations landlords needed more and more grazing land. This need led to the beginning of the "Enclosure Laws," which cut down the land resources of the villagers. Economic opportunities declined for the children of tenant farmers and cottagers. In turn this decline set in motion a considerable floating population trying to support itself through begging or odd jobs on the highways and byways of the country. In the cities the guild system had assumed many characteristics of a tightly held monopoly. Many young men who had gone through apprenticeship training and had advanced to the status of journeyman could advance no farther because the economic requirements for achieving the rank of master became more and more stringent. It is against this background that the English Poor Laws must be understood.

The first of the series of "poor laws" was promulgated in England in 1531. Its main purpose was to regulate begging, not to abolish it. For this purpose registers of the local poor had to be drawn up. If the poor wanted to support themselves by begging, they required a license to do so, but such a permit was to be given only to people who had handicaps caused by physical defects or age. Able-bodied persons were barred from begging. Violators of the law of 1531 were to be punished by whipping.

This first poor law did not confine itself to a distinction between unemployable and able-bodied people and to setting up different procedures of dealing with them. It also introduced the concept of *settlement* into the relief administration which has remained significant to this day. The principle of settlement was embodied in two features of the law of 1531. Those poor who had qualified for a license were assigned a specific location in town where they could solicit alms. Able-bodied poor who were arrested for begging outside their native city were to be returned to it after they had suffered the corporal punishment provided for illegal begging. If they had resided in another place for at least three years prior to their seizure, that locality was considered their settlement and they could be transported there.

By 1536 a more comprehensive poor law had been enacted. This legislation retained the procedures already established with regard to the treatment of people engaging in begging without a license. It seems that a large number of homeless children up to the age of fourteen were roaming about the English countryside at that time. They had either run away from home or had been abandoned by their parents. These children were to be taken off the road and turned over to employers who could teach them a trade. That such family disorganization existed is clearly indicated by a law passed in the seventeenth century by Parliament prohibiting the selling of children to British colonists in America.

The Poor Law of 1536 established a pattern which has remained basic in relief administration ever since. The local authorities were made responsible for the raising of funds to carry out relief programs for the indigent poor. While this law clearly established the principle of local responsibility for the financing of poor relief, it still relied on voluntary contributions of the more prosperous citizens for the necessary funds. The contributions

were to be collected in the parishes of the locality, but the funds were to flow
into a common pool to be set up in each community. The law of 1536 also
created the position of collector of these contributions, who was required to
give full accounts of collections and disbursements.

Experience showed that public poor relief could not in the long run be
financed by voluntary contributions. In 1572 a law was enacted requiring
the localities to levy a *poor tax*. These local taxes remained in effect until
far into the nineteenth century. The first poor laws already contained some
fragmentary provisions with regard to work relief. In 1576 a very important
principle was introduced into the English poor-law legislation: the doctrine
that relief should be normally given in form of work projects. In fact,
certain types of work were mentioned, such as the processing of wool, hemp,
and flax.

This emphasis on work relief eventually led to that well-known institution, the *workhouse*. A law enacted in 1722 formalized that situation.
Already prior to that time local relief administrators had been called
"Overseers of the Poor." This early eighteenth-century law made it mandatory for these officials to establish workhouses to which families or individuals receiving relief were to be transferred. It was permissible at that time
to farm out the actual administration of such a workhouse to private entrepreneurs. In this way considerable profits could be made out of poverty. The
operator of the workhouse would receive a global sum corresponding to the
per capita allocation of relief for the indigent inmates. These people were
put to work and their produce would be sold, often below comparable prices
of private business. To these revenues could be added "savings" in food
and other allowances actually earmarked for the poor This method of running workhouses soon became the subject of criticism. In 1782 a law was
passed forbidding the turning over of the administration of workhouses to
private individuals. At the same time, small local communities were permitted to pool their resources for the operation of a workhouse where the
poor of a number of small settlements could be sent. Despite these administrative reforms, the conditions in workhouses remained extremely bad,
yet this method of dispensing relief continued to exist in England throughout the nineteenth century.

It was shown above that the English Poor Laws from the very beginning stressed the principle of settlement, giving prime responsibility for extending relief to the local community in which the applicant for assistance
had his permanent residence. A second principle of poor relief went hand in
hand with these residence requirements. It is embodied in the *"means test."*
In order to qualify for relief the overseer of the poor had to be satisfied that
the applicants were completely devoid of means of subsistence and could
not be supported either by parents or children. Obviously the strict residence requirement of the early poor laws had a tendency to freeze poor

people into remaining in their native town and villages or in other places if they had lived there for at least three years prior to their application for relief.

In the second half of the seventeenth century, when the first signs of the Industrial Revolution began to have their impact, a greater amount of labor mobility throughout the country became desirable. In 1662 the Law of Settlement was enacted, making it much easier for people to establish residence in towns to which they had moved. In order to understand the operations of this law we must remember that in those days many localities were still surrounded by walls with guarded gates so that people entering or leaving a town could easily be checked. Now, according to this law, local authorities had the right to investigate the financial status and outlook of any person who had entered the city with the intention of taking up residence. Within a 40-day period city officials could investigate whether or not the new resident was able to support himself, as indicated, among other things, by the type of room he had taken. If it was very cheap, then the authorities would conclude that the new resident was not only poor but also had very poor prospects. They could then remove him to the community where he previously had legal residence.

Obviously there were many loopholes in this arrangement, and it became comparatively easy for poor people to get into cities and towns where, after a 40-day period, they would have to be considered as permanent residents entitled to poor relief if they could not support themselves. In order to promote labor mobility and lower their own relief burden, communities were allowed to issue to a poor person who desired to move to a more prosperous area papers acknowledging the responsibility of the home community to grant poor relief to the bearer. In this way entry into towns was made easier and the 40-day period would very often elapse without thorough investigation. Thus a new permanent resident would be added to the population.

While the law of settlement was national in scope, the actual administration of the poor laws rested with the communities. The taxes and budgets for individuals or families on poor relief were determined locally. It was often difficult to put into practice the principle that only people who were unemployable were to be concentrated in workhouses, and that employable people should be assigned to some kind of work. Under the inflationary strain of the wars against France, a law was passed in 1795 which openly acknowledged the existence of a situation that had been a fact for a considerable period of time. Direct relief had been given outside the workhouse to people who could not find employment. Such a development was inevitable unless workhouses were to be expanded to an unreasonable degree. The law of 1795 went one step further by permitting a system of "allowances in support of wages." It directed the local administrators of the poor laws to grant supplementary payments to workers if the wages paid them by their employers were less than the relief budget established for the community. These supplements were designed to bring the total earnings of the worker up to this relief budget. In this connection it is well to remember that these budgets made allowance for the number of children in a family so that larger families would be somewhat better off on relief than smaller ones.

This use of relief funds to bring up wages to the subsistence level enabled the government to continue a wage-freeze policy even in the period of the Napoleonic Wars—during which, as we have seen in Part IV, trade unions were still considered as illegal conspiracies.

It is easy to see why the economists of that era condemned this abuse of the relief system. Actually, it amounted to the subsidizing of sweatshops with public funds. However, this rather obvious point was not raised by David Ricardo. He was more concerned with the fact that the poor laws had a built-in incentive for the creation of large families. In his *Principles of Political Economy and Taxation* (1817), he advocated a total repeal of the poor laws.

In view of the rising public criticism of the poor-law structure, a Royal Commission was established by the British Parliament in 1832 to enquire into the administration and practical operation of the poor laws. Like other such commissions set up later in the nineteenth century to study industrial conditions, this group did an excellent job of investigation. Many witnesses were heard and the study really reached down to details of administrative procedures on the local level. All the findings and supporting data of the enquiry were incorporated in a report of over 13,000 pages. An extract of the voluminous findings was published in 1833. The commission stated that the administration of the poor laws was "destructive to the morals of the most numerous class and to the welfare of all." The Report stressed that "paupers" receiving relief in their own homes seemed to have lost all interest in maintaining a decent appearance and a clean house. Statements of that kind helped to continue the workhouse system throughout the nineteenth century in England, especially because the Royal Commission did not propose the abolition but merely a reform of the poor laws.

In 1834 a law revising the structure of poor relief was enacted. On the administrative plane it brought about primarily a streamlining of the structure. The more than 13,000 local relief units were merged into 568 larger districts. The law also provided for stronger coordination and equalization of relief standards and practices throughout the country. The system of allowances in support of wages was abolished. While the workhouse remained the standard institution through which relief was to be extended, the law acknowledged that this objective might become unenforceable, especially during the frequent depressions characteristic of the unstable economic system of the nineteenth century. Consequently, in cases of "sudden and urgent necessity," direct relief could be given to people in their own homes. To underline the principle that able-bodied people, especially men, should not be given relief, local governments established "yards" where men who otherwise would have to be granted poor relief could report for outdoor employment if they were out of work. Hence, throughout the nineteenth century, work relief was the standard method of dealing with male able-bodied applicants for relief. This historical fact is worth bearing in mind because during the 1930's members of the Roosevelt administration frequently referred to work relief as a specifically American way of dealing with poverty of able-bodied people out of work.

The reform legislation of 1834 did not silence the critics of the workhouse or for that matter of "outdoor relief." But it was not until 1905 that another Royal Commission was set up to investigate the poor laws. As a result of the findings of this Commission the poor laws were abolished prior to World War I or almost a hundred years after they had become a subject of great public criticism. The report of that Royal Commission prepared the ground for the British system of social insurance which was begun with the National Insurance Act of 1911, establishing some measure of health and unemployment insurance. This system was vastly expanded in the similarly named law of 1946, which established a comprehensive program of old-age benefits, thereby completing the rather large edifice of social insurance in England.

20-2. APPROACHES TO RELIEF IN THE UNITED STATES PRIOR TO 1933

The description of the British Poor Laws given in the previous section has great bearing on American approaches and methods to deal with problems of poverty. Basically the same principles prevailed in the Colonies and in the early history of the United States which we already have encountered in the study of the British relief system. For instance, the provincial legislature of New York passed a law very similar to the English Settlement law. This was particularly true of the 40-day period in which indigent migrants could be returned to their home communities. All local communities had to appoint overseers of the poor. This law was reenacted after the United States gained independence.

Soon thereafter an important change was made. As early as 1788 the city of New York was authorized to establish what amounted to a two-year residence requirement. Anyone who had to apply for relief within the first two years after he had come to New York City, could be transported back to his home community at the latter's expense. It should be noted that this two-year residence requirement remained in force until World War II. Only then was this principle of settlement abolished in New York City.

However, the often-heard charge has never been proven that large numbers of Americans from the South and from Puerto Rico abused the dropping of the residence requirement to come to New York in order to "go on relief."

Poor relief was considered to be strictly a local responsibility. The citizens of each community were to decide on the amount of the poor tax and how it was to be paid. This principle of local responsibility continued as a standard until the 1930's. Only then did the Federal government assume financial responsibility for the employable poor who were supposed to be absorbed almost completely by public works provided and financed by the Federal government.

Throughout the period of exclusive local responsibility for relief the British system of workhouses or poorhouses was an important phase of the total public welfare structure. However, as in England, it was impossible to refer all relief recipients to the poorhouses. As early as 1849 the city of New York established a separate department which concerned itself with the "outdoor poor." In the course of time this led to the establishment of a home-relief bureau.

From an early time state governments asserted their rights to supervise local relief activities without, however, interfering with the principle of local responsibility to care for their poor. In 1823 the New York State legislature ordered a survey of relief procedures. A report submitted in 1824 contained a whole catalogue of malpractices such as "farming out" the poor to the care of private persons, unnecessary cruelty in enforcing the settlement laws, and often, lack of a distinction in the treatment of the indigent and of criminal elements of the population. Eventually, the supervisory function of the state government was institutionalized by creating a control agency in 1867. Most of the other states followed the same pattern and, by 1929, only Mississippi, Nevada, and Utah did not yet have state welfare agencies.

While public relief followed largely the British pattern throughout the nineteenth century, private relief activities gained much greater significance in the United States. Many voluntary agencies came into being dedicated to the aid to various categories or groups of the indigent population. Very often they specialized in aid to immigrants coming from European countries. American voluntary agencies soon developed very efficient techniques of fund raising, such as the setting up of committees of wealthy and prominent citizens to head the campaign and carrying out annual drives to raise contributions. These private agencies were able to assist their clients in a more individual and constructive manner than was possible under the poor laws. However, in sharp contrast to current procedures of private welfare agencies, they did not confine themselves to counseling or casework but also dispensed financial aid.

20-3. THE CRISIS OF RELIEF IN THE 1930'S

We have already seen that England abolished the traditional poor laws in 1911 when the National Insurance Act was passed. Actually, social security legislation, especially health, industrial accident, and old-age insurance had been introduced in Germany through legislation in 1885 and 1899. Many other countries followed suit. However, in the United States, there was little interest even on the part of organized labor, in a government-supported social security system. The idea prevailed that in the United States social insurance was unnecessary because the earnings of workers were high enough to carry them through shorter periods of unemployment and to enable them to build up a nest egg for a "rainy day." Besides, in case of real need, the generously endowed voluntary agencies were available to give assistance to those who had become needy. This widespread feeling that social insurance may be necessary for indigent Europeans but not for prosperous Americans explains the fact that, when the Great Depression of the 1930's spread in ever-widening circles, the institutional defense against it were extremely weak. The Social Security Act of 1935, which is analyzed in the next four chapters, came too late to be of substantial help for the millions of people who had lost their jobs in the early 1930's or who had reached retirement age during that period because, at the earliest, only small benefits became available prior to 1940.

A real crisis developed, therefore, soon after 1930 because, in the absence of social insurance the traditional public and private relief system in the United States simply could not cope with the unprecedented mass emergency. The rigid adherence to the principle that local communities were financially responsible for the relief of the poor broke down under the twofold pressures of an unprecedented rise in the number of applicants and a rapid decline in the tax revenues of municipalities. While voluntary agencies stepped up their fund-raising campaigns, the distress caused by the Depression was beyond the scope of private voluntary contributions. This then, was the period when "breadlines" appeared and other makeshift arrangements had to be devised, including loans by private banks to city governments. Some state governments also came to the aid of cities. For instance, the state of New York established a Temporary Emergency Relief Administration in 1931 with an initial appropriation of $20 million. In some cases resources of the newly created Reconstruction Finance Corporation were also used in order to back up local relief situations.

Immediate action was taken by the incoming Roosevelt administration with the passage of the Federal Emergency Relief Act in 1933. This law made it possible for the first time for the Federal government to give direct grants to states for unemployment relief. Table 20-1 shows the extent of the relief operations prior to the start of the social-insurance programs of the Social Security Act of 1935. In order to evaluate the figures given in

TABLE 20-1
NUMBER OF HOUSEHOLDS AND PERSONS
BENEFITING FROM PUBLIC-AID PROGRAMS,
1933–40
(thousands)

Year and Month	Households	Persons in Households
March 1933	5,358	21,035
March 1934	7,236	25,876
March 1935	6,853	24,369
March 1936	6,143	21,109
March 1937	5,892	18,657
March 1938	6,339	19,544
March 1939	7,017	21,256
March 1940	6,188	17,912

SOURCE: National Resources Planning Board, *Security, Work and Relief Policies*, 1942.

the table it is well to remember that in 1933 the population of the United States was 125,479,000 people. While it is possible that double-counting occurred in compiling these data, the information given in the table demonstrates clearly the vast amount of need that existed during the Great Depression.

Following the long-established tradition that relief to able-bodied men should be granted primarily in form of "outdoor work," the Civil Works Administration was established in 1933. Naturally it was difficult to organize a sufficient number of worthwhile projects on short notice. For this reason the CWA came under early criticism for sponsoring "leaf-raking" and similar make-work projects. In 1935 work relief was reorganized and the Works Project Administration (WPA) was set up. Throughout the rest of the period prior to the entry of this country into World War II it became the main agency through which work relief was given. While the majority of the projects under WPA were of the "outdoor" type, about 20 percent of those employed in this program were in professional and service groups. For a time this included the Federal Theater Project and a number of Writers' Projects.

Table 20-2 shows the considerable share that WPA employment had as a means of relieving total unemployment. Although the ratio of WPA employment to toal unemployment was consistently high, the original goal of WPA to absorb virtually all employable but jobless persons was never reached. Actually, such an objective is somewhat unrealistic if the intention remains to avoid make-work types of activities.

It should be noted that in the 1930's people on work projects were counted as among the unemployed. This way of handling public works projects seems to be the only correct method of dealing with them statistically. People on work projects are there because they have neither a job in the private or in the government sector of the economy. They certainly are not

TABLE 20-2
RATIO OF WPA EMPLOYMENT TO TOTAL UNEMPLOYMENT

Month and Year	Total Unemployment (thousands)	WPA Employment (thousands)	Ratio of WPA Employment to Total Unemployment (percent)
December 1935	9,099	2,667	29.3
December 1936	7,120	2,243	31.5
December 1937	8,841	1,594	18.0
December 1938	9,304	3,156	33.9
December 1939	8,257	2,109	25.5

SOURCE: *Ibid.*

public employees. Moreover, since they have no regular work with industry or business, they are unemployed and must be included in overall statistics of unemployment. To count such people as employed would distort any detailed analysis of the labor market and may also be misleading in other ways.

In the 1930's the incidence of unemployment among young people was particularly high. To deal with the problems peculiar to this age group, a special work program was organized under the title of Civilian Conservation Corps (CCC). The age limits for eligibility varied during the 1930's. At one time these ranged from 17 to 28. In 1937, however, it was scaled down to the age group from 17 to 23. Table 20-3 shows the vast scope of the CCC activities.

TABLE 20-3
AVERAGE NUMBER OF
YOUTHS EMPLOYED IN CCC
CAMPS, 1936–40

Year	Employed
1936	415,562
1937	318,664
1938	270,023
1939	279,612
1940	280,129

SOURCE: *Ibid.*

The CCC projects were of the outdoor type. The young men were brought together in camps from where they went out to do jobs in reforestation, soil conservation, and similar activities. In the 1930's young people were also covered in work-study projects under the National Youth Administration (NYA). There were two separate programs. One dealt with some vocational training outside the schools, for instance, in workshops, but also in some types of clerical or semiprofessional work with public agencies. The other program was a student study project supporting young people while attending schools and colleges.

All the activities of the various levels of government discussed so far were outside the vast program of Social Security which came into existence with the passage of the Social Security Act of 1935.

A Landmark Decision On Residence Requirements. We have seen in the first section of this chapter that early poor law concepts focused on *settlement*, that is to say, they made eligibility for relief dependent on *residence*. This centuries-old system was left untouched in the Public Aid sections of the Social Security Act leaving the matter of residence requirements up to the states. Some states, for instance New York, lifted all residence requirements whereas most others continued linking eligibility for aid to prior minimum residence period in that state.

All this was changed by a landmark decision of the United States Supreme Court of April 21, 1969 in Shapiro vs. Thompson. In a six to three decision with Chief Justice Warren and Justices Black and Harlan dissenting, the Court ruled that residency laws making welfare grants dependent upon a stated period of settlement in a particular state or locality are unconstitutional because such restrictions interfere with the right of people to move freely from one place to another throughout the United States.

The elimination of residence requirements in American public assistance programs represents a drastic departure from traditional patterns which were first developed in the English Poor Laws of the 16th Century and were considered by many a necessary protection against claims for assistance of newcomers to a particular community. The decision of the Supreme Court has removed an existing imbalance in the structure of public assistance in the United States. If residence requirements are lifted in some areas, as happens in this country, while they remain in others, this can engender a drifting of population in the poverty sector into areas where they assume relief can be obtained easier and sooner than in their old community. This landmark decision of the Supreme Court will facilitate the formulation of national standards for public assistance which according to the proposals submitted by the Nixon Administration will lead to a substantial increase in public assistance payments in those states where they have been extremely low thus triggering a large scale outward migration of indigent residence of such states.

In his address of August 8, 1969, President Nixon called the present system of public assistance a "colossal failure." In our study of the Social Security Act we will find many areas to which this criticism of the President can be applied.

SELECTED BIBLIOGRAPHY

Abbott, Grace. *From Relief to Social Security* (Chicago, Ill.: University of Chicago Press, 1941).

Epstein, Leonore A. and Alfred M. Skolink. "Social Security Protection After Thirty Years," *Social Security Bulletin.* U. S. Department of Health, Education, and Welfare (Washington, D. C.: U. S. Government Printing Office, August 1965).

Rubinow, I. M. *The Quest for Security* (New York: Holt, Rinehart & Winston, Inc., 1934).

Witte, Edwin E. *The Development of the Social Security Act* (Madison, Wis., University of Wisconsin, 1962).

QUESTIONS FOR DISCUSSION

1. Trace the development of the Poor Laws in England from 1531 to the start of the twentieth century.

2. What special significance can be found in the concepts of settlement, work relief, workhouse, and means tests as they applied to the British Poor Laws?

3. British Economists of the classical school, particularly Ricardo, reacted against the poor laws. What important arguments did these men call upon in their attempts to demonstrate some of the problems created by the poor laws?

4. To what extent have the British Poor Laws influenced our contemporary management or relief payments?

5. The trend toward urban living which came as a product of the industrial revolution has important implications for the manner in which relief programs can be carried out. Why is this so, and what changes did this situation require?

6. What factors accounted for the relatively late introduction of a formal social-insurance program in the United States?

7. Outline the programs initiated in the United States during the 1930's which were designed to reduce the social and economic impact of the depression.

8. In general, do you feel that the programs outlined in the above answer were adequate for the task? Present specific and detailed facts to support your opinion.

9. Discuss the significance of the decision of the U.S. Supreme Court in Shapiro vs. Thompson of April 21, 1969.

An Economic Analysis of Social Security Systems

We have seen in the preceding chapter that poor-relief systems—or public assistance, as it is now called in the United States—make funds available only if applicants prove that they are needy and have no resources of their own. Furthermore, almost everywhere residence requirements were an aspect of public relief administration until 1970. The main difference between public assistance and Social Security programs is that in the latter no means test is necessary in order to establish a claim. Nor is residence of particular significance, except in unemployment compensation. Eligibility for Social Security benefits is based on the number of months or quarters (of a year) of covered employment of the applicant. All that is necessary to substantiate the claim for benefits is to establish that the minimum contributions have been paid. The amount of benefits rises, especially in old-age insurance, with the number of quarters covered.

Under the Social Security system there can therefore be no prying into the private financial situation of applicants. The whole procedure becomes impersonal and standardized. This, however, means that Social Security benefits do not create a condition of dependency on a public agency and its employees for the recipient of the payments. In fact, psychologically speaking, "social security" has lost all the distressing connotations traditionally connected with poor laws or their successors. The Social Security Act of 1935 and its amendments introduced two schemes of social insurance: Federal Old-Age and Survivors Insurance, and Unemployment Insurance. But in addition to these two important programs the law of 1935 also provided for Federal participation in public assistance. These relief programs now have been differentiated to deal separately with the aged, with the aid to dependent children, to the blind, and to the permanently and totally disabled. There also exists the program of general public assistance. This is available to needy persons who do not fit into the special categories of public assistance. The plan of the Nixon Administration to set up national minimum income standards—discussed in some detail in Chapter 25—represents a drastic departure by involving the federal government in all aspects of public assistance and eliminating the various specialized programs mentioned above.

In this chapter we will examine the general scope of Social Security and public assistance and the way in which they are handled in the accounting of the national income. Some economic implications of the vast amount of transfer payments which are generated by these Social Security programs will be examined.

20-1. THE DEVELOPMENT OF SOCIAL-WELFARE EXPENDITURES

One of the great changes brought about by the New Deal legislation was the entry of the Federal government into relief programs. Furthermore, social-insurance systems were established in the 1930's. Table 21-1 shows the rapid rise in the Federal disbursements for welfare in the past thirty years. It should be noted, however, that in Table 21-1, following the accounting practice of the Department of Health, Education, and Welfare, welfare expenditures also include Veterans' programs and Federal aid to education and public housing.

As can be seen from Table 21-1 the concept of "welfare expenditures" is stretched almost to the breaking point. In recent decades "welfare" has often been identified in everyday language with "relief." As we will see in Chapter 25 of this text, for many the "welfare state" is a bad word. Considering this widespread meaning of welfare, it seems quite inappropriate to include Federal, state and local funds for education into the sum total

TABLE 21-1
PUBLIC SOCIAL WELFARE EXPENDITURES, SELECTED FISCAL YEARS
1928–1929 THROUGH 1967–1968
(in millions)

	Total Expenditures from Federal, State and Local Funds				
	1928–29	1939–40	1949–50	1959–60	1967–68
Total	3.921.2	8.795.1	23.508.4	52.293.3	112,399.9
Social Insurance	342.4	1.271.8	4.946.6	10.306.7	42.850.6
Public Aid	60.0	3.597.0	2.496.2	4.101.1	11,135.3
Health and Medical Programs	351.1	615.5	2.063.5	4.463.8	8,037.1
Veterans Programs . . .	657.9	629.0	6.865.7	5.479.2	7,324.5
Education	2,433.7	2.561.2	6.674.1	17.626.2	38,782.4
Housing	-----	4.2	14.6	176.8	415.3
Other Social Welfare	76.2	114.4	447.7	1.139.4	3,854.8

SOURCE: *Social Security Bulletin* (December 1968).

of welfare expenditures. Of course, in another dictionary sense of welfare, education like almost everything else, adds to the general well-being of people. But given the popular connotation it is psychologically wrong even if it may be required by organizational linkages to classify educational activities as basically welfare projects. It is also totally wrong to include social security expenditures into a summation of total welfare spending. As we will see throughout this part of the text social insurance systems are financed by specific contributions of future claimants and beneficiaries of such programs as retirement and survivor benefits or unemployment compensation. Such payments plus the employment taxes levied on employers establish claims of individuals to these benefits. With the exception of a short period in the late 1950's and early 1960's the trust fund, that is to say, the reserves of old age insurance increased continuously because contributions exceeded cash benefit payments. Social insurance systems are as a rule self-financing. They do not require and in fact never have required in the United States annual money appropriations from general tax revenue in order to secure their continued operation. In sharp contrast to public aid programs they do not depend on the yields of general taxes because special compulsory levies earmarked exclusively for these insurance systems are prescribed by law. For this reason the almost $43 billion social insurance expenditures shown for the year 1967–1968 as part of the more than $112 billion total social welfare expenditures do not belong in this series at all just as the $39 billion local state and federal expenditures for education are out of place there. Neither can veterans' programs, although they certainly add to the "welfare" of veterans be justified as a welfare expenditure. They are in fact payments for past wars. If we disallow for social insurance, education and veterans' programs, we find that out of the $112.400 billion "welfare expenditure" shown in Table 21-1 for 1967–1968 at least $88 billion have to be taken out leaving about $24 billion for such programs as public aid, health and medical expenditures, housing and other social welfare. But even this contains overstatements because a great deal of the medical program consists of hospital insurance, for which contributions are being levied as surtax to contributions to old age insurance. Supplementary medical insurance is being financed by contributions of $5.30 per month by recipients of old age benefits. It is, therefore, also misleading to assert that total public welfare expenditures of all three levels of government exceed expenditures for national defense.

It becomes clear that a "welfare state," denoting the "something for nothing" stereotype, is a state of mind rather than an actually significant feature of the American economy. In fact, the two largest items in total welfare expenditures are most tangible signs for the steady progress of labor which we have been able to observe throughout our study of the various aspects of labor economics. For the overwhelming majority of the labor force, income maintenance—in terms of shorter-term unemployment and permanent old-age retirement—has been established through social-insurance systems. While they reduce the disposable income, they build up claims and actual payments for clearly stated cases of unemployment and withdrawal from the labor force at the statutory age. We have seen, furthermore, that despite the still-rising contributions to social insurance the real disposable income of wage and salary workers continued to go up until 1969.

The high expenditures for education represent in part the spread of higher education among more and more young people, including the vast group that used to be referred to as the "working class." We have seen that a close relationship exists between educational achievements and lifetime earnings. The upgrading of vast segments of wage and salary earners into the higher-skilled job classifications which is characteristic of the new emerging structure of the labor force is predicated on this ever-widening base of higher education. In this sense "welfare" expenditures for education are closely associated with increased earnings and rising levels of the real gross national product in the long run.

There is, of course, another side of the coin. Larger contributions to Social Security and higher taxes to finance education also increase the operating cost of the American economy. Moreover, they widen the discrepancies between total compensation of wage and salary earners and salary disbursements which was already shown in Table 5-1. While this condition will not put an end to real growth, without doubt these contributions and taxes are an important factor in the downward inflexibility of the price system of an advanced industrialized society. But this in turn merely shows that everybody is paying for the Social Security and educational systems which are part of total "welfare expenditures." Nor can it be said that to a large proportion this structure "takes from the rich" in order to "subsidize" the poor. The financial sources of welfare expenditures are so widely spread among the total population that they can no longer be encompassed by the obsolete concept of a "redistribution of wealth."

The Social Security Act was passed in 1935. Its main purpose was to put such income maintenance programs as old age and unemployment benefits on a contributory, that is to say, insurance basis and to use Federal-State funds in addition to local expenditures for remaining public aid programs in support of the aged, the blind, the crippled and of dependent children. Table 21-2 shows the development of public income maintenance programs for the first thirty years of the operation of the Social Security Act. In the period 1934–1935 prior to the passage of the Social Security Act, the greatest part of income maintenance expenditures went to public aid in form of general and special types of public assistance. The second largest amount, more than 10 percent of the total, was spent for veterans' pensions and compensation.

The fiscal period 1964–65 presents an altogether different picture.

TABLE 21-2
PUBLIC-INCOME MAINTENANCE PROGRAM EXPENDITURES AND INDIVIDUALS
RECEIVING PAYMENTS, SELECTED YEARS, 1934–65

Program	Annual (Fiscal Year) Expenditures (millions)				
	1934–35	1949–50	Recipients	1964–65 (preliminary)	Recipients
Total expenditures	$3,827.7	$10,041.9		$39,096.8	
Cash payments, total.........	3,706.7	9,209.5		36,074.8	
Social insurance	318.9	4,677.8		27,437.1	
Old-Age, Survivors, and Disability Insurance		784.1	2.743	16,962.3	19.80
Railroad retirement........		304.4	370	1,128.6	886
Public employee retirement	210.0	743.4	580	4,595.0	2,075
Unemployment insurance and employment service		2,311.5	2,121	3,047.0	1,393
Workmen's compensation (excluding medical care costs)	108.9	433.2		1,205.0	
Temporary disability insurance (excluding medical care costs)		101.2		499.2	
Veterans' pensions and compensation	390.2	2,092.8	3.314	4,076.3	5.053
Public aid (excluding medical care costs):					
Special types of public assistance	102.4	2,075.6	4.877	4,127.8	7.073
Other	2,895.3	363.3	.337	433.6	778
Medical services, total........	121.0	832.4		3,022.0	
Workmen's compensation..	65.0	193.0		570.0	
Temporary disability insurance		2.2		55.0	
Veterans' health and medical·care............	56.0	585.9		1,100.0	
Vendor payments under public assistance........		51.3		1,297.0	

SOURCE: "Social Security Protection After 30 Years," *Social Security Bulletin* (August 1965), Table I.

Public-aid expenditures which in 1934–35 were at the $3 billion level had risen 30 years later only $4.5 billion. However, now the largest proportion of public assistance was in special types of programs, such as aid to dependent children, whereas general public assistance had dropped to $433.6 million.

A comparison of social-insurance payments of the period 1949–50 with fiscal 1964–65 demonstrates the very rapid rise in Old-Age, Survivors, and Disability Insurance payments. Compared to that the increase in disbursements in unemployment insurance was not substantial, although actual unemployment was about 200,000 people higher in the latter period.

It should be noted that all social-insurance programs shown in Table

20-2 are financed by contributions which are deposited in trust funds set up for these schemes. On the other hand, public-aid programs and veterans' pensions are financed out of general taxation.

While the development of the Social Security systems and the participation of the Federal government in local welfare programs has eased the burden resting on states and cities with regard to relief spending, in recent years there has again been a significant rise in state and local expenditures for public welfare. Table 21-3 shows this.

TABLE 21-3
STATE AND LOCAL EXPENDITURES FOR PUBLIC WELFARE
SELECTED YEARS
1927–1967
(in millions of dollars)

Fiscal Year	Public Welfare	Fiscal Year	Public Welfare
1927	.151	1948	2.099
1934	.889	1958	3.818
1938	1.069	1967	8.249

SOURCE: *Economic Report of the President* (January 1969), Table B-69.

Table 21-3 shows an escalation of the public welfare expenditures. They more than doubled in the decade after 1958 although the price index went up only by about 16 points in the same period. In the Economic Report of the President these expenditures correctly do not include state and local expenditures for education. The latter increased in the same period from about $16 billion to $38.2 billion.

The increase in public welfare expenditures runs counter to the expectations and high hopes which were entertained when the Social Security Act of 1935 was written. It was assumed at that time that public aid programs outside social insurance could be kept small, especially once a condition of full employment was established. Although unemployment was kept even during short recessions at a very low level compared to the 1930's, public aid programs, as can be seen from Table 21-3 increased rather than declined. In this connection it is also important to note that in 1951 and in subsequent years large groups which had not been included in old age insurance originally were brought into the system so that virtually the total labor force of the United States is now being covered. Despite these extensions of social insurance the public aid rolls even for "old age assistance" a program supplying in full or partial income maintenance for people 65 years and over whose other income, either from private sources or from old age benefits is less than local assistance standards for aged couples, dropped only imperceptibly from 2.183 million in 1962 to 2.073 million in 1967. This was far less than the decline in recipients in general assistance which dropped during the same period by 118,000 people, thus reflecting the impact of full employment.

Of course it could be argued that without social security programs which are financed by contributions the burden of public welfare expenditures would be far greater. Even so two facts have to be considered: first, public welfare expenditures financed by taxes of state and local government and the Federal government, far from decreasing have kept going up even in periods of a "heated up" economy. Secondly, the ability of state and local governments to raise revenue for these public aid programs is severely restricted by the high level of Federal taxes which in turn have been stepped up as national defense expenditures began to rise steeply after 1965.

21-2. SOCIAL-WELFARE EXPENDITURES AND THE INCOME FLOW

At the beginning of this chapter emphasis was placed on the great difference between social-insurance systems and other public-welfare schemes from the viewpoint of the individual who, when making his claim for insurance benefits no longer has to undergo a means test or satisfy residence requirements. We now turn to the macroeconomic aspects of social insurance.

Social-welfare expenditures constitute the most important component of the *transfer payments* accounted for in the receipts and expenditures of the gross national product. Commensurate with the rapid increase in this type of spending, transfer payments including interest and subsidies increased from $37.1 billion in 1960 to $47.5 billion in 1964.[1] Now a great part of these transfer payments were not raised by general taxation but by specific levies on payrolls for Old-Age, Survivors, and Disability Insurance (OASDI) and state unemployment insurance. The welfare program outside the social-insurance system must, of course, be financed by general taxation. In this section the financial structure of Social Security, especially social insurance, will be analyzed further.

A social-insurance system, properly conceived, tends to be self-supporting. That is, past and current contributions are supposed to be sufficient at any given moment to meet the current claims of those entitled to benefits. This objective has been met by the two main social-insurance schemes in the United States since their inauguration through the Social Security Act of 1935. At no time was it necessary for Congress to make additional budgetary appropriations to these systems in order to continue paying the statutory benefits earned by persons covered under OASDI and unemployment insurance. The ability of social-insurance systems to

---

[1]*Economic Report of the President* (1965), Table B-7.

develop this status of self-support is one of their greatest advantages. While legislation is required from time to time to make adjustments in benefit rates, social insurance can largely be kept out of politics as long as there is no need to make specific budget allocations for it each year. In contrast, annual appropriations remain necessary for all welfare expenditures other than those under social-insurance schemes.

In the fiscal years 1960–61 through 1963–64 benefit payments exceeded slightly the receipts from contributions in OASDI. In 1964–65 there was again a substantial excess of receipts over benefit payments. The slight deficits were due primarily to a liberalization of certain provisions of the law permitting older people with comparatively few quarters of covered employment to qualify for benefits. As shown in Table 21-4, the substantial

TABLE 21-4

STATUS OF THE OLD-AGE AND SURVIVORS INSURANCE AND DISABILITY
INSURANCE TRUST FUNDS 1937–1969
(thousands)

Receipts	
Net Contribution Income.	$219,404,555
Transfers from	
general revenues	552,931
Net Interest	11,530,226
Expenditures	
Cash benefit payments	197,022,617
Rehabilitation services	
for disabled	1,090
Transfers to railroad	
retirement account	4,032,304
Net administrative expenses.	4,365,849
Assets at end of period	
Invested in U. S. Government securities	23,654,328
Cash balances	2,411,523
Total assets.	26,065,852

SOURCE: *Social Security Bulletin* (June 1969).

reserves accumulated by the system since its start in fiscal 1937–38 were more than ample to take care of these small discrepancies between receipts and expenditures. The sizable interests credited to the system in addition to current contributions helped to bridge this gap.

The total assets of the OASDI trust fund shown in Table 21-4 represent a small decline from the peak that the trust fund had achieved in fiscal 1955–56. However, the downward trend in the trust fund was reversed in the period 1963–64 and combined employer-employee contribution rates are slated to rise from 7.7 percent in 1966 to 9.7 percent in 1973. Furthermore the maximum covered earnings have been raised from $4,800 to $7,800 a year. This increase in the covered earnings corresponds to the steady rise in wages and salaries and is necessary to keep benefits in old-age insurance at a somewhat more realistic ratio with prior earnings.

Unemployment compensation is a much smaller scheme in terms of over all funds and expenditures. In fiscal 1964–65 about $2.4 billion were claimed in benefits, but at the end of the period $7.6 billion remained in the state accounts of the unemployment trust fund. Actually, then, the ratio of the trust fund to payments is more favorable in unemployment insurance than it is in old-age benefits.

Let us now return to an analysis of Social Security contributions and benefits as they relate to the income flow. In the initial years of operation of old-age and unemployment insurance the trust funds accumulated very fast. In old-age insurance the ten-billion dollar level was reached in fiscal 1947–48 and in 1953–54 that fund had doubled. This rapid accumulation of reserve was due to the fact that contributions exceeded each year by far the benefit payments. In 1964–65 contributions exceeded payments by about $600 million. However, with the increase in benefits and the rising number of beneficiaries, the wide gap that existed between collections and disbursements in old-age insurance will not return. The purpose of the trust fund will be as it was in the early 1960's—to make up temporary imbalances between benefit payments and contributions.

21-3. TRANSFER PAYMENTS IN SOCIAL SECURITY

The share of transfer payments in the gross national product has risen steadily in recent years. In 1954 the total gross national product was $363.1 billion and transfer payments amounted to $21.5 billion. In 1968 the gross national product had risen to $860.7 billion but transfer payments had more than doubled, reaching $70.2 billion in that year. The largest single item within the aggregate of transfer payments are trust-fund receipts and expenditures. Other transfer items are payments to veterans and their families and also net interest paid by government. We are concerned here only with those transfer payments which refer to social security. Table 21-5 shows recent developments.

TABLE 21-5
CONTRIBUTIONS TO SOCIAL INSURANCE, 1962 to 1969
(in billions of dollars)

Year	Receipts
1962	19.9
1963	22.1
1964	23.5
1965	24.6
1966	28.5
1967	35.8
1968	37.9
1969	44.0

SOURCE: Table B-63, *Economic Report of the President* (January 1969).

As can be seen in Table 21-5 receipts of social security contributions have increased fairly rapidly in the 1960's. As a result surpluses have reappeared in old age insurance and have continued to rise very sharply in unemployment insurance. In 1962 the trust fund in unemployment compensation was 7.3 billion; it had risen to 11.7 billion by 1968. The rapidly rising contributions to social security as the largest component part of transfer payments requires further analysis of its economic impact.

In old age insurance to which hospital insurance has been added contributions are shared equally by employee and employer. Furthermore, the self-employed also have to make contributions. In employment compensation only the employer has to pay these contributions.

Now the economic effect of the burden of transfer payments is entirely different for employers and for employees. The employer's share in contributions is an employment cost on top of the total compensation of employees. He will consider these outlays as operating expenses and they will be part of his cost and price structure. On the macroscale the employer's contributions are part of the cost of operating the economy. For employees the contributions to social security placed upon them are a withholding in addition to income taxes which reduces the disposable income. The higher the contributions to social security rise the greater is the gap between total compensation of employees and wage disbursements. In 1962 the respective figures were $323.6 billion and $296.1 billion resulting in a gap of $27.5 billion. In 1968 total compensation had risen to $513.6 billion and wage disbursements were $463.5 billion. This created virtually a $50 billion gap coming close to 10 percent of total compensation. Of course, this is only one side of the picture. The other side is represented by the conversion of these transfer payments into cash benefits for old age insurance, hospital and related service benefits and unemployment compensation. It has, therefore, been argued that transfer payments have a neutral effect on the economy and that even if they are very high they are merely transferring part of the total aggregate income flow from one sector of the economy to another. Very often the opinion has been voiced that this redistribution of income is actually a strong support for the economy as a whole because it enables maintenance of income of segments of the population who have lost their earning power through old age, sickness or temporary unemployment. The economic effect of transfer payments requires some further considerations.

One school of thought points to the social-insurance system and to other aspects of Social Security, such as special public-assistance programs as "Built-in Stablizers" contributing to a good measure towards the elimination of severe economic fluctuations. It is maintained that the much steadier performance of the American economy after World War II owes a great deal to the cushioning effects of social insurance. There is, however, considerable reason for doubt. Inasmuch as no modern society will permit large numbers of people to become utterly destitute who have lost their ability to earn an income by reason of unemployment, sickness, or old age, the alternative to social-security systems is certainly not the abandonment of potential beneficiaries. It would, however, be a tremendous extension of general and special public-assistance programs. Such measures would have to be financed out of current tax levies. It follows that the real difference between having or not having social insurance is institutional and social rather than strictly economic. As we have seen, social insurance is preferable from the viewpoint of individual recipients and also of cost of operation, because it is far easier and cheaper to administer than public assistance which must inquire into the financial status of each applicant.

The objection could be made that under social insurance there are a considerable number of beneficiaries who do not really need these payments and therefore would not automatically be eligible for public assistance if insurance schemes were not available. Unfortunately, this argument has little validity in terms of the largest social-insurance scheme, old-age benefits. In 1962 there were just over 18 million beneficiaries in Old-Age, Survivors, and Disability Insurance. It was estimated that of these about two-fifths were below the poverty margin despite their benefits.[2] On the other hand, 25 million of the 73 million wage and salary earners and self-employed persons were covered also under private group pension and deferred profit-sharing plans. Nevertheless, especially for employees whose earnings during their productive years were substantially above the maximum covered earnings—$4,800 until the end of 1965 and $6,600 thereafter—old-age benefits with or without additional private pensions or income will add up only to a fraction of their former earnings, in most cases far less than 50 percent of the former disposable income. The gap is, of course, smaller for those whose income during their participation in the labor force was relatively low.

These aspects of old-age insurance must be taken into account in assessing the economic impact of Social Security transfer payments. The contributions to OASDI are levied in form of payments equally split between management and labor. In 1964–65 they amounted to $15.9 billion. Half of that amount, to be paid by the employer, is part of the total compensation of employees which is not disbursed to them. The other part is included in the gross earnings of wage and salary workers and is withheld at the source. The employer's half of the contribution will of necessity be incorporated into the price of the goods and services sold. The employee's half represents a curtailment of the income that wage and salary earners

---

[2] "Social Security Protection After Thirty Years," *Social Security Bulletin* (August 1965), p. 10.

would otherwise have at their disposal. Inasmuch as people who are regularly employed at prevailing wages have in the overwhelming majority sufficient disposable income to cover the necessary expenditures corresponding to a generally high standard of living, the part of the income transferred from their gross earnings to Social Security lessens their ability to engage in discretionary spending. It is spending of this type, however—for cars, boats, household appliances, travel, and education—which has a high employment multiplier.

In the transformation into benefits payments, of part of the gross earnings withheld from people covered by old-age insurance, the character of aggregate spending of the recipients of these benefits undergoes a significant change.

Owing to the sharply reduced income of the population in retirement, even of those who remain above the poverty level, the propensity to consume will approach 100 percent. In fact, actual levels of spending may lead to a certain degree of dissavings on the part of those in the retirement group who were provident enough to accumulate some funds earlier in their lives for just such purposes. Nevertheless, the impact of this aggregate spending primarily for the basic necessities on the economy and on employment levels will not contribute toward a substantial rise in business activities. On the other hand, the employer's share in the contributions will add to the factors making for a great deal of downward inflexibility of prices.

The preceding analysis is not an argument against social insurance. However, its intent is to caution against misleading rationalizations that try to elevate social insurance from a fair and efficient system of dealing with the loss of permanent or temporary earning ability to a "weapon" in the fight against recessions or even more severe downward trends of the economy.

Another aspect of this situation will become more noticeable as more and more people join the ranks of beneficiaries and the scheduled increases in contributions and benefits take place. This means that the steady increase in transfer payments and especially their main component part, old-age insurance benefits and contributions, will continue. By the very logic of the national-income accounting techniques this will give a steady boost to the gross national income figures. However, this "growth" of the GNP is hardly of the type to generate significant increments of employment. In fact, the prospect offered here is for a greater growth of the insurance and welfare sector than of the economy at large.

While social-insurance systems cannot have the stimulating effect on the economy often attributed to them, their impact on the financial structure is considerable. The greater the levies for social insurance become, the more pronounced will be the differences between administrative budget receipts and expenditures of the Federal government and cash receipts and expenditures. For instance, in the fiscal year 1964 the administrative budget receipts amounted to $89.5 billion, whereas the cash receipts reached $115.5 billion. While budget expenditures exceeded receipts by $8.2 billion, thereby creating a deficit of this magnitude, the excess of total expenditures over total cash receipts was only $3.8 billion. In a way, then social-insurance systems have a tendency to strengthen the cash position of the Federal government. Furthermore, they build up trust funds. These will be analyzed in the next section.

21-4. TRUST FUNDS IN SOCIAL SECURITY

We have already seen that soon after the passage into effect of Social Security legislation in 1935 trust funds accumulated rather rapidly in old-age and unemployment compensation. The more recent status of the Old-Age, Survivors, and Disability Insurance trust funds was shown in Table 21-4. With the enactment of the 1965 amendments, a steep rise in these funds is expected. Table 21-6 shows estimates of the development of these funds based on the expected higher contributions and benefit payments.

TABLE 21-6
ESTIMATED BALANCES IN OASIS
AND DSI TRUST FUNDS
1967 THROUGH 1972
(millions)

Year	OASIS	DSI
1967	$18,856	$1,721
1968	19,881	1,880
1969	23,495	2,052
1970	27,759	2,246
1971	32,155	2,464
1972	36,704	2,714

SOURCE: Robert J. Myers and Francisco Bayo, *Social Security Bulletin* (October 1965), Tables 5 and 6.

The projected doubling of balances in OASIS and DSI Trust Funds between 1967 and 1972 brings again to the foreground the issue of financing social-insurance programs. When Social Security trust funds accumulated at a rapid rate in the 1940's, critics demanded a change over to a "pay-as-you-go system" of raising the necessary amounts for yearly benefit disbursements. In the context of the 1940's, in which this question was debated with some heat, it would have meant low current contributions. But this policy merely would have shifted a much higher burden to employers and wage and salary earners in the 1960's and 1970's. This shift would have been particularly noticeable in the period covering the fiscal years 1960 through 1964. It was at that time that the method of accumulating trust— that is, reserve funds—in social-insurance systems demonstrated its soundness. In those years statutory benefit payments exceeded current receipts. If trust funds had not been available, Congress would have been confronted with a dilemma: it would have been compelled either to vote for a deficiency appropriation in OASDI or to cut benefits. It is precisely the function of a trust fund to prevent the rise of such undesirable alternatives. Nor can it be said that the very substantial levies, amounting to $15.5 billion in fiscal 1963-64, were lost to the income stream or that the trust fund itself represents, as it were, a huge frozen asset. In fact, we encounter here a second line of criticism of the method adopted by the Social Security Act of financing social-insurance programs.

The contributions collected for social insurance are received by the U. S. Treasury. Old-age, Disability, and Unemployment insurance must at all times have cash on hand in order to meet the disbursements for at least one month. From the very beginning of the social-insurance program the excess of current receipts from contributions and current cash requirements have been invested in special, nonnegotiable U. S. Government securities. To illustrate, the total assets of the OASIS trust fund in May 1965 were $20.4 billion, of which $18.8 billion were invested in U. S. Government securities and $1.6 billion represented cash balances.

The government securities represent the receipts for social insurance. The incoming funds are merged with other cash receipts of the Federal government to the extent that they are not required for cash balances shortly to be paid out in benefits. As we have already seen, one of the side-effects of social-insurance programs is to bolster to a considerable extent the cash position of the government. The cash coming in from Social Security contributions may currently be spent for purposes of government not even remotely connected with Social Security. The government securities deposited with the trust funds constitute, as it were, an I.O.U. from the Treasury Department to the Social Security Administration. In case of need, as in the early 1960's, these special nonnegotiable government securities can be cashed in by the Social Security Administration. For this reason these securities which are owed by one government department to another are part of the gross national debt. In 1964 the debt held by U. S. Government investment accounts amounted to $60.6 billion; total public debt of the Federal government was $318.7 billion. It is clear, then, that any accumulation in trust funds, actually representing excess of cash receipts in social insurance over cash disbursements, increases the gross national debt.

Furthermore, the ratio between the total gross public debt and government-held debt is changing rapidly. In 1945 only 10 percent of the total gross debt was held by government accounts. In 1964 this ratio had doubled to more than 20 percent. In fact, whereas the total gross national debt between 1945 and 1964 rose only from $278.7 billion to $318.7 billion, or $40 billion, the government-held debt increased by $33 billion. This highlights the still-increasing significance of social-insurance systems not only for the cash balances of government but also for the public debt itself.

In social-insurance programs whenever the excess of receipts over expenditures for benefits is considerable, the economic impact of cash disbursements by the Federal government derived from these receipts for general purposes of government may well be more significant than the aggregate expenditures of beneficiaries.

It is important, however, to bear in mind that the inevitable expansion of the social-insurance sector within the economy does not contribute to economic growth, although it adds to the gross national product. Social-insurance programs represent a great improvement over older methods of poor relief and public assistance. To a much greater extent they retain the independence of beneficiaries. In this sense they are progressive but in economic terms they should not be mistaken as being dynamic.

SELECTED BIBLIOGRAPHY

Brinker, Paul. *Economic Insecurity and Social Security* (New York: Appleton Century Crofts, 1968).

Burns, Evelyne M. *Social Security and Public Policy* (New York: McGraw-Hill Book Company, 1961).

Gagliardo, Domenico. *American Social Insurance* (New York: Harper & Row, Publishers, 1949).

Haber, William, and Wilbur J. Cohen. *Social Security Programs, Problems and Policies* (Homewood, Ill.: Richard D. Irwin, Inc., 1962).

Turnbull, John, C. Arthur William, and Earl J. Cheit. *Economic and Social Security* (New York: The Ronald Press Company, 1959).

QUESTIONS FOR DISCUSSION

1. Using Table 21-2 as a reference guide, account for a indicate the significance of the relative changes in the breakdown of public expenditure as in cluded in this table.

2. A part of public-welfare and social-insurance payments are financed out of general taxes, and a part are financed out of contributory trust funds. Indicate the components of each category and note to what extent this distinction is meaningful.

3. Social-insurance programs are generally conceived in order to provide at least a limited income for those individuals, who because of age, illness, or other reasons are unable to sustain themselves. Does the present Social Security system fully meet this objective?

4. On balance, Social Security payments and collections have tended to cancel out. Is this de facto system of "pay as you go" social insurance good or bad? Why?

5. Present the arguments for and against Social Security payments as a system of "built-in stabilizers." Give your own position in the matter.

6. Indicate the nature and monetary management techniques for the Social Insurance Trust Fund.

7. The management of the Social Insurance Trust Fund has important implications for our understanding of the Federal debt structure. Indicate the nature and significance of these implications.

8. The next decade will bring some significant changes in the structure and magnitude of social-insurance contributions and payments. Indicate the trends likely to appear and interpret their possible effect in terms of macroeconomics.

Chapter

22

Old-Age and Survivors Insurance

The old-age insurance program is by far the largest scheme in Social Security. It also has been expanded almost continuously since its inception in 1935 to the point where it now covers virtually the total labor force of the United States. Originally, only the wage and salary earners who had been covered were eligible for retirement benefits. But already in 1939 widows, mothers, and children (where husband's death occurred before age 65) became eligible for benefits. In 1950 the coverage of old-age insurance was extended in a significant way. Up to that time only people in an employee status were included in social insurance. Now the self-employed were taken into the program. Furthermore, large numbers of employees hitherto exempted because they worked for nonprofit institutions were added. The Social Security Amendment of 1965 extended the coverage to self-employed physicians who up to that time had been opposed to their inclusion in order to retain a posture of consistency in their opposition to medical-care insurance, or—as they insist on calling it—"Socialized Medicine." With the adoption of "Medicare," discussed in Chapter 24, this attitude was no longer meaningful.

Over the years the OASDI underwent this continuous widening of its scope until it reached the status of an almost universal system. There were other significant changes of the original scheme also. The Social Security Act of 1935 provided for retirement at age 65. Now the retirement age has been lowered for women as well as men to 62, and widows can receive somewhat reduced benefits as early as age 60. The children's benefits under the earlier provisions normally stopped at age 18. The 1965 amendment extends benefits to eligible children in the age group 18–21 if they are attending school.

The Social Security legislation of the 1930's contained a gap which was causing great hardships. We refer to such cases in which a wage or salary earner became totally disabled long before he had reached retirement age.

If such a disability had been caused by an accident on a job covered by workmen's compensation, the partial or total loss of income could be compensated by the awarding of benefits. Workmen's compensation also provides payments to widows and children. If, however, the disability was not job-connected but was caused by a disabling illness, there were no ways of dealing with the grave consequences of such a condition other than general public assistance with all its implications of a means test.

In 1956 disability insurance was established as a scheme connected with OASIS. This new OASDI is available to totally disabled persons. Benefits are based on the earnings of the disabled person prior to the onset of his disability. In 1965 hospital insurance was added for people 65 years and older. The OASDI grew to OASDHI. As a result of the increase in the labor force and the extension of coverage in old age insurance there has been a steep increase in the number of people who are actually covered. This will be shown in Table 22-1.

TABLE 22-1
ESTIMATED PAID EMPLOYMENT AND COVERAGE IN OLD AGE, DISABILITY
AND HOSPITAL INSURANCE, 1940–1968

Month	Eligible for Coverage		
	Paid Employment (including self-employment)	Coverage in Effect	
		Total Number	As Percent of Paid Employment
December			
1940	47,100	30,400	64.5
1955	65,700	56,200	85.5
1965	74,500	66,400	89.1
1966	77,000	69,000	89.6
1967	77,900	69,900	89.7
1968	79,400	71,200	89.7

SOURCE: *Social Security Bulletin* (June 1969), Table Q-2.

As can be seen in Table 22-1 there remains only about 10 percent of the people in paid employment who have remained outside the coverage of OASDHI. The largest group consisting of 2.6 million were employees of Federal, state and local governments which had not been taken into the coverage. Another large group about 1.5 million consists of self-employed with earnings of less than $400 a year and another of those employees of nonprofit organizations who did not avail themselves of coverage which was opened up to them by the 1950 Amendment to the Social Security Act.

22-1. OLD-AGE INSURANCE BENEFITS AND RETIREMENT

Prior to World War I there was little talk of mandatory retirement. Life expectancy of people over 65 was far shorter than it is today and many people continued in employment until they were no longer able to function as a result of increasing physical or mental disability. Compulsory retirement was introduced after World War I in a number of Civil Service systems in Europe in order to accommodate war veterans desiring appointments in government agencies. Soon the practice of retiring older employees spread to the private sector of the economy, especially in countries which already had systems of old-age insurance.

The OASIS as set up in the Social Security Act of 1935 actually had a double purpose. It intended to provide minimum income for elderly people who at that time had in many cases lost most of their investments or had become dependent on their children, on charity, or on public assistance. At the same time, however, this social-insurance program was also designed to create incentives for retirement in order to increase the turnover of jobs and to provide more employment opportunities to younger people. Both objectives have retained their validity.

A person of retirement age can receive old-age insurance benefits only if he or she has actually retired from the labor force. However, this requirement applies only to people up to age 72. If people of that age or older have earnings from employment in excess of what is permitted to beneficiaries in the "younger" old-age brackets, they can retain them fully. The reason for this rule is the assumption that only very few people of this advanced age will still be employed so that their continued participation in the labor force will not, to any measurable degree, decrease employment opportunities for younger people.

The strength of the intent of the law to induce retirement from the labor market of people eligible for old-age insurance benefits was shown during the deliberation of the 1965 amendment. Up to that time beneficiaries were allowed annual earnings of $1,200 without suffering any deduction in their benefits. This permissible amount of earnings was raised only to $1,680. For all additional earnings between that amount and $2,700 a year, $1 in benefits is to be withheld for each $2 of annual earnings. That is, if a person actually earns $2,880, $600 is withheld from the annual benefit payment. For earnings of more than $2,880, a dollar per dollar deduction would be withheld.

While annual earnings are used in order to establish the amounts which have to be withheld, the beneficiary can receive full insurance payments for each month in which he had no more than $140 income from employment, including self-employment. In view of the great pressure on the labor market exercised by the large numbers of graduates from all school levels, the policy of inducing retirement and checking on its observation seems to be fully justified. The same considerations also induced the legislators to lower the retirement age to 62. At the same time, collective labor contracts have expanded already existing company-pension schemes to include incentives to retirement prior to the statutory age of 62 or 65. Again, in this area the main reason was the desire to increase the job turnover.

Beneficiaries up to the age of 72 must satisfy the Social Security Administration each year that they are actually retired or that their earnings did not exceed the limitation indicated in this section. It must be stressed, however, that this policy will bring about hardships to a large number of individuals if benefits plus permissible other income do not really enable old people to spend the rest of their lives in modest comfort.

22-2. SCOPE AND ADEQUACY OF OASIS AND DI

We have seen in the preceding section that 90 percent of people in paid employment are eligible for coverage for old age, disability, and hospital insurance. This represents a tremendous extension of coverage over the initial period of this scheme of social insurance in which in 1940 only 64.5 percent of the labor force was included. This extension of coverage in which preferential treatment was given to people who belonged to the higher age brackets in 1950 has led to a rapid increase in the total number of beneficiaries. This rise was accelerated further by the optional early retirement at the age of 62 which is now available to men and women. An additional factor in the expansion of the rolls of beneficiaries is the greater life expectancy of people 65 and over. On Table 22-2 the

TABLE 22-2
PRIMARY BENEFICIARIES IN OASIS
(Selected Years)
(in millions)

Month	Total Number	Beneficiaries		
		Without Reduction for Early Retirement	With Reduction for Early Retirement	
			Number	Percent of Total
December				
1958	6,920,677	6,351,854	568,823	8.2
1963	10,263,331	7,662,499	2,600,832	25.3
1968	12,421,371	7,433,671	4,987,700	40.2

SOURCE: *Social Security Bulletin* (June 1969), Table Q-5.

rapid increase in the number of beneficiaries will be shown. It must be remembered, however, that the figures given there refer only to primary beneficiaries in old age insurance. It does not include wives' or husbands' benefits, children, widowed mothers, widowers and widows' and parents' beneficiaries. Table 22-2 shows that a considerable proportion of claimants are availing themselves of the opportunity to retire at the age of 62 although this brings about a permanent reduction in their monthly benefits. For instance, in 1968 average monthly benefits without reduction would have amounted to $107.70. After the reduction it was $85.67. Women are more willing to retire at the age of 62 than men. In 1968, 53.4 percent of the female claimants were early retirees whereas only 30.3 percent of the men chose retirement at that age.

Actually more than 10 percent of the total population are receiving income from the old age pension system. In order to demonstrate the full scope a breakdown of the total population involved in OASIS will be shown in Table 22-3 for the last month of 1968.

TABLE 22-3
TYPES OF BENEFITS IN OASIS, DECEMBER, 1968

Total	24,560,374
Retired Workers	12,420,742
Disabled Workers	1,295,300
Wives and Husbands of	
Retired workers	2,645,407
Disabled workers	253,198
Children of	
Retired workers	518,635
Deceased workers	2,490,398
Disabled workers	786,636
Widowed mothers	504,916
Widows and Widowers	2,937,867
Parents	31,596
Special Age-72 Beneficiaries	675,679

SOURCE: *Social Security Bulletin* (June 1969), Table Q-14.

So far in this section we have dealt with the scope of old age insurance which has been widened over the years to the point that 90 percent of the labor force are covered and that, as we have shown in Table 22-3, over 24.5 million people were receiving benefits either as retired workers or as wives, widows, children, or parents of primary beneficiaries. Now we must turn our attention to the question of the adequacy of the benefit formula and of the actual benefits to which people are entitled in old age or disability insurance. There exists, of course, a close relationship between components of the formula and the monthly benefits which are granted.

Generally speaking earnings are covered only up to a maximum amount per year. The benefit is based on the average of earnings during the total period of coverage after 1950. For instance if in the last ten years prior to retirement a wage or salary earner had a yearly income of $9,800 a year, only $7,800 can be used for computing the benefits. That is to say that all earnings above the ceiling are outside of coverage for social security. There is no growth factor which could be applied to narrow the gap between benefits and past earnings. In the United States in the past an upward adjustment of maximum covered earnings was always lagging behind the actual rise in aggregate wages and salaries. Congressional procedures do not lend themselves to speedy adjustments. For instance, the maximum covered earnings in the period 1951–1954 was established at \$3,600 but at that time 75 percent of the families already had an income of \$3,000 and more. Over the years maximum earnings were raised rather slowly by Congress. In 1967 it was proposed to lift the maximum earnings to \$10,800 a year but Congress allowed for only \$7,800. But at that time 50 percent of the families already had an income in excess of \$7,974. While family income cannot be identified exclusively with the earnings of the principle bread winner, the comparisons just made show that the lag which was becoming pronounced after World War II has not been overcome. When Congress raised maximum covered earnings to \$7,800 it also increased monthly benefits to a maximum of \$218.00. But this is an empty promise for the 1970's and 1980's. This maximum amount can be reached only if a claimant has been in the \$7,800 group long enough to establish this amount as average earnings. It has been calculated that under the 1967 law it would have taken until about the turn of the century for beneficiaries to become eligible for the maximum benefits. Actually average benefits awarded to retired workers in 1969 were less than half of the maximum benefits written into the law in 1967. If we allow for wives' benefits which add 50 percent to the benefit of retired workers this means that a married couple obtaining this average benefit award in 1969 would still have a benefit income of less than \$2,000. Average earnings in the total private economy in 1969 were about \$6,000. It follows that retirement plus wives' benefits together would amount only to slightly over 30 percent of the prior earnings of the period immediately preceding retirement. For the retired worker alone the benefits would be only just about 20 percent of average yearly earnings in the total private economy.

In the fall of 1969 the Nixon Administration proposed an across-the-board increase in retirement benefits of 10 percent. Congress went beyond it and late in 1969 legislated a 15 percent increase in Social Security payments beginning with January 1970. But since 1967 when the previous adjustment of benefits had been made the Consumer Price Index had risen from 116 percent to 128 percent. Prices continued to rise in 1970 so that even the 15 percent increase voted by Congress merely enabled beneficiaries to retain the meager purchasing power which they had in recent years. Proposals are being made to restructure the old age insurance system by raising the earnings ceiling. The figure of \$10,800 which was frequently mentioned late in the 1960's seems to be becoming rapidly obsolete because wages in current dollars continue to rise at a rate of more than 6 percent per annum.

When Old Age Insurance was introduced in the Social Security Act of 1935, the benefits were not designed to provide a complete replacement of the former earnings of the recipient. Two additional sources of income of the aged were expected to supplement the insurance benefits; income from individual savings and retirement benefits from employers. However, the Old Age Insurance payments were originally geared to a level of 30 percent of the earnings. Despite the seven amendments to the Social Security Act providing for higher benefits, the replacement effect of benefit payments has been stabilized on the 20 percent level. At the same time rapidly rising prices in recent years have eroded not only the purchasing power of the benefit payments themselves but also of the two other forms of income expected to enable the aged population to maintain a moderate standard of living above the poverty level. Despite numerous extensions and increases Old Age Benefits in the 1960's and 1970's provided a less favorable ratio and replacement with regard to earnings than in the 1940's. In fact the system far from improving has lost ground and makes a lesser contribution to the income maintenance of retirees now than was the case when the law was enacted.

It should be clear from the foregoing paragraph that this chronic lag cannot be cured by attaching a cost of living escalator to Social Security benefits. We have already seen in Chapter 9 that such wage clauses have been discontinued in many union agreements in favor of a general system of automatic wage increases scheduled at stated intervals during the duration of a contract. They will take place even at a time of price stability. It can easily be seen, therefore, that especially in periods in which the economy is operating normally and not in the overheated condition of the late 1960's, the discrepancy between average wage levels and social security benefits would continue to grow to the disadvantage of the millions of beneficiaries.

In the affluent economy of the United States the structure of old age insurance, dating back to the 1930's, far from reducing the scope of poverty has not prevented the condition whereby 22.2 percent of all families with a head 65 years or over were poor in 1966.[1] This is more than double the incidence of poverty of families with a head of the family less than 65 years old. That is to say that the transition from employment to retirement means a substantial decline in income and the descent into poverty of a considerable number of people who before their retirement were not in that category at all. To illustrate, in 1966 there were 7.689 million families with a head aged 55 to 64 of whom 800,000 were poor. In the same year there were 6.929 million families with a head of 65 years and over of whom 1.538 million were poor. For at least half of these 22.2 percent of the old population the expectation that their other income, together with Social Security benefits would prevent their remaining or falling into poverty was not realized.

[1]Mollie Orshansky, "The Shape of Poverty in 1966," *Social Security Bulletin* (March 1968), Table 7.

The great difference between earnings from employment in the years preceeding retirement and benefits is brought about by the adherence to the concept of "average earnings" during the duration of covered employment with the sole exception of permitting the dropping of the five lowest years of earnings in the computation of total covered income. Another modification was that lower covered earnings prior to 1950 could also be disregarded under certain circumstances. Now most of the male beneficiaries will have had a 40 plus period of years during which they were covered for old age insurance. Most women will have fewer years of coverage. But according to the method of computing average earnings for virtually the full period of coverage, the benefits of people ending up eventually in the maximum covered employment bracket whatever it may be at the time of retirement, will be weighted down by decades in which they found themselves in lower wage classes. This condition is aggravated by the fact that ever since the 1940's wages and salaries have moved up continuously, in the latter part of the 1960's at annual rates of about 6 percent. These increases which up to 1965 at least reflected annual rises in productivity widened the gap between last pay levels and monthly benefits even more. Under the current system retired workers are excluded from the general productivity and income gains of the economy. Here, progress for those under 65 supported by rising efficiency and output turns into severe economic retrogression for those 65 years and over. Such an unfavorable result was not foreseen and perhaps not foreseeable in the 1930's when the Social Security Act was written. In those days prices were low compared to the 1920's and they were stable. As a result there was very little movement in earnings. Now, if this condition would have continued, the old age benefits while still not ample would not have been such a small proportion of the last earnings as they are today for the majority of covered people above the lowest wage category. The question arises whether in the American economy of our age which must be kept growing, the average earning concepts used for the computation of benefits devised in the 1930's should be permitted to operate in the entirely different setting of the 1970's. The answer is an unqualified NO. There are feasible alternate methods of maintaining a system of old age insurance on a benefit level which is far closer to former earnings than is the case today under the Social Security Act. We will study this in the next section.

22-3. METHODS OF "DYNAMIZING" OLD-AGE INSURANCE

As we have seen in Part III, employment stability at or near full employment requires continuous growth of the GNP at a high rate. Hence, aggregate wages and salaries as well as wage rates must continue to rise because they are the most important factor in consumer spending. Furthermore, productivity is certain to continue rising each year. If old-age insurance benefits remain tied to *past* earnings, as they are even under the stepped-up maximum covered earnings of $7,300, to an ever-increasing degree they will get out of line with current income of wage and salary earners still in the labor force, and also with the consumer price index. It must be said, therefore, that there is a high degree of built-in obsolescence in the American old-age insurance program. A study of old-age insurance systems in other highly advanced countries shows that this situation is not inevitable.

Canada, like a number of European countries such as Switzerland, has had since 1951 a national system of old-age pensions covering the total old population regardless of previous employment status. Rather low flat rates were paid to every person 70 years and over having had a certain minimum residence in Canada.[2] In the course of the years these rates were raised from an original $40 per person—that is, $80 per couple—to $75 in October 1963. A Canadian couple 70 years or over, therefore, has been receiving since then a monthly combined pension of 150 Canadian dollars. This compares favorably with the average primary benefits plus wife's benefits of $121.23 which, as we have seen in Sec. 21-2, were due a married couple, both 65 or over, receiving benefits for the first time in May 1965 in the United States. On the other hand, it must not be forgotten that these pensions start only at age 70. However, a retirement test is not required in order to establish eligibility. Seen in a longer-run prospective, this flat-rate pension system is subject to the same type of erosion that is operating inexorably on American benefit formulas. In order to overcome these unfavorable effects, a new Canada Pension Plan was enacted in 1965. It introduces a contributory OASIS. In the initial ten years this legislation provides for a flexible pension index according to which the old-age pension based on the legislation of 1951 will be continued for those already eligible. For those working throughout the period 1967–76, previous earnings will be made the basis of computing benefits and will be subject to a revaluation of 2.5 percent for each $100 of monthly earnings. Thus the benefits that can be claimed by eligible people in 1975 will be substantially higher than the flat pensions in force at $75 per month since 1963. However, these pensions will continue so that combined with old-age insurance based on the legislation of 1965 they will represent a substantially increased total income for recipients of the combined pension. In 1975 single beneficiaries with average monthly earnings of $400 will receive total monthly payments of $175. This will be about the same as projected *average* benefits in the United States even after the 1969 increase of 15 percent.

For the period after 1976 an entirely different system of computing old-

---

[2]See Daniel S. Gerig and Robert J. Myers "Canada Pension Plan of 1965," *Social Security Bulletin* (November 1965).

age insurance benefits will go into effect. They will be based on an "Earnings Index." Broadly speaking, this will be a statistical device which will help keep old-age benefits more or less in line with increases in wages and salaries as they are reported under Canadian income-tax regulations. Since this system will go into effect only after 1976 it would be highly conjectural to predict what benefit rates will be established on the basis of the earnings index. It is clear, however, that such a scheme will overcome the great shortcoming of the current old-age insurance system in the United States by readjusting pensions each year to the level of current earnings of those still in the labor force.

The Canadian law provides for a stepping-down of the current retirement age of 70 to 65 in 1970. Contributions to the Canada pension plan, to be levied from employers and employees, started with a combined rate of 7.7 percent in 1966 and are scheduled to rise to 9.7 percent in 1973. However, the $75 a month flat-rate pension will be financed as before out of general taxation.

Old age insurance in **Germany** goes back to the 1880's when it came into being simultaneously with compulsory public health insurance. Originally the system was devised only for manual workers but included from the very beginning domestic employees. Actually this initial social security system was a combined retirement and disability insurance. The benefits are still called "Invalidity Rents." At the age of 65 invalidity did not have to be proven, it was assumed to be sufficient to warrant retirement. But in case of earlier disability benefits could be granted if a medical examination established the fact that the worker was no longer able to perform his job. Contributions had to be paid by the employer through the purchase of invalidity stamps at post offices. These stamps were pasted into books issued to the insured. The book provided enough space for stamps covering two-year periods. A minimum of five books is required to establish full coverage. From the beginning widows of the recipients of invalidity rents and minor children were eligible for survivor benefits. Just before World War I old age benefits were also introduced for white-collar employees. However, for this group which is still rapidly increasing due to the continuing labor force transformation, an entirely separate, centralized insurance institute which is located in West Berlin was established. From the very beginning contributions, split 50–50 between employers and employees, were much higher than for blue-collar workers and accordingly monthly benefits also amounted to substantially higher monthly figures. Furthermore the maximum covered earnings extended from the beginning to the upper reaches of middle income. In 1969 maximum covered earnings were extended to all salary earners. As became apparent to everyone in the 1960's, the German Mark (DM) was undervalued in relation to the dollar. A conservative estimate would arrive at the conclusion that the maximum earnings covered under the German white-collar system would be at least the equivalent of $10,800 which was proposed but not accepted by Congress in the 1967 Social Security Amendment.

The two German old age pension systems survived the inflation after World War I and after World War II. However, the manual worker insurance did face deficits after World War II because it had become imperative to increase monthly benefits whereas accumulated contributions of pre-war periods had been eroded by inflation. The white-collar insurance fared substantially better due to their investments in mortgage loans and other assets which were better protected against a decline in value through inflation.

When after the stabilization of the currency in 1948, it became necessary to put both systems on the basis of the new monetary unit, the suggestion to merge the blue-collar and the white-collar old age insurance into one system like that established under the Social Security Act was rejected. One argument was that the white-collar system although committed to far higher benefits was in much better financial shape than the blue-collar system. The latter required subsidies from the Federal Government even in the later 1960's. One reason for the continued financial weakness was that the blue-collar system lost every year about 100,000 insured workers through their promotion into white-collar occupations. In this way contributions declined while benefits increased due to the rising number of people 65 years and over. In 1969 it was decided that the white-collar insurance should contribute substantial amounts each year to the blue-collar system to compensate it for the loss of blue-collar insured persons and the resulting drop in contributions.

Originally the German old age system was structured very similarly to the American plan as embodied in the legislation of 1935. Benefits were based on covered average earnings. It must be remembered, however, that in the white-collar system covered earnings reached into far higher levels than is the case in the United States. However, when the time had come to adjust the German system to the post World War II situation, a commission of experts from universities who had received the assignment to review the principles underlying German social security analyzed the problem within the context of macrodynamics as developed in Part III of this text. They stressed in their findings which became known at the "Professors' Report" that a number of growth factors must be applied in order to achieve a satisfactory benefit formula. Past earnings are still the basis for the computation of the basic monthly retirement income. But this income is not frozen. The rents have become "dynamic rents" because they are kept with certain time lags in a constant relation with wage levels. The dynamic rent principle implies that benefits should rise with productivity, current wages and the Gross National Product.

Each year a specially designated committee of experts is called upon to assess the changes in general levels of wages and salaries. They must then reach a conclusion with regard to the percentage increase of all old-age insurance benefits which are to be kept continuously in line with the plateau reached for the income of those still employed in the labor force. In recent years this situation has sometimes led to very substantial increases in old-age insurance benefits, occasionally reaching 9 percent or slightly more in a single year. These increases of the employed and the retired workers incomes were at all times in excess of upward changes in cost of living. They represent, therefore, an increase in real income which the rather vast proportion of the German population on retirement pay was able to participate in under this system of dynamic rent.

Table 22-4 will show the relation between wage level increases and old age benefit increases from 1959 through 1965.

TABLE 22-4
WAGE AND BENEFIT INCREASES IN THE GERMAN OASIS

Year	Wage Increases (percent)	Benefit Increases (percent)
1959	5.1	6.1
1960	8.9	5.9
1961	10.2	5.4
1962	8.7	5.0
1963	6.1	6.6
1964	8.1	8.2
1965	8.0	9.4

SOURCE: *Research Report No. 13*, U. S. Dept. of Health, Education and Welfare: "Old-Age and Sickness Insurance in West Germany in 1965."

The effectiveness of this dynamic principle can be shown in the substantial rise of the amount of monthly pensions in German Marks. In the blue-collar system benefits rose from 144.50 in 1959 to 223.00 in 1965. In the white-collar system the increase was from 231.60 to 371.10. It should be noted that the growth factor is being applied to all pensions in force, not only to newly awarded benefits. If we compare the average monthly pension in the white-collar system in 1965 with the $78.00 which was the average old age benefit for a retired worker under the American OASIS we come to the reluctant conclusion that in terms of purchasing power, based on the conservative 2:1 real ratio between dollars and marks the average white-collar benefits in Germany were $2\frac{1}{2}$ times higher than American rates and the difference in purchasing power in monthly benefits for blue-collar workers in Germany was at least $1.25 in their favor as compared to American beneficiaries. In the meantime benefits in the United States have risen but so have the pensions in Germany.

Naturally especially the German white-collar pension system requires high contributions. They were raised in the 1960's to 16 percent of the gross earnings to be shared equally by employers and employees. The German system, therefore, imposes 6 percent more in terms of contributions than the maximum levies contemplated in this country for OASIS for the years 1973–1975 which will be 10 percent to which have to be added 0.65 percent for hospital insurance. However, this difference is somewhat reduced if we consider the extremely high corporate allocations for private pension plans which we have shown in Table 9-3 of this text. If we take this into account, total public and private contributions to employee pension plans in this country are not substantially lower than those in West Germany.

The Canadian and the West Germany experience cannot be dismissed with a statement that the introduction of a growth factor for all retirement pensions in force cannot be adopted in the United States because it would be "inflationary" or would unduly increase employment cost. It should be added that this dynamic principle is entirely different from the frequently made suggestion that a cost of living escalator should be attached to the benefits. This really would be missing the point of the dynamic rent system. A cost of living escalator would of course be better than the current situation in which monthly benefits are frozen while the consumer price index continues to rise, a condition sometimes retroactively and ineffectively remedied by belated legislation. But the Canadian and German system make it possible for the retirees to participate in the overall gains of the system and actually share in the increase in real income. Anyone who maintains that this cannot be done in this country is underrating the strength of the American economy if well managed and operating under rational social priorities.

SELECTED BIBLIOGRAPHY

Epstein, Leonor A. "Income of the Aged in 1962: First Findings of the 1963 Survey of the Aged," *Social Security Bulletin.* U.S. Department of Health, Education, and Welfare (Washington, D.C.: U.S. Government Printing Office, March 1964).
Palumore, E. "Work Experience and Earnings of the Aged in 1962," *Social Security Bulletin.* U.S. Department of Health, Education, and Welfare (Washington, D.C.: U.S. Government Printing Office, June 1964).
Trafton, Marie C. "Earnings of Older Workers and Retired Worker Beneficiaries," *Social Security Bulletin.* U.S. Department of Health, Education, and Welfare (Washington, D.C.: U.S. Government Printing Office, May 1965).

QUESTIONS FOR DISCUSSION

1. Outline the principal later modifications to the Social Security Act of 1935 with respect to the question of old age insurance.

2. What stipulations does the Social Security Act make about retirement age, additional earnings, and the related conditions which must be met by the recipients of old-age insurance?

3. Aside from the specific aims of the Social Security Act, that legislation had some very important additional aims which are significant in terms of labor market conditions. What are their aims, and what are the implications thereof?

4. In 1967, significant changes in the Social Security Act would seem to have important implications for the future. To the best of your ability, analyze these implications in terms of macroeconomics.

5. What are some of the important shortcomings of the American system of social insurance?

6. Outline the principal features of the German and Canadian versions of old-age insurance programs, giving special attention to the relative advantages of each in comparison to the American plan.

7. In light of your answer to Question 6, formulate a brief but specific approach by which the American plan could be significantly improved.

Chapter

23

Unemployment Insurance

Unemployment compensation was introduced in most countries a considerable time after other social-insurance programs, such as old-age benefits and health insurance, had already been inaugurated. One reason for this lag was the difficulty of dealing with unemployment in terms of an insurance scheme. Even today, as we shall see, unemployment insurance can only cope with relatively short periods of unemployment.

In the United States unemployment insurance was introduced in the Social Security Act simultaneously with old-age insurance in 1935. However, although both schemes are contained in the same law, the structure provided for unemployment compensation is entirely different from that of old-age insurance. The latter scheme is entirely Federal and is operated by the Social Security Administration down to the local level in field offices. Unemployment compensation is operated by the State Employment Services. More important even is the fact that the Social Security Act of 1935 merely established a framework for unemployment-compensation systems by creating a situation which for all practical purposes compelled state legislatures to enact unemployment-compensation laws. This was done by introducing a Federal payroll tax on employers in order to finance unemployment compensation with the proviso that if states levied a similar tax, this tax could be used to the extent of 90 percent to offset the Federal unemployment tax liability. The remaining 10 percent is earmarked for administrative expenses. These funds are sent to the Federal government and are administered by the Bureau of Employment Security. The state employment services have to submit their budgets to this Federal agency. In this way the Federal government is in a position to exercise a great deal of control over the personnel procedures and the operations of the state employment services.

Immediately after Pearl Harbor the Executive Office of the President took over the operation of the state employment services. Soon they were integrated with the Manpower Commission, which was also in charge of the draft. In this way the manpower policies of the war economy could be coordinated, especially the handling of cases of deferment of essential workers. Following the end of hostilities in World War II demands were made for an immediate return of the public employment services to the states. The appeal of this "states' rights movement" was so strong that objections voiced by the Administration were overruled. Actually, however, the very strict control over state budgets outlined above remained in the hands of the Federal government and is exercised by the Social Security Administration, Bureau of Employment Security. One part of this administration is the United States Employment Service (USES), which plays an important role in standardizing procedures of the State Employment Services.

23-1. THE GENERAL SCOPE OF UNEMPLOYMENT COMPENSATION

While coverage of old-age insurance has been extended steadily since the enactment of the Social Security Act of 1935 to the point where it is all-inclusive, the coverage of unemployment compensation has been extended very little. Obviously, the self-employed cannot be covered by unemployment compensation, which must be limited to the large segment of the labor force having employee status. Furthermore, the rather considerable number of people working in small businesses employing only one or two workers are not covered by unemployment compensation in most states. In many states, however, the minimum employment is still four or more, as in Illinois, New Jersey, Texas, and West Virginia. On the other hand, some states cover even one-employee firms. Among these states are New York, Pennsylvania, and California. Table 23-1 shows the great discrepancy be-

TABLE 23-1
TOTAL WAGE AND SALARY WORKERS AND
THOSE COVERED BY UNEMPLOYMENT
INSURANCE 1963–1967
(thousands)

Year	Total Nonagricultural Wage and Salary Workers	Employment Covered By Unemployment Insurance
1963	56.702	48.434
1964	58.332	49.637
1965	60.832	51.580
1966	64.035	54.739
1967	66.030	56.341

SOURCE: *Economic Report of the President* (January 1969), Tables B-27 and B-26.

tween the total number of wage and salary workers and that of the workers covered by unemployment insurance in 1963.

Covered employment as shown in Table 23-1 includes wage and salary workers participating in state unemployment compensation systems, those Federal employees taken into unemployment compensation in 1955, and programs for railroad retirement and unemployment compensation for ex-service men. The inclusion of the latter group explains the great increase in covered employment between 1955 and 1967. Whereas in 1960 about 8 million nonagricultural wage and salary workers were not covered by unemployment compensation, the gap in 1967 was 9.7 million. However in terms of percentages the gap dropped from 14 percent in 1960 to 10 percent in 1967. We must realize, however, that in both years agricultural workers are excluded from the total. If we "think the un-thinkable" and include farm laborers, still numbering 1.3 million in 1967, the gap, of course, becomes much wider. One of the main reasons for the discrepancy between total wage and salary earners and those covered by unemployment insurance is the fact already mentioned at the beginning of this section that in a large number of states, employees in firms not em-ploying more than four workers for at least 20 weeks a year are excluded.

In 1969 the Nixon Administration proposed an extension of coverage in unemployment compensation which was enacted in 1970. However the proposal to include farm workers was defeated in the House Ways and Means Committee. On the other hand coverage of nonfarm workers was extended to about 4 million wage and salary workers hitherto left out. If we add to those not covered by this decision the 1.2 million hired farm workers, then there will still be about 12 million wage and salary workers left outside unemployment compensation. This is in sharp contrast to the all-comprehensive old age and survivor insurance systems now existing in the United States. The Committee also raised the amount of covered earnings which is scheduled to reach $4,200 in January 1972. Provisions are also made to extend the benefit period by 13 weeks whenever either the national unemployment rate or that of a state exceed 4.5 percent of the work force during a period of 3 months. This is a much-needed improve-ment. Whenever unemployment is increasing persistent unemployment especially of 26 weeks and more tends to rise sharply because employers immediately raise their employability standards when labor becomes somewhat more abundant. As we will see in the next section of this chapter the assets of unemployment insurance are enough to support such improve-ments in the benefit period. To finance these changes, Federal taxes on em-ployers were raised to 0.5 percent on covered payrolls.

The extension of the benefit period would reduce to some extent the great discrepancy between total unemployment and the number of re-cipients of unemployment compensation. For example, unemployment in 1967 was reported as averaging 2.9 million people. For the same year in-sured unemployment averaged 1.27 million people.[1] It follows inevitably

---

[1]Economic Report of the President (January 1969), Tables B–22 and B–26.

that there is a significant discrepancy between unemployment rates as a percentage of the civilian labor force and as a percentage of covered employment. The first rate was 3.8 percent in 1967 and the latter was 2.7 percent. For this reason figures of insured unemployment are of limited value in accounting for total unemployment. Actually, insured unemployment figures lose much of their significance in periods of large-scale unemployment because a considerable number of those unemployed will have exhausted their benefits even if they are extended to 39 weeks. They remain unemployed but become invisible in the total picture of unemployment-compensation statistics. In fact, insured unemployment may decline while total unemployment continues to rise.

Unemployment-insurance statistics while unreliable with regard to total unemployment are nevertheless useful for spotting trends in employment. This is particularly true of the weekly reports on initial claims in unemployment insurance. If these claims rise in a particular week over initial claims in the corresponding week of the preceding year, or if the reverse relationship exists for these two dates, it is fair to assume that unemployment in general is either rising or falling.

The impending increase of covered earnings in unemployment compensation to $4,800 will eliminate one of the greatest shortcomings of this social insurance system which had been permitted to continue far too long. The original intention of most state compensation laws was to assure weekly compensation benefits which would be 50 percent of the previous earnings. In 1945 already weekly benefits had dropped to 41.6 percent of prior weekly earnings. In 1963 they had declined to 34.6 percent. Average weekly benefits increased from $18.77 in 1945 to $43.43 in 1968. Now if you consider the consumer price index we see that there was a virtual doubling of prices between 1945 when the index was 62.7 percent on the basis of 1957 to 1959 = 100 and 1968 when the index was 120.9 percent. This clearly indicates that unemployed persons receiving benefit payments at the average level for the nation as a whole are worse off than they were in the 1940's.

In recent years many states have raised maximum benefits substantially. In some states, for instance in Connecticut, Illinois, and Indiana, dependents' allowances have been added. In the first-mentioned state this could bring weekly benefits up to a maximum of $90.00 for a family with six dependents, at which point no further dependent benefits would be granted. New York and California have maximum benefits of $65.00 a week but there are no dependents' allowances in these states. In many other states maximum benefits are substantially lower than those prevailing in the states just mentioned. This is particularly true of Texas, Virginia, Oklahoma, and most of the other Southern and border states. It should be noted, however, that the two newest of the United States,

Alaska and Hawaii, have very high maximum rates for unemployment benefits.

While there is great diversity in weekly unemployment benefits there is far greater uniformity with regard to the maximum benefit period which in most states is still 26 weeks. However some states with low maximum benefits, for instance, Oklahoma, have lengthened the benefit period to 39 weeks. On the other hand we encounter a 22-week maximum in South Carolina.

The great diversity in weekly benefits and even in the benefit period is due to the fact that according to the Social Security Act the several states were given the right to write their own unemployment compensation laws. However, the resulting diversity has actually led to great inequities for people who happen to work in one state rather than another. In 1969 President Nixon proposed national standards for unemployment benefits bringing them back to the original intent of the law which assumed that benefits would be about 50 percent of the weekly earnings of the unemployed in all states. He also suggested a lengthening of the benefit period to 39 weeks in situations where persistent unemployment of a significant scope was developing.

Unlike contributions to old-age insurance, which are shared equally by employers and employees, contributions to unemployment insurance are levied only on the employer. This different treatment is derived from an ideological and theoretical approach to unemployment insurance as it prevailed among some of the original pioneers of social insurance in the United States. We will encounter the practical consequences of these ideas in the financial analysis of unemployment insurance.

23-2. FINANCIAL STATUS OF UNEMPLOYMENT INSURANCE AND THE ISSUE OF EXPERIENCE RATING

Because of the large-scale exclusions from coverage in unemployment insurance of wage and salary workers and also the legal limitations of the duration of the benefit period, the trust fund for unemployment insurance in the United States has been maintained in sound shape. In 1960 5.6 percent of the civilian labor force was unemployed; in the same year insured unemployment was only 4.8 percent of covered unemployment. Throughout the period since the inauguration of unemployment insurance, wide differences have existed between total and covered unemployment. Nevertheless there are periods when benefits paid out of state accounts exceed contributions collected. This ratio between collections and benefits changes rapidly with even small increases and decreases in covered unemployment.

As can be seen from Table 23-2 the balance in the trust fund at the end of a calendar year declined from $6.9 billion in 1958 to $5.8 billion in 1961. It was not until 1963–1964 that the balance returned to the level of

TABLE 23-2
FINANCIAL STATUS OF UNEMPLOYMENT INSURANCE
1958–1968
(in billions)

Calendar Years	Total Assets	Invested in U.S. Gov't. Securities	Deposits and Transfers	Interest	Withdrawals for Benefits	Balance at End of Period
1958	7.2	7.1	1.6	0.198	3.5	6.9
1959	6.9	6.9	2.1	0.178	2.3	6.9
1960	6.6	6.6	2.3	0.194	2.7	6.6
1961	5.8	5.8	2.5	0.176	3.5	5.8
1962	6.3	6.3	2.9	0.173	2.7	6.3
1963	6.7	6.7	3.0	0.194	2.8	6.6
1964	7.4	7.4	3.0	0.225	2.6	7.3
1965	8.6	8.5	2.9	0.266	2.2	8.3
1966	10.2	10.2	2.9	0.329	1.8	9.8
1967	11.2	11.2	2.7	0.398	2.0	10.8
1968	12.3	12.1	2.5	0.460	2.0	11.7

SOURCE: Table Q-18, *Social Security Bulletin* (June 1969).

1958 but since then there has been a steep increase to the all time high of $11.7 billion in 1968. In the first year of the period shown in Table 23-2 insured unemployment as a percentage of covered employment reached the post-World War II high of 6.4 percent. After a small drop another high at 5.6 percent was reached in 1961. Since then insured unemployment as a percent of covered unemployment has dropped steadily to a low of 2.2 percent. It should be noted that even in that year of an "overheated" economy total unemployment as a percentage of the civilian labor force was 3.6 percent. The developments after 1965 seem to indicate clearly that when the economy is reaching full employment, unemployment covered by insurance is declining faster than total unemployment which also considers those not covered by unemployment compensation. The rapid increase in trust fund balances at the end of calendar years after 1965 shows the ability of the system as set up at present to build up substantial reserves in a short period of time. On the other hand reserves are being utilized, it seems, whenever covered unemployment reaches 5 percent or more of insured unemployment. But due to the 26-weeks' standard limitation of benefit periods and the lagging behind—despite recent increases in some states—of average weekly benefit payments, the decline in balances during periods of some unemployment is at a slower rate than the increase in these balances in periods of full employment.

The rapid accumulation of assets in unemployment insurance occurred while the maximum covered earnings in unemployment insurance remained limited to the anachronistic pre-World War II level of $3,000 a year. In 1969 it was proposed to lift this ceiling and to take in about 5 million more wage and salary workers who were excluded from unemployment benefits in the original law. It was further proposed to create the possibility of extending the maximum benefit period from 26 to 39 weeks in periods of more persistent general unemployment.

The proposed changes leave intact the right of states to levy lower contributions to unemployment insurance from employers who have a good record of employment stability but collecting a higher rate up to the maximum of 2.7 percent from firms with a high labor turnover contributing to unemployment. It is, however, necessary to re-examine the validity of the assumptions which originally led to the adoption of the optional *experience-rating system*.

The ideological root of this scheme is to be found in a doctrine widely advocated by experts in social insurance in the 1930's that only employers should be liable for unemployment-insurance contributions because they cause unemployment by laying off workers. This argument, which was translated into the employer only principle in unemployment insurance in the United States, was amazingly näive even for the 1930's. It assumed that employers were in some way "guilty" of generating unemployment by lay-offs, completely overlooking the fact that firms try to maximize profits at all times—a policy which implies the desire to employ as many workers as are warranted by an optimum relation between input and output. These relations are determined by impersonal market forces and usually do not create individual or collective guilt. Nevertheless, this ideology was extended to the theory and practice of experience rating of contributions to unemployment conpensation.

The basic reasoning of this scheme of flexible rates is that employers will be deterred from laying off workers if they then have to pay a higher rate of contribution to unemployment insurance. Conversely, employers will be encouraged to retain workers in exchange for the reward of having to pay only a minimum rate of contribution. It should be stressed that this line of reasoning assumes extreme marginalism in decision making with regard to the number of workers employed in a given period of production. Inasmuch as the range of contributions normally is between 2.7 and 1.0 percent of payrolls up to about $3,000 a year per worker, it is extremely difficult to see at what point an employer could be either penalized for laying off workers or rewarded for not laying them off—if the additional contributions or savings in contributions are compared with savings in total employment cost in the first and additional employment cost in the latter case.

In practice, the system rewards stable industries that experience only small fluctuation in employment due to the steadiness and relative inelasticity of the demand for their product. On the other hand, firms operating in a more unstable market with wide swings in the levels of demand and employment are punished for being in an unstable industrial group rather than in a more stable one. Furthermore, experience rating favors big business for the simple reason that large firms can afford the luxury of not fixing their employment schedule exactly at the margin, whereas smaller firms must come much nearer to it in their employment practices.

In the 1930's this system of experience rating, whereby an employer's contributions would either be raised or lowered according to his record of employment stability or layoffs, was known as the "Wisconsin Plan" because that state had introduced it. When the Social Security Act was before Congress, vigorous attempts were made, without success, to write experience rating into the Federal law. But since the Social Security Act left to the states a great deal of leeway with regard to the actual system of unemployment insurance they wanted to enact, the several states were free to adopt either uniform contributions or experience rating. In the beginning most states adopted uniform contributions. But when the unemployment-insurance trust fund began to rise and unemployment remained low during the 1940's, eventually all states introduced one or the other system of experience rating. The inducement to do so was very great because experience rating meant some savings to large numbers of firms under those favorable conditions of the labor market.

The objection to experience rating made in those days—that it is difficult to administer because the employment records of a very large number of firms have to be watched—is no longer valid in the present era of automated data processing. However, the main criticism of the system remains relevant. It is that experience rating cannot be a significant factor in the stabilization of employment, while it most certainly leads to an endemic financial weakness of the structure of unemployment insurance in a recession. Uniform contributions to unemployment insurance can very well be combined with flexibility. If, in a period of protracted full employment, reserves in unemployment insurance seem to rise too fast, it would be possible to lower the contribution. But this should be done uniformly and without jeopardizing the soundness of the system and its social efficiency in the long run.

23-3. SOME SUGGESTIONS FOR IMPROVEMENT IN UNEMPLOYMENT INSURANCE

We have seen that the Social Security Administration of the Federal government exercises direct control over budgets, personnel policies, and procedures of the public employment services—which, however, remain state agencies. Actually a very high degree of standardization has been achieved in the use of forms and statistical methods. The Social Security Act of 1935 opened the way to this development because it required that unemployment compensation be paid through state employment services. An organic link between the administration of unemployment compensation and of public placement services was therefore established from the beginning. However, on top of this rather firm and uniform administrative structure there now exists fifty different sets of unemployment-insurance laws which, as we have seen, vary widely even in contiguous labor markets extending over the area of several states. A reexamination of the current American system of unemployment compensation might start, therefore, with an inquiry whether this cumbersome legal structure of unemployment compensation should not be replaced by a uniform Federal law. Such legislation could provide a standard minimum-maximum benefit period, identical rules with regard to waiting periods and the number of quarters required for eligibility for unemployment compensation. Furthermore, it could establish flexible but uniform rates of unemployment-compensation contributions throughout the country.

Such a review seems imperative also on grounds of administrative efficiency. As things stand now, unemployment-compensation payments create some problems in the large number of cases in which people reside in one state and work in a neighboring state. In the course of time these initially difficult situations have been straightened out by routine procedures. Nevertheless splitting up of employment compensation into fifty state systems—plus the one in Puerto Rico—is a factor discouraging labor mobility, especially if people want to venture out and accept employment in a distant part of the country.

The most important effect of such a plan would be the merging of the state accounts of unemployment-insurance reserves into one general trust fund. In this way a much better distribution of risks in unemployment insurance could be achieved. The incidence of unemployment varies considerably in different sections and states of the country. Under the present system some states may be in danger of running out of their reserves in a period of recession, whereas others may continue to have considerable surpluses which they do not need. Actually the funds even now flow into the Federal treasury and the unemployment-insurance trust fund holds the same type of nonnegotiable debt that is also held by the old-age insurance system. This merging of the state accounts would also have the advantage to states more likely to endure large-scale unemployment of not having to increase their contributions to unemployment insurance as a response to the great drain on their reserves.

Even if the political obstacles to the realization of such a more rational and efficient system of unemployment compensation remain unsurmountable, there is much that could be improved within the framework of the current Federal-state system. Abolishing of experience rating, advocated for many years by most specialists in this field, and an introduction of a uniform rate of contributions require only an amendment to the Social Security Act. Along with such reform legislation the 10 percent Federal withholding from contributions to unemployment insurance could be reduced to 5 percent. Experience has shown that this 10 percent originally earmarked for the administrative expenses of the state employment services represented an overestimate of the actual budgetary necessities and allocations. In fact, unspent balances in these administrative funds piled up so fast after World War II that at one time Congress empowered the Social Security Administration to use them to assist states where unemployment-insurance reserves began to run low. While this stopgap measure served to highlight the inadequacy of the separate state funds in unemployment insurance, it also demonstrates that 5 percent is entirely ample to meet the cost of administration of unemployment compensation. The 5 percent saved in this way could be added to the contributions to unemployment compensation destined for the payment of claims. Within the framework of the original 3 percent total contributions to unemployment compensation, this would mean that the rate to be paid for benefits would rise from the present maximum of 2.70 to 2.85 percent. If and when Congress concerns itself with unemployment compensation and decides on uniform rates, 2.85 plus 0.15 percent ought to be set as the normal maximum rate in order to assure adequate benfits and administration.

Such rates, which as already mentioned were proposed by the Nixon administration in 1969, would be necessary if the actual situation in unemployment compensation were to return to the original intentions of the legislators in the 1930's. At that time weekly benefit rates were set to represent about 50 percent of the last earnings of the recipient. It was thought that such a level would enable the unemployed and their families to live through shorter periods of unemployment without too much deterioration in their basic economic position. As wages rose after World War II and the amount of covered earnings in unemployment compensation lagged further and further behind, the ratio between average weekly benefits and average weekly wages became less and less favorable. For instance in 1945 the ratio still was 41.6 percent; in 1963 it was down to 34.6 percent. In order to restore a better ratio the maximum covered earnings ought to be raised to what they are now in old-age insurance. Actually there is no reason why these two systems of social insurance should operate with different maximum earnings criteria.

At best, unemployment compensation can deal only with shorter-run unemployment. Persistent unemployment, especially of the type which engulfed so many millions of employable people in the 1930's, cannot be handled within the framework of such a program of social insurance. However, the experience of the early 1960's showed that an extension to a 39-week benefit period proposed again in 1969 is feasible during a recession. Inasmuch as the underlying condition with which unemployment insurance has to deal is subject to sudden changes on the labor market, it can be expected that the new provision to extend benefit periods to 39 weeks when unemployment exceeds 5 percent will strengthen the effectiveness of unemployment insurance.

From the very beginning the Social Security Act established a close link between unemployment compensation and placement activities. This will be discussed in detail in the next section.

23-4. UNEMPLOYMENT INSURANCE AND THE LABOR MARKET

Unemployment-insurance payments are not predicated on a means test and can be claimed on the basis of covered earnings, yet benefits can be paid only to people who are in the labor force but currently unemployed. For this reason unemployment-insurance payments are contingent on an initial and continuing state of unemployment on the part of the recipient. Furthermore, these payments can be made only to people who are able and willing to work. That is, people who are temporarily unable to work due to sickness cannot claim benefits. The criterion for willingness to work is, however, quite liberal. Generally people will be cut off from unemployment benefits if they refuse to accept a job not too distant from their residence or earlier place of employment in the state, provided that the new job to which they have been referred by the public employment service is in the category of their regular employment pattern.

While the waiting period in unemployment compensation has been reduced in most states to one week, it is considerably longer when employees quit their jobs on their own account or if they are discharged for cause. The extension of the waiting period for people who leave their jobs voluntarily is necessary in order to discourage an excessive turnover in employment. In the latter case the longer waiting period operates as a penalty for people who have lost their employment through faults of their own. This, of course, does not bar a discharged employee from protesting against such a discharge by evoking grievance procedures or trying to get judicial relief.

Extended waiting periods exist in a number of states also for workers on strike, as we have already seen in Sec. 16-4. This rule seems to contradict the very concept of unemployment compensation for the simple reason that workers on strike are not unemployed. They forgo employment and income for the time being in order to bring about more favorable conditions of work and pay when they resume work with their current employer. Furthermore, the expectation of being able to collect unemployment-compensation benefits after a waiting period of 17 weeks can be a factor in prolonging strike situations. Whenever unemployment compensation is paid to workers on strike, social-insurance funds are actually being used to subsidize one side in a labor dispute.

Because unemployment insurance can be paid only to people without jobs who are available for referrals to employers, the public placement services are an indispensable part of this program of social insurance. Nevertheless, as we have seen in Sec. 11-8 the public employment services are quite far from monopolizing placement activities on the labor market. While they can compel the unemployed to come to interviews with placement offices, and to follow up leads given to them as a condition of continued benefit payments in case no employment materializes, the public placement service has no way of inducing employers to fill their vacancies through its offices.

This should not lead to an underrating of the role that public employment services play on the labor market. In Chapter 11 we have shown that increasingly the public employment services are being used to participate in special manpower programs designed to reduce hard core unemployment. However, in view of the vastly improved financial status of unemployment insurance even while it continues to levy far less than maximum contributions the question is raised whether funds could not be used on a larger scale not only to enable formerly employed people who have been displaced to be retrained and find new jobs but also to finance programs at least in part which are designed to increase the employability of young people whose training is now supported by projects emanating in the Office of Economic Opportunity. There is no doubt that from the very beginning the "war against poverty" while ambitious in objectives was underfinanced. At the same time vast surpluses were piling up in unemployment insurance trust funds which were not available for urgently needed additional programs designed to eliminate pockets of unemployment and prevent their increase in a period of general full employment. The flow of funds into the reserves of unemployment compensation should not be sterilized but used in a prudent way to reduce present and future unemployment.

SELECTED BIBLIOGRAPHY

Becker, Joseph M. *Shared Government in Employment Security* (New York: Columbia University Press, 1964).

Klein, Philip A. "The Role of Benefits in Meeting Expenditures During Unemployment," *Quarterly Review of Economics and Business* (Chicago, Ill.: University of Illinois, Summer 1965).

Lester, Richard A. *The Economics of Unemployment Compensation* (Princeton, N. J.: Princeton University Press, 1962).

QUESTIONS FOR DISCUSSION

1. Outline the main features of the Social Security Act as it pertains to the question of unemployment compensation.

2. The system of unemployment compensation is such that a relatively large number of workers are not directly covered. Which workers fall into this category, and what are the implications of this lack of coverage?

3. Differences from state to state with respect to several key issues in unem-

ployment compensation are quite evident. What are the more important differences, and what implications can be drawn from these differences?

4. What is the nature of the financial structure of the system of unemployment
compensation with respect to contributions, payments, and trust-fund management?

5. The "experience-rating" system of contributions to unemployment compensation has been criticized on several grounds. What is the nature and intent
of this system, and what are the specific criticisms which have been made
against it?

6. Outline the features of an inclusive plan whereby the present system of unemployment compensation could be made more efficient and workable.

7. What are the primary functions and characteristics of public and private
employment agencies?

8. An efficient labor market requires a certain amount of built-in flexibility.
Does the present system of unemployment compensation add to, or detract from
this flexibility?

Medical Care for the Aged and the General Problem of Health Insurance

The system of social insurance established in the United States through the Social Security Act of 1935 differed in one important respect from legislation already existing in other advanced industrial nations. It did not provide for health insurance for wage and salary earners. Seen in the context of the international growth and development of social-insurance systems, this shortcoming was hard to explain. In some countries such as Germany, health insurance had been among the very first programs to be established when social security legislation began in the 1880's. When the Social Security Act was under consideration in Congress in the 1930's there was an abundance of experience with health-insurance systems in other countries. The same was true, only more so, on the numerous occasions when the Social Security Act was amended over the years. But only the Social Security Amendments of 1965 introduced a substantial program of health insurance and that only for the aged.

While this was a giant step forward designed to relieve a situation which had become extremely critical and completely incompatible with an "affluent society," an academic study of this legislation should not confine itself to a descriptive analysis. The discussion must be extended to an inquiry into the overall adequacy and efficiency of the present American system of dealing with medical costs in terms of what is known from experience in other modern countries about health insurance in general. Actually the Social Security Amendment of 1965 leaves the majority of the American population outside of health insurance and dependent on the very limited services and benefits of voluntary health "insurance." Only the population age 65 and over is eligible for Medicare and the lowest income group can receive "Medicaid" if they pass a means test.

A rapidly increasing segment of the population is eligible because of age. No means test is required for the elderly eligible for hospitalization and other medical services under Medicare for which they have made monthly contributions. But for those under 65 claiming medical services under "Medicaid" a condition of *medical indigence* must be proven. Before we will study the details of the beginning of public health insurance for some groups within the American population it is necessary to investigate the current practice of dealing with the cost of medical services, the operation of voluntary systems of health insurance, and foreign experience with public health insurance or national health services.

24-1. A SURVEY OF THE DEVELOPMENT OF MEDICAL CARE EXPENDITURES

Prior to the rapid growth of voluntary health insurance, especially group insurance covering shorter periods of hospitalization and part of the cost of surgery, there were two segments of the population in the United States that did not have to worry about medical expenses—the very rich and the very poor. Wealthy persons obviously are able to pay whatever bills were incurred by them for all kinds of medical service. On the other end of the income scale, people totally dependent on public-assistance payments and those whose earnings are so low they cannot meet the cost of treatment or hospitalization, were and still are treated in clinics and hospitals at the expense of local welfare departments. Naturally those not on welfare have to undergo a traditional means test in order to establish eligibility for free treatment. Even in those cases, however, they must pledge repayment if possible after recovery.

In the American tradition, no one has been denied necessary medical procedures or hospitalization on the grounds of poverty or inability to pay. Annual drives to raise funds for hospitals for improving equipment, plants, and services emphasized this social aspect of medicine. Generous giving for such charitable purposes became a splendid American tradition.

However, an ever-increasing proportion of the population became ineligible for free use of facilities for medical treatment and hospitalization. Increasingly, people moved out from poverty levels to lower-or-middle-income ranges. This was particularly true of blue-collar workers above the unskilled-labor category and of many echelons of service and white-collar employees. While all this represented substantial social progress and a great gain for labor, it moved millions of families and individuals into income brackets that were considered high enough for them to meet their own cost of medical care.

Very soon this led to many serious individual and family situations for the simple reason that medical-care expenditures had been rising continually and steeply, as is shown in Table 24-1.

Of the total amount of national health expenditures in 1967, 67.2 per-

TABLE 24-1
MEDICAL-CARE EXPENDITURES
SELECTED YEARS 1950 TO 1967
(millions of dollars)

Year	Total Medical-Care Expenditures
1950	$12,867
1955	18,036
1960	26,973
1965	40,591
1966	45,006
1967	50,655
1968	57,103

SOURCE: *Social Security Bulletin* (January 1970), Table 5. By Dorothy P. Rice and Barbara S. Cooper, "National Health Expenditures, 1950–67."

cent was spent from private resources for health services and 32.8 percent for Federal, state and local health facilities. The greatest item of expenditures was for hospitals. Table 24-2 will give a breakdown for the year 1967. In 1968 these expenditures had risen another $3 billions.

TABLE 24-2
EXPENDITURES FOR HOSPITALS, 1967

	All Hospitals	General	Tuberculosis	Psychiatric
Total	$17,946.2	$15,570.0	$79.5	$2,296.7
Consumers	8,752.0	8,439.8	10.5	301.7
Public.	8,854.2	6,790.2	69.0	1,995.0
Federal	5,548.7	5,257.8	1.5	289.4
State and local	3,305.5	1,532.4	67.5	1,705.6
Philanthropy	340.0	340.0	—	—

SOURCE: *Ibid*, Table 3.

If we compare the expenditures for hospital care in 1968 of $20,451 billions to those in 1950 we will see the tremendous financial problem which is created by the cost of health services. In 1950 total hospital care of all facilities, private and public, amounted to $3.845 billion. Nor was this type of increase of medical expenditures confined to hospitals. In 1950 $2.5 bilion was spent for physicians' services; in 1968 total spending for such services had risen to $12.6 billion, a rise of $2.4 billion in one year. Of course, a comparison of two years so far apart as 1950 and 1968 must take into account changes which have occurred in that period. The first factor is represented by the increases in the population which naturally is stimulating the aggregate demand for hospital and other health services. It was calculated[1] that 17.9 percent of the increase in national health expenditures

[1]Source: See footnote to Table 24-1.

is attributable to the growth of the population, 48.2 percent additional increases represent rises in prices and the remaining 33.9 percent are attributable to other items which have tended to increase total national health expenditures. However in an economic assessment of the cost trend in medical care it is important to realize that in the 1960's the index of medical care consumer prices has outrun the general price index at an accelerating rate. In 1950 medical care cost in terms of 1957 to 1959 = 100 stood at 73.4 percent as compared to 85.8 percent for food. By the end of the decade the relation already was reversed with medical care at 104.4 percent and food at 100.3 percent. In the 1960's medical care costs simply ran away from all other items on the consumer price index as will be shown in Table 24-3.

TABLE 24-3
INDEX OF ALL ITEMS OF CONSUMER PRICES AND OF
MEDICAL CARE, 1960–1968
(1957 TO 1959 = 100)

Year (average)	All Items	Medical Care
1960	103.1	108.1
1961	104.2	111.3
1962	105.4	114.2
1963	106.7	117.0
1964	108.1	119.4
1965	109.9	122.3
1966	113.1	127.7
1967	116.3	136.7
1968	120.9	144.6

SOURCE: Table B-45, *Economic Report of the President*, 1969.

The development shown in Table 24-3 explains why total medical care expenditures are claiming an increasing share of the gross national product. In 1950 4.4 percent of the G.N.P. was spent for health care. By the late 1960's medical expenditures already claimed almost 6 percent of the gross national product. A comparison of the G.N.P. and of medical care expenditures in current dollars takes care automatically of population and price increases. Thus the shift to medical care in total expenditures demonstrated here stands out in its real significance. If the trend of the 1960's is not being contained in the 1970's, this escalation would claim ever-increasing shares of national expenditures in the decades to come.

Of course, the argument is being advanced that the rapidly-rising medical care expenditures are merely a reflection of the tremendous advances which are continuously being made in medical research, knowledge, specialization and practice.

In addition to the steady rise in the cost of medical care resulting from continuous improvement in knowledge and in procedures, other explanations for this behavior of prices of medical care must be mentioned. The purely administrative cost of hospitals, always rather high, has been increased further by the necessary raise in wages of the lower echelons of hospital workers. While this could no longer be put off, the rise in this type of employment cost was immediately reflected in higher charges of hospital services.

Another source of increased medical cost is the method of establishing fees under voluntary health insurance. Actually doctors are free to charge whatever they assume is a fair price for surgical and other services, and voluntary insurance covers a certain amount or proportion of the bill.

Still another set of causes is in the area of the pricing of drugs. The pharmaceutical industry has justified rather high prices for certain products by the need for allocating research costs to manufacturing and selling costs. Furthermore, new types of prescription drugs just reaching the market after approval by the Food and Drug Administration and by medical associations start out with a limited volume of sales. When demand for these drugs increases prices are often lowered. Generally speaking, the price of drugs contributes to the rising trend of medical-care expenditures.

24-2. VOLUNTARY HEALTH INSURANCE

Even with the Social Security Amendment of 1965 the population of the United States under the age of 65 will have to content themselves with "voluntary" insurance under the Blue Cross and Blue Shield Plans which are closely controlled by the medical profession. For the population over 65 public hospitalization has been established through the 1965 Amendment to the Social Security Act. In addition old age beneficiaries over 65 can participate through monthly contributions of $5.30 in Medicare covering treatment by doctors in offices, their homes and hospitals and other medical expenses exceeding $44.00 a year. Nevertheless as will be seen in Table 24-4, people 65 years and older are to some degree maintaining coverage in voluntary health insurance plans.

As can be seen from Table 24-4 a very high percentage of the population—82.8 percent—is enrolled in the hospital care plan. Almost half of the population of 65 and over is also participating in that private, voluntary system. As we go down the line on Table 24-4 we find decreasing percentages of participation especially in the items, physicians' office and home visits, and prescribed drugs. The standard period for hospital care is 21 days but this is subject to extensions usually at reduced insurance payments so that the balance has to be made up by the insured patient. The short duration of fully paid hospital care and the far lower coverage rate for doctors' visits and drugs, places most voluntarily insured persons in the United States at a distinct disadvantage compared to the far more com-

TABLE 24-4
ESTIMATED ENROLLMENT IN VOLUNTARY HEALTH INSURANCE
DECEMBER 1967
(in thousands)

Type of Service	All Ages		Under Age 65		Aged 65 and Over	
	Number	Percent of Popu- lation	Number	Percent of Popu- lation	Number	Percent of Popu- lation
Hospital care................	162,853	82.8	153,768	86.5	9,085	47.8
Surgery	150,396	76.4	142,828	80.3	7,568	39.8
In-hospital visits.............	122,570	62.3	116,665	65.6	5,905	31.1
X-Ray and laboratory examinations..............	92,480	47.0	88,926	50.0	3,554	18.7
Physicians' office and home visits................	78,565	39.9	75,785	42.6	2,780	14.6
Dental care..................	4,679	2.4	4,596	2.6	83	.4
Prescribed drugs.............	71,201	36.2	69,363	39.0	1,838	9.7
Private-duty nursing.........	76,080	38.7	73,857	41.5	2,223	11.7
Visiting nurse service	81,772	41.6	79,302	44.6	2,470	13.0
Nursing home care	18,754	9.5	15,873	8.9	2,881	15.2

SOURCE: *Social Security Bulletin* (February 1969). Louis S. Reed and Willine Carr, "Private Health Insurance in the United States, 1967."

plete and longer coverage under public health insurance schemes in other countries.

Nevertheless the status of voluntary health insurance as shown in Table 24-4 reveals striking improvements in the coverage of the population of the United States within the span of one generation. In 1940, only 9.3 percent of the population of all ages is estimated as having had voluntary hospital and surgical insurance. As we have seen by the end of the 1960's this had risen to over 80 percent as far as hospital care is concerned. Private health insurance is not only underwritten by Blue Cross and Blue Shield: increasingly insurance companies have entered the field so that actually by 1967, 57.4 percent of the hospital care was handled by insurance companies.

We have seen at the beginning of this chapter that total medical care expenditures have increased at an accelerating rate in recent years. This is also reflected in total premium income and benefit expenditures of the Blue Cross-Blue Shield Plans and the increasingly important insurance company schemes. This development will be shown in Table 24-5.

Private voluntary nonprofit operations or insurance company plans must operate in the black at all times and they have done so as is shown in Table 24-5. In fact, both in the Blue Cross and the Blue Shield plan claims expense as a percent of subscription income dropped in the period shown on Table 24-5. For Blue Cross the claims expenses declined from 94.3 percent of income to 91.6 percent; in Blue Shield they dropped from 89.2 percent in 1962 to 84.7 percent in 1967. As a result

TABLE 24-5
PREMIUM INCOME AND BENEFIT EXPENDITURES OF
PRIVATE HEALTH INSURANCE, 1962–1967
(in millions)

Year	Premium Income	Benefit Expenditures
1962	7,411.1	6,343.8
1963	8,053.6	6,979.3
1964	8,983.6	7,832.1
1965	10,001.3	8,728.9
1966	10,564.1	9,141.8
1967	11,105.3	9,544.8

SOURCE: *Social Security Bulletin* (February 1969), Table 15. See Footnote on Table 24-4.

reserves grew rapidly for both plans in the same period. In Blue Cross the reserve funds increased from $455 million in 1962 to $798 million in 1967. The corresponding figures for Blue Shield are $267 million and $509 million. One striking difference between the Blue Cross-Blue Shield plans and the insurance company programs is the great gap in operating expenses. In 1967 the nonprofit group had operating expenses of $326 million dollars whereas the insurance companies reported $559 million. Their operating expenses represented 13.1 percent of premium income whereas Blue Cross had only 4.5 percent and Blue Shield 10 percent operating expenses as a proportion of the income. As a result of the high operating "expenses," insurance companies showed a net loss from their health insurance policies although their claim expenses in 1967 were only 93.6 percent of their premium income. This extraordinary performance justifies doubt on the common assertion that the private sector can handle certain economic problems more efficiently and at lower cost than the public sector. If we recall at this point the development of private company pension plans which was discussed in great detail in Sec. 9-4 of this text, the question about the alleged natural superiority of privately organized projects in the field of income maintenance and health expenditures has to be raised with increased urgency.

The Blue Cross-Blue Shield covers total costs for people in the lowest income groups. However, especially as far as surgical services are concerned as well as doctors' visits even if they are included in coverage, there is no limitation on the bills which can be sent by the doctor to the clients. The Blue Shield will pay the doctor a fee for operations which has been agreed upon with the medical association. But whenever doctors feel that they are entitled to more and that the client can pay more, they will charge according to their own judgment. It can be inferred from the development of physicians' fees that whenever the payments to doctors by the insurance companies are raised, the total doctor's bill, charged to the patient, will increase also. This voluntary health insurance system has a built-in cost escalator, whereby total physicians' fees are going up whenever their compensation for their services from voluntary health insurance is being increased. This explains why total expenditures for physicians' services increased from $8.7 billion in 1965, to $12.6 billion in 1968. Very belatedly it was discovered that at least in Medicare and Medicaid ceilings ought to be placed on total doctors' fees.

The American voluntary health insurance system as presently constructed is completely under control of the medical profession. Its cost performance raises the question whether the system has not become openended, continuously reinforcing elements of price escalation of medical care expenditures. Granted the fact that increased population and far greater utilization of facilities and services must lead to an increase in medical expenditures, the problem of escalation of medical costs above and beyond these growth factors remains with us.

Another cost-push factor in medical expenditures is the rising outlays for research and medical-facilities construction. They rose from $937 million in 1955 to $3.4 billion in 1965. Table 24-6 will give some details of this development.

TABLE 24-6
COST OF MEDICAL RESEARCH AND CONSTRUCTION; SELECTED
YEARS 1955–1967
(in millions)

Years-Type of Expenditures	1955	1965	1967
Total	937	3,381	3,770
Research	216	1,469	1,775
Construction	721	1,912	1,995
Publicly owned	370	521	628
Privately owned	351	1,391	1,367

SOURCE: Table 5, as indicated in Footnote to Table 24-1.

Expenditures for medical research and construction have increased their share in total medical spending from 5.2 percent in 1955 to 7.4 percent in 1967. The greatest increase occurred in research which in 1955 claimed only 1.2 percent of the expenditures but twelve years later represented almost half of the total spending, namely, 3.5 percent of overall research and construction spending. The cost of research and construction are worked into the charges made to patients and are recouped in this manner. The same, incidentally, is true of prescription drugs whose prices also embody, according to assertions of the producers, the cost of research. Without research, medical progress like any other type of progress is impossible. The figures given in Table 24-6 indicate, however, that in recent years there has been such an acceleration of research activities and cost increases that the question might very well be asked whether the traditional method of financing research through the device of increasing hospitalization and medication charges to individual patients is still consistent with the expenses generated in the persuit of the technological and scientific revolution in medicine. If such expenses could be controlled by appropriate committees of legislative bodies with their investigatory powers it might be possible to channel funds into medical research in part from general tax revenues and subjecting the vast expansion of research activities to some questions with regard to their relevance for medical practice.

While costs of medical care are rising rapidly and tend to claim a larger part of the national income, a redeeming side of the picture has been pointed out frequently by the medical profession. Modern drugs and treatments have reduced the average period of hospitalization, so that while the charges per day seem to be high indeed, the total cost is less. By the same token, doctors point out that "miracle" drugs, in addition to shortening periods of illness, enable them to handle a far greater load of patients than would otherwise be possible.

Progress in medical science and practice and the high percentage of enrollment of the American population in voluntary health insurance, especially Blue-Cross-Blue-Shield have vastly contributed toward an improvement in health standards. But skyrocketing national health expenditures under the present system of medical economics have not lowered the infant mortality rate in the United States to a rate approximating that of Sweden, Great Britain, West and East Germany, and France, to mention only these countries. It is true that the higher infant mortality rate in the United States is connected with the greater proportion of the nonwhite population in this country. But this is an explanation, not an excuse.

While the voluntary system of health insurance is preferable to not having any system at all, the question whether it is the best of all possible systems is no longer asked merely by "radicals." The Social Security Amendment of 1965 established some features of public health insurance for people 65 years and older. They will be discussed in Sec. 24-4. But since 1965 the realization has been spreading gradually that the present system of having voluntary insurance for those under 65 and compulsory insurance for those over 65 makes little sense. At the convention of the American Medical Association in 1969 there was greater evidence of the acceptance of public health insurance by some doctors than on previous occasions. However, the Association still visualizes a compulsory system which would be administered, as is the fact today with voluntary insurance, at least indirectly by the medical profession alone. There is no doubt that this is not the last word in the rapidly evolving great debate in the United States on the recent trend in medical care expenditures and what it means to the economic and social conditions under which the majority of the American people live even in this period of affluence. The points about foreign experience with public compulsory health insurance which will be made in the next section are designed to contribute to this discussion.

24-3. FOREIGN EXPERIENCE WITH COMPULSORY HEALTH INSURANCE

Generally speaking it must be said that the United States, probably like most other countries in the world, has fewer hesitations about utilizing and usually improving on foreign technological breakthroughs, for instance rockets, than about benefiting from the experience of social arrangements and institutions in other national and political settings. For this reason the literature in the area of comparative social security systems is somewhat limited in this country. However, there have been some notable improvements in recent years. In 1965 the Joint Economic Committee of the 89th Congress released a paper, No. 7 "European Social Security Systems." In the following year the U.S. Department of Health, Education and Welfare released its research report No. 13 on "Old-Age and Sickness Insurance in West Germany in 1965."

First a clarification of terms is necessary. For a long period of time the American Medical Association insisted on labeling any system of medical services which was not either entirely private in terms of doctor-patient relations or regulated to the exclusion of any outside agency in the form of private voluntary health insurance as "socialized medicine." This generalized term was applied also to public health systems set up in countries which at least when this branch of social security got underway could not by the furthest stretch of the imagination be labeled "socialistic." In fact, when old age and health insurance was introduced in Germany in the 1880's the Socialist party in that country was outlawed. One of the main motivations inaugurating social insurance was the political desire of the government to demonstrate to the working class that they did not need a Socialist party because the government was looking out for their interests. Of course this was paternalism.

Socialized medicine in the true sense of the word exists, naturally, in socialistic countries especially in the Soviet Union. Under this system medical services are financed out of general tax revenues. Medical practitioners, admittedly operating on a high level of professional skill, are employees of the public health administration. In every district there is a medical center in which doctors with various specializations are stationed as well as diagnostic and other treatment facilities. People living in this district must apply to this center in order to obtain medical services. They must accept referral to specialists, and doctors have no possibility of refusing service to a particular patient. In fact, there is under such systems no free choice of doctors. It has always been asserted that this destroys the "private and confidential relationship" between doctors and patients characteristic of the American practice. Apparently it has not interfered with high standards of medical practice in the Soviet Union.

Now it is simply not correct to assert that this fully socialized system is the only alternative to the present American structure of medical care. The British National Health Service System stands in between fully socialized medicine and systems of private and public health insurance. Unlike the latter the British Health Services are financed as in the Soviet Union out of general tax funds. They are not part of National Insurance. Hospitals in Great Britain with the exception of some university and research hospitals are under the direct supervision of the Ministry of Health. On the other hand medical doctors are not employees of the government. If they so desire they can stay outside of the National Health Service and establish themselves in private practice with no limitation on their fees. A number of doctors have availed themselves of this option, especially specialists including psychiatrists. However, the overwhelming majority of British doctors participate in the scheme. They do not receive a fixed salary but are given fees based on the actual number of cases and the type of services they have rendered to clients. As a result the incomes of individual doctors may vary considerably. There also exists a free choice of doctors by the patients. In Britain as well as in Belgium and Italy there have occurred in recent years conflicts between doctors and public health administrations on the question of the adequacy of fees. But nowhere has there been a demand for the repeal of the National Health Service System. It was introduced by the first post-war labor government. When the Conservatives took over again they maintained it intact and concentrated on carrying on minor changes such as the imposition of nominal fees for doctors' prescriptions.

The Soviet and the British systems, while differing in many respects, have in common the fact that they are outside of social insurance. However, in many other countries health insurance was one of the very first schemes of social insurance introduced. This was true particularly of the German system which received at the beginning the odd name of "Sickness Insurance" which it has retained.

Like old age insurance, sickness insurance in Germany started out as a compulsory public system for the lower income groups. Over the years coverage was continuously extended to cover higher and higher income brackets. However, vast groups of the labor force such as independent proprietors, professionals and Civil Service employees do not participate in the system. They have set up a large number of voluntary sickness insurance associations often offering more services than are supplied by compulsory health insurance. The latter is far more comprehensive than the standard benefits available under private voluntary health insurance in the United States. Hospitalization can be granted for 26 weeks; all the

diagnostic and surgical services are included. Furthermore, doctors' visits
at home and at the office are covered as well as all prescriptions. As in
England doctors are not employed by public health insurance institutions.
They retain independent professional status and negotiate collectively
through the Medical Association with the health insurance system concerning their fees. Doctors are free to treat noninsured patients and charge
them whatever they feel is right. If a doctor decides not to participate in
the local health insurance panel he can stay out and engage exclusively in
private practice. Patients have a free choice of doctors from the panel.
Usually doctors indicate on their shields to what panels of the health insurance system they belong.

Now it must clearly be understood that the German system of compulsory public health insurance is not run by the government. While there
has always been a Federal health office, raised to the Ministerial level
after World War II, this government department is not concerned with the
operation of health insurance. Supervision rests ultimately with the Federal department of health and is concerned primarily with enforcement of
the law and consideration of new legislation. In order to understand the
structure of German health insurance which is at the same time compulsory and outside the government it is necessary to mention briefly the Continental European institution of a "public law association" which actually
goes back to medieval legal development. What it amounts to is compulsory membership of individuals in a group serving public purposes. For
instance, farm owners on the banks of rivers would be compelled to enter
an association designated to engage in flood control or river regulation.
The fact of location in a given area established the obligation of joining this
group and participating in its activity through labor or monetary contributions. The fact that a state or national law prescribed membership in such
an association did not make such a unit part of the government structure.
However, such public law associations were given the right to levy contributions backed ultimately by the enforcement power of the government.

As has been pointed out in the report of the HEW mentioned in the
first paragraph of this section, health insurance in Germany had a historical
background in voluntary funds set up by craftsmen's guilds and similar organizations. But when it was decided to establish a national system of
health insurance the system of a "public law association" was selected.
That is to say the Sickness Insurance Law identified the groups of wage and
salary earners which had to be covered. This was done primarily by establishing maximum earnings which, however, in German practice meant
that employees earning more than the maximum did not have to pay contributions and could not become eligible for benefits. With the continuous
rise in maximum earning levels the proportion of the labor force covered
by public health insurance has been rising continuously. The law also pre-

scribes the minimum benefits which must be supplied by health insurance. Now this legal structure became one of the most important features of health insurance in Germany and in countries like France and Italy which adopted similar systems. The law compelled communities and counties to set up health insurance funds. These local institutions, however, are controlled by the local contributors to the fund who elect representatives. The insured wage and salary workers as well as the employers are compelled to contribute select delegates to an administrative committee which sets policies and supervises the operations of the local health insurance fund. As a result contributions are determined for each health insurance fund by these representatives. The full time administrative staff is appointed by this committee. The policy governing relations between the fund and the local medical association are also set by the committee. The same is true of the cooperation of the fund with public and private hospitals.

In sharp contrast to private voluntary health insurance in the United States which is dominated by medical doctors to the exclusion of the insured beneficiaries and the government, the German system of compulsory health insurance is an interesting case of local self-government of those immediately concerned with the cost and benefits in compulsory health insurance. This has not prevented a substantial increase in costs of medical services but it has kept the practices and cost factors under firm control. It must then be said that this system is far more democratic than the private health insurance system in the United States in which the insured people have not even a channel of communication to those who run the various "voluntary" plans. There is one other important difference which has kept costs and prices of medical services under control: medical doctors participating in the panel of health insurance funds cannot send additional bills for their services to those insured patients even if they are able to pay more than the fee prescribed by the health insurance system. The fact that the cost of prescription drugs is also covered enables insurance funds to control prices to some extent. In short the old system of self-government of the insured recently called "participation" has removed many of the self-reinforcing cost escalators which are as we have seen in the previous section are part of the private American system. The European experience also shows that it is simply not true that compulsory health insurance would require the setting up of a new huge Federal bureaucracy. Granted that the concept of a public law association cannot be fitted into American constitutional and administrative law, and that therefore public health insurance probably would have to be carried out by local agencies operating under the Federal-state legal framework, an examination of the cost records of private voluntary health insurance in the United States simply does not confirm the assertion that a private system could handle medical care costs cheaper than one which is based on social security legislation. In fact there is strong reason to believe that the private system as it has operated in the last twenty-five years tends to increase costs faster than government programs would.

With the Social Security Amendment of 1965 some uncertain steps have been taken in this country towards public health insurance. At best this system is transitional in character. We will examine this in the next section.

24-4. HEALTH INSURANCE FOR THE AGED

One aspect of the advance in medical science is the steady increase in life expectancy. As a result the population of 65-year-olds and over is increasing at a significant rate. Since the vast majority of people in that age group suffer a very substantial loss in income upon retirement, they are confronted with a particularly difficult situation: cost of medical care keeps going up, while incomes of the 65-and-older group are frozen in this country. Furthermore, it is precisely this age group that is most likely to run into protracted periods of illness.

Frequently the plight of individuals in this age category was passed along to their children who were active in the labor force. In most states family-support laws required employed children to contribute toward the support, and especially the medical expenses, of their parents if their income exceeds certain moderate limits.

These conditions had made it clear for some time that legislation was needed to protect at least the 65-and-over population against the loss of assets and savings caused by protracted illness, and to enable them to maintain a minimum adequate income even while disabled through illness. The American Medical Association, which over the years had made tremendous efforts to defeat general health insurance—which it labeled "socialized medicine"—could no longer prevent the enactment of Medicare.

The 1965 amendments to the Social Security Act have added a new title dealing with two health-insurance programs for persons 65 years and over. One plan deals with **hospital insurance,** the other with medical insurance for the services of physicians at home and for additional medical and health services outside of hospitals. Both plans adopted the sound principle that beneficiaries of health and hospital insurance should make a contribution of their own. A patient must pay $44 toward the total cost of hospitalization arising during a first 60-day period of stay in such an institution. If the stay extends longer than the next 30 days, the patient must pay $10 a day for each day after the first 60 days of hospitalization. However, the total coverage for one continuous illness cannot exceed 90 days. It should be noted that this is a tremendous improvement over the 21-day coverage in voluntary hospital insurance. While that coverage can be extended to a total of 180 days under certain circumstances, the average daily amount covered by voluntary insurance is so little that protracted stays in hospitals under the Blue Cross plans are almost economically prohibitive for most people.

Of special importance for aged people is the post-hospital extended-care feature of hospital insurance. For each spell of illness requiring hospitalization of at least three days, patients can receive additional care for a period of 100 days—for instance, in a nursing home. The first 20 days of such care are free; for the remaining 80 days of extended care the patient would pay $5 a day, a mere fraction of what is charged by nursing homes.

Aged persons requiring diagnostic services can receive them after having paid $20. They also have to pay 20 percent of the total cost for each diagnostic study.

Post-hospital care can also be given to aged persons in their own home. After they have been discharged from the hospital or from a nursing home, they are entitled to 100 visits to receive nursing and other health services by a qualified person assigned to them by a recognized home health agency. However, such services at home must be supervised by a physician.

These post-hospital services enable a large number of aged persons, who up to now could not be taken care of elsewhere, to leave hospitals. In this way the case load of hospitals is somewhat lessened and so is the strain on personnel and medical facilities. These changes should in turn bring about an improvement in the operation of private nursing homes, which will have to comply with personnel and other standards of care established by public authorities in order to participate in these programs.

Hospital insurance is financed by contributions levied on the employees which are scheduled to rise gradually to 0.8 percent of the payroll in 1987. It should be noted already at this point of our analysis that the levy for hospital insurance does not benefit currently employed persons subject to contributions to old age and disability insurance but only those who have retired.

In the first three years net contributions to hospital insurance totaled $9.3 billion. Disbursements for hospital and related service benefits amounted to $8.8 billion in the first three years of the operation of the hospital insurance system. In addition to the contributions the Federal government has transferred to the hospital insurance trust fund $1.4 billion to provide for hospitalization benefits for persons 65 years and over who are not covered by OASDHI. As a result of these transfers the total assets of the hospital insurance fund amounted to $1.9 billion by January 1969 although the excess of contributions over hospital service benefits in the initial three year period was only about $500 million.

In the first two years of hospital insurance for the aged 11.8 million people received hospital treatment under this program. The average amount reimbursed to hospitals per claim was $537.00. Other services such as out-patient hospital diagnostic and home health care required only small amounts per claim, $12.00 and $69.00 respectively.

The original financial plan for hospital insurance for the aged merely stipulated an increase in the rate of contribution to OASDI. No separate fund was to be set up and the expenses arising from Medicare were to be taken from the Old-Age and Survivors Trust Fund. The opposition against this merging of old-age insurance and Medicare funds which arose in Congress was very well founded. Actually, the outlays for health insurance for the aged are very difficult to forecast. The possibility could not be discounted that this new program, necessary though it was, would face an undue strain on the limited reserves of OASDI even after the rather drastic increase in contributions scheduled to start on January 1, 1966. In the final version of the Social Security Amendment of 1965, a separate hospital insurance trust fund was set up in the Treasury Department. To this fund will flow that part of the contributions to OASDI which will be specifically earmarked for hospital insurance. Based on an annual-income ceiling of $7,800 hospital insurance rates will rise according to the schedule shown in Table 24-7.

TABLE 24-7
CONTRIBUTION RATES TO HOSPITAL INSURANCE

Year	Percent
1966	0.35
1967–72	0.50
1973–75	0.55
1976–79	0.60
1980–86	0.70
1987 and thereafter	0.80

SOURCE: *Social Security Bulletin* (September 1965), p. 11.

The low contribution rates for the initial years of hospital insurance seem to have been sufficient to meet the benefit claims created for people over 65 under the general title of hospital insurance.

Hospital insurance and extended care for the aged does not cover the services of physicians, including radiologists and psychiatrists. Neither does it include the cost of surgery or anaesthesia. If persons 65 and over want to insure themselves against the expenses arising from these services, they can make use of the second program provided by the 1965 amendment.

While hospital insurance for the aged merely requires that they pay $44 for each case of hospitalization, the **medical-insurance** plan established in 1965 in the Social Security Act requires that persons aged 65 can enroll in this program by special application and pay $5.30 a month, which is matched by a similar amount paid by the Federal government out of general funds. The latter point is of great importance. It means that the Federal share in medical insurance is not to be financed out of specially earmarked contributions but from general tax receipts.

Medical insurance will generally cover 80 percent of the cost of physicians and surgeons services rendered in a hospital, clinic, doctor's office, in the home of a patient or in a nursing facility. Furthermore, this insurance covers home health services up to 100 visits a year under the supervision of a physician. These types of services do not require prior hospitalization as is the case with post-hospital services at home mentioned earlier. X-ray and similar treatments are also included in medical insurance, as are iron lungs, oxygen tents, the purchase of hospital beds for use at home, and ambulance services. Not included are dental services or devices. Out-of-hospital treatment of mental, psychoneurotic, and personality disorders of the aged are restricted to a maximum outlay by the insurance plan of $250.

There is no doubt that Medicare represents great progress and over the years should make vast improvements in the medical and economic aspects of caring for the aged population of the United States. Actually, it will place this numerically growing segment of the older population on equal terms with comparable groups of people in other advanced countries which have known general health insurance for many decades.

Whereas hospital insurance is financed by a surtax on contributions to old age insurance, Medicare is based on monthly payments of $5.30 by those recipients of old age benefits who have voluntarily agreed to join the Medicare program. A very large percentage of this group joined up, not without very active publicity work of the Social Security Administration which urged all people eligible to enter into the program. For those currently receiving benefits the $5.30 is withheld from their monthly check.

Medicare premium income is supplemented by Federal grants matching the receipts from the contributions roughly on a 50–50 basis. Total receipts in the supplementary medical insurance trust fund between July 1966 and January 1969 amounted to $3.74 billion. Expenditures for medical service benefits under Medicare amounted to $2.7 billion. Administrative expenditures of about $380 million had been incurred. After about two and a half years of operation the total assets in the medical insurance trust fund had risen to $430 million.

As with hospital insurance, Medicare for the aged has proved to be entirely feasible although in the latter program the government is contributing to the expenses in a substantial manner.

The Social Security Amendment of 1965 also enables the states to initiate public support programs for individual expenditures for hospitalization and other medical services for people under 65 years of age. A number of states have availed themselves of this opportunity and have initiated "Medicaid." In this way they have become eligible for Federal matching funds to finance this program. It was, however, up to the states to formulate their own concepts of eligibility for Medicaid. As mentioned at the beginning of this chapter, this required an establishment of an income ceiling and the application of a means test to claimants under 65. It is in this area rather than in the programs for the aged that serious difficulties arose shortly after the inauguration of Medicaid. For instance in New York State medical indigence was presumed to exist wherever a family of four had an income of $6,000 or less per year. Naturally a considerable proportion of the population became eligible and began to obtain free services of doctors and of health facilities. In 1969 the income ceiling was lowered to $5,000. As a result a large number of people who had benefited from Medicaid fell outside the program and again had to pay for medical services not covered by the standard Blue Cross-Blue Shield plan. It would have been much better to start out with a lower ceiling and raise it after some experience with this project had been gained rather than starting out with a high ceiling and then cutting off people who had been counting on the continuation of the original scheme. But these difficulties can be classified as "growing pains."

The worst feature of Medicaid is that late in the 20th Century and in sharp divergence from the practice of almost all advanced industrial nations it subjects a significant segment of the population, which is above the poverty level and in its overwhelming majority is regularly employed, to a means test as a pre-condition for obtaining free medical services. This feature of the current American system of dealing with health expenditures is a clear indication that the 1965 Amendment to the Social Security Act can be considered only as a preliminary move in a larger inevitable attempt to come to grips with soaring health expenditures in a manner more consistent with general modern experience and practice.

The current system in the United States abandoning the population under 65 either to "voluntary" private health insurance in which the insured have no say at all, or offering to the less privileged but nonpoor in a technical sense, the prospect of having to face a means test while establishing at the same time public health insurance for those over 65, is incoherent, highly cost-ineffective and utterly inconsistent with an affluent society claiming high achievements in rational management of business and of certain lines of scientific research.

The jerry-built structure of American health insurance, partly private and practically uncontrolled and partly public is clearly destined for a complete overhaul. The present state of affairs in health expenditures is attributable to a great extent to the success that the American Medical Association and its Political Action Committees have had in intimidating voters, members of Congress and succeeding administrations to the point that for a considerable time any advocacy of public health insurance was considered politically suicidal and was filed away as "unthinkable." When the financial burden of caring for people over 65 threatened to destroy not only the savings of that group but also those of their children liable for their support, hospital insurance and voluntary medical insurance was introduced for that age group. Very soon quite a number of medical practitioners discovered that public health insurance, far from damaging the earning capacity of doctors, opened up new sources of revenues. As in the initial phases of almost any program, there were abuses and in 1969 the Internal Revenue Service became interested in the tax returns of doctors who had earned more than $25,000 a year in fees from Medicare and Medicaid. While this certainly does not reflect on the ethical standards of the medical profession as a whole, these occurrences show clearly that the often-repeated argument against public health insurance, that such a system would pull down the income of physicians, lower medical standards to general mediocrity and discourage young talented people from entering the profession, have no foundation in reality.

What is needed at this time is a very comprehensive study of the total administrative and financial and cost structure of health services in the United States by experts operating outside the medical establishment. One of the first projects of the Rockefeller Foundation early in this century was a survey of the standards of teaching prevailing at American medical schools at that period of time. The findings brought about sweeping changes in medical education. The claim of the medical profession that "laymen" are not qualified to judge medical problems and procedures is true only as far as the professional practice of medicine is concerned. But this exclusion of outsiders cannot go into areas of the economic aspects and consequences of the current cost and price structure of health care in the United States. It cannot veto cost effectiveness studies and fundamental considerations about the operational efficiency of the present system. A complete evaluation of the American experiences with health expenditures in the last generation must be made in which professional accountants, economists, and sociologists ought to participate. If we continue the current patch-work system of occasional changes, we may discover before long that while we have learned how to cure many diseases we have also created the conditions for increasingly threatening chronic malfunctions in the social and economic aspects and operations of medical care problems.

24-5. TOWARDS A UNIVERSAL HEALTH INSURANCE PLAN FOR THE UNITED STATES

The conclusion reached in the analysis of the current state of voluntary and public health insurance in the United States in the preceding sections of this chapter is increasingly shared by important segments of the American people. A Committee for National Health Insurance has become active with I.S. Falk, Professor Emeritus of Public Health of Yale University, as technical consultant. The purpose of this committee is to advocate the setting up of a universal health insurance system in the United States in which the population under 65 as well as over 65 would participate. This would eliminate the current dual structure whereby those under 65 are voluntarily insured in the private sector and only those over 65 are being taken care of by public health insurance. The plan under discussion by this committee would cover in a comprehensive way the costs of personal health care to the exclusion of drugs and dentistry. While the latter costs are also excluded in many foreign health insurance schemes, prescription drugs are usually included in the benefits. Financing would be through a payroll tax with employers and employee contributions split on a fifty-fifty basis. The Federal government would also make an annual contribution to the cost out of general tax revenues. While the National Health Service in Britain is financed completely out of general tax receipts the fact ought to be considered that in some other countries general public health insurance is self-supporting and does not rely on yearly allocations out of a national budget.

There is little doubt that eventually a comprehensive public health system will emerge in the United States superseding the present unwieldy and illogical structure. However such a national scheme will fail unless it introduces a separation of power between the administration of health insurance and the medical profession. There also should be a representation of the insured on local levels so that the people who are contributing will be in a position to have a say with regard to the delivery of medical care to them. Under no circumstances should such a national system turn over the administration to the Blue Cross. The record of that organization especially the geometric rise in cost and contributions do not recommend this course of action.

24-6. WORKMEN'S COMPENSATION

The start of general public health insurance was long delayed in the United States, yet, as in other nations in the process of rapid industrialization, industrial accident insurance was introduced at an early time under the name of workmen's compensation.

Factory inspection revealed the prevalence of great hazards to the health and safety of workers. Safety codes were drawn up for use in business enterprises and were enforced by state agencies. Originally, however, workers who suffered an accident while working were in a most unfavorable position. Some courts held that anyone who knowingly accepts employment—say in a powder factory—is aware of the risk he is taking and must be solely responsible for any injuries sustained as a result. Soon, however, the principle of employers' liability developed. It implied that the employer must take normal precautions to protect workers against industrial accidents. Hence in case of a mishap the employer was considered responsible if he had been negligent in enforcing the required safety measures. However, the burden of proof was still on the injured worker or, in case of death, on his survivors who might be suing for damages. Very often in these suits employers countered the charge of negligence with the assertion that the worker had contributed to the accident by his own carelessness—or by intoxication. In all cases the need to sue the employer proved to be most burdensome to workers and a just settlement was often delayed for a considerable period of time.

Workmen's compensation laws took industrial-accident litigation out of the regular courts and set up special procedures and boards to deal with the resulting claims. The principle of employers' responsibility was fully recognized. In order to meet damage claims, the employer can in most states select three methods: he can (1) take out insurance with a state agency set up for this purpose, (2) also insure himself with a private company, or (3) proceed on the principle of self-insurance. The latter course is suitable only for very large companies disposing over vast resources.

Workmen's compensation payments vary according to the injury that the employee suffered. In case of total disability, employees in most states are entitled to a compensation of 66 2/3 percent of the former average weekly earnings. If there is only a partial disability enabling the injured employee to return to work in a job in which his weekly earnings are considerably less after the accident, a partial disability payment can be awarded.

Workmen's compensation covers the cost of surgery and hospitalization. In case of fatal accidents, survivors are entitled to substantial payments which, however, in most cases will be paid out in form of monthly compensation benefits.

One good by-product of workmen's compensation legislation has been the great concern of industrial management in the United States for safety of operations. In many plants safety records are posted which indicate the number of days in which no industrial accidents have occurred. There is also a strict enforcement of safety rules such as the wearing of helmets and of goggles. Among the most dangerous operations is mining. Despite all the progress that has been made, serious accidents causing many fatalities are still occurring in mines here and abroad. There have been frequent complaints that in some states the enforcement of safety regulations in mines was somewhat lax. In response to this criticism Congress passed the Mine, Health and Safety Law in 1969. It introduces mandatory Federal health and accident prevention standards. The former include obligatory chest X-Rays for all miners at the expense of the company. Furthermore it introduced Federal disability benefits for about 50,000 former miners who had been afflicted by the "black lung." Prior to this legislation these people who had incurred a serious occupational disease had not been eligible for workmen's compensation.

SELECTED BIBLIOGRAPHY

Ball, Robert M. "Medical Prices and Their Control" *Social Security Bulletin* (March 1969).

Corning, Peter A. "The Evolution of Medicare . . . From Idea to Law" Office of Research and Statistics, Research Report 29, Social Security Administration, 1969.

Fisher, Paul "Old Age and Sickness Insurance in West Germany in 1965" Office of Research and Statistics, Research Report No. 13, Social Security Administration, 1966.

Greenfield, Margaret. *Medicare for the Aged.* Institute of Governmental Studies (Berkeley, Calif.: University of California Press, August 1964).

Klarman, Herbert E. *The Economics of Health* (New York: Columbia University Press, 1965).

Reed, Louis S. "Private Health Insurance in the United States, An Overview." *Social Security Bulletin,* U.S. Department of Health, Education, and Welfare (Washington, D.C.: U.S. Government Printing Office, December 1965).

QUESTIONS FOR DISCUSSION

1. Outline the factors which contributed to the final adoption of the Medicare program in 1965.

2. In detail, outline the features of the Medicare plan adopted in 1965.

3. The financing of Medicare may place a considerable burden on the Social Security Trust Fund. Why is this so and what measures have been taken to offset this possibility?

4. In your opinion, are there any apparent shortcomings to the Medicare plan of 1965?

5. Outline the nature of the British system of National Health Services and point to any advantages such a plan has in comparison to the United States program.

6. Contrast the British system of National Health Services with the German system of health insurance.

The Welfare State

The field of labor economics cannot be fenced within the confines of shops and offices. It covers all the economic factors and conditions shaping the total life situation of wage and salary workers. Education gains increasing significance not only for the intrinsic values of the skills, knowledge, and understanding it is expected to convey to students, but also for the earning capacity of people. Furthermore, whatever financial security people may enjoy in their later years is determined by the way in which they can accumulate credits for benefits while working. To a very large degree then the material welfare of people depends on their ability to work. While working most of them acquire in addition to wages and salaries claims for such payments as unemployment and old-age insurance benefits, and private pensions. Because the overwhelming majority of people today are included in a still-expanding Social Security system; and because a considerable number of persons receive various forms of public aid—with the Federal government concerned about elimination of inequalities in education—the concept or image of the "welfare state" has arisen. It still remains ambiguous and is misunderstood by many people who are inclined to attribute high tax rates to "relief expenditures" rather than to national defense in an age of progressing technology.

Welfare economics as propounded, for example, in the works of Knut Wicksell and Arthur C. Pigou preceded the actual emergence of the welfare state by some decades and actually had as its primary objective an analysis of the conditions under which an optimum allocation of resources could occur in a more or less perfectly competitive market system. Intervention by the state, while not totally excluded, was to be kept to a minimum. However, welfare economics was concerned about inequalities and the resulting insecurity for many, and sought to develop concepts and policies designed to obtain optimum conditions for all participants in the market society.

When the Federal government was compelled to intervene massively in many sectors of the economy during the Great Depression, many people grew apprehensive about this development. The welfare state became almost a derogatory term and "cradle-to-grave security" was roundly denounced. In the early stages of the operation of the Social Security Act this type of criticism was addressed even to this new system of social security. Generally speaking, the welfare state was depicted as destroying initiative and self-reliance while conditioning large masses of people to feel entitled to "get something for nothing." Nothing could be more misleading, as will be shown in the following section.

25-1. THE WELFARE SECTOR AND THE GROSS NATIONAL PRODUCT

The stereotype just referred to—whereby people in the vast majority receive a benefit without having contributed a previous equivalent established by their own work record—simply does not correspond to the hard facts. We have already seen in Chapter 21, Table 1, that current administrative practice classifies as social welfare expenditures, programs and institutions which are at best only remotely connected with the popular concept of "welfare." This is true of all social insurance programs which are financed by contributions of employers and employees. Even hospital insurance for those over 65 comes under this category. A properly conceived system of public health insurance as outlined in the previous chapter is, of course, also outside the welfare system properly understood. It would also eliminate the "welfare" aspects of "Medicaid." That neither educational expenditures nor veterans' programs should be classified under the misleading title of welfare needs repeating before we address ourselves to Public Aid which in the true sense of the word is a relief program necessitating some sort of a means test in order to establish eligibility. A means test remains even if as has been the case recently in some large-scale welfare administrations, applicants for relief are permitted to sign a brief statement asserting that they are without means of support. This has brought about a simplification of administrative procedures because the case worker does no longer have to engage in painstaking investigations of each and every application trying to verify the alleged case of need. Instead random checks are made as it was customary for income tax returns prior to the time that a far greater percentage was put through computerized examinations. Preliminary studies have shown that this new system does not produce more false claims than the old one. It is, of course, true that many people are more sensitive to cheating by reliefers than they are to many other malpractices which disadvantage average consumers, or to overruns in military expenditures costly to the taxpayers.

It is, therefore, necessary to relate *public aid programs*—not "social welfare expenditures"—to the Personal Income in order to gain a better

TABLE 25-1
PERSONAL INCOME, SOCIAL INSURANCE BENEFITS AND PUBLIC ASSISTANCE
SELECTED FISCAL YEARS—1940-1969

Years	Total (in billions)	Social Insurance Benefit as Percent of Total Income	Public Assistance as Percent of Total Income
1940	$ 78.3	2.1	3.4
1945	171.1	1.7	.6
1950	227.6	3.0	1.0
1955	310.9	4.1	.8
1960	401.0	5.8	.8
1961	416.8	6.4	.8
1962	442.6	6.3	.8
1963	465.5	6.3	.8
1964	497.5	6.1	.8
1965	538.9	6.1	.7
1966	587.2	6.2	.7
1967	629.4	6.8	.8
1968	687.9	7.1	.8
1969 (Sept.)	759.8	7.2	.9

SOURCE: *Social Security Bulletin* (December 1969).

perspective of the size of the problem. Table 25-1 will relate public aid to the Personal Income.

Table 25-1 shows a significant change in the structure of the American economy. In 1940 which still was a depression year public assistance payments claimed the highest percentage of personal income in the whole period shown in this table. At the same time social insurance payments were low because the Social Security Act at that time was only five years old. Social insurance payments as a percent of the personal income have risen steadily throughout the 1960's although at a slow rate. In 1969 they claimed 7.2 percent of the total personal income whereas public assistance payments still were less than 1 percent. It is true that toal public assistance money outlays climbed rapidly. In 1966 they amounted to $4.3 billion, in 1968 they had risen to $5.7 billion. The greatest proportion of this increase was in Aid to Dependent Children which rose from $1.849 billion in 1966 to $2.823 billion in 1968. While on the macroeconomic scale this meant merely one tenth of 1 percent increase in public assistance payments, from 0.7 to 0.8 percent, it is easy to see why the rapid rise in these payments especially in large metropolitan areas created so much concern. These developments were one of the reasons why in 1969 the Nixon administration proposed introduction of a guaranteed minimum family income. This project would supersede the present specialized public assistance programs. The new income guarantee will be discussed in Sec. 25-3.

Although public aid programs represent an extremely small proportion of the G.N.P., they have been rising fairly rapidly from $3.6 billion to

$6.4 billion between 1965 and 1968. This increase occurred at a time when the American economy was operating at a full employment level. The rising concern about public aid programs is to some extent occasioned by the impression that the rise in these expenditures seems to be unaffected by long protracted prosperity. This has given rise to the demand for reforms which will be discussed in Sec. 25-3 but it is necessary to study first in some detail the public aid programs set up by the Social Security Act of 1935.

25-2. PUBLIC-AID PROGRAMS: THEIR DEVELOPMENT UP TO 1969

As we have seen in Chapter 20, one of the oldest principles of public relief is that its programs should be financed and administered by local authorities. When state and city governments were no longer able to cope with the mass problems of distress generated by the Great Depression, the Social Security Act of 1935 introduced the financial participation of the Federal government in special programs of public assistance. The two main areas covered by these programs are old-age assistance and aid to families with dependent children. In addition to these programs the law provided aid to the blind and since 1950 aid to the permanently and totally disabled. Even today, however, the Federal government does not participate in general assistance. This relief program is available to people under 65 who have no means of support. For instance, people who have exhausted their benefit period in unemployment insurance and who are without funds and unable to find employment may be eligible for general assistance.

Since old-age insurance became effective only in 1937 and then only with extremely low monthly payments, the overwhelming majority of people 65 and over who had no income or assets of their own had to be cared for by old-age assistance. The peak year in this program was 1950, when about 2.8 million people 65 and over were protected by old-age assistance. At that time 3.5 million people of the same age group received old-age insurance benefits. In 1967 the number of recipients in old-age assistance had dropped to 2.1 million, whereas the beneficiaries under OASDI had risen to 25.3 million. It is clear then that old-age assistance is declining at a fairly rapid rate and that in the years to come it will shrink to a small program of public aid.

The reverse seems to be true of the second specialized program of public aid—aid to families with dependent children. The purpose of this program was originally to provide assistance to families who had lost the earnings of the main breadwinner through the death of the father, or through incapacitation or for other reasons. One of these could be "desertion." Increasingly, however, aid was also given to female heads of households with children, very often from unknown or even a number of fathers. It is easy to see why this program became subject to heavy criticism, although nobody could deny that the families in question were in dire need of some form of public assistance. Table 25-2 shows the rapid growth of this program of special public assistance.

TABLE 25-2
AID TO FAMILIES WITH DEPENDENT CHILDREN, 1961–1967
(thousands)

Year	Families	Total Recipients	Children	Payments (millions)
1961	916	3,566	2,753	$1,148,838
1962	932	3,789	2,844	1,289,824
1963	954	3,930	2,951	1,355,538
1964	1,012	4,219	3,170	1,496,525
1965	1,054	4,396	3,316	1,644,096
1966	1,127	4,666	3,526	1,849,886
1967	1,297	5,309	3,986	2,249,673

SOURCE: *Social Security Bulletin* (December 1968), Table M-23.

It was indicated earlier in this chapter that the public-aid programs of the Social Security Act, and particularly the one whose rapid growth has been shown in Table 25-2, are at best marginal to the field of the economics of labor. However, the doubling of payments of aid to families with dependent children in the short span of time between 1961 and 1967 is of major concern from a more general viewpoint of economics. Here we are confronted with a growing sector of poverty which seems to be unresponsive to a general decline in unemployment and a rise in economic well-being. It is in this area that the specter of two-or three-generation relief families is looming and with it the continuous reproduction of poverty. The problem is aggravated by the uneven incidence of such relief cases among racial groups and in various parts of the country. Whereas in 1963 for the nation as a whole 42 out of 1,000 children under 18 were receiving this aid, the average was much higher in some states. Among these are New York with 57 per thousand, Pennsylvania with 58. The highest rate in continental United States was 130 per thousand in West Virginia. In Puerto Rico it was 139.

In view of the trend in the number of cases and expenditures in this program, substantial investments in preventive and rehabilitation programs possible under the Economic Opportunity Act of 1964 certainly would be no waste of money. One example would be "Operation Head Start" through which children from deprived homes can be brought up to the verbal and general behavior level of children from somewhat higher-income groups, so that they can start their formal schooling without the usual handicaps. The growth of this type of poverty is not inherent in the "welfare state," especially if such programs can attract highly qualified and trained people who are dedicated to a responsible and sober treatment of these problems.

In contrast to the public-aid program, general public assistance has remained almost stationary. In 1961, 411,000 cases came under this category; in 1967 there were 352,000. It must be realized, however, that general public assistance until now was a public aid program in which the Federal Government did not participate and which had to be financed out of state and local funds. This may account to some extent for the huge size of the A.D.C. program shown in Table 25-2. Naturally welfare departments operating on tight budgets will have a tendency to have as many cases as possible in special public aid categories where the Federal government provides matching funds. This tendency has in the past been enhanced by administrative practices whereby relief could not be granted to families with a man present. Such a policy tends to encourage desertions or the dropping out of males from the sight of the Census Bureau. Increased sharing by the Federal Government and policies designed to create incentives to change from a relief status to employment may prove to be effective in putting brakes on the rise of public aid expenditures in the midst of prosperity. These alternatives to the situation as it developed under the Social Security Act of 1935 will be discussed in the next section.

25-3. THE REFORM OF PUBLIC AID PROGRAMS

By the late 1960's it had become clear that the structure of social security as conceived in the 1930's required a complete overhaul. It had been the assumption a generation ago that social insurance, after an initial period starting out necessarily with low benefits would be adequate to raise the income of those entitled to insurance payments at least above the poverty level. The expectation that the vast majority of people in the labor force could earn enough credits during their lifelong employment to be assured at least minimum income maintenance after their retirement has not been realized, for considerable segments of the population over 65 who were not poor before their retirement are pushed down into the poverty sector. As was shown in Chapter 22 this is due to the obsolete and static structure of old age insurance which cannot be patched up by occasional increases in benefits such as the one voted in 1969. But apart from that it is true that social insurance has reduced substantially the number of people on public aid programs and this was one of the reasons for inaugurating this form of social security in the 1930's.

We have seen in the preceding section that public aid in the 1960's commanded at most 1.4 percent of the G.N.P. But this low percentage does not convey the seriousness of the problem connected with public aid in metropolitan areas where there is a concentration of poverty and also rural parts of the country which have suffered from mechanization in agriculture and the closing down of high cost industrial operations. Hence, the financial impact of public aid on local governments and the psychological fallout from the accumulation of the poor in urban districts is far greater than the macroeconomic rank of public aid programs. For this reason it was increasingly difficult to just let the public aid sector continue along the lines established in the 1930's.

There is growing awareness of the dangers inherent in this deteriorating condition. Proposals were being formulated to counteract this threat of a dual structure. One of them is the suggestion of a "negative income tax" put forward by Professor Milton Friedman. Basically this would come to the assistance of families in the lowest income groups. Using $3,000 as the poverty line, a family of four earning only $2,000 a year could claim $2,400 in personal exemptions plus $600 in standard deductions. Hence the difference between actual earnings and what could be claimed in exemptions would be $1,000. While there are some who would subsidize such poor families with a negative income tax to the full amount of $1,000, Professor Friedman would limit the tax to half of the difference between exemptions and actual earnings—in the example given, to $500. Furthermore, he proposes that this type of negative income tax should take the place of current public aid programs.

There is no denying that such a plan has some attractive features. One of them would be the simplicity of administering it. On the other hand, such a scheme, far from overcoming the dual-structure tendency of the American economy, would actually strengthen it. The recipients of public aid would be largely deprived of counseling and rehabilitation services now available to them through their contact with public and private welfare agencies. The older population would also be losers, because such a mechanical scheme would weaken the drive for a continuous updating of old-age benefits and their integration with general wage developments, as outlined in Chapter 22. Furthermore, such a seemingly simple technical approach to the problems of poverty would impair public awareness of the need to continue the war against poverty and to go on with a fight on many fronts against the multiple aspects of this phenomenon.

Similar schemes allocating somewhat larger income to poor families have been suggested by Edward E. Schwartz and Robert Theobald.[1] The former proposes a Federally guaranteed minimum income which could be obtained in the following way: every head of a family or an individual expecting to have less than this minimum in the year to come could claim on a form a "family security benefit" which would be the difference be-

---

[1] Robert Theobald, ed.: *The Guaranteed Income*, Doubleday 1967.

tween his actual income which might be zero and the Federally guaranteed minimum income. Robert Theobald has an even more ambitious concept of a guaranteed income. It should be ample enough to "provide the individual with the ability to do what he personally feels to be important."[2] To observe that this is a highly ambiguous statement which would be extremely hard to translate into policies and monetary values is only one of the criticisms levied against Mr. Theobald's presentation. The other one would be that he has not updated his understanding of the employment effect of automation. He still adheres to the idea that this will create "massive unemployment." We have seen, however, throughout this text that actually automation has speeded up the labor force transformation from manual to white-collar and professional workers and has so far not generated unemployment outside of the agricultural sector.

While guaranteed income plans which should not be confused with guaranteed annual wages discussed in Chapter 9 of this text have been widely discussed in recent years the reform proposals formulated by the Federal government in August, 1969, do not follow through with such vast and somewhat vague schemes. The main purpose of the new plan is to establish *Federal standards* for the determination of public aid budgets. In this connection it would also change the old system sanctioned by the Social Security Act of 1935 that general public assistance is exclusively the responsibility of local and state governments. The setting up of national standards is intended to lessen substantially the great differentials in public aid allowances existing between the States. The traditionally low levels in Southern and Southwestern states have contributed in the past to the migration of many poor and disadvantaged from these areas and their convergence on huge metropolitan areas. The Federal standard proposed by the Nixon administration would provide an annual income of $1,600 to a family of four.

This $1600.00 a year minimum for a family of four represents the new national standard for public aid. It eliminates the glaring discrepancies between the very low standards of some parts of the country and the much higher grants given to indigent families in most industrial states of the nation. Furthermore in a sharp break with traditions going back to the poor laws of England the Federal government will assume the cost of this minimum income. In this way a sharing of the Federal government in General Public assistance will be introduced whereas up to 1969 the Federal government subsidized only the programs set up for specific categories such as old age assistance and aid to dependent children. The latter program which had come under so much criticism is to be discontinued and combined with the new general system of minimum income maintenance.

[2]See Theobald, *op cit*, pg. 103.

On April 20, 1970, the U.S. Supreme Court ruled that state laws prohibiting A.D.C. to families where a man was present were unconstitutional. This ruling eliminates the disruptive effects of such welfare practices.

We have already seen in the preceding section that under the system prevailing until 1969, there was a built in "incentive" for welfare administrators to shift as many people as possible to ADC. Now that the Federal government is willing to participate in public aid programs by assuming a burden of $1600.00 a year for a family of four for all categories of relief recipients, a better balance between the various programs, reflecting more adequately and honestly the real situation of welfare families can be expected so that the former distortions in the relations between these various programs will be eliminated. This healthy development will be enhanced by the discarding of the unrealistic ruling established by many states that unemployed men do not qualify for public assistance.

The introduction of a national minimum income standard financed by the Federal government has been linked with two provisions which are designed to create incentives for relief recipients to become self-supporting. The first plan makes it mandatory for able-bodied relief recipients to seek employment, for instance by registering with the public employment service or special agencies designed to find jobs for hard core unemployed or to participate in job training activities. It should be noted that the effectiveness of such programs is predicated on the maintenance of extremely high levels of employment, probably below the four percent unemployment rate. But quite apart from this, these innovations establish a close connection between relief recipients and the institutions of the labor market and therefore must be considered a step in the right direction.

The other program deals with the working poor and those people on welfare who up to recently had no incentive to look for work even part time because their earnings were deducted in full from their relief allocation. Under the new scheme, earned income of $720.00 a year will be retained completely by the family without suffering any reduction of the basic $1600.00 a year annual benefit. As the earned income reaches $2000.00 the benefit will be reduced $960.00 so that total income will be $2960.00. The cut-off point will come with an earned income of $3920.00 per annum.

It should be noted that a wage earner in a family who works 2000 hours a year at the federal minimum wage of $1.60 an hour would still receive benefits in the neighborhood of $300.00 a year under this proposal. Here we see that the new incentive plan has also some pitfalls. Very great care must be taken that this new system does not in fact turn into a subsidy not only of relief families but also to employers continuing extremely low standards of pay. It seems inevitable that the work incentive system so rightfully introduced into public aid administration will lead to a substantial upgrading of federal minimum wage standards. Unless incentive plans for relief recipients and minimum wage standards are adjusted in this way, the work incentives while improving the conditions of the poor may in fact tend to enable substandard sectors of the economy and sweatshops to continue on under such a protective umbrella.[3] This however should be avoided at all costs as will be stressed in the next section.

In evaluating the innovations, the advantages and their pitfalls, it cannot be overlooked that the proper functioning of social-insurance systems and of programs of public aid is predicated on high levels of employment. Only if employment and earnings are high will there be a continuous large flow of contributions into the Social Security trust funds. If unemployment increases, more and more people will be left unprotected by social insurance either because they have exhausted their benefit periods in unemployment compensation or because they have lost their jobs long before becoming eligible for old-age benefits. This will tend to escalate the applications for public aid at a time when tax revenues supporting these programs are likely to decrease because of a falling of the national income growth rate.

It is clear, then, that even in this last third of the twentieth century the basic guarantee of minimum levels of social security does not reside in the elaborate legal and financial structure of social insurance but in the ability of a modern industrialized system to maintain itself as closely as possible to the levels of full employment. We have seen above that the welfare state is not a scheme whereby people get something for nothing. But just because it is increasingly based on a flow of contributions it is dependent on a generally good state of the economy. Sir William Beveridge's statement during World War II (when he submitted his report on Social Insurance and Allied Services at the request of the British Government) that full employment is a prerequisite to a satisfactory system of social insurance is just as true in the 1970's as it was in the 1940's.

25-4. LEADS AND LAGS IN THE ECONOMIC STATUS OF AMERICAN LABOR

We have seen throughout this volume that in the last two generations American labor has made great strides forward. Prior to World War II, the practice of collective bargaining was extended to millions of workers who up to that point had not been incorporated into the structure of organized labor. This development, as we have stressed continuously, benefited also the unorganized wage and salary workers. At the same time the Social Security Act of 1935, with its important extensions in 1939 and in 1950, introduced rather belatedly some programs of social insurance into the United States.

[3]See also the discussion in Sec. 7-3 of this text.

These institutional innovations in the field of labor established a firm basis for the great progress which was made in conditions of pay and work in the United States after World War II. Collective bargaining did not only assure workers of continuous wage increases which kept ahead of rising prices until the final years of the 1960's; more important in terms of status and security was the elaboration of the wage structure through fringe benefits. These substantial advances of labor occurred against the background of an economy which only infrequently departed from macrodynamic levels of full employment. However there is another side of the coin. In pointing with pride to the achievements of labor as is the wont of certain labor leaders, there is often a tendency to play down and deemphasize certain glaring lags.

As we have seen in this part of the text there is no program of American social security which can be termed adequate or comparable to the best systems operating in other highly advanced industrialized countries of the Western world. In view of the boundless ability of the American economy to produce, a second or third best social security system is not good enough for this country. But unfortunately this is what we have at the present time. This situation detracts from the high earnings and other advantages that American wage and salary earners receive while they are working.

There are two great challenges which the American economy must meet successfully if it is to prevent a gradual erosion of the great gains and progress which has been made by American labor. The first is a successful transition from full employment facilitated by continuous high level spending for national defense to full employment supported by forward projection of nonmilitary national goals in housing, health, education, irrigation, pollution and generally return to a more healthy natural and urban environment. This objective does not require additional spending but rather a transfer of public spending from destruction goods to contruction goods.

The second challenge can be characterized by the old slogan of eliminating "Poverty amidst Plenty." When this description was formulated in the 1930's it meant primarily the task of showing up the economic position of farmers and of providing employment opportunities for millions of people with adequate education and occupational experience. Today poverty amidst plenty refers not so much to economic but to deep rooted social lags. It is connected not only with the burdensome economics of expanding educational systems but with their inability to prepare all graduates with sufficient elementary skills to enable them to compete on the labor market; it refers to hard core unemployment especially among the youth of minority groups. Finally, it is related to the obsolescence of traditional methods of public administration in general and welfare administration in particular.

If these lags are not overcome in the 1970's, the American economy stands in danger not only of perpetuating but of aggravating a dual structure whereby a majority of the people will remain in the prosperity sector, and a minority compressed into urban ghettoes is frozen into a hopeless situation of deprivation and poverty. The avoidance of such a development is not the specialized job of social workers or for that matter of technicians and administrators of social insurance and public assistance programs. Unless these problems are taken up within the framework of a general analysis of the social and economic processes of our post-industrial society they will not receive the intellectual and academic priority they need.

25.5 THE PERILS OF SUCCESS IN SOCIAL POLICIES

As modern industrialized society developed, labor has been both an object and a prime mover in progressive labor legislation and in economic policies designed to assure economic progress. Although the popular concept of the welfare state is largely based on a distortion of the real structure of contemporary social security, there is another aspect to this term which has greater significance. In a more generic sense a welfare state, properly understood, symbolizes the collective conviction of a society that social and economic progress is not the automatic by-product of increases in production, productivity, and the greater affluence represented by the flood of material goods and services. Rather it is assumed that even if, in the initial stages of this rapid economic advance, things moved ahead spontaneously, it becomes increasingly necessary to stimulate and guide economic progress as higher and higher plateaus of economic well-being are sighted and approached. In this sense the welfare state is the expression of a continuous concern for the maintenance of a steady advance of the economy on the widest possible front. It implies full-employment policies, collective wage determination fitted into the goals and requirements of economic growth, and a continuous revaluation of the Social Security system. Beyond the purely economic sphere the welfare state also embodies concern about the scope and the value of education and the attempts to involve in the educational progress the largest number of people without lowering aims and standards.

While much of this type of welfare state has been institutionalized by such laws as the Employment Act of 1946, the Social Security Act of 1935 and its amendments, a mere institutionalization of welfare policies in the broadest sense of the word is not enough. To be effective they require continuous impetus emanating from groups within society.

Here certain difficulties arise. Movements such as organized labor which started out in opposition to the establishment inevitably become part of it once their original goals have to a large extent been realized. There is then a built-in tendency of formerly "radical" groups toward a slowdown of their dynamism and a blending into a general middle-class consensus. This development is only natural but it can become dangerous if it leads to a general ossification of organizational behavior. If this sets in, gaps are likely to open again between those who have been received into the established order and those who have been rejected by it. Thus a new dynamism may develop which may be either destructive or constructive.

The labor movement certainly must be considered as an example of a constructively dynamic group which has changed the structure of society as it existed in the nineteenth century. In this volume the economic structure of the problems confronting labor in the later part of the twentieth century have been described and analyzed. But if the progress of labor is to be maintained, and if newly arising problems are to be solved, continuous research and action are needed in the general area of labor. Labor economics can render a service by providing insights into these structures. But here as elsewhere real progress is the joint product of theory and practice.

SELECTED BIBLIOGRAPHY

Budd, Edward S. *Inequality and Poverty* (New York: The Macmillan Co., 1966).

Elman, Richard M. *The Poorhouse State* (New York: A Delta Book, 1967).

Moynihan, Daniel P. *Maximum Feasible Misunderstanding* (New York: Free Press, 1968).

Mydral, Gunnar *Beyond the Welfare State* (New Haven: Yale University Press, 1965).

Reissman, Frank *Social Class & Social Policy* (New York: Basic Books, 1965).

Schoor, Alvin L. *Explorations in Social Policy* (New York: Basic Books, 1964).

Theobald, Robert, ed. *The Guaranteed Income* (Garden City, N.Y.: Anchor Books, 1959).

Titmuss, Richard M. *Commitment to Welfare* (New York: Pantheon Books, 1965).

Will, Robert E. and Vatter, Harold G. *Poverty in Affluence* (New York: Harcourt, Brace & World, Inc. March 1970).

QUESTIONS FOR DISCUSSION

1. Carefully interpret the data in Table 24-1, giving special attention to the factors accounting for the changes which can be observed in that table.

2. Why may it be said that the Welfare State is a "state of mind" rather than an actually significant feature of the American Economy?

3. Outline the various programs of public aid as provided for the Social Security Act and its amendments.

4. Analyze the redistribution effects the social insurance payments and public aid programs provided for in the Social Security Act.

5. What is a "dual-structured" economy, and why should such an institutional setting be avoided?

6. Give an overall evaluation of the social-insurance system as it exists in the United States today.

INDEX